Last of the Flying Clippers

Last of the Flying Clippers
The Boeing B-314 Story

M.D. Klaäs

NX 18601

Schiffer Military/Aviation History
Atglen, PA

DEDICATION

This book is dedicated to my brother, Gregory Alfred Klaäs, and to my best friend ever, Walter Donald Shaw, the latter of whom also underwent many a clipper-collecting experience(s)—all in memory of our youth when we two traveled by old electric *Red Line* streetcars and buses, either in rain or in sunshine, to many a dingy and musty downtown Los Angeles magazine shop for our many picture-gathering hours while searching diligently to find clipper memorabilia, and a time unbeknownst to me to be the very beginnings for this book.

Book Design by Ian Robertson.

Copyright © 1997 by M.D. Klaäs.
Library of Congress Catalog Number: 97-81405

Printed in China.
ISBN: 0-7643-0562-X

We are interested in hearing from authors with book ideas on related topics.

Published by Schiffer Publishing Ltd.
4880 Lower Valley Road
Atglen, PA 19310
Phone: (610) 593-1777
FAX: (610) 593-2002
E-mail: Schifferbk@aol.com
Please write for a free catalog.
This book may be purchased from the publisher.
Please include $3.95 postage.
Try your bookstore first.

CONTENTS

Acknowledgments

The beginnings for this book actually originated in 1951 when, as a young teenager, I chose, as a subject, to write a general history of U.S. commercial aviation for a school English paper. In preparation, I sent a number of letters to various airlines who, in turn, mailed me an extensive amount of public relations-related handouts. In the sorted pieces from Pan Am were two glossy photographs of the 314, one of which showed the ship's posh salon that resembled a cabin aboard a luxury yacht or one found aboard a first-class club car. Fascinated, and hard to believe that such ambiance once existed aboard commercial aircraft, I began to explore and delve into the history of the 314 Clippers. Airliners in the early 1950s were far removed from such elegant interior arrangements. Thus began a long and wonderful hobby that has prevailed to this day. Some people collect stamps. I collected 314 data from which evolved this book. Through the years, and by and through the patience, understanding and fine cooperation of many people, it has been possible to achieve my goal. To my knowledge, all have since retired with a few having become deceased. To those still with us and to those who are not, I remain indebted to the following:

Marilyn Phipps, Historical Services, Boeing Aircraft Co., friend and aid who contributed so much to make this book what it is. Without her constant concern and many times "to the rescue," I could never have achieved the indepth study I so desired.

Additional appreciation is also extended to former Clipper Capt. Edward Matthew Black; Clipper Capt. William Meyer Masland; Ann Whyte, former staff associate, Public Relations, Pan Am; and the late Gordon S. Williams, Boeing Aircraft Co., who supplied unprecedented amounts of valuable information and photos; and to my witty, delightful editor and life-long friend Elaine diBello Bradish, the soul who kept my fast-jotted writing legible.

Credit as well is due to five close friends: Reel and Doris Blaylock, Rita Daniels, Phyllis ("Krizzie-babes") Krizmanich and Norma K. Wallace, who so often encouraged me not to "abandon ship."

A special note of thanks is also most deserving to the following for their admirable contributions over the years, some of whom supplied fascinating anecdotes so much enjoyed, expected and appreciated by ardent, historical aviation readers:

Delio R. Alonso, manager, Airlift International, Inc., San Juan; Hank W. Arnold, aviation historian; William J. Bachran, Pan Am PR representative; Wellwood E. Beall, chief 314 project engineer; Clipper Capt. Kenneth V. Beer; Frederic Bemis, assistant manager, Los Angeles International Airport; Bart Benedict, freelance writer, research, public relations consultant; Howard Bingham, chief FAA information officer; Clipper Capt. Gilbert B. Blackmore; John Borger, Chief Pan Am engineer; James S. Boynton, director, Boeing News Bureau; E. W. Bradford, LCDR, U.S. Navy; Barr Braman, U.S. Air Force historian; Pan Am Second Officer William O. Buchanan; Marion L. Buckner, librarian, San Diego Public Library; Clipper Capt. John Curtis Burn; Pan Am Second Officer Ferguson J. Byars; Suzanne Caster, librarian, *San Francisco Chronicle*; John M. Chapman, vice president, Universal Airlines, Inc.; T. E. Scott-Chard, BOAC reference officer; Chester Catfield, Boeing editorial staff chief; Carl M. Cleveland, Boeing PR director; Lt. F. E. Coghlan, pictorial branch, U.S. Navy; R. E. Cohen, specialist, U.S. Dept. of Commerce; Eric Collins, U.S. Navy legislative and technical information director; Brian A. Cooke, vice president, World Airways, Inc.; Lt. Cmdr. D. M. Cooney, chief U.S. Navy Magazine Book Branch officer; Mrs. Howard M. Cone, wife of late Pan Am Capt. Howard M. Cone; A. E. Cormack, aviation records assistant, Royal Air Force Museum, London; Pascal Cowan, Pan Am manager, Pacific Division; Peter T. Craven, finance director, World Airways, Inc.; BOAC Steward Patrick E. A. Griffin; Fearine G. Crockett, assistant FAA control system's registrate; Robert E. Cummings, World War II historian (Gen. MacArthur specialist); Clipper Capt. Jack H. Curry; Eleanor Jean L. Dabagh, librarian, Honolulu Public Library; Clipper Radio Operator Col. Walter M. Dalglish; Edward J. Daly, president, World Airways, Inc.; Robert Demme, Pan Am PR representative; J. Doig, Convair/General Dynamics service parts manager; Pan Am Steward Roy L. Donham; Lt. M. R. Dumas, U.S. Coast Guard PR officer; Pan Am Steward Gene E. Dunning; G. T. Eccles, U.S. Navy chief of records and data processing; Virginia E. Felker, U.S. Navy assistant PR officer; Pan Am Technical Chief Pilot Scott Flower; Clipper Capt. Robert Ford; A. W. French, Pan Am curator; E. French, BOAC assistant reference officer; Paul Friend, chief Pan Am photographer, Atlantic Division; Mary Edith Fry, technology librarian, Seattle Public Library; Peter J. Gilbert, aviation enthusiast, Empire State College, N.Y.; Lt. Col. C. V. Glines, U.S. Air Force Magazine & Book Division chief; Clipper Capt. Harold E. Gray; Bonnie Grover, FAA Records Branch assistant; Clipper Capt. Haakon G. Culbransen; Gerard E. Hasselwankder, U.S. Air Force assistant historian; Col. Grover Heiman, Jr., U.S.

Acknowledgments

Air Force Magazine & Book Division chief; Cmdr. W. H. Hile, Jr., U.S. Navy Records and Statistics chief; Bob Hope, comedian/actor; Clipper Capt. Robert ("Bob") C. Howard; Jack Isabel, General Dynamics/Convair Division News and Information manager; Stanley Kalkus, U.S. Navy Library director; P. J. Keith, Fuller Lacquer & Paint manager, Los Angeles Branch; BOAC Capt. John Cecil Kelly-Rogers; Robin Kinhead, Pan Am PR representative; C. C. Knapp, Oakland Airport assistant manager; Nick A. Komons, FAA Agency historian; Lt. Col. Harvey M. Ladd, U.S. Navy Magazine & Book Division assistant; Pan Am Second Officer Thomas F. Laughlin, Jr.; Althea Lister, former Pan Am curator; Michael J. Lombardi, Boeing Aircraft Co. historian; Mrs. Julian (Mary "B") Longley, Sr.; Lt. Cmdr. A. L. Lonsdale, U.S. Coast Guard Public Information chief; Ted Lopstkiewicz, CAB Information Office officer; Capt. F. Kent Loomis, assistant U.S. Navy director, Naval History; Clare Boothe Luce, *Time-Life* heiress; Eleanore M. Lynn, Maryland Public Library librarian; Harold Mansfield, former Boeing Aircraft Co. PR director; Ilona Massey, actress; Clipper Capt. Steven McCrea; E. H. McGregor, FAA General Operations inspector; M. E. McKee, CAB Safety Bureau aasistant; Lt. Cmdr. M. A. Michael, U.S. Navy Public Information officer; William R. Mockler, community relations director, Port of San Diego; J. P. Murray, Boeing vice president; John H. Newland, Boeing News Bureau assistant manager; B. H. Norman, U.S. Navy information assistant; Lenore Norman, New York's Landmarks Preservation Commission's executive director; Fred Nott, Pan Am historian; Harold S. O'Dougherty, engineer project manager, Hughes Aircraft Co.; Marian C. O'Donnell, librarian, San Francisco Public Library; David T. Parsons, Pan Am PR director, Atlantic Division; Mike Pavone, 314 flight engineer chief; R. L. Pittman, assistant FAA control system's registrate; F. Lopez Porta, Pan Am PR manager, Latin American/Eastern Division; George B. Pottoriff, Pan Am PR representative; Donald M. Ratledge, BOAC's information chief; Lester G. Robinson, FAA aircraft registration branch chief; Robert J. Russell, 314 construction worker, Boeing Aircraft Co.; Hisako Sakamoto, library technician, Hawaii Public Library; George S. Schairer, Boeing aerodynamacist, Boeing Aircraft Co.; John F. R. Scott, Jr., aviation director, Friendship International Airport, Maryland; Rosemarie A. Serafin, Pan Am PR representative, Atlantic Division; Richard L. Singley, aero-philately historian; Edward E. Slattery, CAB public information officer; Roland Smith, journalist and third husband to Jane Froman; George Snyder, 314 stress engineer, Boeing Aircraft Co.; Michael Stanley, Pan Am photographer; Bonnie L. Stoll, FAA records division assistant; Leon H. Tanguay, CAB Safety Bureau director; G. L. Thompson, U.S. Navy PR officer; Capt. W. K. Thompson, Jr., U.S. Coast Guard public information chief; Clipper Capt. Harold Lanier Turner; Tom Wheeler, PR manager, World Airways, Inc.; Bruce Whitaker, vice principal, Los Angeles Unified School District; S. Roger Wolin, Pan Am PR manager, Latin American/Eastern Division; William L. Worden, manager, Boeing International News Service; and A. O. Van Wyen, chief U.S. Navy Aviation History unit, Washington, D. C.

Acknowledgement is also due the following agencies and organizations for their invaluable support through the years of 314 Clipper research:

Associated Press (*AP*); *Baltimore Sun*; Boeing Aircraft Co.; British Overseas Airways (now British Airways); Oviatt Library, Calitornia State University of Northridge (CSUN); Civil Aeronautics Board (CAB); Department of Aviation, Baltimore, Md.; Federal Aviation Agency (FAA); General Dynamics/Convair Division; Glen L. Martin Co.; *Hilo Tribune Herald*; *Honolulu Advertizer*; Honolulu Public Library; *Honolulu Star-Bulletin*; *Los Angeles Herald Examiner*; Los Angeles Public Library; *Los Angeles Times*; *National Geographic*; *Newsweek*; *New York Daily News*; *New York Herald Tribune*; New York Landmarks Preservation Commission; New York's Port Authority Commission; New York Public Library; *New York Times*; Pan American World Airways System, Inc.; *Port Washington News*; Royal Air Force Museum, Hendon, London; San Diego Port Authority Commission; San Diego Public Library; *San Francisco Chronicle*; *Seattle Post-Intelligencer*; Seattle Public Library; Sikorsky Aircraft Corp.; *The Baltimore Sun*; The Curtis Publishing Co.; *The Saturday Evening Post*; *The Seattle Star*; *Time/Life, Inc.*; *United Press* (*UP*); United States Air Force; United States Coast Guard; United States Navy; Warner Brothers Studios; and World Airways, Inc.

1

Purpose for Design

"Fifty years from now people will look back upon a Pan American Clipper flight of today as the most romantic voyage of history."[1] So wrote the late Clare Boothe Luce, international celebrity and a former U.S. ambassador to Italy, following a roundtrip trans-pacific air cruise aboard Boeing-built Model B-314 flying boats in 1941.

Many years have come and gone since that writing, but there are numerous veteran air travelers still about who well recall when Boeing's flying ships ruled the vast oceanic air lanes of the world. The 314s provided an intriguing story for and after the infancy of international commercial flight during a time when our globe was storm-swept into war.

Glamorous and romantic, the 314s are now part of America's aviation past. Within the span of elapsed time since their conception, the memory of those winged, ship-styled sky liners has become eroded. Today's air-minded public gives little credence to the prestige once held by the mighty 314s — to their contribution and expansion of world-encircling commercial air travel. The word "clipper" that once symbolized the great transports of sea and air has long lost its air-equated meaning over the years that for a period of time defined the now defunct Pan American Airways (Pan Am) and its "System of Flying Clippers."

In the 1930s, and through the mid-1940s, when one mentioned the word "clipper," the noun usually referred to a marine-operated aircraft of immense size. It expounded the type of vehicle used for travel prevailing high above the vast oceans connecting various continents. Today, dictionary-wise, "clipper" ascribes to either a tall-masted ship designed in the 1800s on the U.S.'s east coast by Donald McKay, or in specifying a type of tool or method used by a barber to trim hair or an instrument used to cut back hedges.

Pan Am's eximious quality for the word-usage stemmed from the historical accounts and praises awarded McKay's square-rigged sailing ships that once plied the seven seas in the 19th century. It was first adapted by Pan Am in November, 1931, when the then U.S. First Lady, Mrs. J. Edgar Hoover, christened a Sikorsky-built S-40 amphibian the *American Clipper*, the U.S.' first four-engined over-water aircraft.

Despite the dictionary's word-change-meaning, as related to the bygone flying boat era, Pan Am retained the descriptive adage for all their future-owned aircraft. Since Sept. 21, 1935, as ruled by the Federal Court, District of Washington, D.C., it became illegal for any commercial venture to apply the word "clipper" to their product(s) without written approval from Pan Am. This ruling was reaffirmed on June 21, 1951, in the case of Pan Am versus Clipper

First plane named a clipper by Pan Am is christened by President Herbert C. Hoover's wife at the Anacostia Naval Air Station in Washington, D.C., on Oct. 12, 1931, while Juan Terry Trippe (left) holds bouquet of red roses he presented earlier to the First Lady. The craft, a Sikorsky S-40 amphibian, was the first in the series of long-range, sea-spanning flying clipper ships. (*Photo Courtesy: Pan American World Airways*)

Low-cut parlor chairs and divans dominated the Do-X's swank cabins, all remembered by Trippe who later insisted on near similar styling aboard his flying clipper hotels. (*Photo Courtesy: U.S. Archives*)

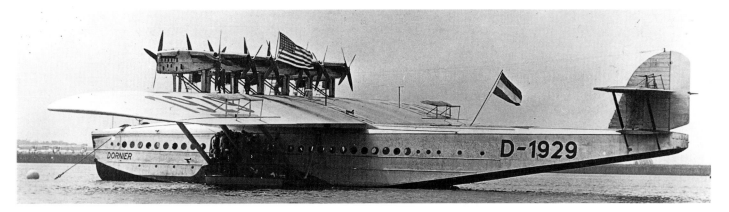

Germany's colossal Do-X, shown moored at New York's North Beach in 1931, mirrored the coming of 314 commercial transoceanic aeroplane service on a regular schedule eight years later. (*Photo Courtesy: United States Navy Archives*)

Van Lines, Inc., and B & B General Storage Warehouse, Inc. In Pan Am's favor, the decision was handed down in the U.S. District Court, Eastern District of New York, Civil Case No. 10673, which decreed by law that "clipper" had become a registered Pan Am trademark and therefore could not be visually equated to any article or service not so mandated by said airline.

The credit for applying "clipper" to Pan Am planes originated with and by Juan Terry Trippe (1899-1981), founder, president and former chairman of the airline. As with everything Trippe did for his enterprise, there was always a sound reasoning behind his authoritative decision-making power. With great ambition and foresight, he was dedicated to opening the world to commercial flight regardless of the cost or obstacles involved — a highly shrewd intellectual given a keen sense of financial, industrial commerce and trade-type negotiating techniques.

Trippe, a Yale graduate, had a deep-rooted philosophy as to the structuring of his great empire. As a youngster he had traveled afar on the great Cunard ocean-floating palaces with his parents. He was fascinated not only with shipboard life but with ships in gen-

eral. When Trippe launched his enterprise in 1927, the spirited capitalist had developed a format for his ambitious career — his endeavor to operate a flying business based on a nautical theme. By the late 1930s Tripppe's dream had expanded to the point of having flying clipper ships winging throughout the Caribbean, Central and South America and across the expansive Pacific. In late 1935, during the establishment of the great Pacific air route to Manila and beyond, serious attention was turned towards conquering the Atlantic by airplane. What futuristic, heavier-than-air[*] boat would rule this sector of the world had yet to be decided upon or built.

As of 1936, one evident fact was that the line's present flying ships were incapable of the stringent U.S. Government payload requirements necessary to operate across the Atlantic. Since all transoceanic Pan Am operations were U.S. mail subsidized, the payloads were figured by both the airline and U.S. Government as being enormous between the U.S. and Europe. Passenger traffic alone would be demanding and more than the already established transpacific route between San Francisco and Manila, and, therefore, a

[*]apposed to lighter-than-air that referred to dirigibles or blimps.

Sikorsky-built S-42 was Pan Am's second model-type flying boat that was also used to survey both Pacific and Atlantic Oceans for the M-130 and B-314 services. Shown is the noted *Brazilian Clipper* (later renamed *Colombia Clipper*) that operated on Caribbean and South American air routes. (*Photo Courtesy: Pan American World Airways*)

Richly appointed compartments and watertight bulkheads styled after surface-going vessels as seen aboard an S-42 gave an added assurance of safety to those who dared to fly. The technology to span oceans by air had come of age. (*Photo Courtesy: Pan American World Airways*)

Curtained-off M-130 suites foreshadowed the unparalleled luxury later experienced aboard the more grand B-314s. (*Photo Courtesy: Glenn L. Martin Aircraft Co.*)

new aircraft had to be designed and built to meet the Atlantic's anticipated heavy mail and passenger demands. All of the outlined calculations for a new airliner had been thoroughly analyzed by Pan Am immediately following the inaugural 1936 passenger service across the Pacific. This route was maintained by three Glenn L. Martin-built M-130 flying boats, the *China, Hawaii* and *Philippine Clippers*. Space for 800 pounds of mail per flight was then required by government contract, a subsidy that kept the airline afloat. Total gross weight of an M-130 was set at 52,000 pounds, and if more mail was carried, a reduction in passengers had to be made. The mail came first.

Pan Am officials had been stunned when Trippe announced preparations for the conquest of the Pacific in 1934 rather than the Atlantic. In fact, all personnel had been prepared for Atlantic organization. They had expected that the next bid for an ocean-spanning aircraft was for the design of a liner to be used between New York and London. Much to everybody's astonishment, the Pacific was opened up first through Trippe's foresightedness and Martin's production of the M-130. European landing rights for the U.S. were unavailable in 1934, and the technological development of a plane big enough to handle the Atlantic's operational mail and passenger loads was marginal. Trippe, always a secretive man in his business

Glenn L. Martin's legendary M-130 *China Clipper*, seen over San Francisco Bay, advanced Pan Am into its third stage of over-water, four-engined flying boat clipper ships. The Martin planes were found difficult to operate and considered less efficient than the more advanced Model B-314. Shortly after Japan attacked Pearl Harbor, *China* was transferred to Miami, via Los Angeles. En route, Capt. M. C. Weber took the boat over and into Arizona's Grand Canyon so transferring airline personnel aboard could view the canyon's many colorful clay walls. Unusual, and a bit more adventure added to its historical flying career, the NC 14716 not only had flown to Macao and Hong Kong but in and out of the gorges of the majestic Grand Canyon as well! (*Photo Courtesy: Pan American World Airways*)

directives, understood this aspect. He was chief and would act accordingly.

The biggest block to regular heavier-than-air commercial transport service over the Atlantic was in acquiring foreign landing rights. Britain simply would not agree to a contract unless she in-turn could offer an equal service to the U.S. The French, like the British, also held firm for a reciprocal operation.

Interestingly enough, Pan Am did have a plane that could have carried an adequate load factor across the Atlantic by mid-1934. However, no landing rights were forthcoming from the eastern side of the Atlantic. It was at that point when Trippe began to focus on the Pacific.

Trippe's transoceanic dreams rested at first on the 1934 delivery of Igor I. Sikorsky's S-42 flying boat, ten of which were built for the airline. The liner was a four-engined craft that had a cruising speed of 160 m.p.h. with a gross weight of 38,000 pounds. She was a highly successful plane for the time and particularly noted for her large picturesque portholes for passenger viewing. But since there were no immediate and foreseeable landing rights to be granted from abroad, the S-42 was put into survey work on the Pacific. Months slipped into years and by 1936 the S-42 was considered obsolete for the heavy traffic she would have had to bore across the Atlantic. Trippe knew how difficult it was, and would be for some time to come, to deal with the British and French. So it was that in 1934, when the S-42 was first introduced, the line concentrated its efforts in spanning the Pacific and improving their Latin American Division (LAD) operations out of Miami, FL, with S-42s.

As for conquering the Atlantic, Pan Am had desires to do so as early as 1929, two years after the line began flying between Key West, FL, and Havana, Cuba; but, as stated, little headway was achieved. In 1930 talks were opened with the Bermuda government for landing rights to the island's Hamilton Harbor, even if Pan Am lacked planes with efficient range and a suitable payload capacity. It was, however, a hopeful sign leading to the first step into establishing flights over the Atlantic. While talks continued, Pan Am turned elsewhere — to the Caribbean and further south concentrating heavily on the Latin American countries.

While negotiations dragged on, Trippe continued with his planning of Atlantic routes. In 1933, Col. Charles and Anne Lindbergh charted two futuristic routes for Pan Am's third-staged goal of world operation in a single-engined Lockheed Sirius floatplant. More than 30,000 miles later the famed couple had surveyed a northern route, via Newfoundland, Labrador, Greenland and Iceland. Landing rights from England were not necessary, for at that time the sites were not under Parlimentary Jurisdiction.

A second mapping, known as the "southern route," between the U.S., Azore Islands and Portugal, was also planned. The Lindbergh's return trip back to the U.S. was via Africa, the South Atlantic, South America and north to America. Unknown to the Lindberghs, and for that matter to Pan Am officials, was that the South Atlantic crossing was later to become a third crucial air link between the free world and warring Europe. In-turn, the originally surveyed southern route would eventually become the mid-Atlantic or "Blue Ribbon Route."

Lindbergh's Atlantic-encircling trip was dubbed the "Jelling Expedition" after the *S.S. Jelling*, a supply ship chartered by the airline to store supplies and act as a home base for the noted aviation hero-and-wife team. In command of the surface vessel was Maj. Robert A. Logan, an early northwestern Canadian surveyor.

While Lindbergh, acting as a technical advisor for Pan Am, and Anne left the ship and flew aloft for a day's work, Logan and his crew kept busy charting possible landing sites for the future clippers. Their chartings, along with earlier 1931-32 weather studies of the Arctic and mid-Atlantic sections, were cross-checked and put aside for the times ahead. All data was kept up to date until Pan Am was awarded Atlantic service in 1939. The pertinent weather notations and charts were kept astride under the leadership of Dr. Vilhajalmur Stefansson, a renowned Arctic explorer who began work

Poised atop a beaching cradle at its snow-covered Baltimore, MD, Martin plant, the Pan Am-rejected M-156 "Super Clipper" awaited another trial run prior to its sale and shipment to Russia. (*Photo Courtesy: Gordon S. Williams*)

Consolidated's clipper bid rested with its PB2Y-1, a model considered by Pan Am as being too small in passenger capacity but later accepted and built for the armed forces. (*Photo Courtesy: Convair Aircraft Corp.*)

with Pan Am in 1932. Through Stefansson's efforts, expeditions in Greenland were financially backed by the airline to study and chart air and ice conditions for safe flying as the area was mapped for a possible air base link to Europe. During this time period the practicalities of air science were deemed feasible, but the landing right fiascoes that involved government red tape continued to be unsettled. It seemed Pan Am's coffee breaks did not jive with Imperial Airways' tea time, and Air France was only beginning to add an irritant lemon taste to America's and England's competitive, commercial air supremacy brew.

England's hesitancy to grant Pan Am landing rights became more strained in 1935. Imperial was giving serious thought to her country's air superiority regarding Atlantic service. The British line, through the British Government, had ordered a fleet of 39 streamlined flying boats far advanced in aeronautical design as compared to anything the U.S. had. They were conceived by Arthur Gouge of Short Bros., Rochester, England, and designated as S-23 Class C Empire flying boats. The liner was a high-winged, four-engined monoplane with outward floats that expelled in its mein any clewline struts and wing supports so familiar to America's S-42s and the soon-to-be exonerated M-130s.

Gouge's S-23s resembled a fine yacht with varied compartments implementing clean lines and deep-upholstered wing-back chairs. The transports even bolstered a "promenade deck," a port mid-sectioned area where passengers could stand, grasp onto a chromed, ship-styled handrail and peer out at leisure through three large square-shaped portholes. A gimmick to attract seasoned travelers, the space nonetheless became a popular feature — an above-the-clouds novelty. England's air marvels well demonstrated how luxurious large over-water planes were becoming.

As fine a plane as the S-23 was, it fell short of one major factor — range! With a cruising speed of 164 m.p.h., the 24-passenger, 18-ton flying boat could fly only about 760 miles with 2,500 pounds

of mail and cargo and 600 gallons of fuel. But she was England's only challenge to the Atlantic. Time would tell if the pristine S-23 could be improved upon or completely changed to include not only a better range, but also a much higher load factor, and, possibly, more passengers in more commodious compartments. Meanwhile, S-23s were put into regular Empire service in the Mediterranean in October, 1935. Within a few months they were rolling out of the Short Bros.' factory and making runs throughout the English Empire, including trips to Malaya in the Far East from whence they acquired their accepted public name, "Empire Class Flying Boats."

While the S-23s gained public acceptance overseas in 1936, Trippe and his board of directors ordered query letters to be sent to various U.S. aircraft manufacturers requesting if the construction of a large flying boat bigger and better than anything the airline had in service could be built. Already, a German dirigible, the *Graf Zeppelin*, was carrying mail and passengers across the South Atlantic between Germany and Brazil, a service begun in 1931. In addition, Germany's Lufthansa was also carrying mail over the South Atlantic with Dornier-built planes being catapulted off ships on the high seas. Although the planes lacked range, the catapult system proved successful in that it shortened the water gap between continents to meet the Dornier's range. In 1936, Air France and Lufthansa signed an agreement for a mutual mail service across the South Atlantic, thus strengthening the air ties between Europe and the lower Americas.

While Lufthansa and Air France concentrated heavily on developing the South Atlantic run, Pan Am and Imperial Airways knew the true impact of air service lay in the north, a route to link the old and new worlds. Both airlines were well aware that whoever connected the two continents first with regular, heavier-than-air air mail and passenger flights would gain worldwide prestige and also reap the lion's share of international air service.

By the time Air France became interested in the North Atlantic connection, war interrupted its effort to compete. Two four-engined

Sikorsky's speedy S-44 boat was also turned down by Pan Am for its lack of passenger seating and space for large loads of cargo and mail. Remaining S-44, shown during a late 1960s takeoff from Avalon Harbor, Catalina Island, is preserved at the Bradley Air Museum, Windsor Locks, CT (*Photo Courtesy: Avalon Air Transport*)

marine liners, the Latècoére 302 and the huge L-631, came too late for the challenge. The L-631 was to have carried 46 passengers 3,500 miles non-stop. She was powered by six engines at a cruising speed of 185 m.p.h , weighed 72 tons and had a wing span of 188 feet with a hull length of 142 feet. Other French designs were also produced, but Adolph Hitler's Third Reich seemed to stymie any progressive commercial air advancement for France's transoceanic commodity. There were models, such as the L-300 and the six-engined L-523, that became either reconnaissance planes for the French Navy before France fell to the Germans in 1940, were confiscated by the enemy, or were hidden by the Free French before Hitler's invasion.

France, it was noted, may have competed well with Britain and the U.S. in the air race for scheduled North Atlantic passenger and mail service. In 1930, French aeronautical engineers had developed the L-521 *Lieutenant de Vaisseau*, a six-engined, 104-foot long flying boat with a 162-foot wing spread for the South Atlantic service. Capable of carrying only 20 passengers on long ocean hops and 76 on shorter flights, the 37-ton, double-decked monster came to the U.S., via Africa and South America, in the early 1930s. While at Pensacola, FL, it was badly damaged when a storm struck the port. Her tour suddenly ended, France's hopeful was dismantled and shipped home where she was later rebuilt to try for the North Atlantic run in 1939.

Between ocean tries, Paris' aviation elite, like those in and around London, continued to deny Pan Am landing rights. An expressed attitude within the heiarchy of France's air-minded circles was why should they, the French, have to link their foreign provinces in South America, via the U.S., if they could do so without having to negotiate with the U.S. for landing rights? Air France

Wellwood E. Beall in fashionable dress, 1939. His unique clipper conception brought Pan Am to its zenith of airborne luxury and world acclaim unparalled in the course of international aviation. (*Photo Courtesy: Boeing Aircraft Co.*)

officials believed it could single handedly reap large air profits with just a South Atlantic service rather then with a reciprocal U.S. agreement to operate flights across the North Atlantic. The only item blocking the French was a capable airliner that would show a reasonable profit. Their L-521 bad to be loaded down with 36,000 pounds of fuel that eliminated nearly all weight loads for mail and passengers. Turning back to the drawing boards, France's Air Ministry-sponsored program struggled for some time to come up with the L-631. But it was too late — Hitler was at the backdoor and the finished product was dismantled and hidden long before Nazi helmeted forces marched into Paris.

About the only other European country awakened to the early efforts of transatlantic flying — especially across the South Atlantic — was Italy. In 1927, Gen. Francesco de Pinedo, an Italian marquis and skilled aviator, commanded a 1924 Italian-built S-55 flying boat named *Santa Maria* from Rome to the U.S. Pinedo left Italy on February 8th in the craft designed by Alessandro Marchette, chief engineer for Italy's Savoia Aircraft Co., and flew down the coast of Africa, across the South Atlantic to South America and north to the U.S. where the plane was destroyed in a crash. Pinedo had to wait for another S-55 from Italy before continuing back to Rome.

In United Airlines dress, the late 1930-designed DC-4E prototype is seen over Los Angeles during test flight. Liner paved way for futuristic transport landplanes that doomed the great flying boats. Because of the project, which coincidentally had the same type triple-finned tail and aft suite as the 314, Douglas turned down Pan Am's bid for the possible construction of a flying boat clipper model. (*Photo Courtesy: United Airlines*)

One year later, Italian Air Minister Gen. Italo Balbo headed a squadron of S-55s to the U.S. Then in 192O, Capt. Arturo Ferrarin and Maj. C. P. del Prete, famed Italian aviators, set a non-stop record between Rome and Touros, Brazil, in their Savoia-Marchetti S-64 after flying a distance of 4,466 miles in 51 hours and 59 minutes. The flight brought Italy into air prominence. In December, 1931, Balbo led another formation of 14, double-hulled, catamaran-styled Marchetti planes from Rome to Rio de Janeiro. A North Atlantic run, via Holland, Ireland, Iceland and Canada, was conducted starting July 1, 1933, with 24 Marchetti planes to Chicago and New York. The round-trip flight, commanded by Balbo, covered more than 12,000 miles. Regardless of all the Italian flights made in the late 1920s and early 1930s, there was never an attempt to establish a commercial service. At the time interest primarily lay in setting records and achieving fame with a relatively new mode of travel. The Italian-constructed aircraft were not of mercantile quality; their twin hulls were only 54 feet, two inches long and stratified by a wing span of 79 feet, four inches. They were powered by two push-'n-pull Fiat A-24Rs that produced 700 horsepower at a maximum speed of 147 m.p.h. with a service ceiling of 13,775 feet. By the time World War II erupted, Italy, under fascist ruler Gen. Benito Mussolini, was conducting a mediocre and non-competitive landplane service over the South Atlantic between Gambia (now Senegal) and Brazil.

Germany's 1930 headline-making try to conquer the Atlantic with heavier-than-air service began with its titanic 900-mile-range Dornier Do-X flying hotel. Conceived by Dr. Claudis Dornier, former designer for the Zeppelin Co., Friedrichshafen, Germany, the 1929-built sky giant was powered by 12 Curtiss Conqueror, water-cooled, push-'n-pull-mounted engines. Constructed of corrugated light alloy sheeting, the Lufthansa-assigned flying boat had a wing span of 157 feet, five inches and a hull length of 131 feet, four inches, with a wing area of 4,887 square feet.

Capable of carrying 100 passengers in unaralleled luxury, Dr. Dornier's 134-m.p.h. behemoth fell short of the Atlantic's answer to heavier-than-air service shortly after she was launched. Problems and long delays plagued the liner during a preview tour to the U.S., via Portugal, Africa and South America. She was nearly destroyed at Lisbon, Portugal, due to an engine and wing fire, and her hull was later damaged by a high wave while moored at the Canary Islands. If that was not enough, she was struck by lightning in August, 1931, after reaching New York. It seemed success was against the boat throughout the 740-day trip. But the true failure rested in the plane's engine power and in its wooden-pitched propellers that disqualified the Do-X for holding its high maximum gross weight of 114,600 pounds. Significantly, the debacles of the flying boat proved a good try for the Atlantic, but the machine was proven too inadequate and doomed to failure by 1932.

The world's air-minded public was still waiting for an Atlantic air service when the eight letters of a probing nature were mailed to U.S. aircraft manufacturers by Pan Am's Franklin Gledhill, chief

Trippe, about 1950, and who when a child built model airplanes and propelled them with rubber bands through New York's Central Park, was America's quintessential airline businessman whose world air empire nearly encircled the globe at the advent of World War Two. (*Photo Courtesy: Pan American World Airways*)

purchasing agent, in early 1936. The typewritten sheets requested the design and building of an Atlantic sky giant as never before deemed possible — an aeronautical challenge of the highest order. To promote interest, Pan Am offered $50,000 as a prize to the winning bidder.

To be sure, the selected aircraft firm whose designed ship would bear Pan Am's winged globe logo would have to achieve far more than meeting just a payload factor for the anticipated heavy mail and passenger loads over the Atlantic. Gledhill's statements demanded that the new airliner have superb long-range luxury appointments for passengers and crew during long flights. Other specific requirements included a high seating capacity, improved fuel efficiency, increased range ratio and a monumental amount of horsepower needed to meet the demands. If the builder of the future clipper could meet the line's firm requests, then Pan Am was willing to negotiate. Competition became keen.

In early March, 1936, Robert Minshall, Boeing Aircraft Co.'s chief engineer, was called into conference at the plant's executive offices in Seattle and shown the airline's letter dated February 28th. Minshall's first reaction was in the negative based on the fact that acceptance for a design would hamper the company's shaky engineering financial power.

Money was scarce. America was just beginning to drum itself out of a devastating depression. Cash reserves at Boeing showed only $582,000 in 1934. Then the following year, $275,000 was tied up when a prototype Model 294 bomber was destroyed in a test flight after the company was awarded a contract from the U.S. Air Corps to construct a new lethal air destroyer. Since the crash, the majority of slightly increased 1934 funds were in limbo during the redevelopment program for the four-engined bomber known as "Project X," and to Boeing officials as the "Experimental Bomber, Long-Range, Design One," a nomenclature for the gargantuan XB-15 which eventually unfolded as the acclaimed B-17 Flying Fortress. In addition to the money squeeze, Minshall believed an extensive area of the Boeing plant grounds would have to be improved upon in order to construct such a mammoth air boat as indicated by Gledhill's letter. Also, the layout and construction tasks alone would call for an excessive number of engineers and general assembly workers that would have to be hired. Minshall disfavored Pan Am's bid believing it to be too much of a costly gamble for his company.

Boeing's President Claire L. Egtvedt disagreed with Minshall's tabulated cost figures — that Boeing should at least give the boat program a fair shot; for whatever firm did design and build the new commercial flying boat was not only assured of international praise and recognition but would, in-turn, be granted future design work within the escalating aviation-building market. Egtvedt told Minshall to proceed with a plan design and that if he needed more manpower for his department that it would be given.

Minshall recalled a young man that had been lent to his division from the company's sales office back in January, 1936. He was Wellwood E. Beall* (1906-1978) who had just completed detailed, engineered sketches of an enormous flying boat that had racked his brain since late 1935. Beall's endeavors were excellent enough to cause talk of a promotion within the engineering department.

An impeccable dresser, Beall had started work with Boeing in 1930 as an instructor of aeronautical engineering and stationed at the old Boeing School of Aeronautics in Oakland, Calif. In 1934 he became an engineer salesman, held the position of Far Eastern Manager in Shanghai, China, for two years and then returned to Seattle in August, 1935.

While quartered in Shanghai's *Cathay Hotel*, Beall's wife Jean jokingly chided her husband for having doubts about air transportation that would soon link America and the Far East. About the same time as Jean's remarks were made, the S-42 *Pan American Clipper*, under command of Capt. Edwin C. Musick, then Pan Am's leading pilot, was surveying the mid-Pacific for the forthcoming M-130 service. At first Beall believed it to be years away before

regular air flights over the widest ocean would be established. The young engineer who was in Shanghai for a successful sale of P-26 Peashooter fighters to China was bugged by Jean's remarks. The long trip home by surface ship made Beall think of a massive plane that could cut the time by more than half — an ocean liner that could fly!

Back in Seattle, and during what spare time he had between his regular job, raising a family and flying as a hobby, Beall slaved over his dream ship at night, first on his home's dining room table and then on an office drawing board. He sketched out what later was said to be an exhalted machine that was "...not the product of trial and error experimenting."[2] Beall, like his contemporary U.S. aircraft designers, was a pioneer and, at times, considered overdaring. He lived in an era during which he, and others like him, would, in quantum jumps, improve plane structures, power plants and aerodynamics. Ahead lay many challenges. It was once said of Beall that he had "...a mind trained in engineering skills plus a creative facility of high order and had been able to see the boat in his mind's eye, complete in every detail, before he sat down to put his first sketch on paper."[3]

While Beall skillfully committed to paper what his mind transposed into visual statements, Jean now and again took to peeking in at her husband's efforts and remarked that the profile view of the drawn fuselage resembled a whale, the cetacean order of mammal

Dynamo André A. Priester was Pan Am's secret force behind the development of the 314. He was both admired and disliked by many a crewman for his stern rules and set ways. (*Photo Courtesy: Pan American World Airways*)

*Became Boeing's senior vice president in 1952 and retired from the company in February, 1964, to work for McDonnell-Douglas.

marine life. Besides her whimsical remarks and strong encouragement, Jean, having been an interior decorator, helped to formulate the plane's varied cabin color schemes in order to boost Beall's presentational drawings later given to Boeing executives for review.

Regardless of the aircraft's whale look and Jean's color scheme, Beall's fascination with a large commercial flying boat had turned into hard determination to produce. From approximately September, 1935, through June, 1936, the strong-willed engineer was not distracted from his sketching and revamping processes to reach his goal. Beall had to create through his mastered abilities, to settle what stirred in his mind ever since his return from China.

Drafted onto paper were components from the existing XB-15 bomber and many of its long-range features. Absorbing the huge landplane's technology, Beall was able to compute stress loads and needed horsepower to concoct what he believed to be Pan Am's desired aircraft. As he figured and drew out the dream boat, Beall studied other large seaplanes to guide him in his minute computations, especially the S-42 and M-130 models.

One of Beall's neatly penciled pages, dated March 27, 1936, recorded a fraction of what he was thinking at the time — thoughts focused towards using the XB-15's 149-foot wing span design: "Increase span by adding 26 inches to body width,"[4] he wrote. In essence, Beall had taken the XB-15's wings and applied them to a wider ship-styled fuselage. With the sketches nearly completed, Minshall called for Beall to once again show him the impressive plans. Then other plant executives and technicians were requested to review the work. What followed became a monumental series of meetings centering around altering Beall's rough ideas into the first formal blueprint forms. The time-consuming task started out as a risk for Minshall, but he was soon assured that what Beall had created could be a money-making proposition for the company. At that point Pan Am was notified and asked for an extension on the deadline date for submitting a proposal. It was granted and Beall was appointed chief commercial engineer in 1936.

Once the blueprints were completed Boeing was ready to submit its proposal. The commitment was typed up and mailed to Pan Am on June 22, 1936. A section of the cover letter stated, "Said Boeing Aircraft Company is a wholly-owned subsidiary of this Corporation and we hereby agree, on behalf of this Corporation and its successors and assigns, with you and your successors and assigns, that if such agreement is entered into by you we will cause Boeing Aircraft Company and/or its successors duly to perform and fulfill all of the terms and provisions of said agreement to be performed on the part of Boeing Aircraft Company."[5]

Both letter and documented proposals were signed by Egtvedt and Evan M. Nelson, assistant secretary and witness to presented exhibits.

While Boeing rushed to catch up with the bidding, other leading aircraft firms had long since responded to Pan Am's plea. Sikorsky engineers had drafted into blueprint form a forceful craft of incredible specifications and speed, an aeronautical achievement based on past, successful knowledge and experience. Sikorsky's proposed boat, the S-44, would have a 124-foot wing span with a hull length of 70 feet, three inches, and was to be powered by four Pratt & Whitney 1050 powerplants. The ship's swift-looking lines complimented her 3,000-mile range at a speed of 200 m.p.h. with the ability of carrying 40-day passengers or 16 sleepers plus a five-membered crew. The liner was extolled by Sikorsky as flying the fastest of speeds with a maximum load over the greatest of distances.

Consolidated Aircraft in San Diego came to the fore with what they called the XPB2Y-1, a large four-engined flying boat that evolved from the famed Catalina line, the twin-engined PB-Y amphibian later used by the U.S. Navy and Royal Air Force (RAF) during World War II as a rescue and reconnaissance plane. The XPB2Y-1 had also been built for the military, the prototype of which was ready for tests in December, 1937. Consolidated, like Sikorsky, was not new at constructing flying boats. The former, later named Convair, had, by 1930, put into production the Commodore, a reliable twin-engined transport used by Buenos Aires Airlines (NYRBA) and Pan Am for flights between the U.S. and South America. Additional seaplanes also bore the Consolidated mark.

To meet Pan Am's 1936 deadline date, Consolidated hurled forth a rushed commercial version of their XPB2Y-1. Although striking in appearance, the boat did not have the range of Sikorsky's S-44 and hence was turned down by Pan Am. The model, however, was later modified for the military and became the PB2Y Coronado, a transport capable of carrying 44 people plus a crew of five.

In Southern California, Douglas Aircraft Co. rejected Pan Am's request for a marine-type liner as they were in the process of developing the then large DC-4E for American, Eastern, Trans Continental (now Trans World) and United Airlines. Interesting too was the fact that Pan Am, besides extending its financial arm out for a new flying boat, had agreed to pay 11 percent for underwriting the one million-dollar fee to Douglas for building the DC-4E experimental model later sold to Japan. Trippe had been toying with the idea of incorporating landplane service with existing flying boat routes. But by late 1938, the triple-tailed DC-4E prototype had run into unexpected costs and Eastern, Pan Am and TWA pulled out, leaving American and United (the latter being the instigator of the DC-4 project) holding the bag. Pan Am and TWA then turned to Boeing who then constructed the four-engined, 148,000 pound B-307 Stratoliner, the world's first pressurized transport. Five luxury 307 landplanes were delivered to TWA in 1940 with three going to Pan Am. Pan Am placed their craft on the Caribbean-South American routes while TWA operated their share between New York, Chicago and Los Angeles.

Although landplane service — as we know it today — was to eventually dominate the world's airlines, transoceanic flying in the late 1930s was strictly maintained by flying boats due to the lack of ground facilities within the major countries and at the many

England's S-23, used mainly along its Empire routes to the Near East, fell short of competitive transatlantic service due to its lack of payload and range capabilities. (Photo *Courtesy: British Overseas Airways*)

steppingstone islands. What airports were available were scarce, and those that did exist were inadequate in runway length to accommodate large land-based airliners that would have to be built to cross the wide oceans. Major seaports of the world were the 1930's answer as they offered less expense to facilitate than did their counterparts. In addition, the big box-shaped flying boat hulls provided for more commodious spacing than did the cylindrically-shaped landplane fuselages. More freedom of movement was afforded passengers and crew within the flying boat design despite the slowness of speed and hence greater length of time in which to reach a destination. The psychological safety effect upon passengers while soaring high over great expanses of water was enough to maintain the flying boat design.

One by one, aircraft engineers and designers completed their deadline drafts and journeyed to New York for review and dragged-out conferences. Heading Pan Am's technical staff as chief engineer was Ándre A. Priester (1891-1955), known as "Mr. Airline himself."[6] It was Priester's extensive experience with aircraft design and mechanics that helped determine what company would be the winning bidder for the transatlantic clipper.

Conservative Priester was a perfectionist and often disliked by some associates as well as by many clipper crew members. Being Pan Am's operations chief, his main priority was overlord to any plane design accepted by the airline. He battled with construction engineers in having them meet current safety standards and programmed each of the plane models, beginning with the S-40, into flying laboratories as a means for studying and implementing improvements for each succeeding model. Priester had a mania for extreme orderliness within the realm of passenger safety as related to aircraft performance and efficiency. It was Priester who organized Pan Am's early pilot-training program, including the 1934-35 hotel format on the Pacific Islands of Oahu, Midway, Wake,

Guam and Luzon. A Pan Am PR statement read in part, "...his plans were so perfectly worked out that when the operations began he did not find it necessary to leave his office to supervise them."[7]

Like Trippe, Priester was extremely shrewd. While assisting his boss build an air empire, the zealous Dutchman searched to find the best solution to all problems at hand. Born in Krian in the Netherlands East Indies, the ranking executive served in World War I as a first lieutenant with the Royal Netherlands Army. After the war Priester studied aircraft maintenance and basic plane construction for a year and learned to fly from British war ace Capt. Hindcliff. In 1920 Priester went to work for Royal Dutch Airlines (KLM) for five years. Within the first sixth months he became assistant operations manager. Interested in long-distance flight, and believing the U.S. was becoming the leader in aircraft construction and commercial flight, Priester sailed for New York in 1925. For two years he worked for the former Atlantic Aircraft Co. as an air transport specialist and operations manager for their small airline operating between Philadelphia and Washington, D.C. Two years later he joined Pan Am after being introduced to Trippe by Anthony Fokker of the Fokker Aviation Corp.

As stated by another Pan Am PR release, "...over a casual Coca Cola in a drug store that there began a discussion between the two men which lasted far on into the wee small hours of the next morning. When the discussion ended, Trippe had found the man to handle the technical problems of his projected international, overseas airline. And Priester had found the niche in which he could at last put into actual practice his ideas of fast, efficient and safe air transport over the longest distances and the greatest obstacles the world had to offer."[8]

By the late 1930s Priester was well-admired for his ingenious skills devoted to civil aviation performance. His precise and firm manner usually proved right in the end, even though, at times, he had been heavily bucked by other qualitative engineers concerning the construction of Pan Am's long-range aircraft. He hammered away at the manufacturers until they were often on the brink of utter frustration over what the airline deemed necessary regarding superb in-flight operations. Priester assured Trippe that Pan Am liners would maintain superior safety standards, speed, range and a high degree of economy.

Priester's authoratative manner and sensible knowledge in safety pursued until his downfall within the line's hierarchy and death from a heart attack at the age of 64. While with Pan Am he had fostered unique developments for commercial flight that included long-range navigational techniques, operation and servicing. He pulled for more efficient fuels and power plants and established the strict schooling to train multiple crews similar to those of sea-going lines. The latter was in conjunction with Trippe's philosophy — to run an airline on a ship-like basis.

Clipper interiors, another Priester concern, were perfected through his office. The S-40, S-42 and M-130 models had been patterned after the posh accommodations found aboard surface ves-

From the XB-15, viewed while on a test flight outside Seattle, came forth the daughtered 314 Clipper as seen by the bomber's wing and nose design. (*Photo Courtesy: Boeing Aircraft Co.*)

sels. Originally, for example, the Sikorsky cabins were divided by bulkheads, their hatches equipped with portholes and watertight latches like aboard early Cunard liners. Overheads were of polished walnut paneling. The S-40 went so far as to have an ocean liner's salon-styled standing ashtray and an exposed life preserver hung in the aft lounge. As for the M-130s, they were extolled for their two private suites (rarely used because of the costly fare) that could be set up in the lounge's aft starboard section through the use of curtains. This was, in 1936, the jet-setters' way of elegant flying, even if there were no jet planes!

The ultimate of Priester's ship-like program was evident in the way passengers and crew embarked or deplaned a clipper. In order to step on or off a Pan Am flying boat one had to walk across a Priester-conceived gangplank sided by canvas and handrails . The sight was like boarding or leaving a ship. Pan Am's entire operational arrangement encompassed ship-like efficiency, safety and comfort. Priester maintained extremely high standards despite the periodical cries such as it can't be done, or, but it will take time. Always stern and to the point with aircraft manufacturers, Priester's firm demands for a new clipper were stipulated to Gledhill who in-turn prepared the bid request-style letters. The requests out-equalled any plane to date. What flabbergasted aircraft manufacturers was the almost unreachable goals called for by Priester. Four basic demands were required, the first of which required the development of an air transport that could travel at least 2,400 miles non-stop with a headwind of 30 m.p.h., and could cruise at 10,000 feet at 150 m.p.h. with a 10,000-pound payload. The second factor insisted on a craft that could be operated with great efficiency with a minimum amount of fatigue to the crew, coupled with an extreme maximum of maintenance safety in the air and while on the water. Third and last claims were that the manufacturer provide for the best pas-

senger and crew comfort for long-range flight and to design a ship that would be as inherently safe under the existing knowledge of materials, equipment and science of flight.

Though precise and to the point, the bid seemed a bit farfetched for the day's technology. It had only been nine years since Lindbergh, known as the "Lone Eagle," flew the Atlantic non-stop, a few flight hours that hurled the aviation world towards new horizons. Then, in 1936, Priester shot for another incredible feat described as, "...the most vital designing job of the generation."[9]

As Priester patiently awaited the various blueprint presentations and the meetings to follow, Beall's dream ship took on a more concrete appearance. Minshall, to meet the extended deadline, aided Beall with 11 engineers. The compatible team began turning a Shanghai idea into reality! It was said that while feverishly working out the final prints that Beall now and then would break the tense atmosphere with his wisecracking and wide smiles. One co-worker told an interviewer that conversation of a heavy nature was not Beall's way — that he was more of a listener than a talker. Yet all knew and respected his strong assurance of self and his knowledge of mathematics. Every man under Beall's supervision admired his sound, tactful manner and wise decision-making policies.

Beall, born in Canon City, CO, and who became Boeing's chief engineer in June, 1939, first became interested in engineering when his father, a metallurgical engineer, gave him a set of drafting tools when a teenager. The technical skill achieved from the equipment aided him during his four years of study at the University of Colorado. Fascinated by Lindbergh's flight to Paris, aviation began to take on a more serious roll in Beall's life when he enrolled at the Guggenheim School of Aeronautics at New York University. Mingled between studies, Beall designed an advanced cantilevered monoplane with a detailed finery given to wing flaps. His model, utilizing new structural and aerodynamic concepts, led to a winning prize awarded him by Wright Aeronautical Corp.

While grinding his nose to the books, Beall earned enough side money to support his education by doing extensive research work for the Guggenheim Foundation. He also conducted numerous commercial tests at the university's wind tunnel laboratory. With a bachelor of science degree in mechanical engineering and a graduate degree in aeronautical engineering, Beall went to work at the Boeing School of Aeronautics in February, 1930, teaching mathematics, drafting and aerodynamics. Six years later he was completing the almost endless task of blueprinting the concept that would soon leave the drawing boards and hopefully go into production. But first there was a sale to be made.

In New York City other manufacturers that agreed to bid for the clipper project had submitted their proposals. Sikorsky was notified that his design fell short of Pan Am's needs. The S-44 had met the range and speed requirements, but the boat was far too small; it did not carry the amount of required passengers in relation to the payload quota. It was not unlike Priester to be heard saying, "too short, too small, too slow,"[10] and always in a terse tone.

However, this did not stop Sikorsky from going ahead and building the prototype S-44 which was completed in 1937. The U.S. Navy had become interested in the speed bird and had started to acquire an air armada of seaplanes and flying boats by the late 1930s.

When the archetype XPBS-1 was delivered she became a patrol bomber and was dubbed by the Navy as the "Flying Dreadnaught." Three more S-44As were later constructed and sold to a newly established airline, American Export of the now defunct American Export Steamship firm.

The same fate awaited Consolidated's clipper efforts — too small. When the bid went under it wasn't considered a great loss to the San Diego-based firm because the military had originally contracted for the PB2Y-1. Following modifications a fleet of Army Air Corps and U.S. Navy Coronados were soon flying as patrol aircraft and government transports.

Martin's entry, the M-156 "Super Clipper," was rejected by Pan Am because the cubic footage within her 91-foot-compartmented hull did not meet the requirement for unprecedented crew comfort. The earlier M-130 ships had extremely cramped quarters for flight officers, many of whom had experienced immoderate degrees of fatigue and other medical oddities while cruising hours at a time over the Pacific. Since the M-130 was studied as a failure in this regard, much improvement by Martin was required. Although very appealing in her wing span of 156 feet and 190-m.p.h. cruising speed, the 46-passenger M-156 was considered nothing more than a one-foot longer version of the M-130. The final say for any acceptable Pan Am plane design rested (as it did until 1963) with Lindbergh. Trippe had entrusted "The Lone Eagle" with this unique decision-making authority in the early 1930s shortly after the air hero went to work for the airline. It was said that Lindbergh's consiencious mind was well- likened to Priester's firmness when it came to accepting a new transport plane.

Earlier, Lindbergh had nearly turned down the S-40 design because, in his opinion, it was just an enlarged version of the S-38, a small twin-engined amphibian used throughout the Caribbean and as far south as Panama by Pan Am starting in 1926. The *Spirit of St.*

Louis flier was dismayed with the S-40 plan in that he had expected a more progressive engineering feat from the Sikorsky plant. Akin to his daunted feelings towards the S-40 were his final contentions also concerning Martin's bid. The M-156, Lindbergh believed, was just a M-130 copy, and, for a progressive airliner, it was a total disappointment from the earlier and stupendous M-130 quality begun in 1934.

Because of Pan Am's rejection, only one M-156 was built in 1937. Dubbed the "Super Clipper," the boat was test flown, taken apart, crated and shipped to Russia. Communist air executives had become eager to purchase the twin-tailed American loser for service in the Ukraine. Hence, the flying ship was sold and sent to the former "iron curtain" country with the joke tag, "Soviet Clipper." The once Atlantic air contender remained in Russian service carrying hundreds of passengers until scrapped for needed World War II metal in 1944.

By mid-1936 Pan Am had narrowed down to Boeing. Other aircraft manufacturing firms, including Douglas and Lockheed, responded in the negative. Former commitments or financial restrictions limited them to take on a clipper project of immeasurable risk.

Determined to succeed, Beall packed up his prints, a booklet of technical writings and flew off to New York in early June, 1936. With him aboard a United Airlines DC-3 were Egtvedt and Ralph L. Cram, a Boeing aerodynamicist expert assigned to Beall by Minshall. Egtvedt, who helped steer the project into its present state, went along to give the sales pitch while Cram acted as the liaison officer regarding the finer details of dynamic air flows related to the plane's control and general attitude. Beall was to make the formal presentations that covered the proposed liner's structural and over-all operational qualities and interior arrangements.

Once in New York, the rumbling and thumbing through sheets of prints and prepared statistical data began within Pan Am's Chrysler Building headquarters. A bit anxious, but with a steady hand, Beall unraveled his efforts for viewing by Priester, Gledhill and other airline executives. Questions and answers followed. Seemingly preordained by Beall's efforts, officials of the winged globe company were more than pleased — they were astonished at what lay before them. Scaled drawings envisioned a massive four-engined transoceanic flying boat that superseded Pan Am's greatest expectations for operational efficiency and safety.

Designated as the Model B-314, the double-decked boat was so large that its engines could be accessible during flight via wing passageways. Briefly scanned, Beall's marvel was 106 feet long with a wing span of 152 feet, then the largest plane — should it be accepted — ever to be built in the U.S. The prints showed a craft comparible in size to France's L-521, but far more streamlined.

Along with her fine lines the 314 rated a cruising speed of 175 m.p.h. at a maximum speed of 190 m.p.h. with a calculated 3,100 mile range (4,000 maximum.). Beautifully appointed cabins and staterooms accommodated 74-day passengers and 40 by night plus

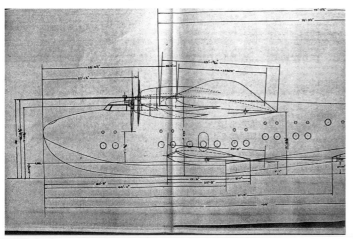

Standard portholes were first planned for the 314 as seen by this 1936 Boeing-produced blue print drawing. (*Photo Courtesy: Boeing Aircraft Co.*)

a standard crew of 10. The gross weight was set at 82,500 pounds that included a cargo capacity of more than 10,000 pounds. Beall's clipper was exceeded in size only by the impractical Do-X and Russia's ANT-20 *Maxim Gorki** and ANT-20bis, two huge landplanes built in Moscow in the 1930s. Mentally captivated, Pan Am's judges continued to be amazed as they poked over the plans and writings to spot additional facts and figures relating to the proposed clipper's specifications, power performance and updated interior arrangements and equipment.

Approximately two or three days were spent in New York before Beall, Cram and Egvedt flew back to Seattle. Anxiously awaiting word on their bid, a Postal Telegraph wire finally arrived:

"REFERRING TO YOUR LETTER DATED JUNE TWENTY SECOND NINETEEN THIRTY SIX SUBMITTING AMONG OTHER THINGS FOUR COPIES OF PROPOSED AGREEMENT RELATING TO YOUR MANUFACTURE AND SALE TO US OF BOEING MODEL THREE F0URTEEN FLYING BOATS YOU ARE HEREBY NOTIFIED THAT WE HAVE TODAY EXECUTED SUCH AGREEMENT WHICH HAS BEEN DATED TODAY=PAN AMFRICAN AVIATION SUPPLY CORP."[11]

With victory in hand, and sessions regarding compromising on varied ameliorations of the chosen liner slated for construction, all improvident corrections were in time polished off to satisfy both parties. The joint-approved contract called for a possible six additional craft. The latter was a hedge on projected growth as to the volume of anticipated mail and passengers to be carried across both the Pacific and the then up-coming Atlantic runs.

Already a slight backup in waiting lists for passage across the Pacific on M-130s was taking place. To immediately offset the problem while waiting for the 314s, the airline started a vigorous advertising (PR) campaign that suggested to the traveling air public it might consider taking an ocean cruise to Hawaii, and from the island port pick up the clipper for points westward. Since the flight between San Francisco and Honolulu was the only overnight journey aloft over the entire Pacific, fewer passengers could be carried on the first leg of the trip due to the amount of space taken up by the wide and lengthy berths. Some of the new 314s would, Pan Am projected, alleviate this thorn. Therefore, an agreement clause for an optional six models was written into the contract as a safe guard for Pan Am's unknown future requirements.

Boeing's 314 production announcements were sent out to mass media editors for public release by the air manufacturer's News Bureau Manager and Public Relations Director Harold Mansfield on September 26th, two months after Pan Am and Boeing agreed to all the negotiated provisions and had signed the contract. When the final papers were prepared for official file print on August 6th, and the news of Boeing's construction plans for the clipper released, mankind had recorded another epic in the transitional stage of historical events within the field of commercial aviation.

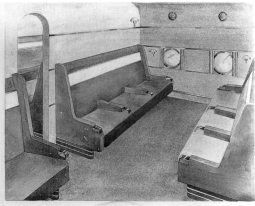
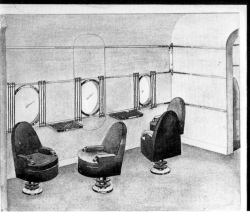
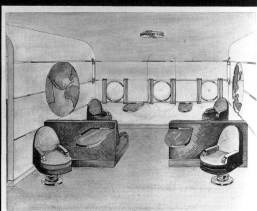

*Powered by eight 900-horsepower M-34FRN, 12-cylinder, Vee-tyre engines mounted to a 206-foot wing spread, it had a fuselage length of 107 feet, 11 inches, and was destroyed on May 18, 1935, after a mid-air collision with a heavy loss of life. The ANT-20bis, built to replace the *Gorki*, was of similar size.

October, 1936, 314 cabin (top) and lounge (lower) renderings by Boeing artist John T. Jacobsen indicated a flying ship of immense size. Squared-off lines and a more complimentary modern-appointed interior prevailed in the final product. (*Photo Courtesy: Boeing Aircraft Co.*)

2

Birth of a Liner

Plant layout and construction plans for the big boat began in earnest immediately following the signed contract. Flying boat assemblage was quite a change from Boeing's usual landplane construction, the then latest being the twin-engined 247-D transport and XB-15 dubbed the "Big Brother" to the 314. Boeing had not been in the seaplane business since 1925 when the company made final deliveries of their Model 204 single-engined floatplanes. In 1925 the comany built the famed PB-1 twin-engined Navy patrol boat that broke a number of freight-carrying records. Prior to that the company's Model C, a 1919-constructed floatplane, inaugurated U.S. air mail service between Seattle and Victoria, B.C., Canada, on March 2, 1919. By the time the 314 came along Boeing had constructed 2,000 planes of 62 different varieties.

Towards the end of July, 1936, Egtvedt and his staff had taken stock of what was needed to construct the 314. New facilities, equipment and tools were called for. Studies revealed the building of a final assembly dock; a flight test platform (barge-style) and ramp; a communications and towing launch for testing of the finished product; additional drop hammers and storing areas for the handling of lead and zinc dyes; newer machine belt-driven equipment for turret lathes, milling machines and disc-and-belt shapers; a complete sheet metal working station equipped with the latest tool designs, such as hand brakes, squaring shears, metal folders, screw and drill presses, band saws, rivet squeezers and guns, electric drills and the like; and two large plants to house 70 engineers and 1,930 workmen.

Chosen for the main assembly building was "Plant No. 1" which was eventually situated next to the narrow Duwamish Waterway that wound its way down and into Elliot Bay, a segment of Puget Sound. In order to handle the clipper project, Boeing had to move a portion of its bomber construction into extended plant facilities. Work modification for the then known "big job" was spread out between "Plant 1" and "Plant 2," the latter being a relatively new facility that stood as high as a five-storied building with a 200 foot-long sliding door. It was built for the 16-ton YB-17 bomber line which evolved out of the XB-15 and measured 204 by 304 feet with an enclosed space of more than 400,000 square feet. Clipper wings, the outer two engine nacelles and cowlings were produced in "Plant 2," whereas the 314 hulls, inner nacelles, sponsons and tail sections were assembled elsewhere throughout the 20 multi-manufacturing field shops. The boat's varied and odd-sized sections, coupled with the lack of one large plant space, necessitated the additional places of work.

Assembly Building No. 3, Plant No. 1, where it all began, housed partial construction of one of the U.S.' most popular and remembered airliners. Site was situated alongside Duwamish Waterway and is no longer in existence. (*Photo Courtesy: Boeing Aircraft Co.*)

By early February, 1937, the first jig to hold a 314's hull frame was erected in building No. 3, Plant 1. Note wood-planked flooring. (*Photo Courtesy: Boeing Aircraft Co.*)

One of Boeing's many-employed 314 engineers at work on "Drawing 15-4415" of clipper frame station 53 in 1937. (*Photo Courtesy: Boeing Aircraft Co.*)

The second 314 stage of development began when two scale models of the future flying ship were built by the tool and dye department. One model was of the hull in one-tenth actual size and the other of the entire plane in a one-twenty-fifth dimensional replica. Upon completion, both were sent to the National Aeronautics Control Administration (NACA) seaplane testing grounds at Langley Field, Va. The first model was placed in a long narrow tank and towed for simulated water runs while the other model was simultaneously hung in a wind tunnel for air flow studies, a recorded first for dual air-model-testing. Movies of the tests were made for engineering calculations. A one-fourth-sized model of the wing was also run through NACA's wind tunnel.

Most important to the success in balancing the water-towed model was finding the exact positioning of the two hull-attached hydrostabilizers called sea-wings. For correct righting water stability of the hull model the two small stubs were joined amidship on either side of the fuselage to replace the conventional wing tip-style pontoon design. Varying angles to the hull were tried on the model for best continuity in surface movement and smoothness of ease in balance. NACA's measured degree of angle for the sea-wings, prematurally selected as the actual hull model tests later proved, was the "dead rise," a higher upward slant on the front

leading edges with a sharper decline towards the back lines. Water model testing was conducted by Starr Truscott, chief NACA engineer, and John M. Allison, junior NACA engineer, of the Langley Memorial Aeronautical Laboratory. Tank testing was concluded by the two men on Sept. 16, 1936.

Boeing had selected sea-wings rather than pontoons for six reasons: the wings themselves offered better righting and maneuvering (taxiing) conditions; they provided space for the storage of fuel away from the hull; they were easier to make turns in the water in any normal wind velocity; provided for a more seaworthy structure in rough water; were structurally sounder and safer than pontoons; and the stubs acted as boarding ramps for crew and passengers. The only disadvantages were the sea-wings added more weight, produced aerodynamic drag and allowed heeling angles in cross winds when the ship was operating at slower water speeds.

Sea-wing selection was made long before the final contract was sealed. At first Boeing was hesitant on using the wing-type buoyance design, cautious only in that they might be held libel for infringement on seven patents then in existence that revealed similar construction. The earliest of the patents was recorded by Dornier in 1917, and used on many of the company's water planes including the Do-X. In order to clear itself from any possible future court action, Boeing contacted Charles L. Reynolds, a Seattle-based patent attorney of Reynolds and Reynolds, and son of Henry L. Reynolds, former assistant examiner tor the U.S. Patent Office, Washington, D.C.

Reynolds made a thorough investigation. He reported his findings to Boeing in a letter dated June 25, 1936. Among the seven existing patents Reynolds listed, only Dornier's gave any immediate thought for concern. Patent No. 1,591,475 of July 6, 1926, and based on Dornier's original 1917 patent, had seven more favorable years to go as of 1936. The registered design was similar in style to

Hull model water bouyancy tests were conducted by Boeing in March, 1937. (*Photo Courtesy: Boeing Aircraft Co.*)

Boeing's intentions: short wing stubs mounted above the hull's water line in a diagonal, continuously decreasing chord direction. Further inquiries were then made that eventually solved the international inequity produced by the Nolan Act which extended the time for making a patent application in the U.S. following the close of World War I.

Finding themselves in the clear without intent to infringe, Boeing's Vice President of Production Fred P. Laudan was told by the company's administration to set up the manufacturing schedule for the Model 314. With all miniature model tests registered as being satisfactory, and the results forwarded to Boeing from NACA, the green light to produce was given. Countless design details, including changes since the contract was signed, were marked into proper blueprint positions. After studying the plant layouts, materials, manpower and time, Laudan set the confidential master production schedule. He estimated that "Boat No. 1" would be ready for her first test flight on July 21, 1937, and therefore arranged for delivery to Pan Am on September 21st the same year. "Boat No. 2" would be delivered on Nov. 15, 1937; "No. 3" on Jan. 5, 1938; "No. 4" and spare parts on Feb. 20, 1938; and "No. 5" and "6" on April 5th and May 15, 1938. Many unforeseen delays would make Laudan's schedule plan read like a fairy tale!

In the early 314 construction stages Boeing introduced the shipyard method by using full-scaled metal templates (drawings on white-coated aluminum sheets taken directly from the shipyard-type loft where hull contour lines were laid out full size) to supplement the conventional shop blueprints. Another of Boeing's innovations originating through the 314 construction was to drill and rivet together the hull's multiple bulkheads by means of a large traveling drill apparatus that seated drillers as it moved along on wide-spaced tracks. Men and machine were straddled above the

Massive beaching cradle for 314 was float-tested at a dry dock facility at Seattle's Lake Union in November, 1937. (*Photo Courtesy: Boeing Aircraft Co.*)

placed and fitted bulkhead frames so that drilling procedures were efficiently performed with perfect vertical alignment. Electric spot welding for seaming joints in non-highly stressed sections was another Boeing invention when piecing together the 314's Alclad aluminum wing form. All exterior pieces were precisionally cut to form and electrically spot-welded before being attached by primed rivets to the wing frames,

Prior to "skinning," the securing of final aluminum sheets to both hull and wing frames, the plates were first given a coat of cadmium and then anoxized for sealing against corrosion. Under the direction of Finishing Shop Foreman Al Halvorsen, a thin layer of cadmium, a soft metallic element, was electrically melted and thinly plated onto the aluminum skins. Element-exposed surfaces were then sent down the creative shop's line and electrically anodized in glass-lined tanks semi-filled with aluminum oxide. Special reels were devised beforehand to hold the metal in place while it was anodized. Once the first clipper was assembled, the entire exterior surfaces were sprayed with two coats of aluminum lacquer which gave a shiny, sleek finish. Interior frame work and sheeting were sealed with two coats of aluminum varnish. The internal joints and seams in the hull and sea-wings were previously made watertight by means of a flannel material that had been impregnated with clear varnish and sealed with an industrialized non-friction tape. Then came the last sealing of aluminum varnish.

Two great keel jigs, called "docks," lined "Plant l's" 500,000 square-foot floor where the 314 hull frames were assembled. Each dock was set in steel and concrete, the first ready for use in early 1937. Each dock measured 115 feet long by 36 feet wide and 27 feet high. For final tail, wing and sponson assembly, Boeing developed an outdoor dock for launching the completed liner. The latter was surfaced with wood planking and had, in addition to a regular flat pier paralleled to the plant's floor line, an inclined ramp also set

Kenworth Motor Truck Corp.'s 15-ton-structured steel 314 beaching gear was 16 feet wide by 22 feet long. It is shown undergoing a static 50-ton test. Additional flotation tanks were later installed to gear's sides. (*Photo Courtesy: Boeing Aircraft Co.*)

One bulkhead and wing spar frame section of steel and aluminum alloy on full-scaled template was pieced together by means of the specially designed and moveable drill jig which ran along outer rails, April, 1937. (*Photo Courtesy: Boeing Aircraft Co.*)

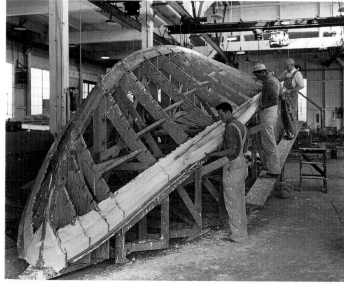

Under the direction of Jack Elswick (extreme right on plank), two workmen help form 314 hull bottom mock-up used to make drop hammer dies for clipper's forward hull section. (*Photo Courtesy: Boeing Aircraft Co.*)

in concrete where the 314s would be guided atop a short rail that led down to the Duwamish Waterway by the use of electric winches and cables.

Curtailed by the mass building of bombers and clippers, Boeing sub-contracted for the construction of the cradles needed to haul the flying boats into and out of the water for major and general servicing during their years of operation. Kenworth Motor Corp. of Seattle, specialists in building sturdy industrial trucks, buses and trailers, was selected for the job. Kenworth and Boeing signed a five-paged contract on April 29, 1937, for 12 dollies based on Boeing specification manual D-1648 through which a wooden test model was built at about the time the small clipper models were undergoing NACA testing. Each rig was priced at $7,000, and the contract called for 20 percent down before work was begun.

Under the direction of Kenworth's Chief Engineer James W. Fitch, each of the steel beaching gears had eight hard rubber ramprail wheels that measured 16 feet wide by 22 feet long and weighed 15 tons. V-shaped to fit a 314's hull bottom, the first and then largest flying boat cradle in the world was land-tested with a 50-ton load of wood and lead weights equaling more than a 314's weight. On Nov. 2, 1937, the dolly was lowered into and out of Lake Union near Seattle by a 36-ton crane to test the cradle's two large floatation tanks for correct water buoyancy. The static road testing was done on October 28th at Seattle's Terry Ave. and Harrison St., a location then occupied by the Great Northern Yards.

At the conclusion of the tests the cradle was towed by truck back to the Kenworth plant where it was taken apart and inspected. No yielding of steel or failure of any structures was found. Six engineers, three from Kenworth, one from Pan Am and two from Boeing, witnessed and recorded all three test phases. Kenworth

proceeded in construction and in time shipped the first six cradles to Pan Am's home bases in Baltimore, Port Washington and San Francisco at the airline's expense.

In July, 1937, Elswick put finishing plaster of Paris molding over 314's hull bow mock-up for the drop hammer dye process. (*Photo Courtesy: Boeing Aircraft Co.*)

In June, 1937, Plant No. 2 Wing Shop Foreman Ernest Orthel (left) and Shop Clerk D. P. Adams held a P-26A wing spar to compare against the 314's structured span likened by some employees as that of a bridge trussing. (*Photo Courtesy: Boeing Aircraft Co.*)

spection work as mandated by the bureau for an acceptable U.S. commercial air transport. While Quick was busy recording sea-wing results, the 314's 49 foot-long horizontal tail stabilizer took on an awesome size in another section of "Plant 1." The form's surface was greater than the total wing area of a twin-engined, 14-passenger Lockheed Lodestar, a small but popular air carrier of the day.

Surrounding the first two 314 hulls, which neared completion by late September, 1937, was a maze of scaffolding trussed up from three and one-half carloads of heavy lumber. Stretched around each clipper were five levels of gangways. Combined, they totaled one-half mile in length, were three feet wide and connected by 300 feet of stepladders at various levels.

Boeing's first two 314 creations were so large that toward the end of 1937 the liners were referred to as "flying hotels." Others claimed them as "flying palaces!" Some who viewed the first two clippers under construction questioned anything as massive and weighty as what was before them would ever fly. Many faces of security-controlled visitors who wandered through the plants on guided tours for the first time, such as World War I Flying Ace Eddie Rickenbacker, showed great astonishment. John Borger, a young Pan Am engineer selected by the airline as their Atlantic Division's 314 project engineer, exclaimed as he walked into "Plant 1," his eyes drawn as though by a magnet to the two hulls locked in their jigs, "Jesus Christ!"[12]

As big as the 314 seemed on paper, the more grand it became as the boat-shaped hull progressed in size. Both wings for the first clipper built, assembled in five sections, added to a large scale. The two wing spars for one 314, joined later as a unit and made up of bolted and riveted duraluminum to support the incredible wing span, stretched 59 feet in length. They were basically composed of a channel of square tubing. Weight for the hull from top center to bottom of keel line was 19 feet, while over-all height from top of tail to

Dimensions of the first 314 soon became astronomical — even more so when the eye began to pick up and transmit to the brain the huge shapes of massed steel and duraluminum that began taking on a solid form. First came the center fuselage and hull sections built mainly of steel. Embodied into a single unit, they were assembled upside down simply because it was the easiest manner in which to construct.

Finished in April, 1937, the two-ton steel center frame consisted of, besides the outer duraluminum-covered and inner two truss-type bulkheads and V-shaped mid-hull bottom, the middle wing spar joint and the two inboard engine housings. Fore and aft monocoque-contoured hull fittings were then added to complete the 314's fuselage. Simultaneously assembled side by side, and similar to the methods in building surface ships, the assembled parts for two clippers were then moved into the two keel jigs.

Dressed in its Alclad covering, the mid-section of the first 314 was completed on June 26th to await its connection to the other bulkhead and longitudinal stringer-constructed parts. Across the way in the forward portion of "Plant 2," double port and starboard wing-trussed-type spars were placed in their jigs to undergo installation of ribs, compression struts, a layer of corrugated aluminum plating and an anodized layer of smooth outer sheeting, nacelles and engine mounts. Steel tubing was used for the mounts that were cut to length, ground down to proper shaping and then clamped into position where numerous welds were made. Surfaces were then machined smooth, sand-blasted and plated.

Both sets of ailerons for the clipper were also completed by late July. One sea-wing at that time underwent a final leakage tank test supervised by Raymond B. Quick, chief inspector for the Bureau of Air Commerce. Quick was in charge of all testing and in-

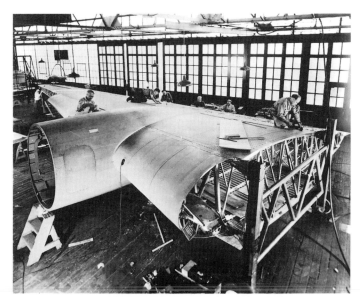

Starboard wing of first clipper built takes shape in Plant No. 2. (*Photo Courtesy: Boeing Aircraft Co.*)

By Oct. 5, 1937, the 314's trailing wing-edged ribbing was completed and attached to forward wind-lifting panels. (*Photo Courtesy: Boeing Aircraft Co.*)

A sight that stunned plant visitors was of the 314's center section in August, 1937, with its upper steel wing spar and engine nacelle housings just prior to its man-rolled move into hull assembly jig for attachment to forward and rear fuselage sections. (*Photo Courtesy: Boeing Aircraft Co.*)

keel measured 27 feet, seven inches. The hull beam was 12 feet, one-half inch. Total exterior surface of the blocked and tapered ship was one-tenth of an acre, or 4,000 square feet with an additional wing area of 2,867 square feet composed of square tubing, channel ribbing and Pratt-trussed spars.

Beall contended, "And it did look big, even to those of us who had been with it from the inception of the design. But we shared none of the lay visitors' skepticism as to its ability to fly. The art of aeronautical engineering has advanced to the point where it is possible to design a plane to fill a given job and predict quite accurately the plane's flight performance before its throttles have even been opened. Hence, we knew that the airplane would fly, and fly well, and that at most it would require merely some amount of adjustments in its many mechanical details and functions. These would be worked out in the airplane's actual flight test program to make it fulfill the high standards that had been set for it."[13]

From crude, urgent planning came forth another of man's wonders.

When Beall first started to plan the immense clipper he took into consideration one of the first principals of good design: take what you have and go from there. Since sound and practical knowledge leans towards what has taken place in the past, Beall went back to study the old PB-1 fuselage as well as the Sikorsky and Martin clippers. Analyzed at his private residence, the basic boat-styled V- bottom, first designed by American aviator and plane builder Glen H. Curtiss, was redrawn in an enlarged version both in length and width to fit the lower section of the XB-15's fuselage. Combined, the comprehensible formula dictated the final 314's hull.

The bottom part of the great flying boat had a pointed rear step and an athwartship main step located midway down the length of the hull. It was found by past experience, as tested and built by

Curtiss-designed flying boats, that a tapered rear step reduced aerodynamic drag which gave the V-bottom hull excellent water-running characteristics. This allowed for the installation of a water rudder thought to be necessary according to NACA's model testing. The rudder was attached to the aft vertical point line of the athwartship step and believed, at the time, essential to any and all water craft, and therefore a must for the big 314 in her taxiing and mooring maneuvers. Strangely enough, the square marine control mechanism was later eliminated after having proved worthless in its purpose for design. But during the early, theorized testing the addition was believed important, for if large surface-going vessels had rudders so too must the 314!

Giant cavern-sized 314 engine nacelles lined Boeing's Sheet Metal Shop by September, 1937. (*Photo Courtesy: Boeing Aircraft Co.*)

Trussed up in a web of scaffolding, the first clipper undergoes alloy sheet metal skinning in late 1937. (*Photo Courtesy: Boeing Aircraft Co.*)

Center framing that housed lounge shown in jig just before securing to other hull parts. Note boat-shaped bottom. (*Photo Courtesy: Boeing Aircraft Co.*)

Beall and associates knew, as based on Pan Am's major demands, that the 314 would require a near undeveloped source of power. This in turn forced engineers to design a wing and engine nacelle structure to dazzle even the most imaginative soul. The structural solution to carry such thrust was already formed and tested in the XB-15's wing. It had been put through every stress-testing program known to date. One whole panel built for examination purposes was given numerous load tests. Eventually the pressured conditions led to the planned panel's destruction by extensive lead weights in order to finalize all approved calculations.

The XB-15's wings were so encompassing in size that an in-flight mechanic was able to crawl through the inner structures via catwalks that extended out into the nacelles. This unique feature, located along the wings' inside leading edges, was an added safety measure in that minor power plant repairs were possible while the plane sped through the atmosphere.

Priester insisted that the 314 maintain the XB-15's wing tunnels — a prime feature for transoceanic flight. However, there was one major problem that had to be resolved. A new and more powerful engine was needed. The XB-15's four Pratt & Whitney R-1830 engines were under-powered for the huge bomber giving a total of only 4,000 h.p. for takeoff, far under what was required for the 314.

Luckily for Boeing, Priester had earlier approached Wright Aeronautical Corp. of Paterson, N.J., for a more advanced engine. Wright had just gone through a successful program with the U.S. Army testing their new Double-Row Cyclone GR-2600-A2 power thruster. It was then offered to Pan Am and Boeing in the nick of time. Boeing at first hesitated but soon realized that the 14-cylinder Radial, twin-ignition valve-in-head power achiever was the only mechanical wonder then available. Beall wondered if the four Wrights, weighing considerably more than the total loaded weight

of a 10-year-old B-80A transport, could maintain a fully loaded 41.5-ton clipper in flight. Tests proved it could, but only through use on smaller military aircraft where one GR-2600-A2 put out 1,500 h.p. for takeoff and 1,200 h.p. for cruising at 2,100 rpm at 4,400 feet. Wright stood behind their product and Boeing and Pan Am engineers had no recourse — to push on or delay the 314 project. There was no postponement; Wright's past reputation as a reliable producer settled the matter.

Wright made no public announcement until March 3, 1938, that their then highest power-rated engine would be used commercially.

In a PR release, Wright stated that four of the engines for one 314 generated "as much power (6000 h.p.) as 10 of the 12 Curtiss Conqueror engines which powered the Do-X, and twice the power for takeoff."[14] In addition to the clipper's use, the U.S. Navy had also selected the GR-2600-A2 for their contracted Martin-built Mariner twin-engined patrol boats.

Beall's earlier decision that four engines were ample enough to lift his cantilevered, high-wing monoplane into the air was carried forth into the preliminary design requisite. However, as compared to past clipper models where engines and wings were suspended high over hulls, the 314's engine and wing mounts were

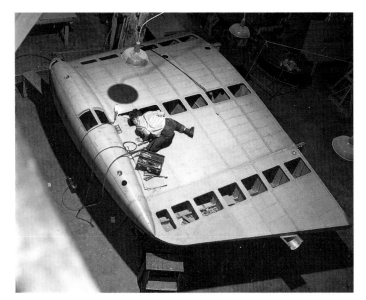

Massive port sea-wing nears completion that also stored two large fuel tanks. (*Photo Courtesy: Boeing Aircraft Co.*)

molded together and the latter attached directly to the fuselage. Each gigantic and protrusiled engine housing, similar to an XB-15's, measured five feet, nine inches in diameter and could, for size comparison, hold four men comfortably.

Curved to correspond with the power shells, and located just forward of the wings' leading edges, were hinged doors that opened out and down to rest in a horizontal position. The hatches provided a working platform for future Pan Am ground crew when the ships were docked or beached. The sturdy openers were but a larger design feature carried over from the M-130s. Extra light weight collapsible working frames were also stored inside a clipper's wings that could be attached to the outer sides of each engine casing by mechanics for additional platforms for forward work near the props.

One of the biggest problems faced by Beall was how to keep the weight of the near all-metal plane down versus the amount of fuel to be stored aloft for great distances. Any savings in fuel weight, it was figured, would be against the savings in structural weight. The total amount of fuel was set at 4,300 gallons with a maximum oil tankage of 300 gallons.

It was Priester who needled Beall and his men to increase the ship's total gross weight from 37 to 41.5 tons. His applied pressure needled the minds of Boeing's men to make concessions in design that eventually led to the 314's emergence as the near perfect plane she was.

Externally speaking, the 314 was to have "clean lines," the visual appeal as seen in a Douglas-built DC-3. Free-form contours in wings, tail and hull were necessary to undermine the otherwise great weight problem that would have confronted engineers in aerodynamic design. In solving the weight predicament, the 314 was given a cantilevered wing with an aspect ratio of 8.05 for the balance between aerodynamic and structural considerations. It was positioned where it neatly intersected the hull and tapered in both

plane and thickness, thus eliminating the old plank-type span found on the S-40, S-42 and M-130 clippers. The latter two models had neck supports which joined wings and hulls supported by a maze of clew lines and braces that added up to an excessive amount of extra weight and drag. Beall's 314 wing design introduced a new concept for flying boats by offering a low profile drag with a high left-drag ratio for cruising. The extensive eagle-like span was also easier to construct in that the same contours were given to both upper and lower surfaces.

In order to maintain the low profile air resistance when in flight, the paired appendages incorporated a split-trailing-edged wing flap that supported the 314 in her lift coefficiency. For landings, a deflection of 60 degrees with full flaps was incorporated. A flap angle of 20 degrees was figured for takeoff under a useful load of 33,955 pounds (15,402 kg.) with a power-loading of 13,75 pounds h.p. (6.24 kg/h.p.).

Wing tips were finely tapered with enclosed flotation tanks to help keep the flying boat on an even keel while sloshing through wind-tossed surfaces. In the event the whale-like hull dipped on a rough surface, it could not, in theory, capsize as the sea-wings and

One of two 600-gallon gasoline wing tanks under final soldering by Boeing's acetylene torchman Samuel H. Tompkins. Four similar tanks, each of 750 gallons capacity, were installed in the two hydrostabilizers. (*Photo Courtesy: Boeing Aircraft Co.*)

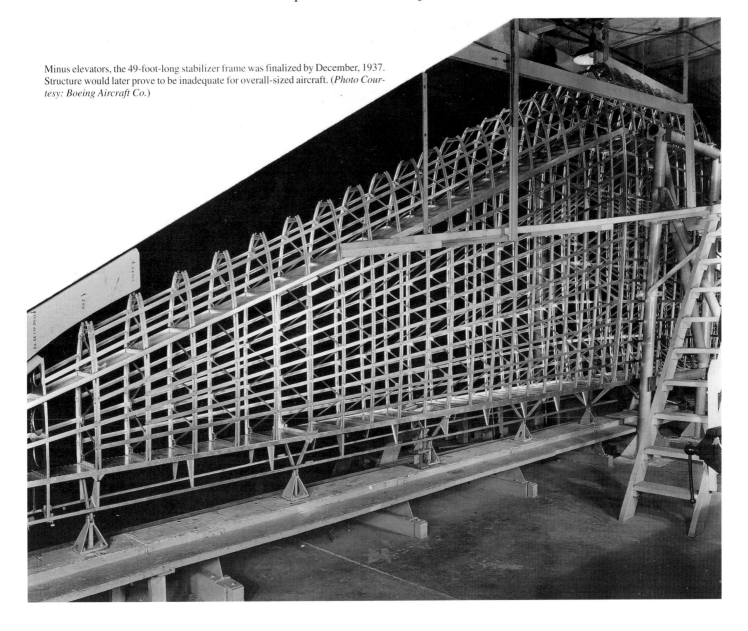

Minus elevators, the 49-foot-long stabilizer frame was finalized by December, 1937. Structure would later prove to be inadequate for overall-sized aircraft. (*Photo Courtesy: Boeing Aircraft Co.*)

flotation tips would automatically right the otherwise floundering liner.

Wing trim and control tabs, made of aluminum tube-and-channel framing with doped canvas covering, solved the engineering task for control surfaces and flight control. Four "Frieze" -type ailerons (two per wing and each supported by three hinges) were used in a semi- irreversible gear to reduce any yaw and were attached directly to the main cable system within the hull. Each aileron had a trim tab that was divided in half along each wing span so as not to bend or bind the hinges when the wings deflected in flight. Trim tabs, acting as a separate unit, were utilized on the ailerons.

The 314's wing elevators were so large that by regular 1930's aerodynamic conventions they would have been very difficult to control manually. Special tabs were connected to the fabric-covered elevators that linked them to the control system. There were four tabs (two per wing), with one set to master the trim and the other for control. These expedient and ticklish installments were activated by means of "spring links" that, when maneuvered by the captain or first officer, automatically adjusted the tabs and elevators to the desired angle. Trim tabs gave assurance of equal aerodynamic balance through their various settings.

Each elevator was based on the "mass" and "static" balance principals that offered 85 percent of the clipper's in-flight stability. A captain's manual use for elevator control was required for the remaining 15 percent. "Static" balance was accomplished through a weight placement located dead center of the hull and wing intersection while "mass" balance was distributed at the tip of each elevator. Both of these important counter placements for weight load kept the plane on as much a longitudinal flight level despite varied weather conditions. The grueling effort put forth by Boeing toward lift and balance resulted in the most advanced aero-engineering job at that time as related to wing size and its corresponding elevator control system.

When the U.S. Army began testing Wright's engine, Cram became preoccupied with studies as to what type of propeller should sustain the clipper's flight. Turning to Hamilton Standard, the company that fitted out blades for the XB-l5, Cram asked for efficiency and thrust data on Hamilton's latest prop design. Once received, Cram studied efficiency curves for cruising, high speed level flight and takeoff that reflected excellent performance calculations when the prop was combined with Wright's power source. As with Wright, Pan Am financed Boeing for all controls and necessary equipment including the props.

"It is recomrcnded that every effort be made to obtain the Wright R-2600-A2 for Model 314 with 5.3 gearing," Cram wrote in his Nov. 27, 1936, propeller study, "and that Hamilton Standard, 3-blade, constant speed, full-feathering propellers of 14-foot diameter with blade design 6159 be purchased."[15]

Shortly thereafter, Hamilton Standard was sub-contracted to produce the multi-sets of variable pitch screw props to impel the clippers forward at their top and normal cruising speeds of 190 and 150 m.p.h. Only a slight modification was in order before the props could be accepted by Boeing. The round shank section had to be redesigned as it faired too far out from the hub to allow for engine cooling while the ship taxied on the water. Correction was made when the blade airfoil was brought closer to the hub and the coweling ends flair-vented for cooling. Hamilton's molded and polished steel prop had a central hub with three radiating blades that twisted in a manner so that they formed a part of a helical surface. Except for size they were nothing new in the aircraft business.

Upon learning of the standard-type prop to be used, Priester became totally dissatisfied — not with the product, but with its efficiency limitations, especially since Pan Am was footing the prop bill. After immediately working out an engineering campaign with his New York-based staff, Priester flew to Seattle to consult first with Boeing and then later with Hamilton Standard. He demanded from both companies a mutual effort for the creation of a hydro-static, full-feathering mechanism — a device that could shut down a troubled engine without having to worry about a slow, windmilling and uncontrollable prop. Such a hazardous and bothersome state could be eliminated Priester believed. He demanded "feathering," the ability to halt a prop in the air by use of a switch that activated the blades from a flat-faced surface to turn inward which, in-turn,

Similar to hand-finishing a Rolls Royce, skinning of 314's stabilizer called for exact splicing of alloy-sheeting and precisioned drilling, a novelty of the day. Clipper's tail unit had an area much greater than a wing of an earlier-produced Boeing 247 transport. (*Photo Courtesy: Boeing Aircraft Co.*)

caused less air drag. A cut engine and stilled prop would enable an engineer to work more safely while making minor repairs in flight.

Hamilton engineers first told Priester that after exhaustive and verified testing on his behalf that his prop demands were considered impractical.

"Not by my figures,"[16] Priester retorted!

Pan Am's dynamic personality got his design. From that day forward, and until the end of prop-driven aircraft, airplane designers around the world incorporated the executive's impeccable ingenuity. The first four 314 tractor thrusters shipped to Boeing for installment combined the Priester-fostered hydromatic mechanism with variable pitch that included a new braking, full-feathering system.

As the 314 ship-styled construction continued, minute planning was also given to the boat's posh interior that entailed Pan Am's requirement of establishing outstanding luxury appointments for passengers and crew. From the very start Beall stipulated that the flying ship was to have two decks, one for flight operations that included a crew's sleeping quarters, mail and cargo holds, while the lower deck was to be entirely devoted to sumptuous passenger accommodations . The clipper's planned interior arrangements soon became the epitome for luxury aloft.

3

Luxury Aloft

Spacious and opulent in its layout, the 314's passenger deck was an engineering delight — a combination of mind work and handicraft accredited to both Pan Am's and Boeing's endeavors. Divided into 11 compartments, the square-shaped lower-decked hull cabins had an awe-inspiring ambiance as they teared upwards towards the stern. An over-all effect of shipboard life, plush in every aspect imaginable, was evident. Priester was sure of that fact!

Begun in late 1936, and completed in mid-1937, was a scale-sized interior mock-up made of plywood and cloth and assembled on the lower level of Boeing's engineering department. Two dummy compartments, one of the lounge and the other a standard stateroom, were amassed and furnished with all approved fineries. Other mockp sections included the flight deck, wing cargo compartment and the men's and women's dressing rooms. In another assembled area were the galley and spiral staircase dummies furnished only with plywood fixtures which allowed Boeing and Pan Am engineers to plan, test and finalize all appropriate interior detailing.

All cabin appointments and arrangements were directed by Pan Am engineers in conjunction with Norman Bel Geddes, famed industrial designer. Geddes, a former New York theatrical set artist of the 1920s, and who later opened a Manhattan-based studio lab, became a leading figure in the esteemed Art Deco-style movement.

Credited for coining the word "streamline" in relation to architectural, industrial and interior fashions, Geddes was contracted by Pan Am in late 1936 for his practical, yet artistic solutions in designing cabin and galley layouts relevant to safety, compactness, comfort and general appearance. His previous and striking work on the M-130s was well akin to the advancement of American aviation "Modernism."

Geddes' M-130 furniture, upholstering and bulkhead lining was designed for efficiency and had zippered seams for instant removal during over-all maintenance. In-flight dishware was another of Geddes' understanding of detail. Used by various airlines, the plates and saucers had vacuum bottoms that clung to tables in rough weather. His chief concern for commercial air products was based on new space economics relating to light weights, more functional and feasible items and materials and for, in general, any product that would be a time saver for converting day cabins into flying bedrooms. Mere decoration was not Geddes' way—streamlining was! Function over design was always a prerequisite with Geddes as seen in the 314 layout.

Within each of the clipper's standard passenger compartments, called staterooms, were low-slung divan-type seats. To keep weight down, furniture frames were made of duraluminum and porthole

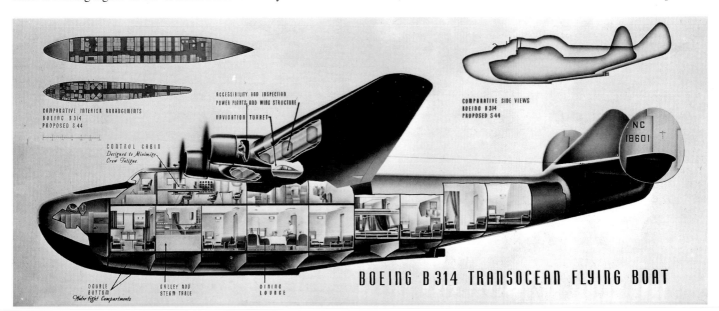

Scaled 314 deck plan indicated unparalled luxury, a magnificent interior equated to a flying hotel. Boeing Clipper is compared in size and roominess to earlier-rejected Sikorsky S-44 boat. (*Photo Courtesy: Pan American World Airways*)

panes of a plastic stronger yet lighter than glass. Cushions were overstuffed with a newly developed softness made from curled Australian horsehair mixed with latex, while a light weight carpet of varied hues covered the entire passenger deck.

Soundproofing was kept at a reasonable level using a new "Dry-Zero" insulating material that consisted of spun glass, wool and felted kapok, the latter being a substance made from silky pod fibers taken from the tropical ceioa tree. The use of these fibers, similar to the type used by explorer Rear Adm. Richard E. Byrd in his ice-locked shack in the Antarctic, allowed sound waves to pass through the porous fabric and, in-turn, acted as a heat insulator. The light weight material was fastened to outer bulkheads, overheads and stateroom partitions that allowed for easy cleaning removal.

Once the 314's Geddes-designed furnishings were approved by Pan Am, arranged for shipment and further testing by Boeing, the airline sub-contracted Howard Ketcham, a New York color expert, to coordinate the ship's interior hue scheme. Selected in 1936, the cabin colors had to reflect light as well as to give a visual airy look. If too drab, a psychological effect of closeness and mental state of boredom for passengers and crew was assured during long flights. Then, if the colors were too bright in intensity, the glare would redden one's eyes . Only after many scientific studies was

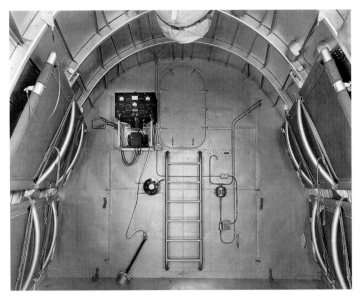

Aft view of anchor room with folding crew bunks and additional communications radio set. Accommodation ladder led up to hatch that opened to bridge between pilot seats. (*Photo Courtesy: Boeing Aircraft Co.*)

Ketcham finally satisfied with the hues he named as being "skyline green, Miami-sand beige" and a semi-deep shade labelled in the honor of the airline called "Pan American blue."

The 314's passenger deck was simple in concept and extremely elegant in appearance. Beginning forward in the bow, just aft of the anchor room, was stateroom A. It measured 12 feet across by seven, one-half feet in length and seven, one-half feet in height that seated 10-day passengers. To starboard were two facing rows of three-abreast davenport-styled seats. To port, separated by the main aisle Pan Am called the "promenade," were four additional-grouped luxury seats. Each divan was fashioned with a removable arm rest, low cut and extremly wide. All were adjustable-backed-cushioned and plushy upholstered in an all-wool, tan-dyed tapestry fabric in a cross-check pattern with a weight of 1.75 pounds per square yard. Arm rests and cushions were trimmed in turquoise-green leather to match the pale "skyline green" bulkhead and overhead paneling and the deeper shade of turquoise-colored carpet called "Reseda green." At the outer two bulkheads were two 12-by-17-inch square picturesque portholes centered between the forward and stern-facing seats. The panes had a thick inset frame made of a durable plastic ("Pontalite") finished off with green lacquer to compliment the cabin's hue range. Coordinated by Geddes and Ketcham, the materials had been sub-contracted through the manufactures of Johnson & Faulkner, Inc., and Schumacker & Co. of New York .

Against the main bulkhead that divided stateroom A and the anchor room, and dead center with the promenade, was one of two drinking fountains aboard the clipper. These built-in flows with disposable cups were, by past experience, necessary to alleviate a steward's burden of having to constantly keep his passengers lightly refreshed at the most inconvenient and onerous times. The stand,

Bow compartment looking forward was referred to by crew as the anchor room that was used to store extra mail and luggage. Note upper-secured and packed life raft, hung life saver (right), anchor (left) and mooring line (center). (*Photo Courtesy: Boeing Aircraft Co.*)

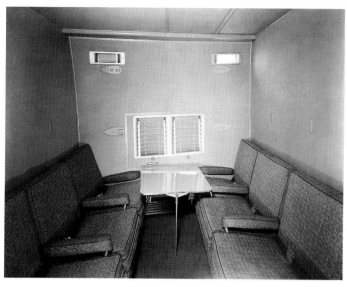

Upper-standing drinking fountain and stewards' lower cabinet separate seat groupings at forward end of stateroom A. Behind bulkhead was bow room available only to crew from upper deck. (*Photo Courtesy: Boeing Aircraft Co.*)

Starboard side of stateroom A with removeable table. Slit windows offered view for upper-berthed passengers, the assemblages of which are seen stored beneath the seats. (*Photo Courtesy: Boeing Aircraft Co.*)

finished off in black walnut, also served as a steward's vanity cabinet.

Originally, all passenger deck portholes were round in design, but changed to the square shape when Boeing began to alter the plans. Design-wise, the square portholes were more compatible looking to the ship's interior box-like lines. And, as with the first-planned windows, the horizontally striped curtains that were to have been used gave way to a more classic shade design. According to Pan Am, Priester, upon learning of the curtains for window shades, vowed his disapproval. He made a special trip to Seattle from New York, saw the porthole-curtained mock-up and voiced his negative

Port side, stateroom A. Forward compartment narrowed in width due to inward angles of bow. This viewed section was later turned into a galley extension and all of cabin a crew's off-duty relaxing station. (*Photo Courtesy: Boeing Aircraft Co.*)

opinion. The standard pull-type drapes were just not up to a yacht-like appearance — not grand enough for the 314! On Oct. 18, 1937, the porthole drapery change was made from Richard E. Thibaut, Inc., to Claude D. Carver Co. on East 48th St., New York. Carver's result was an accordian-pleated roller shade made of a washable "Tontine" material and dyed to match Ketcham's multi-compartment bulkhead lining colors. Once more Priester was satisfied!

Above the stateroom A's starboard davenports near the overhead, as found in all the standard compartments, were two rectangularly shaped portholes that allowed for extra daylight to flood the cabin and offered upper-berthed passengers a window to gaze through. Also in the after half of the overhead was a slide-fastened hatch that allowed for crew and ground mechanics to inspect the plane's forward cable controls. To port was another upper-positioned berth porthole. Each standard stateroom slept six passengers during night flight — four on the starboard side in two uppers and two lowers in cross sections to each other and two per port side in one upper and one lower in a bow-to-stern direction.

An average time of 30 minutes was required by two stewards to prepare and change a day-arranged stateroom into a snoozing bedroom. Between the seat cushions and frames were additional upholstered bed supports the length and width of one whole seating section that acted as the base for upper berths. Pulled out, they were attached 35.5 inches above the day seats and hinged to bulkhead brackets covered by plates during day travel. While the main seat cushions remained for lower berth endurance, the four-inch-thick back cushions became upper berth mattresses.

Full-length berth curtains of royal "Pan American Blue," with stitched numbers and airline insignias made of leather, encircled each larger-than-Pullman bed. Starboard arrangements measured

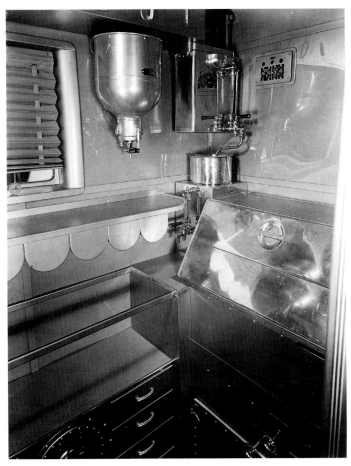

Streamlined Art Deco-styled galley looking forward was small in space but eloquently designed to hold all alimentary elements. In corner is seen juice container, automatic coffee maker and, to right, lidded steamer. (*Photo Courtesy: Boeing Aircraft Co.*)

No space-crimping here as aboard today's jet airliners, the men's posh and roomy restroom was part of station B across from galley, starboard side. Opened door exposed toilet. (*Photo Courtesy: Boeing Aircraft Co.*)

seven feet, four inches long by 38 inches wide while the port sets were six feet, three inches long and 32 inches wide. Each berth was equipped with a pillow, starched sheets, a light blue wool blanket, shoe bags, garment pockets, dark blue-enameled balsa wood coat hangers and a ventilator, call button and reading light. Terms such as "Sky bus" and "tourist class" were unheard of in Beall's and Priester's 314 world. There was only one class of travel aboard the new clipper, and it was fit for a king!

Aft of stateroom A was situated compartment B that encompassed the galley, men's restroom and stair well that connected to the upper deck. At portside was the eight-foot-long by five-foot-deep galley which housed provisions for two main meals, an abundance of intermediate snacks and assorted beverages along with an ample and varied supply of cocktails and mixes. A removable waist-high door contained shelves for storing glasses, liquor and mixes and could be rigged across the galley's entrance to form a standing bar.

Fashioned by Geddes, the galley's bulkheads, overhead lining, doorway trim and cabinets were lined with metallic, beige-lacquered Vinylite plastic sheeting for easy cleaning. Gray- colored linoleum covered the deck which was reduced to a mere four-by-four-foot

walking space by the time cabinets, counters and other accesories were installed. Positioned in the upper left corner was a one-gallon-capacity drip coffee maker while across the steward's station, and past a porthole fitted with a beige, venetian-style blind, was a built-in 10-by-12-inch aluminum sink equipped with hot and cold-running water, the latter coming from a 115-gallon tank concealed behind the overhead. Below the sink was housed a 16-gauge aluminum ice box complete with six and. three-eights-gallon ice tank. To the right of the galley's entrance was a combination stove/steamer unit with a lid and having two cast kerosene burners. A weight saver, the double unit scaled at only four pounds and held one quart of kerosene used to heat water for bouillon, tea and for steaming vegetables.

One of the most unique galley features was the advanced 16-gauged aluminum cabinet designed to contain all food for one hot meal. The entire electrically heated and shelf-lined insulated box was removable for airport stocking. Other galley equipment included two electrically operated one-half-gallon aluminum thermos jugs with lids and pouring lips to prevent spilling (used for soup and juices); two 12-by-15-inch aluminum platters; a two-tiered tray rack; four vertical dish racks for holding 200 fine china plates; two glass

Looking towards bow, gentlemen's toilet is to right while to left is seen the first and last standing urinal ever installed aboard an aircraft. A novelty, it surprised many a male passenger. (*Photo Courtesy: Boeing Aircraft Co.*)

and cup racks; one saucer rack; eight drawers; a slop bin; three steward lockers for keeping important papers and passenger passports; three store bins; and three pull-out shelves. More than 1,031 miscellaneous serving items, ranging from 10 pairs of sterling salt and pepper shakers, to 350 Gorham-sterling hotel-style flatware pieces in the "Moderen" pattern, to, amongst other items, a sterling-plated tea set, were stored in the small but well-planned galley. All kitchen supplies totalled 235 pounds, while foodstuffs and other gastric-related quantities was estimated in the 256-pound range. Every item, from eating utensils to food products, had their proper storage space.

Along the promenade, just outside the galley, were two folding steward seats. Directly across the "Miami-sand beige"-toned compartment, with its "Tango rust"-carpeted aisle, was the stair well hidden from view by a royal "Pan American blue" curtain. Although off limits to passengers, the stair conception connecting two decks later impressed many a traveler. The mere idea of flying aboard a double-decked airliner in the late 1930s gave thought to what immense sky-liners were yet to be foreseen.

Within the passageway, mounted to the extreme aft starboard bulkhead, was a steward's call-board incorporating a flight-deck interphone system, plus a 56-station call-in panel lined with signal lights connecting all cabins. To the left of this board was a door that when opened revealed the men's fashionable dressing room. Done in maroon-colored Vinylite-sheet-plastic wainscoting with "Miami-sand beige" upper-lined fabric and gray linoleum decking, the streamlined furnishings included a steward's locker, a dental counter with two duraluminum wash basins with hot and cold-running water, two mirrors sided by four Art Deco-styled light fixtures, two razor outlets, a drawer, soap and towel dispensers and, believe it or

not for the first and only time aboard any built plane, a standing urinal!

Beall, not commenting about what could happen if being used during an unexpected rough weather encounter, remarked on this almost laughable feature: "This will no doubt be an interesting innovation to the male passengers "[17] To the extreme forward right end of the compartment was a black walnut-paneled door that opened outwards to disclose the out-of-the-plane dump toilet.

Aft of station B was a standard stateroom which also seated 10-day or six-night passengers. Seat cushions and arm rests were welted with a rust hue to match the "Tango rust" carpeting that complimented the "Miami-sand beige"-colored bulkhead lining. Overhead, as installed in all cabins, was a dome-shaped light fixture that could be dimmed or brightened by a steward using a set of galley switches adjacent to the galley's drip coffee maker.

Stepping astern through a corrugated, metallic beige-lacquered "Pontalite"-trimmed doorway was the beautiful Art Deco lounge, or cabin D. This was the social gathering place used by passengers for card games, additional reading, writing and for dining. Simply laid out with its clean lines, the six-portholed grand salon was the width of a standard stateroom and 10.5-feet long, or 860 cubic feet. To port were two corner chairs with bulkhead-hinged pull-down tables finished with black walnut. Centered between was a quadruple seating arrangement with a removable table for access to one of two main entrance and exit hatchways. The starboard side had two additional quadruple groupings per corner and was also fitted with removable, black walnut tables reinforced to withstand 200 pounds. Between these two groupings, mounted in the outer bulkhead, was another main hatchway. Centered overhead were two cylindrically shaped light fixtures.

The cozy and stunning star-specked-upholstered lounge was the social gathering place for the rich and famous. Note small step ladder between divans to egress or embark through main hatch centered on outer bulkhead. (*Photo Courtesy: Boeing Aircraft Co.*)

Stateroom G, port side, between cabin F (right) and special compartment, the latter being a two-stepped higher room. Cabins, except for the suite, were the same but varied in hue schemes. (*Photo Courtesy: Boeing Aircraft Co.*)

With window and companion way trimmings yet to be installed, stateroom G, port side, is arranged in upper and lower berths similar to those found aboard first class Pullman rail cars. (*Photo Courtesy: Boeing Aircraft Co.*)

Inviting with its "Tango rust" carpeting and silvery "Miami-sand beige" bulkheads, the lounge was located directly amidship. With special upholstering by sub-contracted Richard E. Thibaut, Inc., of New York, the seats had the Art Deco look of famed 1930s furniture designers Hendrick Van Koppel and Taylor Green. Striking with their chrome, tubed frames and medium blue cushioning, the seats' fabric was different from any other standard cabin upholstering and duplicated only in the aft bridal suite. Back cushions were splashed with five white six-pointed stars set against a double, wavy-like milkyway vertical design of 26 closely woven black and chartreuse-colored thread lines.

The lounge's furniture was designed to be interchangeable from an 11-person daytime seating capactiy to the more formal 14-person dining arrangement. It could also be converted into sleeping accommodations for six persons in three upper and three lower berths. In time Pan Am decided to forego the bother of rearranging the chairs since many passengers considered the cabin a 24-hour recreation center — a place in which to converse, enjoy cocktails and to play cards and other games. Generally, but not always, it was kept in the 14-person dining order.

When meal times rolled around, especially dinner, the two stewards politely requested all passengers to exit the lounge. Once cleared, the three larger tables were covered with imported Irish linen and set with fine Lenox-made china, heavy crystal water goblets and the sterling flatware. Stewards gave final touches by adding standing linen napkins, vased flowers and printed menus. In a matter of minutes a cozy lounge had become an elegant salon not unlike a fine French restaurant. The only lacking items, it seemed, were an array of flickering candles.

Prior to the evening's meal many passengers enjoyed the cocktail hour in their staterooms where small tables were set up and attached to the outer bulkheads just beneath the portholes. Atop the linen-covered tables were placed trays of hors d'oeuvres and selected drinks. Then came the sumptuous cuisine.

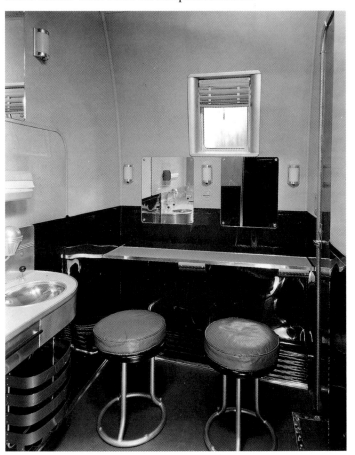

Sparkling anew in its Art Deco-appointed splendor, the women's powder room highlighted primping stools as well as other fine female amenities. (*Photo Courtesy: Boeing Aircraft Co.*)

Against the outer lounge bulkheads were triple-set portholes with beige-colored shades. The two middle panes were part of the main hatchways. Beall had devised a more flexible enplane and deplane system. He knew that for secure and stable 314 buoyance at bay on often changeable wind-conditioned harbors, a clipper would be moored to docks in diifferent positions. And because of the seasonal winds, the flying boats would be either tied down with a nose-outward direction or latched profile to a dock. Regardless of the mooring angle to a float (dock), a main entrance to a clipper was always available for enplaning and deplaning passengers and crew. Both hatches opened outward about three and one-half feet above the lounge's deck. Beall's careful placement of the doors ensured the passengers would first enter the plush salon to simulate boarding an ocean liner. A small folding aluminum two-step re-movable ladder was hinged to the bulkhead that enabled passengers and crew to step up and out or down and into the flying boats. This same light weight fixture was also used to assist passengers into and out of upper berths.

Walking through the lounge's rear doorway was stateroom E that also held 10-day passengers and six at night. It was finished in the "Miami-sand beige" color scheme. Up two steps at the compartment's aft doorway led into standard compartment F, and further astern into stateroom G, both cabins of which were com-pleted in the refreshing "skyline green." Each cabin sat 10-day and six-berthed passengers. Up another two steps was the "special" compartment situated to port that accommodated only four-day or two-night passengers. Rendered in "skyline green," the compact stateroom was labelled "special" in that it could be reserved for a party of four and, if desired by the occupants, concealed for extra privacy through the use of a full-length draw curtain of Royal "Pan American blue."

Across from the "special" compartment was positioned the second self-serving drinking fountain. To the left of the water spout was a door that opened to a lady's spacious powder room, its lower bulkhead paneling done in "Pan American blue" plastic wainscot-ing to contrast with the upper "Dry-Zero," beige-colored fabric and gray linoleum decking. Against the forward bulkhead were an alu-minum sink with running hot and cold water and a mirror. Along the outer bulkhead was a bolted dressing table having a beige "Micarta" top and sided by two swivel, turquoise leather-covered primping stools. As in the men's room, four Art Deco light fixtures and two square plate mirrors were attached to the bulkhead to ei-ther side of a porthole equipped with a beige-colored shade. Art Deco-designed receptacles for towels, kleenex and other items were also installed.

In the aft left corner of the powder room was a black walnut-lined door that closed off the small toilet room. Canned water for the two toilets and urinal came from used wash basin water. When a toilet seat was raised, or the urinal flushed, an individualized cyl-inder filled each tank with water and flushed clear all waste mate-

Looking aft through what was termed the "special compartment" can be seen the second-mounted drinking fountain (left), an emergency ladder (left rear) which reached upper-roofed hatch, and two steps leading to suite's door. (*Photo Courtesy: Boeing Aircraft Co.*)

rial — dumped overboard to dissipate into the air. Used galley sink water was simply drained out.

The bridal suite, more often termed the "deluxe compartment," was the lower deck's last stern cabin. Up another two steps from the "special" compartment was another door that opened outwards to reveal the suite's dernier cre in furnishings. Against the far up-per-curved tail bulkhead, and facing forward, was a three-cushioned davenport that made up into an upper and lower berth arrangement. At each end, between the outer bulkheads, were built-in black wal-nut side tables with lower-positioned magazine/book shelves. A love seat added a touch of finery against the starboard bulkhead just beneath two portholes. Forward of this decor was a deeply uphol-stered occasional chair angled towards an interchangeable coffee table also capped with black walnut.

At the suite's port side, against the forward bulkhead, was a combination dressing and writing desk sided with a leather, beige-colored primping stool, two lights and a mirror. At the right for-ward corner a table top concealed a wash basin. A shallow-depthed wardrobe closet with hangers was also included as was an Art Deco-

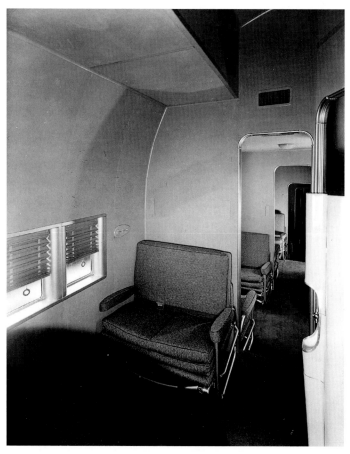

This picture-angled shot, taken from suite's doorway looking down through "special compartment" along promenade towards lounge, gives visual effect to the grand luxury once found aboard 314s so much enjoyed by the hundreds of passengers who flew aboard the liners of sea and air. (*Photo Courtesy: Boeing Aircraft Company*)

Simplified in appearance, the bow's forward hold had exposed riveted hull plating. Originally, Boeing engineers wanted to place the galley in the bow for better airflow garbage disposal, but Pan Am said no. The airline desired that the kitchen be closer to the lounge when serving hot meals. So instead, the space was used to house a six-foot-long, 91-pound stainless steel anchor with a fixing power of one-twentieth of the gross weight of the plane (4,000 pounds). Also stored in the hold were two "sway buckets " (wing anchors) that could be attached to ropes tied to hooks halfway out on the wings' undersides for added buoyance in rough water; 150 feet of three-inch Manila rope used as a tethering line; and a large tank of oil to calm a given perimeter of sea water around the craft in the event of a forced mid-ocean landing. Additional pieces of equipment included extra May Wests, bulkhead-hooked life preservers, life rafts, a bell and fog horn, an emergency radio set and four folding bunks for off-duty crew. Near the very tip of the bow was an upper mooring hatchway used by the crew for docking procedures. When opened, two cleat poles locked into place for securing tie lines. To port was a large Dutch door used for the loading of extra mail, air express and luggage and provided an opening to secure additional tie-downs. In-all, the anchor room was a more advanced version than found on earlier clipper models and afforded crews more freedom of movement.

Upstairs, and to the rear of the bridge and flight-deck, were two five-foot-long storage cabins, each with a 20-by-20- inch deck hatch used to assist ground crew in the loading of mail. Placed directly over the lounge, each of the holds measured 87 cubic feet. The first hold, reached from the flight-deck through an ironing board-shaped hatch in the deck's rear bulkhead, was bracketed off on either side of the center passageway by wire-meshed cages that held stacked and tied-down mail and freight. The port-caged hold door could be secured with a padlock for the storing of valuable cargo.

Atop the clipper, and dead center of gravity between the caged holds, Beall planned the tear-shaped celestial dome, an astro-viewing hatch encircled with six portholes and named the "blister" by Pan Am crew. A three-step ladder was connected to a small aluminum platform from where a navigator took his sightings of the sun and stars with a sophisticated bubble sextant, a fine instrument that implemented an artificial horizon "spirit" for aiding in course direction. Opening upward, the glass-enclosed hood allowed for the loading and unloading of extra mail and express.

Situated further aft was the crew's quarters that provided the airmen with three extra bunks, built-in wardrobes and drawers for their overnight gear and other personal items. In an isolated spot was a bin that contained a second emergency radio. Two small hatches in the outer bulkheads opened to the drift sight stations where two more hatches could be removed from the wings' undersides near the trailing edges. From these small openings a naviga-

styled towel dispenser. All furniture was upholsterod in the star-studded lounge fabric flashed against "Miami-sand beige"-hued bulkheads contrasting with the "Tango rust" carpeting. Built into the rear bulkhead, above the davenport, was an inspection hatch for viewing and servicing the tail's control cables.

Unknown at the time to Boeing and Pan Am, the suites would later be occupied by military brass and heads of state during the early days of the forthcoming world war. In the meantime, however, they were created for the rich and famous - - glamorous ocean liner-like cabins affording the best in world air travel.

To the extreme forward end of the ship was the 13-foot-long anchor room with a holding capacity of 3,400 pounds (density of 8.5 pounds per cubic feet based upon its 400 cubic-foot capacity). Here was stored all mooring equipment -a utility post for nautical operations when moorings were underway. An aluminum staircase was originally designed to connect with the bridge, but for space-saving measures a bolted bulkhead ladder was installed that led directly upwards to a watertight hatch located between the bridge's pilot seats.

tor calculated the aircraft's drift using a pelorus, a device at the center of a compass card about which was fixed a rim calibrated in degrees.

About four feet up from the deck in the crew's quarters back bulkhead was another crawl hole that led into a divided 16-foot-long baggage hole that measured 134 cubic feet. Total luggage weight was estimated at 4,851 pounds as averaged by the 77-pound weight allowed per passenger. Additional mail and cargo could also be carried in these two overhead compartments, especially when passengers were reduced in number for the allowed 34-placed berth occupancy. A second upper-hulled hatch was also provided for the loading of luggage.

Load figures, including passenger and crew weights, ranged between 9,100 to 21,000 pounds per trip depending on the calculated miles flown. Pan Am's 314-pound variance was based on the range versus the total weight factor. For instance, for 2,500 miles of flight, 9,100 pounds of payload could be transported; for 1,750 miles, 15,000 pounds; and for 1,000 miles, 21,000 pounds and so forth. This was charted on a 100 percent passenger, crew and storage-hold weight capacity for either day or night flying with the between scale of miles versus weight factor figured accordingly.

Many months following the delivery of the first six 314 models there appeared numerous Boeing and Pan Am PR releases, aviation articles and magazine picture captions containing inaccuracies as to how many passengers and crew a 314 could transport per flight. The occupancy figure went as high as 89 in the published media. This figure was even stated by Beall in the early stages of the model's development. The reason was based on the fact that Pan Am wanted each boat certified by the newly established Civil Aeronautics Association (CAA) as an 89-place monoplane in order to carry additional crew for in-flight training. If the 89 figure had been enforced strictly as a commercial (passenger and crew) ven-

Once occupied only by the rich, famous and nobility of state, the opulent tail suite's accommodations included, among other things, abundant space to lavishly entertain a group of fellow travellers. Looking aft to starboard is seen love seat, cornered book shelf and stand and star-studded divan section. Out-of-view to left was positioned a wash basin and an occasional chair. (*Photo Courtesy: Boeing Aircraft Co.*)

ture, then the suite would have had to become a standard stateroom seating at least eight people and the lounge switched into a 14-placed stateroom along with an additional permanent flight crew of eight. However, despite the addage of crew for training purposes, the high 89 figure was never put into play except in print. Designed for the ultimate in air transport luxury, a 314 carried a total of 58-day passengers on shorter hops (as between New York and Bermuda) and only 34 within the berth-arranged cabins for longer overwater flights which, in turn, generally allowed the hull's mid-section to remain as a social daytime lounge and for an evening's dining salon.

4

Safety over the Seas

With as many people as it was programmed to carry, great care was given to include the latest safety factors when building the 314. The most outstanding inherent safety feature was that the model was a flying boat which had a prime advantage over landplane construction in the event of a downing at sea. A flying boat could outfloat any land-based plane, and for this reason made prospective passengers feel more at ease when traversing an ocean.

Earl Jensen, second Boeing aerodynamicist 314 hull designer under Beall, likened the 314 to a surface-going ship. In the hull bottom, beneath the anchor room and passenger cabins, were 10 watertight floatation compartments. If ever a 314 was to strike an object below the water line — and the planes often did — water would only seep in as far as the watertight decking. The degree of flooding could be checked through opened hatches located along the promenade beneath the carpeting. This double-bottom, watertight safety feature was considered fundamental within Priester's strict program for air boats operating under the Pan Am flag.

Each floatation compartment was vented by a forced air system in the event of damage. A continuous air flow within any damaged tank was supplied by two vent valve connections for positive and negative air pressure that acted as a pumping device to keep the water pressure low, especially if two or more hull sections were flooded.

Access to the four engines during in-flight maneuvers was, without question, one of the most acclaimed safety devices ever devised for prop-driven aircraft. All of the 314's valves, tanks, majority of plumbing for engine lubrication, hydraulic oil, deicer fluid, water vacuum and fuel line apparatus were accessible while soaring high over the seven seas. According to Beall, if a difficulty arose early enough it could be corrected before a state of extreme danger came to fore. Periodic flight checks of engines were not uncommon.

Wing passageways were nothing new in the aircraft business but considered essential to Pan Am's safety requirements. The unsuccessful Do-X had in-flight power accessability, but it came to an abrupt end when more powerful engines were installed, thus doing away with the house casings between fuselage and wing that protected an engineer from the elements as he climbed a small ladder to reach the original Siemens-Jupiters power plants.

Far advanced as compared to the Do-X's engine accessibility design, the 314's power plants were reached directly from the hull and wing connections. Small, oval-shaped hatches with viewing

Strong-willed efforts by all engineers, and backed by the best of craftsmen (some of whom are seen nearly encased behind scaffolding at 314's prow), ensured a flying ship to be inherent with all-advanced safety factors known at the time. (*Photo Courtesy: Boeing Aircraft Co.*)

Wright's air-cooled Cyclone engines were the most powerful and reliable at the time the 314 was conceived, thus allowing for the multiple, safe journeys across oceans and continents. (*Photo Courtesy: Boeing Aircraft Co.*)

Absent of sea-wings, the cradled clipper shows its many emergency exits provided in the plane's design. The larger squared openings along the fuselage grouped in pairs give evidence to the size of exodus provided in each cabin. Exit panels were installed shortly after picture was taken on Aug. 25, 1937. (*Photo Courtesy: Boeing Aircraft Co.*)

Main heating duct, seen between upper storage-hold and plane's roofing, and its applicable solution to perform correctly, was a tricky problem to solve for such a huge aircraft. (*Photo Courtesy: Boeing Aircraft Co.*)

portholes were located at the rear portion of the clipper's flight-deck. Opening inwards, XB-15-type catwalks extended outward towards each of the engine nacelles. A flight inspector had to crawl along the catwalks to reach the engines. The mere thought of one grappling about within the wings of a 1930s flying machine well-expressed the fast-paced course aviation was taking. Never in the history of aviation was the marvel of such rapid development seen as with Boeing's creation and its fabulous inner-wing structural design. Behind each intricate engine system rested a stainless steel firewall plate that could be removed by unbolting its two sections for access to more engine parts. The casings were another added safety feature to contain any possible fume leaks or inner-engine fire within the forward-positioned mounts and to keep them from reaching the wings' passageways. Also, in the event of a failure within one of two 600-gallon-each wing fuel tank's fuel-fed pumps, all engines could be kept in motion through the supply of only one tank. An auxiliary cross-feeding system, operating from a different engine pump, excelled the needed fuel to the otherwise impared source(s) of power. A hand compressor called a "wobble pump" also provided for the lapsed function of the two electrically operated pumps if the latter failed to transfer fuel from the sea-wings' storage tanks to the upper wing tanks, and hence to the engines. The largest pump equipment for fuel transfer was contained in the 314's hull bottom directly below the lounge's decking. At least one pump was guaranteed to function at all times.

Further safety measures built into the wing structure included propeller, wing, tail and engine carburetor deicer systems along with the feathering prop installment specified by Priester. Wright's and Boeing's propeller systematics assured the highest of flight safety during winter months, especially above and through the most

unpredictable conditions of the North Atlantic. Two 20-gallon tanks contained denatured Ethylene alcohol and 15 parts of C.P. glycerin that was stored behind each of the outboard engines. Electric pumps,

Bow of first 314 depicts built-in foothold accommodation ladder that acted as an added safety measure for crew when precariously involved in line-casting maneuvers. Opened Dutch-door's lower inside paneling was also corregated for better footing — one more safety measure that evolved from the 314's detailed planning. (*Photo Courtesy: Boeing Aircraft Co.*)

Every conceivable safety and comfort item(s) was thoroughly thought out as seen by the mock-up arrangement for steward seats near mocked galley entrance along promenade. (*Photo Courtesy: Boeing Aircraft Co.*)

tors which kept a constant power revolution for maintaining correct altitude.

Such innovative thinking also led to Priester's demands for the clipper's full-feathering prop design. A switch on the engineer's panel activated a four-way selector valve that started the remotely-controlled pump. When kept down, the switch activated a solenoid action, a magnetic force derived by a charge through a tubular coil, until a pressure point of 400 pounds per square inch was reached. At that point the troubled engine's prop was feathered. To unfeather, the engine was restarted with the solenoid switch. In the unfeathered state, the power plant was kept to a minimal force of output. If not timed to a reduced power, as found during the ship's testing period, too much hydraulic oil could enter the troubled engine's crank case. An excessive amount of hydraulic lubricant caused a "slipping" engine.

Aligned with the many 314 safety features was the heating system, which at first was a major problem for such a large plane. Beall wrote, "One hazard and a source of grief on nearly all aircraft is the heating."[18] If not designed correctly, fumes could enter the fuselage resulting in a low or high heat factor at high altitudes that in turn could pose a hazard. The 314's heating system was minute in mechanical assemblage and, according to Beall, "rather unusual."[19] Air for the vent system was heated in three exhaust stack stoves on the port engines. Exhaust pipes were installed on the stoves and resisted cracking or burning out.

manipulated by rheostat knobs on the engineer's flight panel, opened or shut off the valves which held or released the anti-freeze solution via a hub-placed "slinger ring" device that automatically coated each blade while in revolution.

Deicer systems for the wings and tail were also electrically controlled through a vacuum process, a suction created from pumps on engines 1, 2 and 3 that produced deicing along the front edges of the wing and tail surfaces. Consequently, any ice that formed eventually broke off and fell away. Black boots, long stretches of rubber fitted along the leading wing and tail edges, were later attached. When electrically heated, the rubber expanded and cracked away the ice.

Not least in importance was the carburetor deicer system. At the time the 314 was being built, many aircraft, including commercial models, were without this significant advantage. One Imperial Airways S-23 crash at sea in early 1939 was linked to the lack of this type of installation. The 314's carburetor deicer system was simple in concept. A small tank was built into the center wing area that housed pure alcohol. When necessary, a pump released the fluid through an aluminum alloy tubing to each of the engines' carbure-

To keep weight down, interior porthole lining was made of a light plastic-like substance as were the plexiglass viewing panels. (*Photo Courtesy: Boeing Aircraft Co.*)

One key safety installment in case of pipe failure was "the positive pressure on the hot air and the depression in the exhaust system that would produce a differential pressure so that any leakage would be from the ventilating system going into the exhaust system,"[20] Beall continued.

If a stove did burn through, a set of by-pass valves were manually operated as a "fusible link" that enabled the troubled stoves to be terminated. Also, a vent carbon monoxide analyzer, located at the engineer's station, detected exact amounts of CO concentration. It the element was too high the instrument automatically shut down the heating system and in turn activated the panel warning lights. The exhaust-heated, hot-air ducts handled a volume of 170,000 cubic feet of air per hour that maintained a comfortable 70 degrees Fahrenheit throughout the 314's interior. The controlling thermostat was located in the lounge with a protective cover and set by the chief steward.

Even the 12-24 direct volt single wire electrical system had a built-in safety measure. Two generators, each of 80-ampere, 15volt power, were linked to two larger 12-volt batteries, the latter of which could be charged by one or both generators. The power supply for radio and lighting was kept at 12 volts to insure that current could be drawn from either battery if the other one went dead. A small auxiliary battery, powered by a gasoline engine, was used as an emergency supply to ensure a communications syatem at all times. Radio safety was instigated by splitting the radio equipment into three separate locations aboard the clipper: anchor room, radio operator's station and crew's quarters.

During hull construction all parts of the fuselage were treated for vibration and flutter tendencies. Any faulty materials were coded and later modified to prevent structural failure. The same vibration tests were given to all engine, nacelle, wing and tail components.

To insure safety against explosive fumes that might have collected, all electric motors used to drive fuel pumps were enclosed in a ventilated, fume-tight box and tested by the U.S. Government's Underwriters Laboratories for complete satisfaction and final approval. The hull was free of any fuel tanks in order to protect cabins from fumes. Gasoline, still one of the greatest threats to air passenger safety, was stored in the wings and sponsons. Each sea-wing, measuring 20 feet, 4 37/64 inches at its widest root base, and tapering out to a little more than 13 feet, had five airtight compartments. The first hold was next to the hull and shielded by a steel plate that separated it from the second and third sections which held 2,124 gallons of fuel. Any leaking fumes were kept isolated and retained from entering the hull by the plating. The outer two tanks were additional floatation cells, visible bulbous tips, which aided in keeping the protruding seawings from being submerged for any length of time when an unlateral positioning of the hull occurred in rough seas.

Along with the basic built-in safety mesaures were the emergency provisions strategically placed throughout the plane's interior, such as life rafts, vests and the like. The ominous thought of a

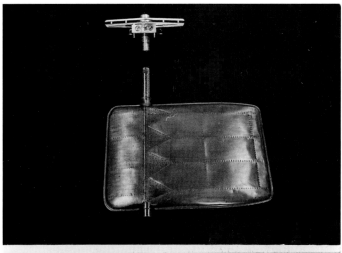

9930-16   Water Rudder Assy. - Dwg. 6-5971

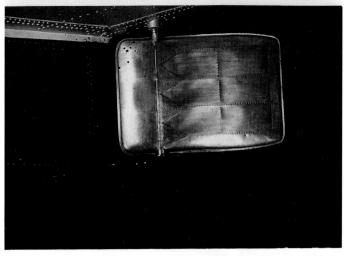

9930-28   Water Rudder Inst. - Dwg. 6-5971

The 314's rear-hulled water rudder was first thought to give the ship a better safety edge in surface navigation but later eliminated when found operationally insufficient. (*Photo Courtesy: Boeing Aircraft Co.*)

sudden downing at sea was always a possibility, and every safety precaution was taken to ensure human life. When the first 314 was launched it was hailed by aeronautical authorities as the safest overwater airliner ever built. In order to win the public's confidence in safety over the seas, the clipper's protective devices were extolled by both Boeing and Pan Am through one of the biggest PR campaigns ever master-minded in the late 1930s. Words, however, did not win the CAA's approval; the extensive testing that perfected all safety measures was the final mandated criteria by which the clipper was accepted for scheduled service.

Thirty emergency exits were blueprinted into the design of the ship. All staterooms had a port and starboard window exit and the suite had one on the starboard side. A lever, when pulled inwards and up, released a 19-by-24, 3/4-inch section of the plane's bulkhead. The ejected window panels provided for even the most robust of passengers an ample opening to safety.

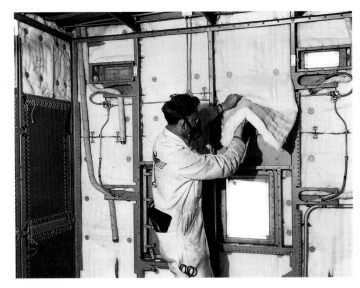

A Boeing technician carefully lines hundreds of yards of bulkhead soundproofing fiberglass for the comfort of passengers and crew against engine noise. Padding was an improved item from that used on earlier flying boat models. (*Photo Courtesy: Boeing Aircraft Co.*)

The all-steel, 14-foot-each diameter Hamilton Standard propellers incorporated Pan Am's demand for full- feathering features, another leading safety factor built into the Boeing Clipper. Looking on during prop installment is test pilot "Eddie" Allen in dark suit, extreme lower left. (*Photo Courtesy: Boeing Aircraft Co.*)

Passengers and stewards were also able to escape via the forward staircase that led up to the flight-deck's multiple exits. In the "special" compartment was a 10-rung ladder permanently mounted in the cabin's rear starboard corner which led to a 20-by-25-inch auxiliary overhead hatch. Other exits included engine nacelle openings, navigator's turret, and lounge and anchor room hatchways.

Boeing engineers, besieged by Priester's forceful insistance for more advanced safety features, planned for two large rectangular side-sliding porthole panes within the cockpit (bridge). Designed mainly to open for plane-to-shore verbal and hand-signal communications when at bay, the windows, when opened, offered a quick escape for the two commanding pilots. Over the captain's port seat was a padded 25-by-26-inch hatch that provided the chief officer with a 390-degree outside view during mooring procedures in stormy or foggy weather when visibility was poor. It also offered one more human exodus from a possibly fast-sinking liner.

All material used in upholstering, carpeting, bulkhead and overhead lining and blinds was sent to the Caledonia Fire Preventive Co. in New York for flame-proofing. Slightly more than two dozen types of fire resistant chemicals were laboratory-tested and treated on the cloth samples under the guidance of the company's director, Henry E. Kramb, before one chemical was authorized for the 314's varied-type fabrics.

Placed beneath each passenger seat was a Pan Am-designed and tested life jacket. Eight collapsible life rafts that held 12 people each were stowed near main exits in cabin overheads, while two were concealed in the upper canvas-covered wing sections. Just above the sponsons, within the under main wing panelings, were 40 additional life vests. From outside the plane, a canvas portion of the locular wings could be ripped open by crew members while positioned atop the stabilizers. One raft encased a water distiller, sail and navigational instruments. Other safety devices included signal lights, ring buoys, raft-towing lines, a bucket and axe, first aid allotments and a "Very" pistol to shoot off flares.

Beall's Model 314 was as near perfect in design as one could imagine for the day, and was equipped with top of the art safety features. Boeing's aeronautical engineer later exclaimed, "...at least some of these avenues would be available for use in case of an accident on the water, no matter what position the aircraft assumes."[21]

5

Flight-deck Operations

Today, hundreds of international air carrier jets land and take off every hour of the day throughout the world, the largest of these being the Boeing B-747 series. Many of these sky monsters, weighing some 712,000 pounds each at takeoff, are handled by only two flight-deck crewmen per liner within a small and somewhat cramped cockpit while the majority of ship operations is conducted through advanced and sophisticated technology. The mastering of flying by hand-on-yoke approach, at least concerning commercial aircraft, is becoming a lost art.

In the past glory years of scheduled international flight, beginning with the great but small clipper ship fleet of Pan Am, it took

The only known 314 stair well picture in existence shows the semi-spiral structure in its early-staged mock-up completed by Boeing in September, 1936. Off-limits to passengers, connector led to crew-manned flight-deck. (*Photo Courtesy: Boeing Aircraft Co.*)

up to ten, and sometimes more, qualified officers to control the 314 over the great expanses of sea. Each crewman had mastered his particular flight trade that ranged from pilot to navigation to engineering to radio communication and stewardship. By the late 1930s it had become a fine art to achieve and wear the gold and silver-winged insignia on the lapels of Navy blue and white uniforms and to be part of a clipper command during a very unique era full of high adventure, romantic travel and wondrous thrills — a time when man and machine had blended into one operational commandship enveloped with the early grandeur of world flight.

It all began on Oct. 28, 1927, when three Wright Whirlwind engines, each producing 240 h.p., were at full throttle when they helped to lift a rumbling, wooden wing Fokker F-VIIa/3m landplane into the skies from Key West, Florida, to Havana, Cuba. Two squeezed-in crewmen acting as pilots, radio operators and navigators, and a third man as the mechanic, swung the primitive-looking Pan Am-marked Fokker low over the deep blue Caribbean to establish the first international, commercial U.S. over-water airmail service. An eight-seat passenger operation was inaugurated a short time later.

What began as a small task soon developed into a far-reaching airline industry uniting North, Central and South America into a strong tie of partial world air commerce and trade. As the line stretched its routes farther south to include Rio and Buenos Aires, so too grew the size of the aircraft used.

With the lack of airfields throughout the southern hemisphere, Pan Am turned to twin-engined amphibians and later to larger flying boats capable of carrying hundreds of pounds of mail and cargo and greater amounts of passengers. Hiring more men to fly the flying boats entailed additional detailed over-water training. Thus began a program that eventually led to the 314's multiple crews. Initial training was handled through a trial-and-error process as based on — and besides the skill of flying an aircraft — admiralty law, theory of sailing and mooring techniques. In the air the planes were considered aircraft, but when on the water they were maneuvered like surface-going vessels. A surface/flying laboratory, involving precise scientific studies and evaluation, evolved which eventually led to the conquering of the Pacific and Atlantic Oceans.

Conducting certificated, commercial aircraft through an ongoing merchant marine sort of system was deemed necessary, according to Trippe when he wrote and later stated in 1941, "Static

Clipper flight-deck was modified after the shown XB-15's layout. Beall, an excellent engineer, followed the first principal of good design: "Take what you already have and go from there." (*Photo Courtesy: Boeing Aircraft Co.*)

Un-mounted dais-placed bridge seats expose first 314's rudder pedals for captain (left) and first officer (right) in this March 30th, 1938, photo. Watertight hatch between stations gave crew access to anchor room. Captain's auto pilot control is seen in lower left corner. (*Photo Courtesy: Boeing Aircraft Co.*)

conditions, typical of the tropical sphere of our (early) operations, had required the use of radio telegraphy rather than voice communication. As a result, the standard Pan American Airways crew had always consisted of a least two pilots and a radio operator. Now, the use of four-engined aircraft led us to add a fourth member to the flight crew, an engine specialist. To insure accurate navigation across our trans-Caribbean sector, we undertook to adapt celestial navigation to air transport purposes and to increase the range of our radio direction-finders. We also extensively supplemented our weather service organization to provide improved weather analysis for this overseas flying."[22]

The only well-established merchant marine sailors of the air were the crews that operated the great flying boats of Pan Am — a mastering of techniques that culminated with the 314's multi-stationed control room, and which, in the end, came to fulfill an everlasting glory. Hence, manipulating an aircraft in the same manner as an ocean liner had reached its zenith with the last of the flying clipper ships, the Boeing Model 314.

Nine Reseda green-carpeted steps within a semi-curved, tuquoise-painted stair well led upwards to the 314's magnificent control room. Designed after the 1936 Pan Am contract prerequisite, "...efficiency of crew operations," the living room appearance

By early January, 1939, as shown, the flight-deck was completed. From left to right is navigator's station, bridge, opened stair well hatch, radio operator's post and, in deep right corner, engineer's quarters. (*Photo Courtesy: Boeing Aircraft Co.*)

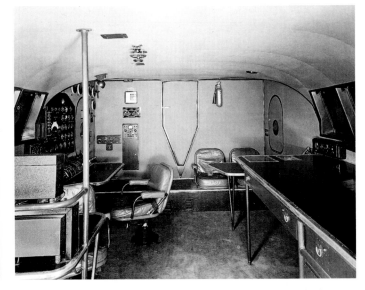

From left to right looking aft was control room's radio communication's center, engineer's post, captain's conference station and navigator's table. Centered ironing board-shaped hatch opened outwards for entry to mail bins, navigator's astrodome post and crew's bunking quarters. (*Photo Courtesy: Boeing Aircraft Co.*)

Master's bridge post or station featured the same control panel dials as at the copilot's post. Equipped with plush seat upholstered in red-dyed pig skin, skippers had ample room to cruise the giant clipper. Large porthole to left of the yoke could even be opened during flight. (*Photo Courtesy: Boeing Aircraft Co.*)

gave the impression that the area was yet another luxurious passenger lounge. Green-colored bulkhead and overhead linings, with a matching deeper green carpet and aft-positioned porthole blinds, were of the same soundproofing material as found throughout the lower passenger deck. The "super cockpit," as it was sometimes referred to, measured 21 feet, four inches long, by nine feet, six inches wide and six feet, one inch high. Epitomized as the last word for crew luxury aloft, the 314's crew quarters remains unprecedented in size and comfort — even when compared to the latest jet airliners.

Bridge was simple in controls when compared to today's whale-bodied jumbo jet cockpit displays. Note flexible yoke gear and large-viewing portholes. (*Photo Courtesy: Boeing Aircraft Co.*)

Twenty-five years after Pan Am's 314 demise, and during a transpacific flight aboard a Pan Am B-747 between Los Angeles and Tokyo, Capt. Stephen McCrea, a former 314 officer, spoke about the roominess afforded crew members on a 314: "Yes, I remember those planes well. The flight-deck was very large and gave us plenty of room to walk around and stretch our legs. Builders of planes like this one (B-747) don't consider the crew like they did in the past. Passenger comfort comes first today, but it's not so bad. The flights are much shorter now, and we (crew) don't tire as much as we did in the old days."[23]

And the 314 flights were long! It took nearly a week — with stops — to fly the Pacific and sometimes, due to bad weather, a week or so to cross the mid-Atlantic. In the early Sikorsky and Martin-built flying boats, crew members found themselves cramped within limited flight quarters. Excessive vibration of the M-130's control panels and poor ventilation often made some of the crew extremely air sick and fatigued by trip's end. Therefore, through the strict 314 building criteria and numerous suggestions for improvement by Pan Am crews, the 314 project was utmost in providing flight officers with every conceivable aid at the time, not only in instrument equipment, but in comfort as well.

Terms such as aft, fore, bridge, bulkhead, captain, first officer, deck, galley, port, starboard, steward and the like had been in common usage by Pan Am by the time the 314 came about. Based on Trippe's philosophy of a ship-running airline, many of the maritime-stylized words were coined by Pan Am for operational use and have since been taken in and used by other airlines, domestic and international. But it was through the 314's cockpit activities that these now mainstream terms were utilized to coexist with the "ships of the air."

Forward of the control room was the bridge. Encircling the space were seven different-sized portholes. To port was the master's or captain's post, often called the "Watch Officer's Station." In a deco-cushioned red pig skin-upholstered chair, equipped with a raisable arm rest for easy entry and egress, the master officer maintained course in accordance with flight data correlated by other crew and passed directly on to the bridge. Before each trip the master would correlate pre-flight data supplied him by ground operations that covered weather, altitude, plane's gross weight versus cargo and passenger weight distributions, and to log and examine all such procedures. A visual inspection was then carried out over the 314's entire airframe. Once aboard, controls were unlocked, examined and the altimeter set. Inter-cabin phone circuits were tested and all four propellers placed into low pitch position. Each prop was then turned four complete revolutions without using the ignition boost switch. Then the captain's overhead emergency hatch was tightly secured. Following came notification to all personnel that "cast off" was in order.

Detachment of mooring lines came next. Usually the third officer, or another crew member as directed by the captain, was positioned in the bow's hatchway to assist with the nose mooring line

Starboard-positioned radio center and flight engineer's stations had, as did other posts, deep-upholstered, leather-swirling chairs. Engineer's panel monitored engines, oil temperatures and gas consumption. Power was controlled by both the on-duty engineer and bridge officers. (*Photo Courtesy: Boeing Aircraft Co.*)

Engineer's instrument board was easily removed. Capt. Ed Black told of a behind-panel story when crews coming in from South America, and having passed customs at the last stop in San Juan, often stored bottles of rum in the panel's large cavity. At end of trip men placed rum in flight bags and went free without another check. (*Photo Courtesy: Boeing Aircraft Co.*)

and to hoist sea anchor upon a hand signal from the captain via one of the bridge's forward portholes. In turn, ground crew freed the 314 from the float and signaled the master that the liner's other mooring lines were removed and that the ship's additional hatches were secured. The flight engineer was then informed, either by hand or phone signal, to start engines 2, 3 and 4 in that order. Throttles were set at between 600 and 700 rpm and the ship slipped away.

Following one propeller revolution per engine, the master's command for "booster" and "priming" was given and increased until oil temperature was set. The latter was repeated until all power plants and their individual oil gauges registered correct pointings. Panel instrument operation was visually monitored and flaps maneuvered and left disengaged. When power reached about 700 rpm, the master ignition switch was again tested and the order for checking individual engine switches and spark plugs was issued.

Communication with the water launch was then put into effect. The Pan Am boat pilot informed the captain by phone that the sea-runway had been surveyed for floating debris and that surface traffic, if any, had been cleared. If the water course was void of hazards, a high-speed taxi order was given and engine run-up tests administered. Carburetors were monitored for accurate acceleration, first with engines 2 and 3 and then 1 and 4. The command signal for lift-off and directional flap use were then systematized. Set into the wind, the clipper's throttles were ordered open.

With the liner striking forward, the captain, as he does to this day, controlled the throttles and control surfaces. The first officer manned the flaps and the short-range radio telephone for communication with the launch. Lift-off power was registered at 1500 h.p. per engine at 2400 rpm with a 42.5 inch manifold pressure. Approximately 30 seconds from the time full power was applied, the

314 broke surface after about a half-mile run. Just after takeoff, the captain would usually hold the clipper just above the water until an air speed of 105 knots was reached to assure safe maneuverability in the event one engine suddenly quit. Meanwhile, the flight engineer observed the cylinder head temperatures and oil and fuel pressures from his board.

At 105 knots, each engine was throttled back to 1200 h.p. and maintained at this ratio by the flight engineer up to 1,000 feet. Then, the throttles were cut back to the climb rating 900 h.p., giving a speed of 110 knots which was held until the clipper reached its preselected cruising altitude.

During a normal climb to the planned ceiling (usually between 8,000 and 10,000 feet), a visual check by the captain of engines 1 and 2 was made. The second officer, one of three fully qualified pilots aboard, was then ordered to make a ship inspection, report back to the captain, and then record his findings into the ship's log book. When the 314 had gained its planned altitude, the signal for "level off" was given and all throttles set after which the automatic pilot gyros were adjusted and engaged.

Once course was maintained, the master was free to leave his post and to turn the command over to the first officer. Free to wander, a check of other station activities was usually made to insure or alter the flight plan as based on unexpected conditions that might have come to fore in the oral or written reports made out by the flight engineer or second officer since departure. If all was well, a master often times — as did other officers during "off-time watch" - - refreshed his memory at a post for the on-going courses demanded by the airline hierachy. During the station checks, any variance of power or other minor problem(s) that arose were quickly dealt with. If a major problem occurred, and was found unsolvable,

Looking forward, upper deck's aft cargo bins are seen to left and right. Mail was stored in unseen-padlocked cages. Gold and precious gem stones were stored here on many a flight. (*Photo Courtesy: Boeing Aircraft Co.*)

steamship's grand salon, a "captain's table" was reserved in the formally set dining room. The selection of guests had to be few in number due to the limited quadruple seating spaces. This often made for a difficult decision on the commander's part as to whom of the many noted passengers he wanted at his sitting. Usually those who occupied the clipper's deluxe suite were given first priority. Once the choice was made, the purser was told and the invitation sent out. The first and second officers usually presided at the second and third sittings.

Throughout the flight the captain acted as an administrator, an executive who issued commands as deemed necessary. During landing procedures the master, by Pan Am decree, took back full flight control. His first order commanded the crew to prepare for landing. Again, a spark plug test was made and the automatic pilot disengaged.

All bridge instruments were master-tested and the first officer was directed to use calculated flap control if a second approach was found necessary. Wind and water condtions were transmitted by sea launch to either the first officer or to the captain. If normal, the 314 was brought directly into the wind at 70 m.p.h. with bow slightly up until touchdown was made. If the sea was somewhat rough, the clipper was set down into the wind parallel to the swells.

the order of "turn-around" was given, a rarity in 314 operations. When all system checks were reported as being "on track," the clipper was continued on course with one of three cruising ranges at a speed conducive to the maximum miles per gallon of fuel consumed.

Before any departure, the meteorologist and dispatcher informed captains as to which cruise range to use. There were three: "Long Range," the method for getting the greatest miles per gallon, and generally used tor extensive flight hours; "Standard Cruising," the normal pattern without stressing engines speed (overworking and heating of power plants) and consuming fuel at a higher rate; and "High Speed Cruising," which called for the increase of engine rpm when time was a critical factor, such as when suddenly having to change course to avert an unexpected storm, to arrive at the destination before a storm, or for any other variables that required the minimization of the original estimated flight time. Each cruise setting was determined after figuring miles versus time and the fuel needed as related to the total plane's gross weight prior to takeoff. While under any flight cruise pattern, the more fuel used the more the gross weight had, of course, to be reduced. Towards the end of any trip the power output was decreased, but only to the point where the engines could not be allowed to run rough.

Usually an hour or two after lift-off, and at a time of choosing, the captain, following strict airline protocol, went below deck to briefly mingle with the passengers. Normally, those who could afford to travel by clipper were of the VIP category which called for every courtesy possible. Part of this in-flight etiquette was geared to the Trippe philosophy where, as aboard an ocean liner, the captain catered to the elite and the wealthy. In the evening, as in a

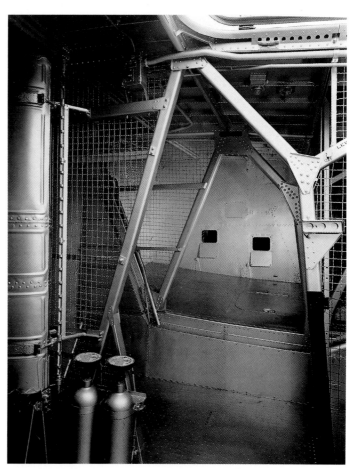

Cargo holds viewed from starboard hold to port-stationed bin. To right is profiled stepladder and rung seat for navigator's use when taking sightings through astrodome. (*Photo Courtesy: Boeing Aircraft Co.*)

Harbors provided for plenty of room previously scanned by launches as the sea-runways extended far beyond today's longest landplane runways.

Once on the water the commander taxied the ship to the dock where one of the last orders of the trip was given to the engineer to stop engines. Flight controls were then secured into the locked position and the captain usually sent the third officer to the bow to engage the mooring hook. A final check of casting lines was made both on shore and from the clipper's outer topside. Permission was then granted for passengers to disembark with the crew following in line led by the master. Such were the basic functions of the captain during a routine 314 flight. As for the flight stations within the control room, they were simple in design yet complex in purpose.

Forward of the captain's seat was the somewhat simplified-looking Lord engine and instrument panel board mounts where six flight instruments were mounted behind circular glass panels. The indicators recorded airspeed, rate of climb, altitude, banks, turns, flight direction and horizon positioning. The varied set was duplicated, but in reverse, at the first officer's starboard side of the bridge's panel. In the center, between the dual-arranged instruments, were mounted the gyro pilot and engine-rating gauges which included two dual tachometers and two compasses, a clock, outside air temperature gauge, two pressure ratings for the gyro pilot and an instrument vacuum gauge. The gyro pilot's remote controls were situated at right angles to each other beside each of the two adjustable bridge seats. Near both chairs were two small wheels that controlled the elevators and rudder. When the gyro was engaged, either the captain or first officer could operate the 314's elevators, or any degree of turn, by simply rotating the wheels to the desired setting.

Mounted to the left and right of the captain's and first officer's seats, and against the outer bulkheads, were control stands for dual and manual operation of elevator, aileron and rudder trim tabs (each supplied with indicators), plus four throttles, a master fuel mixture control, master automatic manifold pressure regulator and a master prop speed switch. Synchronization of other engine adjustments were left to the flight engineer.

Regarding the master controls in the bridge, according to Beall, "...all the engine controls available to the pilots, except the throttles, are master controls; that is, controls which function at all engines simultaneously. Individual throttles are, of course, necessary to the pilots for maneuvering on the water. An attempt has been made to relieve the pilots of as much work in connection with the power plants as possible and, for this reason, the full control of the power output at any time by means of their master controls. The same applies to the mixture and automatic manifold pressure controls."[24]

Overhead, and just above the bridge's portholes, was the electric switch control panel for wing flaps, engine and booster starters, and switches for the master ignition. Navigation and taxi light switches, wiper control and heater and duplicated wing flap ignition knobs were located on the first officer's upper side. Two additional radio and interphone panels were placed below and forward

of the described control stands (one set near the pilot). Each pilot had before him an identical half circle-shaped control column mounted to a torque shaft-bearing wheel. The master's wheel included a button that when pressed lighted up the instrument board for night flying, while on the deck near the torque shaft rested two adjustable rudder pedals. Beneath the main control panel, and dead center of the bridge, was a watertight hatch built into the main forward bulkhead. By stooping down and crawling forward between the pilot seats, an officer could unlatch the hatch, descend a ladder, and enter into the bow's anchor room which housed mooring lines, anchor, extra off-duty crew bunks, life preservers and any additional mail and baggage.

At castoff time, and coordinated with the master's commands, the first officer's duties were to check the controls, check all radio equipment, turn both vacuum valves on and set trim tabs in neutral position, set altimeter, give signal for securing all hatches and test full range of flaps. During the warm-up period — and at the captain's command — the first officer turned all engine ignition switches on naming them aloud as he did so. When all power plants were activated, the props were operated in low pitch and the automatic Sperry pilot system scanned and then disengaged until the clipper was airborne. An intercom message to the stewards below was addressed so they could inform passengers to fasten their safety belts.

During the taxiing period to the sea-runway, the second in command kept a keen eye on the water and informed the captain to steer clear of any floating obstacles. Meanwhile, spot checks were conducted by both pilots from the bridge's side portholes. After the turn into the wind, a pause before takeoff was given while the master ran each engine to run-up speed as the first officer again checked the flight controls, unlocked the empennage tabs and, if ready, acknowledged aloud the master's signal, "ready for takeoff."

Looking past mail cages to rear is seen crew's sleeping quarters. Note body belts atop bunks. Above is part of astrodome. Beyond resting quarters were extra cargo bins and luggage holds. (*Photo Courtesy: Boeing Aircraft Co*)

Chapter Five: Flight-deck Operations

Opened port hatch (right) at rear of control room exposed inner-wing catwalk that allowed a flight engineer to crawl deep into wings to engines for minor in-flight repair work. (*Photo Courtesy: Boeing Aircraft Co.*)

Following lift-off, and the start of climb, props were shifted to 2300 rpm and the manifold pressure set during rpm change and then lowered every 1,000 feet gained. A periodic visual scan was given engines 3 and 4. Once the liner reached its cruising altitude the first officer set the rpm to 2100 and once more visually checked all engines. Ground radio contact was maintained every 15 minutes. When the master chose to leave his post, the first officer took the captain's seat to act as on-watch officer. Two of the most important responsibilities of the first officer was to insure proper aircraft loading and that an inspection be given the craft before departure.

Normal landing duties for the first officer included the setting of all fuel mixtures and regulating props at 2100 rpm. A signal to stewards that the ship was about to land was issued and then the flaps operated to their correct down position. If a second approach was necessary, the flaps were retracted and another lookout given for surface debris. Once at the dock, all throttles were advanced on engines and ignition switches turned off following the stoppage of each prop's revolution. The master switch was then turned to the "off" position and the hatches unlocked.

Just aft of the bridge, and separated by a pull-type curtain used to keep the control room's night-flying light glare from entering the bridge and disturbing the pilots' vision, was the operational center that included posts for the radio officer, flight engineer, captain's conference station and navigator. Directly behind the first officer's seat was a deck hatch. When opened upwards, the main stairwell connecting the two decks became accessible. For security purposes, and for allowing for more walking floor space, the near kidney-shaped hatch could be lowered from a hinged position and locked.

Aft of the well was positioned the radio operator's post. A pigskin-covered swivel chair faced forward to a large table bolted to the outer bulkhead, its inner edge connected to leg supports and to a stanchion braced between the overhead and deck that gave a shock-proof support for the sensitive radio equipment secured across the forward table section. It was at this station that the radio operator made continuous contacts with both ground and ship-based personnel through the use of transmitters and receivers. It was the radio officer's responsibility to also furnish the captain, navigator and flight engineer of any incoming reports on weather changes and to directly supply the navigator with radio bearings. The latter aided the navigator in his plotting which in turn allowed the flight engineer to conserve fuel if a change of course had to be calculated for additional mileage, such as detouring a sudden storm. Assisting the second officer was the famed Directional Finder (DF), a radio-wave system developed and perfected by scientist Hugo Leuteritz in the 1920s and 1930s for Pan Am's over-water services. Tuning in on the DF allowed the captain to keep the clipper on course. Atop the hull, and over the radio station, was the teardrop-shaped DF antenna. Attached to the interior overhead, and just to the left of the radio operator's forward facing chair, was the DF control knob. Static eliminator devices, resembling insect feelers, were mounted outside and above the bridge's forward portholes.

The radio post was equipped with a double Bendix-made transmitter and receiver (a third set was stored for emergency use), a set of earphones, a small adjustable lamp and an inter-cabin phone. In the event of any well-wishing bon voyage cables received for passengers, the coded messages were first deciphered, dispatched to the captain for clearance and then passed on to the purser for delivery.

Aft of the radio operator's station, near the back starboard corner of the control room, was the flight engineer's post. A same style swivel chair faced into another table braced to the outer bulkhead. Above the desk was a shock-mounted board containing 26 power plant instruments. The first set, called "autosyn," included two dual tachometers, two dual manifold pressure indicators, three dual fuel quantity gauges, two dual fuel-flow indicators, two dual fuel-pressure indicators, two dual oil-in temperature indicators, two dual oil-out temperature gauges and two dual oil pressure indicators. Other instruments included two dual air-fuel ratio indicators, two carburetor air temperature indicators, one potentiometer that registered engine cylinder temperatures, one carbon monoxide mount pinpointing any C0 in the heating system, one clock, one gyro-pilot pressure calculator and one vacuum gauge.

Harold Mansfield, then Boeing's public relations and advertising director, wrote, "Actually, the 26 instruments served the function of 62 different indicators: 21 of them are dual indicators, each registering from two different engines, and one is a precision potentiometer (measures electromotive forces) connected with a rotary switch to give temperature readings from 16 sources, the heads and bases of the two master cylinders on each engine."[25]

The engineer could control each engine individually through the use of automatic manifold pressure regulators, fuel mixture, cowl flap, prop feathering and speed control. A synchroscope, an instrument which indicates that engines were timed simultaneously, gave a light warning when engines were in synchronized rhythm. Easy to reach throttles for hand-operated fuel pumps were located beneath the table. Six fuel system controls (hand wheels) were to the right of the main board.

Mounted on the aft control room's bulkhead was an indicator showing if any water was at the bottom of the fuel tanks. On the same back panel was the main electric fuse box and pressure controls for the engines' fire extinguisher system. Electrical switches and engine priming buttons were incorporated into a panel to the left of the engineer's board that also contained a bank of warning lights. Through the use of all these instruments, the prime duty of the flight engineer was to maintain accurate calculations through flight data supplied him by the captain and navigator for setting correct power thrusts as related to the exact amount of fuel needed (consumed) from any given point of time to another as calculated during the monitored time period within the course of flight.

Before a trip began, and prior to casting off, the engineer checked shore battery charges and put the battery switch to its "off" position. The plane's heating system was then turned on and the water indicator checked. Carburetor, thermocouple and temperature switches and engineer-to-captain phone connections were then tested as was the warning light panel system. The main autosyn gauges were switched to "on" and the fuel and oil gauges monitored. Next, the tank selector valves were set and the master battery switch turned on and the shore battery disconnected.

Quahog-shaped firewall seals off power plant from No. 3 nacelle, the latter so big it could seat four men comfortably. (*Photo Courtesy: Boeing Aircraft Co.*)

When all passengers were aboard, and the captain informed the crew that the clipper was prepared to be cast away, the engineer set each engine selector valve to start the power plants along with their fire extinguisher switches to the "on" position. He then waited for the captain's command to turn engines 2, 3, 1 and 4. When all were started, the hand pump for fuel pressure build-up was put into effect and the priming of each engine on the captain's order was then manipulated. Oil pressure gauges were checked and the captain was notified of each engine's correct temperature. Cowl flap testing followed while props were spun. Instruments were again checked, especially the oil pressures and vacuum gauges. Next came the deicer equipment check followed by fuel gauge monitoring to ensure that each wing tank was half full. When the latter reached a proper temperature reading, the engineer once more contacted the captain by phone to report that all engines were proper for taxiing, his eyes constantly giving spot checks to each engine head temperature gauge .

During taxiing, cowl flaps were fully opened and fuel mixture set. Engine head base and oil temperatures were closely observed and engines controlled to maximum taxiing rpm. As the clipper was posed for takeoff, and the captain revved each engine, the engineer set all fuel valves to "on" and checked to see if the cowl flaps were fully opened. Oil temperature and fuel pressure gauges were again monitored during the run-up of engines. With the master's takeoff signal given, the engineer responded in same if all instruments were found normal. Picking up speed, all gauges were carefully scrutinized by the flight engineer. At takeoff, climb and leveling-off periods, the engineer synchronized the rpm, regulated cowl flaps and fuel mixtures and transferred fuel from tanks to engines when required. Then began hourly readings and constant instrument checking.

When the clipper reached its destination, and the captain informed all to prepare to land, the engineer responded back to the bridge from his post, "prepare to land." The fuel pump transfer switch was turned off and the engine rpm was again synchronized. Cowl flaps were adjusted to their proper positions while the engineer waited to hear from the captain if a second approach was neccessary. If so, the cowl flaps were once more manipulated while a constant monitoring of all gauges at the engineer's post was put into effect.

Once on the water, fuel mixture controls were turned off and engine rpm set for taxiing. At the dock the engineer waited for the master's command to stop engines and did so through phone message or hand signal. All electrical equipment, mixture fuel valves, master battery switch and plumbing terminals were terminated. The engineer's last maneuver was to close all engine cowl flaps.

Emphasized was the ruling that since the master, first officer and flight engineer had interconnecting controls, a three-way cabin radio was considered of the utmost importance, especially due to the great distance between the flight engineer's post and the bridge. During the critical times of takeoff and landing, a communication between the three officers was always kept open. If a sudden emergency developed, such as loss of power or engine fire, a complete set of procedures was instigated by means of a communicative and operative double-check system between the flight men. If a minor breakdown of power occurred while in flight, the engineer could use one or two of the wing passageways to check the source of failure. Between June, 1939, and June, 1941, a total of 431 in-flight 314 engine-related repairs were made during both Pacific and Atlantic Ocean crossings. If it had not been for the 314's accessibility to engine housings, many of those flights would have had to have been aborted, demanding a return to base. Hatchways opening to wing passageways were located in the aft two corners of the control room. They were equipped with viewing portholes, a precaution against entering a wing if extensive flames, smoke or fumes engulfed the inner walkway.

Across the cabin from the engineer's station was the captain's office having a hinged table that could be lowered or raised from the outer bulkhead and braced to the deck by a leg support. Two jump seats, mounted on tracks along a raised running board against the rear bulkhead, were used by the captain and any of the officers for flight conferences regarding trip procedures or changes therein, emergency calculating or for any disciplinary action deemed necessary. Both seats could be shifted and locked into place anywhere along the cabin-width track and also provided for additional seating during takeoffs and landings. For more discreet talks, a pull curtain, hung from the overhead, enclosed the office area for more privacy.

Forward of the master's station was the navigator's post, the last station in the 314's control room. A seven-foot long by two and one-half-foot wide chart table for displaying two full-sized navigational charts was mounted to the port bulkhead. To the left of the table, and positioned on the bulkhead, were the Very signal pistol and shells to be used in the event of a distressed ditching, an encasement that housed an altimeter, air temperature gauge and an air speed indicator. The calibrated Gatty drift indicator was attached to and just below the table's left edge. Placed behind glass and atop the table's back surface were the 314's master aperiodic and countercheck compasses.

Two map drawers were installed beneath the table and a long horizontal and adjustable fluorescent lamp was anchored to the rear of the table. Just above were two extra large portholes that allowed for a flood of light to enter the room during day flights. A duplicate set of portholes was located at starboard at the radio post. Just aft of the bridge, and between the navigator's table, were three locker cases for storing marine reference books, charts, maps, the clipper's log book, reading material for off-duty crew and the delicate chromometer and bubble octants used to position the 314's route.

Navigation techniques in the days of 314 operations were quite crude compared to the more sophisticated electronic means used today. Clipper navigators worked under what was called the "dead-reckoning" approach. The mind was the computer that analyzed measures of a compassed course through the use of celestial devices at hand to chart the sky highways as they related to the winds at various altitudes affecting the flight. The navigator had to use three separate posts to collect the celestialized information.

First, the navigator took his sightings from the astrodome atop the hull between and dead center of the out-stretched wing panels. Location findings were measured through the use of a bubble sextant to ascertain latitude and longitude at any given altitude. Once obesrved and recorded, the navigator left the astrodome and proceeded to the drift sight station(s) in the wing(s) where wind velocity and drift calculations were made by means of flare droppings and use of a pelorus. Returning to the control room's navigation station, all data was calculated and compass-charted onto mapped sheets with fine navigational instruments kept in a velvet-lined box.

Final bearings were then passed on to the bridge and flight engineer's station.

Navigation by dead-reckoning was, at times, imprecise. A probable position was determined as much by the navigator's judgement as by the scientific tools of the period used to calculate a given location, especially if a clipper was locked in clouds for a great length of time and the navigator could not, therefore, rely on flare droppings to figure the degree of drift. An officer's mind had to be as near exact in charting a course as the scientific materials he relied on. A bad dead-reckoning could lead to a possible perilous adventure; but then Pan Am crews were "tops" in their trade -too well-trained for such an error. In fact, clipper crews were so articulate with their trades that shortly after the U.S. entered World War II, Pan Am training courses were integrated into the U.S. Naval air program for teaching air cadets how to pilot, navigate and communicate aboard large and long distance flying boats, from Consoli-dated-built Catalinas and Coronados to the later gigantic 82.5-ton Glenn L. Martin JRM-1 transport.

Last of the posts aboard a 314 was the lower-decked galley known as the steward's station or purser's post. Though not classi-fied as officers, the two stewards assigned to each flight were responsible for determining the total foodstuffs per trip, catered to passengers' every whim, set the dining salon with the fine china, linen, sterling flatware and flowers, served snacks, cocktails and meals and made up and took down berths. They polished shoes and cleaned restrooms. They were also accountable for all luggage taken on and off the clippers and assisted travelers in currency exchanges and in visa and passport preparations before reaching foreign ports of call. And, if for any reason a layover occurred at some remote island, stewards were, in addition to all their other duties, required to act as social directors — to provide games and events for their otherwise bored and often times anxious passengers.

Hatch-styled astrodome, located dead center between wings, was also used by ground crew to load and unload mail and cargo. The six window-paneled bubble was referred to by crews as the "blister." (*Photo Courtesy: Boeing Aircraft Co.*)

6

Clipper Crew Training

Establishing one's self as a Pan Am flight officer was, during the 1930s through the mid-1960s, the most esteemed commercial aviation career in existence. The Master Officer was top in rank and chief pilot — an expert in all phases of flight, radio communications, engineering, navigation and, of course, piloting. As captain, he was also well-versed in the history of ports and countries to which the clipper was flying. A master was a former post-graduate student and a veteran of numerous flight hours, many of which were spent in the military. Usually he was an officer in the U.S. Navy or U.S. Army Air Corps reserve. As a master, he was bestowed by Pan Am with a degree equivalent to a marine captain's ticket entitled "Master of Ocean Flying Boats," the first of which was awarded to Capt. Harold E. Gray, chief Atlantic Division-based master during the early years of 314 reign. Trippe had given his ranking pilots absolute authority in all airborne operations as based on the master's qualifications in business administration, international marine law and extensive flying experience under the Pan Am flag.

Retired Capt. Edward Matthew Black, past 314 fourth officer who worked up the ranks to a 314 first officer flying the Atlantic, summed up early clipper captainship and what it stood for when he wrote in early 1994, "The old-time captains of Pan Am were all distinquished gentlemen. I became a good pilot, I think, from what I learned from them. Without exception, the captains at that time were the cream of the world pilot group. I am proud to have known them."[26]

Next in line was the First Officer who ranked second in command. He lacked mastership only in pilot course work or accumulated flying hours before becoming a full-fledged skipper. By the time a man became a first officer he had specialized in all flight-deck operations, international maritime law, was proficient in at least one foreign language other than English, and understood all book rules and regulations concerning international transportation. From the time an air cadet was accepted by Pan Am to the time he became a captain, five to seven years had elapsed. He then had to fly for approximately four years as a senior officer before being awarded the rank of "Master of Ocean Flying Boats."

The Chief Radio Operator was a specialist in radio communication, a college graduate and had accumulated Pan Am flight experience and was also knowledgeable in geography. He usually took extra courses in engineering, the next step to becoming an assistant flight engineer. During each flight, the radio officer transmitted the clipper's bearings on the half hour from data supplied him by the navigator. Every hour a log report was filed on flight progress that related to winds, weather and any other varied conditions that affected the flight path. Clipper radio training was usually undertaken at Pan Am's Coconut Grove Radio School in Miami, headed by Robert C. Wilson along with a staff of six instructors, two of whom were women.

On the average, radio students were accepted into Pan Am's radio school with past experience in fields other than aviation. Incoming trainees had to learn dead-reckoning and celestial navigation, radio history and theory and the airline's multi-equipment repair shop course. An operator was required to send 25 words a minute and rated as a senior officer only after two years of in-flight experience along with having earned his radio telegraph license through the Federal Communications Commission (FCC) and had increased his word-sending and receiving abilities up to 30 words a minute. In addition to the initial training program, radio operators were constantly monitored once a month on the "radio jeep," a ground training device used for programming problems in direction finding.

With five off-duty crew elsewhere during a night flight, officers are seen at their prospective posts, each working up the ranks to become an esteemed "Master of Ocean Flying Boats" captain. Schooling and strict training qualified such men as the most admired and envied crew within the field of commercial aviation. (*Photo Courtesy: Pan American World Airways*)

A glimpse into what it was somewhat like to have earned a 314 radio officership is gleaned from the experience of Col. Walter M. Dalglish. As a young lad he enlisted into the U.S. Army Air Corps in the early 1930s and was soon schooled in a radio course at Chanute Field, IL. Leaving the Air Corps in 1939, and after having served as a radio operator in Maryland, New Jersey, Ohio, and then at Bolling Field in Washington, D.C., Dalglish was employed by Pan Am. At that time he was proficiently skilled in code-sending, installation and adjustments of field radio and telegraph equipment, electricity and magnetism theory, elements of radio, circuits and radio and telegraph equipment problem-solving testing, knowledge of radio nets and procedure and basic radio practice.

A letter from the airline dated March 6, 1939 reads, "This will acknowledge receipt of your application for employment as Radio Operator with Pan American Airways. At the present time we have a vacancy which your qualifications, as stated in your application, indicate you will be able to fill. It is suggested that you arrange to report to Baltimore for a circuit test immediately.

"It is understood, of course, that this is to be at your own expense and does not obligate the Company to employ you in the event you fail to qualify under actual operating conditions."[27] The letter was signed by Pan Am's Baltimore Municipal Airport Division Communications Superintendent W. T. Jarboe, Jr., a past radio operator on the earlier M-130 Pacific Division-based *China Clipper*.

At the time of employment with Pan Am, Dalglish held a 1933-earned Army Air Corps' degree in technical radio mechanics and operation, a 1935 degree in radio electronics — the latter awarded him while stationed at Fort Monmouth, Oceancort, N.J. — plus a temporary February, 1939, FCC's Second Class Radio Telegraph Operator's license given him in Washington, D.C. , and made permanent in February, 1942. After joining Pan Am, Dalglish first manned the radio shop at the line's Baltimore 314 base. In January, 1940, he became an assistant radio operator on the clipper flights to and from Lisbon. And his training didn't stop. In early 1941, he earned a degree in practical radio engineering after completing an introductory course of study.

Dalglish quit Pan Am in 1942. In August, 1943, he continued on with his operator's career to earn another degree after completing 20 hours of classroom and laboratory study and practice in celestial navigation at the Buhl Planetarium in Pittsburgh. His work for the Federal Aviation Administration following Pan Am took in air traffic control at airports in Washington, D.C., Boston, Cleveland and Pittsburgh. The much admired and respected gentleman retired from the aviation field in 1956 to be employed by a private company designing sophisticated filing systems.

Regarding his time with Pan Am, Dalglish wrote in December, 1993, "We were required to be proficient with the DF used for approaches. In my case, we did it on a Stinson landplane over a beach area at Bridgeport, CT. There were two masts at the station. After an initial run on the station to get the 'feel' of it, the captain pulled

To sit at this post required years of higher education in radio communications, telegraph sending and receiving along with a knowledge of celestial navigation. On top shelf from left to right were tuning amplifier, remote radio control and direction finder unit. Lower grouping included radio receiver and double-boxed transmitter. Telegraph key is seen atop table, lower right. (Photo Courtesy: Boeing Aircraft Co.)

the blinds on me so I couldn't see out at the station's antenna. I made 19 straight aporoaches right between the two masts. The captain said, 'That's enough Walt!' We returned to the airport at North Beach (later LaGuardia).

"On my first flight on the run from Lisbon to Horta in the Azore Islands, I was asked to make the first foot ceiling. With the usual caution we made a run of it to get the feel, then proceeded and broke out of the clouds at 500 feet and landed. The DF was highly accurate and I had confidence in it."[28]

From Chief Radio Operator we go to Chief Flight Engineer. One who gained such rank was definitely a college graduate who had mastered all aspects of flight engineering and radio communication and one who continued with navigation courses leading towards the next rank up as assistant navigator. The engineer was responsible for all mechanical operations of the clipper, from the loading manuals for oil and fuel and the amounts specified for the flight to the actual participation in the plane's inspection and general servicing before departure. A "Jack-of-all trades," the engineer's log contained on the average some 7,300 notations relating to a round-trip flight following the monitoring of his 41 separate instruments, engine throttles, carburetor settings and fuel supply valves.

One became a flight engineer for Pan Am as a graduate of aeronautical engineering or by working up the ranks through aircraft and engine mechanics and schooling. Regardless, each man had to additionally train in Pan Am shops to familiarize himself with the intricacies of engines, propellers, instruments and other mechanical accessories dealing with the clippers. A combination of schooling and in-service shop experience was necessary before one was checked out as an assistant engineer. At least one year was also required in working in a maintenance hangar in order to complete the necessary in-service time. The "on-line station" period, as it was called, encompassed studies covering engine and plane service, propeller and accessory overhaul, instrument mechanics and thorough plane inspection. After passing exams on each, a graduate apprentice engineer that desired flight duty was put on a waiting list and, in time, became an assistant (second) engineering officer. After accumulating a year or two of flying time under a ranking engineer's observation, and coping with ground studies between flights and other studies dealing with air emergencies, marine equipment, company policies, clipper manual procedures and CAB regulations, the last step was achieved — becoming a Chief Flight Engineer.

A clipper's navigator was known as the Second Officer. Also a college graduate, he was required to have passed all exams in radio communications, engineering and navigation, and was involved in post-graduate study aiming to become a first officer. The celestial observer, usually a former flight radio technician and engineering officer, was an in-training senior pilot. During each trip the captain, as he did with a third officer, gave him a brief assignment at the controls for training credit. Proficient in radio theory and practice, the second officer mastered his tools that included the sextant, the octant, chronometer, slide rule, pelorus and drafting apparatus used in dead-reckoning and in DF computations of elapsed time differentials since the flight's beginning as balanced against the plane's speed in relation to wind directions and drift calculations.

Next in line was the Third Officer. He too worked towards becoming a master of flying boats. His title was equivalent to the highest-ranking junior pilot aboard a 314. He was usually involved in final navigation courses and working upwards to become a first officer, lacking only study or required flight hours, or both, to acquire the latter status. His main duty was primarily to serve as a relief officer for the co-pilot and to perform any duties so assigned him by the captain or "boatman" as he was called. Second priority was to assume boatswain during cast-away or anchorage tie-downs.

Last, but not least, was the Fourth Officer. At the bottom of the pole, he too was an in-pilot trainee and working up the ranks so described. Usually very young, the last uniformed 314 officer often was required by the boatman to prepare the 314's center of gravity weight and balance manifest load calculations and in the aiding of stewards with such items as informing passengers about emergency procedures shortly after each takeoff and assisting them on how to fill out their custom inspection papers before landing. The more varied the job, the better the experience. The fourth officer was always at the captain's call.

Any young man (26 being the average starting age) who wanted to become a captain had a strenuous time before achieving his dream - the highest pilot rank then attainable in the commercial field of flight. Pilot officers were seasoned veterans of years of expert aeronautical enlightenment, found to have superior judgment and entered Pan Am knowing that they would again have to start their flying careers from the bottom up. Some were former barnstormers, a few former World War I cadets.

It seemed more time was spent at a ground facility and in classrooms than in the air while aiming for the most demanding of air professions. Usually three months after acceptance, an applicant was placed aboard a clipper as an apprentice pilot. Between the long periods of waiting for flights, the in-pilot trainee studied his subjects and worked at a base to grasp the standardized and varied aspects of flying boat ground operations, from beaching gear procedures to scraping seaplane hull bottoms and filing down propellers. Reporting to a field by 4:00 A.M. for more than a full day's work was not considered unusual.

In addition, a thorough knowledge of seamanship was also necessary when striving to become a Pan Am master. A flying boat was subject to all the governmental and natural laws that applied to ocean-going ships. Since the clippers were fitted with marine gear, such as bilge buckets, fog horns and sea anchors, much attention was given to water operations. Long hours in square knot tying, fresh water stilling, life raft safety and other seaman-type tactics were taken into account. With everything mastered, a clipper captain's education was still not considered complete. To keep astride of his profession he periodically took advanced courses, took constant pre-flight physicals and refresher pilot checks in the Link Trainer, a ground simulator used for instrument flying testing. From a general two-year study session as apprentice pilot to junior pilot, second-class, on to junior pilot, first-class, then to senior pilot and on to master pilot, the high standards of experience and demonstrated practical skills seemed endless. And always there was the stiff curriculum of subject matter and competition with fellow flyers that one had to contend with.

Periodic instrument training in the link Trainer for all flight pilots on the Atlantic seaboard was done at LaGuardia Field in New York and at Pan Am's clipper base outside Miami adjacent to Biscayne Bay. Other training facilities were located in Baltimore, San Francisco, Seattle and at the Texas-based headquarters in Brownsville and in Lima and Rio in South America (the latter three mainly trained men for DC-3 and B-307 Stratoliner landplane operations). Between 15 and 18 hours were spent in a session which ranged from blackboard diagrams and lectures to intensive Link maneuvers and instrument instruction aboard a single-engined Stinson monoplane or Rearwin trainer. Both aircraft were equipped with instruments and controls like those found aboard a clipper.

Enclosed in darkness by means of drawn curtains, and while the instructor flew the plane, a Pan Am officer worked with the dials and knobs during the blind flying session that simulated approaches in fog where reliability of instruments and radio were essential. Experienced and apprenticed pilots had to pass sessions in such categories as basic Link and Stinson academics, DF, company procedure checks, instrument rating, airline rating, instrument theory, meteorology (a pilot had to receive and copy 100 words per minute of broadcasted weather information over a radiophone), practical radio navigational aids and the appropriate use of a navigation tool called the Mark VII, a compilation of celluloid discs within discs showing graphs and figures. The Mark VII was comprised of a circular slide rule against a moveable plotting board and used to solve mathematical and navigational problems.

One unusual training base was the Pan American Foreign airport (PAFA), so-called because of its land-based center rather than a standard water port. The transpacific training station, established in the fall of 1942, was located at Sherman Field in Walnut Creek, CA. It was set up away from Pan Am's Treasure Island clipper base in San Francisco so training procedures would not interrupt regular travel schedules and where more room was available to build a trainee dormitory. As with other bases, the PAFA headquartered a qualified staff that taught complex instrument flying skills through the use of the Link and small landplanes. Pilots, as at all bases, were taken through courses in air speed indicators, rate of climb, turns and banks, artificial horizon, radio, radio beams and DF to master a clipper on a given course through clouds, fog and storms.

A personal insight into the type of training given Pan Am pilots, a stiff program instigated by the airline eight years before the 314s were introduced, came from the late Capt. William M. Masland, a former 314 Master of Ocean Flying Boats. With his abundant knowledge and fond memories of days of old, Masland provided an insight into that seemingly endless training task that began out of the clipper base at Dinner Key, Miami:

"Most of us who entered the company at that time were Navy hotshots. I had been on the old carrier *Langley*, for example, and knew all about it — or thought I did. Pan Am wasn't so sure. They put every last one of us into a hangar at Dinner Key, and there we stayed until we earned our A and E mechanic licenses, even if it took two years which, in come cases, it did.

Engineers, some of whom were former aircraft mechanics, were the masters of clipper operation and in-flight repair. Hatchway to right of gaged board opened to wing's starboard catwalk. (*Photo Courtesy: Pan American World Airways*)

"Following this stint, we were then sent to the radio shops and told to stay until we had earned our commercial radio license. This was not the phone license that takes a few hours of home study, but the license required for radio telegraph operation on commercial circuits, copy 20 words a minute of cipher, know the ins-and-outs of five different types of equipment, and so forth.

"After these exercises, we were turned loose on little two-man trainers out in the sticks to operate as copilot, mechanic and radio operator. My stint was in Port of Spain, Trinidad, running across Venezuela and to Baranquilla on the mouth of the Magdalena. The ships we flew were either a Sikorsky S-38 or S-41, both of them twin-engined amphibians. This was an excellent school for do-it-yourself operation. We serviced, maintained, repaired and improvised our way across country as wild as you will find. Facilities were often no more than a couple of Indians with a drum of gas and a hand pump, or a dugout canoe with some five-gallon tins in the bottom and another dugout with the passengers.

"But this was only the start. We ran a series of courses at home in our spare time and took periodic exams. Successful passage of the first series raised us from the status of apprentice pilots to junior pilots. After completing the circuit, which had included time in the engine overhaul shops as well as the hangars and the 'morning runup' crews, and followed by a year or so in an out-based operation like the one I mentioned in Venezuela, we then went to an ocean division. Here we started all over again at the bottom.

"First assignment was as junior flight officer. These ships, at the time the M-130 *China Clipper*-type, were close to marginal as to load. We carried a crew of seven. It was the junior flight officer's job to relieve each of the others in turn; first the captain, then the first officer, then the radio operator, then the flight engineer — an hour for each in turn. Then you had an hour off for yourself, but you used it to understudy the navigator. He had an extra octant and an extra chart for your use.

"Eventually you navigated a crossing from Alameda, Oakland, to Manila or Hong Kong under the eyes of a checked-out navigator. If successful, you were then moved up a grade. As in so many other areas, we followed the practices of the ships rather than the railroads.

"While this was going on, you were also studying and taking other exams. Among others, there were four oral tests held at Alameda. My exam in meteorology would be tycical. It was given by a Mr. Clover, the chief meteorologist. It took three hours; he asking the questions and I hopefully providing the answers.

"All-in-all there were about 100 exams before you had run through the course from apprentice pilot to first officer to Master of Ocean Flying Boats. They ran through the area of navigation, starting with charts and projections, plane sailing, Mercator sailing, celestial navigation (including cosine-haversine method), to admiralty law, aircraft structures and strength of materials, power plants and fuels. Other exams included at least one in foreign language, the history and culture of the countries in which you were flying, the history of Pan Am, and on and on and on. It all came in handy before we were through. I have been at the local met office with my navigator making my own forecast and my own flight plan while the first officer was loading the ship, the engineers beating out some needed fittings at the local blacksmith shop, and the two stewards baking their own bread in an oven they had constructed on the beach. Then we loaded fuel out of a surf boat, loaded the plane to our own specifications, and were off — often to a place none of us had even seen before, and sometimes to a place no one had ever flown before.

"This was all very hard work. Like a sailing-ship captain, you were never off duty. But it was also a lot of fun. There were sometimes long hours of high tension. And then there were days or nights of great beauty; a night at sea in the Gulf of Paria with a dead engine and rising winds, five night-flying hours on three engines across a jungle with a rained-out destination that had no navigational facilities and everybody shooting at you, especially your friends! Or, there were quiet nights at anchor in the remote part of Angra dos Rein ('the anchorage of the kings') on the Brazilian coast or, farther north, in the deserted San Mateus River, or on anchor watch on a cold, clear night in the Persian Gulf with the stars hanging as low overhead as the lamps in a mosque.

Tabulation of watch lists, and about 8, 000 hours of data on crew sleep, indicated that if you kept going and did not spend too much time in port refueling, or in making short hops, one could continue on almost indefinitely. Once a man learned to accommodate himself to watch-on, watch-off work, you had no problems."[29]

Capt. Marius Lodeesen, 35-year veteran with Pan Am who logged 30,000 air hours, or three-and-a-half years aloft, briefly recalled the difficult clipper-training days at Coconut Grove:

"When I reported to Pan American...I was unmarried, and a naturalized American citizen. I had a master's degree in aeronautical engineering, flown two years with the fleet as a naval aviator and I spoke several languages, including a smattering of English. For the job awaiting me I was ill-prepared.

"'So, you're one of the new wheelholders,' Mr. Richardson said to me as he looked me over from head to foot through his thick spectacles. 'Come with me,' he said, 'and I will make you a swaggerstick.'

"I followed the foreman through the hangar, dodging past and underneath wings, floats and hulls to a work bench. Richardson produced a foot-length of copper tube, stuck a piece of cable in one end, crimped the end shut and frayed the wire cable so that it resembled a brush. 'This is your tool,' he said. 'I'll show you how to use it.'

"He took me to one of the flying boats, a two-engine affair, painted silver, with many ugly red spots on the hull and struts. Richardson pointed to the spots. 'Here is where the inspectors found corrosion. Scrape the paint down to the bare metal. After the in-spector okays your work, brush them with red oxide. The painter comes around to spray them with aluminum.' He turned around and through his glasses his eyes looked evil. 'Do a good job and I will promote you to cleaning bilges with paint remover.'

"I must have done a splendid job for the following week, Rich put me on stripping bilges.

"Miles of scraped flying wires and half-a-dozen bilge cleaning jobs later, I found myself assistant to 'Rabbi' Poss, the expert in laying walkways on the topside of boat hulls. It's similar to covering a sailing boat deck with canvas except that instead of painting, 'Rabbi' soaked the canvas in a tarry substance and then ran a hot flatiron over it. After a job like that, you could have stuck both of us to the ceiling."[30]

The type of training described by Masland and Lodeesen was of the kind that led to the world's most respected aviation jobs. Many captains had their own fan clubs and were sought out around the world and asked for their autographs. Being the first airmen to regularly traverse the oceans in commercial aeroplanes, they were considered to be rough-'n-ready but gentlemen at heart. In essence, they were America's cowboys of the air!

Probably the best-known Atlantic Division Clipper pilot was Capt. Gray. A superb mathematician who was always fascinated with solving complicated equations, Gray first learned how to fly while a cadet in the U.S. Army Air Corps. By the time he was 34 years old, Gray had become Pan Am's senior pilot on the Atlantic's "blue ribbon" route and chief check-out pilot officer at LaGuardia's 314 clipper base.

Capt. Gray was born in Guttenberg, Iowa, and attended the University of Iowa, Brooks, and later the University of Detroit from which he graduated with a degree in aeronautical engineering. After setting up his own consulting engineering firm, the pilot worked for an early U.S. (Ford) airline and was one of the first American pilots to be checked out on Ford Tri-motors. Two years after he joined Pan Am in 1929 (tenth pilot to be hired), he earned his master's degree in aeronautical engineering. Flying first to Mexico, and later out of Miami where he was placed as senior pilot, Gray was transferred to the Pacific Division. He made 14 round trips to the Orient commanding M-130s before being sent to the Atlantic Division in 1937 from where he headed five Sikorsky S-42 round-trip survey flights to Europe preparatory to 314 service.

By 1941, Gray's work was primarily involved with checking out new pilots for Pan Am. In his simple, undecorated office on the third floor at the airline's hangar at LaGuardia was a multitude of information on the 50 transatlantic pilots under his jurisdiction. The multiple fold-book file listed captains' comparative flight times, night-landing records, semi-annual instrument check ratings, certificates and other pertinent data. Gray also maintained the pilot "Schedule Board," his own design made up of squares that related such pertinent information as flight schedules, names of clippers to be used for given flights, layover and vacation periods for the crews and so forth. In March, 1944, Gray, in addition to being LaGuardia's Pan Am operations manager, became head administrator of maintenance, meteorology and communications when the offices were streamlined and consolidated into one department. His principal staff representative was Capt. Arthur E. LaPorté, a commander who made 314 history when he inaugurated regular, heavier-than-air air mail service eastward to Europe in 1939. The chief pilot position vacated by Gray in 1944 went to Capt. Audrey D. Durst, another early Pan Am skipper. Gray's career continued to rise with Pan Am. In 1947, he became manager of the Pacific-Alaska Division, then the airline's president in 1964, and later chairman. He died of cancer on Dec. 23, 1972, at the age of 66.

The last personnel stationed aboard a 314 were the First and Second Stewards. The former, referred to as Chief Purser, had to have at least two-to-four years of college, be knowledgeable in topography and, if on the Atlantic run, be able to communicate in at least three languages. Some stewards spoke eight or nine! Also required were extensive training periods covering theory of flight, food economics, first aid, emergency procedures, marine tactics and local and foreign travel regulations. Former hotel or steamship experience as a porter, waiter or chef was a prerequisite to hiring, as was good grooming, a warm personality and an interest in people. The difference between first and second rating was based on the number of air hours accumulated with Pan Am. Stewards were the only members of the crew to slightly alter their uniforms just prior to welcoming passengers aboard. Uniformed jackets and hats, the same issued to flight-deck officers, were removed. In their place stewards donned short, high-collared white jump jackets trimmed in black cloth — the same as seen on waiters in the finest of restaurants or aboard first-class ocean liners.

Extra officers were put aboard 314s during long flights for watch-hour changes or for in-flight training. The additional crew members were either junior pilots or supernumerary personnel of all ranks. Many were aboard to pick up extra air time, relief officers or for check-out ratings. At times up to 15 men made up a single 314 flight crew. In-all, a ship-like operation had been well-planned and put into effect long before the 314s came about. Known as the "Multiple Flight Crew," the scientifically trained crew had grown in number after Pan Am realized it needed specialized assignments when operating four-engined equipment. The line's primary personnel requirements in flying the big ships, beginning with the S-40 in 1931, were six-fold: expert flight control, piloting, navigation, efficient power plant control and maintenance, communications and superb passenger service.

Two days prior to any 314's transoceanic departure from the U.S., 185 mechanics and inspectors labored through three eight-hour shifts to check 1,500 different 314 items as required by Pan Am's routine round-trip maintenance program. The crew selected to fly a particular run would report the day before and give the ship a test flight accompanied by mechanical specialists, inspectors and

service engineers. As for the crew, according to Capt. Black, they too were rigorously checked out prior to each trip. Pre-flight physicals were a must — complete to the state of stool-taking as the men would often be gone for weeks on end, especially during the diabolical war years. Officership rules were so strict that crewmen even had to stand for inspection before their captain prior to boarding. If shoes were not shined, uniforms unkept or growth of beard showing, they were immediately replaced. At the Atlantic Division, disciplinary action soon followed in Capt. Gray's office with first a warning and if not amended could, in the future, lead to dismissal.

Once the aircraft was approved for flight and accepted by the captain, the flight plan was formulated. First came the study and charting of the final weather map and its methods that equated air mass and its relation to the flight planning. A second chart reckoned with known upper air conditions at altitudes ranging between five and 12,000 feet, while the third graph illustrated the conditions the captain could expect en route.

Compiled, the base's meteorologist and second officer were able to divide the projected route into zones that blocked areas of known winds and storms. The flight pattern was then established at various altitudes or altered (new route) depending on the forecast of clouds, freezing altitude temperatures and wind directions and their velocities.

Following the captain's approval, the clipper's first officer charted and computed the allowed payload and registered it in the Weight-and-Balance Manifest that determined the location for passengers, mail, express and cargo as related to the plane's c.g. for favorable takeoff, flight cruise and landing.

A 314's c.g. was determined by the gross weight of the plane when fully loaded. A summation of all weight was then indexed and could not exceed the maximum allowable gross weight of 84,000 pounds. The balance point of the aircraft was determined by adding the total index units of individual weight categories, such as weighing-in all passengers and crew, mail, cargo, baggage, fuel, oil, water, food, bedding, life jackets, rafts, and the like, and then relating them to the gross weight of the clipper. Calculated, the sum was projected on a graph (loading schedule form) that revealed the clipper's c.g. weight range (allowed between 25-30.7 percent of the 314's Mean Aerodynamic Chord -MAC — for takeoff and landing, and from 17.65-30.7 percent MAC for flight).

When completed, the third officer gathered local and foreign government clearance forms required for each flight and placed them on file in the terminal with a duplicate set placed aboard the aircraft. While this was going on, the stewards determined what they needed. Bedding, food stuffs, utensils, china, table flowers, linen and such were taken into account and listed on a order form.

Completed 48 hours before departure, stewards also checked and reported to the captain on needed government import and export declarations. First-aid kits, life jackets and rafts were inspected and cleared by the stewards. Then the total weight summation was

Charting a 314's course called for exact principles of navigation that took in the studies of ship-like celestial navigation. (*Photo Courtesy: Pan American World Airways*)

ucts were forbidden. Through trial and error, cream fillings, custards and breaded chops were also never on the preparation order lists because they did not withstand high altitudes. Chosen for the hot meals were chicken, braised roasts, steak, plain chops, potatoes and steamed vegetables without heavy sauces. Fresh fruit and simple desserts, such as ice cream, baked pies, or pastries were always a commodity as they had proven airworthy aboard earlier clipper model flights.

Once in the air, the flight-deck crew worked around a aystem called the "howgozit" (how goes it) curve developed for Pan Am by Capt. Gray. It was a constant, informative fuel reserve coding that was relayed to the ground flight watch and used to chart the amount of fuel needed to complete the trip or return to port of origin. This data was based on five curves: plotting miles versus gallons under current flight operations; gallons versus total miles to destination; while the fourth and fifth curves gave miles versus gallons on three engines — to continue on course or return to base. The "point of no return" (halfway mark) was also charted.

Each "howgozit" curve was drawn on a chart by the first officer who maintained a record of the plane's fuel consumption at any given point of time as relayed to him by the flight engineer. Any deviations were indicated to the captain and showed if the clipper was satisfactorily completing its original flight plan or whether some condition, such as a change of wind velocity, was raising fuel consumption and at what particularly alarming ratio.

A log, such as those kept aboard sea-fairing vessels, was always at hand on the 314's flight-deck. Recorded were the ship's flight history and maintenance records that included total flight hours and miles flown. Capt. Masland referred briefly to 314 log books when he wrote in 1965:

"The logs of the ships may still be about, but bit by bit we reduced the content. Originally they were kept in the same form and with the same amount of details as the log of a surface ship. An engineering firm, such as Ernst and Ernst, came in and changed the entire concept. But, as I say, some of these logs may still be around, and the older ones at least would contain information where the ships had been and when."[31]

Whereas over the years Pan Am had developed a methodical crew-training institution to coincide with its ever-improved scien-

formulated and given to the first officer for inclusion into the final payload manifest.

All food served aloft first came from local markets or catered hotel services, and later from the line's own airport commissaries. The selection and gathering of all produce and meats was supervised by a top-rated chef who usually was a former flight steward. Two hot meals were normally planned per flight — sometimes more depending on the length of the journey. The basics were lunch and dinner. Breakfasts were light and consisted on the whole of only sugar rolls, fruit juices and coffee or tea. Between lunch and dinner, snacks of fresh fruit and sandwiches were served as was high tea with assorted French pastries and tiny sandwiches. When Pan Am introduced its own base kitchens, stewards had to arrange all food and remove bones from meats to lessen weight. What had to be cooked was partially done so on the ground and then packed and frozen. The food was taken aboard in trays where the rest of the cooking was done on the combination stove-steam table after being removed from dry ice.

Planned long before a flight, a consulting physician guided chefs in their pre-flight menus. Pan Am's in-flight menu research and development program pioneered what and what not to serve passengers during long international trips. Small amounts of not-too-rich foods kept passengers' stomachs at ease and helped in avoiding airsickness. Pork, beans, cabbage and other gas-forming prod-

tific over-water operations, Boeing Aircraft Co. so too instigated its own 314 training program in 1938. Known as the "familiarization of aircraft," Boeing programmed leading Pacific and Atlantic-based Pan Am flight crew and ground maintenance personnel into the operation and care of the Model 314.

As the first of the new clippers neared its final stages of completion, an elaborate and comprehensive study course was formulated and put into practice. Room 30 in Boeing's Administration Building became a lecture and study hall for numerous Pan Am employees. The program had been encouraged by Pan Am's Andre Preister and co-sponsored by Earl Ferguson who headed the instructional school. Ferguson, who co-piloted the Model 314 during its testing period, was also an engineer and a leading expert in the flying boat's engine installation, fuel system, power plant controls, prop installation, flight control surfaces and floatation statistics. Thirty-year-old Ferguson, a native of Seattle, had attended the University of Washington from which he graduated in 1932. Before joining Boeing in 1930 as an engineer, Ferguson enlisted in the Navy where he began flying at Pensacola and then later at the Marine Flying School at Quantico, Va.

Assisting Ferguson at the Boeing School were seven of the plant's leaders: Berger Anderson, loading weights unit senior; John K. Ball, stress of strength and load factor engineer and 314 hull specialist; Harold Brown, 314's electrical chief; Cram; Ed Duff, head clipper project engineer in construction and servicing; E. G. Emery, senior engineer of equipment and furnishings (including navigation facilities, instruments and de-icing system); and Nate Price, development chief of 314 heating and ventilation.

The first of three scheduled sessions began on April 11th and ended ten days later. The first two courses were a testing ground for those that followed. At the end of each lesson, communication skills on 314 principles were verbally analyzed and resolved by both the instructors and the pupils. Modified, the two original courses were set into a final preparatory form of instruction — a two-way comprehensive and understanding communicative pattern of thought for the future study programs given airmen and mechanics who would fly and maintain the 314s. Courses that followed acquainted a few senior flight men and chief ground-check personnel with the 314's design, construction and general operating performances. The knowledge was then passed on to other Pan Am men stationed at the clipper bases.

Beginning courses started with a complete inspection of the construction site and with the first Model 314 (used as a laboratory), and ended up in Room 30 with two to six classes per day that took in five hours of lectures and concluded with open round-table discussions. Exams were given at the close of each course. Attending the first series of instruction were C. D. Wright, Pan Am's Atlantic Division's chief flight engineer; R. W. Beecher, Pacific Division's second flight engineer; A. del Valle, Pan Am's Boeing resident engineer; George Nash, Pan Am's chief 314 inspector; T. R. Runnells, leading 314 radio installer; Harold Homan, Atlantic

Division's chief of plane service; and Harry Keister, Pan Am's apprentice engineer. A 56-page diagrammed manual, designed by Ferguson and associates and printed up by Boeing, was used as the textbook. It gave pupils detailed instructional material to follow as covered by the lectures.

Boeing's second school sessions began on May 4th and continued for six days. Present were Capt. Gray; Carl Green, Pacific Division's chief flight engineer; G. M. Smith, leading flight engineer instructor at Pan Am's Alameda school; Dr. R. Gregor, Atlantic Division's chief inspector; and again Wright, who acted as an observer in order to fully acquaint himself in all 314 subjects before giving instruction to other Atlantic Division-based personnel.

A third class started on May 11th and was the beginning of the formulated and stylized course offering at Boeing for the numerous flight men and mechanics that had to delve into the clipper's operational procedures. Additional courses were offered at other plants across the country that produced 314 parts, such as at the Wright, Hamilton Standard, Holley Carburetor and Pioneer Instrument factories.

It was during their stay at Boeing when Capt. Gray and other clipper crew members wound their way up the first 314's staircase and stepped for the first time into the boat's flight-deck. Stunned, they were more than delighted with the spaciousness given to the command center. Its design had started in concept in Priester's New York office. Form letters had been mailed to Pan Am crews about the same time the airline sent out bids for the development of a bigger clipper. The 1936 questionnaires and comment spaces contained information regarding the advantages and disadvantages of then present operating factors within the Sikorsky and Martin clipper cockpits. Crew members responded with their complaints and the compilation of returned letters was formulated and studied. When Boeing placed its 314 bid with Pan Am, the gathered information from various crews regarding the future flight-deck design was sent on to Boeing's engineering department as it was to other bidding aircraft builders.

Among the prime requests taken and studied from pilots and crews was that the future clipper should provide for more room and comfort per flight officer station. With such strong recommendations for a better aircraft control center (cockpit), Boeing turned to a larger XB-15-styled arrangement and built a full-sized mock-up flight-deck from wood and other dummy equipment. Numerous alterations were tried and mulled over until the final plan was set and put into full production when Pan Am accepted Boeing's bid.

As for the programming of the multiple crews that were to fly the 314s, Priester had affirmed such a plan as early as the mid-1930s. This was told in 1936 to Capt. Lodeesen, then third-ranking officer on the M-130 boats. Following a transpacific flight to Manila from San Francisco, the Martin-built *Philippine Clipper* was anchored out in the Luzon Island's harbor. The threat of a typhoon was at hand. Priester, who had just completed his first Pacific inspection air cruise, decided to remain aboard for the night while crew mem-

Master pilot (left) and navigator confer over a weather change dispatch received by radio officer while seated at a 314's captain's office. The ability to make correct in-flight decisions called for the best of schooled minds. Some skippers were likened in fame to Lindbergh. (*Photo Courtesy: Pan American World Airways*)

bers kept vigil. While waiting word on the strom, Lodeesen and Priester began to talk to pass time. Sitting next to each other in the darkened cockpit (lights had been turned off to conserve the batteries), Lodeesen recalled part of their conversation:

"Priester talked about the future. Of the huge ships which would one day be criss-crossing the oceans, planes much bigger and faster than our M-130 clipper. 'The captains of these ships,' Priester said, 'will be somewhat like the masters of ocean liners, running their ships from the bridge. Perhaps they will not fly the planes them-

selves any more than a master mariner handles the wheel, but they will have a flight captain who is also the executive officer, leaving to the commander, the decision-making and the running of the flight.

"'That's what we are training you fellows for,' he said quietly.

"A picture took shape in my mind of ships charged with the poetry, the grace of fluid air and charging seas, the mightiest creations man had ever known.

"You'll do it, Mr. Priester.

'Do what?' he asked.

The impossible, tomorrow!"[32]

7

First Launching

By early 1938, the first 314 had neared full construction. With two aft and fore sections joined to the hull's midsection, a heavy double coat of Dupont silver lacquer was applied by spray gun to the fuselage and its extremities which gave the clipper a smooth surface that blended together the numerous skinning parts and rivets. The V-bottom was then painted a Dupont "Yacht Black DeLux" as were the sides up to the water line where a fine red pinstripe was added. Then the Kenworth-built dolly was slipped beneath the 314's keel. Creaking and rumbling atop her cradle, the shiny product was eased backwards by means of an automated pully and cable system until just the rear portion of the hull cleared Plant 1's sliding doors. Hours later two huge outdoor-placed cranes constructed from four pole pine logs common to the northwest lifted the horizontal tail

stabilizer into place where it was bolted and smoothly faired to the hull. Next came the more than 15-foot-high metal-skinned vertical fin which was also hoisted upwards and locked into place.

On February 13th, minus her wings and sponsons, the completed fuselage, with its cantilevered tail unit, was moved out of the factory and onto the concrete and wooden-planked dock. Gleaming in the sun in her gallons of silver lacquer, the streamlined hulk was viewed as resembling a sheik's yacht without masts, rigging or sail. Split-leveled rows of different-sized portholes gave the appearance of a four to five-storied vessel — a dream expanse likened to a surface steamer with numerous cabins about to be crafted into sectioned places of luxurious comfort. On hand as the huge hull was moved backwards were a dozen newsreel and press pho-

Nearing Assembly Building No. 3, Plant 1 roll-out time, Feb. 12, 1938. (*Photo Courtesy: Boeing Aircraft Co.*)

Good enough for a magazine cover, the backwards roll to the outdoors was stilled by Owens' camera, February 13th. At near same time, U.S. Commerce Department granted American Export Steamship Co., Pan Am's rival for transatlantic air service, temporary permits to fly liners to Black Sea, Germany, Egypt, Italy and Portugal. (*Photo Courtesy: S. D. Owens/Boeing Aircraft Co.*)

A whale of a tail is seen mid-point across the Duwamish as caught by Gordon S. Williams, a young freelance photographer working his way through college as a journalist. (*Photo Courtesy: Gordon S. Williams/Boeing Aircraft Co.*)

tographers. One front view shot of the 314 by photographer S. D. Owens appeared a month later on the March 14th issue cover of *Time* magazine.

Within the next few days hydrostabilizers and the four-part wing spans were attached to the mid-hull and wing joints. Taken from Plant 2, the wing sections were hoisted high by the wooden cranes and carefully joined by hand to the fuselage. Scaffolding used inside Plant 1 for the first clipper was then moved outdoors and reassembled around the plane like a cocoon to provide engineers and mechanics simultaneous access to all parts of the ship whereupon final fittings, aileron installations and paint touchups were accomplished. Assisting Boeing's technicians were engineers from Wright and Hamilton who teemed in the final and delicate placements of engines and props. A beehive of activity, the scene resembled a ship-building yard rather than an aircraft plant. Artisan

Ted Tagholm of the Finishing Shop gave one of the clipper's last exterior touches in April when he painted the "Boeing Bug" logo onto the 314's tail fin with Dupont's "International Orange" paint outlined in black.

Finally, in the latter days of May, 1938, the labyrinth of lumber was removed. The fist 314 stood alone atop her dry-docked cradle. Her markings were simple. A deep blue paint to protect pilots' eyes from sun glare covered the top of the bow from the cockpit down to the nose's mooring hatch. Across the top of the wings in near span was a wide band of the "International Orange" paint for identification purposes in the event of a future mid-ocean ditching. The brightly colored stripe, it was believed, would be easily spotted by crews of searching aircraft. Every Pan Am over-water clipper had such markings. Other 314 addages included large bold letters and numbers of NX 18601 (NX-O1) in black paint beneath the port and

Once outdoors next step was to finish cockpit and install control cables, engines, props, sponsons and wings. (*Photo Courtesy: Gordon S. Williams/Boeing Aircraft Co.*)

Looking like a beached cetacean, 314 is cradled in launching slip alongside a rain-swept dock. (*Photo Courtesy: Boeing Aircraft Co.*)

Port wing is joined to inner-built stub, early March, 1938. (*Photo Courtesy: Boeing Aircraft Co.*)

upper starboard wings and tail fin. The letter N stood for "number" while the X abbreviated "experimental." The last digit in government licensing recorded the order of construction.

Poised like a polished gem, the NX-O1 reflected to all those standing about that soon, without a doubt, the liner would rank as the world's foremost commercial "queen of the skies." A speculative announcement from a Boeing executive was printed in an aviation magazine of the period which indicated that the new transoceanic airliner would be named the *South Sea Clipper*. There was strong belief behind the statement, for England at the time had still refused Pan Am Atlantic service landing rights except for a mutually 1937-settled reciprocal run between the U.S. and Bermuda. If the stubborn stand was not settled soon and permission granted to Pan Am, Trippe had all intentions of placing the first 314 on the Pacific. Survey flights to the south of Honolulu, and in particular to Auckland, New Zealand, via stepping-stone islands, were underway with an extra gas-tanked S-42 boat. Once established for commercial service, a 314 would be used on the new route and, at the same time, somewhat relieve the M-130s of already existing heavy passenger and mail loads on the trek between San Francisco and Honolulu. Hence, the rumored NX-Ol's christened name was thought to be compatible with the area it might serve — the South Pacific.

Lights burned late into the wee hours of the morning of May 31st at Plant 1. Final preparations before launching were evident as spotlights glared down onto the outside dock while the clipper's own interior glow radiated forth from the many tiered windows along the hull. Beall's moment of elation was near at hand when the sun finally peered bright over the horizon. For the next 11 hours final checks of all operational equipment were given that entailed checking compartment and fuel tank watertightness, even fuel flow,

manipulation of all controls and the scrutinization of flight equipment.

At long last the licensed NX-O1 was cautiously inched down the wooden-planked apron on a short rail track at 5:00 A.M. under the guidance of a tug stationed aft in the waterway and by a shop-operated pully within the plant. Brief stalls were conducted for calculating correct water line angles as the mammoth machine was slowly slipped backwards and entered for the first time into one of her two natural elements. With ease, the attached cradle beneath the hull that bore the tonnage settled its majestic load four feet into the water. All went according to plan and without incident.

R. B. Bermann, a former staff writer for the *Seattle Post-Intelligencer* newspaper, and assigned to cover all events relating to the 314's public debut and early trial runs, wrote, "Twenty years of dreams and plans found their culmination when the great Seattle-built clipper was launched...

"The clipper represents so many 'firsts' that any one trying to describe her is in danger of running out of superlatives."[33]

As the silver-reflected behemoth was parted from her submerged cradle, four men in two rowboats controlled ropes attached to the 314's wings to help balance the ship's cumbersome attitude until she was safely afloat. While two mechanics rowed the dinghies beneath the roof-like wings, the two other technicians stood in the small picket boats and grappled with the ropes that were tied to sea-anchor hooks built into the liner's undersided wing panels. Slowly, the flying boat was pulled in reverse by a tug and taken further out into the narrow Duwamish Waterway. A queen of the skies was born!

Waiting portside, and aft of the plane's stoppage point, was a barge and a second tug. The tugs, facing opposite directions to one another for braking purposes, were then tightly secured to the 110-foot-long barge. Boeing had contracted and paid for the shoreman's

A mighty spread for a mighty sky-sailing ship, March 15th. (*Photo Courtesy: Boeing Aircraft Co.*)

The 314 gets her ailerons while atop apron-connected launching pit. (*Photo Courtesy: Gordon S. Williams/Boeing Aircraft Co.*)

equipment from the Puget Sound Port Authority to ferry their latest creation to lower water levels. While secured sideways to the barge's mid-section to insure clearing the extensive wing span through a somewhat narrow waterway, and heralded by blasts from the *Christie B's* and *Dolly C's* tug whistles, a slumbered queen glided effortlessly away from the launching site. Several thousand spectators watched from the banks of the Duwamish and from surrounding hills as the proceedings continued in good order under the direction of Laudan. Beall, Egtvedt, Minshall and prominent airline representatives also witnessed the grand event.

The tricky journey down the Duwamish had been well thought out and planned. A 10-hour stop was made a few hundred yards down river at the West Spokane Street Drawbridge. The tug-escorted conveyance of the clipper into the West Waterway of Elliott Bay had to wait until 3:30 A.M., June 1st, for the incoming tide which allowed the convoy safe passage through the narrows and locks. That night, while the 314, barge and two tugs were at anchor near the bridge, the plane's engines were tuned, their roar more ear-piercing than that from a pack of howling coyotes on a moonlit night. Wrapped in sleeping bags, Laudan and a guard crew spent the deep night hours aboard the NX-O1.

At 5:00 A.M., the assigned test crew boarded the boat for the last hour's journey to the open waters of Elliott Bay. They included co-pilot Earl Ferguson, mechanical engineer Bud Benton, flight en-

gineer Mike Pavone, Wright Aeronautical engineers W. C. Lundquist and Frank J. Wiegand entrusted to record engine operations, and nationally acclaimed chief test pilot Edmund ("Eddie") Turney Allen. A slight man of medium height and build, and having an extensively receding hairline and trim mustache, Allen was not new to the 314 project. The then U.S.' leading test pilot had been with

By May 26th, 314 was externally complete, her working cocoon of scaffolding about to be dismantled. (*Photo Courtesy: Boeing Aircraft Co.*)

"Eddie" poses with his ship just before launching. (*Photo Courtesy: Boeing Aircraft Co.*)

High-in-the-sky Tagholm puts final paint dabs of Boeing's bug logo to 314's portside rudder, placement of which was soon after interchanged with liner's painted tail license numbers. (*Photo Courtesy: Boeing Aircraft Co.*)

the undertaking since its inception and was known for high work standards, self discipline and skillful test flying.

Allen was born in Chicago, IL, in 1896, and grew up in the city. He had spent one year at the University of Illinois when World War I erupted. Enlisting in the U.S. Infantry he was later changed to the Signal Corps of the new aviation branch upon learning that the former offered little chance for him to enter officer training school. Following pilot, instructor and instructorship training, Allen was shipped to England. At Marthlesham Heath he studied military plane testing, the beginning of a lucrative career. At war's end Allen returned to the U.S. and resigned from the Army at McCook Field, Dayton, Ohio. His first civilian job was the monumental task of being the first test pilot for NACA at Langley Field. Allen's quest for knowledge returned him to the University of Illinois in 1919 for one year and then to Massachusetts' Institute of Technology to study and master aeronautical engineering.

Then, so Allen thought, came a time for relaxation. Having a zealous desire to learn to fly gliders he joined a glider club (MIT) that traveled to France and Germany. During his first trip abroad he suffered a broken nose and multiple bruises in a wind-swept crash. Following three months in a German hospital the infatuated aero-

nautical enthusiast returned to the U.S. in 1923 and became a freelance test pilot. Allen worked for various aircraft companies while earning his civilian test pilot license. In 1925 he flew for the U.S. Post Office airmail service bouncing aloft in World War I vintage De Havilands out of Salt Lake City, Utah, and Cheyenne, WY.

For Allen, a seemingly carefree person (wild cats never stop looking for prey), the job of flying mail was one of high stakes while being constantly jolted aloft in unpredictable weather without a radio and while frantically trying to make some sort of course on an air-devil's route not completely marked by guiding ground lights. By the grace of God and his seat-of-the-pants flying, plus expert past knowledge of handling such craft, Allen'a scarf kept stiff with the wind!

In 1927 Allen Joined Boeing Air Transport (BAT), the predecessor of United Airlines established March 28, 1927. He flew BAT's Boeing Model 40As between the newly-established Chicago and San Francisco air mail milk run to soon become one of BAT's leading pilots. During what spare time was available, the brave and temerarious Allen shuttled between San Francisco and the Boeing plant where he freelanced in testing such noted Boeing-built planes as the Model 83 and 95, tri-motored 80 airliner series, Model 203 trainer and the famed Monomail. Between his tight scheduling was time spent with Thorp Hiscock, a forerunner in aviation radio equipment design. The combined talent and efforts of Allen and Hiscock led to the development of the first radio telephone system devised for aircraft.

By the time the 1930s came to past, Allen was doing more freelance test flying. He hopped about working for Douglas Aircraft (test flew their DC-1 and DC-2, the latter a baby sister to the DC-3), Northrop Co., Chance Vought, Curtiss, North American, Sikorsky, Eastern Airlines (acted as chief engineer for a short while), and Pan Am to aid the early airline's development program as a consultant engineer and to check out pilots for the line's Caribbean and South American runs. By the late 1930s Allen was back with Boeing as a free-lance test director for the XB-15 "Super Bomber."

Little did Allen know on an early morning in June, 1938, as he sat in the clipper's bridge, that in less than a year (April, 1939) he would end his free-lancing to became a full-time employee of Boeing. Within 11 months he was appointed by Egtvedt as Boeing's Chief Research Director of Aerodynamics and Flight Research, and, at the same pace, continue as chief test pilot of the company's newly established Flight Research Department. The latter assignment eventually led to flight analysis of the B-17 and B-307 Stratoliner. At a black tie banquet held in New York on Jan. 26, 1940, the Institute Of Aeronautical Sciences honored him with a standing ovation upon his receptance of the first "Chanute Award" for " . . . outstanding contributions to methods and procedures in flight research in connection with airplane design and operation." The to be annual award was for those who contributed the most within the field of aeronautical sciences and was in memory of Octave Chanute, a civil engineer who built gliders and encouraged the Wright Brothers to pursue their efforts of mechanical, propelled flight.

In October, 1940, Allen was chosen one of 20 top American aviation figures assigned to the CAA by then Assistant Secretary of Commerce Robert H. Hinckley as an advisory member to guide the department in solving current problems and future growth of airlines, aircraft manufacturers, aeronautical technicians, private flying, commercial flight schools, technical air publications and other related aviation organizations and groups — all on a non-compensatory basis. Allen had mastered the theory of flight so well that he could talk for hours about the materials and workmanship that went into the planes he had tested, as well as give advice to manufacturers for design proficiency and financial practicability.

Allen was chosen by Boeing executives to test the 314 as early as 1937. His efforts were backed by months of laborious hours of studying how the largest commercial plane in the world would actually perform according to the rigid drawing board statistics sought by her purchaser and chief designer. He spent hours at the wind tunnel and water basin test sights to analyze the model's results under various conditions simulating the actual 314's in-flight performance as well as on rough and smooth water surfaces. Studies included the clipper's attitudes when faced with possible upsets during sudden water turns or in the puncturing of her floatation compartments. Hundreds of blueprints of the flying boat's control system and its activation procedures were memorized by Allen, as were blueprints diagramming the plane's oil and fuel lines, hydraulic and vacuum systems to operate the tail's and wings' auxiliary airfoils, plus a thorough examination given to diagrams depicting the 11.5 miles of voltage wiring needed to manipulate the big boat through its elements of sky and water.

Even before Allen knew he was to test the super clipper, and prior to attending the plant's required 314 school courses tor those involved with the ship's development, he had familiarized himself

Prismed in light, the jewel-like dream ship is launched. (*Photo Courtesy: Boeing Aircraft Co.*)

Afloat at last, the mass of aluminum and steel is guided towards barge (right) for long haul to Elliott Bay. (*Photo Courtesy: Boeing Aircraft Co.*)

with the materials required to build the transoceanic beauty following his testing of the XB-15. The past experience of aircraft testing and barnstorm flying — and the knowledge gained therein — had payed off. Boeing's choice for the 314's first captain, and the publicity entailed, soon ranked Allen as the world's foremost test pilot. Overnight he was a hero and an idol to aviation-minded teenagers — a true-to-life "Tail Spin Tommy!"*

So it was that on June 1, 1938, Allen found himself helping to wind the silver 314 down to Elliott Bay. Leading the pack with a hawser attached to the barge was the specially designed *Panair* launch, a near duplicate to the ones that were seen in harbors touched by Pan Am's service and used for patrolling the line's sea-runways. En route down the Duwamish central radio communication was quartered in the launch. Messages between Boeing engineers in the white-painted *Panair* to tug pilots were flashed back and forth to ensure a safe navigated run to open water.

Near mid-morning the barge, arranged to be the temporary base from which the clipper was to be tested, was anchored in the shelter of Fauntleroy Cove that flows into Elliott Bay off Duwamish Head. Allen, who had accredited 6,700 flying hours to his fine record, was about to begin testing his 13th aircraft. Meanwhile, the race to bridge the Atlantic with regularly scheduled commercial airplane service was narrowing. Competition between the powers of Europe (England, France and Germany) was growing at an alarming rate. Pan Am could do little but sit on the sidelines and observe the progress while continuing its open-door sessions with Britain — an effort of hope that might bear fruit, but all at a snail's pace!

In England, Short Bros. was in full production of their larger Empire-Class flying boat, the S-26G. Having a range of more than 3,000 miles with a sizeable passenger and mail load, the craft was to be put into service by 1939. It was Britain's competitive answer

*Hollywood's noted movie series of the 1930s that revolved around the adventures of a fictitious test pilot named Tommy.

to Pan Am's 314 Atlantic service. However, England was not waiting until 1939 to try and start a regularly scheduled air mail service to North America. Montreal, Canada, would be the destination. There would be no hassle in having to acquire U.S. landing rights .

In late 1937, Major R. H. Mayo of Short Bros. developed a "piggyback" experimental mail service for Imperial Airways using a small four-engined S-20 floatplane attached to the top of a larger S-21 flying boat. One aircraft alone could not meet the range factor. By flying out to sea so the S-20 *Mercury* would detach from the mother ship *Maia* to continue the long Atlantic journey. Tested in January and February, 1938, the first successful crossing to Montreal was completed five months later with a full payload of mail and newspapers after a flight of 20 hours and 20 minutes. Not quite the answer for passenger service, the interlocking concept for large mail loads was, however, continued elsewhere on England's Empire routes until the outbreak of World War II.

France, on the other hand, had many types of large flying boats, but all were considered impractical for Atlantic service. Yet at the Latècoére factory a magnificent flying boat was under construction. Known as the L-631, it could fly 3,730 miles nonstop at 185 m.p.h. using six 1,650-horsepowered Gnome Rhone engines. With a wing span of 188 feet and a hull length of 142 feet, the giant

A night's rest under spotlight near Spokane Street Drawbridge. (*Photo Courtesy: Boeing Aircraft Co.*)

weighed 72 tons fully loaded. Originally planned for flights across the South Atlantic, France came to believe that such a craft would be more feasible for the North Atlantic competition. Ten L-63ls were scheduled for production. Their interiors far surpassed even the 314s with Art Deco-designed bars lined with chromed and deeply upholstered stools and chairs adjacent to spacious lounges and high-fashioned staterooms curtained off from the main aisle for additional passenger privacy. War, however, would temporarily stop their production.

Serious consideration for North Atlantic service was begun by the French in June, 1937, when a French shipping company, French Line, joined hands with Air France to create Air France-Transatlantique. Survey flights were periodically conducted across the Atlantic until Aug. 28, 1939, with the L-521 *Lieutenant de Vaisseau Paris* between Portugal, the Azores and Bermuda. Rebuilt since its earlier 1930s storm-damaged incident in Florida, the plane's interior rivaled even the upcoming 314's. Each of the 12 private suites were furnished with a shower. But as in the past, a substantial passenger and mail load was against the L-521's range capabilities despite its 145 m.p.h. speed with six tractor-pusher Hispano-Suiza Ybra engines each rating 850 h.p.

Germany, on the upsweep to enter the passenger and mail air race, began survey mail flights over the North Atlantic with the Blohm und Voss HA-139 floatplane in 1938. Catapulted from the German ship *Schwabenland*, the four-engined *Nordwind* began a scheduled-like mail operation between the Azores and New York. Also, in May, 1938, a prototype Dornier Do-26 was test flown to increase the speed and range for the German mail run. Prepared to go into full operation by 1939, the small four-engined Do-26 flying boat flew nearly 200 m.p.h. for an astonishing 5,000-mile range. The combination mail and passenger service, however, rested with the 1938 drawing board stage of the sleek Blohm und Voss BV-222 Wiking six-engined flying boats later used by the Luftwaffe as patrol and troop transports during the war. Weighing over 100,000 pounds at takeoff, the ultra luxury flying boat could carry 24-day

or 16-night passengers. The 150-foot, 11-inch-winged giants with their 157 m.p.h. cruising speed were ready for Lufthansa service in 1940, a bit late but well illustrating the European race for weekly Atlantic airplane service.

By mid 1938, about the time the 314 was to begin its testing phase of operation, England's and France's political relations with Germany had become extremely strained. Not until the middle of 1939, however, was Trippe relieved from Germany's intervention in the heavier-than-air transport race across the Atlantic. The U.S. Government had, by that time, assured Pan Am that regularly scheduled Lufthansa air service would not be granted.

More startling in the rush for North Atlantic plane flights was the sudden interest and development of proposed transoceanic commercial landplanes by France and Germany. Air France's Inspector General Messieur Codos advocated the use of landplanes over flying boats. Far ahead in his thinking, Codos foresaw swifter service with the use of landplanes that could fly at greater altitudes with pressurized cabins. Subsequently, through his vigorous persistence, three unpressurized landplane models were built; but again the fear of German invasion put an abrupt halt to their commercial use.

Germany's technological ingenuity and skill had built, test flown and had ready a 26-passenger Focker-Wulf GW200 Condor landplane named the *Brandenburg*. If the Third Reich had been given license for operation to the U.S. in 1938, Germany would have stolen the show and crippled the many cost-paying years Pan Am put forth to convince the general public about safety over the seas through the use of flying boat design.

Recorded by a democratic press, and taken as a PR stunt, Germany nevertheless foreshadowed the use of commercial landplanes over great spanses of water. In early August, 1938, German Capt. Alfred Henke and a crew of three flew the Condor non-stop from Berlin to New York in 24 hours and 58 minutes, a record flight that stunned the air market world. Three days later Henke and his men returned the speedy, four-engined plane to Berlin in 19 hours and 55 minutes. Despite the fine achievement, the Atlantic air race was still in the running with Boeing's 314 in the lead.

Morning moorings, Fauntleroy Cove, June 1st. (*Photo Courtesy: Gordon S. Williams/Boeing Aircraft Co.*)

8

"It's Up!"

Skies of blue domed overhead as the clipper lay tightly secured to the mildly swaying barge. The long and arduous testing was about to begin. The early programmed stages were scheduled to last about four days and covered engine tuning; maneuvering and control characteristics of the plane at low speeds using the water rudder; yawing and rolling tests; 360-degree turns in a 10-knot wind; flap-down taxiing tests; engine and oil-cooling monitoring; sailing techniques; spray studies; maneuvering in dead air with two engines out; and stability and cross-wind taxiing. Next in line were planning speed studies that entailed time checks to get the 314 on step using minimum velocity; skipping; control forces and effectiveness in turns in cross winds; yawing and rolling manuevers; stability at given speeds from 20 to 80 m.p.h.; tab angle tests; and trim possibilities relating to spray characteristics.

"Test No. 1," set for engine run-ups, was scheduled for the afternoon, followed by taxi runs near Alki Point located west of Fauntleroy Cove in Puget Sound. Lundquist and Weigand were at their posts on the flight deck waiting to begin engine recordings. Watching from afar, either from shore or aboard numerous sea-fairing boats, were reporters, Department of Commerce representatives, Boeing and Pan Am officials, noted suppliers of 314 equipment and crowds of the general populace. Then it happened!

Tugboat *Dolly C* positions temporary base barge towards anchorage as communications *Panair* launch stands by to begin 314 testing. (*Photo Courtesy: Gordon S. Williams/Boeing Aircraft Co.*)

While all looked on in anticipation to the glory that was to take place, the first defect showed up. It was almost comical in that what occurred brought an abrupt cancellation to the day's testing. The clipper's spark plugs had gone bad. But at least the NX-01 floated nicely!

Thursday, June 2nd, proved more fruitful following spark plug changes. Once again at dawn Allen and his crew clambered aboard the 314 to begin what they hoped to be the first phase of testing — to again rev the engines and proceed to run the ship through its initial taxi runs.

Joining Allen were two additional crewmen: Cram, who acted as chief overseer of 314 test recordings, and Harry West, a leading Boeing electrician. A mass array of special and sensitive equipment had been temporarily installed in the control room that ranged from temperature and pressure gauge markers to vibration recording apparatus. A "Sperry-M LT" panel to monitor 27 of the clipper's vibration points was also installed within the wing's mail compartment, while pressure and temperature equipment were positioned at the captain's conference station. All temperature and pressure gauges gave readings from 88 different clipper areas. More than 11 variances of precisioned instruments were, in time, utilized simultaneously throughout the testing period which included the use of the 58 permanently installed items located at the various officer stations. The flight-deck had become known as "a flying laboratory."

Canvas covers, stretched around the forward engine cowlings to keep the chill and moisture from seeping into the otherwise exposed engine housings, had been removed by ground crew. Allen then flicked the engine switches to the on position, but the power plants just coughed and spat. Three of the four power sources didn't start because the batteries had become low in charge and couldn't activate the primer solenoids, boosters or starter motors. Engine No. 3 eventually thundered to life and spun its prop as white exhaust poured aft and upwards into the wind. The engine was operated long enough to build a charge that activated the other power thrusters.

When all four mounts had burst into action, engine run-ups between high and low pitch were conducted until noon while the clipper's stern was moored to a buoy and the prow made fast to the *Panair* with a lead line to keep the liner braked and from pulling away from the stationed barge. Crowds had congregated on shore

Tuning of engines opened testing program, Elliott Bay, June 1st. (*Photo Courtesy: Gordon S. Williams/Boeing Aircraft Co.*)

and aboard numerous boats just as they had the day before as the sound of the clipper's engines reverberated across the water.

Cast-off was at 4:00 P.M. when the first of slow speed taxi tests began. Three U.S. Coast Guard picket boats and the *Panair* cleared the way as the clipper swished across Elliott Bay and into Puget Sound. Doing 10 knots, the ship began to yaw in rougher seas. Allen applied rudder control but the tail's vertical-hinged surface could not compensate for the angular motion that deviated the plane from her course. When speed was cut the flying boat heeled between three and five degrees. She did the same in turns at slow speeds, yet remained laterally stiffened at 10 knots. Allen instructed Weigand, seated at the engineer's station, to open throttles to 1,500 rpms and the bow started to lift easily and smoothly. The elevators were then tested and responded positively, as did the rudder control — the latter improved at the greater speed.

Exactly 1.05 hours of preliminary taxi tests were given when more problems developed. Large amounts of oil were needlessly used as it passed to the vacuum pumps to operate the flaps and rudder. Then engine plugs became fouled and a number of exhaust couplings were lost. Additional engine tests programmed for the day had to be cancelled.

Allen reported that more taxi runs were necessary to determine correct rudder control as related to the ship's lateral stability. That night at his home Allen scrutinized the day's findings and prepared for another series of tests. Far out in the darkened water, while moored to her makeshift base, the NX-01 bobbed about with the tide as the blanket of night swept the gold sheet of day to the west.

"Test No. 2," Friday, June 3rd, was a continuation of Allen's recommendations to conduct further taxi runs for a better rudder control and righting stability at given speeds. The morning hours were spent figuring how the 314 could be given a much lower center of gravity for better control. Her hull was given a lead ballast used to offer an equivalency of a fixed load — a given weight rep-

resenting passengers, mail and cargo — calibrated into the gross weight of the plane when fitted with luxuries.

While the men planned for the afternoon's testing, and the clipper refueled from portable gas tanks secured in place atop the barge, a mass array of the general public excursioned around the barge in a swarm of boats. Private aircraft circled overhead, some of which were seaplanes that landed and taxied alongside the moored clipper. One U.S. Navy floatplane from the not-too-distant and anchored battleship *HSS Mississippi* puttered beneath one of the NX-01's far-stretched wings like an ugly duckling next to a swan. Boeing's and Pan Am's 314 publicity reports, printed by the journalistic media of the day, had spread far and wide. The clipper's progress made top news.

Shadows began to create silhouetted forms along the shore line when the flying boat was cast loose from its barge base to begin a 48-minute testing period. The 314's gross weight was set at 55,674

Varied tests at high speeds left behind many a bridal-trained wake as seen by this June 5th run. (*Photo Courtesy: Gordon S. Williams/Boeing Aircraft Co.*)

pounds as compared to the previous day's 56,154 pounds. Without any misgivings, all engines sputtered to life. Engine No. 3 was run at 1,500 rpms for 10 minutes to measure oil flow. A few minutes before 6:00 P.M., Allen moved the boat out into the bay trailed by the three Coast Guard picket boats while the *Panair* dashed ahead to clear surface traffic. The *Kalakala*, a ferry filled with commuters from nearby Bremerton, a small town directly aligned with Seattle across Puget Sound, slowed down as the spectacle buoyantly skimmed past. *Kalakala* passengers were given a free ticket to a one-time action air show of historical value.

Hitting between 35 and 38 knots at 1,500 rpms in a 20- m.p.h. wind, the flying boat did not plane, but rudder use was recorded as being negative. When Allen slowed the craft down to 30 knots, the ponderous flying boat could not be held on a center course by using just the rudder control. The test pilot had to differentially gun the outboard engines to maintain the line of direction.

Yaw stability was found neutral at, but negative under, 35 knots. Lateral stability registered negative at three or four degrees without centrifugal forces in a non-beam wind.

One taxi test required taking the ship through a cross- wind turn at a speed of around 30 knots when the NX-01 started to raise up on her step, a time of applied power when a flying boat stiffens in a horizontal position in line with the water's surface and just prior to takeoff. In comparatively open water, and past Alki Point, the commander turned the plane into the wind, raced the engines and sped away. Suddenly Allen began to have difficulty handling the ship. The strong cross-wind was too much for the plane and its ill-dispersed fuel weight balance.

Heading toward reference points Smith Cove and the lee of Magnolia Bluff, the clipper heeled to starboard in a beam wind of 20 knots. The right sea-wing became swamped, the main wing's starboard tip and more than half the outboard aileron cut into the deep, green-shaded water spewing aft a cascade of spray. Instantly, Allen reacted; he raced the downed wing's engines and popped the submerged structure from the water. Too much starboard power then lurched the NX-01 to port, nearly throwing the other wing tip deep below surface. Hundreds of spectators, including Beall and Priester, who were standing in the *Panair*, watched in horror. Instantly Allen cut all engines and the 314 came to a splashing halt just as the tipsy bulk of metal heeled once more to starboard.

A shaken Allen ordered three nerve-racked and life-jacketed crew members out the celestial dome and onto the wing while the other four men sat inside the outer starboard engine nacelle to try and balance out the unstable 314.

Allen stood in the clipper's opened bow's mooring hatch and waited as the skipper of *Verna*, a nearby trawler, lent a dory and some deck hands to help attach a hawser to the plane's two nose bollards. After Boeing's chief test pilot secured his ship he looked for possible wing damage. Finding none, Allen reported that only the tail pipes on engines No. 3 and 4 had run too hot — that the

Another look at the wake left by the Clipper's passing.

vacuum pumps again exhausted too much oil and that five new exhaust couplings were lost at sea.

With such statements completed in the log, the men sat like "Lilliputians" on the wing waiting for the lame "Gulliver" to be towed back to the barge by the *Panair* crash boat. A filtered sun, trying to pierce its rays through a thick overcast, slowly sank below the western horizon. Another 314 testing day had come to a close.

Reasons for the unexpected dunking were surmised by both crew and Boeing engineers. All of the fuel had been stored in the overhead wing tanks making for a top-heavy aircraft. With both sea-wing tanks empty, the strong Pacific winds swept the 314 off balance and caused her to heel. Two hydrostabilizers had too high an angle, a deadrise slant when attached to the hull that added to the instability of the clipper at certain speeds. Even when plant engineers estimated the sea-wings would eventually have to be lowered for a better righting angle, the present angle of the stub wings was found not that critical for any immediate alteration. Correction of weight distribution for the next test was executed when 2,600 gallons (1,300 pounds) of gas was poured into the sea-wing tanks. A lower center of gravity was achieved when a ton of lead was placed dead center within the hull's passenger deck.

Allen told Boeing executives that more taxi tests were needed to study the 314's rudder control and its lateral stability effects. Saturday, June 4th, was spent replacing couplings, pin-pointing the solution to fuel storage imbalance and more engine calculations. The next day, without rest on the Sabbath, "Test No. 3" was conducted with a gross weight of 74,984 pounds. A bit of a stickler was noted when engine No. 1 wouldn't start after a primer solenoid stuck. The problem was quickly resolved.

Taxiing out for the day's event, Allen hit 25 knots with the boat at 1300 rpm in a six-m.p.h. wind. He applied full right rudder and the clipper turned 45 degrees off course. Holding the rudder tight to the right, the ship oscillated back to its correct run line and did the same when full left rudder was enforced. It was found unstable up to, but stable past, a 10-degree angle at 25 knots.

Maintaining the same speed, Allen used full ailerons with rudder control in a wide circle to a point where the leading edge of a dipped sea-wing kicked into the water. Coming down-wind across the Sound at a reduced speed of 20 knots at 1500 rpm, the 314 could be held on course through rudder use only. After two minutes into the third phase of the taxi tests, Wiegand told his captain to stop engines as No. 4's exhaust tail stack had run too hot (All four stacks were later replaced with a more efficient product.)

SEATTLE POST-INTELLIGENCER—*The Quality Newspaper of the Northwest*—SATURDAY, JUNE 4, 1938

As Wind Tipped Big Clipper on Test Run

WINGS AWASH!—The Boeing Clipper lifting her right wing out of the water off Smith Cove after immersing it during a practice run. The plane was not damaged by its experience and taxiing tests will continue today, with just a bare possibility that the maiden flight will be taken.

Local media, national magazines and radio broadcasts covered clipper's first heart-throbbing wing-dipping event in Puget Sound. (*Photo Courtesy: Seattle Post-Intelligencer*)

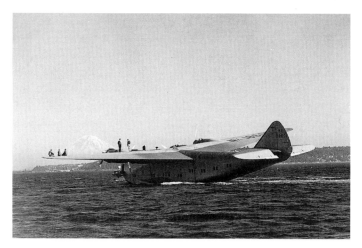

Following close-call tipping some of crew scrambled atop port wing to help balance out ship while waiting rescue towing. (*Photo Courtesy: Boeing Aircraft Co.*)

Once the stack had cooled, Allen struck up the power plants and used a full right rudder to complete a turn in a down-wind heading with engines No. 1 and 2 running 1500 rpm, while Nos. 3 and 4 were throttled momentarily to 1300 rpm. During a turn the leeward sea-wing's leading edge became somewhat submerged and shot water over its outer bulb tip.

With the turn completed, Allen hit 60 knots and kept the 314 on course only through a high degree of rudder use. Increasing speed to 72 knots, the clipper oscillated while maintaining a relatively good directional heading using limited use of rudder. Aileron control was found to be average, but tab was not sufficient enough for Allen to get complete control unless the ship was brought up on her step. Next came a successful upwind turn followed by a down-wind course on step in a 20-m.p.h. wind after which the control was passed to Ferguson to head the ship back to base.

Fifteen miles of straight line taxiing to West Point was behind them when the starboard wing suddenly went down during a turn to momentarily dip its tip. Water swallowed the leeward sea-wing. The NX-01 was controlled again only through the use of opposite wing engine power. With the switches cut to the "off" position, and riding dead in the sea, both sea-wings were inspected for a possible answer to the mind-boggling lateral instability that should have been improved with the added sea-wing fuel load. Water was found in the port sea-wing's inboard tank and Allen and crew believed at first that possibly a plate had been torn or sprung during the constant rough water pounding. No damage was spotted, but over time moisture had seeped through loosened plates. As for the second dunking, the crew thought a blast of wind had spun the aircraft about. It was later determined that Ferguson, unfamiliar with handling such a big air boat, had gunned the wrong pair of engines while making a simple turn when using the differential power technique.

Fifty miles of taxiing and five hours of hard work ended at 2:30 P.M. when the 314 was reanchored at its floating base. She had been towed home by the *Panair* and prepared for the next test-ing session scheduled for Tuesday, June 7th, to determine rudder control and yaw stability at high taxi speeds, and to have engines and control accessory performances checked. June 6th involved roll stability tests near the base. With dead engines, the clipper was balasted with lead weights, first to starboard and then to port to record how far an angle she would roll before reaching a critical mark. Allen contemplated on taking the NX-01 into the air during the next outing of June 7th. It was a most anxious time for Beall — his dream ship was nearing its first flight.

Engine No. 1 was again difficult to start at the beginning of "Test No. 4" on the morning of June 7th due to a deficient primer solenoid. Repaired, the clipper was cast off with a gross weight of 74,984 pounds and taxied out to sea. Again the liner heeled strongly to starboard in a four-to-six-m.p.h. port beam wind.

Allen, cruising the plane between four and six knots, swung the ship down-wind to clear a large vessel and then returned to planned course. He became alarmed when the flying boat again listed to starboard from wind on the port beam. The sharp angle caused the leeward sea-wing to plow into the ocean and force water forward. What Allen couldn't understand was why, in a low wind, the wing dipped so much on this test and hadn't under similar taxiing conditions during "Test No. 3" when the plane was at a lower gross weight.

Arduously trekking north, the clipper was piloted in the west-to-port wind until it was clear of Duwamish Head. Every time Allen increased speed above six knots, the starboard sea-wing dug into the water and built up forward waves. When windward engines were throttled more than the leeward two it was difficult to keep the bow out of the wind and remain fixed on the northern course. The action caused the slipstream of air to lift the windward wing which tended to accentuate the starboard listing.

Unable to solve the predicament, Allen turned the clipper into the western wind and increased speed to 25 knots. All went well for awhile. The NX-01 stiffened laterally until Allen had to turn it out of the wind to avoid Alki Point, and down went the starboard wing. Determined to find the cause for the weird tilting, all engines were cut and the 314 brought to a stop to roll and sway with the waves. Like the day before, fuel tanks in the sea-wings were inspected. Everything checked out, including the overhead wing tanks. But an extra 110 gallons of gas had been placed in the starboard wing tank by ground crew. Allen's verbal reaction was never recorded!

Engines were restarted to resume the taxi tests and the flying boat was directed toward the lee of Vashon Island due west of Seattle. Allen needed the lee of the island to get out of the direct western wind to accomplish a tight turn on the step between 55 and 66 knots. The first fast turn out of the strong wind was successful. Throttles were cut back after the turn was completed and the 314 settled down into the water off her step. For a second turn, Allen brought the plane up to 55 knots and raised the hull where lateral stability was improved. At the fast speed an attempt to turn south and cruise parallel to shore was met with more frustration. Man's air machine started to list to port. More tries with the unbalanced fuel load were made until Allen decided it too dangerous to continue the effort to accomplish a second turn.

A low speed turn was made with flaps down and inboard engines cut to sail the plane past the lower section of the island. With flaps raised, the 314 was turned and sailed back towards Seattle across the Sound. About half way Allen idled the craft while the *Panair* drew near to allow Beall to board for test observations.

Approaching the eastern shore, Allen turned the ship at nearly zero speed. The wind picked up, and with correct rudder control and engine thrust the clipper seemed to be pushed by nature's force in any direction the captain wished to take his ship. But the sea's semi-calm state didn't last long when winds became violent and the surface suddenly frothed with an exceeding amount of driftwood.

Allen decided to discontinue further tests and opted to sail to port parallel to shore from Alki Point to Duwamish Head. Once away from the lee of Vashon Island, and back into the powerful winds, the 110 gallons of gas was divided and transferred from the starboard wing tank to the sea-wing outboard tanks.

Sailing became nearly impossible when the wrathful winds and seas lashed at the clipper from the west. Inboard engines were started and a turn to the north was attempted but impossible to accomplish. Allen's fears of an unbalanced ship were intensified when, in trying to make the pivot, another leeward list was encountered. Instead of a tight turn in the battering winds, a wide, two-mile-long radius around Duwamish Head and into Elliott Bay was made. Any earlier ideas of getting the NX-01 airborne were dashed by the weather. Skimming the waves en route back to the barge, the boat was run up to 65 knots on her step when she began to porpoise, a serious 314 problem first noticed and later corrected by having to alter the design of the hull bottom. Allen had to reduce speed to 50 knots before he could stop the bouncing.

While Allen cruised the clipper home, Ferguson watched for any additional driftwood that could possibly damage the hull. Once in the safe haven of Elliott Bay the clipper's engines were throttled back and the ship was taxied downwind to the barge and subsequent mooring. The day's disappointments were expressed by those watching and closely monitoring the clipper's daily events, a day expected by some to be the one when the NX-01 was to have flown aloft. Some people, including those of the press, had anticipated that the first flight was to have been the same day as the launching. This supposition, however, was contrary to Allen's thinking:

"...the clipper was far from ready to fly when she was eased down the ways at the Boeing plant," the test pilot later wrote. "Indeed, the testing program bore more resemblance to that of a Zeppelin or an ocean liner than to the popular conception of a new airplane's trials — the notion that a test pilot just 'gives her the gun and sees what she will do.'

One of the chief reasons I was given the job of testing the new Boeing clipper is that I am afraid to take risks... But the test pilot obviously does not balk at necessary risks in probing the unknown characteristics of a new-type airplane, so that other pilots will know it is safe for them to fly. What I mean is that an experienced test pilot analyzes the problems presented by a new ship and solves them step by step, more often than not eliminating the main chance involved by solving the individual factors composing it, or by taking advance precautions to render the risk harmless if it finally does develop."[35]

Boeing's test pilot was not about to take the 314 into the air during its first four trial runs until he was sure he and his crew were completely at ease with the plane's precise synchronization of gaged power, handling characteristics and acceptable water stability through rudder and aileron control, the period of which each en-

Single fin-tailed 314 was a common sight along Seattle's waterfront before first flight. (*Photo Courtesy: Boeing Aircraft Co.*)

gine was given a two-hour monitoring and much of the run-ups at full throttle. Between each power plant testing and adjustments were further studies to insure that the engines would support the aircraft's lift. It was what the ship could or could not do, versus what she was expected to achieve on paper, that concerned Allen and crew. Only after the first four-day tabulated reports did Allen determine that a takeoff, climb and cruise flight could take place; but again only if water stability properly coexisted with an 80-m.p.h. charge, which was substantially above the plane's minimum takeoff speed in a maximum wind of 15 m.p.h.

The only item that concerned Allen the most was the lack of complete rudder control — the vertical tail surface lacking enough planing surface to maintain correct course in adverse cross winds. There was no foreseen danger in letting the clipper fly, but Allen realized the ship would eventually have to have its tail modified. Earlier wind tunnel tests of the single tail fin model had proven incorrect for the final full-scale performance of the aircraft. While the 314 was being built, some people, even aviation-minded teen-agers involved in model building, had commented to Boeing that the 314's single vertical tail assembly seemed less than adequate to support the clipper's in-flight control. Yet Boeing engineers, re-canting later, recalcitrantly stuck by the original Langley Field model wind tunnel tests.

All of the preceeding had taken place by the late morning of June 7th. There were plans to take the clipper out for an 80-m. p . h. afternoon taxi run, but more harsh and unexpected winds swooped through Seattle and turned Puget Sound into a tossed, white-capped body of churning water that caused an alternated yank-and-pull-like strain on the 314's hemp mooring ropes that were held taut to the barge. An underside port wing eye-bolt sea-anchor hook used to secure a wing line snapped. The crew, finished with lunch and waiting for the winds to calm down to resume testing, hurried back to board the pitching flying boat.

Finally, up and away into a rain-spattered sky. (*Photo Courtesy: Boeing Aircraft Co.*)

With thoughts of clearing the 314 away from the barge to avoid denting, Allen became aware that repairs for the ruined bolt fas-tener were imperative since it was one of the main securing locks that moored the clipper to the barge. Allen hoped the sea would calm down enough so that he might try for a takeoff and fly the ship to Lake Washington, east of Seattle, where the majority of tests were to occur. There the water was more docile, a place where re-pairs on the bolt catch could be more easily accomplished.

"...we had to cut her loose from our work barge in Elliott Bay because it was the safest thing to do,"[36] Pavone later remarked.

In good order, the clipper sloshed away from her trappings while Allen battled the sea to keep his ship from being severely damaged by running aground on shore. At 5:00 P.M., as quickly as the winds had viciously errupted, they fell to a mild seven m.p.h. Although the hour was late, "Test No. 5" was initiated.

About 5:40 P.M., Allen warmed the 314's engines and taxied the ship, laden with a gross weight of 67,659 pounds, towards Seattle's downtown waterfront. People in droves gathered behind the fenced shoreline as the Coast Guard picket boats and the *Panair* churned their water blades to lead the way. Turning west, the boats and the clipper headed towards Alki Point in the seven m.p.h. north-to-east cross-wind that struck the NX-01's port beam. Speed was increased to 30 knots that resulted in a starboard list. Allen cut to 10 knots and the flying boat stabilized. Then a down-wind turn was made at an extremely slow speed. Completed, a course was set for Restoration Point on Bainbridge Island. Power was increased to 70 knots and the 314 raised up on her step and began to porpoise. Control was marginal; Allen had to use differential power to main-tain course, so throttles were closed and the 314 settled back down into the water and was taxied at slow speed to the center of Puget Sound. On-step-taxiing that day was considered by Allen as being too dangerous.

Small waves lapped at the clipper's water line as the plane was slowly turned into the wind at zero speed. The flight crew were at their assigned stations and somewhat uncomfortably strapped into their seats with bulky parachutes and life preservers tied to their upper torsos. Ferguson was at the first officer's station next to Allen in the bridge. Their extra garb made it most unpleasant, but it was the rule when testing a new plane to wear protective gear. Behind the pilots sat Lundquist at the captain's conference station. Wiegand was posted at the engineer's post while West sat at the radio operator's station. Cram was positioned to starboard next to Lundquist in a jump seat. All aboard were well-prepared for a pos-sible takeoff after .85 hours of taxiing.

Many wondered if Allen was going to do it this time—lift the clipper away from its first holding element. There was little if any time for the crew to contemplate such an event as they were only thinking of another high speed taxi run and the monitoring of all instruments.

"My companions," Allen wrote, "knew precisely what I planned to do and were letter-perfect in what was expected of them. I had told them that if I was satisfied with the ship's behavior on the 80-m.p.h. surface test, it would turn out to be the clipper's take off run. Otherwise, I intended to throttle down, let the ship settle back into the water and taxi back to our moorings."[37]

Straight ahead was an unobstructed 10-to-15-mile visibility. The wind blew directly down Puget Sound. Engines were set on idle — the NX-01 was poised and ready to strike out. In motion with the waves, the flying boat rocked buoyantly atop the licking water. Allen was to control the plane and Ferguson, if needed, would assist in applying extra steering and rudder pedal force, along with holding the correct throttle settings to give engine power synchronization. Instrument and engine readings were watched by Lundquist and Wiegand, and if Allen did lift the clipper it was Wiegand's task to cut back all power speed from 2300 to 1900 rpm. Full power was set at 2300 rpm with a 42-inch manifold pressure. All of the electrical instrument recordings were supervised by West while Cram acted as general overseer of flight operations. Special attention was focused on the clipper's rudder control at the high speed, the aircraft's trim setting, cowl flap operation, engine cooling, ship's stability and any occurance of porpoising.

A quick review of each crew member's responsibilities was discussed before Allen swung around in his seat and faced forward. Debris clearance information was received from the far-off *Panair*. Ferguson patiently sat alongside his commander waiting for orders and keeping his eyes glued forward and down into the water looking for floating debris of any kind. The path ahead looked clear despite a heavy overcast. A light rain was falling.

Allen took the engines off idle. Throttles were slowly pushed open. The ship seemed to stick for an instant, then a slapping of waves against the lower hull was heard as the 314 moved forward, its keel dug deep into the water. Engines increased their crescendo and the automatically pitched propeller tips spun 165 m.p.h. Sucked air pushed the clipper onward, momentum gained with each passing second. Beall and other officials followed alongside in the launch and picket boats on a parallel course while a small plane droned low overhead.

Seattle Post-Intelligencer cameraman Clarence Rote and newsreel photographer Charles R. Perryman had chartered a plane flown by Lana Kurtder to photograph and film one of the 314's standard taxi tests. Unaware of what they were about to record, the men began to angle their cameras down upon the moving clipper. Kurtder flew the single-engined plane in circles above the 314 when the latter turned into the wind. Perryman later recounted:

"Down below, the big plane was boiling along, leaving a wake like an ocean liner. Suddenly her pilot gave her the gun, and the four motors opened up with a roar that sounded like all the hurricanes in history rolled into one."[38]

At the helm, Allen stared ahead. Waves began to smack harder on the plane's undersides. Wham, wham, wham went the hull as the liner spliced through the surface, its windows swaddled with a first takeoff spray. Increased wave action rolled nicely away from

End of first flight after first landing, Lake Washington, June, 1938. (*Photo Courtesy: Boeing Aircraft Co.*)

the hull and beneath the sea-wings, the resulting spray becoming evanescent aft of the tail. Allen glanced at the air-speed meter — the needle was nearly at the 80-m.p.h.. mark. The 314 wanted to lift. Allen held the wheel firm and kept the ship atop the water, the keel just cutting the surface. Right and then left rudder was applied to test for effectiveness of control and yaw stability. Both directions were satisfactory.

Lateral control was affected when Allen cocked right and left ailerons. As he fingered the right aileron, the right wing started to dip, with the same result when the left aileron was activated. The giant obeyed its master — lateral control was excellent. Elevators were tried next and proved even more effective as the 314 raced along at her takeoff speed across the sea-runway to leave behind a bridal-like train of mist. At that point Allen realized it would be safe to fly the clipper.

"Almost imperceptibly, I lifted my restraining grip and let her take the air."[39]

Perryman and Rote fumbled with their cameras in the small plane's cabin. Below, the clipper's tail went down slightly as the bow bid a momentary farewell to her gripping fulcrum. From one of the speeding picket boats came an exhuberant yell, "It's up!"[40]

For a second she was, and then the clipper once more whacked the surface.

"She's down again," an official further exclaimed![41]

But not for long. A splash and the 314 was airborne — touched surface a wee more and then lifted to dash away in poise and grace, her bow directed towards Magnolia Bluff. Shouts of joy rang out from the three patrol crafts left far behind on the clipper's fifth test run and the start of its "Test Flight No. 1." Rote and Perryman began to click and roll their cameras. Perryman said of the takeoff:

"Then, so quickly that we barely had time to get our cameras trained on her, daylight showed between the hull and the water, She was in the air after a taxiing run that seemed less than a quarter-mile! She soared onward like a big graceful swan, flying just above the water. The pilot let her climb very gently. She looked like a big flying hotel with all her windows .

"Kurtder gave our plane the whole throttle while Clarence and I worked our cameras like mad. But it was like chasing a cyclone.

"She went over the horizon like a silver streak and left us alone in the sky."[42]

The NX-01 was kept at 10 feet for about a mile so Allen could bring her right down if anything drastic occurred. The air-speed indicator swept past 90, 95 to 100 m.p.h. Propellers gyrated and whined, their sound disturbing to the ears of the crew despite the soundproofed control room. It was the tips of the props that caused the ear-splitting scream. They were turning 2,300 revolutions a minute — faster than the speed of sound!

Allen shouted to Weigand, "Synchronize engines at 1900 rpm!"[43] His voice was lost to the noise. A microphone was at the captain's reach to contact Weigand, but Allen was afraid to let go of the yoke. Twice more he yelled out his command. Twice more he could not even hear his own voice. Instictively, Allen reached over to use his own master throttle which lowered the noise. The four tachometers had reached marks of 2000, 1950, 1850 and 1900 rpm.

"Synchronize at 1900," Allen once more called out to Weigand.

"Right, 1900," Weigand confirmed.

"Give me thirty-two inches manifold pressure," the commander addressed Ferguson.

"Thirty-two inches manifold,"[44] Ferguson answered, his eyes focused on the instrument panel before him.

The NX-01 was held straight and just off the water for about a minute after lift-off until the engines were synchronized and the manifold pressure was uniform. Lundquist recorded all engine temperature readings with the 24-point thermocouple switch from the time the ship graced aloft using full horsepower to when each power plant was set at 950 h.p. Immediate in-flight testing repeated some of the ship's ground tests, such as trim angles, stability, rudder control and the like.

"Are your engine temperatures OK," Allen again yelled out.

"Engine temperatures all satisfactory,"[45] Lundquist called back.

Allen allowed the clipper to climb with controlled ease. Up, up, up went the liner to 203 feet. The clipper was free in her natural element — so beautiful in her bigness and streamlined mein as she soared through the sky. The rain continued to slash at the bridge's forward-paned portholes.

During the climb Allen used aileron control to examine just how much force he needed at the wheel during the plane's flying speed. He rocked the massive flying boat from side to side and all went somewhat satisfactory. There was a noted touch of "stiffness" to the control cables due to their newness within the expansive wings.

Lateral stability was then tested when each wing was dipped 15 degrees to determine the force needed to hold the appendages down against the plane's own tendencies to right itself. Directional and longitudinal stability were tried with the elevators and tail rudder. Although longitudinal stability was found to be satisfactory, the directional was not. The clipper, nearly as she had done on the water, began to yaw — a deviation from the straight path of operation. Allen had to fight the controls to keep the 314 straight on course by applying an extensive five-degree tail rudder. At first he believed the excessive yaw was due to "over-controlling," but soon traced the problem to the lack of tail rudder.

Slowly climbing to 2,000 feet for an assured safe height, assymetrical power, the alternating shift (cross-gunning) of port and starboard engines, had to be given to swing the 314 around. It was assured the clipper lacked vertical tail surface to adequately control the mammoth airliner in a tight turn. A slow, wide, 10-mile radius bank was then executed called a "grandma turn." The sleek 314 flew south over the west shore of the Sound, past its old water moorings, Boeing Field and then headed east. While over the city, and making its conservative turn to begin a landing approach to the 17-mile-long by four-mile-wide Lake Washington, the smog had become so thick that Allen flew blind for about 15 seconds. It was at this point that Cram came forward to the bridge and stood between the two pilots to further discuss the plane's contractive controls. Soundproofing had given a definite quiet to the flight-deck after the engines were tuned. A normal conversation was held between Cram and Allen as the former talked about his inner wing inspection tour after takeoff when the plane had leveled off — that each power plant functioned perfectly. Cram also reported in the log that there was no exhaust manifold overheating or cowling malfunctions and that the apparatus for engine cooling was "on line."

Engines were then throttled to test the ship in a power-off glide. The clipper responded in good fashion to her commander's slightest touch and remained maneuverable and stable through the use of the servo controls (air balances) that aided Allen in the power-off glide.

Coming in at the north end of Lake Washington on the final approach, Allen pushed the button that lighted a sign that read "landing" on the engineer's board.

"We're landing," Allen called out. "Is it all right to throttle the engines ?" The question was directed to Lundquist as the power plants were highly compressed and were being operated at a high temperature. They could have been damaged if cut too quickly.

"Engines OK for landing,"[46] Lundquist replied.

Power was throttled from cruising speed to 110 m.p.h. Yaw stability was noted to have improved at the lower descent speed when the clipper leveled off at 800 feet altitude before reducing to 80 m.p.h., the same speed used for takeoff. Lined up with the western shore in a north-to-south landing, the 314 was eased straight in with flaps up; for Allen knew if he had used flaps, the speed would have been cut further to 68 m.p.h. — a speed too slow that could have possibly caused a stall resulting in a sudden list or drop. Rudder control was also noted to have improved at the faster landing

Crowds (left) greet reposed flying boat, Matthews Beach, end of "Test Flight No. 1." (*Photo Courtesy: Boeing Aircraft Co.*)

speed. Just above the water the majestic queen of the air flattened out horizontally to the surface line.

"Those last few feet and inches seemed interminable," Allen later said. "Actually, we had been on the water several seconds before anyone aboard realized that the clipper's first flight was over, so smoothly had the big ship returned to her denser medium. It was probably the best landing of my entire flying career, and I joined in the incredulous and exultant cheer which burst spontaneously from the lips of my companions."[47]

And it was a perfect first landing. The 314 split the waters of the lake north of the village town of Laurelburst so easily that the spray couldn't be seen from the bridge's portholes. Water and hull first met at the ship's mid-section with tail a bit down. Rote focused his lens on the 314's starboard side and flicked his camera's shudder as Kurtder flew the tiny private plane north in the opposite direction of the queen's settling, marking the end to the 38-minute flight. Kurtder had flown the photographers to the lake area after the 314 out-distanced them over Puget Sound. It was at Lake Washington that Perryman and Rote knew where to get the next set of camera action shots to cover the impressive 314's first bout with the sky.

Forced outward from the clipper's hull was a big swell that eventually dwindled in size once the plane's keel depressed itself deeper into the water after the power was cut back. Allen carefully slipped the liner towards the float and dock specifically built for the 314 testing program. Mooring facilities were at Matthews Beach, then a semi-resort located at the north western shores of the lake which included a small house dubbed by Boeing ground crew as "Shanty No. 1." The base, supervised by company employee Walter Way, had been leased by the aircraft firm from Seattle's city government. It was not the typical beach one relishes for leisurely bathing with shade umbrellas, esplanades and finely grained particles of white sand. Matthews Beach, now part of a state park, was almost uninhabited at the time — a scenic spot nearly untouched by man and enmeshed with tall reed grass that resembled an early North American Indian wild rice swamp. In June, 1939, it became a terminal site for Pan Am when the S-42 *Alaska Clipper* inaugurated passenger air service to Alaska through the Inside Passage.

A mere handful of inquisitive people greeted the 314 as she glided to a halt and was warped to a buoy near the dock. Announcements of the clipper's triumph were flashed over local radio stations. Soon countless automobiles streamed to the lakeside, via a nearby road. By the time Allen and crew stepped off the clipper and taken ashore by a motored dinghy, hundreds of people were standing about to catch a glimpse of the renowned test pilot while being interviewed about his latest sky adventure. Newspaper reporters and radio commentators crowded around the crew for first-line stories while ground mechanics from "Shanty No. 1" clambered in and about the 314 like a swarm of ants.

"She 'feels' fine," Allen smilingly related to those about him. "There are still a few minor adjustments to be made — but she's a great ship. I didn't begin to use all her power at any time. I got up about as far as Everett" (a town on the Sound 25 miles northeast of downtown Seattle) "and then turned back"[48]

Tested during the short flight were the plane's trim, engine cooling system, control qualities and cowl flap operations, vibration tendencies, structural effects as opposed to increasing speeds related to control stiffness, stability and general engine operation and yaw stability. Control forces in normal turns, propeller and engine controls, engine temperatures and other functional systems connected to fuel, electrical and hydraulic equipment were also monitored. During the landing a check was made of the plane's speed with effects on control, stability on the step, distance to cease planing, porpoising, the effect of water rudder use, lateral and yaw stability and control at slowing speeds.

A humorous side note to the end of the flight was given when Allen was told he had been in the air only 38 minutes as compared to what he believed was an hour's sky-breaking event. As accurate as he was as a test pilot, Allen's wrist watch was off! The master of flight only conceded to the accurate timing when he was told that both takeoff and landing had been officially clocked.

Unable to continue on with the interview, Allen departed the scene to write and submit to Boeing his log report of the day's activities. He was pressed for time. At 9:00 PM., after being accompanied to the airport by Beall and Minshall, Allen, Ferguson and Cram boarded a United Airlines DC-3 for San Francisco. The three men held conference the next morning with Pan Am representatives at the airline's Pacific Division headquarters regarding future 314 testing. Discussed were some of the 314's problems, one of which was the rudder that Allen had found discouraging. Following the one-day meeting, Boeing's salient test men boarded a 3:45 P.M. plane for the return trip to Seattle.

Further clipper tests were rigid and complex that assured an airline delivery delay. Only after Boeing and Pan Am were satisfied with the flying boat's performances could the clipper undergo additional comprehensive and detailed U.S. Government's Department of Commerce testing. Then and only then would the Model 314 be accepted into the commercial realm of international flight.

9

Mastering a Queen

At dawn on June 8th, while Allen, Cram and Ferguson were in San Francisco, the NX-01 was towed from Matthews Beach to the Sand Point Naval Air Station located less than one mile south of the temporary clipper testing base on the same side of the lake. Having a beaching ramp, the 314 was hauled out of the water on the cradle that had been shipped to the Navy's depot. For the next eight days the clipper was checked and given a new coat of black paint on her hull and sea-wing bottoms.

"Test No. 6" was put into effect on June 15th to again determine rudder control with a 81,892-pound gross weight during taxi runs and turns up and down the lake. Control was still found to be negative. The next day during "Test No. 7," and despite insufficient rudder control between 40 and 50 knots in cross-wind taxiing, and while making on-step turns, aileron and elevator use was found satisfactory between 50 and 60 knots. However, during the next few days of testing the 314's tail rudder was still considered a major problem. In one 60-knot turn, using full rudder and full throttles

on the inside engines, and half throttles on the outside plants, the flying boat refused to come out of a bank. It was at that point that Allen knew the single tail rudder was inadequate for the hull size and span of the wings.

As Allen continued with testing, Boeing engineers began a small model-towing testing on the lake with the addition of a small fin attached to the miniature model's hull bottom. It was believed that such a full scale attachment would aid the 314's directional stability during taxiing and takeoff runs. What was needed, however, was a new tail! Scrapping the fin idea, Beall and his staff gave attention to tail modification while 314 taxi tests continued to further record control, stability and yaw at different speeds.

Following "Test No. 10" on June 28th when some S turns were easily made with a minimum load of 56,016 pounds, but control again found marginal while taxiing between 35 and 40 knots, the 314 was taken back to Matthews Beach. There she stayed for more than a month moored to a float until Boeing studied a new tail on a

Beached for primping, Sand Point Naval Air Station, Lake Washington, after first flight. (*Photo Courtesy: Harold Slack/Boeing Aircraft Co.*)

Power of engines could be heard for miles around as NX-01 streaked up and down Lake Washington in near perfect form. (*Photo Courtesy: Boeing Aircraft Co.*)

model within the latest 250-m.p.h. wind tunnel complex at the University of Washington from whence many of the clipper's engineers had graduated. In early August the 314's original tail was unbolted, sawed off and lifted away by a wooden crane atop an old flatbed truck owned by the Eyres Co. of Seattle that had been contracted to assist Boeing in the tail change.

Roger H. Callarman, a Boeing inspection worker with the firm since 1929, was given the job of loosening the tail. "The foreman," Callarman recalled 15 years later when asked about his most unusual assignment during the years with Boeing, "handed me some

drawings, pointed to the clipper and told me to go saw off the airplane's tail... I didn't know what the new tail would be like at the time. But I picked up my hacksaw, laid out the station line and started sawing."[49]

Without a tail, and while waiting for the modification underway at Boeing's engineering department, the NX-01 was anchored off shore where testing of engines and other vital parts continued.

There was no time to waste, even minus a tail! It had been impossible to return the 314 to the Seattle-based plant for the tail modification because the second 314 occupied the factory's apron space.

Two ranking airline flying boat advisors, Boeing technicians, a Wright Aeronautical Corp. engine expert and CAA flight crew made up the first 314's U.S. Government testing team as they posed at Matthews Beach on Nov. 22, 1938, following first CAA test flight. From left to right stand Pan Am Capt. R.O.D. Sullivan, Julius Barr, Harry West, Ed Yuravich, Joe Boudwin, F. J. Weigard, Pan Am Capt. Jack Tilton, Allen, A. Berdeman, G. C. Miller and Ralph Cram. Not in photo was CAA's George W. Haldeman. (*Photo Courtesy: Boeing Aircraft Co.*)

An imperfect tail is removed, Matthews Beach. (*Photo Courtesy: Gordon S. Williams/Boeing Aircraft Co.*)

Engine tuning continued while 314 waited for new tail design, June, 1938. (*Photo Courtesy: Gordon S. Williams/Boeing Aircraft Co.*)

On August 12th the new empennage was towed atop a barge to Matthews Beach. It consisted of a long horizontal stabilizer with two outer egg-shaped fins, each measuring 13 feet, nine inches tall, by 11 feet, eight inches wide at mid-point. Installation work was immediately begun after the Eyres-owned vehicle was backed up close to the clipper's stern. Once positioned, the truck's crane then hoisted the tail off the barge and set the huge, cumbersome mass of metal and doped canvas into place whereupon it was bolted and faced off after master control cables were reattached. Thirteen days later the NX-01 continued with its major testing program on the lake. Surface water operations with the new tail were marked as greatly improved, but not to the point of acceptance. Allen also recommended that for better water running characteristics that the 314's attached sea-wing angle to the hull be slightly altered which in-turn called for more lake model towing.

The first takeoff and in-flight run with the new tail was made during "Test No. 12" on August 31st. Rudder control was found

Sleek but not perfect! (*Photo Courtesy : Boeing Aircraft Co.*)

marginal and the clipper's pitch angle during landing figured to be irregular. Seven more takeoffs and landings were made, but not much improvement was indicated despite changes in speed and angles of climb and descent.

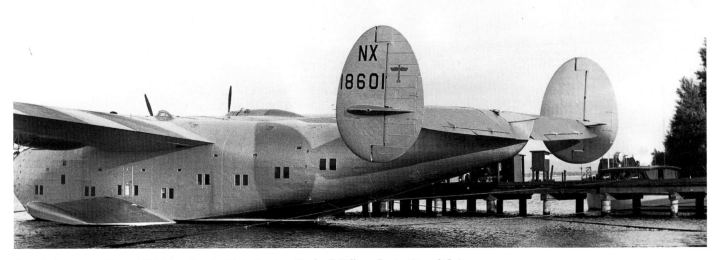

A new look to new problems off Matthews Beach. (*Photo Courtesy: Gordon S. Williams/Boeing Aircraft Co.*)

Allen (left) and Boeing's Chief Engineer Minshall discuss clipper tail problems at firm's main engineering department, 1938. (*Photo Courtesy: Boeing Aircraft Co.*)

Mooring and maintenance of clipper was handled at Lake Washington's "Shanty No. 1" by a dedicated and hard-working ground crew headed by Walter Way, rear center. (*Photo Courtesy: Mike Pavone/Boeing Aircraft Co.*)

Between "Test No. 12" and "13," the clipper was flown to the town of Winslow, west of Seattle across Puget Sound, for sea-wing alterations. Model test reports and Allen's notations pointed to an immediate change. Previously, when the 314 rose to her step, the sponsons' trailing edges didn't clear the water well enough which caused a drag disallowing an even keel of balance in cross winds that in turn produced scary wing dipping. It was thought that if the aft edges of the sea-wings were freed of bow waves during takeoffs and landings, a better righting angle of the ship could be maintained.

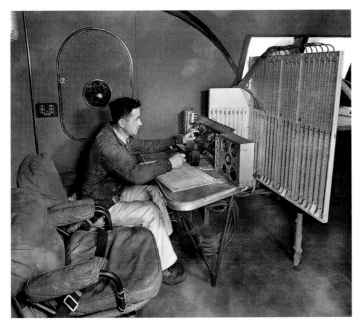

Mike Pavone, Boeing's first in-flight engineer, monitors test-installed pyrometer at aft captain's office. Positioned forward was a temporary board indicator equipped with manometers that measured various engine pressures. (*Photo Courtesy: Boeing Aircraft Co.*)

Winslow, at the time, was a small, quaint fishing village. Coved by water and pine, the rustic town was noted for its historical Marine Railway and Ship Co. that had constructed windjammers beginning in 1903. From the waterfront's old drydock came five-masted schooners, such as the *Vigilant of Honolulu* that transported lumber between Puget Sound ports and the Hawaiian Islands. It was here in Winslow that for one week the 314 occupied the drydock once used to build the full-rigged ships of historical trading value. Resting on her cradle sent from Sand Point, the NX-01 underwent hull painting and sea-wing changes. The clipper, by that time, had accumulated 250 miles of taxiing plus a number of takeoff and landing runs. By September 8th the alterations were completed. The hydrostabilizers' forward edges were decreased three degrees and each sponson was extended outboard six inches to improve yawing between 20 and 60 knots while taxiing across water. It was through this trial-and-error process that the 314 became perfected — one of the most complicated aircraft engineering tasks undertaken in the 20th century. A *Queen Mary* of the skies was being mastered!

By September 9th the clipper was back at Matthews Beach to resume the testing program, her wings once more spreading a rippled umbrage upon the deep-shaded waters of Lake Washington. That morning an American plane record was set when the NX-01 was taken into the air with a heavy load factor of 77,500 pounds. Beall was aboard and he and the other nine-man test crew felt the ship bounce several times before it shot aloft — the skipping first believed to be the result of a lag in the control system possibly due to an improper weight loading. Not until much later was the problem traced elsewhere.

While cruising in near cloudless skies, Allen began to manipulate the twin rudders that started the clipper into a banking turn found somewhat difficult to correct. Although not considered seri-

Pan Am's Chief Pilot Gray steps forth from 314's main port hatch. Gray was a continued on-sight inspector during the long performance period. (*Photo Courtesy: Boeing Aircraft Co.*)

ous, Allen realized that the reinstallation of the tail's central fin would make for better flying — that three fins might solve the clipper's on-water and in-flight control problems.

Two days later, on Sunday, September 11th (overtime had become routine for Boeing employees assigned to the clipper project), Allen took the 314 up with a gross-weight flight load of 82,500 pounds that became a world's record for a commercially built plane—a mark surpassed only by the unsuccessful Do-X and Rus-

sian-built *Maxim Gorky*. Empty weight of the 314 was set at 47,500 pounds while 35,000 was made up of lead shots, fuel, water balast and crew. In comparative terms, the NX-01 — the first plane to do so — not only carried her own weight, but also that of more than an empty DC-3!

During "Test No. 17," which began the following day with the same gross weight, Allen, while bringing in the clipper for the first of two planned landings, fought the controls while trying to raise the ship's elevators to reduce the fast speed of descent. The 314 smacked hard into the water and bounced 10 feet into the air and then shot 20 feet more on the second touch with the surface to become nearly uncontrollable. The same incident occured during the clipper's second landing of the day, an indication that porpoising had become the plane's second greatest problem.

The first "Consolidated Flight Test Report" was submitted to Boeing's executive board presided over by Egtvedt on September 20th at Boeing's 200 West Michigan Street headquarters. Prepared by Allen, Beall, Cram and other 314 technicians, the typed document pinpointed the liner's faults and the corrections needed for passage by the Department of Commerce and by Pan Am. Allen spoke first regarding takeoffs, landings, stability and control characteristics. Cram followed with statistics that ranged from general performance to cruising and landing speeds. Beall's lengthy analysis came last with reports on power plant installation, instrument ratings, gyro pilot functioning, heating and electrical systems and fuel-dumping studies.

Over-all, the majority of problems and solutions needed for correction were minor and easily attainable. The two major concerns were complete rudder control and the severe porpoising attitude during the majority of takeoffs and landings. Allen stated that the 314's tail rudder control remained a problem for lateral stability while on the water and in the air. He also recommended that the

A queen of the air gets final tail fin, Matthews Beach, while famed test pilot, standing to left with hat, looks on. (*Photo Courtesy: Boeing Aircraft Co.*)

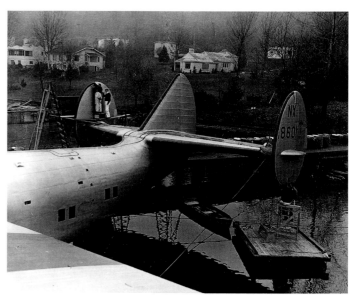

An early morning Lake Washington fog nearly shrouds background as ground crew finalize rubber de-icing boots to massive empennage. (*Photo Courtesy: Boeing Aircraft Co.*)

On-step water-chopping, Lake Washington, with a tail that works! (*Photo Courtesy: Boeing Aircraft Co.*)

sea-wings be possibly given a V-bottom to the outside bulb tips, or that the undersides be smoothed out along with an extension of the aft trailing edges. Further testing was ordered; and although none of Allen's sea-wing suggestions were used, the rear bottom sections of the hydrostabilizers were given a teardrop-shaped horizontal directional fin unit. Model tests proved these afforded even water flow stability and also increased firmness of lift during high taxi speeds when getting the 314 up on her step.

Porpoising was blamed, so Allen first thought, for the lack of a "technique" to be used in handling the ship. Man had made a fine machine and now it was man that had to learn how to handle it — so it was believed when attacking the skipping problem. Some

porpoising was later eliminated by reducing takeoff speed from 80 to 70 m.p.h. using a free elevator plus a 20-degree angle flap. The landing speed would also be reduced to 70 m.p.h. with flaps up and tail slightly down to avoid an on-the-step touchdown that almost assured the bouncing.

"It is only the skip or bounce out of the water at high speeds that is difficult to control,"[50] Allen reported. The awkward and dangerous porpoising was later traced to the 314's underside lines, but not until after the first six flying boats were put into regular service. Only after a near crack-up at the Azore Islands in 1939 was pressure put on Boeing to modify and correct the aft V-bottom step. It was, after all, not the 314 captains who had to master a manner of

First soaring with final tail modification. Allen was at the controls. (*Photo Courtesy: Boeing Aircraft Co.*)

Time off at Winslow for a fresh under-hull lamp black-coating and general maintenance. Beaching giant was very time-consuming. (*Photo Courtesy: Boeing Aircraft Co.*)

Numerous day and night hours were spent confined within the NX-01's control room discussing ship's progress. From left to right were Allen, Yuravich and Haldeman. (*Photo Courtesy: Boeing Aircraft Co.*)

With eyes focused towards the NX-01, a concentrated Allen, unaware a character-type photo portrait was being taken, balances himself against *Panair*'s cabin top en route to the moored clipper for test flight around and over Burien City. (*Photo Courtesy: Richard Hubbell/Boeing Aircraft Co.*)

performance essential to expertness of execution upon touchdown, but rather it was the Boeing engineers of the period who had to alter the hull design.

Longitudinal stability of the aircraft was given a high mark whereas directional and lateral stabilities in the air were not. There was too much yaw, a side-to-side swaying during directional flight that eventually resulted in a severe uneven movement called a "Dutch Roll" from which the Model 314 never fully recovered. Allen called for more tail surface for improved airstream flow that would drastically reduce the ship's lateral and directional in-flight imperfections and in-turn give better control.

Those attending the September meeting concurred that when the 314 acquired a third fin, that the extra weight, however minimal, would help balance the ship's hull to where an 82,500 gross-pound weight load would enable the plane to meet its 70 m.p.h. landing requirement and aid in correcting skipping on touchdown. Following the meeting, Jack Kylstra, acting 314 engineer put in charge when Minshall and Beall turned their talents to other Boeing designs, was sent a confidential memo ordering him to prepare Boeing's aerodynamics section for an engineering layout plan for major 314 changes. Included was the call for the immediate release of materials for the fabrication of the center tail fin to be completed on or before October, 1938.

Allen and crew calculate a successful double port, dead-engine tryout high over Burien City, November, 1938. (*Photo Courtesy: Boeing Aircraft Co.*)

Because of the unforeseen inherent problems in the early design stages, a supplemental contract agreement with Pan Am had to be issued on Jan. 20, 1937, that granted Boeing an extension of three months for every aircraft delivery. And by the end of September, 1938, Boeing was again eight months behind according to the supplemental agreement.

Kylstra sent a confidential reply to Beall on September 22nd with a copy to Egtvedt regarding the final authorization for tail modification:

"As much engineering overtime as practicable; including Saturdays and Sundays, will be expended on this item."[51]

On October 12th, the clipper acquired her last empennage addition at Matthews Beach with incidental changes to the hull and stabilizer. The central fin was of the same style as the original, but instead of being all metal, it was sheeted with stretched canvas over an aluminum frame of nine horizontal supports to minimize weight and was without rudder. Its purpose was to correct the improper degree between lateral and directional stability of the aircraft when on the water and in the air. The outer two rudder-equipped fins allowed for proper pilot efficiency in directional water and flight control. To reduce porpoising from the adverse tail weight, throttles were cut back just before touchdown. Sometimes, in later tests, it worked and sometimes it didn't; but even though cutting back on the throttles was no guarantee against a bounced landing, the action taken was a plausible explanation — a "technique" — to speed up another delay in the 314 construction and testing process.

Gordon S. Williams, then a part time photographer for Boeing while working on his BA in Journalism at the University of Washington and hired full time by Mansfield in 1941, recalled the 314 tail modification period:

"...a cartoon appeared in the *Aeroplane*, a British aviation magazine. They had a cartoon of a Boeing engineer explaining to another chap about a huge flying boat with six or eight vertical tails and saying something to the effect that 'as we begin testing we'll

A seemingly precarious-perched flying dynamo is prepared for final weigh-in at Winslow. (*Photo Courtesy: Boeing Aircraft Co.*)

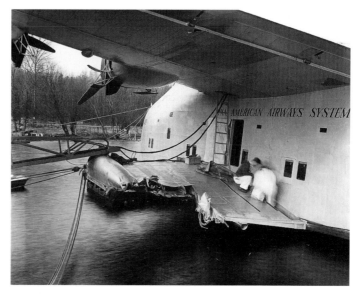

A wounded queen undergoes repairs after stalled landing incident. (*Photo Courtesy: Boeing Aircraft Co.*)

remove tails one at a time until we have the correct combination.' C. G. Grey, the cantankerous editor, always liked to poke fun at the Americans, so I'm sure the cartoon was his idea."[52]

More tests followed. First came taxi runs, takeoffs, climbs, cruising and landings. Beall later remarked:

"The final design of the empennage has produced excellent flying characteristics, resulting in an aircraft which will stay almost dead on course for protracted lengths of time and yet has the lightness of control of a pursuit plane."[53]

More than five months of grueling work was given the 314 during Boeing's testing program. The flying 314 laboratory results were compiled from the clipper's scientific and precisioned instruments stationed on the NX-01's upper deck. Report forms, tabulations and charts were taken from the ship's complex mechanisims by way of 261 electrical-type stethescopes (detector devices). They measured temperature, vibration, pressure and instrument panel movements. Continuous recordings were mapped out from the various flight-deck stations.

Before each test run, Boeing's crew took aboard graph charts marked off into hundreds of squares that equated to special instrument readings at given intervals of operation time. In a typical two-hour period, as many as 600 coded references were usually accumulated on the charts to scientifically validate that all the ship's equipment, design and construction was to specification. Any deviation from the latter was promptly dealt with from a special division within the Boeing engineering department. Refinements in any of the clipper's installations were acquired from the accurate knowledge revealed by the many charts sent back to headquarters.

On October 26th, the NX-01 was flown to Winslow for a week for paint touch-ups, have new dump valves installed and weighed for final specifications prior to the CAA testing program. Directing the drydock procedures was Chris Ericksen, yard foreman for the

Winslow Marine Railways and Ship-building Co. As the clipper was hauled up on a cradle designed to accommodate wind jammers, and slipped onto her own beaching gear, Ericksen told gathered reporters:

"Here at the yard I have seen the passing of the sailing ship and the development of steamship transportation, and now they've brought us a clipper ship of the air! It makes me feel as though I've really graduated."[54]

When the NX-01 was put on the scales on the early morning of November 2nd, the weight increase was only 260 more pounds, an error of one-half of one percent of the 52,000-pound empty weight. If the total weight of the plane had been above the terms contracted for with Boeing, payload and passenger weights could have been effected. Beall remarked, "Strange as it may seem, we have been able, even with the changes in tail surfaces, to meet our design payload; not only that, but the weight of the aircraft on its actual weighing was within approximately 50 pounds, or about one-tenth of one percent, of the estimated empty weight."[55]

Critical to Boeing was the fact that if the 314 had been so much as two percent overweight, Pan Am could have acquired the clippers at a reduced price, or even worse, cancelled the entire order. If the former had occurred, the NX-01 and her sister ships could have been purchased at a flat rate of 40 dollars per pound, an astronomical money loser for Boeing.

Boeing's 314 trial testing came to a close on November 3rd. All test data consisted of what the manufacturer said were three sections: taxiing, flight operation and computing and adjustments. Thirty-two distinct test programs, each divided into numerous individual items that usually entailed a full day's work load, had been manifested in the NX-01's log. More than 450 miles of taxiing, 80 takeoffs and landings and approximately 5,000 miles of in-flight operations were affirmed. Three additional weeks were given to

studying propeller vibration and installation of bulkhead lining, carpeting and other interior furnishings shipped to Matthews Beach — all approved, right down to the recommended use of 1/3000-inch-thick toilet paper for the first airplane to use a water-flush, dump-toilet tank designed and supervised by Beall that took nearly a year to refine.

Completely satisfied with its testing program, Boeing transferred the NX-01 to the CAA in November for government testing. In its glorified, final triple-finned tail form, the 314 had some 50,000 parts, excluding 15,230 bolts and about one million rivets. The 3,500-mile-range airliner, illuminated by 150 electric bulbs, required 17,500 square feet of engineering drawings and 385,300 square feet of blueprints and other plans, that if laid out flat would have covered 15 acres. Nearly 13 miles of wiring was used in 400 conduits as was 3,000 feet of plumbing tubing, enough of the latter to equip 12 standard, five-room houses. The 4,000-square-foot hull surface (one-tenth of an acre) enclosed 5,000 feet (60 city blocks long) of control cables. There was enough fiber glass soundproof padding and cabin lining to upholster 160 automobiles and enough rubber in the wing's and tail's de-icing boots to make 120 innertubes.

Shortly after November 14th, Kylstra was notified by the CAA's Seattle regional office of the board's nine-man team assigned to handle the 314. Heading the group was Joe E. Boudwin, CAA board executive and senior aeronautical engineering inspector. Eighteen days later a total of 11 men had been assigned to undertake the government's phase of testing, two of whom — acting in an advisory capacity — were Pan Am's Capt. Robert Oliver Daniel ("ROD") Sullivan, top Atlantic Division pilot, and Capt. Jack H. Tilton, Pacific Division's senior flight officer.

Although the government's testing was not as extensive as Boeing's, hundreds of items were charted and catalogued for the department's files in Washington, D.C. Various provisions were made as well as minor structural adjustments, such as an improved hinge after a hatch blew open during a test dive as did sections of deicer boots calling for installation changes.

Eight different CAA tests were accomplished by the beginning of December, one for every two days since November 22nd. Twenty-one hours of in-flight observation occurred in the first two and one-half weeks of CAA testing. An average of two and one-half hours was figured by engineers for each flight. Through the various tests, future Pan Am captains were directed never to exceed 211 m.p.h. during flight. Gliding speed was marked at 234 m.p.h. which was lower than Boeing's original 251-m.p.h. concept. Cruising was to be held at 158 m.p.h. if flaps were used. One of the last crucial government-sponsored tests called for a water run on the rougher surfaces of Puget Sound when the NX-01 was required to hit a four-foot-high wave head-on during a 70-m.p.h. turn to test for hull strength while operating on heavy seas. The clipper passed the test well with only slight denting to the chine which was quickly and easily repaired.

Dolly C edges barge-secured second Model 314 built down locks to Elliott Bay. (*Photo Courtesy: Gordon S. Williams/Boeing Aircraft Co.*)

Chapter Nine: Mastering a Queen

In early December, one CAA flight set an unofficial world's record for aircraft at that time when the NX-01's maximum 82,500 pound weight was carried into tho heavens with one engine inoperative. Allen climbed the clipper for the CAA test crew to 8,000 feet at 50 feet per minute and later recorded that the 314 could have climbed even higher.

While the CAA carried forth with its program, the second 314 built was eased into the Duwamish Waterway on December 6th at 4:00 A.M. Painted blue and white Pan Am logos (winged globes) were seen on the NX 18602's (NX-02) prow sides. Blue letters reading "Pan American Airways System" also showed above the clipper's main entrance and egress hatchways. Towards mid-afternoon the NX-02 reached Elliott Bay after a four-hour-long tug and barge excursion trip down the Duwamish whereupon taxi runs were conducted by Allen. The following day the ship was flown to Matthews Beach where shoreline viewers admired not one but two 314s, their size captivating the slightest of imaginations. Naive "Tailspin Tommy" movies of the day would never again capture the hearts of aviation-minded fans as much as would the up-coming giants of the air. The slogan, "Flying high, wide and handsome" had, unlike the early barnstorming days, moved on to a more serious, scientific state of affairs.

On Jan. 13, 1939, Allen, following another round of taxi runs on Elliott Bay, flew the third 314, NX 18603 (NX-03), to Lake Washington to join the CAA's "Project 314" testing fleet. A month later a near disaster occurred. Ferguson, with a flight career of 1,400 hours, was at the controls of NX-01 during the cold, ceiling-unlimited morning of February 20th. Aboard were four other Boeing crew members, three company technicians, one CAA representative and eight Pan Am observers. At the north end of the lake with a less than two-m.p.h. wind, Ferguson gave the clipper a 60-degree angle of flap for a power-off, stall-speed-landing test. The diagonal descent was too steep for the plane's low-geared speed and the ship suddenly dropped. Ferguson leveled the ship off just above the water, but the flying boat stalled and heeled 15 degrees to port whereupon the sea-wing struck the water.

Quick reaction by Ferguson averted a crash when he immediately righted the plane for a porpoised landing. One-fourth of the sponson was ripped away, the broken pieces bouncing off the water and striking the port wing's lowered flap causing further damage. A fast taxi run to base was executed, and when the engines were cut and the ship came to rest all aboard and on shore were surprised that the liner hadn't lost much righting buoyancy. The incident, although serious, proved the 314 was a floating fortress.

Although photos of the damaged clipper were taken by Boeing — and repairs ultimately made — both the snapshots and written-up accident report were never released to the news media. A public relations cover- up was issued to safeguard against possible nervous jitters of soon-to-be first-time Atlantic air travelers. Two quick changes as the result of the accident were the increase of the 314's off-power gliding speed from 70 to 80 m.p.h. when using a 60-degree flap in a low velocity wind, and the switching from permanently attached sea-wings to more easily removable-type structures.

The loss of a 314 at that time would not only have caused further delivery delays, but extensive amounts of money to Boeing and Pan Am, especially during the time when the U.S. was still struggling to recover from a great depression. And a 314 dollar tag was not cheap — it was staggering within the late 1930's money market.

Pricing of a 314 began in 1936 when Pan Am first teased aircraft bidders with a $50,000 out-of-the pocket bonus prize package to the company who could deliver a new flying ship as based on their stern demands. And, in addition to the bonus, a minimal $485,000 across-the-board payment was offered to the winning bidder (Boeing) by the airline as well. Once Boeing was selected, cost-bidding terms between the Seattle-based firm and Pan Am was then set at $618,908 basic market price per ordered aircraft along with a contingency clause for six additional clippers if later needed by the airline.

Boeing had figured that since the XB-15's wing, tail and flight-deck could be adapted to a flying boat, half of their 314 research expenses would be cut in half. If that money was tight for Boeing, it was on these grounds of general research cost reductions that the aircraft manufacturer was able to gamble, bid and win the contract. Pan Am held back $100,000 per ordered craft but payed Boeing the remaining cost for the first six boats.

With the price figure agreed upon by both parties, Pan Am went about its business to help finance the new planes — to reimburse itself for the payable unit price owed Boeing. When the 314s fell behind in production and testing scheduling by 13 months, the airline was given an opportunity to study and incorporate a new financing plan.

Devised and put into effect in January, 1939, the winged-globe line pioneered its formula of 314 cost to an aviation equipment trust financing program. Pan Am put up $2,500,000 for the 314s in certificates at four percent to two New York City banks. Another million dollars in certificates was sold to an insurance company. Cash-wise, Pan Am paid only 30 percent to Boeing and the certificates, when sold, payed off the remaining 70 percent.

Equipment trusts were, upon maturity, to last five years, or the equivalent life span of the 314s. Boeing, on the other hand, speculated at least a 10-year expectancy on their air boats and the payments by the airline would have ended after five years for the total amount of securities issued. The owner's financing approach was mirrored after the dealing arrangements used by the railroad industry when they were about to acquire new equipment — referred to in the trade as the "Philadelphia Plan." At a four percent return until the certificates were sold, Pan Am came out roses, or at least as far as the basic funds owed Boeing were concerned.

The question that remains is, who purchased the securities from the banks and insurance company, and for what guarantee on their part(s)? One reliable and former Pan Am official, Los Angeles Public Relations Manager R. L. Sloan, declared as late as 1964, "Hell, those old Boeing boats were backed by the U.S. Government from the outset and don't let anybody say otherwise! They (government) knew war was coming and they would need the big planes when it came..."[56]

Above and beyond the builder's price were Pan Am's extra overhead and write-off costs. Additional payments, for example, were sent to the Howard Ketchum Firm and to Norman Bel Geddes' Studio for their colorful and functional compartmentalization studies and acquired fixture arrangements as charged to the 314's enclosed dimensions. Other finance expenses had to be payed Hamilton Standard and to additional sub-contracted outlet companies — costs considered beyond Boeing's basic price tag.

Boeing later testified they had gone into the red when the first six ships were completed. The costs per hull, wing and tail frames came to $804,925.73 while total contracted engines, propellers and other related equipment for the six 314s was figured at about $756,430. This revealed a grand total of $5,586,034.33, or close to one million dollars per clipper.

The first 314 to have its experimental X removed from the license plate was the NX-03. In place of the X was painted a C standing for commercial acceptance. Next in line was the second 314 built and finally the NX-O1. She was forced to keep the X painted on her wing and tail surfaces until the CAA ironed out all remaining requirements.

Finally, on Jan. 25, 1939, the CAA, through the Department of Commerce, awarded the Model 314 a *A-704 Certificate of Airworthiness.*

Third sister ship, NC 18603, joins first two built at Matthews Beach, January, 1939. Site is presently a much-visited Washington State Park resort without much rememberance to past 314 testing development. (*Photo Courtesy: Boeing Aircraft Co.*)

All testing reports were turned over to the CAA flight test board and in turn sent on to Washington, D.C., where they were scrutinized by the CAA's Aircraft Airworthiness Section headed by L. V. Kerber. After extensive review, Kerber authorized the 314's temporary certificate with the permanent one allotted only after Pan Am operated the Model 314 for a specified number of hours before allowing for the transport of passengers and mail.

With Boeing, the CAA and Pan Am representatives thoroughly satisfied with all testing procedures and results, and with a certificate on file in Washington, D.C., an ocean for regularly scheduled airplane service was waiting. Boeing's "Project 314" was ready to meet that Atlantic challenge.

10

Interlude

About the time Boeing realized they were losing money on the six-contracted 314s, Pan Am too began to have financial problems in the Pacific, and in a disastrous way. Desiring a branch line extending south from Honolulu to the "Land Down Under," the airline had acquired survey landing rights from the New Zealand Government back in November, 1935. A regular service, however, was not immediately granted. Pan Am lacked intermediate island landing facilities and, more importantly, long-range, profitable equipment. By March 11, 1937, full commercial rights were issued even though Trippe and his men had just begun to develop and explore plans for the South Pacific route as directed by Pan Am's Harold Gatty, an Australian-born navigator.

In charge of the first survey flights was Pacific Division's Senior Capt. .Edwin C. Musick, one of the world's most respected pilots. Second to Lindbergh in air-hero worship due to the notoriety dished out for him by Pan Am's PR releases and press reports while he trained crews for transoceanic flight and commanded the line's inaugural airmail service across the Pacific in late 1935 with the *China Clipper*, Musick had built a reputation unequalled by any airman in commercial air circles. He had become so famous that *Time* carried his picture on their December 2, 1937, covers.

Hopefully given the adequate plane from Boeing by December, 1937, and following the survey flights, a regular service was scheduled by Pan Am in order to meet New Zealand's agreement demands. When Boeing informed Trippe of the 314 construction delays, the wise airline president continued to muster forth with his South Pacific flight studies. Musick had not been pleased with the port-of-call harbors during the first two survey trips conducted in 1937. Believing that the original trunk line to remote Auckland could be worked out, Pan Am ordered one last survey study. The proposed 314 stops at Kingman Reef and American Samoa (Pago Pago) were to be re-examined.

Musick departed San Francisco on December 13, 1937, piloting the past-titled S-42B *Pan American Clipper II* to Honolulu. Renamed the *Samoan Clipper*, the flying boat had been altered to allow for a substantial gasoline load for the long island-hopping route to Auckland. Eight large tanks capable of holding 1,020 gallons of fuel for 2,800 miles were stored in the once luxurious passenger cabins.

Flying out of Pearl Harbor on Jan. 9, 1938, the 19-ton Sikorsky ship started its 4,498-mile jaunt to Auckland, via Kingman Reef

With a hull filled with extra fuel tanks for the long-ranged flight, Capt. Edwin C. Musick controlled the S-42 *Pan American Clipper* (former *West Indies Clipper*) west past incompleted *Golden Gate Bridge* for first route-proving flight to Honolulu and back, April 16, 1935, and later across Pacific. (*Photo Courtesy: Pan American World Airways*)

Musick, who's fame reached almost every American home, takes a break to sit in co-pilot's seat during an S-42 Pacific survey flight. He would not live to reap the glory of a 314 command, but opened the way for the Boeings to the land down under. (*Photo Courtesy: Pan American World Airways*)

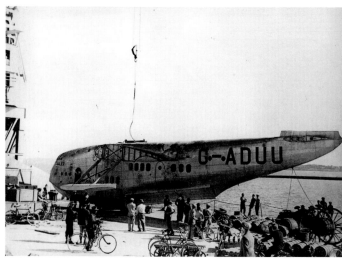

Samoan Clipper (former *Pan American Clipper II*), moored in Auckland during first inspection flight to New Zealand, is prepared for return flight to Honolulu. Loss of ship and crew stalled Pan Am's South Pacific attempts until advent of 314s. (*Photo Courtesy: Pan American World Airways*)

Another beached whale-like bulk captivates workers and tourists alike as *Cavalier's* fuselage was taken from sea by crane and lowered to dock where she was pieced back together. The lack of boat's range prohibited Imperial to fly S-23 from England to Bermuda. (*Photo Courtesy: British Overseas Airways*)

and American Samoa in the Polynesian antipodes. After again charting Kingman Reef, the S-42B was continued on to Pago Pago, capital residence of American Samoa. The harbor there is a pictorial spot surrounded by 1,500 feet of lush-planted mountains, a land where one fantasizes to get away from it all. But for a flying clipper it was a precarious spot to approach requiring meticulous skill in navigation to skirr over the wall of 2,150 ft. Mount Matafao and then precipitously drop for a landing onto the small inlet's turquoise-colored surface. It was here that Musick wanted to triple-check before having Pan Am commit itself to establishing a permanent and costly base. Generally, Pago Pago was not a good port — a tiny barren atoll vulnerable to typhoons—and the harbor was considered below average in size and safety for any large scale flying boat passenger operations.

Departing Pago Pago at 5:30 A.M., January 11th, following more survey studies of the port, the seven-man clipper crew headed the NC 16734 south towards Auckland for the 1,793-mile flight. Aboard was stored some freight made up of auto and tractor parts, China war newsreels and projectors and some crated clothing. No mail was stored despite authority given by the U.S. Post Office. Thirty-eight minutes later a transmitted call to Pago Pago's ground operator told of an oil leak in No. 4 engine — that it was shut down and the plane would return to port after dumping gas. A heavily fuel-laden craft was dangerous to land, and doubly so with the tricky approach to Pago Pago's harbor. Fuel-dumping was not in an advanced stage of technology and therefore not permitted by the Bureau of Air Commerce for U.S. passenger-carrying transports.

Removed from freighter in parts, hull of Imperial Airways' S-23 *Cavalier* is towed to Bermuda's air facility whereupon liner was reassembled for reciprocal service to U.S., 1937. (*Photo Courtesy: British Overseas Airways*)

Musick, it is believed, thought that since the *Samoan's* flight was not commercially orientated that to relieve the ship of the added fuel weight was his constituted decision.

While between 14 and 24 miles out at sea at 10,000 feet northwest of Samoa, Musick, or his first officer, started to lower the ship's flaps. Whirl-winded and trapped fuel fumes caught against the flaps were ignited, either by friction from the electrically operated auxiliary wing leverage or by the aft flowing, 40-foot spark stream leaving the engines' exhaust pipes. Like a shooting star in slow motion, as witnessed by a local native, the $320,000 clipper, dubbed in the past by Pan Am crews as "The Flying Gas Tank," fell to sea in a fireball of wreckage and human flesh. Debris from the downed, gross-weighted 41,936-pound ship fell in pieces. Partially recovered clothing, punctured with holes, was saturated with dualumin powder, suggesting a powerful explosion. Following a lengthy investigation, Musick, with 13,200-credited air hours, and crew were figured blameless; but political and influential outcries during the aftermath were tinged with Pan Am monopolistic tendencies tinged with dangerous overtones.

Voices in Washington, D.C., began to state that the airline was forging ahead too fast with blatant disregard to air safety standards and an unconcern for human life by using old and ill-equipped aircraft along an unprepared and unsafe route in order to avoid any future competition entanglements — like with Britain regarding Atlantic service — that may arise between New Zealand, and in particular with the Australian Government. This apathy towards a new air route was strongly backed by powerful and conservative Grover Loening, a past Pan Am board member, pilot and aircraft builder known for his late 1920's Loening Air-Yacht amphibian design.

Loening had given his strong opinion to the Washington press where it appeared in print. He sternly believed that Pan Am was expanding its services at a pace that could not be matched by the progress of American air industries for the building of safer passenger-carrying planes. Although the mounted pressure against

Trippe eventually quieted down for a time, the Department of Commerce had no alternative but to suspend the airline from any further survey flights to the South Pacific. The route was shut down for two years until the advent of the bigger and safer 314, and not allowed to open again until the Boeing liner had proved its worth across the Atlantic and Pacific.

Meanwhile, Pan Am had time to plan for a new stepping stone-island airway path through the South Pacific.

Hardest hit by the *Samoan Clipper* disaster were the New Zealanders. They wanted a connecting air route to the U.S. Besides giving them a regular air mail service north, such an operation in turn would bring an influx of tourist trade. Though loyal to Britain, New Zealand officials did not politically feel the same as did the Austrailian Government regarding a reciprocal air service to the U.S. Britain had pressured Australia into thinking that a mutual airline system was necessary in the South Pacific just as it was proposed for the Atlantic between England and the U.S.

The government of New Zealand showed its disappointment and profound sadness by the loss of Musick in what he was doing for them and for commercial flight by building a radio station in his memory. They also established the "Edwin C. Musick Trophy," an award to be given each year to the firm or person who contributed the most for improving or developing techniques in air safety.

Barely adjusting to the *Samoan Clipper* tragedy, Pan Am incurred a greater hit six months later. On July 29th (.July 28th, EST), the M- 130 *Hawaii Clipper*, the ship that inaugurated transpacific passenger service over the Pacific on Oct. 21, 1936, was lost without a trace while flying west between Guam Island and Manila. In command of "Trip No. 229" was experienced Capt. Leo Terletsky who had 9,200-accredited flight hours, 1,014 of which had been spent aboard M-130 aircraft. Also aboard were six male passengers and eight other crew members plus 1,138 pounds of baggage, cargo and mail.

Despite an extensive sea and air search, nothing of the clipper was ever found. It was as though Terletsky had flown the M-130

Airway hands across Atlantic between England and U.S. were partially bridged with reciprocal S-23 and S-42 services to and from Bermuda and New York. Here America's *Bermuda Clipper*, under command of Capt. Sullivan, arrives from New York on Hamilton Harbor, June 18th. (*Photo Courtesy: Pan American World Airways*)

into outer space. Trippe strongly believed the Japanese Imperial Government had something to do with the incident. It was well known that diplomatic relations between the U.S. and Japan were far from compatible and that the "Empire of the Rising Sun" was not exhuberant about America's new air service, a vital communication's system to any country facing near hostile relations.

In November, 1945, two months after Japan's formal World War II surrender, Pan Am publicly announced that two Japanese nationals were apprehended in 1935 for trying to sabotage the M-130 inaugural air mail service to Manila. American FBI agents arrested the saboteurs aboard the *China Clipper* at Alameda on the eve of its departure just as the men had begun to tamper with the ship's sensitive DF system. Then six weeks later the *China Clipper's* hull bottom was torn open during a taxi takeoff run by mysteriously placed rod iron spikes later spotted just below the surface and anchored into cement pylons within the sea-runway channel.

Along with these incidents, and to further disrupt clipper flights, Japan refused to cooperate with Pan Am in giving continued weather data around the area of the Far East. Japan felt the commercial flights were an intrusion into their predominately held territory of Micronesia and their established Pacific military bases. Perplexed by the latter problem, Pan Am turned to the U.S. Naval Intelligence Division for assistance. In conjunction with the Navy Department, radioman John Cooke, Navy-trained in cryptology and meteorology, and who spoke and wrote fluent Japanese, was sent to Guam as Pan Am's chief ground radio operator. By listening to goblin-like messages, specialist Cooke shortly deciphered the Japancse code so that accurate weather reports could be furnished to clipper airmen, thus maintaining safer flight schedules.

Another obvious Japancse dislike for the clipper flights was the quick communication service they offered to U.S. and allied government officials and world newsmen. For instance, in December, 1937, Norman Alley, world cameraman of the "Newsreel" series, so popular at the time in American and Canadian theaters, rushed film of the devastating Japanese air attack on the American gunboat *Panay* to Washington, D.C., by clipper. Alley and his reel of the *Panay's* sinking in China's Yangtze River was sent by destroyer to Manila where the *China Clipper* had been specifically ordered held up for the prized cargo. Once in the U.S. capital, and after a private viewing was held for President Franklin D. Roesevelt and Secretary of State Cordell Hull, an immediate apology was forwarded by Japan along with a $2,214,000 indemnity payment. Quite plainly, the swift clipper service was not admired by the embarrassed Japanese Government.

When the *Hawaii Clipper* disappeared without a trace, a possible theory as to a Japanese in-flight takeover was secretly raised (the term "hijack" was not in vocabulary use in 1938). Japan was in need of a large aircraft capable of flying great distances and had shown great interest in the S-42 and M-130 models but were de-

nied plant inspections when the flying boats were under construction. To thwart any future clipper tamperings, and possible takeover, by the Japanese, all clipper flying boat bases in the Pacific were placed under heavy military guard. At the Boeing plant, 314 upper decks were secured against unwanted intruders by means of the lockable deck-floored hatches. The raisable devices were equipped with a snap latch and multi-tumbler locks that could be deadlocked from the flight-deck side and reopened from the stair well side only by means of a secretly guarded key unknown to anyone but the crew. Pan Am was not about to take any chances with their new Pacific-stationed 314s!

The disappearance of the *Hawaii Clipper* marked the third four-engined clipper-class flying boat loss with fatality. The first occurred in mid-April, 1936, when a South America-bound S-42's hull broke open after Capt. Wallace Culbertson, who was hitting 50 m.p.h. across Port of Spain waters, lost control when a clipper's pontoon struck a small boat that had crossed into the sea-runway, throwing the S-42 into a wide arch. Two of the 22 passengers aboard, including a steward, were trapped and drowned in the fast-sinking plane. Jose Iturbi, world renowned concert pianist and conductor, survived despite severe wrist injury when a fellow passenger trod upon his hands after he fell in the darkened cabin while trying to exit the plane.

But it was the *Hawaii Clipper's* last flight that stung Pan Am the hardest. There were only three M-130s that kept the Pacific Division in operation. With profits based on contracted government mail and cargo revenues, the airline soon found itself crippled when the NC 14714 vanished. Weekly Pacific service was hampered and the mail and cargo loads became backlogged, thus allowing for fewer passengers — their weight replaced with larger mail and cargo loads. It took a week for a Martin ship to cross the Pacific one way, and after three round-trips, or about 390 hours of service, the planes had to be overhauled at Alameda, a time-consuming necessity. The two remaining M-130s could barely make a turn-around on the Pacific run and be properly maintained when the profit signs began to drop, despite the replacement for a time by Pan Am of a Latin American-based S-42 on the Manila-Macao-Hong Kong route following the Musick crash, and then later in 1941 by another S-42 also renamed the *Hong Kong Clipper*. The Sikorsky boats were used to relieve the M-130s from duty beyond the Manila point.

Passenger revenue came second to Pan Am's yearly net income. It was not the passenger service that Pan Am relied upon for substaining a profitable business, but rather the government subsidies provided through mail and cargo. Martin flying boats could each carry up to 30-day passengers or 18-overnight sleepers, yet the majority of those transported up to the time of the *Hawaii's* tragic end were less than what the ships were decked out for. Only the rich, government and military personnel, business executives and the airline's official employees were afforded the expensive journeys.

Chapter Ten: Interlude

To keep the Pacific Division operating, Pan Am leaned heavily on her LAD profits. Of the nearly $1.2 million LAD had acquired for the year 1938, $75,000 was all that was left by December 31st. The rest was spent on keeping the Pacific Division operational.

Financially troubled, the line's San Francisco headquarters was losing around $95,000 a month and was placed on 60 percent flying status. In desperation, Pan Am turned to the U.S. Post Office for assistance in providing more mail funds. But Trippe realized that the Pacific Division's salvation rested with the 314s; for one 314 would be capable of carrying twice the load in passengers, cargo, express and mail as an M-130. And because the 314 was late in the first delivery, Pan Am as a whole became over-extended with patience. In addition, there were the problems to contend with and to resolve with the British regarding the Atlantic service.

Trippe signed an agreement with Imperial Airways' Manager George Woods-Humphery for a mutual transatlantic service on Jan. 2, 1936. Two clauses were stipulated: that service could not begin by either party until each was prepared to do so, and secondly that the arrangement be set between Pan Am and Imperial Airways only. Such an agreement upset German and French politicians. Germany's Lufthansa and France's Air France were highly interested in a transatlantic service to America and protested to London authorities. The agreement was then questioned by both U.S. and England Governent officials. In Washington, D.C., Pan Am was beginning to be accused of violating the "Sherman Antitrust Act," a law inacted in 1890 against big businesses creating monopolies.

Other problems followed. The U.S. Post Office refused to grant Pan Am a transatlantic air mail contract on the grounds that the contract would go to the lowest bidder — that there had to be at least one other American contender. Seeing that Pan Am was the only U.S. airline capable of offering such a service, Trippe was stumped. In addition, landing rights from Canada and Ireland for the northern route to Europe were still needed, along with permits from Bermuda and Portugal for the southern route. The delays dragged on into months while officials fussed and fussed.

Finally, on Feb. 22, 1937, after much hard negotiating, Imperial Airways, through the British Air Ministry of England, awarded Pan Am its permit to operate to and from Bermuda, England, and Newfoundland. Within two months Canada and Ireland granted their permits, as did Portugal.

The agreement with Portugal for landing rights at Lisbon via the Azores (Horta) was made separately by Trippe and set up exclusively for Pan Am. Again, a strong hint of antitrust was evident, yet such unlawful oddities did not concern Portuguese officials. Portugal, not in the transatlantic race, saw only the riches in trade that would be provided by Pan Am.

Next came the reciprocal survey flights between Imperial Airways and Pan Am, and the start of the regular, reciprocal passenger and mail flights between New York and Bermuda. On May 25, 1937, Capt. Gray lifted the S-42 *Bermuda Clipper* away in a light rain at 10:16 A.M. from Port Washington, N.Y., for the first inspection flight to the resort island. Leaving Hamilton at the same time for New York was Imperial's S-23 *Cavalier*. Imperial had shipped their S-23 model to Bermuda from Kent, England. Upon its arrival earlier in the year, the assorted sections and parts of the plane were reassembled and the interior fitted out with the line's reknowned luxury items.

Both flying boats reached their destinations the same afternoon with Gray arriving first with the faster S-42. He completed the 775-mile flight at 3:36 P.M. in the Great Sound off Darrell Island, a short distance from Hamilton and a future port-of-call for the 314s. En route, the finest prepared meal was served to the observers on linen-draped tables — all but a mere touch of finery to the par elegante service later provided passengers aboard the 314s .

Return flights were made the next day. Gray left at 10:37 A.M., Bermuda time, and landed back at Port Washington at 4:07 P.M. Following four more survey flights by Capt. Sullivan, regular joint service between New York and Hamilton was begun June 18th by Sullivan with two flights per week offered by both airlines. In the first year of operation, the *Cavalier* alone carried 1,200 passengers. Her sumptuous interior and English-styled catering was a big draw for tickets.

In preparation for the transatlantic reciprocal service, Trippe ordered ground crew personnel to their assigned sites at Shediac,

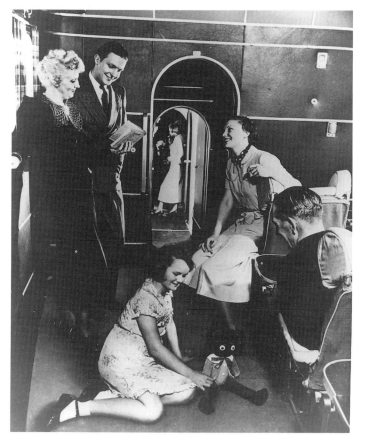

Fastidious travelers who flew on the *Cavalier* expected the ultra in comfort, such as enjoying the well-advertised "promenade deck" as viewed looking forward to bow's smoking salon. English service included the serving of afternoon tea and crumpets. (*Photo Courtesy: British Overseas Airways*)

New Brunswick; Gander, Newfoundland; Foynes, Ireland; Southampton, England; Lisbon, Portugal; and Horta, capital of the Azores. Everything seemed finalized for survey flights and the eventual, regularly scheduled plane service.

On June 25, 1937, Imperial conducted a flight across the North Atlantic, a struggle even with stops. The S-23 *Caledonia*, piloted by Capt. A.S. Wilcockson, flew 1,990 miles between Foynes and Botwood in 15 hours, eight minutes. Loaded down with large fuel tanks within the hull, and bucking strong headwinds, rain and fog, the *Caledonia* continued on at low levels to Montreal, Canada, arriving June 8th. The following day the flying boat squatted down at Port Washington.

Pan Am's S-42A *Pan American Clipper III*, later destroyed in Brazil, made the reciprocal survey flights under the command of Capt. Gray. From June 25, 1937, to, and ending on, September 3, 1937, five flights were conducted, the first four round-trips between ports along the northern route (Shediac and back, then to Botwood and back, then to Foynes and back, and then to Southampton and back) with the last conducted across the mid-Atlantic between Port Washington, Marseilles, and Southampton, via Bermuda, Azores, Portugal and return. During the same months the English flying boats *Caledonia* and *Cambria* made round-trip inspection flights as well.

Even though one of the British flights made by the *Cambria* made a record crossing between Botwood and Foynes in 10 hours, 36 minutes on September 27th-28th, the recorded results of Imperial's trial runs for S-23 scheduled passenger flights tended to be in vain. The impoverished S-23 just couldn't make a qualitative passenger and mail load without the extra fuel tanks that filled up a large portion of the ship's otherwise reserved passenger cabin space. Though sleeker and roomier in design as compared to the S-42, Britain's hope for a successful transatlantic airliner couldn't compare with the Sikorsky boat in its range and load capabilities.

The S-23, having a gross weight of 40,200 pounds, battled hopelessly against the Sikorsky's 40,000 pounds, a 2,000-pound increase since the S-42 first appeared in 1934. The useful load of a S-23 was only 16,200 pounds while the S-42A was marked at 17,800.

There didn't seem to be that much difference between the two planes; both had to have extra fuel tanks stored aboard for the Atlantic crossing. But Imperial was well aware of the soon-to-be 314 and Pan Am's intent. No sooner would the Sikorsky ship inaugurate America's service over the northern route with a minimal passenger and mail load when Pan Am would turn around and introduce the incomparable Boeing liner that would be twice the size of a S-23. At that point there would be no more competition. The S-23 could never fair well with the 314's luxury prestige or load ratio. Also, the S-23 would be England's only available transoceanic craft around for some time to come because of Europe's deteriorating political state with Grermany, despite the layouts for a bigger and more efficient flying boat, the S-26.

Due to the S-23's poor load factor for long-range flight, Woods-Humphery again stalled Trippe for starting a regular aeroplane service. Hard-boiled in business practices, England's Air Ministry chief held to his originally signed agreement of 1936 stipulating that a service could not begin until both parties were able to do so simultaneously. Frustrated and slightly disgusted with its first Atlantic tryouts, Imperial was forced to cut off its end of the agreement, thereby forcing Pan Am to cancel any immediate steps it had arranged for regarding Atlantic flights. The reciprocal service clause had forced the postponement.

By the summer of 1938, Germany and France, who had been given U.S. authority for survey flights to the American continent, began making experimental trips to New York. Trippe was anxious and kept badgering Woods-Humphery by letter and phone for the right to start a service; but Imperial needed at least a year until they developed a larger and more powerful aircraft suitable for the reciprocal service and a stronger competitor for the superior American-built over-water transports.

This second delay caused U.S. officials to take a stronger look at the 1936 agreement. Once more the "Sherman Antitrust Act" came to fore causing great stress to Trippe. Wanting to be fair and fearing a possible scandal, Woods-Humphrey recanted and turned to the Air Ministry for amending the agreement. In January, 1939, Pan Am was graciously granted full rights for a route to England on the condition that Imperial could do the same when ready. Trippe agreed without restraint. To appease the outcries of antitrust, and the fear of prosecution, Trippe in turn revoked his airline's exclusive right to Portugal. The nearly explosive issue was defused and Pan Am achieved a victory on the eve of delivery of its first 314 Clipper. Fate was not so kind to Woods-Humphrey. England's Air Ministry called for his resignation!

Clearing up one problem led to Trippe facing another troublesome matter — to stop American Export Steamship Co. of New York from going into a competitive, transatlantic airline business. American Export Lines (Amex) was a highly profitable company offering steamship service to the Mediterranean. By 1937, the company had visions of developing an airline modeled after the successful Pan Am line. Amex figured that the majority of future overseas travel might rest with planes rather than with ships. To reap some of the harvest, Amex's President John M. Slater believed that some of their profit should be spent in aircraft rather than in purchasing newer and costlier ocean liners. Hence, American Export Airlines was founded in April, 1937.

Amex launched their newly acquired six-man crew Consolidated Catalina PB-Y on June 20, 1939, at the Battery in New York City. The ship was christened *Transatlantic* by Mrs. John H. Towers, wife of Adm. Towers, chief planner to have the U.S. Navy fly the Atlantic in 1919. Through his leadership, Albert Cushing Read commanded the first successful crossing to Lisbon and Plymouth, England, with a Curtiss NC-4 flying boat.

License to fly passengers and mail over the Atlantic from New York to Marseilles, Southampton, Lisbon and Rome was again applied by Amex to the CAA on May 9, 1939, and in turn given a temporary certificate. That summer, three round-trip survey crossings were made with the PB-Y amphibian under command of Capt. P. J. Byrne. In the meantime Amex opted to buy three S-44 flying boats, the Sikorsky ship Pan Am rejected in place of the 314.

With competing airlines for the Atlantic run, the U.S. Post Office reopened transatlantic air mail contract negotiations. Pan Am bid the lowest and was given the major share of mail to be carried. A maximum compensation was set by the CAA at $12,454,400 for the carrying of mail to Europe. It was based on two round trips per week over the northern and southern routes as fixed earlier by survey flights with the S-42A-type aircraft. Minimum loads were based at 1,600 pounds per crossing. The compensation to Pan Am was figured on a trip basis while the $2,454,400 represented the yearly payment beyond that which could not be raised. Final contract details were worked out with the U.S. Post Office and put into effect in May, 1939.

At first Trippe protested to the CAA that Amex was competing with his airline in an unjust way. He said it was unfair for a commercial operator to use two modes of transportation — sea and air. Amex countered that Trippe was monopolizing through the 1936, two-way-only agreement with Imperial Airways and by the Portugal pact where no other American airline, other than Pan Am, could land at the Azores or Lisbon for 15 years . The battle began, one that raged on for nearly two years.

What was a bit upsetting to Trippe was Amex's Sept. 12, 1939, inquiry to Boeing showing interest in purchasing 314s. Fred B. Collins, Boeing's sales director, suggested to Beall, who was in New York at the time, to contact Amex's Sales Manager D. G.

Richardson regarding possible sale. In Trippe's favor, however, a contract arrangement between Amex and Boeing never developed because Amex would have had to wait too long for a 314 since Pan Am had priority over the first six-ordered models with an option for an additional six.

Amex was not the only outsider keenly interested in purchasing 314s. Japan, as it had done with the S-42 and M-130 models, came forth with a serious offer to buy one 314, supposedly to study and manufacture a similar plane for their country's airline, Japan Air Transport, or for constructing a large marine-type patrol bomber.

Collins informed Beall of Japan's interest the same time Amex approached Boeing. Representatives from Mitsubishi, one of Japan's leading aircraft manufacturers, had contacted Collins. Manufacturing license rights and delivery entanglement eventually terminated the possible sale. Collins told Beall that the 314's shipment to Japan in its component parts could not be accomplished and that a ferry flight by Boeing was out of the question. Collins also doubted strongly if Pan Am or the U.S. Government would be cooperative in such a sale, especially after Japan's earlier M-130 DF tampering incident in late 1935.

Concentrating more on his plan to outwit Amex rather than to worry about outside 314 sales, Trippe put forth an effort to try and buy out Amex by offering stock in his airline. The competitor was willing but the arrangement was blocked and turned down by the CAA. Corporate power continued to blaze forth when Slater gave his arguments in defense of Amex's existing airline to the Justice Department and House Merchant Marines Committee. Thirteen months of cross-fire from both sides continued from the time Amex first filed for its certificate with the CAA.

On June 6, 1940, the last oral debates from Amex and Pan Am lawyers were heard by the newly estiblished CAB. In July, Trippe was notified that he was overruled when the CAB, in the interests of the American people, found it just and right for the operation of more than one American airline to compete for the Atlantic air routes. Competition was the American way of life and President Roosevelt signed the final authorization papers granting Amex its right to proceed with planes over the Atlantic and return.

Disappointed and upset, Trippe figured that the government, and in particular President Roosevelt, was cozen to his airline's progressive program, a service to Europe only one year in its development. Trippe did not give up the fight.

In early 1941, hundreds of millions of dollars was geared by the House Appropriations Committee, some of which was amassed for airmail service, and rested on what was known as the "Treasury and Post Office Department's Appropriation Bill, Fiscal Year 1942."

If passed, and there was no doubt it would not, $1,299,736 was to go to Amex for subsidizing the airline's mail load over the Atlantic. If Trippe and his influential cohorts could defeat the clause for appropriations to Amex, he could once more stall Amex for starting Atlantic flights. Pan Am needed all the subsidy it could get; it was

S-23's bridge, as was the S-42's and M-130's, was somewhat cramped and antiquated by the time the 314s came about, the latter having more commodious and streamlined quarters. Note rolled-up sun visor blinds mounted along side windows. (*Photo Courtesy: British Overseas Airways*)

an international carrier extending throughout the Caribbean, South America, the Pacific and Atlantic.

Trippe well knew that when the war in Europe was over — not realizing at the time that the U.S. would soon be involved — that many airlines, including foreign, would emerge and compete for air traffic across all oceans and not just the Atlantic. In 1941, to forestall the beginning of the onslaught, he mustered all the support he could for granting his still relatively young airline the Treasury subsidies required to sustain his far-flung empire. Many of Pan Am's earlier air mail contracts were also on the verge of expiration. When renewal time came about, more money was needed due to the inflational cost of air mail prices since the original contracts were put into effect. To acquire additional subsidies from the appropriation's bill, and to head off Amex from acquiring a substantial amount, is all that it took for Trippe to again fight back. A corporate battle was rekindled.

Amex and Pan Am lobbied hard against each other in Washington, D.C. Antitrust and monopoly overtones were once more brought to light against both parties. Officials in favor of Amex stated that there was enough public available for the operation of two airlines. Opponents declared that Amex was as much, if not more, a monopolizer in controlling a ship line and then an airline as well — an infringement on the airline industry and that the two lines should be kept separate. If Amex got its way it was estimated the company would steal 90 percent of the traffic to Lisbon with its ships and planes combined.

Backing Amex, however, were nearly all the agencies in Washington: the CAB, Post Office, Navy, State and War Departments. Each had their own reasons as to why a second airline would be

beneficial to the U.S. The Navy and War Departments, for example, deemed it advisable for national defense purposes while the State Department foresaw another airline helping to spread American commerce and good will to as many foreign ports as possible.

But it was Trippe who stopped Amex in her tracks. As a key witness, he appeared before the Senate in early May, 1941. He reduced the battle tactics to simple arithmetic. Amex, not yet having its S-44 equipment, and being only in the infancy of airline development, would cost the Treasury Deoartment a reputed $21,000 per round trip in subsidy cost for carrying mail as compared to the already well-establised Pan Am Atlantic time schedule which was based on a lower bid and hence cost only $9,000 per round trip.

The Senate Committee debated and passed in favor of Trippe. Then Pennsylvania Senator James J. Davis changed his mind and the vote went against Pan Am. The air appropriations money, in favor of Amex, was sent to the full Senate for approval.

There on the floor another debate took place when Trippe's operational costs versus Amex's costs was again hashed over. The final vote was set 44 to 35 favoring Pan Am. Trippe had not only challenged the U.S. Government to financially sustain his airline, but he temporarily broke Amex's back and then went on about his business in healing and directing America's greatest international air carrier. He was a man to be admired and respected, not only by his employees but by the American populace in regards for what his clippers — in particular the 314s — would do in aiding in the prosecution of World War II.

Amex, though halted for a time, was not foiled. Slater proceeded to develop his airline, for the company had its certificate to operate as authorized by the CAB. Picking up the pieces, Amex pressed on for the delivery of the S-44 boats.

Loss of M-130 *Hawaii Clipper*, seen docked at Wake Island, was a blow to Pan Am's Pacific operations, and in turn put the line on alert to thwart any possible future-suspected Japanese sabotaging. (*Photo Courtesy: Pan American World Airways*)

11

New Bases for New Clippers

After landing rights had been granted Pan Am in early 1937, full-fledged plans went forth into the construction of foreign and domestic Atlantic Division bases along the planned northern and southern routes. Shediac, New Brunswick, a Canadian province, was chosen as the first northern fuel stop. A small building was erected along with a pier and a gasoline pump line to feed 100 gallons per minute to the S-42 survey plane and later 314 clippers. A DF tracking station was also built. At Gander Lake, Newfoundland, a second but larger base was built when a thick forest was cleared for future landplane service. Four runways were carved into the hardened soil and sided by hangars, a small hotel accommodating 90 passengers and crew, plus a tourist thrift shop. The marine terminal and customs office were constructed on the edge of the lake sided by another long pier. The third stop was set up at Foynes on the 10 mile-wide Shannon River where a radio station was assembled along with a fueling float. To this day the site remains a museum to the early days of transatlantic flight and houses the original ground radio equipment and other clipper-related artifacts. Eastbound air travel along the northern route terminated at, and shared with, the long-established Imperial Airways' Southampton seaplane base in England where a boat train provided transportation to and from London.

Bases were first set up in Bermuda on the southern route and later in the Azores and Portugal. Darrell Island, near the capital of Hamilton, was chosen for its deep, wide channel where flying boats could safely set down and lift off. A pier, gas line and mooring equipment were installed as was a small DF and radio station adjoining a white shack used for customs and attached to a tall con-

trol tower. Pan Am flags, as seen at all bases, were hoisted high for all near to see.

If Imperial Airways' Woods-Humphrey and the Air Ministry had not granted Pan Am landing rights to Southampton and Bermuda, Trippe had no recourse but to bypass Bermuda and fly his clippers directly to Lisbon, via the Azores. Future 314s could easily make the journey eastward due to their range, but the return trips took up more fuel by the constant bucking of strong head winds. This meant that westward flights would have to be stripped of nearly all passenger and cargo weight in order to make the homeward journey, a profit-losing enterprise as mail had to be carried under U.S. Post Office subsidy contract issued before the August, 1938, "Civil Aeronautics Act" (CAA). Trippe would have ruled for the latter as a last resort and sacrificed return trip costs to get some of his 314s over the Atlantic, the reason why the Azores were at first so desperately needed as a prime fuel stop. The nine-grouped islands, 1,000 miles west of Portugal, are the only land points, besides Bermuda, that lay between New York and Portugal in a near direct line.

In 1933, Pan Am had sent their Budget Director C. H. ("Dutch") Schildhauer to the Azores to study and chart a possible landing site but returned with a poor finding. All nine islands rose sharply from the sea. The best site available was at Horta on Fayal Island. Yet even Horta was not safeguarded against heavy swells that always churn and go as high or higher than three feet during winter months. Shortly after "Dutch" returned to the U.S., Charles and Anne Lindbergh found the same poor conditions when they surveyed the volcanic-formed islands.

In 1937, while negotiations were still underway with Imperial Airways, Trippe sent oceanographer States Mead to study the swells and tides around Horta. His reports, after some months of study, revealed a strong possibility that nature's currents and waves could delay flights and trap clippers in port for weeks, but that a base, even at the high cost of cancellations or delays, could be achieved. Affirmed, Horta was chosen as a fuel stop. A hotel to house passengers and crew caught in a storm-related layover was put into the planning stages.

Once established and the service began, 314 captains dreaded the Horta stop during winter. They were forced to use full throttle outside the only concave bay of sorts to get their heavily loaded 314 bellies away from the choppy seas. The Boeing ships were allowed a five-mile scan of sea-runway when whisking off into the

Tons of supplies shipped hundreds of miles were required to build foreign clipper bases as exemplified by the toil exerted at the Pacific's 314 Canton Island stop-over. (*Photo Courtesy: Pan American World Airways*)

Like so many of Pan Am's base camps, Canton's was desolate, primitive yet efficient. (*Photo Courtesy: Pan American World Airways*)

western wind. At the opposite end of the run rose ragged 7,000-foot-high Pico Mountain. A skilled and experiencod captain was needed to swerve a 314 sharply and yet as gently away as possible from the towering promontory just after leaving the water with a heavy load of cargo. Skill was required the moment a 314 broke surface to the time a captain started to bank his clipper, and, at the same time, maintain correct balance and control during the simultaneously fast and pivoted climb. Such flying tactics became routine at Horta.

To service the clippers at the Azores' capital, Pan Am engineers designed special tenders. A 55-foot tanker was specially outfitted with a stern-positioned coupling that enabled refueling in calm waters. In high seas the 314s were towed around the island where swells were usually lower. This was, of course, time consuming, costly and usually called for a flight layover. At bay in Horta's harbor was stationed a 50-foot enclosed boat used to transfer passengers and crew to and from shore. It also acted as an emergency pickup launch in the event of any unforeseen mishap.

Journalist Harvey Klemmer wrote in 1941 about the precautions Pan Am put into force at Horta, "The company has pursued a cautious policy and has not allowed its planes to land in rough water. That has meant long delays. Passengers have been held up, eastbound at Bermuda and westbound at Lisbon, for as long as two weeks or more, while the company's meteorologist watched the waves at Horta.

"I have made the clipper crossing three times, and I can testify to the extreme precautions the airways people exercise at Horta. Planes are not supposed to takeoff if the waves are more than 30 inches high.

"I remember one trip when we plowed, at 100 miles an hour, through waves that looked twice that high. We all held our breaths as the great ship tore the waves to tatters and finally leaped from the sea to shave the side of a cliff and spiral off into the dusk on the long hop to Bermuda.

"On my last trip, in April, our skipper executed a maneuver which I have never before seen. He took off on a curve. He started behind a breakwater, gave her the gun as we reached the open sea, and, swinging wide to avoid the cliff, took off in an arc. It was a beautiful job of piloting."[57]

Jim O'Neal, former 314 officer, stated in 1994, "Any one who remembers the 'old boat days' is aware of the many delays caused by the swells of Horta, Fayal, in the winter time. Frequently, there would be two B-314s, and occasionally three, stuck there waiting for the swells to abate.

"It had been determined, how I do not know, that takeoffs could be made when the swells were two, occasionally three feet, but not when they were three, occasionally two. There was, of course, no scientific way to measure them, the go or no-go was dependent on the judgment of the captain.

"I happened to be on a crew with two captains, to the best of my recollection, Audrey Durst and Pat Nolan. Twice a day we would go out in a motor boat to estimate the height of the swells. Along with us was the famous Charlie Lunn, head navigator of Pan American Airways, Atlantic Division.

"For three or four days running one captain judged the swells as one, occasionally two, a go, and the other captain three, ocasionally two, a no-go!

"On the last day, Charlie shook his head sadly and whispered to me, 'One captain fine. Two captains, no good!'"[58]

Lisbon's base, Cabo Ruivo Airport, was established on the city's north shore of the Tagus River and located 11 miles east of the estuary where the Tagus meets the Atlantic. Imperial Airways' seaplane base (flew boats in and out of Lisbon to and from England, Africa and the Far East) was too small and too busy to share with

The grandest of all terminals built, especially for the 314s, was LaGuardia Airport's *Marine Air Terminal*, New York. (*Photo Courtesy: George Valentine Enell And Assoc., Inc.*)

MAT's 1940 dedication drew a big throng while *Yankee Clipper* stood by for departure. To left is Atlantic Division's main maintenance hangar and adjoining beaching ramp. (*Photo Courtesy: Pan American World Airways*)

Trippe's radio-aired speech opened *MAT*'s festive ceremony as dignitaries and general populace crowded the podium. (*Photo Courtesy: Pan American World Airways*)

Pan Am and thus had its own facilities adjacent to the Pan Am terminal.

A plot of land chosen as the first European stop en route to Marseilles, France, was somewhat run down when Pan Am and Lisbon authorities officiated for the remodeling. Europe's longest seaplane dock, extending nearly a full block out into the Tagus due to extreme low tides, was built and equipped with fuel lines and mooring equipment. A terminal, hatched from an old abandoned Christian chapel, and adjacent to a dilapidated mill, was given a new life. In time the stone-faced chapel was converted, not into a shrine, but into a small reception room with benches, counters and side quarters for the storage of mail, cargo and baggage. It would be this quaint, white exterior-painted structure where many nationalities would later flock, not for prayer, but ironically to be blessed as being among the select few out of teaming thousands to acquire passage on the 314s in fleeing warring Europe.

At the extreme eastern end of the southern route, in Marseilles, 314s shared Air Frances' seaplane terminal.

Atlantic Division bases had to be built as well on the U.S.' east coast. While larger combination land/sea airports were under construction in Baltimore, Md., and New York's North Beach property, Trippe turned his attention to develop a temporary base aside Manhasset Bay, Port Washington, N.Y., on Long Island Sound. Foreseeing the future of his airline, Trippe had purchased the land site in 1933 from a defunct American Aeronautical Corp. that had gone under following the 1929 market crash. A pier at Manorhaven Airport was put into position along with a white-painted shack used as the terminal. A large old hangar serviced the boats. Pilots came to dislike this port because of low tides and winter ice flows, a troublesome waterway to sail and moor their clippers.

Further south was Baltimore's new Municipal Airport. A huge hangar and marine terminal were built for Pan Am through city, state and Federal funds. Baltimore politicians were more than pleased to serve the new air clippers, for it would be just like in the old days as reflected in the proud heritage the city had in harboring the once great sailing ships a century before. The airline gave not only a big boost to post-depression commerce trade, but prestige as well to the city's populace in that it provided the city with its own overseas airline base. For some time Pan Am 314s were serviced in Baltimore following every round trip as demanded by Priester's firm program. The international flying clippers were soon to become the pride of America's supremacy — the U.S.' merchant marine of the air.

Topping all eastern seaboard airdromes was the 558-acre North Beach Airport (grew to 630 acres by 1967) constructed at Queens County, North Beach, N.Y. In 1929, the small port was called the Glenn H. Curtiss Airport after the famed aviator and plane designer. In 1935, the city's Mayor Feorella LaGuardia, after studying the city's and Post Office's needs for a larger airline depot, leased the privately owned site and then took full control in 1936. Surveys were made, and on Sept. 3, 1937, President Roosevelt approved expansion plans. Federal funds were granted through the "Works Projects Administration" (WPA), a legislative act sponsored by Roosevelt to give jobs to workers during the depression. The $40,000,000 cost was divided between the city and Federal governments.

From the original 105 acres acquired by the city, the new port grew to 558 acres when part of Flushing Bay was filled in with city-dumped trash. Working three shifts a day, six days a week, 5,000 men toiled on for two years. By 1939, 23,000 workers were

New York's Mayor LaGuardia was guest of honor at *MAT*'s opening. (*Photo Courtesy: Pan American World Airways*)

on hand to rush for completion. On October 15th, Mayor LaGuardia and Postmaster General James A. Farley dedicated the airport at a ceremony where some 325,000 persons gathered to hear the speakers. Dignitaries arrived from Washington, D.C., Canada and elsewhere aboard chartered planes. Seven new DC-3 airliners were lined up in a row in front of the landplane's *Domestic Terminal Building* while one mile away on Bowery Bay, in front of the unfinished seaplane terminal, the 314 *Yankee Clipper* rode at ease. The new airport was hailed as "built for tomorrow and our children's children."[59]

However grand the renamed LaGuardia Field's land-based port was, it was the seaplane facility that stole the hearts of millions after it opened its doors to traffic on March 31, 1940. Commissioned as a New York historical landmark in 1980, the *Marine Air Terminal* (MAT) was designed and built by the architectural firm Delano and Aldrich. Constructed in the round with three protruding, spokelike wings, the *MAT* sits to the west of the now defunct *Domestic Terminal*. The facility, including the nearby 314 maintenance hangar the size of two football fields, beaching ramp and passenger and crew dock cost $7,500,000 to build. Erected with the same type of materials used in building the land terminal, the MAT's natural-rubbed brick was capped with a frieze of gold-leafed flying fish encircling the upper portion of the building. Leaping from imaginary blue waves, the fish symbolized the adventurous fun awaiting those about to embark on a thrilling transatlantic journey.

When first opened at 11:00 A.M. with threats of showers, 300 special guests arrived for a luncheon inside the MAT's huge Art Deco-styled rotunda. Dedication ceremonies followed outside where 5,000 reserved seats were set up near the hangar where the *Atlantic* and *Dixie* 314 *Clippers* rested on their beaching cradles. Seven hundred policeman stood guard while another 100,000 spectators gathered behind a nearby fence

Part of the ceremonies was to have included the first arrival of a 314. But because of poor visibility, the inbound *American Clipper* from Bermuda was cancelled. It didn't arrive until the next day. Just after President Roosevelt sent a special telegram offering his official blessings from the White House, the crowd moved as close to Bowery Bay as permitted. The first 314 clipper to depart from the *MAT* was ready for takeoff.

Not all went as hoped for the MAT's opening day. A wife of one of the passengers became outraged when she learned she could not follow her husband aboard the 314 to kiss him good-bye. She screamed her protest at Pan Am clerks that only drew unfavorable attention. Adding insult to insult, a man burst into a rage when his letter was turned down from going into the 314's 3,000-pound mail stock. At the last minute he had rushed to the counter asking if his letter could be sent aboard. It was too late. The man was denied his request and told his mail had to clear customs due to war-time restrictions. What followed pierced the eardrums of all standing by!

Shortly, the sound of one bell was heard and Capt. Charles A. Lorber walked out with his crew to the moored *Yankee Clipper*. At the sound of two bells, seven men and two women passengers followed suit, one of whom was Winifred Sperry Tenney, widow of Lawrence Sperry, pilot and son of the gyroscope inventor.

Just before 3:00 P.M., the *Yankee Clipper* taxied across Bowery Bay and into Rikers Island Channel. The starboard wing went down in the strong wind as the liner headed towards far-off Bronx-Whitestone Bridge. At 3:09 the clipper, in salute to the new airdrome, roared back into view high over the *MAT*. Her first stop was to have been Horta, but instead the *Yankee* flew north and landed at Port Washington. It was reported that weather conditions forced the 314 to carry an extra 1,000 gallons of gas, and because the fuel lines were not yet completed at the MAT, the *Yankee Clipper* was taken to Port Washington for the needed fuel. Plausible, but doubted by some as to the reason for the unscheduled landing, the 314 was back in the air at 4:52 P.M. for the long Atlantic crossing.

Following the ceremonies, the MAT's personnel settled down to routine business. Visitors and passengers alike praised the three-tiered, wedding cake-like terminal's expansive interior. In essence, the MAT was, and remains, an architectural jewel. Its main Art Deco entrance doors of stainless steel and glass, grilled by stylized winged globes set in the transoms, faced an elongated, elipse-shaped parking lot and opened to a foyer of dark green marble walls sided by potted palms. Five more steel doors graced the way to the grand rotunda crowned by a skylight. In the middle, and periodically placed along the continuous decor of marble walls, were mahogany benches, each end studded with hand-relief-carved propellers. Atop a platform, encircled by a ticket counter, was a huge, perforated and shiny aluminum globe, Pan Am's symbol of international flight.

To the sides, and in the round to conform with the building's shape, were three long check-in counters. High overhead, and spaced wide apart on the back walls, were three signs: "Pan American Airways," "Air France Transatlantique" and "British Overseas Airways"

(BOAC — Imperial and British Airways were united into BOAC when Parliment allowed the Air Ministry to form one overseas airline on Aug. 3, 1939). The latter two counters and offices were closed. War had come to Europe, and two months after the MAT's opening France fell to Hitler's invading forces.

Near Pan Am's station, three full-scale 314 compartments were on public display. They were part of the original mock-ups used by Boeing in designing the clipper and later shipped to New York at Pan Am's request and expense. First of the mock-ups — all sections were open on one side and roped off — was set up in a combination seat-and-berth arrangement. Next was the simulated lounge shown at meal time with tables covered with the same type linen and fine china used aloft. The third and last connecting mock-up showed a standard day-seated stateroom, all arranged as a PR tactic to illustrate to passengers, and to visitors who could only imagine, as to what it was like to fly aboard a 314. Small printed signs described each section.

Behind a nearby information counter were two lighted brown and green wall maps marking 314 Atlantic routes. Miniature metal 314s were moved periodically throughout the day to trace for interested viewers the progress of the flying boats as they cruised across the Atlantic. Mounted clocks gave the times from the point of departures to the times of estimated arrivals.

General business offices were located behind each counter space. To the left of the entrance, off the rotunda, was a swank dining room and newsstand. A modest-sized customs room was near the terminal's back doors where passengers and crew had to first report and clear before flight time and upon arriving.

Contiguous with the MAT's customs office was a small room used by newsmen for interviewing officials and the famous before or following a clipper flight. On a rear wall hung a massive picture of a 314 cutaway, a backdrop for those being interviewed and seen later by millions of movie buffs when Alley's newsreel frames flicked across countless screens across the U.S. and the world. Such was the case when the media approached Republican Statesman Wendell Wilkie after he arrived home by 314 in 1941, deplaned and walked into the MAT. Wilkie had gone to England for a report on President Roosevelt's "Lend-Lease" assistance program for war-embattled Britain.

Encircling the rotunda within the MAT's upper level were headquarters for Pan Am's General Manager Col. J. Carroll Cone, former U.S. Air Commerce director. Meteorologist and flight-crew-planning stations were also provided as was a tourist and passenger "Skyline Terrace" that overlooked the dock and land terminal to the east. A control tower apexed the *MAT*. To the rear, and facing Bowery Bay, a long copper-roofed sheeprun-type canopy and fenced walkway stretched a great distance from the right of the terminal. Numerous personalities of note from around the world would be photographed by newsmen to appear in periodicals, newspapers and Alley's reels. Reporters were always assured of good copy while at the MAT.

MAT's rotunda, circa 1943, embodied the period's Art Deco form of architecture. Inner-circled counter quartered customer information and inter-connecting airline ticketing offices. (*Photo Courtesy: Pan American World Airways*)

To the left and in front of the MAT's entrance stood the then world's largest airplane hangar specifically built for the 314s and for the bigger flying boat clipper ships that never came to pass. Four 314s could be worked on at one time after being dry-docked and rolled into the structure. Additional security was provided by the 25-ton, electrically operated doors. In front of the edifice, and facing the expansive parking lot, were administration offices directed by Operations Manager Schuldhauer and Chief Atlantic Division Engineer Edward McVitty.

Some two years after the *MAT* was opened to the public, an expansive 12-foot-high, 235-foot-long mural depicting the history of flight was completed by American artist James Brooks. Entitled "Flight," and then the largest painted mural in the U.S., Brooks had been commissioned through the WPA program to design a mural. After four years of research, sketching, drawing and painting, the master piece was unveiled on Aug. 18, 1942. Focused into the last panel was a striking 314 rendering. Brooks got the idea to incorporate a clipper into his work while sitting outside the terminal eating his lunches and watching the giants soar overhead as they came in to land or while taking off. Art critics and the general public responded favorably to the modern style composite done in warm reds, blues and greens. Texas-born Brooks' work still adorns the curved walls within the spacious rotunda.

Exactly 2,818 miles to the west in San Francisco was the Pacific Division's new million-dollar state-funded base, Port of the Trade Winds. California State officials in Sacramento wanted Pan Am to represent the golden age of commercial air development at the 1939-40 "Golden Gate International Exposition." Part of the WPA $14,000,000 funds was geared to build Treasure Island, a man-made fill that extends north of Yerba Buena island located between Oakland and San Francisco. Alameda, the old M-130 clipper base that housed a small hangar, sea-ramp, passenger terminal and dock,

Last of the Flying Clippers

was abandoned in favor of a new base. The move was made to the newer facilities on Jan. 23, 1939, while Alameda was turned back to the Navy, the property of which was granted to the airline on a lend-lease arrangement. On Feb. 5, 1934, the *China Clipper* opened service out of the new base.

Colorful and glamorous, passengers arrived and departed from a near fairyland where the ultimate in Art Deco architectural expression and splendor pierced the sky. Temporarily prevailing on the exposition grounds were, for example, massive creations entitled *Tower of the Sun*, *The Court of Pacifica* with its so- called *Fountain of Western Waters*, *Court of the Moon* and *Treasure Garden*, the latter backed by the *Hall of Air Transportation*, one of two hangars that housed general aviation exhibits along with an animated light map that electrically traced a clipper's course along and over the 9,000-mile Pacific route to Hong Kong. At the southeastern end of the island was a beaching and launching ramp constructed for the M-130 and mighty 314s. Close-by was an additional hangar, fueling facilities, a dock and spacious walkway connecting the float and pier to the *Hall of Air Transportation* temporarily used in part as the main terminal during the two-year faire.

At night the palace-like Art Deco monuments were flooded in multi-hued and articulated rays of light while fountains spewed forth in rhythmic profusion. It was man's tomorrow-land, especially evidenced by a dozing "take-me-afar" moored 314 radiating its own windowed cabin lights. The liner, not open for guided tours for security reasons, advertized dreamy destinations to far-off Oriental lands.

The late P. J. Keith, former Los Angeles Fuller Paint purchasing and production manager, said of Treasure Island and the 314 clippers, "Fuller Paint sponsored a luncheon for all west coast managers at the island's airport dining room. It was in 1939 during the Exposition. We were having drinks and lunch when someone in the room called out, 'Here comes the clipper!'"

"All of us got up and went to the windows to watch the Boeing land. There were very few big planes in those days and the clipper was really something to see. It was a beautiful sight — she came straight in with her tail a bit down."[60]

Before the Exposition closed in 1940, the white-painted Art Deco-designed *Administration Building* was turned over to Pan Am for its main terminal. In its spacious lobby was housed another 314 interior mock-up and a huge globe that centered the main floor space.

While Pan Am's new bases were being established for 314 service, the line continued to scout for more feasible landing spots on the delayed South Pacific route between Honolulu and Auckland. Kingman Reef and Pago Pago were definitely out. If Capt. Musick had past trouble getting an S-42 in and out of the small harbor at Pago Pago, then landing and lifting away a more than 41-ton 314 would be nearly impossible and considered extremely dangerous .

Looking further south, the next best location was located in the Phoenix Islands, a cluster of coral atolls 1,913 miles southwest of Honolulu and just past the equator. A study by airline experts was conducted in Washington, D.C., in late 1938, and to everyone's amazement no country had ever set claim to the islands, even though a century before American sailing ships used the Phoenix chain to load guano, a seafowl digestive by-product used for fertilizer. The extensive distance from the Hawaiian Islands was not a concern as the 314s could easily make the trip. A Pan Am survey team was sent to chart out Canton Island within the grouped atolls. Meanwhile, Trippe ordered a group of his officials to Washington, D.C., to ask the State Department to take legal action in proclaiming the island as an American territory .

In Washington, D.C., it was learned that the U.S. Navy was already mining coal at Canton for its steamships. Having a U.S. edge for claim, Trippe then asked the Navy to send a battleship to block off the harbor from the British and Australian Navies who were also in the area searching for an air base site for their governments' proposed reciprocal air service to and from the U.S.

Hardly having a battleship available for such a minor tactical ploy, the U. S. Navy did, however, dispatch a small submarine chaser to guard the harbor's entrance. In contrast, when the Australian Government heard about Trippe's plans they sent a cruiser to Canton to claim the island for themselves. Aboard was an official postal clerk who would, by virtue of authority, stake the island as part of England's and Australia's empire. Unon arrival, the cruiser anchored outside the harbor and a party went ashore where they were met by shoveled and pickaxed Pan Am and U.S. Navy workmen.

Following verbal arguments that must have sounded like lines from an old cowboy movie before the big shootout, the Australians backed off, but not before concessions were made to allow the postal official to remain on Canton. A small shack was built for him by the cruiser's seamen who hauled ashore fabricated sidings and other supplies before steaming away over the horizon.

Capt. Charles A. Lorber (center front) and crew in winter attire group for press photographers at boarding of *Yankee Clipper*'s first *MAT* departure, March 31, 1940. (*Photo Courtesy: Pan American World Airways*)

Caught in a cross wind, Lorber-controlled *Yankee Clipper* wing-dipped on Bowery Bay shortly after leaving *MAT*. (*Photo Courtesy: Pan American World Airways*)

Setting up house on the opposite side of the island from where the Americans were established, the postal clerk remained to himself like a marooned hermit having nothing to do with or to say to his human counterparts. Periodically, Australia sent the clerk supplies.

His only outside touch with the world was through a two-way radio supplied him by the Australian Government. The nearly rejected soul stubbornly stuck to his post like Custer at his last stand, except without any authority to stop Pan Am's progress. It wasn't until early 1939 that the U.S. and Australia, through Great Britain, finally agreed after much wrangling to share Canton for a mutual seaplane base. The joint-term arrangement was to last 50 years.

Second and last stop to Auckland on the clipper route was signed with less difficulty. A pact with France was initiated for landing rights at French-ruled Noumea, capital of New Caledonia, some 1,989 miles south of Canton. Another 1,124 miles southwest of Noumea was Auckland.

On April 29, 1939, the chartered freighter *S.S. North Haven* departed San Francisco, her holds stocked with construction equipment and expedition materials for the building of DF, radio and weather stations, docks and hotels for Canton and Noumea. The ship was the same one used to haul thousands of dollars worth of supplies (some 6,000 tons) to establish bases and hotels on Midway, Wake and Guam Islands in 1935 for the M-130 clipper service across the Pacific. Everything from bed linens to kitchen sinks were shipped south. The last of Pan Am's foreign ports had been accomplished for 314 flights across two past-foreboding oceans before the outbreak of war.

While the 314 bases were taking shape, the U.S. Government set about to regulate the fast development of transcontinental and transoceanic airline companies. Designs for new airliners and routes

to operate them on were leaping forward at a rate uncontrollable for the U.S. Air Commerce and Post Office Departments to handle together. On Aug. 22, 1938, the "Civil Aeronautics Act" was passed by the House and Senate. It had, before passage, been known as the "McCarren-Lee Bill for the Regulation of Air Commerce."

Prior to the passage of this bill, under the "Air Commerce Act of 1926," any person or persons who complied with safety standards could start an airline. However, such airlines could only hope to successfully maintain a business operation by getting subsidies from the U.S. Post Office by means of bidding for mail contracts. In the past there had been no requirement to hold a certificate to operate a flying service to carry passengers on an inter-state, public convenience basis. The U.S. Air Commerce had only imposed safety regulations, a periodical inspection of aircraft and granting of routes to be flown.

The new bill broadened safety regulations and subjected all airlines to economic regulations like those imposed upon public utilities, and so forth. At the same time, the 1938 act eliminated mail contract bidding and gave to airlines permanent certificates of authority to transport passengers, cargo and mail, but only after the lines had proven their worthiness of merit through public hearings. In essence, this was similar to a so-called grandfather clause that allowed airlines to own franchises — to operate on routes that existing companies had satisfactorily flown on before the 1938 airlaw enactment.

There were three official headings (groups) — a tripartite agency — under the passage: "Civil Aeronautics Authority," consisting of a five-member board having quasi-judicial and quasi-legislative powers; a three-member "Air Safety Board" to investigate accidents, causes and making recommendations against reoccurances of same; and "Administrator of Civil Aeronautics" whose branch set regulations for civil routes to be flown and granted landing sites and navigational facilities. The "Air Safety Board" was abolished in 1940 and, effective June 30th that same year, became a five-member team apart from the CAA known as the "Civil Aeronautics Board (CAB), an independent regulatory commission.

According to the CAB, the board's main function was to regulate the economic aspects of U.S. airlines, both domestically and internationally, through certificates; to establish rates and control over inter-locking relationships; to monitor entry of foreign airlines into the U.S.; to work with the U.S. State Department in obtaining and granting reciprocal air rights with foreign countries; the setting of safety standards for all aircraft, private or commercial; and the authority to suspend or revoke certificates along with investigative authority involving accidents.

Previous to the establishment of the CAB under the 1938 act and 1940 reorganization plans, legislation was passed in late 1937 to create the U.S. Maritime Commission, a government body stemming from the 1936 "Merchant Marine Act," which granted government subsidies for surface-going lines, thus doing away with U.S. Post Office contracts for the shipment of mail. Multi-millionaire Joseph P. Kennedy was appointed by Roosevelt to head the commission for 75 days before becoming U.S. ambassador to England in December, 1937.

Because of the fear that powerful and growing Pan Am would monopolize overseas passenger and mail service, and in turn cripple steamship operation within the future, Kennedy pressed to regulate Pan Am under his new authority. Supposedly he wanted to be equally fair to both modes of travel. Figures released by the Maritime Com-

mission showed that when Pan Am began its transatlantic service that one-fifth of 20,000 passengers would probably journey by air.

Trippe stood his ground and lashed back to support his upcoming 314 service over the Atlantic. Through lobby practices, the airline chief worked to include a clause into the "McCarren-Lee Bill." If passed, the "Civil Aeronautics Air Act" would have the only jurisdiction for regulating mail subsidies and new routes for all airlines, including Pan Am. Desiring to keep air and sea regulations separate, Trippe personally said no to Kennedy's plans. The clause was later passed with the new 1938 air-act bill. Once more Trippe had scored for his 314s' Atlantic flights.

A bad turn of events — the fate of destiny and its resistless force — spelled another transoceanic disaster on Jan. 31, 1939. This time the ace of spades was turned against Imperial Airways.

British Capt. J. R. Alderson lifted the S-23 *Cavalier* away from Port Washington in the early morning hours for a routine air cruise to Bermuda with three other crew and nine passengers. Four hundred miles out a 12,000-foot altitude the flying boat flew into a severe cold front clogging engine carburetors with ice and forcing the plane to ditch in rough seas. Upon hitting a third swell the hull broke in two. For 10 hours the 10 survivors formed a ring and helped each other to stay afloat in shark-infested waters until rescued by the crew of a passing oil tanker.

Downing of the *Cavalier* forced the CAA to take necessary measures in aircraft design and in turn regulated for tighter safety standards for over-water aircraft. When the cause of the mishap was established, the 314 was again checked for proper carburetor performance. Also mandated by the CAA was that all future ocean-

Crash of *Cavalier*, shown earlier en route between New York and Bermuda, further crippled Britain's attempt to maintain a strong and profitable airline operation on Atlantic and gave flying public an added fear to over-water safety. (*Photo Courtesy: British Overseas Airways*)

going airliners maintain enough life rafts to ensure the safety of all plane crash survivors. Pan Am stipulated that their emergency equipment and survivor provisions aboard clippers excelled CAA mandates. Four days after the *Cavalier*'s demise, an article supporting Pan Am's safety standards appeared in the *New York Times*.

Being that it was the first crash of a commercial plane in the Atlantic, newspapers and periodicals featured the event. The coverage stirred public reaction to the point where it was questioned if it was safe to fly across oceans. Both the *Samoan* and *Hawaii Clipper* fatalities lingered in the minds of many.

Samuel Goldwyn Mayer Studios (S.G.M.) in Los Angeles grabbed at the publicized story and proposed a movie entitled *Thirteen People Went Flying*. The S-23 crash and SGM's plans couldn't have happened at a more inconvenient time for Pan Am. The line was on the threshold of starting 314 Atlantic flights and upgrading its floundering Pacific Division. After word reached Trippe about SGM's intent, pressure was induced to have the studio cancel their *Cavalier* account as based on the possible damage it may have on America's leading role in transatlantic air travel. In the long run, however, Hollywood would not totally bend to Trippe's request.

In 1940, the movie *Foreign Correspondent* was released starring Laraine Day and Joel McCrea and co-starring Herbert Marshall and George Sanders. Towards the end of the spy-gripping film directed by the master of suspense Alfred Hitchcock, all leading characters are fictiously shown flying to America aboard an S-23. During the flight sequence the flying boat is viewed shot down by a German gunboat rather than being forced down by engine failure. Consequently, as with the *Cavalier*, the plane crashes into the sea and breaks apart. Marshall, playing the enemy agent, swims away to terminate his existence in exactly the same manner as the *Cavalier*'s Steward Robert J. Sponce did in real life.

England couldn't replace the *Cavalier* for its Bermuda service. Cunard White Star Line, England's leading steamship company and general agent for Imperial Airways in Bermuda, announced in early March, 1939, that the airline had intended to bring in a S-26 advanced model named the *Champion*. After completion of tests at the factory, the plane was to have been flown to Bermuda from England, via Portugal, Africa, South America and the Caribbean. It never came to pass. Tensions in Europe precipitated England's need to keep the flying boat — one of a few desperately needed — for its Empire routes to the Far East rather than to maintain a service not directly related to the urgency of a war crisis. Therefore, Britains's reciprocal run of regular, scheduled passenger and mail service between New York and Bermuda on a peace-time commercial basis was ended until after the war. Pan Am continued its contracted flights to and from Hamilton with the S-42A *Bermuda Clipper* as well as with the new 314s, to eventually, for a time, become the world's only airline operator across the entire Atlantic and Pacific Oceans.

Six days after the *Cavalier*'s downing, the first 314 clipper was turned over to Pan Am after having completed its U.S. Government test trials in Seattle. An age of unheralded, heavier-than-air transport luxury in the skies was about to begin.

12

Public Debut

Winter overcast blocked out the sun when the NC-02 lifted majestically from Lake Washington for the last time on the early morning of Jan. 27, 1939. Ferguson acted as bridge master alongside Pan Am's Capt. Tilton, who performed second officership. Boeing's construction number 1989 was destined for Treasure Island to replace the lost *Hawaii Clipper*. Black markings reading "No. 18" appeared on the 314's bow and central tail fin. The stenciled numbers stood for the 18th four-engined aircraft owned by the airline. Also aboard were Pan Am and Boeing representatives that included Beall as well as an unofficial amount of express packages that had been stashed in the ship's mail bins.

First and last planned stop en route to San Francisco was Astoria, OR, located at the estuary of the Columbia River that marks the border between Washington and Oregon. There Pan Am and Boeing arranged for the plane's sales transaction to avoid paying heavy Washington State sales tax. Upon arrival Beall and party were taken to shore by launch and then by auto to a specified bank office where a multi-conference phone connection was made to U.S. Air Commerce officials in Washington, D.C., and to Pan Am's New York Financial Trust Co.'s officials who had gathered at the airline's headquarter offices. Pan Am's Chief Purchasing Agent Gledhill, who had arrived in Astoria earlier, handed Beall the last $100,000 check

due on "No. 18." Beall then handed Gledhill a blank piece of paper — he forgot to bring the clipper's title certificate with him after having mistakenly left it onboard the aircraft. Beall and Gledhill returned to the flying boat after phone arrangements were completed whereupon the title of ownership was officially signed over to Pan Am.

On January 28th the NC-02 was flown on to San Francisco under Tilton's command. The ranking captain who had replaced Capt. Musick had been checked out on the 314 at Boeing's flight school and at Lake Washington. All equipment aboard was monitored during the flight path along the Pacific coastline until she landed off Treasure Island in the late afternoon. For the next few days the clipper was used for schooling Port of the Trade Winds' ground crew in 314 beaching procedures and mechanical care. Then on January 30th, "No. 18" began its first of 16 airline trial flights to familiarize Pacific-based flight crew. All tests were short versions of the ones given in Seattle. Capt. Tilton took the plane into the air for a four-hour flight that included flying with two stilled engines. When the crew went to restart No. 3's power plant, the prop refused to turn over at maximum speed and the day's test was cancelled after only two hours aloft. The minor problem marked the beginning of many 314 bugs that eventually had to be worked out.

Testing of the second 314 built continued the next day when a nagging problem began to persist. The ship porpoised during all takeoffs and landings. Captains learning how to handle the 314 under Capt. Tilton's supervision thought it to be their fault and would have to master a technique as prescribed by Allen and Boeing. Priester, who had flown out from New York, was aboard many of the airline's trial runs out of San Francisco. Also present to help acquaint Pan Am crews was Beall.

Priester soon became disenchanted about the poor takeoff and landing attitudes and remarked to Beall that Boeing would have to resolve the problem without interrupting the line's scheduling of 314 service. By February 6th, as with the two remaining M-130s, NC-02 had a new look. As her nose pointed outwards from the hangar's entrance prior to another test run, two six and one-half-foot-long by four-foot-high wavy American flags were seen painted on either sides of her bow as accomplished by Paint Shop Chief Victor Freeland and his assistants Jim Ayres, Gerry Edlgridge and Frank Christiansen. Clipper "No. 18" was the first of three 314s to have the artistic wavy flag pattern imprint while the rest of the

Beall, about to ascend ladder carrying pouched 314 turn-over papers, boards second 314 built with other Boeing and Pan Am officials before sunrise, Lake Washington, for delivery flight to Astoria. (*Photo Courtesy: Boeing Aircraft Co.*)

Ferguson (left) turns *No. 18* over to Capt. Tilton at Astoria once Pan Am presented Beall with 314's price check. (*Photo Courtesy: Boeing Aircraft Co.*)

Boeing fleet would be masked and sprayed with a flat, square-type cosign. Over time the labor for the former was to become too time consuming and thus too expensive to maintain. Additional flat flags were descried on all 314 wings and beneath sponsons. The Atlantic Division began its 314 American symbol-painting on Aug. 28, 1939, the applications of which were for a reason other than to boast America's air supremacy.

A *San Francisco Chronicle* news reporter aimed his camera high and snapped a picture of NC-02's latest art work as the boat rested upon its cradle. He was told by a Pan Am spokesman that the flags were "...for protection in foreign waters." It was obvious that American and Japaneae tensions were on the increase and the painting of flags was a bold, visual statement to Japan — as well as to Germany at the Atlantic Division — not to tamper with the aircraft. It was, in part, an extension of tighter security given to all Pan Am aircraft as well as to all their U.S.-based bases backed by secret FBI surveillance.

Capt. Tilton was to have been in charge of all 314 break-in flights within the bay area and to have commanded the "shakedown" flight to Hong Kong later in the month, but a sudden appendicitis attack sent him to nearby *Palo Alto Hospital* for an emergency appendectomy. Taking his place until he recovered was Capt. William A. Cluthe, second ranking pilot for Pan Am on the Pacific. Cluthe, who joined Pan Am in 1930, had been an ex-Navy pilot for

12 years and an instructor eight years before he decided to become a commercial pilot. He was first assigned flight duty out of Miami and then transferred to the Pacific Division in December, 1936. Cluthe commanded the *China Clipper's* first air mail flight to China (Macao) that departed Alameda April 21, 1937.

While plans were being formulated for the first 314 transpacific flight, the Atlantic Division's first 314 was fueled and flown out of Matthews Beach at 7:30 A.M., February 10th. Boeing's plant production number 1990 ("No. 17") was piloted by Ferguson who took the plane to Astoria where it was payed for and turned over to Capt. Gray. Shortly after NC-03 lifted away the skies turned bad. Boeing's Flight Engineer Pavone said, "...all hands sweated out the delivery flight to Astoria when the weather socked in after we were well on our way."[62]

Once over Astoria, Ferguson circled the clipper until a break in the stormy clouds allowed for a safer landing while coming down in pouring rain and strong winds. Upon touchdown "No. 17" heeled to port slightly, damaging the wing. Repairs had to be made at Treasure Island after the $100,000 check was turned over to Boeing. Capt. Gray and his seven-man crew departed shortly thereafter to arrive in San Francisco at 4:00 P.M. the same day. For the next few days following the minor wing reconstruction, brief check-out flights were conducted before starting the long hop to the east coast, via San Diego, Galveston, New Orleans, across Florida and north to Baltimore.

With all its 16 trial runs completed, "No. 18" departed Treasure Island on February 23rd at 3:00 P.M. for its shakedown cruise over the Pacific. Inside the 314's wide cabins sat four CAA observers and seven Boeing and Pan Am representatives, one of which was Beall. The clipper's holds were stocked with cargo and mail, the latter made up mostly of covers for aero-philatelists.

Some 17 hours later the 314 was set down at Pearl Harbor. On February 24th, the clipper, with its 12-man crew and non-paying passengers, left for Midway, Wake, Guam, Manila, Macao, and Hong Kong, arriving at the latter's Klong Toi base on March 3rd. At each stop base ground crew were instructed on how to moor, fuel, load and give general maintenance to 314 aircraft.

Manila was reached March 4th on the return trip, and on March 6th the clipper departed for the 1,600-mile hop to Guam. "No. 18" was to have stopped only at Guam and Honolulu on the return flight, but 45 minutes after flying past Wake an engine was shut down after trouble developed. Capt. Cluthe turned the 314 around and brought it safely down at Wake on three engines with an 80,000-pound payload. It was an unexpected test of the 314's capabilities and all aboard marvelled about the ship's fine performance. With a repaired engine, "No. 18" was flown on to Honolulu.

Against a setting sun with silhouetted palm trees swaying in warm trade winds, NC-02 pulled her hull free from Pearl Harbor on March 14th and sped east in an orange-streaked sky. Seventeen hours later after an 18,000-mile journey, the 314 glided down on white-capped waters off Treasure Island. Hypothetical safety drills,

Swift-lined *No. 18* nears San Francisco off Marin County during delivery flight. (*Photo Courtesy: Boeing Aircraft Co.*)

flight-deck operations over a wide body of water, equipment test-ing and ground crew introduction procedures were completed and logged when the flying boat taxied to her dock at 11:00 A.M., March 15th. CAA officials, saying their good-bye to Beall and others, pro-ceeded on to fly back to Washington, D.C., to file their reports for granting Pan Am authority to schedule 314 passenger flights across the Pacific. Only the engine failure and some porpoising on land-ings hampered the otherwise near perfect trip.

As "No. 18" was soaring across the Pacific, the first clipper built, construction number 1988, was cleared to join the Pacific Division. She finally left her Lake Washington seri on March 2nd, made a brief stop at Astoria and then was flown to Treasure Island. Pan Am's "No. 19" would have been turned over to Pan Am earlier if it had not been for the poor landing incident that nearly tore her port sea-wing off in late February that resulted in further sponson manufacturing and testing.

Capt. Tilton, who had recovered from his operation, and Pan Am's veteran Capt. J. H. Fetters acting as first officer, docked "No. 19" at Port of the Trade Winds at 3:25 P.M. with nine other crew aboard. The next day the ship began its two-week airline taxiing and bay area flight runs. For one day NC-01 was taken into the *Hall of Air Transportation* and placed on exposition display. Spec-tators, however, were not allowed to tour the interior due to the usual security precautions.

Capt. Gray brought "No. 17" into Baltimore on February 23rd. Date wise, the 314 was late in arriving. The wing repair in San Francisco, Pan Am's testing phase and the lack of proper fueling facilities at ports-of-call en route to Baltimore, prevented an earlier arrival. Once in Baltimore, a week was spent giving the NC-03 some minor repairs as well as the same type Pan Am testing given the previous two-delivered 314s.

Early in the morning of March 3rd, "No. 17" roared off the Patapsco River for a short flight to Washington, D.C., where the

First Lady Eleanor Roosevelt christened the flying boat at a gala-prepared ceremony. The Atlantic Division's Paint Shop Chief G. C. Gwinner had removed the "No. 17" title from the bow and tail within the cavernous Baltimore hangar and replaced the markings with black-painted words *Yankee Clipper*, a name forever engraved into the annals of aviation history.

Flying low over the domed U.S. Capitol, the clipper dipped its wings in salute before Capt. Gray alighted the sparkling liner at the Anacostia Naval Air Station's Tidal Basin next to the Potomac River. A flag-draped barge was positioned into place where the 314 was secured. Three thousand people sat and stood along the Tidal Basin's shoreline when the First Lady and other dignitaries arrived. Among the many noteables were Gen. H. ("Hap") Arnold, U.S. Army Air

Tilton circles *No. 18* over and past Port of the Trade Winds and Treasure Island's Golden Gate Exposition. White edifice directly below 314's bow later became clip-per base's passenger terminal. A Commodore flying boat is also seen in bay used to train clipper pilots and crew. (*Photo Courtesy: Pan American World Airways*)

Outbound past *Golden Gate Bridge*, *No. 18* begins shakedown 314 flight to Far East. Beall was aboard. (*Photo Courtesy: Pan American World Airways*)

At rest at tropical-lined Pearl City base, first stop along ocean-mile-stretched inspection trip, Feb. 24, 1939. (*Photo Courtesy: Pan American World Airways*)

Corps chief; Edward J. Noble, CAA chairman; and Trippe, who presented Mrs. Roosevelt with a bouquet of long-stemmed red roses just as he had done with the former First Lady (Mrs. Hoover) when she christened the U.S.' first four-engined over-water S-40 ,the *American Clipper*, at nearly the same spot in October, 1931.

With two hands, Mrs. Roosevelt, wearing a red, fur-lined coat over her dress and donning a red hat to match, gripped a gold wire-wrapped champagne bottle filled with water collected from the seven seas brought in from a distance of 37,000 miles. Stepping forth and standing on the raised podium to reach the *Yankee Clipper's* prow, the First Lady stated, "...I christen thee *Yankee Clipper*."[63] She then swung and whacked the bottle against a temporarily placed cablelike bow device attached to protect denting the liner's nose. Samples of

the seven seas spurted forth striking the First Lady's face and drenching the front of her coat, the crackling sound of which was nationally heard through *CBS* and *NBC* radio hookups. Of the millions across the country who heard the broadcast were a few hundred Boeing employees who were allowed to gather outside Plant 1 during their lunch hour. Company officials had arranged to have a radio sound truck to park near the plant's main gate.

Voicing into microphones, Trippe spoke, " . . . ten years ago, from that same heritage that produced the sailing clipper ships, the nation's businessmen provided the capital and the nation's industry provided the constructive genius to bring forth the *Yankee Clippers* of the air, which have again proved their superiority over all competitors.

No. 18 breaks stilled Pearl Harbor waters upon landing off Pearl City, first 314 flight across the Pacific. (*Photo Courtesy: Pan American World Airways*)

Manila, fifth stop across Pacific, is reached during breakdown air cruise. Wooden terminal (upper left) was fire-balled by PAA's Regional Manager Rush S. Clark to keep it from advancing Japanese troops following Pearl Harbor attack. (*Photo Courtesy: Pan American World Airways*)

"Commanded, like their predecessors, by American captains, manned by gallant crews, they have — in 10 short years — brought our country from last to first place on the airways of the world..."[64]

Nearly an hour's worth of speeches followed before Gray and his crew flew some of the prominent guests over the capital. Mrs. Roosevelt deferred her trip until the second flight and just before the NC-03 was taken back to Baltimore to conclude Pan Am testing. On Monday, March 13th, Capt. Gray whisked the clipper to Port Washington where workmen had barely finished completing the line's third docking facility on the eastern seaboard. Planned by the airline as a publicity stunt, and to acquaint Atlantic Division ground crew with the latest clipper model, Gray brought the flying boat down off Manhasset Isle where the ship remained for nearly three days. Three thousand special guests visited the Manorhaven Airport after receiving invitations through the mail to tour the plane.

Thousands of other spectators gathered nearby as Gray was presented a key to the city by a town delegate after stepping ashore.

More than 100 public officials, airline associates and media reporters were flown over Manhattan and the New York World's Fair in airline-sponsored courtesy flights the following day. The mighty NC-03 was seen as a harbinger for the more glorious times ahead in the never-ending saga of commercial flight. What the *China Clipper* did for Pacific ports, the *Yankee Clipper* would do for Atlantic ports. With a roar of mighty engines, debonair ace commander Gray then took the NC-03 back to Baltimore on the afternoon of March 16th. Final preparations for the first 314 Atlantic flight were put into motion.

Before the *Yankee Clipper's* christening and starting out over the Atlantic on its shakedown flight and port inspection trip, the airline rushed for an approved and necessary renewal landing application right with the French Government. Legal documents had to be legalized and passed. By late February all was in order to operate an American air service to the foreign Republic on a six-month grant as negotiated through the U.S. State Department. A more permanent authority to fly to French soil was held back by the French as based on their reciprocal service. War, however, would soon disolve the latter and also close the door to Pan Am's operation to and from Marseilles .

Meanwhile, at Pan Am's Pacific Division headquarters, 314 activities paralleled the Atlantic Division's developments. The markings of "No. 19" were erased from NC-01 and replaced on the bow with the words reading *Honolulu Clipper*. Also at the Treasure Island base, NC-02's edifice "No. 18" was effaced to state *California Clipper*, names approved by Pan Am's board of directors in New York. All 314 titles, with the exception of one, were limited to two words.

Selected to fly the *Honolulu Clipper* on her shakedown cruise to the Orient on March 16th was Capt. Kenneth V. Beer who was

Passengers enplane NC-02, Treasure Island, for first transpacific 314 service flight. Exposition's *Tower of the Sun* is to far left. (*Photo Courtesy: Pan American World Airways*)

Capt. Gray steers *Yankee Clipper* over U.S. Capitol before alighting for ship's colorful christening ceremonies. (*Photo Courtesy: Pan American World Airways*)

born in Salt Lake City, Utah, in 1903. Graduating from Stanford in 1926, Beer returned to the university's business school for an additional year before enrolling into the Army Air Corp's training facility at Brooks Kelly Field whereupon he graduated a year later as a second lieutenant, becoming a reserve officer. Beer then applied for work as a pilot with Pan Am and was hired on April 19, 1929. He was the 19th flyer taken in by the airline and first flew Fokker F-10 landplanes between Miami and Puerto Rico for two months and then was transferred to Brownsville to fly Ford Tri-motors to and from Mexico and Central America. Five years later he was again transferred back to Miami where he began the arduous training of learning to fly the boats. Following a three-year stint he was sent to the Pacitic Division where he earned his mastership following two round trips across the Pacific piloting M-13Os.

The *Honolulu Clipper's* first transpacific flight was planned not so much to break-in the clipper as it was to instruct new captains and officers in extensive over-water 314 operations. Besides Beer and a 10-man crew was one Boeing official and four Pan Am inspectors who departed Port of the Trade Winds at 5:00 P.M. for the long trek to Hong Kong. When the NC-01 reached Manila on March 26th, CAA officials in Washington, D.C., informed Pan Am that the original "No. 18's" shakedown reports were cleared for allowing 314 passenger service. A wire was sent to the Philippines,

Seven seas' bottled water wets First Lady at NC 18603's christening. Event was nationally broadcasted. (*Photo Courtesy: Pan American World Airways*)

and on March 27th, at 3:28 P.M. PST (7:28 A.M., Manila time), Beer took to the air with 30 paying passengers and two extra crewmen. Among the first scheduled 314 passengers were 20 members of a Chinese football team returning home to Singapore via Hong Kong. With 45 people, including the crew, mingling about in the 314's plush inner hull, Pan Am reported that the trip to Hong Kong was, at the time, the largest human payload ever carried on a commercial, heavier-than-air aircraft.

The return trip to the U.S. also marked the first one-way Pacific-paying passenger flight with a 314. Beer and crew left the NC-01 at Manila on the return voyage. Another crew brought the clipper home one week after its departure from Hong Kong. Only a handful of paying passengers were aboard when the ship alighted on San Francisco Bay off Treasure Island.

Tragedy struck again when the *Honolulu Clipper* was only three days out en route to the Far East. Catastrophic to many, the calamity was a blow that wrenched the hearts of Boeing employees and fellow Pan Am comrades into deep sorrow. A part of the 314 story had also come to a close. Cram and Ferguson, along with eight other Boeing engineers and Netherland Government officials, were killed on March 18th in the crash of a new 307 Stratoliner landplane during a test flight near Alder, WA. Part of a wing and tail of the airliner had broken away while the plane was in a dive at 10,000 feet.

Eleven days following the 307 crash, wealthy Willard Shepherd, owner and president of a Los Angeles-based tractor firm, and his wife were enjoying Treasure Island's exposition grounds when they noticed a great deal of activity taking place at the clipper port. After leisurely strolling over to the hangar area they learned that a clipper was being prepared to fly the first-paying 314 westbound passengers across the Pacific and would depart later in the day.

"Any accommodations left," Shepherd asked a Pan Am ticket agent.

"Yes, still room,"[65] was the answer.

Life's spur-of-the-moment joys — if one had the money and the time — sparked the Shepherds to pay $278 each for a one-way flight to Honolulu, an $82 reduction from the M-130's earlier charge.

The epochal 314 westbound Pacific passenger air cruise left Treasure Island at 5:17 P.M. A large crowd stood nearby to watch and cheer as Capt. Tilton cut the *California Clipper* through the water and flew the flying boat off towards the open sea with his 10-man crew and 25 passengers aboard.

Three days earlier in Baltimore, the Patapsco River waters churned and sprayed aft from the 4,200-gallon gas-fueled *Yankee Clipper* as it sped away in a 40-second surface run to mark the first 314 Atlantic crossing. Departure had been without ceremony despite several thousand onlookers who had gathered on the 10-acre marine base at the 360-acre Baltimore Municipal Airport to observe the departure. Overhead a Condor landplane circled the port so its occupants could watch the clipper head for Horta, 2,448 miles to the east. It was piloted by Clarence Chamberline who flew Charles

Last of the Flying Clippers

Gray and crew gather for picture-taking, Port Washington, prior to *Yankee Clipper*'s inspection flight to Europe. (*Photo Courtesy: Pan American World Airways*)

Levine to Germany in June, 1927, that established Levine as the first official passenger to fly the Atlantic.

Capt. Gray was in command of the 12-man crew during the NC-03's inspection flight to four continents not including the ports at the Azores and Bermuda. Below-deck sat nine observing non-paying passengers representing Pan Am, Wright Aeronautical Corp., Boeing, the CAA, U.S. Mail Service, U.S. safety Bureau and U.S. Navy, Army and Coast Guard. The latter three departments indicated military interest in Pan Am's 314s.

Four-hundred miles out to sea Gray reported all was well. By 10:30 P.M., EST, the *Yankee Clipper* had flown 1,377 miles under a star-filled sky, its navigator using Arcturus, Spica, Polaris, Sirius and Capella for bearings. Then, 17.5 hours after leaving Baltimore, and with a tail wind that boosted cruising speed to nearly 160 m.p.h., the NC-03 was landed at the Azores. For the next three days ground personnel were trained in handling 314s along with refueling techniques from the airline's *Panair V-A* ship. On March 30th, the clipper was taken on to Lisbon and then to Marseilles on April 2nd. Adverse headwinds, however, altered the course and Gray instead first landed the ship at Biscaroose on a large lake before going on to Marignano near Marseilles. It was at Biscaroose, near the Bay of Biscay, that Air Transatlantique had anchored its boats for service to the U.S.

On April 4th, the NC-03 was flown 588 miles over France and the English Channel to Southampton. Customs officers stepped from a launch onto the *Yankee's* port sea-wing to enter the craft after it had been secured to a buoy in the harbor. At that moment a *Associated Press* (AP) news photographer in another boat aimed his camera to capture the scene. Ironically, the photo was the one selected to initiate a perfected method of transmitting pictures by wire. The so-called "wirephoto" was sent to New York from London by *Western Union Cable* where it appeared in U.S. newspapers just hours after tbe *AP* reporter had delivered the unique shot.

A long Easter weekend, coupled with an English bank holiday, delayed the 314 from continuing on with its base inspection flight until April 11th when she was flown the last 351 miles to Foynes where a night was spent at the passenger-prepared *Dunraven Arms*. The flight had covered 5,753 miles since takeoff from Baltimore. From Foynes the return trip began with a three-hour trip back to Southampton, to Lisbon in nine hours, and on to Horta, Bermuda and Baltimore. A cold rain greeted the flying boat as it touched down to complete its 11,017-mile inspection trip at 12:41 P.M., EST, April 16th. All had gone according to plan except that at each port the welcoming dignitaries with their lengthy speeches hampered Gray and his crew in their work to school ground personnel in 314 operations and in calibrating DF radio equipment. Gray had also noted that the liner had porpoised during the majority of its port landings.

In all, the NC-03 had been gone 22 days. Three and one-third days were spent aloft during the exultant sea and air voyage. President Roosevelt invited Gray to the White House to give a firsthand report whereupon the master air captain presented Roosevelt with a model of a sailing ship. The large hand-carved Azorian fig wood piece, housed under glass, was made by a monk and given the president for his personal ship collection. Indirectly, the model had become the first unofficial air express item shipped over the Atlantic.

Twelve days prior to the *Yankee's* maiden Atlantic flight, the fourth 314 built was delivered to Pan Am. Capt. Sullivan took delivery of Boeing order No. 1191 at Astoria on March 14th and ferried "No. 20" to Baltimore via the same U.S. southern route flown by the NC-03 on its delivery flight. Following Pan Am's trial runs, "No. 20" was pressed into immediate-paying passenger service between Port Washington, Baltimore, Bermuda and return.

Sullivan skippered the NC-04 for the Atlantic Division's inaugural twice-weekly[*] 314 passenger flight to Bermuda on March

[*]Thrice-weekly round-trip service was initiated in April, 1940.

Yankee Clipper sits idle on Tagus River while Gray and crew receive warm welcome by Portugal dignitaries during ship's shakedown flight. (*Photo Courtesy: Pan American World Airways*)

An American flag blows in strong breeze and rain atop NC 13603 as liner skims into home-ported waters to end long inspection trip to and from Europe. (*Photo Courtesy: Pan American World Airways*)

29th. "No. 20" carried 74 passengers and crew and left a few hours ahead of the Pacific Division's NC-02's first round-trip passenger flight over the Pacific. By the end of April, "No. 20" had carried 643 paying passengers between the U.S. and Bermuda. The crash of the *Cavalier* left Pan Am to handle the heavy traffic. Between the S-42A and 314, 3,614 passengers were transported to and from Darrell Island in 349 trips during the month of April. An influx of American-Bermuda business ventures were given as the reasons for the demanding and increased air service. Pan Am's traffic was up 156 percent over the same 1938 period with 1,095 people carried on the New York-to-Bermuda route in the first quarter of 1939.

Waiting lists became long. "No. 20," to aid the 34-passenger S-42A *Bermuda Clipper*, came to the rescue none too soon. It had become evident that more passengers desired to fly to and from the warm island resort during the 1939 Easter vacation period when it was publicly announced that 314 flights would be offered. Traffic soon became so heavy on the Port Washington-Bermuda run that an extra long customs counter — reported by Pan Am as the "world's longest" — had to be installed within Port Washington's marine base hangar so Customs Inspector William Mitchell ("Uncle Billy") and staff could speed up the checking process for the stacks of luggage confronting them after each flight.

In spectacular 314 glory, fifth ship built was put into round-trip service between U.S. and Bermuda before its gala christening. By the end of 1939, 314s had made 100 Atlantic crossings carrying 1,800 passnegers and some 40 tons of mail. (*Photo Courtesy: Pan American World Airways*)

As Trippe smiles (left) and Capt. Sullivan peers out side cockpit window, another keel is doused at a massed gathering. (*Photo Courtesy: Pan American World Airways*)

Paint Shop Foreman Gwinner worked through the night of April 24th and into the early morning hours of the following day putting 15 one-foot-high black letters spelling *Atlantic Clipper* on the NC-04's bow plates. The former "No. 20" was to be christened along with the dedication of the new Baltimore Municipal Airport. The special events had taken a full week of preparation. A fresh coat of black paint was applied to the NC-04's undersides as supervised by Division Engineer Ed. W. McVitty in conjunction with the maintenance departments. Mike MacDermind, carpentry shop chief, was put in charge of manufacturing hundreds of wooden posts to rope off the expected thousands of attendees who would flock near the front of the clipper's hangar, site of the christening ceremony.

Inside the hangar, while Gwinner stood on a rigged platform under glaring lights doing his artistic lettering applications, maintenance cleaners walked along the NC-04's upper hull and wide wings with buckets and scrub brushes soaping and washing down the clipper until it shined like a jewel. Other ground crew cleaned and polished windows and vacuumed out the interior. Work was completed as the sun started to rise. Then, nose first, Pan Am's beauty was moved into place near the hangar's opened doorway and a platform constructed near the flying boat's prow. State colors of black and gold bunting encircled the stand and upper podium. A planked stairway was positioned forward of the ship's starboard sea-wing that enabled celebrities to reach the upper stage.

A scorching 90-degree heat soon enveloped the city and base. The temperature was a bit cooler inside the clipper terminal where a special "Aviation Day" luncheon was held to commemorate the event and from where Trippe voiced a 2,106-word speech praising the people of Baltimore for establishing the first major east coast transatlantic air base tied to Pan Am's achievements regarding international flight. Trippe stated in part:

"...It was here that Baltimore's aviation pioneer, the late John Hambleton, and I discussed the first plans for what has now come to be the Pan American Airways System. And it was from Baltimore, in 1926, that we set forth in the first tri-motored airplane to be seen in this country to survey America's first international air route from Key West to Havana, the pioneer 90-mile overseas operation that has been expanded in 10 years to the 54,000-mile American international air transport system.

You will be interested to know how Baltimore came to be the first transatlantic air terminal. Ten years ago, Imperial Airways made a detailed survey of Atlantic coastal ports. Because of its natural operating advantages, the British engineers selected Baltimore as the logical terminal for a service to Bermuda, the first section of an air route to Europe. Later Pan American engineers confirmed the natural advantages of Baltimore as a transatlantic operating base.

Framed by the *Oakland Bay Bridge*, *No. 18* is prepared for a California sunshine christening, Treasure Island. (*Photo Courtesy: Boeing Aircraft Co.*)

Chapter Twelve: Public Debut

They found at Baltimore an ice-free harbor, well protected waters, and weather which would permit a year 'round operation.

"History has repeated itself here — for the *China Clipper*, first to take the United States' air mails across the broad Pacific Ocean to the Philippines and the Orient was built at Baltimore, the same port that saw the *Ann Mc Kim*, first of the famous sailing clippers just 100 years before, square her sails and point her bow for far-off China.

"Again today, at Baltimore's transatlantic air base, ride at anchor the Super-Clippers designed for the final conquest of the North Atlantic. In their aerodynamic advancement, in their technical performance, and in their accommodations for passengers, they represent new standards for the entire aviation world. They are fit and ready — for the next great step"[66]

At the close of Trippe's speech, and following the luncheon, 2,000 invited guests filed outside and over to where the *Atlantic Clipper* sat on her cradle. Once the guests were seated in metal chairs, and while thousands more stood behind barrier ropes, Trippe left his place of honor and approached the rostrum lined with microphones. He first introduced Robert O. Bonnoll, president of the Baltimore Association of Commerce, who praised Pan Am by stating in part, "...The events of today mark another epoch in the economic history of Baltimore. We are on the threshold of a great new development in aviation when regularly scheduled crossing of the Atlantic Ocean by air is about to emerge from the experimental stage into an almost commonplace actuality. These great new Pan American clippers will sail high above the ocean which only a few years ago carried the famous Baltimore clipper ships from this port to the ports of the old world. It is a significant time for America and for the world, and we, of Baltimore, are proud to have a part in it..."[67]

At the conclusion of five long speeches, one of which was by Howard W. Jackson, Baltimore's mayor, Trippe escorted the wife of Maryland's Senator Millard E. Tydings up the long stairway to the bunted stand. Wearing a print dress, gloves and wide-brimmed hat with feather, Mrs. Tydings turned and spoke into the microphones, "I christen thee *Atlantic Clipper*, and may all your flights be happy ones."[68]

With her right hand, Tydings smashed the gold-meshed, beribboned bottle of champagne against the black keel just beneath the 314 's nose and was then handed the standard Pan Am christening bouquet of red roses. Capt. Sullivan, standing in the 314's bridge, his upper torso extending through the opened overhead hatchway, placed American and Pan Am flags into holding brackets just back of the clipper's forward windshield. A band struck up the "Star Spangled Banner." For the next three hours at a minimal charge, more than 2,000 people were escorted in small groups through the liner's interior and the hangar's mounted displays of engines, work stands, rope racks and the like that encompassed the workings of the marine base.

Across the U.S. in San Francisco, and west to Hawaii, Pan Am had arranged for two additional and simultaneous 314 christenings. In the city of the Golden Gate, strung from tail to bridge with marine flags that signaled *California Clipper*, the NC-02 was poised on the sun-drenched apron's launching railway at Port of the Trade Winds. Mild temperatures prevailed as the clipper's gleaming hull pointed inward to a high platform draped in state colors of brown, green and white bunting. A soft wind swept over the channel, the distant background swept by the blue-gray greenery of Yerba Buena Island.

Only 1,000 luncheon and ceremonial invitations were mailed out due to the limitation inspection rights enforced at the base. Security was extremely tight at the base. Some of those attending the simple but impressive ceremony were U.S. Army Maj. Gen. A. J. Bowley, commander of the 9th Corps Wing; Leland Cutler, president, Golden Gate International Exposition; U.S. Postmaster William J. McCarthy; and Angelo Rosse, city mayor. Pacific Division's Manager Clarence Young presided.

McCarthy stated, "...With the going into this important service of the *California Clipper* and her new sistership, the *Honolulu Clipper*, there is reached a new stage in Pan American's development of the world's standard of international air transportation, which today not only crosses the Pacific and is now projected over the Atlantic, but also serves some 40 countries and colonies from one end of the Western Hemisphere to the other..."[69]

President Roosevelt's personal representative to the exposition, George Creel, spoke through local and national radio hookups, "...As we look out over the world today — a world convulsed by hates and greeds — a world on the brink of war that may well spell the end of civilization — how is it possible for us not to see the evil consequences of those narrow, bigoted isolationist philosophies that

With a prow aglow in name, old glories and line logos, Mrs. Alexander, second from left, is flanked by Mayor Rosse (far left) and Clarence Young and wife before whacking NC 18602 with bubbling, state-produced champagne. (*Photo Courtesy: Phil Stroup Photography/Pan American Airways*)

refuse to recognize the absolute interdependence of modern life, and are deaf and blind to the necessity of international amity based on peace and justice and orderly trade.

"Starting here today, therefore, let us make the high resolve that this *California Clipper*, now about to be launched so proudly, will carry our friendship and faith to every land to which it wings, and so bring back to us the same precious cargo in fullest measure."[70]

"...As I look over this 41.5-ton ship of the skies," Mayor Rossi said, "now about to be given the name *California Clipper*, I realize that the time has come for all of us to cease forever being skeptical or doubtful about what the future of air transportation holds... The *California Clipper*, as it stands here today, is definite proof that we are on the threshold of even greater aviation achievements than those which we have witnessed in the recent past... I wish happy landings, and many of them, to the *California Clipper*."[71]

Speeches continued hailing the clippers of old and new, and, in a small way, how the 314s represented America's peaceful interests abroad — the winged ambassadors of good will. San Francisco's Junior Chamber of Commerce President Frank Dolan, Jr. then presented Young with a commemorative plaque of the NC-02's first flight over the Pacific. When Dolan finished his brief oratory, Young took the arm of elderly Honorary Sponsor Mrs. Wallace M. Alexander, wife of one of Pan Am's directors, and walked with her up the long stairway to the christening stage. Wearing a striped spring suit, jacket, gloves and veiled hat, Alexander held onto her head's raiment with one hand against the strong breeze and crashed a bottle of California champagne with the other against NC-02's prow following her words, "I name thee *California Clipper*."[72]

The bottle, wrapped in gold-mesh wire, partly broke to fizzle out its contents in a frothy, bubbling spurt. Amidst smiles and chuckles, Young handed Alexander a red-ribboned bouquet of red roses on behalf of Trippe. A band started to play the "Star Spangled Banner," followed by the strains of "California, Here I Come."

Like the launching of a surface ship, the clipper — to the thrill of all on hand — was guided backwards by a tractor down the ma-

Capt. McGlohn (far left) and crew receive flowered leis from local Hawaiians at NC 18601's formal debut, Pearl City. (*Photo Courtesy: Pan American World Airways*)

rine railway and into the bay. Moored to a float, 600 of the special guests were allowed to roam through the flying boat's elegant compartments. Another special day in aviation history soon came to a close.

Missing out on the planned thrice-christening precedence was the *Honolulu Clipper*. Gusty headwinds between Midway and Honolulu prevented Capt. R. H. McGlohn from landing on schedule to keep the appointed ceremonial rendezvous. The hour was late when the NC-01 taxied up to the dock at Pearl Harbor. Passengers and crew deplaned and the special event was postponed until the following morning.

The early hour ritual of April 26th was the most picturesque and romantic ceremonies given to baptizing a 314. Fleecy clouds drifted lazily overhead as invited guests and a large crowd began to re-congregate on the palm-shaded courtyard lawn surrounding Pan Am's hotel and terminal. Pleasant sounds from the "Royal Hawaiian Band" softly exerted dreamy island music to conclude with the enchanting "Hawaii Poni" when the wife of Pan Am's Honolulu-based Manager L. Reis opened the gala ceremonies.

Capt. McGlohn and his 10-man crew stepped across a canvas-sided gangplank and into the clipper and then walked back out onto the wharf as though they had just arrived and smartly lined up at near attention alongside the ship's bow. Mrs. Reis proceeded across the lawn and down the dock to bid welcome. She was escorted by then Governor Poindexter and his daughter, Helen, who was to christen the clipper, and a Hawaiian court of ladies dressed in tropical garb and carrying redolent orchid leis.

One by one the crew took off their ship-styled hats as individualized and distinguished greetings were exchanged and while the women placed perfumed flowers over the crew's heads which draped their necks and broad shoulders. Salutations completed, Reis, carrying half a coconut filled with its milk, turned to Helen who held a palm frond. Dipping the extended tip into the proffered liquid, the honor maid raised the leafy branch and shook it lightly to the four winds. Then dipping the palm again into the shell, Helen touched the side of the clipper to formally christen NC-01 *Honolulu Clipper*. Nature's formed cup was in-turn offered to McGlogn who took a sip and passed it on to his crew who repeated the toasting ceremony.

Chanting to the strums of Hawaiian music, the troupe and crew left the dock to assemble in the shade of a large hau tree near the water's edge where speeches were conducted. Honolulu's Mayor Charles S. Crane gave the principal address:

"Through the past four years we have watched these mighty ships of the air as they continued their unerring flights between Honolulu and the Mainland as well as between this city and the Orient. We have seen these ships change in design and grow with increased horsepower and additional carrying capacity. Each of these new types of equipment has brought additional features which typified the latest progress in the art of aeronautical development. Today we have had the honor of seeing one of these modern flying palaces christened as the *Honolulu Clipper*, named in honor of our city.

It has been a signal honor to all of us here that this great craft should, on its flights which constantly traverse the Pacific Ocean, carry this designation which symbolizes the fact that in all air transportation operations, Honolulu is really the 'Hub of the Pacific'... To the captain and members of the crew of the *Honolulu Clipper*, we extend our aloha and assure them of our constant interest as well as our best wishes for their continued success."[73]

A band played the national anthem, ensued by an invitational Hawaiian luau held on the hotel's lanai. Later in the afternoon, and behind schedule, the NC-01 was stocked with cargo, mail and passengers and rumbled across Pearl Harbor to speed in poetic fashion through the open straits and into the air for its flight of pagentry to San Francisco.

13

A Ceremonial First

On the fifth day of the fifth month of 1939, the fifth 314 built was delivered to Pan Am at Astoria. Capt. Cluthe ferried the ship on to San Francisco where it was detained a month after tail structure failure was found during a hull inspection. Repaired, the NC-05 "No. 21" continued its journey to Baltimore where she was briefly broken in on the Bermuda shuttle run and then groomed for a very special flight — a ceremonial first. Any proposed plans for a christening were dashed following the craft's west coast delay. Given the name *Dixie Clipper* to commemorate the U.S.' historic South, the liner became the *Yankee Clipper's* rival when Pan Am employees began to wager bets on which ship would extoll in historical flights. The *Yankee* was in the lead, but the *Dixie* was about to strike forth for a scheduled heraldic flight set for June 28th.

Prior to the *Dixie's* headline-making trip, the magisterial CAA's precautionary directorship decreed that on the new Atlantic routes between five and seven one-way crossings, or four roundtrips, as granted Pan Am on May 18, 1939, that had to be established before regular passenger service could be inaugurated. The agency's predominant decision was to ensure that all operational standards were well-formulated and decisively mandated as safe. Until such flight numbers were completed, Pan Am was free to start regularly scheduled air mail flights to and from Europe.

Capt. LaPorté whisks aloft *Yankee Clipper* for the first-scheduled, heavier-than-air air mail service to and from Europe, May, 1939. Before the gala departure LaPorté told press, "I guess maybe I naturally feel a little pride at carrying the first regular mail across the Atlantic, but as far as the actual flight is conerned, it's old stuff to me. I've made 50 crossings—that is, 25 round-trips—across the Pacific, and that's a much longer drink than the North Atlantic." (*Photo Courtesy: Pan American World Airways*)

Lindbergh's 12th anniversary of his 1927 non-stop solo air crossing of the Atlantic was dedicated as "Aviation Day," the date selected to fly the first scheduled heavier-than-aircraft air mail to Horta, Lisbon and Marseilles. Capt. LaPorté lifted the *Yankee Clipper* from Manhasset Bay, Port Washington, shortly after 1:08 P.M., May 20th. Stashed aboard the NC-03 was 1,804.18 pounds of mail, four boxes of marigolds destined for the Queen of England, 14 crew and three airline observers. A letter cost 30 cents for half an ounce.

Prior to departure LaPorté was ordered to participate in advertising the event by cruising the *Yankee Clipper* over the New York World's Faire and circling the faire's *Aviation Building* during its dedication in honor of Lindbergh's anniversary. When the *Yankee* came into view, her powerful engines were heard for miles around, especially by the nearly 100,000 people who were reported on "The World of Tomorrow" grounds that day, 1,000 of whom were gathered near the *Aviation Building* containing the latest developments in aeronautical science.

Near the compound's entrance was situated a platform where the new CAA Chairman Robert Hinckley and other officials sat and waited for the NC-03. Mayor Fiorello H. LaGuardia was to have officiated, but being energetic he had, instead, gone to Port Washington for a private clipper tour and to bid farewell to LaPorté, crew and passengers. When the *Yankee Clipper* taxied away for takeoff, LaGuardia rushed to his waiting car and ordered he be whizzed back to the faire. Zipping along at 70 m.p.h. with sirens blaring to beat the NC-03 to the fair grounds, LaGuardia was seen as anything but calm.

Hearing the 314's engines and looking up to see a speck become an enormous sky-wonder of man's extraordinary power of invention at 2,000 ft., Hinckley hastened towards a radio transmitter and receiver installed on the *Aviation Building's* outside platform. Capt. LaPorté circled the giant liner and dipped its wings in salute. What followed was a bit humorous when Hinckley began communicating with Laporté:

"On behalf of the city of New York and the aeronautical groups and officials gathered here, Capt. LaPorté and you others on the plane, we too salute you. This is an auspicious moment, not only in aviation history, but we believe in the relations between the United States and Europe. We want you to understand..."[74]

Either because LaPorté was receiving poorly or because he was tired of political hogwash, he interrupted Hinckley and broad-

at 70 m.p.h.!

Arriving at the Azores the following day, a six-hour delay was encountered while Azorian postal employees and clipper crew frantically stamped 23,000 first-cover letters. That evening with mail back on board, the NC-03 arrived at Lisbon, and the next day, May 22nd, reached Marseilles where more mail was catche-stamped and then on to Southampton. Retracing the ports-of-call, LaPorté returned to Port Washington on May 27th at 3:57 P.M., EST, with 2,024.73 pounds of mail, much of which had been hauled aboard in sacks at Lisbon, Horta and Bermuda. The first scheduled round-trip aeroplane foreign mail service flight over the Atlantic was logged and historically recorded for future aero-philatelists.

Twenty-six days later, June 17th, Capt. W. D. Culbertson was put in command of the first non-revenue "preview press" flight to Europe and back using the southern route. Aboard the grand *Atlantic Clipper*'s 3:34 P.M. departure from Port Washington were, besides Culbertson, 10 crew and 16 special press and broadcasting representatives. With 609.73 pounds of mail stashed aboard, the NC-04 was refueled at the Azores and arrived at Lisbon the next day. That night, against the slopes of pastel-dotted buildings, passengers and crew ate and rested at the chic *Aviz Hotel*, a former palace of 20 rooms that had been renovated for Pan Am transits through the courtesy of the Portuguese Government. Weary-eyed passengers were awakened at 5:30 A.M. when they dressed, ate breakfast and were taken to Cabo Ruivo Airport at the east end of town where they soared aloft at 8:04 A.M., Lisbon time, June 20th, for an eight and one-half-hour flight to Marseilles.

Two days later the *Atlantic Clipper*'s westbound flight left the French port for Lisbon. Few spectators saw the clipper off at 9:05 A.M., French time, on June 24th, with 257.42 pounds of mail stashed in her holds. Nearby, the French flying boat *Ville De Sainte Pierre* was moored on the Tagus following a round-trip survey flight over the mid-Atlantic.

gave up his speech efforts as he looked towards the flying boat, stating, "Proceed to Europe Capt. LaPorté — proceed with the mail."[78]

Capt. LaPorté stopped the circling, leveled the ship off, shot it to a higher altitude, banked, leveled the boat out again and flew it eastward whereupon it dwindled to a mere speck and then out of sight. Mayor LaGuardia was still being ground-cruised somewhere

Non-revenue press and radio clientele board NC 18604 at Port Washington for 314 preview service flight across Atlantic. (*Photo Courtesy: Pan American World Airways*)

Yankee Clipper is off to inaugurate aeroplane air mail service on northern route between U.S. and England. (*Photo Courtesy: Pan American World Airways*)

En route to the Azores First Officer W. D. Winston spotted four whales — the mammals unaware that a silver cetacean was flying above and past them. At Horta the total 7,000 inhabitants of Fayal Island greeted the NC-04 and the four press women aboard the clipper were given bouquets of hydrangeas, the profusely growing flower of Horta. While the *Atlantic Clipper* was refueled, the air guests were taken by car to "High Point," a spectacular location offering a panorama view of the city, sea and clipper below. Then it was off to the *Amor di Patria Club* for cocktails, gifts and speeches.

At 5:32 P.M. the NC-04 spat through moderately heavy seas for a long and laborious takeoff with 4,170 gallons of fuel stored in her wings and sponsons. For two hours the plane bucked headwinds and overcast and then broke into clear weather where stars radiated their brilliance about the heavens. In the lounge, strung with decorations, the "captain's dinner" was a festive occassion followed by an "amateur ship's concert." At 11:43 A.M., June 25th, the *Atlantic Clipper* landed at Port Washington establishing a westbound record when bypassing Bermuda to the north.

Weather reports forecasted poor conditions when regularly scheduled aeroplane air mail service was inaugurated on the northern route on June 24th. Capt. Gray winged the *Yankee Clipper* away from Port Washington after the ship had been flown in from Baltimore with 2,543 pounds of mail. In addition to the 12-man crew, 20 all-male, non-paying passengers were listed for the 9:21 A.M. departure. "Number One" passenger was Trippe who was en route to England and France to speak on reciprocal British and French air operations as well as on Pan Am's present Atlantic progress. Other passengers represented the CAA, U.S. House of Representatives, the Senate, U.S. Post Office, U.S. War Department, U.S. Coast Guard, the White House and Pan Am.

Capt. Gray's first scheduled stop was Shediac where the *Yankee Clipper* was landed at 4:04 P.M. Fog was so thick at Botwood, second stop, that the clipper, originally timed to stop for only one hour, was held up for three days at Shediac. When the weather cleared, Gray flew the boat on to Botwood and then to Foynes, arriving June 28th at 3:00 P.M., Eire time.

Flying between Botwood and Foynes, Trippe was sitting in the lounge talking with a few of the official guests when stewards brought in a lighted birthday cake, glasses and champagne to celebrate their chief's 40th year. At 6:04 P.M., Foynes time, June 28th, Gray took the clipper on to Southampton where edgy passengers and a concerned crew were again confronted with fog so dense that the clipper couldn't be seen from the ground until she sat down on the night waters after three passes over the harbor. Sea-runway lights guided the monster in after Gray made an instrument landing at 8:39 P.M., British time, the first night touchdown made by a transatlantic commercial airliner. Thirteen hours and 41 minutes of flying time was recorded in the NC-03's log since takeoff from Port Washington four days earlier.

Eighty-year-old U.S. State Department passenger Walton Moore said of the crossing, "We took off from Botwood early and covered 1,900 miles without any trouble whatever. We reached Ireland at the fixed time, just as though we had been traveling by train.

"There seems to be nothing that can stand in the way of air travel with all these comforts."[79]

British official Sir Frances Shelmerdine officiated in the welcoming of Trippe and party when they stepped ashore from a launch and were taken to London by the Royal train used a week earlier by the King and Queen. On July 2nd the *Yankee Clipper* was back in the U.S. after flying the same route with the same passengers, mi-

With backup music by Port Washington High School band, part of *Dixie Clipper*'s crew to fly first, regularly scheduled airplane passenger service over Atlantic sat and stood for press pictures. Heading team was Capt. Sullivan (seated far left) and First Officer Gilbert Blackmore next to Sullivan. (*Photo Courtesy: Pan American World Airways*)

nus Trippe, along with 925 pounds of mail. Climax to the trip came when passengers formed the "North Atlantic Pioneers." James Rowe, President Roosevelt's secretary, was appointed secretary and treasurer and given the 314's international flags used at the ports-of-call. In turn, Rowe presented the United States' ensign, Pan Am's house flag, Canadian, Newfoundland, Irish and English flags to the *Smithsonian Institution* in Washington, D.C., where they were put on public display behind a glass-enclosed case along with other flight memorabilia.

The long-awaited time for regularly scheduled, heavier-than-air aircraft revenue passenger service over the Atlantic was now set. A one-way fare was $375 and $675 for a round-trip, with one-half more the one-way ticket price (one way) for occupancy of the deluxe suite. When the *Atlantic Clipper* made its press flight the waiting passenger list had risen to 400. By June 28th it had extended to 500.

Will Rogers, America's beloved comedian actor, was booked for the first flight. His reserved seat was passed on to the next in line on the waiting list when he was killed along with famed aviator pilot Wiley Post in a 1935 floatplane crash during a takeoff near Point Barrow, Alaska. The clipper's seat space went to W. J. Eck, assistant to the vice president of the Southern Railway System. Eck's name had been on the priority roster since 1931.

It was a clear, warm day when several coach buses rolled from New York City into Port Washington's limits just before 2:00 P.M. carrying 22-ticketed passengers, photographers, press reporters and luggage. The near cloudless day was not only historical for Pan Am and the world's aviation industry, but more momentous for the residents of Port Washington. A semi-holiday was declared by the town's Chamber of Commerce and the main street was decorated as though there was to be a parade. Thousands of onlookers swarmed about the small terminal when the police-escorted buses came to a stop.

Photographers clicked their cameras and bulbs flashed inside the Pan Am terminal while reporters continued to query the small number of prominent personages about to embark the *Dixie Clipper*. Outside, near the dock and standing in blue and white-colored uniforms, the 85-piece, twice-awarded national champion, Port Washington High School band played to the crowds. Capt. Sullivan and eight of his 11-man crew — two stewards were already aboard the clipper — were asked to pose for a group picture as were the passengers. Eck bragged about being offered $5,000 for his prized ticket.

Port Washington's Rev. William J. Woon gave a brief benediction and blessing for a safe voyage. Chamber of Commerce President John J. Floherty then handed Sullivan three separate scrolls stating cordial salutations for the mayors of Horta, Lisbon and Marseilles. They were signed by Port Washington's Public Relations Committee.

Two bells were rung at 2:30 P.M. that signaled the crew to board. At 2:44 P.M., engines were switched on while waiting passengers were given boutonnieres, corsages and souvenirs consist-

Among passengers to traverse Atlantic for first aeroplane-scheduled flight were Mrs. Whitney (seated third from left) and Betty Trippe to right of Whitney. Donovan is standing third from right, second row. (*Photo Courtesy: Pan American World Airways*)

ing of first flight-monogrammed sterling silver cigarette cases. A single bell then sounded for passengers to enplane after the last of the luggage pieces and 416.8 pounds of mail had been lugged aboard. Among the noted passengers to stroll down the long pier were attorney Col. William Donovan, later appointed by Roosevelt to head the Office of Strategic Services (OSS), early origins of the U.S. Central Intelligence Agency (CIA), and multi-millionaire and short-timed Pan Am president and financier Cornelius ("Sonny") Vanderbilt Whitney and wife, as well as Trippe's spouse Betty Elizabeth Stettinius.

"Write me a letter," a girl yelled to her mother as the latter walked to the waiting clipper.

"I'll be back before the letter,"[80] responded the waving elder.

Gusts of backlashing winds caused by the spinning props forced passengers to hold onto their hats as they stepped from the float, over the gangplank, onto the port sea-wing and through the *Dixie*'s hatchway and down into the lounge where Stewards Bruno Candotti and John Salmini directed them to their assigned staterooms and seats. Clara Adams, New York socialite and noted world air traveler, occupied the tail suite while Betty and the Whitneys sat in a forward compartment. Meanwhile, the band had struck up "Flying Down To Rio," theme song from the 1933 movie musical starring Dolores Del Rio and featuring, for the first time together as a dance team, Fred Astaire and Ginger Rogers. The song was symbolic in that the film extolled the S-40, Pan Am's first clipper-named aircraft. Grand salutes were also shot off by four yacht clubs.

After cast-off, Capt. Sullivan taxied the NC-05 away that soon disappeared from view behind a tree-lined bend. Manhasset Bay was filled with sailing regatta streamed with bunting and flying pendants. Except for distant cheers and the sounds of motor boats, it was almost quiet — the 314's engines nearly stilled by distance. Suddenly a great roar was heard by well-wishers shortly after 3:00 P.M. when the winged hotel appeared over tree tops. Climbing, the *Dixie* was banked and circled over the thousands of gauking spectators below only to vanish from view to the east over the Atlantic.

Once the ship was leveled off at 8,000 feet, Candotti and Salmini walked through the compartments to distribute printed passenger lists, an old ocean liner tradition. At one point Capt. Sullivan came below to have a cigarette in the lounge and to answer questions regarding the flight. He was noted to have been an extremely cordial and "grand person" with a sense of wit and at the same time to maintain an air of superiority. The master boatman was born in Missiouri on March 25, 1893, and learned to fly at the U.S. Naval Air Station in Pensacola, FL. In 1929, while a lieutenant in the Navy reserve, he joined Pan Am and soon became one of the line's ranking pilots. Knowing every flying boat technique in the book, he was sent to Seattle in 1938 to assist Allen with the 314's sailing maneuvers.

With takeoff excitment over, passengers settled back in their divan seats to read, chat or play cards. Those in the lounge experienced a bit of high tension when one of the two main boarding and egress hatches clicked open and banged continuously against the doorway's lining until a steward managed to grab the inward handle on the hatch and secure it shut. No one had become alarmed. Lawyer and passenger Julius Rappaport had brought aboard a bottle of liquor and invited Betty and a few others to the suite for a drink. Stewards provided glasses but ice was unavailable — its weight considered to be an unnecessary extravagance Regularly served cocktails were not offered on clippers until later. Priester's rules had forbade it as based on medical reports. One drink at high altitude is equivalent to two, two to four and so forth. Public pressure and Betty's questioning to Trippe eventually eliminated the ruling.

That evening Sullivan hosted the "captain's dinner" where a four- coursed meal was elegantly served in two shifts. Heavy-stemmed crystal goblets, polished sterling flatware and white Irish linen cloths and napkins adorned the lounge's flower-bedecked

Walking in file to strains of band music, crew board *Dixie Clipper* for first commercial airplane Atlantic revenue flight. By the end of 1939, Atlantic-flying 314s made 100 ocean crossings, carrying 1,800 passengers and some 40 tons of mail. (*Photo Courtesy: Pan American World Airways*)

tables. Passengers and select crew members dined on celery, olives, fruit cocktail *Dixie*, rice consomme, breast of chicken with potatoes and asparagus, strawberry shortcake "Sullivan," and iced tea, coffee and mints. Catering of all food had been provided by the *Lord Baltimore Hotel*, Baltimore, and served on fine, fluted-edged Lenox china rimmed in cobalt and centered with the line's winged-globe seal.

Berths were later assembled throughout the cabins and passengers soon crawled into their private cubby holes. Betty Elizabeth found it difficult to keep warm. Turning up the heat regulator made her curtained-off berth section too warm. Turning the dial down, temperatures became too cool. Regardless of her later comment to Trippe, the control system remained a life-long 314 problem.

Fifteen hours, 55 minutes after takeoff the *Dixie Clipper* was glided down on the rough waters off Horta for refueling. Once ashore, Capt. Sullivan handed out one of the scrolls. Women passengers were given bouquets of hydrangeas and sun hats. Then everyone was taken up the hill in a bus to the *Amor di Patria Club*. One hour and 24 minutes later the *Dixie* was off for Portugal for a six-hour, 44-minute flight. Arriving at 7:14 P.M., Lisbon time, passengers were hurried through customs and taken to the Louis XV-fashioned *Aviz Hotel* in old town where, in the evening, a banquet-type dinner was held. Centering the main table was a 314 model formed out of bougainvillea elegantly perched in a vessel of pooled water. The next morning the clipper departed at 6:40 A.M. for Marseilles following a hotel-served breakfast. After a slight weather delay and a six and one-half-hour flight offering a leisurely lunch at 10,000 feet, the NC-05 reached Marseilles. A total of 42 hours and 10 minutes were logged since leaving New York, 29 hours and 20 minutes of which had been spent in the air. Some passengers, including Eck, returned to the U.S. aboard the *Dixie* as they wanted to be part of the first round-trip aeroplane passengers to be recorded in the annals of aviation history. Betty and the Whitneys went on to Paris, via a foreign airline, to meet with Trippe who was, at the time, holding business meetings with Air France Transatlantique's personnel.

On July 2nd, at 8:20 A.M., Marseilles time, the *Dixie Clipper* began its return voyage by flying first to Lisbon with 13 passengers and only 174.26 pounds of mail. The next morning at 7:55, Lisbon time, NC-05 departed for Horta and then on to Port Washington where it arrived at 12:55 P.M., EST, July 4th, American Independence Day. Total elapsed time for the westbound trip was 52 hours, 22 minutes, of which 34 hours, 46 minutes were spent aloft.

America had won the Atlantic air race for regularly scheduled airplane air mail and passengers service. Betty Elizabeth, Trippe and the Whitneys later returned to the U.S. from Lisbon on the NC-05 with Capt. Sullivan again at the helm. To meet the heavy payload, water was sacrificed for the flight. The insufficient amount put aboard at Lisbon forced the stewards to assist in carrying the bundles of dirty glasses, flatware and china ashore at Horta where they were washed and dried in the station's small customs building.

Pan Am's northern route revenue passenger service was inaugurated by the *Yankee Clipper* on July 8th with Capt. LaPorté at the controls. Along with his 12-man crew were 20 passengers, the majority of whom were noted newspaper chiefs that included James Furay, vice president, *United Press*; Roy W. Howard, partial owner and president, *Scripps-Howard Newspapers*; Mrs. Ogden Reid, part owner and vice president, *New York Herald Tribune*; and John F. Royal, *NBC's* vice president. Pan Am considered the trip to be a mercy flight when, through their combined efforts with the American Express Co., they allowed special passage for an Italian immigrant working for his American citizenship papers to fly to Europe to be with his son reported dying from polio.

Stashed in the NC-03's caged wing bins as it soared away from Port Washington at 9:14 A.M. were 614.15 pounds of mail, much of which was stamped as first covers. The following day the clipper arrived at Southampton at 5:49 P.M., England time, after making stops at Shediac, Botwood and Foynes. The return voyage began at 3:02 P.M., July 12th, with 17 passengers and 410.01 pounds of mail and concluded July 13th at 7:27 P.M. at Port Washington a day before the *Dixie's* heralded arrival.

Pan Am had published and posted their first Atlantic revenue schedules just before the *Dixie's* famous flight. Round-trip crossings along the southern route were offered once a week from Port Washington beginning July 22nd, while the northern route was conducted every two weeks starting on Saturday mornings with returning flights offered the following Thursdays. Weekly sky cruises along the northern course were not initiated until the following month. By late 1940, twice-weekly round-trip flights from the U.S. to Portugal were established, and then three per week along the southern route by late 1941. The time-consuming and difficult struggle to tear through foreign and local political red tape in order to commercially conquer the Atlantic by plane had been resolved.

Last of the first six-contracted 314s was turned over to Pan Am on June 16th at Astoria and ferried to Treasure Island by long-time veteran Capt. Richard J. Nixon. For the next two and one-half weeks Boeing Order No. 1993 was airline-tested in and over the bay area. While in the hangar for general servicing, the "No. 22" title was sprayed out and replaced with the old S-40 name *American Clipper*. Flat and wavy old glory ensigns were also painted on the boat's wings, sponsons and prow sides. Pan Am's New York-based Van Dusen scheduled the NC-06's christening ceremonies to be held in Los Angeles. Dusen notified Col. Young in San Francisco to arrange for all necessary details. By having the 314s christened in as many ports as possible, Dusen believed the effort would create more public attention. There was one problem, however. At the time Pan Am had no docking facilities within the Los Angeles Harbor.

Port of the Trade Winds' Assistant Manager Jack Bonamy flew down to the City of Angels a week before the ceremony to arrange

Bucking propeller gusts, it was all aboard the *Dixie Clipper* as the Whitney's stroll brought up the rear. (*Photo Courtesy: Pan American World Airways*)

for the event. He contacted U.S. Navy authorities for assistance in acquiring a barge and for the construction of a connecting pier with a high-rised christening platform. Coinciding with Bonamy's rushed departure, Young, in turn, contacted Pan Am's Los Angeles District Sales Office officials R. W. Peterson and Bob Stroeike to program for the on-site provisions that included the procurement of bunting, flags and hundreds of chairs. Meanwhile, Young's staff mailed out numerous invitations to honorary guests and speakers. At one point it became so tense that Stroeike was seen holding two phones conversing about the N-06's brief stay at the U.S. Navy's Fleet Air Base, Terminal Island, in San Pedro. While listening on one phone, Stroeike explained through the other how a florist should properly wrap a bottle of champagne so it wouldn't explode and have the glass cut the christener, Mrs. Mark T. McKee, wife of one of Pan Am's board of directors. It became so hectic that Peterson's secretary Helen Niles commented, "...I could have quietly throttled the ancient Greek who first thought up the idea of christening ships!"[81]

The day before the big event, Wednesday, July 5th, Capt. Tilton flew the *American Clipper* to Los Angeles with an 11-man crew. Capt. McGlohn acted as first officer. Aboard as passengers were Col. Young, his wife and two airport traffic staff members who had coordinated the inspection of the clipper by prominent and invited guests during the two-day, one-plane airshow. Because of the lack of an airplane-type fueling station in the area, the NC-06 was sufficiently fueled for its six-planned demonstration flights around the city and for the return trip to San Francisco at the conclusion of the ceremony.

"Golly," one Naval officer said as the flying boat drifted down for its landing on the buoy-marked harbor laid out by the Navy under Bonamy's supervision, "she looks like a whole squadron in formation!"[82]

Last of the Flying Clippers

After docking at the barge following a near three-hour flight down the California coast line, the NC-06 was opened to Navy personnel and to the Los Angeles press. The next day at 11:00 A.M., the clipper was again available for tours until the start of ceremonies beginning at 3:00 P.M.

More than 5,000 people stood and sat in wooden-decked chairs that lined the waterfront. Young, acting as presiding officer, introduced five speakers, one of whom was Los Angeles Mayor Fletcher Bowron, after a luncheon sponsored by the Los Angeles Chamber of Commerce at the *Los Angeles Yacht Club*. At the conclusion of speeches, Mrs. McKee walked down the flag-decorated pier and to the raised and bunted platform. Holding long-stemmed red roses in her left hand and a wrapped bottle of champagne in her right, she christened the NC-06 with a resounding splatter against the *American's* starboard bow. As the champagne trickled down the plane's silver-lacquered nose, a strong breeze blew the ship's flag-strung pendents coding the words *American Clipper*.

Late afternoon hours were reserved for the six demonstration flights accompanied by a squadron of Navy fighters. More than 250 guests were flown over the Los Angeles basin, the first of which carried press and business leaders while McKee and Pan Am's Pacific Division's public relations officer Frances Walton acted as onboard hosts. Civic organizational leaders were aboard the second flight as were Chamber of Commerce board directors. Additional city officials, travel agents, prominent citizens and Hollywood movie celebrities, the latter of whom broadcasted coast-to-coast their immediate reactions of the ceremony and air cruise through an in-flight *CBS* hookup, encompassed the lists for the last four flights. That evening a banquet dinner was sponsored by the airline for travel agents and their spouses at the famed *Biltmore Hotel*.

A large crowd of U.S. Navy and civilian onlookers bid the silver bird farewell the next day, July 8th, as it spun itself a diamond-like sparkle of trailing mist during takeoff and headed north towards San Francisco. What became a problematic but successful showing also ended 314 christenings. Once back at Treasure Island, the NC-06 was beached and serviced for a mid-July transfer to the east coast for Atlantic service. Just prior to her New York flight, former U.S. President Hoover, vacationing in the city of cable cars, was taken aboard and given a private tour.

With regular Atlantic air mail and passenger flights well established, Pan Am turned its attention to the Pacific and its further development of the air route to and from the South Seas at a time when Europe was on the brink of war.

Last of the first six-ordered Model 314s was formally brought forth into public acceptance at Terminal Island, Los Angeles. (*Photo Courtesy: Pan American World Airways*)

14

South Seas Adventure

Harold L. Ickes, U.S. Secretary of the Interior, gave final authorization to Pan Am for setting up their base on Canton Island when he signed the license to do so in March, 1939. Disagreements with Britain over controllership of the coral atoll were resolved earlier in the year through the exchange of notes between the two powers for mutual sovereignty rights. Whoever built a base first, facility maintenance was to be shared by both enterprises. The joint entente allowed for an American and English reciprocal airline service in and out of Canton.

With the way clear to proceed with construction, 5,000 tons of materials were loaded into the chartered freighter *North Haven* at anchor in San Francisco Bay that ranged from lumber and concrete to simple napkins, glasses and bed linen. There were diesel engines to power lighting plants, pumps, radio equipment and refrigeration. Then came an endless array of tools for carpenters, electricians and plumbers. Launches, tractors and sampans followed with tent-housing and food stuffs for the construction crew. Garden seeds for landscaping were also shipped. Heavier equipment, such as tractors, a bulldozer and electrical machinery, were lashed down to the ship's upper deck. A small cabin housed entertainment supplies consisting of library books, cards, games, a motion picture projector, screen and films along with office stationary supplies.

California Clipper's survey crew at Treasure Island before flight to Auckland, surround their chief, Capt. Tilton, third from left, back row. (*Photo Courtesy: Pan American World Airways*)

There were 314,446 separate items, each one marked and keyed to its corresponding blueprinted number. Nearly a year of preparation had gone into the Canton project. Following the survey mission, a set of plans were drawn up and materials ordered. All machinery was double-tested and the equipment scrutinized for compliance. Specialists in tropical sanitation, meteorology, seamanship, construction engineering, medical dietetics, interior decoration, landscape artistry and other professional fields were consulted before the *North Haven* left her pier for the South Seas.

Airport Construction Engineer Frank MacKenzie, chief contractor for the earlier M-130 mid-Pacific bases, was put in charge at Canton. When the *North Haven* steamed away from the State Gold Storage Plant's dock, 47 medically fit Pan Am workers, 10 of whom had previously toiled for the airline along the Pacific island chain, and 42 workmen under the command of U.S. Maritime Capt. Oscar Peterson, were aboard. Six days later, May 6th, the freighter sailed into Pearl Harbor. Twenty-three additional men and more food stuffs — much of it fresh fruit — were added to the lists.

Each of the 42 construction workers signed on were skilled in at least two, three or more building trades. Among the 70-man airline team was a radio operator, his assistant, a chief mechanic and two aids, a meteorologist and a doctor. Chefs, waiters and mess boys were also on the roster.

At 8:00 A.M., May 17th, the single funnel ship dropped anchor far out from the dangerous coral reef and pounding surf at a point near the entrance to Canton's nine-mile-long by five-mile-wide stretch of land. Tides were high and a rare tropical storm with heavy rains pelted the atoll with an intensity never before reported or seen in the immediate area. One large freight barge was lost in the heavy surf as the men fought past the reef and onto shore to observe only low-growing scaevola shrubs and 12 coconut palms. Highest ground was only about nine feet above sea level. Brackish pools of water depressed the land rippled by winds that swept dunes of sand into nature's patterned forms. A crystal blue-green lagoon gave an unobstructed 50-foot view below to the coral and sandy bottom where brightly colored fish darted in and out of the coral. Forgotten and uninhabited for years since the days of massed sails, the only evidence of previous man was a raised and weather-beaten "Radio City" marker and a small permanent lighthouse. The marker commemorated an early 1930's scientific expedition when a 23-second sun eclipse was observed. The lighthouse was a memorial to the first Pan Am expedition. Life was void except for myraid birds, hermit crabs and bands of mice that scurried at the invasion of their territory.

Day after day the *North Haven* inched higher out of the water as her vital cargo was eliminated. The most difficult task was discharging the heavy-duty power plant units that had to be lowered onto ocean-swaying barges. On June 4th the *North Haven* headed north to San Francisco. Within three weeks a temporary radio shack was completed that allowed communication with the outside world. Eventually, power serviced electric lights died away with kerosene lanterns. Five jagged coral heads were blasted apart in the lagoon to set a channel for a sea-runway.

In less than three months, permanent radio DF towers were in place as were a dock, crew stations, warehouses, power plant facilities, airport operations office, a towered radio station, hospital and meteorological station, the latter supervised by E. Brewster Buxton, chief Pacific Division meteorologist. Periodically, the U.S. Coast Guard cutter *Taney* shipped in fresh supplies, mail, newspapers and camera film to the otherwise stranded men.

By mid-September, 1939, the hotel was nearly completed. A second chartered freighter had delivered the 24-room structure in early August. Shipped contents consisted of 80,000 feet of redwood board, 5,000 bags of cement, three freight carloads of composition sheets for roof and walls, paint, floor wax, a ventilation blower and air-conditioning system, doors, 97 primed window sashes, a 14-tubed radio with record attachment, a sound motion picture projector and screen, athletic equipment, two pool tables and other assorted games, bar goods, 48 steel beds (two per guest roorn)) mattresses, dressers, tables, lamps, rugs, desks, mirrors, bedroom and lobby lounge chairs and pictures to hang on the completed walls. A final hotel touch was an eye-catching, 18-inch-circumferenced globe for the hotel's lobby. Miscellaneous items included 10 tons of frozen meats and poultry packed in dry ice and other canned foods to last nine months. Hospital drugs and store sundries were also on the imported list. Perishables, such as milk, vegetables and fruits, were sent aboard the first 314 inspection flight that arrived August 24th.

Clear skies prevailed when Capt. Tilton broke waves with the NC-02 on San Francisco Bay and headed out over the Golden Gate on the afternoon of August 22nd. A mass of press reporters and a large crowd had bid a safe journey to the *California Clipper*. Aboard were 10 additional crewmen and 18 passengers, four of whom were revenue passengers en route to Hawaii or the Orient. The rest were non-revenue, seven of whom were Pan Am employees on routine tours to the Far East or on their way to be stationed in Honolulu or at other mid and South Pacific bases. Official observers for the inspection flight to the South Seas represented the CAA, U.S. Army, Navy, Coast Guard and Pan Am.

Flying south from Honolulu on August 24th, a planned surprise was in store for some of the observers and crew who had not experienced traveling across the equator. When doing so, King Neptune waved his wand from the sea below to appoint Capt. Tilton and former sea kingships aboard to christen the "polliwogs" with fun-filled festivities before alighting at Canton after a 1,913 mile flight. Waddling in the blue lagoon, the clipper remained in port for two days and three nights while crew and observers inspected the base. On Sunday, August 27th, after a slight delay due to unfavorable local conditions, Capt. Tilton thundered the NC-02 across the pear-shaped inlet and raised the clipper's nose skyward after a 30-second, 3,650- foot run and headed towards Noumea. Before landing, the *California* passed the international dateline and August 27th became August 28th.

The clipper base at the broad French port of Noumea was a novelty in that the terminal had once been a 19th century French prison. Still standing were the rugged walls of stone that once held men confined to a life of repentance. One section of the prison was located at the tip of a stone dock. Weather-scarred and roofless, the old edifice was remodled by Pan Am engineers to become the line's administration building and terminal. The ancient dock was repaired and a standard flying boat pier and float were added. A former prison bake house became the storage hall for hundreds of gallons of barreled gasoline to fuel the clippers.

Official 314 dignitaries and crew were well pleased with the base to the point that a detailed examination and a lengthy stay was found unnecessary. Following a cocktail reception and formal dinner held at the governor's residence, the clipper proceeded on to New Zealand early the next morning and arrived late the same afternoon of August 29th (August 30th in Auckland). A reported 50,000 New Zealanders turned out to watch the NC-02 land. Mayor Sir Ernest Davis officiated at the dock when the 314's human cargo sauntered up the long pier. Reporters and photographers from the *New Zealand Herald* surrounded Capt. Tilton, crew and passengers for stories and pictures that filled the pages of the next day's paper. English Capt. J. W. Burgress, a pilot for Tasman Empire Airlines (TEA), a subsidirary of the British Empire air system, was also on hand to greet the arrivals. Burgress' flying boat, the S-23 *Aotearo*,

Placid Noumea waters grace NC-02 on first flight to Auckland. (*Photo Courtesy: Pan American World Airways*)

Chapter Fourteen: South Seas Adventure

Destination Auckland is reached, survey trip, as TEA's S-23 *Aotearoa* sways at anchor. (*Photo Courtesy: Pan American World Airways*)

that had arrived two days before from Sydney after completing a survey flight over BOAC's projected Tasman Sea route from Sydney to Auckland, was moored in the harbor.

Two days later as the *California Clipper* departed for the U.S., German Ju-87 Stukas, Me-11O and He-111 bombers viciously attacked Poland. Two days later World War II was unleashed in Europe. When Capt. Tilton arrived back in Honolulu the war was one day into its lethal destruction. Tilton left the NC-02 at Honolulu to wing another clipper west to Hong Kong. Capt. Cluthe took command of the NC-02 and flew it back to San Francisco carrying with him a New Zealand press letter of friendship to be given to the San Francisco chapter of the American Newspaper Guild.

Fifteen thousand miles were logged when the *California Clipper* glided effortlessly down on San Francisco Bay on the morning of September 6th. She had been in the air 101 hours and 52 minutes during the two-week escapade to wind up the proposed South Pacific route. Nearly a month later, on October 2nd, a CAA hearing in Washington, D.C., was held concerning Pan Am's application for a permanent certificate to operate their Pacific-based 314s to Auckland and back via Canton and Noumea. Immediate operation, however, became snarled in red tape. A number of factors caused a prolonged delay, most of them resulting from the war in Europe. On November 18th Capt. William Cluthe took the NC-02 on a round-trip "proving" run to and from Auckland before Pan Am was temporarily halted in its South Pacific advancements.

Causes for the extensive delay began when Imperial Airways' efforts to maintain a transatlantic air mail service were curtailed on Oct. 3, 1939, by order of the Air Ministry's commandeering of all British aircraft for the prosecution of the war. Three roundtrips were conducted in the summer of 1939 with advanced S-26 G Class fly-

ing boats. When war came, England's commercial planes were desperately needed on the home front to transport VIPs, mail and materials along the Empire routes to Africa, India and the Far East. Imperial's headquarters was moved August 31st from London to Bristol, and the Southampton base switched to Poole Harbor in Dorset. With temporary cancellation of England's attempts at transatlantic air mail flights, tons of posted envelopes and packages began to pile up at Dorset, at the new landplane Whitchurch Airport in Bristol and at other stressed city airports tnroughout Europe. Pressure, therefore, was directly applied to Pan Am, the sole scheduled operator to wing European air mail to the Americas and Canada.

British and French flying boats and European commercial landplanes, crammed with stamped overseas-bound letters, began to fly their canvas-bagged bundles to Lisbon for outgoing clippers. Pan Am became strapped both ways. Clipper mail was up 10 times over expectations to an average of 3,000 pounds per crossing. Weight rose until a load of 13,620 pounds (about half a million letters) was stored per trip. In December, 1940, the *Yankee Clipper* broke all previous records held through the early 1960s when she set out for Lisbon with 13,402 pounds of mail. Then, trying to comply with Europe's and America's heavy mail loads, another complication came to fore shortly after service was inaugurated. Pan Am became irked by British intelligence diligently searching all mail at Bermuda on return trips from Lisbon and Horta. Clippers were nearly always delayed for hours — sometimes a whole day — while postal inspection was made which invalidated flight schedules and interfered with Pan Am's overhaul timing of the 314s.

Because of the British interference with Pan Am's timetables, Trippe opted to bypass Bermuda on return flights beginning March 18, 1940, which in turn meant that the 314s could not carry as many passengers or cargo due to heavy westerly winds between Horta and New York or Baltimore calling for more fuel and lighter loads. What resulted was that more passengers were being bumped for the mail space and weight. Regardless, the flying boats could not keep ahead of the multiplying amounts of outbound European mail wherein rested the crux of the problem in giving up a clipper to aid the South Pacific operation.

In addition, under the "Neutrality Act," where a country at peace could not operate sea or air vessels into ports of a country at war, the U.S. northern air route was cut back to Foynes for a time. Only mail and VIP flights were resumed on Aug. 8, 1940. The Lisbon-to-Marseilles blue ribbon run was also terminated. It was at this point that the escalating conditions of war also began to effect opening the South Pacific service. With pressure on the Atlantic Division's small 314 fleet that consisted of the *American*, *Atlantic*, *Dixie* and *Yankee Clippers* only, Pan Am found it could not loan an eastern-based clipper to the Pacific Division which, in turn again, narrowed the line's expansion plans in the Pacific.

Early long-range route-planning, versus present and future-ordered equipment, had been underestimated by Pan Am at a time when their Pacific Division had just two of the first-ordered 314s. Pacific mail and passenger loads had, to complicate matters more, jumped 39 percent over the third quarter of 1938. To keep pace with traffic demands between San Francisco and Hong Kong, and points between, and to support the two slower M-130s, Pan Am wasn't able to even take a 314 off the main mid-Pacific trunk line for a service to New Zealand. Without more equipment, or a break in the Atlantic's war-forced heavy mail loads, New Zealanders and all concerned had to wait for clipper service.

Adding venom to the mixture was that at the end of 72 hours of flight time — the equivalency of three transoceanic round-trips - 314s were taken out of service for major overhaul. Unlike the constant maintenance given the ships after each flight, an overhaul took two or more weeks of work. Priester's original order for an overhaul after each round-trip soon became history.

Major servicing entailed stripping a clipper's interior. Seats, carpets and bulkhead linings were removed, cleaned and re-flameproofed. The tail was then removed by hoist as were propellers, cowlings and engines. Jigs, like the type used by Boeing, lifted away the unbolted wings and sponsons and the fuselage was raised from her beaching cradle for hull plate-checking and repainting work. All equipment, such as control cables, fuel and electrical wiring, spars and other structural parts, were thoroughly examined and replaced if necessary.

Despite the lack of equipment and the pressure placed on both the Atlantic and Pacific Divisions, it was the U.S. War Department that coerced Pan Am to reopen the New Zealand trunk line in the interest of national security. By mid-1940, conditions in Europe had become a plundered death row of destruction through further Nazi infringements. The blitzkrieg of London had begun on July 14th, and England began to fight for her life in the air over the seas of Dover starting August 10th. France had fallen in June when the Germans overran the "Maginot Line," an underground fortress of battery emplacements built after World War I to thwart future invasions from the north. In the Pacific, Japan too had become a threat. U.S. Secretary of State Cordell Hull and other government leaders demanded that Japan pull out of China and end her aggressive expansion. Standing neutral and stressing its isolation policy, America was becoming threatened on two fronts. If England fell, Germany and Japan, it was feared, would sweep south to join forces and cut off U.S. business ties in the Far East ranked as the fourth largest foreign trade area of the time, as well as severing the trade with the Land Down Under.

Studying the situation carefully with the U.S. Government, Pan Am eventually had no choice but to relinquish a 314 from the already burdened Atlantic Division to form the vital air link with New Zealand. From Auckland, the route was picked up by TEA and Qantas, a cooperative Australian English line, and extended to Batavia where it was linked to Singapore and Manila, via Royal Dutch Airlines (KLM -then called KNILM), that connected to Pan Am's mid-Pacific service. The "great circle route," as it was called, took on military implications in the event of war in the Pacific and the U.S. Government deemed it necessary to close the gap between the U.S. and New Zealand.

At bay in Auckland, NC-06 nears stillness after inaugural air mail flight from U.S. while TEA's S-23s also rest to rear right. (*Photo Courtesy: Pan American World Airways*)

Chapter Fourteen: South Seas Adventure

Pan Am, however, was — at least in the beginning — a bit reluctant to give up one of her eastern-based 314s to begin the regularly scheduled South Pacific service. Pan Am compiled only after relief in the heavy Atlantic mail loads was seen in the near future when England informed the U.S. Government it planned to resume a weekly mail and VIP government passenger service to New York. Aiding the situation was Ireland's neutrality role in the war that gave Pan Am the jurisdiction to reinstate mail service to Foynes on the northern route beginning Aug. 9, 1940. Additional clippers to support both Divisions was also somewhat resolved after Pan Am had activated its option clause in early October, 1939, for more 314s as stated in the original 1936 contract with Boeing. But before negotiating with the aircraft manufacturer, many 314 improvements were mandated, requiring a new contract. By September, 1939, Pan Am had begun to accumulate a list of major and minor improvements for the next six-ordered 314s.

The third 314 flight to New Zealand was programmed for July 12, 1940. The *American Clipper*, having spent just under one year on the Atlantic Division, was flown back across the southern half of the U.S. to San Francisco in early July. With a temporary certificate granted Pan Am by the CAA, the NC-06 was scheduled to inaugurate air mail service to Auckland, via Los Angeles, Honolulu, Canton and Noumea (under Foreign Air Mail (FAM) Contract 19).

Eleven crew members headed by Capt. Tilton attended the 11:00 A.M. ceremonies before departing for the City of Angels. A crowd of thousands watched from the Port of the Trade Winds' esplanade and listened to speeches. In attendance were Mayor Rossi, U.S. Postmaster McCarthy, Col. Young, Great Britain's Consul General Paul Butler, George Creel*, U.S. Government's appointee for the new service, and Trippe who had flown out from New York. The stocky-framed airline chief surprised and shocked the news media when he made the first public announcement of Pan Am's intent to introduce landplane service across both the Pacific and Atlantic - an indication that flying boat operations would soon be curtailed.

"Next spring, a nine-hour service between California and Honolulu will be inaugurated by Pan American,"[83] Trippe stated with assurance. He did not elaborate on what type of aircraft would be used, but it was known that the airline was having talks with Lockheed in Burbank, CA, concerning the pressurized, four-engined tri-landing-geared Excalibur, later known as the L-49 Constellation. Trippe, of course, had spoken a bit too soon, for the L-49 was not rolled out of its Southern California construction plant until January, 1943, and then only for military use until war's end. Trippe wrote a year later following his somewhat stunning announcement:

*Noted World War I journalist appointed by President Woodrow Wilson to open up Washington news to U.S. press houses under the "Committee on Public Information." Correct dissemination of news releases was his goal in establishing a printed war propaganda machine aimed to undermine Germany's morale.

First air passenger service crew to land-down-under from U.S. surround their skipper, Capt. Beer, who officiated at Treasure Island flight-planning ceremonies. (*Photo Courtesy: Pan American World Airways*)

"The aircraft we now are waiting for are by no means offered as 'ideal' transatlantic aircraft. It will be many years before depreciation and not obsolescence will be our concern. We have immediately before us advancing researches in such fields as boundary layer control, exhaust heat utilization and unorthodox power plants, to mention just a few.

"The need for efficiency distinguishes a long-range ocean transport from other civil aircraft. Thus, the latest type short-range landplane — the Douglas DC-3 — can fly 750 miles with 45 minutes fuel reserve, carrying a full load of 21 passengers. For this, a normal assignment, it carries 450 gallons of fuel, weighing 2,700 pounds; this represents only 11 percent of its gross weight or 33 percent of its useful load. By comparison, the Boeing 314 -operating over a 2,400-mile route with four, one-half hours fuel reserve — requires 4,000 gallons (24,000 pounds) of fuel, which constitutes 29 percent of its gross weight and 73 percent of its useful load. If the DC-3's efficiency could be increased one percent, payload would be raised only 27 pounds . If a corresponding one percent increase could be made in the Boeing, however, 240 pounds would be gained, or slightly more than the allowance for one passenger. Such possibilities justify expense and effort for research. Further, their fulfillment is essential to the successful future of transoceanic air transport.

"The advance of aircraft design is in dynamic forward motion. We can, I feel, look forward to 80-pound wing loadings, aspect ratios of 11, useful-to-gross weight ratios of 50 percent. Efficient 3,000 horsepower engines are in prospect. With advances such as these in the offering, who would be bold enough to predict the distant future?"[84]

Last of the Flying Clippers

Stashed aboard the *American Clipper* when she took off at 12:20 P.M. were 28,474 pieces of mail, much of it from stamp collectors for their prized first cover collections. Some of the poundage was destined for Honolulu, Canton and Noumea while other bags were picked up en route at each of the visited ports. The largest amount was bound for Auckland. Fourteen non-paying passengers were also aboard, all either Pan Am and U.S. Government round-trip observers or airline employees en route to the varied ports for stationing.

Reporters, press photographers, radio announcers and a large crowd awaited the clipper when it landed off Los Angeles' Cabrillo Beach following a three-hour flight along the California coast and anchored off the harbor's Berth No. 56 near the new clipper terminal. While the clipper was briefly checked and loaded with an additional 3,478 pieces of mail, the launched-in passengers and crew roamed through the terminal. Small in comparison to Treasure Island's base, the encampment housed a business office, lobby, mail and express room, health and customs section and a radio station equipped with a 400-watt combination radio-telegraph and telephone transmitter that provided a two-way code or verbal communication system between the terminal and clippers en route to and from Hawaii and San Francisco. Flaired with a South Seas decor, the small lobby evoked an atmosphere of high adventure. In the event of heavy fog along the coastline, inbound passengers were assured of a safe landing at an alternate base at Tulare Lake, about 165 miles northwest of San Pedro in the San Joaquin Valley.

After clearance papers were signed allowing the clipper to proceed on to Hawaii, Capt. Tilton lifted the NC-06 away at 4:35 P.M., PST, and cruised 2,570 miles west where early the next morning hula dancers in ti leaf skirts scurried down the dock to bid aloha with masses of flowered leis. A welcoming party served pineapple juice on the line's hotel lanai before heading off for a full day of sightseeing and early evening socials.

A quick service check for NC-06, Los Angeles Harbor, before night hop to Honolulu, inaugural passenger run to Auckland. (*Photo Courtesy: Pan American World Airways*)

Twenty-six thousand letters (five percent) were added to the stacks remaining aboard when the clipper departed July 14th at dawn for the 12-hour, 51-minute flight to Canton. Arriving just before sunset, Capt. Tilton circled the boat over the atoll while he familiarized his crew with the approach and gave the officers a chance to rehearse radio signals. From the air Canton resembled a thin band of white gold set atop an endless blue carpet.

Darkness enveloped the skies fanned by a warm, tropical breeze as passengers and crew were transported ashore by launch. Later, following showers and a brief rest period, a first-arrival dinner was served in the new hotel's dining room. Capt. Tilton, qualified as an American vessel skipper, officiated at the swearing in of base Manager Harold Graves as Canton's postmaster. That night Graves and assistants cancelled and pouched 9,252 letters. The men were up all night to meet the 7:00 A.M. deadline for putting the mail into the clipper's wing holds.

New Caledonia was reached at sunset on July 15th. Thick, black clouds blanketed the skies to hide the golden rays of dusk as the clipper circled over Noumea for radio checks before swooping down through heavy rain for a landing. Whisked to shore by launch, crew and passengers were hastened into cars and taken to the governor's mansion where they sipped glasses of champagne and snacked on hors d'oeuvres while being interviewed by the local press.

Persistent rain and turbulent skies cancelled the next day's departure for New Zealand, thus allowing many to engage in sightseeing. Noumea, before the war, was a small and colorful town. In 1940 it had a total population of 5,000. The main street was filled with barefooted Malanesians with dark, reddish-brown hair capped with white lime used to eradicate parasites that otherwise clung to their scalps. Small shops offered special buys. Imported French perfume was a bargain at $9.80 an ounce compared to the U.S.' $40 price. Another favorite was good French champagne at 65 cents a bottle to the U.S.' $1.25 tag.

Three-thirty in the morning came too quickly. Sleepy-eyed passengers dressed and were taken to the Ile Nou clipper base where the *American Clipper* was waiting with 15,000 more pieces of mail. (A total of 30,408 letters were shipped out of Noumea during the round-trip flight.) The 314 was off at 5:00 A.M. Noumea time.

Drawing up to the dock shortly after 1:00 P.M., New Zealand time, there was no question the NC-06 had arrived at her destination. Tasman Empire Airways' *Aotearoa* and *Awarua* flying boats were moored to port, their raked noses pointing away from shore where thousands of New Zealanders stood cheering and waving. Their faith in an air service to and from America had not faultered.

Zealously welcoming the clipper and its occupants were heads of state and the press. The next day crew and observers held high level business conferences at a harbor board-sponsored luncheon. That evening a New Zealand Government banquet was attended by crew and passengers before the 314 left the next morning with 34,202 Auckland letters and 3,450 pieces of Australian mail for the return trip.

Chapter Fourteen: South Seas Adventure

Heading north, the *American Clipper* landed at Noumea and the next day at Canton where 9,605 more letters were picked up. Capt. Tilton departed Honolulu for Los Angeles on July 23rd. At 4:00 P.M., July 24th, after flying 16,447 statute miles in 102 hours and 10 minutes, the NC-06 was back at Port of the Trade Winds. The flying leviathan had made excellent flying time since the schedule called for 108 hours and 50 minutes of flight time. Despite the rain at Noumea, and a few surveillance passes over Suva Island in Fiji for an alternate base, excellent wind and weather conditions were credited for the good timing. The flight established a record for the carrying of mail when 144,959 pieces were cancelled.

Pan Am refiled an application with the CAA on Monday, July 31, 1940, to reopen, with permanent authority, its 7,952-mile South Pacific route for the transporting of passengers, mail, cargo and express. Fort-nightly service to New Zealand was stated in the requesting form that concluded more than six years of intensive navigational charting and preparation. Taken into consideration were the airline's three successful 1937 S-42 survey flights and the two recent 314 round-trips.

With a new route established west of the original that was abandoned following the 1938 *Samoan Clipper* crash, and with a safe, proven-type aircraft capable of flying long distances, the CAA finally granted Pan Am permission by "certificate of convenience" to conduct the estimated 98-hour round-trip course route in early August. Conditions were that Pan Am would have to fly two additional round trips before regular passenger flights could begin, and that the route be implemented in its entirety and that passengers, cargo, express and mail not be flown just between San Francisco and Los Angeles.

Shortly after the *American Clipper* made headline news at Pacific ports, BOAC's business came to life at the Atlantic Division's MAT. Capt. John Cecil Kelly-Rogers, England's leading commercial ace pilot, brought in the S-26 *Clare* on August 3rd to reattempt resumption of England's interrupted Atlantic air service. Originating at Poole, the S-26 landed on Flushing Bay, via Foynes and Botwood, after an 18-hour and 32-minute flight. British Overseas Airways' new schedule set arrivals for Sundays and departures on Thursdays. The only passenger to step off the *Clare* was later-to-be U.S. secret intelligence director Donovan, Roosevelt's "walking legs." He was returning to the U.S. after flying to Europe aboard a 314 while on a military secret mission for U.S. Secretary of the Navy Frank Knox. Donovan had held private consultations with King George VI, Prime Minister Sir Winston Churchill, England's War Cabinet and Sir William Stephenson, Britain's canny intellegence chief. Together, Donovan and Stephenson formed an international web of conspiracy — a coup di main — full of intrigue and suspense to rout the Nazis from power and dash their claims for world domination.

On August 23rd, the U.S., in an effort to protect herself from unwarranted leakage of government information, and as a further measure of cooperating with Britain, offered restoration of clipper

Steward Roy Donham lifts vegetable steam table's lid in NC-06's galley while preparing fancy dinner for passengers between Los Angeles and Pearl City during initial revenue flight to Auckland and return. Engine No.3 supplied power for galley equipment, and if the source ever failed, so too went the hot meals! Some westbound cruises to Hawaii in strong headwinds took 20 hours, making extra hard work for stewards who had to constantly pamper the clientele. (*Photo Courtesy: Pan American World Airways*)

landings at Bermuda on return trips from Lisbon for the purpose of censoring mail. Stephenson had flown by clipper to New York in April, 1940, and went to Washington, D.C., to talk with Roosevelt regarding the establishment of a cooperative espionage network between J. Edgar Hoover's FBI and England's British Security Corp (BSC). America's further concern for Britain's dire plight against Germany's intent was seen as a joint effort to stopping air shipments of propaganda material being sent to the U.S. from Germany and Italy.

More importantly, Bermuda was to become the center point for searching and confiscating the enemy's mail transmissions of U.S. journals and classified documents microscopically filmed and implanted in the form of dots on envelopes and letters. A few more than 100 English agents arrived at Hamilton in August. Most of them were women. Tight security surrounded the clipper base at Bermuda. Endless excuses for clipper delays were again given passengers and crew while cargo, mail and luggage were secretly probed. The women censors were so well trained that hundreds of envelopes could be opened and resealed without the trace of a tear. Based on tips from Stevenson's organization and the FBI, westbound 314s were often held overnight while up to 200,000 letters were screened and another 15,000 scientifically tested for microscopic dots and messages concealed on the paper. Many innocent looking letters of correspondence were rooted in code with an invisible ink which was developed by Germany's SS intelligence ring headed by Gen. Reinhard Heydrick.

In preparing for a reciprocal espionage system, Donovan was ordered by Roosevelt to fly to England and study BSC's techniques. He left by 314 on July 14th and returned September 15th to present Washington authorities with plans for a U.S. secret service agency that became the OSS starting June 13, 1942. The following case is but one instance in the files of cloak-and-dagger warfare that illustrates how effective the U.S. and British intelligence offices worked together in trying to halt the Axis powers from using clippers as a fast counter-espionage mail communications link:

A Vichy courier left New York on a 314 in November, 1940, with important papers. At that time it was not certain where the French regime of Marshal Henri Petain stood in relation to the Nazis. As such, Vichy messengers were immune to search in peaceful America when U.S. and New York British-based intelligence personnel informed Bermuda that a Vichy agent was carrying vital documents that could possibly reveal Petain's duplicity. At Hamilton the papers were confiscated over strong courier protest. Carefully, the envelopes were opened, contents photographed, resealed and handed back with apologies. Filmed evidence of the assimilated reports were enclosed in red-covered bindings marked "top secret" for Stevenson's and Donovan's united contravalators and revealed ample clues that the Vichy French were siding with the Nazi cause.

Capt. Cluthe skippered the public relations press flight to New Zealand that left San Francisco on Aug. 10, 1940, at 12:10 P.M. by special CAA permission. The *California Clipper* carried 11 crew, 11 reporters representing national news and feature services, six Pan Am construction relief crew headed for Canton, six paying passengers destined for Honolulu, cargo, express and mail. Some of the passengers boarded in Los Angeles before the ship hopped off to Hawaii with more mail and express parcels. One of the passengers who deplaned in Honolulu was the wife of seriously ill Capt. Joel T. Boone, White House physician for three U.S. presidents.

Newspaperman Royal Arch Gunnison, member of the North American Newspaper Alliance, was chosen to periodically write feature articles for the *AP*, *UPI* and *San Francisco Chronicle*. Gunnison and his associates, including *New York Times* Harold Calender and *New York Tribune's* Ansel E. Talbert, continued on around the "great circle route" to Australia, Batavia, Singapore, Hanoi and Hong Kong where they returned to San Francisco a month later by clipper. The trip offered the free press a chance to report on the feelings and aspirations of the people and governments of the countries to which they were flying in relation to the political and socio-economic impact on the U.S. The fear of war with Japan was growing.

Gunnison wrote in his first published story of August 11th:

"On this 'first flight,' several factors will count heavily in observations made. Certainly, never in the world's post World War I history has the South Pacific, inclusive of Australia, Netherlands, Indies, Singapore, Indo-China and Hong Kong, been of such vital political and economic importance.

"In time of peace, as well as in time of military and naval alertness, this route will mean much to the nations bordering the Pacific Ocean. And the fact that it is possible to make the entire circuit in just under one month gives an indication of the speed with which mail and business orders can be whipped around the circuit."[85]

Writing about the 314 Gunnison remarked, "There are only a few of us on this trip and we rattle around like dice in a big cup."[86]

Elaborate entertainment events were held at each port-of-call. The only known incident occurred at Canton when the *Panair* launch went under a clipper's wing and its radio mast poked a small hole in the fabric-lined aileron causing a 24-hour layover until the puncture was patched. Passengers didn't mind the wait — it gave them time to walk around the island, take in some fishing, view booby and bos'n birds at nest and enjoy a swim in the lagoon.

After arriving in New Zealand on August 16th at 2:50 A.M., following 49 hours and 57 minutes in the air since leaving San Francisco, clipper guests were taken up Musick Hill and shown one of the world's finest 1940 aeronautical radio stations named after the late flier. Early the next morning the *California Clipper* returned to the U.S. and the reporters continued on to Sydney aboard a TEA flying boat. Accommodations did not begin to compare with the 314's luxury.

Before regular passenger service was inaugurated, the fifth 314 flight to Auckland was conducted by the *American Clipper* that left Treasure Island on August 24th under the command of Capt. Nixon. Among the non-paying official V.I.P. flight passengers were Los Angeles Mayor Bowron, Alaska Governor Ernest I. Gruening, *Newsweek* Publisher Malcom Muir and "Sonny" Whitney. During each 24-hour period, as on the last circle flight, the party was hosted at cocktail and dinner functions provided by port-of-call city government officials.

When Whitney returned to the U.S. after covering 26,000 miles in 30 days he told San Francisco reporters, "The chief impression from this trip was the very apparent restlessness and the alarm with which all of these people are watching Japan's moves, her increasing attempts at economic penetration with her left hand while she carries a sword in her right. There is no question that it would be a great loss to us if we woke up one morning to find the great resources of Australia, the Dutch Indies and the Philippines diverted elsewhere — also, perhaps, to find that other happily free people like ourselves were free no longer. If these things are not worth making every effort to preserve now, when they still can be preserved, then we may soon have to fight for them with the odds turned very much against us, for every day these aggressive forces are acquiring more territory and greater resources to fight with. The time has come for us to discard the ostrick policy and look at realities, for the question is now raised as to what this force in the Pacific really means to do."[87]

Whitney's remarks unnerved many. Japan was on the war march in China and her imperialistic rising sun was not about to set! Little did anyone know at the time that it would take two nuclear A-bombs to squelch the Oriental aggression.

Shortly after Pan Am's chief financial backer returned to New York, the airline began its regular passenger service to the South Seas. Thousands of curious onlookers, sparked by the well-advertised inaugural flight to New Zealand, once more crowded Port of the Trade Winds' esplanade to view Capt. Beer, his 10-man crew and 15 passengers board the American Clipper. The price tag was expensive — $650 one-way or $1,170 round-trip. A 10 percent discount was offered for a round-trip ticket.

The weather was fair as the NC-06 rode water next to the float, her bow facing out towards the *Oakland Bay Bridge*. Along the dock ground crew rolled carts filled with cargo, mail and luggage towards the warped liner. At 11:30 A.M., September 11th, a bell sounded and Capt. Beer and crew, carrying small duffle bags and black brief cases, strode past the cheering crowd and down the slanted pier to the float and into the rocking flying boat. Two more clangs rang out and passengers followed suit, four of whom had been aboard the *Dixie Clipper*'s inaugural revenue flight to Europe. One of these was Clara Adams, a tall, smartly-dressed woman who had stumped all veteran air travelers. She was anything but a dehort adventurer when it came to air journeys, especially inaugural flights. A New York socialite (lecturer and writer), Adams was a passenger on the first Atlantic crossings of the German-built dirigibles *Hindenburgh* and *Graf Zepplin*, as well as the first S-42 Bermuda flight. She was also one of nine passengers to fly aboard the M-130 *Hawaii Clipper* when Pan Am inaugurated scheduled air passenger service over the Pacific on Oct. 21, 1936. With the restless urge of an Amelia Earhart, Adams couldn't resist the *American Clipper's* voyage to New Zealand.

Coughing white exhaust smoke, the 314's four engines sputtered into motion. Capt. Beer revved each power plant while taxiing far out into the bay before rumbling the ship into a turn and facing into the wind. Clearance for takeoff was radioed to the clipper's crew by the *Panair's* pilot, and a few minutes after 12:00 P.M. the NC-06 charged forward to soar away towards Los Angeles where two non-paying Pan Am passengers disembarked and three more revenue ones were taken on.

That evening at salon tables while en route to Hawaii, passengers were given a souvenir menu. When opened, the left side was reserved for autographs while the right outlined a seven-coursed meal. Between San Francisco and Los Angeles, a buffet luncheon had also been served. Food was plentiful with the dinner meal consisting of celery sticks, stuffed green olives, radishes, assorted nuts,

Maraschino-topped grapefruit, consomme soup, chef salad, grilled filet mignon au beaurre, fresh peas and shoe-string potatoes, ice cream or Duchess cake, sliced cheeses, wafers, assorted fresh fruits, coffee, tea or milk and after dinner mints.

Four days after its departure from the U.S. the NC-06 set down off Auckland. She returned to San Francisco on September 19th. New Zealanders finally had a regular air service to and from the States and the U.S. Government had another pre-war checking system in the Pacific.

Long before any of the six 314 flights to New Zealand were accomplished, Boeing Aircraft Co. was awarded the 1940 "Musick Memorial Trophy" for its advanced state of engineering in 314 design and construction. Six-hundred people, many of them Boeing personnel, attended a black tie "Honors Night" dinner at Seattle's Masonic Temple on the evening of June 21st. Maj. Lester D. Gardner, on behalf of the people and government of New Zealand, presented the tall, shiny trophy, apexed with a metal 314 model, to Boeing's Vice President Minshall. Accepting with pride, Minshall congratulated his company's composite team effort in turning out the first six giant clippers and talked briefly about some fascinating 314 facts in relation to man's technological feats within the 20th century.

"In accepting this trophy," Minshall stated with authority, "I do so not so much in my behalf as in behalf of all those in the Boeing organization who have contributed to building the Boeing Clipper Ships. The design of the clippers required 381,000 manhours of engineering, the equivalent of one engineer working 190 years, and the construction of the ships required 2,500,000 man hours of shop labor, or the equivalent of one man working for 1,200 years."[88]

Regardless of the glory given to the advancement in aircraft design, as seen through the Boeing boats and their magnificent contributions to flight that had just begun to unfold on the air lanes of the world, multiple 314 problems arose unknown to either the news media or to the general public.

Adjacent to a lumber mill and moored S-23 *Aotearoa*, NC-06 is given maintenance prior to its inaugural passenger return cruise to U.S. (*Photo Courtesy: Pan American World Airways*)

15

Resolving the Unexpected

To the dismay of Boeing and Pan Am officials, a series of press-concealed problems with the 314s began in February, 1939, shortly after the delivery flight of NC-02. The majority of the difficulties were minor and easily remedied while others were assessed to be critical structural failures.

Beall was in San Francisco observing Pan Am's operations with the new craft when the first incident occurred on the afternoon of February 2nd. During a cast-off, the NC-02 was accidently crunched against the loading float at Treasure Island prior to an airline test flight. Approximately 30 inches of the aft main step was dented inward one inch. A new chine piece had to be spliced and fitted into place along with the straightening of other lower twisted plates.

The next day Beall was again on hand when a second minor incident pushed in a portion of the NC-02's under plating. Only after ground crew removed the boat from the water did they notice that the clipper's hull rested some three inches away from the front beaching gear pads. Pan Am's beaching crew had improperly fitted the clipper on the dolly. Ten 314 hull stiffeners were badly damaged and had to be straightened and reinforced with additional stringers. Beall blamed the accident on Pan Am's failure to properly school the beaching crew when handling such a huge aircraft as the 314. An irritated Beall wrote in his February 18th report:

"PAA are having some difficulty with their beaching and launching procedures. It is believed that their troubles could be minimized if they weren't so indifferent about it and if they studied the problem a little. Their beaching crew apparently haven't gotten it thru their heads that they are dealing with equipment much larger than they have been used to. In any event, they have improved their beaching techniques a little by adopting some of the suggestions..."[89]

Shortly after Beall filed his report to Boeing, seven minor structural failures within equipment lines and fuel dump chutes were noticed by ground crew. These were easily corrected; but what was more frustrating to both Pan Am and Boeing was the considerable amount of water that had entered the lounge and stateroom C, as well as through four cabin emergency exit panels. Heavy rains since the NC-02's delivery left the lining under the exits and the deck carpeting in the two cabins badly stained. Also the metal trim around many other exits had failed at the corners from excessive vibration. Only after extensive examination was the inward water flow traced to outlet ventilators atop the hull. To help alleviate the problem it was recommended that the ventings be kept closed whenever the

clippers were in port. Regardless of the advice, the Model 314 would never be cured from water entering the cabins, especially into the lounge during wing-dipping in wind-swept harbors.

Such was the case with the NC-03 during her delivery flight to Baltimore. Strong winds and pelting rains made for a difficult landing by Ferguson when he brought the clipper into Astoria. As a result the NC-03 wing-dipped causing water to seep into cabins A, C and the lounge. More serious, however, was the damage sustained by the starboard wing tip when Capt. Gray taxied the liner in towards its moorings. A sudden gale-like gust of wind hit the clipper's port beam to cause the opposite span to dig deep into the Columbia's estuary. Four aileron ribs and three trailing edge wing stringers were twisted, three of which buckled upward aft of the aileron's torque tubing. A second starboard web member, aft of the rear wing spar, also failed as a column.

Still flyable, the NC-03 was taken on to San Francisco where repairs were made by merely straightening out some of the bent sections and replacing those that were broken or cracked. Mildew was also seen along the canvas-lined trailing wing edges. Beall recommended a commercial solvent be used every time a clipper was in for maintenance. Then, when the NC-03 landed at Galveston along its course to Baltimore, Capt. Gray and crew noticed exhaust streaming from No. 2 engine that had discolored the upper portion of the wing behind the power plant's mounting. Similar unwanted

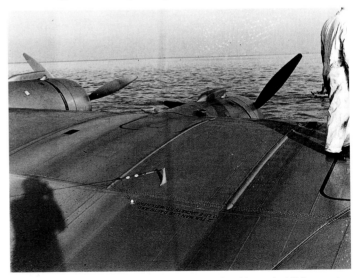

Upper wing oil stains indicated a NC-03 problem after ship reached Galveston during delivery flight to Baltimore. (*Photo Courtesy: Boeing Aircraft Co.*)

suffusions were also later found on the NC-02 when refuse from the galley's dump chute stained the lacquered hull. More streams of deposits were on the port sea-wing and beneath the aft section of the fuselage. Adjustments in exhaust and waste-piping were considered minor and the stains easily corrected by Boeing and Pan Am engineers. More serious concerns involving design and operation of the world's largest commercial airliner soon followed.

The fourth 314 incident occurred just hours atter Gray left Galveston. Coming into Baltimore on what was considered a normal landing, Gray slapped the 314 down hard and the NC-03 porpoised. When taken out of the Patapsco River on her cradle, ground personnel noticed that a section of the 314's mid-hull was twisted and bent upward. Beall caught a plane out of San Francisco to investigate. Whether the NC-03 struck an object upon setting down was not known. Immediate repair work was initiated and completed just before the liner was christened by the First Lady.

In mid-February, Pan Am and Boeing officials underwent a simulated 314 commercial flight to Hawaii in order to completely test the Model 314 and its equipment before placing the flying boats into regular service. The overnight, non-stop mock test flight began in San Francisco under the control of Capt. Cluthe. While flying south to San Diego, Cluthe took the plane out to sea several hundred miles, then north to San Francisco, back down to Los Angeles, again out to sea a great distance and back to Treasure Island. The run covered 1,535 nautical miles and took 13 hours and 43 minutes to complete — similar to a direct flight to Honolulu — with a gross weight set between 78,000 and 79,000 pounds including 2,577 gallons of fuel. Air speed was held between 105 and 112 knots at 10,000 feet.

Throughout the simulated San Francisco-to-Honolulu flight a number of bugs were uncovered by the 12 crew and 12 passengers who were aboard, four of whom were Beall, Priester, Lundquist and John Leslie, chief Pan Am engineer. Three hours into the trip, Cluthe became alarmed when he could only balance the clipper longitudinally by using nearly all the elevator trim tab movements. Down in the lounge Beall and others were enjoying the first in-flight 314 meal. An officer from the flight deck interrupted their meal and told the men that Capt. Cluthe wanted everyone to file immediately forward into stateroom A to help alleviate the uneven attitude.

Cluthe later told Beall he had the plane on auto pilot and was forced to set the trim tab to 20 degrees — a nose-heavy angle — so the ship would balance out with equal pressure on both elevator servo pressure gages. The captain then ordered 600 pounds of spare parts to be moved from the mid-section storage holds to the bow station. Completed, the trim tab was reset to 16 degrees that ensured balance after the auto pilot was disengaged. The problem was later traced to an incorrect loading of the boat prior to take-off.

Freely roaming the cabins, Beall was not surprised by the stewards' complaint that the galley was too small — that they had difficulty in serving the food despite using the port side of stateroom A

"The World's Most Experienced Airline's" *No. 21* was grounded and beached for tail repairs, Treasure Island, while en route to U.S.' east coast for upcoming Atlantic service. (*Photo Courtesy: Boeing Aircraft Co.*)

for additional commissary storage. Beall had long disagreed with Pan Am about the galley's placement but couldn't win the argument. Besides, Leslie told Beall that the airline was considering using cabin A for extra galley and crew spacing. Other irritable malfunctions were noted by Beall during the air cruise. The two stewards were also disgruntled with the garbage chute that blew some of the residue inward to the point where they had to abandon all their in-flight disposals. But Beall stated later that since it was Pan Am's choice of galley placement and sink-drain design that it was, therefore, their problem to correct.

Beall's check list grew with each passing hour. Cabin window shades rattled — the springs inside the rollers were too loose. Other so-called "bird sounds" came from window trims which occasionally slipped from their snap clamps, indicating better clip springs or more snaps. Troublesome items were also found in the glycol (hot water) usage, ventilation and heating systems, port cabin seats, toilets and emergency and control deck hatch trims. On several occasions the glycol's thermal motor slipped into the full cold position and had to be cranked by hand to control. A rod had broken. The poor glycol-functioning caused the water system to nearly scald the stewards' hands in the galley as it had nearly done to others in the men's dressing room.

Further aft, in the ladies' lavatory, the water ran too cold. Beall and others noted that at dinner their food was too cool — the galley's steam table hadn't heated well, yet the water was steaming at the galley sink. In-flight adjustments failed to solve the problems. It was later determined that the galley's steam table and ladies' restroom sink-controlled heaters were starved of glycol that passed only through tubes supplying the galley sink and men's restroom. A work order to cure the ills was put into effect.

Found extremely inadequate was the flight-deck's ventilation system. Insufficient suction in the air outlet ducts was blamed. Due to the lack of proper air circulation, the humidity rose at times to fog the bridge's portholes.

"After about four hours of flight," Beall wrote, "the control cabin (even after cooling off) smelled like the basement of an athletic pavilion."[90] A remodification in vent design remedied the offensive odor.

The heating system on the upper deck was also found to be discouraging. Often times registering more than 80 degrees Fahrenheit, it had to be controlled manually so that a moderate temperature could be maintained. The heat distribution on the passenger deck was also not uniform. Beall put forth a number of recommendations, but the problem was only partially resolved.

Nearly all port-side cabin seats failed when the cushions became inwardly distorted, a sagging caused by lack of bottom support. They became so bad on the flight that it was impossible for two people to occupy them. An aluminum brace beneath the cushions was later installed, a device ordered for all 314s .

Sometime during the night Priester went to the restroom and the toilet clogged. Prior to the flight, an aluminum pin that held the operating valve crank on the toilet lid shaft had shorn and was replaced by a steel pin. Thinking that maybe the pin had failed again, engineers later traced the stoppage to Pan Am's incorrect usage of toilet paper. It was too thick and stuck to the edge of the dump tank preventing the automatic receptacle from turning over. A new hatch handle was also recommended for the bridge's hatch located between the pilots after four persons skinned their knuckles. A harder gage of material for the trimming around cabin emergency exits was also called for.

"...I hope," Beall concluded in his report, "to catch up with all this paper work this weekend, even though PAA are working both Saturday and Sunday."[91]

Like a bad omen, the early troubles only seemed to signal the beginning of a chain of problems that were to plague the 314s.

It was noon, May 25, 1939, when inspectors at the Pacific Division's maintenance shop noticed the horizontal tail structure of the *California Clipper* had buckled on the underside in sections halfway between the center and outer fins. The NC-05, in port and en route to the east coast from Seattle, was in turn examined and similar empennage damage was found. Both ships were temporarily grounded. A telegram was immediately sent to Boeing requesting that they send one of their engineers to San Francisco without delay. The warping was believed caused by strain during accelerations on landings and takeoffs when the clippers porpoised.

Boeing Stress Engineer George C. Martin notified McVittie in Baltimore on May 26th of the condition and enclosed with his cover letter a set of tail blueprints indicating where reinforcements should be made on their Atlantic-based clippers. Martin stated, "The Treasure Island base is at present installing the reinforcements as shown on the enclosed drawings. If you encounter any difficulty to the installations of this reinforcement, please contact the Treasure Island base as I expect to be at this location for several days."[92]

Atlantic Clipper's hull damage was costly and time-consuming to repair following wave-plowed landing off Horta. (*Photo Courtesy: Boeing Aircraft Co.*)

Martin believed high speed landings on choppy waters set up severe vibrations that eventually caused the tails to vertically bend due to the lack of proper structural support when Boeing went through the 314 tail changes. Meanwhile, Pan Am and Boeing engineers began to prepare reports to submit to the CAA while the NC-02 and NC-05 had their aluminum skins removed from their horizontal tail stabilizers that exposed column stiffener failures. Beall, concerned with the Pacific Division's urgent request for an able-minded Boeing spokesperson, sent Martin who left his Seattle office to board a United Airlines DC-3 *Mainliner* for San Francisco. His assignment was to inspect the damage and recommend design alterations.

Within hours after the discovery, the airline sent an emergency radio message to Manila's Cavite Seaplane Clipper Base where the *Honolulu Clipper* was docked and being prepared for flight. Manila's first report back to San Francisco indicated that the NC-01 also had tail wrinkles, and that it would take about a week to finish temporary repair work before the boat could return to the U.S. for major restoration. All 314 clipper tails were fortified four days later.

Exact damage to the NC-02 showed that tail stiffeners on the lower port side had bowed outward and inward while the upper port surface had bent only slightly. The starboard side of the stabilizer was badly buckled on the underside at some stations while other locations were considered only minimally bent. The upper surface showed no signs of distortion. Having less flight time, the NC-05 had similar conditions but less severe on the port underside.

Distortion was hardly noticeable on the NC-05's lower right surface while the upper port and starboard areas showed no visual signs of wrinkling.

A detailed inspection was given the NC-01 upon its return to Treasure Island on June 7th. The temporary repair work done in Manila was rated as good and no further indications of damage had occurred en route home. Distorted stiffeners, not as badly warped as those on the NC-02 and NC-05, were, as done with all 314s, both straightened and reinforced on the upper surfaces to 35 percent strength while 50 percent more support was given to the underside stiffeners. On June 5th, the NC-05 departed San Francisco for its continued ferry flight to Baltimore.

To further test the Model 314's tail stabilizer against warping after repairs, Martin recommended to Pan Am that accelerometers, gauges to record stress vibrations, be temporarily attached to the NC-02's empennage. Boeing had sent a telegram to the Pacific Division on June 1st that gauges and installation instructions were being forwarded the next day. Boeing's Stress Engineer John Ball, called in by Beall in the absence of Martin, had doubts as to the effectiveness of the accelerometers because of their past misleading results under applied loads. He asked that scratch gauges, an improved instrument that yielded precise vibration recordings under load conditions, be installed (four per side) on the stiffeners inside the clipper's stabilizer. It was suggested by Ball that a transpacific flight be made with the gauges under different takeoff and landing conditions at ports-of-call to chart vibrations.

Calculated crew reports were to be forwarded to Seattle for analysis at the end of the round-trip flight.

Pacific Division's Stress Engineer R. W. Beacher notified Boeing on June 2nd that two accelerometers and one vibration gauge recorder were placed on the NC-02 for Pacific "Trips Nos. 229" and "300" as commanded by Capt. R. H. McGlohn. Per Ball's request, eight scratch gauges were also installed upon their priority shipment from Seattle.

Prior to the NC-02's departure on June 6th for a regularly scheduled flight to Hong Kong, Capt. McGlohn tested the clipper on five takeoffs and landings. Martin observed and recorded what he saw from a *Panair* launch. The first two takeoffs and landings on San Francisco Bay were smooth in two-foot waves as was the third takeoff run. But during the third landing a wing started to dip and the tail stabilizer jarred up and down as the ship came in below its mandatory landing speed. She porpoised upon impact. Vibration was noted on the fourth takeoff with little tail movement. The 314

More than half of NC-04's prow had to be replaced at the Baltimore base upon liner's immediate return to U.S. (*Photo Courtesy: Boeing Aircraft Co.*)

again porpoised on landing. The last lift-off was seen as rough with extreme vertical movement of the outer fins, but the landing was smooth. More tests were later given with almost the same results.

Accelerometers and scratch gauges were kept on the NC-02 through September. They recorded vibrations for two round-trip Pacitic crossings and for the August 22nd through September 6th inspection flight to New Zealand. It was during the last trip that the NC-02's stabilizer again failed. Pan Am's Assistant Stress Engineer P. B. Taylor noticed that more stiffeners were deflecting inward and outward. A similar failure began to occur on an Atlantic-based 314.

Once more stiffeners were strengthened on all the 314s by doubling their reinforcements. Arrangements for the latest repairs was carried out through a three-way phone conference between Bill Del Valle, Pan Am's resident Boeing stress engineer, Martin and Taylor. The latest collapses were found at the outboard stations near the fins. Correction of the imperfections called for an extension of the horizontal stiffeners. By September 12th, the 314 tail difficulties had been resolved and the gauges were removed from the NC-02. CAA engineers, studying the perplexing situation from the beginning at Boeing headquarters, gave final approval for all the changes made and once more cleared the ships for commercial service.

In late May, before the empennage problems arose, inspectors found vibration cracks in the NC-05's propeller motor terminal box inside engine No. 2. By the time the tails were being corrected, a cylinder connection in NC-02's No. 4 housing was also found damaged. Martin informed Boeing and Pan Am that a tougher and more durable rubber-type shock mounting had to be installed in all cowlings. Two more problems, though minor in scope, came to fore following a March, 1939, transpacific flight with the *Honolulu Clipper.*

En route across the blue sea, Capt. Beer and his crew were impressed with all but two 314 systems. The navigation table vibrated badly from engine pitch. It was hard for the second officer to draw a straight line, and papers and charts kept sliding about. At Manila, Beer and crew disconnected the table's fittings that secured it to the port bulkhead and deck and installed rubber pads beneath the legs and hung the backside of the table from the overhead with thick strands of elastic. For the remainder of the flight the second officer worked upon a suspended surface free of vibration. Anti-shock mounts were later added to all 314 tables. The galley's garbage chute was also problematic in that it continued to back up by forced inward air that shot refuse across the galley and onto stewards' uniforms. Understanding a purser's totaled frustration, Beer took it on his own to concoct a baffle that created an outward push that temporarily solved the plumbing concern. His idea was later modified into a ramrod that fit tightly into a clipper's sink hole that blocked off incoming air.

One by one the 314 bugs were resolved. The most perplexing and dangerous of all was the continuing porpoising. Priester demanded that Boeing study the problem and come up with a solution. While studies were underway, a near fatal mishap occurred in early May, 1939, while Atlantic Division captains were being checked out on the new 314. Capt. Sullivan bounced four times while trying to bring in his 314 off Baltimore's Logan Field. After the fourth bounce the ship ran out of water and started to come down on land when the skipper, who was more than familiar with handling 314s since the model's Seattle testing period, gained enough full power (air speed) to stay level inches off ground and then slowly climbed away, barely avoiding a flaming smash-up into a freight yard.

Another near serious accident occurred at Horta in late July the same year, again under Sullivan's command. He was returning the *Atlantic Clipper* to Baltimore from Lisbon with a gross load estimated around 72,000 pounds. Aboard were a few leading newspaper publishers and Priester who was on a service inspection tour. Wind velocity and direction, plus a three-foot swell message, was radioed to the clipper before Sullivan made his final, wide-circling descent to settle the craft in fast and flat using a low-angled trim.

Just above surface the clipper smashed into a high swell, shot forward about 175 feet to strike a smaller wave, and quickly decelerated. One flight officer sitting in cabin A, now a crew's quarters, was holding a cup of water he had just poured. Not one drop spilled and no hard jolting was felt by any of the passengers.

Rolling with the high swells, Sullivan taxied the NC-04 to the *Panair V-1* ship to refuel when ground crew noticed wrinkling in the boat's prow. A bad port dent protruded outward just back of the anchor room's Dutch-door near the chine. Passengers were immediately launched to shore. Priester and Sullivan were concerned the press people might see the damage and write blown-up stories that could hinder the line's latest route service.

When the launch was well out of sight, Sullivan, Priester and ground mechanics rushed back aboard and into cabin A where they quickly pulled back the carpeting and opened an inspection hatch. Water was in the hull from a torn plate and had seeped up between crumpled stringers. Maximum deflection was at the forward bulkhead dividing the anchor room and cabin A. Sullivan ordered that the clipper's auxiliary pump be put into operation since no beaching facilities were available at Horta.

A consensus of opinion by those on hand assessed the damage to the striking of the two waves at high speed . There had been nothing wrong with Sullivan's landing — it was Horta's horrid wave action that was thought to be the cause. Stringer clips in the NC-04's hull bottom framework buckled and failed when the ship smashed hard into the first sea roll. The wave-damage theory was plausable, but it did not fully provide for the exact cause of the damage. Some of the men conjectured that the clipper might have struck a heavy floating object that crossed into the sea-runway despite the *Panair's* combing of the area before the landing.

One of the airline's men stationed at Horta told of seeing a considerable amount of whaling deposits recently dumped into the

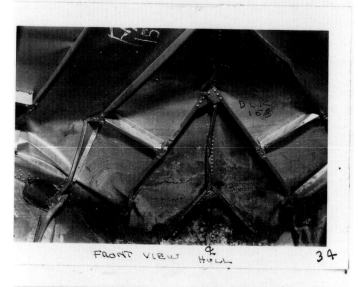

Extensive damage to NC-04's staved-in hull bottom was first noticed by crew soon after the bad Horta set-down. (*Photo Courtesy: Boeing Aircraft Co.*)

314's landing and takeoff area. Large amounts of whale blubber and bone had, in the past, weighed up to 300 pounds. As with an iceberg, only a small portion can be seen above water and was always difficult for clipper crews to spot from the air.

Priester made a long distance phone call ordering another 314 to be sent to Horta with repair equipment. He also requested that his young chief engineer John Borger, who many years later became Pan Am's Chief Atlantic Division Engineer, be aboard. A short time later Capt. Gray, his emergency call crew and Borger sped off in the *American Clipper* and arrived in just under 19 hours of flying time.

According to Borger the temporary repairs given the NC-04 were not extensive. A canvas sling was placed under the damaged hull section to lift the forward end of the clipper out of the water. All of the excess water not eliminated by the auxiliary pump was done away with by more powerful bilge pumps. Then divers went into the sea to rerivet loosened plates while Priester and Borger fastened timbers to the bent stringers beneath the passenger decking. Cement was poured next into the hold to cap the two bilges under cabin A and the anchor room to seal a large gaping hole and to resupport the wood fortifications. In just over a full day's time the work was completed and passengers boarded the *American Clipper* for the continuing journey after being told that the NC-04 was experiencing engine problems.

Before taking the NC-06 aloft, Capt. Gray confirmed with Priester that the accident might also have been caused by porpoising in high seas and that, in general, 314 hulls needed to be strengthened. Priester attentively listened to Gray who he knew to be highly knowledgeable in aeronautical engineering. Gray's 314 hull weakness observation was resupported when the Pacific-stationed NC-01's underside bow frame partially failed following an accumulated amount of flight time. Stringer clips and stringers were found bent and crumpled near the bow's forward keel during a routine inspection shortly after the NC-04's incident. Two months later a stringer clip buckled on the *Yankee Clipper's* keel during what was considered another "normal landing" at Baltimore. Hulls were definitely understrength and Sullivan's unfortunate experience did not go against his otherwise fine record.

The crippled *Atlantic Clipper* lumbered into the air under the fine guidance of Sullivan and crew and came into Baltimore on July 30th with Priester and Borger aboard. At 2:15 P.M. the next day, Boeing Engineer Al F. Kelsey arrived to hold conference and to inspect the NC-04. He was sent by Beall to file a damage report and to recommend aircraft specification changes to thwart any plausible repetition of hull failure. But before Kelsey walked into the hangar and viewed the beached 314, more structural harm had been discovered by Baltimore's ground crew. A center web member near the galley had given way and six additional stringers were found buckled on the port side. A sea-wing was also found to have weakened.

Kelsey calculated that the lower hull stations of all 314s had to be reinforced — or as he stated in the engineering vernacular, "beefed up." In turn, stringers were resupported to frames and longitudinal aluminum tubing along the center bottom lines used for stiffening were also reinforced by angle clips that allowed for higher compression forces. Out of service for some time, the *Atlantic Clipper* resembled a drilled molar before the filling.

"In the list of replacement parts being forwarded," Kelsey wrote in his correspondence to Beall, "there were several skin sheets which will be required but were not listed. After discussing the matter with PAA, they decided they would just as soon make up here what was lacking. I pointed out that they would need some three-eight-inch corrugation, but they were sure they had enough. Apparently there was a miscalculation, for one sheet has just been ordered.

"Believe it has just been decided to make the hydrostabilizer change on NC-04 while it is laid up for bottom repairs. This work will no doubt be started as soon as all the damaged parts have been removed and the men are held up for lack of parts for the bottom repair."[93]

Beall consulted with his engineering staff after Priester demanded that the 314 porpoising be eliminated. Model 314 Stress Project Engineer George Snyder took on further studies to produce a possible solution to the clipper's roll stability when on the water. It was believed that if the clippers had a better righting angle on the surface, that when landing they might stick better into the water and not bounce. By December, 1939, Snyder completed his first report consisting of three possible answers to the problem. The first was to keep sea-wings and install auxiliary wingtip floats; the second to remove sea-wings and add floats with gasoline stored in larger hull tanks; and the third to remove sea-wings and transfer one half of the rule (2,100 gallons) to larger wing-tip floats. Snyder's studies were based on the clipper's present gross weight as related to what was considered a satisfactory roll stability versus wind conditions up to 25 and 30 m.p.h.

Snyder's early theories would have called for drastic changes and more expense loss to Boeing. It was doubted if Pan Am would have accepted wing-tip pontoons. Too many questions would have been raised by the press and the public regarding reasons tor the plane's new look, and floats and their supporting struts were known to cause wind drag and would have reduced the ships' speeds resulting in the consumption of more fuel. The whole concept was a backward approach to the already advanced aeronautical design. It was back to the drawing boards.

Martin sent a handwritten note to Snyder on Jan. 30, 1940:

"Beall wishes us to make a preliminary study of the effect on the center section spars and attaching fittings of increasing the span of the hydrostabilizers by six feet. The idea would be to design the center section spars to be able to take a larger hydrostabilizer at some later date. This study is entirely preliminary. You may obtain the proper work order from Kelsey. When you have selected the plan form you plan to use, we should show it to Beall. The design load on the surface should be boosted by the exact percentage of the increase in total area. Of course the center of loading will also move outboard."[94]

Snyder drafted an enlarged sea-wing with an added area of 7,533 square inches based on a one-inch model scale. Sponson spars were extended six feet on paper and the total weight increase per clipper was estimated to be 350 pounds. The added weight and Snyder's doubt for success made further sea-wing versus float design investigations more complex.

George S. Schairer, an aerodynamacist who joined Boeing's Flight and Aerodynamics Research Branch on June 1, 1939, had learned that aerodynamacist Ernie Stout of Consolidated Aircraft in San Diego used a British-developed model tank technique in solving several of their flying boat porpoising problems. Henceforth, two small 314 models were built by Boeing to test out Snyder's English-related pontoon versus sea-wing theories on Lake Washington. The models were attached to the side of a launch and pulled through the water. Results were invalid due to the lake's choppy surface.

Following the English tank hypothesis, Boeing then shipped their models to Langley Field. Priester ordered Capt. Gray to Virginia to pilot the test rig and to work with Schairer on Snyder's compiled data. Both pontoon and sea-wing alterations were tried, but the results were found to be inadequate.

"The models had wings and could fly when towed," Schairer wrote in 1980 when queried about the porpoising issue. "The models had elevators actuated through remote control by a pilot riding the towing carriage. Takeoffs and landings were made. The models porpoised even worse than the full-scale aircraft. Not much was known then (or now) about the cause of porpoising. There are at least three vastly different types. By cut-and-try process, porpoising solutions could be found."[95]

Schairer next turned his attention to the 314's hull for the key in solving the perplexing misconduct after all of Snyder's proposed changes failed at the NACA testing rig site. Trying different hull modifications with wood adapters, a makeshift form was contoured to a model's keel and fitted to the back of the main step. It worked! The altered model took off and landed perfectly under different testing conditions. A larger 20-inch-long adapter, the only non-alloy material used on the first six 314s (excluding furniture table tops), was tried first on the *Dixie Clipper* that went through extensive testing in June, 1940, under the direction of Priester, McVitty and Borger.

Boeing, absorbing labor and material costs, forwarded Pan Am base engineers information regarding adapter construction and installation plans. Borger stated the additions were added by the airline after the boats came into port for major overhaul. The extensions were made of laminated wood, primed with a water sealer, painted black to match the hull bottoms and bolted into place.

With the aft hull step extended, the 314 porpoising problem became history. Boeing's flying ships performed like the ladies they were originally intended to have been.

While Snyder's reports were being analyzed, and scale models were being built for the testing on Lake Washington, another clipper was badly damaged during a landing at the Azores. Horta had become a dreaded spot on the Atlantic run for Pan Am crews and for those air travelers who frequented Lisbon and beyond.

Sea swells were at their usual smarting high when Capt. Gray brought the NC-05 down on March 21, 1940, with a 72,000-pound gross weight load factor. His normal approach into Horta was parallel to the waves, but the well-respected pilot came in with a cross component, according to Snyder, and the *Dixie Clipper* cracked through two waves that resulted in more structural damage than had been sustained by the NC-04. Not only was the NC-05's underside bow bent and torn, but the leading edges of both wings between the inboard nacelles showed wrinkles that indicated joint failures. To complicate matters, the port sea-wing's upper terminal pins connecting the hydrostabilizer to the hull had shorn while others split to cause inner-spar and metal-webbing distortions and skin wrinkles.

Gray battled the sea to get the 314 to the *Panair V-1* ship. A thorough check of the aircraft was made after passengers were taken to shore. Another 314 soon delivered needed repair equipment and rescued the otherwise stranded passengers and mail.

Helmeted divers went into the water and patched the NC-05's hull. Timbers were placed inside the ship's bilges for stringer and frame support along with two inches of cement to seal the torn holds. The clipper's sea-wing was more of a problem to repair. With the 314's bow raised high enough out of the water on the *Panair's* aft ramp, the sea-wing's shorn taper pins were removed and replaced by pins taken from the rear axle of an old Chevrolet automobile. Gray then precariously lifted the NC-05 away for New York. Upon hearing of the incident, Beall ordered Snyder to the east coast to investigate and detail the damage.

Two typed reports were completed by Snyder, the first of which was sent to Boeing on April 15th. Snyder then sent a memo to Beall:

"I am having Pan American forward all of the taper pins attaching the port sea-wing to the hull to their inspector in Seattle. Some of the pins are apparently slightly understrength."[96]

Overall damage to the NC-05 was extensive but not beyond repair. The port bulkhead frame separating the lounge and galley was twisted when bolts sheared. Upstairs, the vertical door frame between the control cabin and turret compartment was also badly wrinkled and believed caused by wing deflection when the ship spliced through the walls of water. Additional damage was done to the bulkhead dividing the lounge and stateroom C when the upper deck beam and lower port areas buckled. Major skin deflection also marred the port keel area as well as aft of the flight deck windows near the wing connection which indicated that the large load of mail and freight shifted considerably at the time of wave impact.

Wing tip-designed floats to replace hull-attached hydrostabilizers was one of many model studies undertaken by Boeing engineers to solve the 314's porpoising problem. (*Photo Courtesy: Boeing Aircraft Co.*)

Hull bottom damage was most extensive on the port side with a large dent pushing inward along the chine starting from the Dutchdoor to stateroom A. Stringers and extra bearing weight clips buckled and frame supports attached to the keel twisted and failed as well. Channel and gusset connections tying cabin dock-side frame members had warped and rivets near the chine were shorn. Stringer attachement clips below the lounge's deck on the port side were also deformed, their rivets twisted apart due to fuel load tension in the sea-wings. Additional stringers along the entire hull's underside were also bent.

Despite the extensive damage, Snyder wrote:

"...the hull is in pretty good condition. I am surprised at the minimum amount of corrosion in the hull bilges. The hull bottom plates and stringers look very good, especially aft of the front step."[97]

Upper inboard surfaces of the port sea-wing had considerable torsion wrinkles with the worst at the rear rather than at the front leading edge that called for new skin. Removed from the hull by a jig, the hydrostabilizer's front spar was found deformed as were several station stiffeners and rib webs. Large dents appeared on the underside near the bow's tip.

"I expect some difficulty in installing the sea-wing," Snyder continued. "I feel that no difficulty will be experienced in attaching the rear spar and lower front spar pins, but I do expect trouble with the front spar's upper pins. This may be handled by making a special adapter fitting for the upper terminal that will allow for greater misalignment."

Longitudinal stiffeners had to be added to the leading wing edges where torsion wrinkles occurred near the first outboard nacelles and the skin straightened. During his time at the shop, Snyder inspected the *American Clipper* that was in for a general mainte-

nance check. He noticed similar wing wrinkles at the exact locations and recommended that all clippers have their wings resupported.

Snyder wrote a four-page formal report to Division Engineer McVitty on April 17th stating his recommendations for repair. Panels below the water line were to be stiffened where wrinkles appeared and damaged port side frame members given 50 percent more strength than originally calculated at the Boeing plant. Other crushed clips, frames, hull plates and stringers had to be replaced along with the shorn rivets and bolts. Much of the outer skin, especially on the sea-wing, was to be restored with new aluminum sheets. Snyder estimated it would take three to four weeks before the *Dixie Clipper* could again be put back into operation. It took 55 days to complete the repairs! Pan Am's Atlantic schedules, although already cramped, had to be cut back for a time.

Returning to the east coast to follow-up on repair work, Snyder mailed Beall the second four-paged report on April 26th:

"In as much as the airplane was on the beaching gear, and was supported at the rear step and station '1094' (tail), which practically removed all the hull wrinkles except in the region between spars, I did not feel that I could comment on the location of the added stiffeners. As I recall, the appearance of the airplanes before delivery, the skin job was not too good. In conversations with Borger, he stated that a great many of the stiffeners were added simply from the standpoint of looks. Note that the stiffeners were added on both sides, whereas I could not notice any permanent wrinkles on the starboard side ahead of the front spar. My only suggestions regarding the stiffeners were to reduce the size ahead of station '355' (in stateroom B) to section '21- 2369,' and to add the stiffeners between spars and in the chine region between stations '78' (bow) and '198.5' (cabin A).

"I had the opportunity to inspect NC-04 and NC-06 roughly, and noted several instances of similar failures on all airplanes. In conversations with Mr. Gregor, PAA's chief inspector, and Mr. Dean, metal shop foreman, I learned of several other failures common to all airplanes."[99]

Snyder listed 45 weaknesses with recommendations for their solutions. Many of the problems were minor and eventually corrected without much labor or time involved. Some of the difficulties had already been corrected by Pan Am. One inferior reform was given the ventilation system in September, 1939, when passengers had complained about persistent and "disagreeable odors" in the restrooms with scents being carried over into the deluxe and special compartments.

"In general," Snyder surmised, "I thought that the airplanes were in excellent condition, and was agreeably surprised at the condition of NC-05. The damage evident on the airplane was very minimal, considering the high loading to which the sea-wing and hull were subjected."[100]

In late 1940, a more serious Pan Am plight evolved when airline inspectors found a wing spar cord failure on the *American Clipper* between her two port engines. The deficient spar section had to be reinforced. Then, on November 19th of the same year, ground crew at the Treasure Island base discovered a similar port crack on the *Honolulu Clipper's* lower front spar chord that alarmed the CAA. Snyder went to San Francisco to investigate and report on the findings.

"Should any one of these airplanes be lost due to some unknown cause," Snyder stipulated, "the finger of suspicion will point to these cracks, and quite possibly the rest of the airplanes would be grounded until such time as a full investigation could be made."[101]

The NC-01's wing was removed by hoist and all the damaged aluminum sections were visually and photographically inspected. X-rays were taken by the Industrial X-Ray Co. in Oakland which showed more horizontal cracks outboard of the original and not seen by the naked eye. Corrosion of the spar chord tubing was ruled out and the problem traced to heavy wing loading stress. Computations were made to increase the lower chord's strength by adding joint plates capable of withstanding 76,000 pounds and stronger bolts holding up to 77,300 pounds. Tubing was reinforced for a load of 155,600 pounds that called for a strength increase of 48.9 percent over the original stress calculations. Each 314 had its chords strengthened and was thoroughly inspected after every round-trip.

A crumpled *American Clipper*'s wing flap added to early 314 scheduling delays and costs at airline's Atlantic Division in 1939. (*Photo Courtesy: Boeing Aircraft Co.*)

The only other known recorded wing frame problem occurred in late May, 1944. A vertical wing spar support aft of the two port engines of an Atlantic-based 314 was found to have a five-inch crack with multiple microscopic tears. The split member was sawed out for examination and given to Snyder who shipped it back to Boeing's metallurgical lab for examination under a wide field binocular microscope. The main break was traced to metal fatigue while the smaller splits were of intergranular corrosion, a combined point stress fault that gave way to decay over the years. There was no serious repair concern. All defected clipper wing and hull frame parts were replaced during major overhaul.

Beyond the scope of problems directly related to 314 malfunction, there occurred a somewhat absurd incident that added to the expense of 314 maintenance — and to an extended 314 grounding period. In early September, 1939, the *American Clipper* was being pieced back together after a major overhaul inside Baltimore's large base hangar. The liner's starboard wing was being lowered to be reconnected to the inner wing stub when it slipped from the hoist and smashed down onto a working platform. Severe inboard wing flap damage resulted that put the NC-06 out of commission until replacement parts arrived from Seattle. Meanwhile, an investigation showed that Pan Am should have incorporated into their maintenance program the same type of hoisting apparatus used by Boeing when assembling the planes.

Malfunctions in design that became a primary engineering concern during the early stages of 314 service caused some delays and, as stated, a shuffling about of scheduled time tables. Other operational interruptions that occurred during the time to correct 314 faults were attributed to man's error and to the elements of nature.

16

Nature's Havoc and a New Order

Winter months, especially at Horta, played havoc with the seas that resulted in the postponement of many transatlantic crossings. Often 314s would depart Bermuda, fly halfway to the Azores and then have to return to Hamilton when wireless messages informed captains that waves off Horta were too high for landings. Turning about, clippers were flown back to Bermuda for either a long or short layover until Horta's swells had subsided.

"I was once stranded for 10 days in the Azores waiting for the seas to calm down enough for a takeoff to Portugal,"[102] recalled Clare Boothe Luce regarding one of her many travels aboard 314 aircraft.

Predicting the weather over the Atlantic was still in the early stages of development during 314 flight, a far cry from the sophisticated radar and satellite forecasts of today. Only 40 of the 87 scheduled round-trip 314 flights across the Atlantic were completed during the 1939-40 winter months.

On Dec. 23, 1939, the *Atlantic* and *Dixie Clippers* were grounded at Horta for 11 days due to high swells that entrapped 34 passengers, one of whom was Chaim Weizmann, later Israel's first president. The *American* and *Yankee Clippers* were also idled at Bermuda waiting for Horta's seas to calm to continue their eastward trips to Lisbon. Soon word was flashed to Bermuda from Horta that the waves had receeded. Immediately the *Yankee Clipper* departed for the Azores, but shortly after leaving Bermuda waves again picked up at Horta to delay *Atlantic* and *Dixie Clipper* takeoffs.

By the time the *Yankee Clipper*'s captain was informed, he had taken the ship past the halfway mark and had to land at Horta where she too became grounded. Meanwhile, the *American Clipper* was flown back to Port Washington to resume round-trip service between New York, Baltimore and Bermuda. The 34 U.S.-bound passengers stuck in Horta soon became surly. Thirty of them aborted their air passage and boarded an Italian ship to continue their journey while four opted to sit it out until the seas subsided.

Horta fast became a clipper crew's nightmare. On March 5, 1940, Capt. Francis Patrick ("Pat") Nolan, Pan Am landplane-trained in Brownsville, and new to flying boat operations, struck out across the Atlantic for a routine trip to Lisbon. At Horta the 314 was anchored for five days because of the cresting waves. The return flight out of Lisbon was scheduled for March 18th, but again rough seas at Horta delayed takeoff for two more days. Then at Horta the trip was again delayed by high swells until the following day.

An eastbound 314 under Capt. Gray came in as did another westbound clipper following Nolan's arrival. On the morning of March 21st all three 314s taxied out into the choppy ocean for takeoff. Capt. Nolan was first to go. Slashing through the water the clipper bounced three times when a loud snap was heard by the ship's crew. Cutting power and settling back into the sea, the men noticed an askewed control cabin indicating structural failure as well as a cracked aft port window. All three ships returned to port whereupon Nolan's flight engineers found fifty-dollar apiece fairing bolts securing the port sea-wing to the hull had been shorn. Given CAA radio approval, new bolts were machined from an old Model- T's steel drive shaft, and the clipper, with only two persistent passengers aboard, was back in the U.S. on March 27th for major repairs. Nolan's other passengers, mainly refugees, opted to board another Italian surface liner at Horta and were still at sea when Nolan landed the 314 at Port Washington.

Waves around Fayal Island were so high at times that a sense of near terror would grip all aboard. Pan Am Captains Ed Sommers and Tom Flanagan landed their east and west-bound 314s on the opposite side of the island at an inlet called Pym's Bay when wind conditions and lashing swells forced them to use the emergency site. No sooner had they set down when a sudden change in winds placed them, their passengers and ships in great danger. Both crews were told by the base manager to move out. The question was, to where?

Protected only by a breakwater, *Yankee*, *Atlantic* and *Dixie Clippers* sit out a raging sea at Horta's sheltered cove to upset Pan Am's Atlantic-scheduled flight planning, 1939. (*Photo Courtesy: Pan American World Airways*)

Last of the Flying Clippers

Passengers on both ships became tense and apprehensive amid the confusion. Empirical Sommers made a quick decision. Not wanting to tie up two clippers that would again force the airline to revamp its air schedules, and still having aboard the quantity of reserved fuel, Sommers figured he could possibly get off the water and fly on to Lisbon. Extra crew, dismayed passengers and tons of cargo were discharged to lighten the flying boat. Determined to get off, Sommers took the liner out into the raging sea, gave the airliner maximum take-off power and bounced the craft away for Portugal. Once more a 314's hull was dented and stringers bent. A few porthole panes were also cracked as the clipper darted through the tormented, deep-troughed water.

Flanagan made his decision as well. He decided to taxi his 314 30 miles back to Horta on the roller coaster-like surface — a sailing cruise that made the heartiest of his crew feel a sense of unwanted servility for their trade. Two weeks were spent on the island before Capt. Flanagan could get his passengers, crew and cargo away for Bermuda and New York.

Every effort was made by the airline to locate a better refueling port. Capt. Gray had made what was first considered the last desperate attempt by Pan Am to find a more suitable locale in the island chain. He and his crew were ordered to conduct an aerial survey over the other Azore Islands of Pico, San Miguel and Terciera east of Fayal while en route to Lisbon when flying the NC-03 on its early 1939 inspection tour flight to Europe. Gray's efforts proved negative, and the Atlantic-based 314s were doomed to make their winter stops at Horta, a port that could be tricky in the calmest of summer weather.

If the winter months at Horta caused upsetting delays, Pan Am was also perplexed with its eastern U.S. home bases when Jack Frost came to town each year. The winter of 1939-40 along the Atlantic seaboard was recorded as being the worst in years. Ice conditions were so bad at Long Island Sound that the airline was forced to move its operations first to Baltimore, then to Norfolk, VA, and then further south to Charleston, S.C. No sooner had operations been set up in the latter port when below-freezing temperatures forced flights further south to the line's Miami base . Incoming and out-going passengers were transported by train and bus to reach their seaboard destinations. Bowery Bay iced up three times in January, 1942, when the thermometer dipped near the 32-degree mark. Two 314 flights out of LaGuardia had to be diverted to Baltimore.

Winter storms did much havoc to bases, foreign as well as domestic. On Feb. 15, 1942, a hurricane hit Lisbon and swept inland to Spain. The British flying boat *Clyde* was capsized while moored on the Tagus River with the loss of one employee. Pan Am's main float was sunk and 80 percent of the pier destroyed. The stone-faced terminal was also damaged and nine night landing lights and a number of river buoy markers were lost. Thirteen days later a 60-m.p.h. gale struck New York that brought on six-foot-high swells across Bowery Bay that sank the clipper float for the third time and destroyed the pier. Fortunately, 314 service was not curtailed during the two storms. Arriving and departing passengers at Lisbon and New York were taken to and from the clippers by launches until the facilities at both ports were rebuilt.

Another 314 winter drama unfolded at LaGuardia in January, 1944. A near mile-a-minute gale whipped across Bowery Bay that turned the water into a whitecap hell. Five ground crewmen, including Maintenance Inspector Franklin Robinson, serving as night watchmen aboard the war-camouflaged A314 *Capetown Clipper*, were caught by the sudden wind and marooned several hours on the boat some 50 yards from shore. Waterproof bags filled with food were taken to the men in a small putt-putt boat. The 314's sea-wings, coated with ice, were too slick to walk on and the food had to be hoisted through the ship's two-nosed hatchways. Tension built when a relief crew was ordered out after the wind gust somewhat abated. Exchanged hands had to clamber in and out of the rocking plane by grabbing onto a lifeline secured to the plane's mid-section and firmly tied to the putt-putt.

Bermuda, like her Fayal counterpart, could also bring havoc to clipper travel during heavy winter weather. In February, 1942, a 314 en route to Foynes, via Hamilton, Horta and Lisbon, and following a day's delay at Hamilton due to Horta's high seas, developed No. 3 engine trouble some hours after leaving Bermuda. While flying through thick, stormy clouds on a dead-reckoned course, the situation worsened when, after a turn-around to Bermuda, the windmilling prop wore the emergency generator down forcing the captain to shut off other power-operated units to keep up the battery force. During this time the storm engulfed Bermuda and cut off Hamilton's radio station. Beeping in on the island's DF for bearings, and after circling once, the clipper's captain slapped the 314 in for a rough landing and the ship was anchored to a buoy.

Stranded on Bowery Bay in 1944 by strong winds and choppy water were war-camouflaged *Capetown* (left) and *American Clippers*, a sight not uncommon during winter months. (*Photo Courtesy: Pan American World Airways*)

Chapter Sixteen: Nature's Havoc and a New Order

Whipping waters and lashing winds prevented a safe harbor docking. Not even the base's *Panair* launch could approach the badly pitching clipper. Passengers and crew, many of whom were stricken with seasickness, were forced to remain aboard the swaying 314 for the night. Officer, and later captain, George Jorden, then making his first Atlantic crossing after a three-year stint flying the Pacific, found rest on a hard wing's inner catwalk.

Just past daylight the storm came to full force. To the horror of passengers and crew viewing from portholes, a nearby moored PBY amphibian tore loose from its mooring and was wind-swept into the clipper. The PBY's tail struck the 314's No. 4 nacelle, ripping away most of the cowling and brandishing the clipper's underside wing paneling. Just as the crew of the *Panair* launch was able to honker down the wild-going PBY, a second PBY was sent wallowing into the already damaged 314's starboard wing just outward of No. 4 engine to again rake the wing's bottom side. After a week of temporary patch work, the clipper was flown back to New York by Capt. Sullivan for major repairs. En route a bolt of lightning from the defusing storm struck the 314 and burned out its trailing antenna, its transmitter and torched a small hole into a hydrostabilizer.

Whatever adverse atmospheric conditions that confronted 314s flying the Atlantic, the Pacific's weather problems were minimal in comparison. Typhoons and squalls sometimes forced cancellations or detoured the flying ships many miles. A 1941 typhoon caused extensive damage to the Pan Am hotels on Guam and Wake Islands. Passengers and crew aboard an eastbound 314 wondered about their stays during the layovers but were relieved when temporary quarters were made available for them.

About the only main cause of delay during a Pacific crossing was due to a mechanical problem. Worse, was the running aground on a reef at one of the remote islands. Although the buoyed channels were periodically dredged of coral build-up, freakish accidents still occurred. A M-130 ran aground at Wake during low tide, ripping open the hull. Another M-130 accident at Guam wrangled emotions after hitting a reef. The clipper's hull had to be seared closed with 1,000 pounds of cement. Major repairs took up valuable time — a big problem in the maintaining of scheduled service. There weren't enough clippers to fill the gap when one was laid up for a lengthy repair job. The Boeings were no exception.

Capt. Henry Joseph Chase was taking the *Honolulu Clipper* across Guam's Port Apra on the morning of Aug. 16, 1941, when he aborted the takeoff run. Aboard were businessmen, diplomats and foreign correspondents, one of whom was *NBC* reporter Dee Brodin returning to the U.S. from Batavia. Capt. Chase was told by ground personnel that if the clipper was not airborne by a particular spot indicated by an anchored ship in the lagoon, he was to throttle engines, make a 180-degree turn and try for a a second takeoff run. Unable to get off, Chase started to return the NC-01 for the second try when, at low speed, ground the 314 atop a reef. A misplaced buoy took Chase 350 feet off course. Three watertight compart-

ments below the passenger deck flooded and the starboard sea-wing was punctured. It took 14 days to complete all necessary repairs before Chase could fly the clipper out. Passengers were stranded 10 days until another 314 came in to take them on to the U.S.

Pan Am hoped to overcome many problems with its second and improved 314 order. Confirmation of the purchase was publically announced by Whitney and published in the *New York Times* on Oct. 3, 1939. The new 314s had advanced range capabilities. Negotiations for the latest model were firmly established under the jointly signed contract dated Jan. 31, 1940. Called A314s (A standing for improved model), the order listed 188 changes. Some of the alterations were completed on the first six models during overhauls.

The latest modifications were stipulated in the "Request for Specification Change" forms, a list of priority changes formalized by Ball, Snyder and others. All changes were based on additions and deletions of items to improve operational efficiency.

"It is," Boeing stated, "the responsibility of each group leader to maintain familiarity with all items and to be certain that the items pertinent to his portion of the project are recognized as such, irrespective of whether these items are listed under his group or some other group.

"Changes, or deviations from the requirements of the detailed specifications, shall not be made without specific authority of the Chief Engineer's Office in writing. Copies of all approved change requests affecting specification requirements will be distributed to all holders of specifications.

"In case authorized changes require major revision of drawings, it is permissible to change the original order drawing unless it is probable that repair parts for the first series aircraft will be ordered according to the original drawing. In the latter case, a new

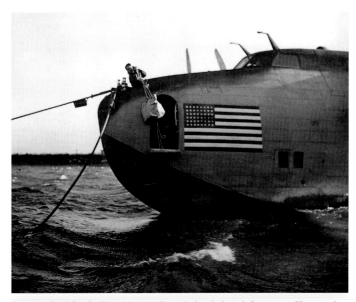

Pouched food for destitute personnel was hoisted aboard *Capetown Clipper* when anchored liner bucked the bad 1944 Bowery Bay wind storm which made New York news. (*Photo Courtesy: Pan American World Airways*)

Coral reefs and mud flats were always a menace to clippers as when ground crew slaved to free NC-01 from a Guam grounding. (*Photo Courtesy: Dee Bredin/Pan American World Airways*)

drawing, or an ozalid, must be used to show the new parts. In some cases the drawing may be such that it can be tabulated, thus eliminating the necessity for a new drawing. Doubtful cases should be taken up with the project engineer.

"If a part used on the first aircraft series is not to be used on the Model A-314, the part on the drawing should not be removed, but should be indicated as '314 only.' Deviations should be clear in this respect in order that the Change Order Unit may correctly bring the drawings up to date."[103]

Minor improvements, from Oct. 25, 1939, to Dec. 12, 1940, began when Pan Am asked Boeing to simplify the heating system control to save weight. The original damper control unit was modified to include the steward-operated automatic dual thermostat that decreased each clipper's weight by nine pounds, but increased the cost to $450 per plane. Navigators and radio operators had voiced discontentment about severe table vibration. Shock mounts were added, a weight increase of four pounds and a $490 price boost per plane. "Gatty" drift indicators were introduced on the 314s on Oct. 20, 1939, a mandated order. They were installed in each wing aft of the rear spar adjacent to the hull, and one was mounted at the rear section of the navigator's table. There were also changes in the manifold pressure control at the engineer's station with a decrease of one pound and a price hike of $335 per clipper. A remote controlled "pelican" hook for ameliorative mooring procedures was ordered and installed on the aft sections of all 314 hulls. Remotely operated by the captain, each hook gave an estimated additional weight of 20 pounds and a $1,525 price tag per ship.

While the majority of the alterations were considered major, some were noted as incidental and ranged from the switching of color schemes for the control room's porthole blinds from a dark green to a lighter shade to doing away with the restrooms' powdered soap dispensers that had a tendency to clog. They were replaced with standard soap dishes, but surprisingly enough raised the price $30 per liner.

The interior, and with only minor alterations, of the A314s were the same as their predecessors. The biggest change was in the positioning of the main forward bulkhead's hatch located between the pilots' seats in the first six 314s built. It was lowered into cabin A after its original location proved precarious for flight men who had to crawl between the pilots' dais, unlatch the door, turn about and step onto a six-rung ladder in order to descend into the anchor room. Since crew members predominately occupied stateroom A for off-duty hours, Pan Am recommended the hatch change in January, 1940. Two steps were centrally assembled against the collision bulkhead leading to the newly designed A314 hatch that reduced the starboard seating to five seats over the original six. Weight was decreased 97 pounds per clipper, yet individually shot the price up $410 (The first six models retained their upper bulkhead hatch). Port seats in cabin A were removed to extend the galley.

Ten more pounds were reduced on each clipper when carpeting was removed from the stair wells, from the step leading to the ironing-board-shaped hatch in the control cabin's aft bulkhead, and from the two bridge's dais platforms. Larger generators and improved electrical circuits were installed on the first six boats and ordered for the A314, as was an improved de-icing system for props, tail and leading wing edges. A revised propeller feathering system was also initiated for the newer aircraft that included a remote control for engine selector valves. All-folding bunks in the crew's quarters and anchor room were removed, saving Pan Am $580 a ship and reducing each plane's weight 84 pounds (Crew used the four starboard berths provided in cabin A).

A higher quality, one-inch-thick bonded-mat fiberglass of flameproof cotton fabric to line interior bulkheads and overheads was ordered from the Owens Corning Fiberglass Corp. The only disadvantage to the latter was the weight increase of 117 more pounds per plane.

Ten-inch-high white headrest covers were placed on all backseat cushions, a solution to cut down Pan Am's cleaning expenses. Dressing room bulkheads for the new ships were bonded with a 40-inch advanced-styled guarding. Other interior revisions included the installment of a better plastic splash panel around each basin; a more powerful converter for the men's electric razors; two additional razor outlets; lucite panels to protect the inside fabric on the main entrance hatches; and a more decorative and silky beige-colored lounge bulkhead lining depicting a global map that symbolized Pan Am's achievement in international flight.

The original sponge rubber used for sealing emergency exit portholes and hatches was found inferior and replaced with an improved substance that reduced metal corrosion caused by salt air and sea spray. Back cushion seams and arm rests on the lounges' low-slung divan chairs had to be reinforced with a more durable leather trim. Even the overhead light bulbs along the promenades were changed to emit a softer glow.

Externally, the A314s were the same as their predecessors except for three minor changes. Eliminated in the A314 model were the two port sets of recessed steps located in the hull between the suite and special compartment and forward near the bow. They were originally designed to assist crew in docking and as an added safety measure to be used to evacuate personnel in the advent of a downing at sea. But in order to use the built-in steps, one needed to tangle with ropes to ascend or descend a 314's port side. Considered by Pan Am as a fluke, the foot holdings were deleted from the A314s. In time, the original six models had their hull steps patched over.

Second and most unnoticeable in external changes was the use of a newer skin rivet for additional watertightness, coupled with lowered labor time when applying or removing outer skin plates during major overhauling.

The third alteration was doing away with all water rudders. Captains found them inadequate when sailing and taxiing the boats. The 314 had proven to be a difficult machine to maneuver on water, and more so when seas and winds were high. When a gust of air hit a 314 broadside, it sometimes became trapped beneath the broad and lengthy wing. Pushing upward, the wind forced the opposite wing down. If the 314's prodigious fuselage had been longer, thus adding more weight and mass against the wind, the wing-dipping problem might not have existed, or, would have, at least, been less of a technical problem.

Dimensional hull improvement was conjectural and the prognostication of a longer boat-shaped hull was not the hypothetical solution to the 314's correct righting angle while on adverse seas. The 314 was the model she was and leading captains, such as Gray, Sullivan, Tilton and others, including Howard M. Cone who made 314 history in 1943, established a set of guidelines to abide by when sailing or taxiing a 314 in strong winds and choppy seas. Capt. Cone wrote a Pan Am pilot manual entitled *How To Sail A Boeing 314*. It was because of Cone's writing that the 314 water rudder was found useless and hence done away with.

By the time the A314 came along, a rule of thumb for 314 sailing and taxiing techniques was firmly established through trial-and-error and much man-wrangling experience. Sailing was applied when working a clipper in a direct downwind and when crossing through air gusts of more than 25 m.p.h. with gross weights set at and above 70,000 pounds, or in winds of 18 or more m.p.h. with a gross weight under 70,000 pounds. The angle of a 314 to the wind was controlled by shutting down three engines. A correct sailing path was then maintained by the amount of power applied from the single-operating outboard engine. Wing flaps could also be lowered to increase aerodynamic drag.

Taxiing a 314 was done with props set in low pitch. If seas were calm, and winds less than 10 m.p.h., any speed under any loading condition could be utilized by the captain. In wave-tossed seas and strong winds, captains often had to send crew hands into the wing tunnels to balance out the ship to prevent wing-dipping and not have to reduce speeds by cutting inboard engines.

Low-speed-taxiing was set at speeds of up to 10 m.p.h. (about 700 rpm, or less, of all four engines). Turns and cross-wind maneuvers were then possible with winds up to 25 m.p.h. with less than 70,000 pounds. Wind velocities over 10 m.p.h. were considered critical to taxiing speeds set between 11 and 19 m.p.h. (about 700 to 1,600 rpm of all four engines). At such speeds, the 314's bow wave started to fall under the sea-wings as the boat began to rise up on its step. Called "off-step-taxiing," such a tactical movement was considered critical in winds over 10 m.p.h. if in a cross-winded state and not headed directly downward or facing directly into the wind.

Reverberating through the water at high speeds above 20 m.p.h. (1,700 rpm of all engines), a 314 could be turned into the wind up to 25 m.p.h. at which point she stiffened laterally on the step. Gross weight for high-speed-taxiing had to be at least 70,000 pounds. Turns could be made only after the first officer told his captain the critical stage was passed — noted when the spray from the ship no longer shot out laterally from under the rear half of the seawings' outer bulbs, but spewed aft under their trailing edges.

"Weathercocking," a state when an abrupt switch of air currents strike the vertical tail stabilizer of an aircraft to knock it into a different heading, was always a deep concern for captains when taxiing a 314. These sudden shifts could be eliminated by keeping the flying boat steadily downwind or upwind by differentially operating the outboard engines. High and low speed techniques were

Found easier to construct upside down, first of the second 314's mid-section takes shape at Boeing's Plant 1. (*Photo Courtesy: Boeing Aircraft Co.*)

used when turning a 314 rather then trying to use the water rudder which, as mentioned, captains found to be only a prodigality and an unnecessary weight factor.

Pan Am's order to eliminate the stern-hinged devices was officially recorded by Boeing on Nov. 22, 1939. Weighing 39 pounds each, and costing $598 apiece, the elimination of the rudder saved the airline $3,588 on the second 314 order. However, such price-saving measures in cutting individual items was offset by newer and more costly A314 structures. Between October, 1939, and December, 1940, there was an approximate $27,544 increase per A314 clipper as compared to an estimated $3,859 decrease. On the average it cost Pan Am some $23,635 more per A314, or $954,635.73 by the time the final price was tabulated.

Boeing'a most noted change order was the airline's call for the installment of improved engines on all 12 boats. Pan Am desired a better payload and range factor in anticipation of an upcoming non-stop route across the South Atlantic between South America and Africa. In October, 1939, Wright Aeronautical Corp. announced the development of their four-geared, 16.9 radial air-cooled Cy-clone 14 engine. Designated as the 579Cl-4ACl, or 709C-14-AC1, a set of four was priced at $4,460 and weighed 7,980 pounds — all at Pan Am's overhead expense. The modified power plants consumed less gas and oil through higher compression pistons, while improved super-chargers and carburetors increased the thrust by 200 h.p.

Requiring 100 less-knock octane fuel over the previous 95 octane-type engine, the biggest advantage in improvement was the 1,600 h.p. offered for heavier load takeoffs that allowed a 314 to leave the water 30 seconds faster than in the past. On long trips the fuel consumption was, at a minimum, .40 pounds per-horsepower per-hour compared with .42 using the 95 octane fuel. The new fuel was lighter and weighed about .15 pounds less per gallon. On a

A hoisted and finished A314 tail awaits structured NC-07's roll-out for placement. *(Photo Courtesy: Boeing Aircraft Co.)*

4,500-gallon load a net weight saving of 675 pounds was determined. With the newer engines, a lighter fuel, say 187 gallons of gas that weighed 1,130 pounds, was consumed in an hour's time. Under the same conditions with 203 gallons of 95 octane fuel that weighed 1,220 pounds, an eight percent improvement was achieved in both fuel weight and the quantity of fuel consumed.

A A314's fuel capacity was enhanced 1,190 gallons when larger gas tanks were devised for all 314s. The two wing tanks carried 600 gallons each while the four sea-wing tanks held 4,248 gallons. Improved statute mile-range was calculated at 5,200 miles that included the reserve fuel. Maximum top speed for the Model A314 was set at 199 m.p.h. over the original 193 m.p.h., while the cruising speed peaked at 184 m.p.h. Gross weight per ship rose from 82,000 pounds to 84,000 pounds.

Wright delivered the first set of four engines directly to Pan Am's New York marine base in late 1940. On Nov. 3, 1940, the *Yankee Clipper* entered LaGuardia's seaplane hangar to become the first of the original 314s altered to A status. The efficaciousness of Wright's accomplished intentions for a better product was summarized many years later by Borger's personal opinion when he remarked, "They were the best piston-driven engines ever built!"[104]

Twenty-five days later the NC-03 was afloat again after several thousand man- hours of modification work, 1,150 of which were spent on three pounds of paperwork. Mechanics had worked around the clock to install the improved engines and bigger props. Each Hamilton H- 6243 blade had a ten-inch radius extension along with an advanced laminar airfoil developed by NACA. The new propellers raised a 314's thrust efficiency 86 percent.

Other work on the NC-03 included the extension of the ship's bottom step, installment of the larger gas tanks and the remodeling of stateroom A. Additional galley storage and counter space was assembled within the forward cabin's port side that did away with the two bulkhead portholes.

Work completed, the NC-03 underwent, as did all other improved 314s, some 100 hours of air-testing covering propeller vibration, engine calibration and fuel consumption studies before being awarded an updated CAB "Approved-Type Certificate." A number of one-to-four- hour crew tests were also conducted before the flying boat was allowed back into regular service.

In early December, 1940, with an additional 1,300-pound payload capacity for a 3,118-mile nonstop flight, the *Yankee Clipper* was flown from New York to Puerto Rico to further test the plane's latest equipment and to inaugurate a nonstop service between the two points after the island's government requested such an air operation. Pan Am was more than willing to oblige since the route was only 1,600 miles compared to the 2,275-mile run via Miami. Twenty-nine men were aboard when the NC-03 departed New York at 23:14 GCT, the first night takeoff made by a clipper out of LaGuardia. Eleven-buoyed lights and two launch-fired parachute flares lit up a large portion of Flushing Bay that guided the NC-03's fast night takeoff across Rickers Island Channel. Capt. Durst was

First two of second 314 lot built had already received final commercial licensing towards end of construction. These liners would not see Pan Am service, however. (*Photo Courtesy: Boeing Aircraft Co.*)

in command along with Capt. LaPorté who acted as Pan Am's chief observer. In addition to the 17 crew, two CAB officials and four Wright Aeronautical inspectors made up the non-paying passenger list. The next 314 to receive an A face-lift was the *Atlantic Clipper*, then the *Dixie Clipper* followed by the *American Clipper*. Modification work on the Pacific-based *Honolulu* and *California Clippers* wasn't completed until after the U.S. entered World War Two.

Boeing's first A314 creaked backwards into the black, glossy surface of the Duwamish Waterway before sunrise on March 17, 1941, under the glare of floodlights. As the sun came up, registered NC 18607 (NC-07) was tied to a barge, towed down the ways and moored in Elliott Bay. En route, the A314 passed under the opened spans of the Spokane Street Bridge during the morning's peak traffic hour. Cars were forced to a halt as drivers and passengers viewed the water show in procession.

It was about forenoon when the NC-07 reached Elliott Bay. The barge was secured to become the temporary base for the new clippers. Atop were fire-fighting equipment, air compressors, two electric generating plants, a gangplank, three gasoline and oil-storage tanks and a conference shack to shelter testing ground crew from the ever-present precipitous weather common to the area.

Testing of the A314 model was not as extensive as those given the first 314s. Since the trial runs were aimed primarily to examine the strengthened hull and engines on more open and rougher water, the Lake Washington base was abandoned. That afternoon trial runs

were begun. The first A314 was unleashed from the barge and made fast to the *Dolly C* tug with a towline. As in past testing, the tug's engine was run in reverse to increase drag while the clipper's power plants were exercised two at a time. It was the tug's job to keep the boat from excessive movement while engines were monitored. However, when full power was unleashed by Allen, the NC-07 went forward and pulled the tug along at 15 m.p.h. By day's end all tests were recorded as being successful.

Two days later, following more technical examinations, the silver-like swan took to the air for an initial two-hour flight. Back at the plant NC-08 was rolled out onto the apron for its wing assemblage, her tail already in place.

While A314 work progressed smoothly within the Boeing shops, so too in grace and speed flew the original six 314s after months of acute problem-solving. Only a select few out of the teeming masses — those who could afford such an air voyage — gracefully winged to far-off romantic lands while millions were left to only imagine what it was like to climb up and away on a 314, the dream ship of the clouds. To have flown by clipper was to have experienced what Pan Am dubbed "A winged Park Avenue penthouse," an adventure in space and luxury mixed with the mistique of war-time intrigue. But in order to keep the grand flying hotels in the air on a regularly scheduled basis, Pan Am's mechanical staff had to devise a new approach in its hangar shop procedures. The initiated ground work program came to be known as "The Quick Turn-Around."

17

"Quick Turn-Around"

On the average, a 314's major overhaul took less than 10 days after every 800 hours of air operation. With only four of the Boeings shuttling across the Atlantic trying to maintain an uninterrupted scheduled service, ground crew engineers and workmen found themselves unprepared for the events such as those that occurred at Horta. Then, to complicate the situation more was the loss of the NC-06 to the Pacific Division in 1940 to assist Pan Am in establishing the U.S.-New Zealand route.

Forced to create a new maintenance plan for keeping air mail and passenger flights at current levels with the small fleet, the airline's Atlantic Division devised the "Quick Turn-Around" — a vital effort to reduce 314 ground maintenance to 48 hours or less. General servicing and major overhauls for the clippers were programmed in two shifts combining men and women to work around the clock. Service at LaGuardia, for example, began with beaching the clippers under the direction of Chief Dockman Stanley Ralph Soulby. Soulby and his team of men were well-trained in seamanship tactics. A former U.S. Navy officer, Soulby once moored dirigibles and, therefore, was well-qualified to handle the large clippers. He joined the Navy in 1908 as an apprentice seaman and promoted to coxswain, boatswain's mate and chief boatswain on gunboats, cruisers and battleships. In 1920, Soulby became a pilot, ex-perienced handling free balloons and dirigibles, and advanced to assistant builder and crew member on the *Shenandoah*, the airship later caught in a squall and torn apart near Marietta, Ohio, on Sept. 3, 1925, that killed 14 men.

After each flight, Soubly found mooring a clipper a constant, on- guard-type duty. First the *Panair VII-A* launch was put into operation to keep surface traffic clear once a 314 set down. When the liner was inside Bowery Bay, a specially designed, square-shaped putt-putt boat was eased under the clipper's tail and attached to a "pull-back" line while bow and tail howzers were connected to shore hooks and maneuvered by means of electrical winches. If the just-landed 314 needed an overhaul or general out-of-the-water servicing, Soulby and his assistant Jim Parker watched for any strong winds that could suddenly whip up to hamper the beaching process. At the same time the men directed the tightening or slackening of lines as they stood on the dock blowing whistles and giving arm signals.

Once a 314 had been secured to the dock and its passengers, crew, cargo and mail unloaded, Soulby ordered his 21-skilled beaching team to begin the "Quick Turn-Around." Three or more white jump-suited inspectors boarded the clipper, and with notebooks in hand carefully examined the ship's interior to determine visually

Beached forward of LaGuardia's Bowery Bay, a ground mechanic gives next "Quick Turn-Around" direction from opened astrodome hatch. (*Photo Courtesy: Pan American World Airways*)

Swung into proper position atop cradle with all lines secured, *Yankee Clipper* is inched forward out of Bowery Bay. (*Photo Courtesy: Pan American World Airways*)

Once atop beaching apron the NC-03 was quickly hosed down to rid excess sea salt residue. (*Photo Courtesy: Pan American World Airways*)

ing ramp. More lines were firmly secured to the clipper and run through a single "sheave block" connected to power winches along a seawall. When operated it pulled the clipper inward towards shore. Soulby guided the 314 every inch of the way by giving more whistles and arm signals.

Once the clipper was aligned bow first with the 100-foot-wide apron, and the launch discharged, 10 men wrangled with sea-wing tackle while power winches made taut a mile of main line. At the apron was the beaching cradle, its protective padding and rollers covered with two pounds of cup grease. Two 50 h.p. Caterpillar tractors and one smaller 25 h.p. McCormick-Deering tractor eased the tonnage down the ramp and into the water. Sea-wing lines were then connected to the cradle which were fed under the sponsons to a tail hook and through a block to men standing on the clipper's hydrostabilizers. Pulling the lines, the men rested the clipper onto the cradle. Once secured, Soulby gave one short blast of his whistle indicating the start of beaching. Inching at three m.p.h., the tractors tugged forward, power winches turned and lines slackened to lessen the load once the 314 and its cradle rode high atop the concrete ramp. The journey from the dock to the beaching apron took an hour while lugging the liner out of the water took only 10 minutes.

Once free of her second element, a steering tongue was attached to both tractor and cradle and the clipper rolled upward to the automatically operated railway. There a check of the cradle's wheel brakes was made to prevent the liner from sliding if a towline broke and where workmen drained off fuel and hosed down the flying boat to prevent sulphation by salt spray and to dissipate any gas spills. Completed, cradle and crane were moved along the the 200-yard rail causeway to the hangar. The use of three tractors and more men saved five hours over older beaching procedures.

Inside the hangar a maze of three-storied work platforms made of cast aluminum and steel were wheeled up against the clipper's

what had to be done. Instrument experts removed loose navigational octants, sextants, parallel rules, stop watches, binoculars and other items and took them to the instrument shop where all were carefully scrutinized for defects and then polished.

Quilted floor mats lined the decks. Clipper furniture was covered with cloth to reduce overhaul time from 144 to 48 hours and to keep workmen from further soiling the multi-cabined airliner. While the latter was underway, the clipper was being towed 300 yards from the dock to the maintenance hangar's angled beaching ramp.

Towing began after tackle lines were attached to the boat's seawings. Float lines were then cast off and a bow howser was tied to the launch. A series of buoys marked the path leading to the beach-

Wash completed, manned Caterpillar tractors tow NC-03's tonnage towards maintenance hangar. (*Photo Courtesy: Pan American World Airways*)

Inside cavernous hangar "Quick Turn-Around" process was fast and complete. (*Photo Courtesy: Pan American World Airways*)

fuselage. Some of the platforms had 24 steps with slide-down poles for quick escape in the event of fire. Inspection ladders, engine and wing nacelle jigs, oil dollies, sheet metal gear and additional servicing stands for overhauling wing and tail surfaces made up fencing that nearly obliterated the 314 from view.

One-hundred and fifty men from carpentry, engine, propeller, metal, paint and other shops began the 1,500 different tasks required for a clipper overhaul. Maintenance orders were correlated by inspectors the moment a 314 landed. Shortly after its arrival, the 314's captain and two flight engineers gave the plane's log and reports of difficulties incurred to Ed ("Mac") McVitty, chief shop engineer under Priester. McVitty and his eight assistants met at a long conference table in his office on the third floor of the operations building next to the *MAT* to hash over flight records with the two just-landed flight engineers. Prompt decisions were made ranging from engine change to galley door hinges that may have worked loose during the flight. Once a clipper engineer complained that a new bracket for a microphone was poorly designed. In a matter of hours a satisfactory replacement was worked out.

All work forms were sent to Shop Superintendent Tommy W. Reid, mimeographed for conference scrutinization and then finalized in the hangar. Usually the last work order was dispatched six hours after a 314 had landed. Work inside the hangar was coordinated by Walter C. ("Pop") Smith, engine service foreman and assistant shop superintendent, and completed under Smith's 23 department foremen. Of the 200 men under McVitty in the hangar, about 50 were supervisory employees, guards and porters. The rest did the actual work on the clippers.

Plane service, the largest overhaul department, was headed by Al Thomas. The second biggest section was the metal shop under W. O. Frank with H. Klein's cleaning, Smith's engine service and Joe Yowell's instrument divisions running third, fourth and fifth. Some outsiders were surprised to learn that the cleaning department ran third. Nearly one-third of an acre of a 314's external surface had to be scrubbed, 71 windows washed and 9,000 square feet of upholstery and carpet had to be cleaned and sometimes replaced. Ground crew wore "dresser shoes," light-soled boots, which kept the workers from tracking dirt and making scratches on the 314s' painted surfaces.

During major overhauls many clipper extremities were replaced due to wear. These included elevators, rudders, engines, propellers and sea-wings (The latter cost some $20,000 apiece to replace). Internal parts, such as gas tanks, oil tanks and water tanks, also had to be periodically changed. New upholstery and bulkhead panelling was kept in the spare quarters. The most common item for change were the engines. If a clipper was desperately needed for a particular run -and there were many — a new power plant was ordered rather than spend hours on one that needed cylinder overhaul. It took about two hours to get a used engine out and down, another 30 minutes hoisting up a new one and two and one- half hours putting it into place. Progress had done wonders over the years. It takes only two and one-half hours to change a B-747's jet engine:

The last procedure in the "Quick Turn-Around" was weighing in a 314 to its empty requirements of under 52,000 pounds (Without interior furnishings a 314 weighed 49,641 pounds). If not properly cleaned before she was placed on the scales, a 314's payload for the next flight could have been jeopardized and that in turn could have caused the elimination of a passenger or two. Before weigh-in, the Boeings were wiped down to remove any accumulated moisture and allowed to air out with hatchways and emergency exits left open. All new equipment, down to a single screw or bolt, was pre-weighed. Anything deleted or added was recorded for weight difference, reported to McVitty and checked by an inspector. Nothing was overlooked! When a 314 was placed onto the scales, two CAA inspectors were usually on hand to scorn so much as a change in a few hundredths of an ounce.

Prior to any weigh-in, a 314 was placed in an angle exactly parallel to the hangar's floor — or in an engineer's vernacular, "zero degree longitudinal trim angle and zero degree heel angle." Jacks were positioned beneath the ship's hull and dolly. Four 85-pound scales, each weighing 20,000 pounds, were placed atop the beaching gear. Jacking equipment was calibrated and subtracted from clipper weight. The 314 was then hoisted clear of her cradle and supported on four scale points. Inspectors walked around the raised boat to ensure that it was not sustained by any other means. The scales were read three times and recorded by Pan Am's Shop Weight and Balance Engineer Don Q. Lampland who was under McVitty's supervision.

Forty-eight hours later, almost to the minute, Soulby and his beaching crew reattached lines to the clipper and dolly. Tractors then backed the clipper out of its shelter to the ramp where it was refueled and eased tail first down the apron into Bowery Bay. While the clipper was in the hangar, Soulby and his men were busy checking dock facilities, buoys, winches, towing lines and tractors.

Chapter Seventeen: "Quick Turn-Around"

Following the "Quick Turn-Around" maintenance work, two monitored flights lasting two and one-half hours were put into effect. The crew selected to fly the checked-out clipper for its next Atlantic crossing were given this task as well as to ground equipment specialists who acted as observers to make sure all flight equipment functioned normally. To save time, clippers were often times towed by launch to a point further out in the bay rather than all the way back to the dock. A manifest of all repair work to be double-checked was given to the captain and flight engineers.

Wearing casual civilian clothing, the chosen crew examined the manifest and began their 314 check-out flights consisting of two phases; testing and recording the calibrations regarding all maintenance work done to the clipper and the practicing of normal pre-departure operations. Requirements called for the 314 to be flown between three and four hours to allow for sufficient time for all checks. The exact timing of a simulated departure under 10 minutes from bay point (dock) was cleared by McVitty.

Engine warm-up was registered for the brief first flight with the clipper loaded to only about 2,640 gallons of fuel which was well under the maximum tank capacity. After lift-off, engineers reviewed the equipment. Some 417 notations were usually made from instrument readings with corrections, if any, written into the duplicate log for ground crew. Calculations were taken from fuel quantity gauges on each engine, cylinder heads, oil points, prestone and fuel temperatures and pressures. Any requests for immediate repairs were noted as well.

Gas and oil transfer valves and pumps were tested for about an hour as were air scoops, heating and electrical circuits. One or two engines were stopped, props feathered and then restarted, an action called "breaking an engine." Any control room equipment found faulty usually caused a 24-hour delay until repairs were made or equipment replaced.

At the conclusion of the 314's maintenance check-out run, the captain returned the ship to LaGuardia, discharged observers and

General servicing, like brandishing props with a protective oil rubdown, insured near 100 per cent 314 safety record. (*Photo Courtesy: Pan American World Airways*)

was off again for a standard pre-departure test flight, at which time the regular crew assigned to the up-coming Atlantic crossing were aboard. In the air stewards checked the lower deck to be sure galley equipment, toilets and sink water functioned. At the helm the captain and first officer flew with blackout curtains ("the hood")

'Round-the-clock hangar maintenance helped keep 314 timetables in check. (*Photo Courtesy: Pan American World Airways*)

snapped to the bridge's windows while they practiced instrument and radio approaches with control tower and launch communicators.

Back at the dock the ship was then loaded with its stock of mail, express, cargo and passenger provisions. LaGuardia Field's "Quick Turn-Around" process was further enhanced starting July 7, 1942, when the effects of war forced the maintenance shops to step up their 314 repair work. Demands of ever-faster transoceanic service made shop foremen request a repair crew to work on clippers moored on Bowery Bay or at the dock for general maintenance. McVitty organized a unit of 22 experts known as the "Line Crew" to change spark plugs, maintain general inspection, cleaning interiors, refueling oil and gas tanks and perform other duties normally done in the hangar — the main purpose for which was to do away with hangar congestion and relieve ground crews for other major work assignments.

Ex-Marine Air Corps Mechanic James E. Hanretta, who worked in hangar plane service and engine shops, was assigned to head the "Line Crew." He and his men toiled in two shifts from 4:00 P.M. to midnight and midnight to 8:00 A.M. When a clipper was not in port, the men prepared for foreign port work or in becoming flight engineers. However, the new team effort did not substitute for the 200-hour major overhaul program, but simply provided an alternate work force not required to do the heavy maintenance that involved the use of cranes and hoists. As soon as a 314 came in that

didn't require an overhaul, the "Line Crew" swarmed over the ship even before passengers and crew disembarked. And when captains made pre-departure tests, a line crewman was assigned to specifically report on engine adjustments, thus saving more valuable time.

Many maintenance records were established following the introduction of the "Quick Turn-Around." In May, 1943, for example, a 314 was taken from dock to hangar in 39 minutes. The following month another record was set when 18 ground crew, trained at LaGuardia's clipper base, demonstrated perfect timing in changing a 314A engine at Trinidad's Cocorite Airport. The *Anzac Clipper* came into port en route to New York with a faulty engine. There was no hoisting or beaching equipment available. Cocorite's Chief Mechanic Otto Johnson called for a floating crane.

One-hundred separate fuel and control engine units were unbolted during the liner's night layover as flood lights illuminated the 314's wing and nacelle. The crane lowered the one-ton Cyclone power plant onto a barge and hoisted a new one into place. Work was completed in 19 hours and 45 minutes. The clipper was then given a two-hour and 25-minute mandatory flight check before it was allowed to take its passengers on to New York. A proud Corcorite ground crew had beat a Bermuda crew's engine change record by nine hours.

With maintenance procedures improved, Pan Am's next 314 effort was to avoid Horta delays and to find a new port-of-call for re-routing westward-going flights during winter months.

One out one in. Fully serviced *South Atlantic Clipper* is ready to depart LaGuardia while forward-viewed and beached 314 begins a "Quick Turn-Around." (*Photo Courtesy: Pan American World Airways*)

18

Bolama

Analyzing maps and studying his huge office-placed globe, Trippe focused in on the western coast of North Africa where he figured an alternate fuel stop could be made besides the one at the winter-blasted Horta station. Hoping that landing rights could easily be granted by Portugal as they had for the first trans-Atlantic service, Trippe zeroed in on Portuguese Guinea. Richard Long, the line's foreign negotiator, was ordered to Lisbon in mid-1940 to open talks whereupon permission was soon granted for 314s to land at Bolama, capital of Portuguese Guinea.

Boeing's fat-bellied-looking cetaceans could easily fly south from Lisbon to the African port, refuel, hop across the pond to either Natal or fly direct from Bolama to the Caribbean and then north to the U.S . Pan Am's latter way meant 4,085 miles more per westbound crossing (more via Natal and Bermuda), and would take three days to do so. But Trippe and his staff concluded that the added distance, and time, was worth the effort to maintain an ongoing winter operation free of major delays. Besides, the second six-ordered 314As would have improved engine power and higher load capabilities. Also, the first six models were being upgraded to A status that would allow any of the 314s to make the extra long journey home.

On Oct. 29, 1940, Pan Am filed an application with the CAB to detour 314s south between Europe and the U.S., via Africa, during winter months. Westbound clippers would fly 1,817 miles due south of Lisbon to land off the Dark Continent. From Bolama the Boeings were to take advantage of the westerly tail winds first navigated by seamen of old and swiftly cruise non-stop to Port of Spain, then north to San Juan and on to New York. Expectations were that more mail and passengers could be accommodated out of Lisbon during winter when stronger northern westbound headwinds disallowed for a fully loaded 314 to fly the range between Portugal and Bermuda. Winter stops at the Azores could be executed only when favorable conditions existed.

Engineers, meteorologists and technicians had been sent to Bolama in November, 1940, to establish the Bolama base. Extensive surveys were conducted by Pan Am for clipper scheduling, via Bolama, on a twice-weekly service beginning December 1st and terminating on April 30th of each following year. President Roosevelt approved the route in January, 1941, but the CAB held back its final approbation until after the first inspection flight was completed. When Chief Meteorologist Herman Campbell sailed

back to New York on Jan. 30, 1941, following his Bolama studies, he informed Pan Am of what the airline could expect regarding the African port's typography and climatic conditions.

The township of Bolama is situated on the 10-mile-wide Island of Bolama and divided by the African mainland by the mile-wide Jeba River. Alligators sun themselves on beaches, and 20 miles outside the town panthers, leopards, antelope and hippopotami roam freely. Monkeys could be bought for a dime, but strict health standards prohibited any exporting of the creatures. Piranha and stingrays swam the Jeba. Clipper passengers found that eggs, oranges

Award-winning photo entitled "Bolama Departure" captured *Dixie Clipper* gaining altitude from Jeba River. (*Photo Courtesy: E. Blackburn/Pan American World Airways*)

and water were extremely scarce. Bottled water, costing 16 cents, was shipped in from Horta. Local well water had to be boiled for cooking and washing use. The only available cocktails in town were sold and served from a shanty called the *Kiosk*. One sat outside beneath trees in a wicker chair and either had soda, whisky or beer. Ice was unavailable until Pan Am shipped in a refrigerator from New York.

Not far from Bolama, with a then majority native population of 4,000 of which 400 lived in town, was one of the biggest Firestone rubber plantations. Every Saturday night the local tribes held custom dances, beat drums, clapped hands and shook stone-filled gourds strapped to their knees. Eventually the gourds were replaced by a thousand empty cigarette tins that had been shipped in earlier to the Pam Am workmen. Only 300 caucasians lived in the area.

One bicycle and four automobiles, owned by the government, made up the town's two modes of transportation. While construction of the small and somewhat crude clipper compound was being built, Pan Am workmen lived in a seven-room house leased from the Portuguese Government. It was the only place, outside of the governor's residence, that had running water pumped in for washing that came from a 300-gallon tank poised atop the roof. Seven-foot-high mounds made by inch-long black and red ants were seen everywhere. Bolama was a touch of Africa at its most primitive state. Within these environmental surroundings, the stationed airline personnel awaited the first 314 flight.

Shortly after the final details were completed at Bolama, a Boeing was scheduled for departure from New York. Bitter cold weather encompassed New York on the morning of Feb. 1, 1941, when the *Dixie Clipper* swooped off Bowery Bay. Aboard the inspection flight were Harold M. Bixby, manager of Pan Am's subsidiary airline in China (CNAC) and general Far Eastern negotiator, Trippe, three CAB route-proving inspectors and a small band of passengers bound for Bermuda. Capt. Lodeesen commanded the 11-man crew to Lisbon while Capt. LaPorté, acting as supernumerary fourth officer, was posted as leading observer. LaPorté was

Clipper crew and ground staff had to maintain high dress standards despite oppressive Bolama heat, humidity and primitive-thatched quarters. (*Photo Courtesy: Pierre Verger, P.P.C./Pan American World Airways*)

placed in the lowest of ranks so as to be free from advanced flight duty so that he could make various observations along the new route.

Stashed in the *Dixie*'s holds were bags of mail destined for Europe that included a load of collectable first-flight covers catchet-stamped with a specially designed U.S.-Bolama stamp. There had been no time for the U.S. Post Office to prepare a formal dispatch announcement from the time Roosevelt authorized the route to the date of departure, so only a short supply of nine series was issued for philatelists through Pan Am's New York offices.

When the clipper arrived in Lisbon the next day without any revenue passengers, Trippe and Bixby inspected both the seaplane and then new landplane airports, the latter being built at nearby Portela. Trippe was most interested in the new port as he planned to inaugurate landplane service to Europe the following year — a plan postponed when the U.S. entered the war 10 months later.

Three days later the NC-05 departed Lisbon at night for the return trip to New York, via Bolama. The first passengers to fly the "crocodile route," named after the ferocious beasts that were often found crawling up onto 314 sea-wings to sun themselves while the clippers were at bay on the Jeba, were U.S. Government official Wendell Willkie, John Cowles, president of the *Minneapolis Star Journal*, and Landon K. Thorne, retired New York banker. Willkie was returning to the U.S. to testify before a Congressional Committee following his U.S. lend-lease tour of Europe by which he had earlier arrived on the NC-03 under Capt. Gray. If it had not been for the new westbound 314 stop at Bolama, Willkie's report to Congress would have been delayed up to 10 or more days due to the forecasted high winds and seas at Horta.

Capt. Gray was at the NC-05's helm as the ship winged high out over the blackened Atlantic as Europe's only city to blare with lights faded from view. Gray had replaced Lodeesen at Lisbon leaving the latter to fly the *Yankee Clipper* back to New York with a lightened load to face between 50 and 60 m.p.h. headwinds past Horta to Bermuda. Gray nosed the *Dixie Clipper* up to 8,000 feet, leveled off and flew the liner south over the trail-blazing route at 150 m.p.h. Most of those on the stripped passenger deck retired early. Berths were limited because of the small weight allowance required by the CAB during a route-proving flight. Trippe and Bixby improvised their own bedding. Chief Steward William Thaler accommodated Bixby with pillows and a set of seat cushions for a mattress, but Trippe, thinking he could do better, put together a group of lounge tables. The next morning, and a bit stiff, Trippe apologized to Thaler saying he was a poor steward and asked Thaler if he would take charge of his bed-making for the rest of the journey.

A tight vigil was kept throughout the trip. During the night Gray often wavered from course to add more trip miles so that Second Officer J. D. O'Neal and LaPorté could record meteorological observations. The weather was good and the flight smooth. At dawn, after a radioed invitation from the Governor of Dakar, Gray made an aerial inspection of the French port in connection with future-

Chapter Eighteen: Bolama

proposed landing rights. Completed, the NC-05 continued down along the African coast to Bolama. Before landing, Gray went under "the hood" to conduct two simulated instrument approaches as demanded by the CAB when establishing a new route. The majority of the German-built ground meteorological and radio equipment used to guide the clipper into port was owned by the Portugese and shared with Pan Am. While Gray circled the flying boat for half an hour practicing approaches, some 6,300 tribes people pounded drums and gesticulated in dance and song to await the touchdown. The celebration and beating of tom-toms had begun days before with each passing hour intensifying in activity and sound.

"Trip No. 262" alighted smoothly on the Jeba to complete its 2,110-mile flight from Lisbon. Gray taxied the boat to a 40-foot-long by 24-foot-wide raft called a "jangada" where it was well secured. On hand to greet the U.S. dignitaries was Pan Am's Chief Bolama Engineer Bill King. As Gray was sailing the NC-05 across the Jeba, King turned to a native friend and asked him what he thought of the big 314:

"Isso nao e um aviao, e um vapor," he exclaimed in Portuguese!" ("That's not an airplane, it's a steamboat!")[105]

Bolama's acting governor, aides, native chiefs and Pan Am basemen welcomed passengers and crew while masses of the general populace gathered about adorned in their finest and most colorful garb. Many carried black umbrellas to shield their bodies from the hot streams of sunlight. Clipper Steward Bruno Candotti, proficient in speaking nine languages, acted as translator during a tour of the base followed by a luncheon held at the governor's mansion where wild hen sandwiches, fruits, African sweets, Portuguese wines and liquors were savored. A native dance added to the festivities.

Early the next morning, Trippe, Bixby, Willkie and others went on a safari pre-arranged by Bolama's absent governor who had journied to Lisbon on urgent business. Taking a steamship to Portuguese Guinea's mainland, the party traveled 60 miles inland into the rugged terrain to hunt for large game. Disappointed, the men returned with just a few bagged ducks. Two months later Capt. Lodeesen, during a layover in Bolama, was the first-recorded outsider to drop a 250-pound leopard, the skin of which was later photographed at the MAT after Lodeesen landed the Yankee Clipper.

The route-proving departure from Bolama occurred on February 7th for the 3,120-mile hop to Trinidad, the longest non-stop commercial plane flight then made in the world. It was for this part of the trip that the Dixie Clipper had been brought up to 314A standards. She had entered the LaGuardia clipper hangar two months earlier for modification work. Her enlarged gasoline tanks, equipped to carry 5,406 qallons against the previous 4,200 capacity, weighed three tons more than a fully loaded DC-3.

Referred to by Pan Am as the "long drink crossing," Capt. Gray alternated between various altitudes and changed course a number of times so his crew could test the route's air currents. Flying between one and 8,000 feet, Gray and LaPorté agreed that the easterly trade winds were more suitable at the mere 2,000 foot level.

Bolama residents gather to view rare sky-bird anchored on Jeba. Loads had to be light for non-stop flights to Port of Spain before final hop to New York's LaGuardia Airport. (*Photo Courtesy: Pan American World Airways*)

Stronger headwinds, like those between Horta and Bermuda, prevailed higher up. The only difficulty encountered during the long flight was communication receivership from LaGuardia due to a heavy rainstorm in New York.

Night passed into day, and without incident the NC-05 came smoothly down upon the waters of Port of Spain where another formal reception awaited passengers and crew. Breakfast was served in the Pan Am terminal while the clipper was refueled and stocked with mail and food for the up-coming and long-established 619-mile run to San Juan. A few hours later San Juan's Governor Guy J. Swope, U.S. military brass and Pan Am employees swarmed the clipper dock to offer their salutations and congratulations while press photographers and newsreel men clicked cameras and rolled film. A testimonial scroll was awarded Wilkie by the Puerto Rican Committee ascribed by the British War Relief Fund that enrolled him into the island's organizational branch.

Bumpy weather was encountered on the last 1,600-mile leg of the trip to New York. A strong wind churned Bowery Bay as Capt. Gray slipped in for mooring at 13:19 GCT, February 9th. Crowded into the MAT's waiting room as the 314A completed the 11,400-mile trip were 87 press and radio newsmen. Some had come as far away as Montreal. Heading the list was a cinematographer from the newsreel company of Norman W. Alley, film dean of historical events.

Upon entering the MAT's customs room, Trippe and Willkie, wearing suits and winter overcoats, faced into pressed microphones to answer a line of questions.

"Bolama is everything you expect after reading about darkest Africa," Trippe toned out. "I think our stay there was about the most interesting day I ever spent in my life."[106]

Talking about European war conditions and the clipper flight home, Willkie remarked about the latter: "Pan American Airways is doing a grand job of flying the Atlantic. I was invited to the control deck during the long flight from Africa and was impressed with the efficiency of the way they work. Their close check on matters of position and meteorology are wonderful. I was glad to be able to come back with them on their route-proving flight. I had a fine trip."[107]

Captains LaPorté and Gray were also interviewed. "The entire operation was okay," LaPorté stated. "I thought I had been everywhere in the world on a clipper, but I really got a big kick out of visiting Bolama. It's perfect."[108]

One reporter turned to Gray: "How was the flight, Captain?"

"Routine," Gray replied, hesitent to say more.

"Did the clipper behave all right?"

"Perfectly. Everything was routine."

"How about those instrument aporoaches at Bolama, then? You'd never seen the place before, had you? Didn't you get a kick out of flying 'blind' over that little spot on the edge of the jungle?"

"No, we'd figured everything out pretty well beforehand. Instrument approaches in Africa are the same as at LaGuardia Field. I'd say the whole thing was routine."[109]

Routine may have been how LaPorté and Gray partly described the trip, but hardly as much for passenger Trippe. Not only did he have a problem with his clipper bedding, but when he went to leave the airport his sedan wouldn't start. It was an anti-climax to the larger and more complex mechanical air machine he had just left. To get the small car motor to turn over for the drive to his Long Island home, Trippe's chauffeur had to acquire a bobbie pin from the Division manager's secretary. Smiling reporters were quick to catch the comical touch that gave them a bit more punch to their copy stories. Within 48 hours after touchdown, the CAB gave its approval for the Bolama service.

Above and beyond all the side human interest accounts put into print by the press, it was the NC-05's accomplishments that

made the top news. When the *Dixie* and *Yankee Clippers* respectively went into Atlantic service, airline buffs followed their history-making events with great zeal. They became the most watched for ships in the world. Many made bets on what ship would be used next in the odyssey of completing another aviation first. In the U.S.' South the *Dixie Clipper* was favored while in the North praise went to the *Yankee Clipper*. Inaugural debates reached a point to where Capt. William D. Winston, who's family heritage stemmed from the city of Winston-Salem and blood-related to the famed North Carolina Winstons, took constant ribbing from airline employees every time he was assigned to take out the NC-03.

Since 1939, the *Yankee Clipper* led the honor's race. She was the first 314 to span the Atlantic, first to survey all Pan Am's European bases and in the carrying of passengers over the northern route; the first to fly regular, heavier-than-air air mail to and from Europe; the first to be scheduled out of the *MAT*; first airliner to set an Atlantic speed and mail-load record; first plane to carry serum and make a night landing; first plane to dip its wings to salute royalty at sea (the Duke and Duchess of Windsor en route to New York aboard the *Queen Mary*); and the first plane to set the 200th commercial Atlantic air crossing.

Then came Bolama. The *Dixie Clipper*, besides introducing paying passenger and air express service to Europe, stole the limelight. She became the first U.S. commercial plane to land in Africa; first to operate on a route linking four continents; first all-metal air transport to fly 3,120 miles non-stop; and first U.S. aircraft to carry passengers and a load of mail across the South Atlantic.

With all the praise and glory going to the two clippers, the question remained: was it advantageous for Pan Am to re-route their 314s during the winter months? A typical flight between Lisbon and New York across the mid-Atlantic took 24 hours whereas

Dixie over Bolama. Price per boat was once reported to be $668,000, but overhead rates raised amount to nearly one million a plane, a costly endeavor in late 1930s. (*Photo Courtesy: George Jervas/Pan American World Airways*)

through Bolama the time was nearly doubled to 42. Often, a two or three-day layover occurred at Bolama as well. Therefore, was it worth the time to sit it out in Bolama or wait out the bad weather at Horta? The answer to these questions, at least as far as Pan Am was concerned, was a positive yes! But for passengers, the trip through Africa could be exasperatingly long if one were in a hurry to reach New York. Yet two or three days in Bolama was not as much a money loser to the airline or as frustrating to passengers as spending one or two weeks at Horta waiting out a storm. The following statistics proved that Pan Am's effort to detour westbound clippers was well worth the financial stakes involved.

From the time the *Yankee Clipper* completed the first, regular-paying passenger Bolama flight a few days after the NC-05's trip to the last winter flight made at the end of April under Capt. A. L. McCullough, the 314s were able to increase their regularity of runs 50 percent in westbound trips to the U.S. than the previous 1940 months of February, March and April. Twenty-one round-trip crossings were made in the two months of 1941 as compared to 14 in 1940. Only four had to be canceled in comparison to 11 during the preceding winter. Because of the new South Atlantic route, 84 percent of all 1940-41 winter flights were completed as compared to only 56 percent in 1939-40.

Passenger traffic also doubled. Between February and April, 1941, 471 passengers flew westbound from Lisbon to New York with only 286 allowed during the same period in 1940, via Horta and Bermuda. Passenger miles flown totaled 3,500,000 due to the longer route in 1941 as compared with 1940's 1,197,098 — an increase of 199 percent. Most important to Pan Am was the carrying of more U.S. Post Office subsidy mail. Poundage increased 85 percent via Bolama, from 45,404 pounds in 1940 to 81,00 pounds in three months time over 33,247 in 1940 — an increase of 146 percent. Combined, the 314s transported more than 165,000 pounds during the winter months against only 78,651 pounds the previous year. The carrying of U.S. and foreign mail jumped 111 percent by April 30th when the Bolama base was shut down until the following winter, leaving only a skeleton crew at the African island.

Meanwhile, Lisbon departures were becoming so secret that night departures were the rule rather than the norm. Just before dusk, 314 captains and first officers would leave early from their crew-housed hotel in Estoril and journey into Lisbon to the British Embassy where, upon arrival, they would slip through a back doorway, up an elevator and into a dimly lit room to receive their coded flight plans—all a cloak and dagger-type of event.

Because of Pan Am's thoroughness in meteorological studies, a near 100 percent schedule for the next four years of round-trip operations across the Atlantic was maintained during the winter months with 314 aircraft. Another problem in the development of transoceanic air service had been eliminated.

19

The Glamor and the Glitz

With surmountable news attention given the 314s in their inaugural flights, the charting of new air routes and the famous personalities carried, one may begin to wonder what it was like, as a passenger, to fly aboard a 314. That question has often been asked by aviation enthusiasts, and at times by even the inquisitive air-minded public who periodically delve into the golden sphere of aviation history following the seemingly millifold of years since the last 314 touched down to end a colorful span as an outstanding airliner of the 20th century.

Meliorative strides in commercial flight have been many since the 314s' historical time slot — much of it to the advantage of passengers. One of these more preferred conditions since the 314 era has been the clipping of time in getting from point A to point B. The world has shrunk since man's breakthrough, his first fillip into unfolding the commercial jet beginning with the British-designed *Comet* in the early 1950s. Where it once took six days to reach Hong Kong by 314 out of San Francisco, the same distance can be covered in a day. And the 24-hour trip to Lisbon from New York has been reduced to five or six hours. Transporting one's self by supersonic means is even faster!

"I took the *Concorde* to Paris and back to New York in November, 1979," related Clare Boothe Luce. "Not at all comfortable, although the trip is mercifully short — three, one-half hours."[110]

Traveling by jet, and eventually by faster modes of aircraft, may be man's answer to a quicker pace for the world of trade negotiations through business transactions, but it is not the average vacationer's delight regarding comfort within the sections referred to as "first class." Where speed has cut travel time a few hours (man will probe for tomorrow's unbuilt machine to nip more), today's airline managements have sacrificed fine accommodations to pack in more bodies. Anything for more dollars! Whatever happened to the idea, "Getting there is half the fun?"

Writer Allen R. Dodd, Jr., wrote in 1973:

"The 314. . .ah, the 314! She set a million youngsters like me to daydreaming on the job, wondering how $28 a week could be stretched to cover a round-trip to Hong Kong.

"The grand tradition is dead, the elite works hard at being just folks, and the tourist now begins his vacation when he gets there and not when he embarks. The luxury was something of a necessity when flights stretched through 60 hours or more. For six hours or less, who cares? If I drop a tear for the flying boats . . . it 's not because they were luxurious, but because they belonged to a time, before in-flight movies, when airplanes had their own built-in excitement."[111]

The 314 was not built for speed, and her jumbo-sized interior for which she was noted hasn't been surpassed by the latest of PR gimmicks full of frills and so-called luxury fads that surround today's airliners. Boeing's lumbering but great boats of the air did not have today's standard rows of cramped seats extending the full length of their hulls common to every jet liner's fuselage that competes against different airlines in relative sameness on the world's air routes. The 314 was unique in style and operating efficiency. She was reliable and extremely luxurious — a "one-class" ship with an ultra deluxe suite and once advertised as "the *Waldorf* with wings" or "the flying palace."

"Those old flying boats were much more comfortable than the transocean-continental planes of today," Luce continued. "They had berths, and one could stretch out and rest or sleep on them."[112]

Berths alone, of course, were hardly what made 314 travel fun and exciting. Behind the mere thrill of flying an ocean was the exhaltation of being a pioneer — the sensation of being absorbed into Trippe's philosophy of operation where one experienced his

For their entire years of operation it was across such-type sea-wings and through such centered hatches that stepped many a famous personality. (*Photo Courtesy: Boeing Aircraft Co.*)

volition for a world empire of "flying clipper ships" offering the most ostentatiously super air service the world has ever known. How long Trippe's dream was to last was unimportant. Possibly he was aware that his monopoly of transoceanic, world-encircling flight would one day die out, as it did, or, be altered to the state of being just one more segment of many international air carriers; for nothing, whatever it may be, ever remains the same. Understanding this, Trippe shot for the moon and took the flying public with him. Everything had to be done on a grand scale. Give all you have and back it up with quality PR tactics. In the meantime, enjoy the excitatory times and the newness involved.

Introduction of the 314 to the world's populace was given the grandest publicity to the point where the M-130 boats on the Pacific were overshadowed. Flying by the latest model in the clipper fleet was a novelty, a stupendous experience and never to be forgotten by the few who did chance to cross an ocean or two by 314 just prior to and during World War II. Clippering became the rich man's avant-garde to navigate one's self from America to Europe, the Far East, the Caribbean or South America, and the reverse. Stepping aboard a 314 was the latest fad — more glamorous than walking across a steamer's gangplank. Boeing 314s were not only the fastest and most convenient way to travel abroad, but considered by the established elite and nouveau riche alike of the day as what now is termed the "jet setters'" way without jets! Flashbulb arrivals and departures were the rage.

Pan Am, as with any big business, relied heavily on publicity for spreading the word of its 314 service debut. Multiple PR statements and photo sessions covering christening ceremonies and first flights were carried forth with vigor under the well-organized leadership of Pan Am's Public Relations Director William I. Van Dusen. Dusen's indispensable efforts brought to the world public the significance of the new transatlantic air schedules and their timing impacts for trade and travel, as well as for the inherent cultural ties bridged by the 314s.

Many of Pan Am's PR 314 pictures that appeared in various publications were the work of Clyde Sunderland, a professional aerial photographer from Oakland. Sunderland was contracted by the airline in the mid-1930s to photograph the S-42 and M-130s, one famous picture of which showed the *China Clipper* passing under the then incompleted Oakland Bay Bridge on its inaugural flight to Manila.

The M-130 was heavily loaded and Capt. Musick couldn't get it high enough after takeoff to clear the structure so instead guided the boat beneath the steel span.

Division press releases on the 314s were mailed out to the mass media like driveway throwaways along with some 3,000 photos with accompanying captions to capture the attention of publishers. *Look* magazine came out with a six-page photo and caption spread in its May 23, 1939, issue illustrating what it would be like to fly the Atlantic from New York to Southampton. Using two New York models posing as passengers, *Look* stated, "Presented here is a pre-

Countless camera bulbs were flashed by pressmen who often were on scene for world's rich and famous upon their U.S. 314 Clipper arrivals. Shot taken at LaGuardia's Bowery Bay terminus, ca. summer, 1939. (*Photo Courtesy: Pan American World Airways*)

view of that momentous first flight, an hour-by-hour picture-log, showing how the passengers will spend their time — what they will see, do and feel."[113]

Fortune, *Life*, *Time* and numerous other periodicals followed suit giving photo and copy coverage to the 314 along with many colorful full-page ads that were sprinkled throughout the varied magazines to entice one to book passage or to just dream of those far-off places reached by clipper.

"Ah yes, those clippers. I remember seeing pictures of them in magazines when I was a boy," recalled Bruce Whitiker, former Los Angeles Unified School District assistant vice principal. "I used to fancy about the romantic places they flew to in the South Pacific. They really were something to view, so big 'n all."[114]

Whopper-sized and impressive, the clippers were just that. Every leading newspaper in the U.S. plastered its pages with daily interest stories revolving around the flying boats' historical achievements. Equal to the printed word was the spoken one. The radio, the second and most enjoyed informative medium, sent out broadcasted specials, many from aboard 314s on their history-making flights.

Plaguing the clippers — stemming from excessive rumors — were extensible mental exaggerations based on their size. Some prospective passengers phoned Pan Am to find out if they could shower aboard the 314. In general, the clipper was publicly imagined to be the "flying hotel" as advertised and boasted of having an actual promenade deck and being completely equipped with private staterooms as aboard a first class Pullman. On a flight out of San Francisco a steward asked a woman passenger if he could take her coat.

"No thank you," she replied. "I'll be needing it later when I go out on the promenade deck."[115]

Last of the Flying Clippers

The 314's very mein exemplified grace, beauty and luxury. Here in A status, the *Yankee Clipper*, minus forward port cabin A windows, lifts off Riker's Island Channel for another of her many flights abroad. (*Photo Courtesy: Pan American World Airways*)

Indirectly, one of the biggest 314 PR promotions was the Dec. 30, 1940, opening of Elmer Rice's New York play, "Flight to the West." Held at the *Guild Theatre* just off Broadway, Pulitzer prize winner and leading playwright Rice stunned audiences with his accurate stage setting of a 314 interior. The play revolved around world conditions at the time and was set aboard a clipper which gave backdrop to, as Rice said, "...a super drawing room, an international sounding board for the exchange of ideas and the expression of hope and faith in a better world."[116]

Rice got the idea to write the play after flying from Lisbon to New York on the NC-04 in 1939 piloted by Capt. Sullivan. Aboard with Rice were *New York Herald Tribune's* Helen Reid and *Baltimore Sun's* Paul Patterson. At the end of the trip Reid and Patterson suggested to Rice that his next play should revolve around a clipper trip across the Atlantic. A year later when the Nazis were sweeping across Europe, Rice found his mind going back to what Reid and Patterson had said . From there the play evolved.

Set designs of the partial clipper interior were by Jo Mielziner and made as accurate as possible. Compartment partitions were only indicated so as not to block the view of the audience seated in the house's extreme right and left-sided seats. Mielziner and the actors had gone to LaGuardia's clipper port to view a 314's interior to sense what it was like aboard one of the famous flying boats.

Following the 80th performance on March 12, 1941, and after raves by critics, Pan Am's Capt. Winston, who flew the *Yankee Clipper* out of Lisbon for New York the day England declared war on Germany, was called on stage. He had attended the last evening's performance with his wife and mother. Standing under the floodlights in the clipper mock-up, Winston was asked to present leading actress Betty Field and cast with a scroll that signified that 300,000 imaginary miles had been flown across the Atlantic. After the curtain came down, Winston was queried as to whether he ever had a group of passengers as highly strung as those who played the roles.

"Sure," Winston retorted. "That ride from Lisbon on the night war was declared when I had a passenger list which included English, German, Dutch, French, Scots and several Czechs, you could have cut the tension with a knife"[117]

Clippers, not extraordinary under the circumstances that prevailed during their time, also had an extraneous collection of oddities during their reign. There were incidents still thought of as quite peculiar and down right outlandishly funny. The story list is extensive and only a few have been pulled for examples.

With a war blazing in Europe, Pan Am officials were flabbergasted one day in late 1940 when their London office received a request from an Englishman who wanted to book three spaces on a 314 out of Lisbon. There was nothing weird about that until the line's agent was told the tickets were for " . . . three of the finest racing horses in the United Kingdom!"[118]

Another time a breeder in Europe wanted to gather all pedigree dogs and clipper them out of harm's way. It was as though somebody told the animal lover that a 314 had been christened *Noah's Clipper*! Pan Am, of course, rejected all such requests only to be further humored by a wealthy fanatic with a record of making long air flights who announced on a 314 that he was God and tried his best to pay $1,800 in cash for a cup of tea.

Somewhat whimsical, yet awkward for a 314 crew, was the trip out of Horta to Lisbon having a bizarre list of passengers aboard. Glaring at each other, but not speaking, were two separate groups of Frenchmen and German naval officers. Once docked at Lisbon, the Frenchmen tried to tip the stewards for the fine attendance rendered while the Germans gave their gratitude by lining up just past the gangplank, clicking their heels and giving a Nazi salute to the deplaning crew. Then there was the fluke when a New York millionaire from Long Island wanted to charter out a 314 for himself and 14 friends. Offering $5,000 apiece, he desired a 314 to be flown to Uruguay and circled over Montevideo so he and his associates could view the German battleship *Graf Spee* counter with the British blockade at the harbor's entrance which eventually ended when the *Spee's* captain ordered Hitler's super warship scuttled.

Other stories on the lighter side were, and still are, charming and delightful to hear and relate. In April, 1941, entertainer Babe Daniels flew to Lisbon on the *Dixie Clipper* and then reboarded another plane for England. After unpacking she noticed she had left her false eyelashes in New York and remained vain to go on stage in London until her coarse, black stick-ons were rushed across the Atlantic on the next clipper. Also told were about the manor house ladies of England who were greatly disappointed to learn that ocean liner-like maids were not part of clipper crews to attend to their personal change-of-clothes layouts for the salon-seated dinners. Or about the English nobleman who sat in a 314's aisle for nearly the entire Atlantic crossing drinking all the available scotch. Another side laugh concerned a male passenger who locked himself in the john and refused to come out until after the clipper landed.

And the stories continued. One witty one occurred after the *Yankee Clipper* came into New York on Aug. 4, 1940, from Lisbon. While taxiing to the dock, a female passenger turned to a fellow male traveler and quipped:

"Well, we've arrived."

Seated nearby was the purser who couldn't resist to intervene with, "Madam, we always arrive!"[119]

Less-startling accounts were noted as well, such as when en route to Lisbon, Capt. Nolan came down from the upper deck and into the NC-04's lounge to inform Mlle. Eve Curie, daughter of Mm. Sklodowska Curie, scientist who discovered radium, the jaw-dropping news, "New York just radioed that your luggage was left on the dock by error."[120]

Along with the extreme publicity, exaggerations and true-to-life stories, a number of Hollywood writers incorporated the word "clipper" into their movie scripts and producers and directors had the 314s exemplified in short, sequential frames to provide an added touch of intrigue to suspenseful and sometimes exanimate plots. Movies such as *Wake Island* (1942), with William Bendix and Brian Donlevy, *Fallen Sparrow* (1943), starring John Garfield and Maureen O'Hara, and *Storm Over Lisbon* (1944), playing Vera Ralston and Erick Von Stroheim, captivated audiences into a world of make-believe and foreign adventure. Even the loin-clothed Johnny Weissmuller and Maureen O'Sullivan had their turns to clipper away in the 1942 fun-packed release, *Tarzan's New York Adventure*.

The 1940 B film *Desperate Cargo* used air piracy for its fast-moving plot. It was the first film to depict what is known today as hijacking — sophisticated thieves who commadeer a 314 during a flight in the Caribbean in hopes of pilfering the clipper's valuable cargo. The film was a mild epilogue in comparison to the terror and treachery that evolved 30 years later and which continues to plague airlines around the world

Hollywood's silver screen carried many in mind to mysterious ports with views of the penthouses of the sky. It was an imaginative way to travel, munching from a bag of popcorn or twisting into a candy bar while one's attention became oblivious to those closely seated about and the heart set to pounding as the projector reflected from the screen a huge shiny ship groaning skyward, the sound of which blared forth from theater speakers. Songs too revolved around the romance of the 314s. Words to the melody "Somewhere Island"

had the blandly pleasing beat of "...moonlight clipper..." added to the lyrics and sung by Freddy Martin's choral group in the 1943 movie production *Stage Door Canteen*.

Highlighting Hollywood's 314 movie enraptures was the Edward Small's high drama *International Lady*, a title that evoked the glamour of clipper travel. Released in September, 1941, the film headlined the striking Budapest-born Ilona Massey, George Brent and Basil Rathbone, better known as "Mr. Sherlock Holmes." Setting the plot was fictitious world-acclaimed pianist and singer Carla Nielson, played by Massey, who, as a Nazi spy, leans for assistance on, and unknown to her, an FBI agent portrayed by Brent to clandestinely get her to America from London to pursue her undercover spy work.

A quarter of the way into the film Massey and Brent are seen flying to Lisbon in a DC-3 to catch the clipper. Minutes later a supposed callboy within Lisbon's mocked, drab terminal announces the clipper is ready for departure. Suspense builds when the camera switches to an outside night-boarding scene as flashes of water reflections ripple across a 314's starboard side. Quickly the film turns to a duplicated lounge, the set of which is done with the finest touches of detail including the clipper's star-studded upholstery. Actors toast glasses of supposed sherry before the imagined takeoff while simulated Tagus River reflections continue their sparkle against cabin bulkheads. Then comes an aerial shot of a 314 over Manhattan, a landing and a disembarkation at the *MAT*.

Small's last clipper frames focus in on Massey, the golden-haired film beauty of the late 1930s and 1940s, dramatizing the clipper's arrival with her piercing gazes and natural beauty-marked chin as she steps from the gangplank while acting press photographers flash cameras. Massey's face is seen through an elegant net veil fashioned over a tall-sculptured hat that accentuated her sensuality and image of the Old World charm that likewise, in the background, graces out the sequential clipper footage.

Other movies also lent to the excitement of clipper travel. *Affectionally Yours* (1941), billing Rita Hayworth and crooner Dennis Morgan, showed a brief shot of a clipper passing over the *MAT* along with a close-up of Hayworth deplaning. Better yet, the unseen and indicated-by-word-only teaser of a 314 briefly emphasized in 1942's *Casablanca* with Ingrid Bergman, Humphrey Bogart and Claude Reins. It's outside movieland's *Rick's Cafe* when the sound of a plane is heard. A twin-engined craft (model) is seen taking off. Reins, playing the part of Casablanca's chief-police commissioner, turns to Rick, admirably protrayed by Bogart, and flatly states, "Plane for Lisbon; you would like to be on it, wouldn't you?"

Bogart matter of factly snaps back, "What's in Lisbon?"

"Clipper to America,"[121] Reins exclaims!

If the movies of the early 1940s fomented audiences with fictionalized, international air journeys, newsreels visually illustrated the real 314 travel. Young boys sat bug-eyed in their seats as the filmed clippers glided into port, sometimes showing their captain idols on the docks. One Texas banker recalled, after viewing a newsreeled 314, how long it would take to pocket money from his meager job for a trip to Europe and back aboard the *Yankee Clipper* piloted by his hero, Capt. Sullivan.

Naturally, to have personally experienced a 314 flight was where the excitement lay. Passenger accounts are few in print. Those that do exist provide tomorrow's airline researchers with a glimpse into the past. Noel Pemberton-Billing, British aviation founder of the Supermarine Works (built flying boats from 1911-14), World War I Royal Navy Squadron Commander and former Member of Parliament, wrote in 1939 about his 314 trip to England. His article, "Are We Too Proud To Learn?," not only praised the 314 but also slapped hard at England's lack of foresight into developing a similar plane for competing against the ever-progressive Pan Am empire.

"To those of us who have struggled since way back in 1908 against ridicule and risk in an endeavour to place this country (England) in the forefront of international aviation, if I may borrow a vulgarism from the country I have so recently left, 'It makes us sick to the stomach.' Unless we are too blind to see or too proud to learn we may yet recover our lost ground in commercial aviation.

"May I remind...that the world significance of this Empire was rendered possible by our supremacy at sea? Surely it is unnecessary to remind them that within the next few years major world significance will pass to that country which holds supremacy of the air.

"I admit that an unusual stress has been placed upon the production resources of our aeroplane manufacturers, but more's the pity, only during the past 18 months, by the condition of unrest existing in Europe. But surely it is not outside the power of a country with our immense financial and engineering resources to create at least a nucleus of efficient Empire air commerce.

"The position being what it is, and from the experience I have gained in the trans-Atlantic passage in a Pan American clipper, were I responsible for the destinies of civil aviation in this country, I would seek powers to buy, if they would sell, or, if not, to charter one of these clippers and use it as a curriculum for the education and inspiration of those who, God help us, are responsible for our commercial airlines or, failing this, I would insist that no man should be allowed to raise his voice in the councils of our Civil Aviation Department until he had made at least one return voyage on an American clipper."[122]

Referring to his 314 trip that set a record of 11 hours, 35 minutes to Foynes, Billing talked of the relative ease afforded him and his fellow passengers. Only one minor incident was noted. One hour out of Port Washington, a passenger was somewhat provoked because he could not get his pet animal from the storage section, and also Pan Am did not carry his particular brand of liquor, even though about half a dozen selections were offered.

"Let me confess," Billing continued, "I myself complained because I could not obtain ginger ale, and I must admit I felt mildly humiliated when the steward informed me that as the freightage value on the glass bottle alone represented approximately two dollars, they would have to charge at least two dollars, fifty cents — that is about ten cents a bottle — to make it commercially possible to carry."[123]

Out of Botwood, turbulence became bad and some passengers, Billing wrote, became mildly airsick. "I should have been affected likewise, because although I never experience that unpleasant sensation when piloting a machine myself, I am anything but a good sailor when flying as a passenger "[124]

Billing was invited by the captain at 3:00 A.M. for a tour of the flight-deck and later reported, "In the forward end of this cabin are two heavy dark curtains and no man, however hard-boiled he may be, could draw those curtains for the first time in the middle of the Atlantic without an emotional thrill. As I looked through, the first thing that met my eyes was a vast sea of clouds, some of them rising for thousands of feet above their base, and right ahead the moon, and above the blue-black sky, the stars."[125]

Because of the great publicity and newness of the 314s, U.S. clipper bases on both coasts were always crowded with tourists or fans waiting to see their idols arriving or departing. Daily Pan Am time tables had equal space in the marine section of newspapers along side printed ship movements until the outbreak of war. An example of the latter is from the *New York Times*, "Shipping and Mails," July 1, 1939:

"Transatlantic - Incoming - July 1, *Yankee Clipper* from Southampton. June 30, due 3 P.M., at Port Washington, L.I. Incoming - July 4, *Dixie Clipper* from Marseilles July 2, due 3 A.M. at Port Washington, L..I. Outgoing - July 5, *Atlantic Clipper* (departs 1 P.M.), from Port Washington, L.I. - Horta, Lisbon, Marseilles.

Ronald Coleman (rear right center), one of U.S.' leading actors of stage and film, relaxes at festive and beautifully served cocktail hour with fellow passengers en route to Europe, cabin E. (*Photo Courtesy: Pan American World Airways*)

"(Letter mail for Azores Islands, Europe, Africa, Asia, Australia, etc., for onward air dispatch from above points.) (Closing 9 A.M.)."[126]

Those who kept track of the daily reports could easily tell where each of the clippers were. For a weekend pleasure, or for those on vacation, it was fun to take an afternoon drive to view the world's most popular airliners. Clippers for Europe left Manorhaven Airport every Saturday and Wednesday at 3:00 P.M., while inbound ships set down on Saturdays and Thursdays at 7:00 A.M. Bermuda-bound 314s departed on Wednesdays and Saturdays at 11:30 A.M., and returned on Fridays and Sundays around 2:30 P.M. Treasure Island-based clippers left every Tuesday between 3:00 and 4:00 P.M, with arrivals the same day at about 10:30 A.M.[*]

Spectators had their biggest thrill watching the affluent stroll down the walkways and then the docks to step into the clippers or reverse. Hundreds of people from nearby Plandome and Sands Point gathered in mid-July, 1939, to watch the *Atlantic Clipper* depart. There was nothing special about the flight except for the prominence of the 16 passengers, just a mere handful of the type who hogged all available seats. Walking across the gangplank and down into the NC-04's grand salon were Carlos G. Bowers, manager of a mine in Bolivia, and the first person from South America to fly the Atlantic by clipper; British Gen. Raymond Browntinel; Whitney Carpenter and wife, world explorers and one of the first white men to cross Arabia with his wife who was the first white woman to do the same; Helen Cornelius, a New York publicity director; Elizabeth Arden, cosmetic entrepreneur; Roger R. Grillon, U.S. sales manager for a Puerto Rico rum distillery; E. Hollingsworth, banker, and wife; Joseph Kahn, businessman; Leon Lebe, rug and tapestry merchant who was aboard the second-to-last flight of the *Hindenburg* before the lighter-than-air ship's fiery 1937 crash; Bernard Schaefer, coffee importer, and wife; Ethel Warner, director of New York's Political Science Academy, Columbia University; and John H. Yeomans, former director of the Port Washington Chamber of Commerce and, at the time, Pan Am's Horta base manager, and wife.

Interestingly enough, the NC-04's Capt. Winston waited 50 minutes for the 16th passenger that never showed — John Cudahy, U.S. Minister to the Irish Republic who had flown to the U.S. earlier on the *Yankee Clipper* to confer with President Roosevelt.

Weather permitting, the crews tried their best to bring in their prized flocks on time. In late August, 1939, Capt. LaPorté landed the *American Clipper* at Manorhaven with film actor Douglas Fairbanks, Jr., aboard who graphically told reporters about Europe's preparations for war. Supporting Fairbanks' account was passenger H. V. Kaltenborn, noted news commentator. The sky clippers were beginning to take on a new breed of travelers — foreign correspondents being rushed overseas to cover the latest international developments. In time there were reporters such as Dudley Anne Harmon,

UPI; Frank Kelly, *New York Herald Tribune*; Helen Kirkpatrick, *Chicago Daily News*; Edward R. Murrow, *CBS*; Ernie Pyle, *Scripps-Howard Newspaper Alliance* and most beloved World War II press writer; Ben Robertson, Jr., *PM* tabloid; Vincent Sheean, *Chicago Tribune*; William L. Shirer, *CBS* out of Berlin; Margaret Bourke-White, *Time-Life* photographer; and dozens more who crossed and recrossed the Atlantic by 314s.

No sooner had reporters finished interviewing Fairbanks and Kaltenborn when they turned their attention to passengers embarking the *Yankee Clipper* for Marseilles. Many were motion picture people. War Correspondent Frank Gervasi, a leading figure with the *International News Service* (INS), also went aboard. Gervasi was on his way to replace *INS*' Arthur von B. trenken, famed two-time medal winner for outstanding photography in China and Spain.

Whereas more press and radio correspondents and government dignitaries began to occupy clipper space, there always seemed to be room for a Hollywood celebrity. Hundreds of female movie fans nearly freaked out when their heart-throb Tyrone Power and actress wife Annabella deplaned the *Yankee Clipper* at Port Washington on Aug. 26, 1939, following a honeymoon abroad. Power and Annabella had occupied the clipper's spacious bridal suite for the trip. The French beauty, wearing sun glasses, head scarf and a mink coat over her traveling attire, became concerned about her family in Pilat, a town about 400 miles southwest of Paris, when told of Europe's worsening state. She and her handsome spouse had not read or heard about any of the world's events during a high seas delay at Horta. Five days after her arrival in New York, Annabella flew back to Marseilles aboard the *Dixie Clipper* in an effort to get her daughter, parents and brother out of France.

Tourists interested in just seeing the clippers rather than who flew on them had more than they bargained for when touring Manorhaven airport in late March, 1940. Two 314s landed near the same time after being caught at the Azores for five days by rough seas. The NC-06 and NC-03 touched down nine minutes apart to join the NC-04 already in port. Later in the afternoon the NC-05 also arrived from Horta. The entire 314 Atlantic fleet was in port. En route, the NC-03 and NC-06 had flown side by side for 2,300 miles, but remained 10 miles apart during night hours for safety precautions. Passengers and crew told reporters that during daylight hours they spotted a number of ships that began an evasive zigzag course of action when the clippers approached.

One reporter from New York dubbed the Manorhaven base as the "Atlantic Transfer"[127] because of the beehive comings and goings. It was just as hectic at Treasure Island, Baltimore and later at the *MAT*. Businessmen, oil men and other entertainers, such as Martyn Brooke (Earl of Warwick) and Noel Coward, British actor, author, playwright and director, called for seats. Just about anyone who was a someone of prominence soon had their names on the "Who's Who" clipper waiting lists. Trunks of French fashions with svelte models to wear them came in on the *Dixie Clipper*, while some American socialites with a touch of snobbery insisted instead

---

[*]Early schedules only; were subject to quarterly changes.

Pacific Division's Purser Roy Donham waits on clientele in 314's fashionable dining salon. Dinners were highlight of clipper trips with some dressing in gowns and tuxedos. (*Photo Courtesy: Clyde H. Sunderland/Pan American World Airways*)

on clippering over the Atlantic to the Paris fashion shows. Listed names of the elite were about as lengthy as those on Santa's Christmas scroll, while others wished and hoped for tickets to be in their Yule Day stockings! John G. Winant, former governor of New Hampshire, and then director of the International Labor Organization, flew by *Atlantic Clipper* as did the gallant Thea Cottone. Wealthy Cottone had flown to Europe for a vacation in July, 1939, and stayed on to volunteer as a registered nurse at the *American Hospital* in Paris after the outbreak of war. She returned in March, 1940, on the NC-04 out of Lisbon for a month's rest before wanting to return.

Often times, during the more pleasant days of 314 flight before Europe and America became embroiled in war, passengers had their choice of which pilot they wanted to fly under. They would call Pan Am ticket agents and ask when their favorite captain was scheduled to take out a clipper. On the west coast there were those like Barbara Hutton, *Woolworth Department Store* heiress, and Ernest Hemingway, master author, who felt at ease with Capt. Joseph Barrows or Capt. John Hamilton, well-established pilots who commanded the earlier M-130 trips across the Pacific. Along the east coast there were followers such as Helen Reid and Byron Price, executive news editor for the *Associated Press*, and later director of Washington, D.C.'s Office of Censorship. Reid preferred flying with Capt. Sullivan, Price under Capt. Gray.

Noel Coward was one who frequently clippered across the Atlantic with an occassional journey in the Pacific. Sometimes getting a ticket for England was not easy. Pulling strings, holding an argumentative attitude and wrangling around red tape through persuasion were the means by which he mustered an early May, 1940, ticket back to his homeland from New York. His assured seat had been postponed for a month. Patiently waiting, Coward finally got

to the *MAT* on June 9th. Fireball actress Tallulah Bankhead and suave actor Clifton Webb were among the close friends who saw him off. Pleasingly enough, actress Madelaine Carroll was to accompany him aboard the *American Clipper*. Similar to Annabella's cause for a return passage to Europe, Carroll was flying to Lisbon and then on to France to financially assist her family and fiance to evacuate. The latest war news terrified her. Beneath the joyous, pleasant-toned answers to inquisitive press reporters and photographers, the deep feelings of departure from the U.S. were sadly felt. Twelve passengers of varying nationalities were about to leave a land of plenty and within a few hours be dropped on a terror-gripped continent where bombs and artillery shells blackened cities and villages and where human suffering prevailed.

Announcement of the NC-06's departure pressed voices into final adieus. Instead of boarding via the long dock, Coward and fellow passengers were taken to the moored clipper by launch. The weather was perfect, the water calm. A sprayed takeoff was grand in the usual smooth manner, and spectactular to see for those left behind. Coward and Carroll extolled the ship's comforts and engaged themselves in deep conversation while sipping cocktails and later feasting upon a sumptuous dinner. There was no turbulence in the clear night sky and Coward later told how they seemed to be suspended in space. Trying to maintain a cheerful atmosphere with fellow passengers, the two entertainers of stage and screen couldn't help but feel sorry for two depressed Frenchmen — their country was crumbling to Germany with each passing hour.

Sunlight began to pierce the darkened sky when the stewards began to arouse those passengers still snug in their berths. A light breakfast was served in the salon before the NC-06 arrived at Horta, refueled and took off again for Portgual. Winging to Lisbon, word was received by the clipper's radio officer that Italy had entered the war with Germany, their troops attacking the south of France. When the shocking news was passed to all aboard, Carroll became concerned and frightened for her loved ones. Others burst into frantic and garrulous audible tones of speech expressing personal anxieties. Lisbon was reached at 7:30 A.M., and, like spokes radiating out from a hub, Coward and Carroll, who, during the long flight, became inseparable friends, went their separate ways.

If flying to a continent enflamed with war was tinged with danger, Coward had another tingling 314 experience in the Pacific a short time later. Eight months had elapsed since he said goodbye to Carroll, a time that took in another round-trip Atlantic flight. Between hard work and long trips, Coward decided he needed a rest. He was in New Zealand and had just wrapped up a long touring engagement in Australia when he booked passage on a clipper to Canton Island to take in some sun. On the afternoon of Feb. 3, 1941, Coward's north-bound 314 landed at New Caledonia. What sunlight was left was spent swimming and strolling. Later he dined aboard the unique Pan Am yacht *Southern Seas* used as a temporary hotel. At 3:30 A.M. the next day, Coward and fellow-traveling companions were awakened for an early takeoff to Canton.

Chapter Nineteen: The Glamor and the Glitz

Headwinds put the clipper three hours behind its scheduled 7:00 P.M. arrival time. Wondering if they missed the small island, and thinking about how long the fuel would last, the tension, according to Coward, finally broke when a passenger called out that lights could be seen below. Many a nose was pressed against portholes as the 314 glided downward to alight on darkened waters.

Coward was left to his solitude in a near vacant hotel when the 314 departed for Hawaii — at least so he thought. A couple of days later an appalling cyclone hit. A New Zealand-bound clipper from Honolulu was caught in the storm and was too far south to turn back. Aboard was Canton's Pan Am manager's wife and newly born son. Hal Graves' wife was returning to the island after giving birth in Honolulu. Five hours past the 8:00 P.M. clipper arrival time the base's manager became shaken. Outside in the blinding storm and darkness churned the crash launch, its beam light revolving shooting rays across the lagoon. Radio messages between clipper and ground were nearly unintelligible during the sit-'n-wait period.

A clear message finally came through from the *Honolulu Clipper*'s radio officer that the boat was about to land. Coward and Graves rushed outside in an effort to view the seemingly lost liner. A roar nearly split their eardrums when the 314 showed overhead in the pouring rain to barley miss the hotel's roof. It disappeared for a few seconds, came back, circled and set down on the lagoon, the outcome of which indicated the expertise in navigational training given Pan Am crews.

For four days the storm pelted the island. The *American Clipper*, bound for the U.S., came in but couldn't depart on schedule. Two over-edged groups of passengers and crew packed the hotel. Meals became staggered. Emergency cots had to be set up. Passengers turned into a miserable and grumpy lot. Finally, on the morning of the fifth-delayed day, the weather became fair enough for the New Zealand-bound NC-01 to get off. Nearly everyone on the island waved as she climbed away. Believing the clipper was well on its way, a sense of ease was felt and enjoyed, but not for long. Two hours later the NC-01 was back with engine trouble and another overcrowded night on Canton was experienced in total frustration. What was to have been a week's stay of calm and quiet for Coward turned out to be a 16-day mad house before he himself could clipper away.

Cyclone encounters and prolonged grounding trials and delays such as Coward's were the exception rather than the rule when traveling by 314. In order to recapture the once golden age of transoceanic commercial flight, we must turn back the clock to a period when stepping aboard a 314 clipper ship was the most highly prized means of transportation available. An imaginary adventure, based on fact, between San Francisco and Hong Kong gives credence to the long lost era of ultra-deluxe transoceanic air travel. According to some aviation historians, traversing the Pacific by flying clipper ship remains to this day the most exciting and romantic commercial air voyage ever undertaken by man.

Ben Robertson, Jr., renowned author and foreign correspondent, was bade farewell by second sister "Boonie" on *MAT*'s observation deck before boarding *Atlantic Clipper* for Lisbon, June, 1940, and then onward to London. (*Photo Courtesy: Mrs. Julian - "Mary "B" - Longley*) "Mary "B" was Robertson's first sister.

With propellers already in revolution, Ben Robertson (extreme lower right) waved to sister before long walk to waiting clipper. He briefly wrote about flight in his best seller book, *I Saw England*, published in 1941. (*Photo Courtesy: Mrs. Julian - Mary "B" - Longley*)

20

Across the Pacific

Resinous Yerba Buena Island-planted eucalyptus trees slightly fluctuated in the mild and preponderant westerly breeze that oscillated through and across San Francisco and Oakland. Below, and just directly north on a clear, chilly afternoon in mid-November, 1940, the *California Clipper* was being loaded with cargo, baggage and mail for another one of its air excursions to the Far East. Reservations had been made far in advance, destination tickets stamped "Hong Kong."

Pacing about inside Pan Am's *Administration Building* terminal were a few news reporters, clerks, well-wishers and the small array of clipperites bound for different ports-of-call along the fine line's blue-ribboned Pacific route. A one-way ticket to Hong Kong from San Francisco cost $760 or $1,368 round-trip, an exceedingly expensive outpouring for 1940's U.S. economy market.

To reach the Treasure Island base, midwest and eastern U.S. residents normally traveled by air. There were three ways to get to the city of the Golden Gate by plane in 1940. United Airlines, then just a transcontinental carrier, conducted a northern route with DC-3 equipment from New York, via Cleveland, Chicago, Omaha, Cheyenne and Salt Lake City. Sleeper service was provided out of Chicago. A second choice was via American Airlines, then too just a U.S. operation, to Chicago and south to Nashville where a change of planes was made and then on to Los Angeles with stops and

All aboard, crew first! Destination, Hong Kong. (*Photo Courtesy: Pan American World Airways*)

north to San Francisco on a United Airlines' DC-3. The final means by air was United from New York to Chicago, change to a Trans-Continental Air (TWA) DC-3 sleeper for Las Vegas and to another TWA DC-3 for the bay city. A slower means of travel was, of course, provided by luxury rail service.

Arriving in San Francisco one or two days before departure offered one a less-hurried and frantic time — a period to give the body a chance to rest and for one to prepare for the long air voyage over the Pacific by doing some shopping. Many transient clipper passengers stayed at the old but fine *Palace Hotel* still standing on Market Street in the city's financial district. Noted for its famed "Palm Court," the hotel was conveniently located near the Oakland Bay Bridge that leads to Treasure Island.

About two hours were required before departure to clear papers and weigh in luggage and bodies, the latter necessary because everything that went aboard a 314 had to have its weight calculated to determine the clipper's center of gravity (c.g.) factor for correct water and air balance. Crossing the bridge from San Francisco, a limousine driver bore to the left, leaving the bridge at the Treasure Island turn-off. Rolling down the causeway, an excellent panorama of the city and bay is afforded. Continuing onward for about a minute the ground gate that once marked one of the entrances to the "Golden Gate International Exposition" came into full view. Beyond, and to the right, rises the large, three-storied clipper terminal (now registered as a historical landmark) capped by a glass-enclosed control tower. To the right is a curved drive where the driver braked at the base of the crescent-shaped edifice's wide-sprawling steps. Red caps greeted the arrival, took bags and vanished behind the white-painted building's Art Deco facade.

Passing through one of many brass and French glass-styled doors, a good-sized hall unfolded with its gracefully curved and chrome-railed staircases poised at the forward end. To the rear was the ticket counter with its upper-painted Pacific route mural. Many in the crowd viewed the large globe mounted in the foyer's central floor space.

A male clerk welcomed passengers and asked for tickets and other traveling documents. Upon receipt they were checked, the tickets taken and papers handed back. Individualized pieces of luggage were taken from the red-capped stock and weighed as were each of the passengers. Only the clerk could see the registered marks so as not to embarrass anyone, especially the ladies!

Chapter Twenty: Across the Pacific

Small blue-zippered overnight flight bags were then issued. Travelers were told to take what they needed out of their luggage for the night and to place the items into the cases cosigned with the line's winged globe logo. Check-in completed, a ground hostess escorted passengers to a medium-sized waiting room where refreshments were offered and where some of the prominent could be interviewed.

Only a handful of personages were listed for "Trip No. 6033." Gathered were a movie star and press agent, a Hawaiian plantation owner and wife, two foreign press correspondents, a foreign courier with a diplomatic pouch handcuffed to a wrist, eight military brass, a southwest building contractor and spouse and three change-of-hand Pan Am ground mechanics headed for Wake Island. Bells soon sounded the times for crew and passenger boardings. Waving and smiling, the revenue-paying adventurers hastened out two east-facing back doors, made a right walkway turn and then a left along the 222-foot-long concourse to the anchored NC-02, her bow aimed south towards Yerba Buena Island.

At 4:00 P.M. (PST), the *California*'s engines were throttled and the liner slipped across the gray-blue open waters of the bay for an 80-m.p.h. lift-off. In a steep climb and wide-arched turn, Capt. Tilton swept the craft past *Alcatraz*, the rock-isle prison holding gangster Al Capone, over an in-bound freighter and then out past the Golden Gate Bridge. A heavy bank of clouds began its roll towards the coast. Further out a higher layer glistened in the sunlight, their billowy palisades reflecting ever-changing pastel hues. First stop was Honolulu, 2,080 nautical miles due west.

Fifteen minutes after takeoff, passengers usually became more at ease. After leveling off, a few explored the ship—to view the many deluxe features they heard or read about regarding the many 314 amenities. A few passengers kept their faces nearly pressed to portholes scanning the sea for ships. Minutes later stewards announced that high tea was being offered in the lounge. An hour later it was cocktails and trays of splayed hors d'oeuvres brought to passengers in their cabins and placed upon accommodation tables hinged from outer bulkheads and covered with linen. Spirits were selected from a 42-choice list that included domestic and foreign-imported beers, ports, wines, cordials and soft and mixed brews ranging in price from 10 cents for a Coca-Cola to 50 cents for a glass of chablis. Mixed libations cost 35 cents each. A favorite "on-the-house" liquor concoction was the "Clipper Cocktail" shaken with rum, vermouth and grenadine and poured over cracked ice.

That evening a formally set dinner was experienced. Passengers ate from bone china, drank from crystal and plucked food with sterling utensils. A noted Pacific clipper meal of the day consisted of relish dishes, mild chicken broth, tossed "Pan American" salad, grilled filet mignon au beurre, stringed potatoes, green beans, hot rolls, ice cream, tarts, fresh fruit and coffee, tea or milk. Amptly sufficed passengers turned to bridge-playing or other games and reading following dinner. Then it was off to bed in Pullman-like berths. From an upper small-sized porthole a passenger viewed a

Cocktails from the galley, a short-lived 314 experience, were served once airborne past Golden Gate between high tea time and dinner. (*Photo Courtesy: Pan American World Airways*)

ship far below, its lights flickering like fire reminiscent of a diamond Cartier brooch set on black velvet. A searchlight threw a beam into the blue of night that set a path of wispy light upwards into the heavens where a full moon peeked through fleeting clouds. In turn, the chief on-watch officer dipped the NC-02's wings three times and flashed landing lights — the surface ship and clipper were exchanging greetings, a long-practiced courtesy of mutual salutes for two ships passing in the night.

About two hours before landing at 8:00 A.M., Hawaiian time, stewards leisurely roamed the compartments and roused everyone not already awake and announced quietly of breakfast. Lounged juices, sweet rolls and freshly brewed coffee helped to open eyes. It was around 7:00 A.M., local Honolulu time, when stewards told all to reset watches and called to port the large island of Hawaii and its 13,835-foot-high Mauna Kea — the pinnacle of which created an island of its own above the clouds. To starboard could be seen the island of Maui.

Capt. Tilton banked the flying boat to starboard. With ease, the NC-02 began her descent. Lower and lower she went until a race along the tops of the clouds broke the want in variety of flying. One second the silver swan was above the fluff in the early rays of golden dawn, and the next under and within the mist where it was dreary and moist. Cabins became warmer. Those still in the lounge were politely ordered to return to their compartments and fasten themselves into their over-stuffed seats.

Approximately 50 minutes flying time later, Diamond Head, Oahu's famed landmark, came into starboard view after the airliner broke into sunlight leaving nimbostratus clouds to the island's highlands. In the distance, Makapu Lighthouse was seen along with the radio station that had kept in touch with the clipper's crew throughout the night starting at the Pacific mid-point or "point of no return." The NC-02 was again banked just north of Waikiki Beach and further lowered over Pearl Rarbor after passing Ford Island and "battleship row."

Splashing in, bow-made waves licked once more against portholes to blot out the last views of touchdown that climaxed 19 hours of flight. Reporters and press photographers from the *Honolulu Star-Bulletin*, and other local island newspapers, were on hand when one of the 314's lounge hatchways was opened to balmy, tradewinds air. With one hand gripping her wide, whitebrimed straw hat, the movie and stage entertainer, in a typical Hollywood-trained pose, hesitated on the gangplank for pictures. She was disembarking for a singing engagement at the *Royal Hawaiian Hotel*. Young servicemen from Fort Schofield, Shafter, Hickam Field and Pearl were among her greeting fans. Three top U.S. Navy officers also deplaned for duty at Pearl. Such military arrivals and departures received little attention until after Dec. 7, 1941.

Walking past the palm-lined quay and manicured gardens of the 45-room *Pan Am Inn* at Pearl City, a full breakfast was enjoyed on the inn's open-aired veranda. Perfume from ginger leis eroded any misgivings arriving passengers may have had about the tropical heat. Continuing passengers took quick showers at the inn and changed to more casual clothing. The rest of the day and evening

Following dinner, passengers, seen looking forward to starboard, sometimes returned to lounge to play bridge or other games before turning in for night. (*Photo Courtesy: Boeing Aircraft Co.*)

were left for discovery. The road to town and Waikiki was very long and narrow through verdant countryside — still peaceful and beautiful before the buildings of Henry Kaiser and other high-rise developers that appeared on the scene beginning in the early 1950s. Shopping, swimming and an early dinner at the old and charming *Royal Hawaiian* was always considered a romantic way to end a perfect tropical day.

Before sunrise, continuing passengers were awakened by young Hawaiian houseboys who worked for the line's inn. Cereals, eggs, bacon, toast, coffee and fresh island fruits were savored in the dining hall while overhead electric-operated fans spun just enough to circulate the otherwise humid and still air. Strums of background Hawaiian music streamed forth from the room's floor-modeled radio console. At 8:00 A.M., departure for Midway Island, 1,126 air miles northwest of the Hawaiian Islands, was executed. Beyond lay stops at Wake, Guam, Manila and finally Hong Kong, the latter five days and 7,567 clipper miles away.

With its hull, tail and wings gleaming like a silver bullet, the most publicized model-built airliner in the world sped across turquoise-shaded Pearl Harbor, lifted its shark-nosed prow and lumbered upward for a nine and one-half-hour air cruise to Midway. Many top-decked sailors waved their white caps in salute as the NC-02 groaned past and disappeared to the northwest.

Getting late, it's time to dress for dinner. Occupants of deluxe suite, as depicted here by models, were normally invited to sit at "Captain's Table," similarly incurred aboard ocean-going liners. (*Photo Courtesy: Clyde H. Sunderland/Pan American World Airways*)

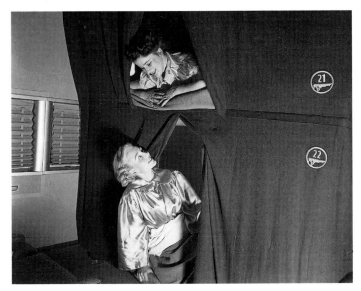

Bed-time berths were wider and longer than those found aboard the world's finest rail cars. (*Photo Courtesy: Boeing Aircraft Co.*)

Aboard the clipper out of Honolulu were two additional U.S. Army officers assigned for Manila service, a Hawaiian shipping magnate and young wife off for an antique shopping spree in Hong Kong, and a Filipino banker, wife and son returning to the Philippines following a month's vacation touring Hawaii. Some still sleepy-eyed passengers stretched out on empty cabin divans with unused berth pillows. More coffee and sweet rolls were again available in the grand salon as the almost unheard of islands of Hauai, Niihau and others passed below the seemingly gliding clipper.

Three hours into the flight the purser announced that fresh fruit, sandwiches and coffee were for the asking; another two hours, a bowl of hot broth or an all-American hot dog. Occasionally one looked out a porthole between card games or reading to see white-

caps in their continuity telling one the sea was running rough. Suddenly, the air became turbulent. Everyone buckled into their seats.

Misty air soon enveloped the clipper to block out the sea below. The ship dropped, pulled up, flew on, dropped, regained altitude and then continued to fly smoothly. Capt. Tilton was riding the NC-02 through a squall. Dark and gloomy was the forecast for the next three hours. Finally the 314 broke through into a hazy sky that eventually became clearer.

Stewards, a bit behind in their schedule, prepared a large buffet luncheon in stateroom A. One of the unoccupied long divan sections on the starboard side was covered with a clean-starched berth sheet. Placed on top were delicatessen spreads of cold meats, fresh fruits and various canned goods. The sheet, covered by the food arrangement, resembled a floral-draped coffin. Over laughs it was dubbed "The Body of the Deceased." Such an amiable way of serving was well understood and appreciated by all. Stewards worked extra hard in setting up the lounge for the formal dinner out of San Francisco. Their more casual approach not only relieved them of additional work, but was considered by many as a unique and welcomed change.

Late in the afternoon the Midway Ialands were spotted in the distance. They are part of a reef barrier that forms an 18-mile circumference, a U-shaped atoll enclosing two land masses known as Eastern and Sand Islands that are close to the 180th meridian and exactly midway around the world from Greenwich Meridian. Sand Island is the larger of the two and is about one and one-half miles long by three-quarters of a mile wide.

Passing over the spectacular reef, Capt. Tilton banked and then skimmed the NC-02 over the deep blue lagoon to check for any floating debris, and then flew over Sand Island, the latter marked by 12 yellow-painted buildings with red roofs, a radio antennae, two water towers and an extensively long pier. Circling back, the

Westbound clippers arrived early in the morning at Hawaii's Pearl City. While passengers normally stayed at the base's *Pan Am Inn* (a few desiring the *Royal Hawaiian Hotel*), crews were housed for the night at Waikiki's *Moana Hotel*. To the right is an M-130 Clipper. (*Photo Courtesy: Pan American World Airways*)

master swooped the plane low over the opposite side of the island growing thick with trees, where, since 1903, the Pacific Commercial Cable Company's relay station was maintained. Then, gently, NC-02 touched into the lagoon, 3,206 nautical miles from San Francisco. As in Honolulu, a rowboat came alongside, its crew having taken a tethering line from the clipper's third officer in the bow hatch to help swing the huge boat into position for mooring to the large and partially housed barge.

Light clothing was the call for the day when passengers felt the blast of heat against their bodies. Dispirited by the near suffocating temperature, they walked up the pier towards the *Pan American Inn* following a short launch ride to shore. Inside the hotel's lobby, with its rattan furniture and touches of Art Deco decor, the heat was less intense due to slow-whirling overhead fans that barely circulated the air.

Signing the register that read like another "Who's Who," the arrivals were shown to their night quarters. All rooms had every comfort of home that contained all-metal furniture finished off in walnut. Traveling clothes to be cleaned were given to Chinese houseboys who also brought in luggage from the tractor-pulled sand sleigh. Usually everyone hit the showers that were only mildly refreshing — partially refined sea water piped in from an outdoor holding tank and reported being "brackish" to the touch. Donning swimsuits and shirts to keep shoulders and backs from sunburning, some passengers went on a tour of the sun-baked atoll.

Fourteen Pan Am men ran the marine station they called "Gooney-land," named after the black and white Laysan albatross that freely roam about. Sand is thick; it's of pure-ground lava and coral and found difficult to walk through. Boardwalks connected the pre-fabricated buildings built in 1935 for the original M-130 service. All drinking water was shipped in. Hot-running water was made possible through the use of windmills and a solar heating system that harnessed both sun and wind.

Ground crew offered all flying guests a guided tour of the compound about an hour before dinner. Leading the way, they took the stopovers across the island to the cable station which, at that time, was run by 23 U.S. Marines. Goonies were everywhere; Midway to this day is a U.S. Government bird sanctuary. Cats and dogs were not allowed on the island. Fearless of man, many goonies followed, clacking their beaks and waddling about. Deep sand-pathed holes were made by another breed of sea bird, the shearwater. The thicket of scrub trees, seen from the air, was filled with other varieties that included boobies, bosuna, canaries, frigates and rails. Many mainlanders were surprised to see that the cable company had cement sidewalks, concrete buildings, a vegetable garden, more than 2,500 tons of imported soil, shipped-in trees and a tennis court for added recreation. Watching out for holes, it was back to the inn and a many-coursed dinner.

Sipping tall cool drinks and pecking at the food because one normally was still heavy from all the "goodies" served aloft, interesting island facts were generally hashed over. Marines, by mid-

Early to rise, its off for Midway Island. Stanley Kennedy, president Inter-Island Airways & Steam Navigation Co., shakes hand with PAA ground attendant. (*Photo Courtesy: Pan American World Airways*)

1941, were beginning to take over the island, and airline passengers would soon not be allowed to roam freely about for security reasons. Midway was directed by a strong-jawed, red-faced Col. Pepper. He was having difficulty with commercial laborers to turn the island into a Pacific military fortress. Builders of barracks, breakwaters, gun emplacements, oil storage tanks and the like, didn't want to stay on Midway for more than three months — even at $600 per month salary. The heat was overbearing and the island was considered very depressing. Uncle Sam's men had to stick it out under military oath at $21 a month. Pan Am alternated their ground-stationed men every six months. Natch, they didn't mind the heat for their pay was much higher!

Unaware at the time, passengers, by early 1941, could no longer be permitted to make a vacationing stopover on Midway or Wake where they had been charged 10 dollars a day (meals included) for singles and $15 for doubles for a two-week vacation. By the summer of 1941, the islands became top-secret military strongholds. Because the soldiers depended on the clippers for their mail, and the clippers on the islands for fuel stops, the commercial sky route through Midway and Wake was kept open. Clipper passengers were hurried into the hotels and not allowed to leave the premises until departure time. Window blinds aboard the flying boats were drawn before the ship's landed or took off. Washington, D.C., officials had become extremely sensitive in guarding their military secrets in preparation for war with Japan.

Before retiring for the night, luggage was placed outside the hotel's doors to be taken back to NC-02. Shoes to be shined were also set out in the hallways, just as passengers had done outside their clipper berths en route to Honolulu.

Four-thirty in the morning came too soon when a hand roughly ran knuckles up and down slatted doors. Saltwater showers were not too pleasant at that hour. Dressed, passengers adjourned to the inn's dining hall where an all-out American breakfast was feasted upon. At 6:30 A.M., the clipper was off for another nine-hour flight to Wake, 1,034 miles southwest of Midway. Stomachs told many to hold back on the quantities of food offered aloft. Breakfast set heavy and another large sit-down dinner spread would be prepared at Wake. Droning through a sky flecked with cumulus clouds, NC-02 crossed a calm sea unmarked by even the tiniest island. She wandered along but was not lost.

Fifty-tive minutes out of Midway number 4 engine began to run rough and was temporarily shut down, its steel prop feathered. A flight engineer crawled out into the massive wing and repaired a broken magneto alternator. In 26 minutes the minor problem was corrected and the engine restarted. The clipper continued to fly at cruising altitude along her sky course to Wake where a permanent repair was given to the faulty power plant during the overnight stay.

Six and one-half hours out of Midway the NC-02 crossed the International Dateline where today becomes tomorrow. First-time day-changers were called to the lounge where a steward had stretched a blue ribbon across the cabin's tango rust-colored carpet. Officiating the ceremony, Capt. Tilton asked each of his non-plenary participants to step forth over the ribbon whereupon they were officially graduated and awarded a captain-signed certificate.

At 2:30 P.M., and having gained a day and two hours, Wake, a coral atoll much like Midway, was approached. A reef envelopes three small islands, Peale, Wake and Wilkes, that, from the air, look like a gnome's legs doing a jig. Later, at dinner, it was learned that the atoll was abandoned until the airline built its aerial road across the Pacific. Where Midway is noted for its birds, Wake is famous for the remarkable selection of tropical fish that fill the wide-channeled lagoon. Many colorful species abound to fascinate oceanographers the world over.

Wake's clipper pier, from which many fish could be seen, jutted 400 feet out into the water in order to pass the shallows. Human bodies seemed weighted from the unbearable heat as they were taken by auto taxi over the long pier's redwood-spiked planking toward the sparsely shaded 45-room *Pan American Inn*, the same type of construction as seen on Midway. Iced drinks were willingly accepted on the wide veranda.

Changing into swimsuits, a few dared to dash off for an ocean dip under the blazing sun. Robert ("Bob") Biggers, Pan Am's Wake manager, suggested they wear tennis shoes -if they had any — since coral is extremely dangerous to walk on. Later a game of tennis on the cemented court worked up a sweat. Then it was back to the lagoon for another semi-cooling swim off the two, one-half square-mile land mass.

One of the most poignant, patriotic accounts involving the Pacific-based clippers was when Clare Boothe Luce wrote of a swim at Wake during her flight to Manila in 1941:

"This time I swim out to the end of the pier where the clipper lies alongside and tread water under the angle formed by its sea-wing. On the underside of the great wing, just above my head, they

have painted a great American flag. It casts its reflection on the clear water. The clear water casts its reflection on the flag, making it seem to wave silkily. The young secretary* paddles out into this Star Spangled grotto. He looks up at the banner that covers him. He makes no comment. Is one required?[128]

Old Glory also waved from a tall mast adjacent to the base's administration building. She was lowered at sunset at the tune of taps. Knowing how early they had to depart, passengers retired shortly after dinner or soon after a stroll along the beach. A quick glance at the room-tabled *Wake Wig Wag*, the island's daily mimeographed news bulletin, brought many up to date on world events. Reported notices were not comforting regarding Europe's plight. Lights out, land-tied passengers drifted off to sleep.

Dawn broke and the *California Clipper* once more was lifted away and headed west for Guam, 10 air hours and 1,305 miles away at 8,000 feet. A few passengers got restless on the fourth day out. They moped in and about their staterooms, paced the promenade — anything to change the monotony of flying. Games became boring, magazines were only glanced at and food seemed to taste the same and didn't appease the foremost thought of getting to planned destinations.

Hopes to spot any Japanese-mandated islands to the north were, at first, enthusiastically tried by peering out starboard portholes. Some felt uneasy about how close the NC-02 was to Japaneae territory. A U.S. major told his fellow-cabined passengers that Guam would probably be the first Pacific island to go under if the "Nips" started a war with America. Again, many passengers gazed out portholes to stare into space as though in a trance.

*Was Anthony Keawiek, one of two personal secretaries to Alfred Duff Cooper, Britain's information officer and later Singapore's coordinator of Far Eastern Defenses. Cooper, wife and party were aboard the same 314 as Luce.

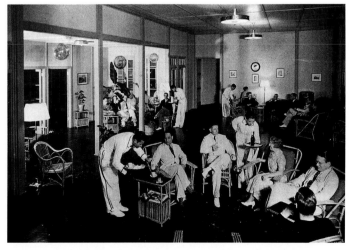

Pre-dinner drinks and hors d'oeuvres were served transient passengers by Philipino houseboys in spacious PAA hotel lobbies along island-connecting route. Japanese fishing buoys, often found washed ashore, hang to left in foyer leading to Midway's dining room. (*Photo Courtesy: Pan American World Airways*)

Thirty-mile-long Guam looked plush, like a continent, compared to Midway and Wake. The island stands 1,300 feet out of the ocean at the southern end of the clipper's approach. Flying low, banana and coconut plantations and rice paddies were seen as were "nip" hut villages. Capt. Tilton flew the clipper ten miles up the western coast, circled the plane over the U.S. Marine barracks near Sumay, and brought the sky liner down in the coral-infested Port Apra. Engines were cut next to the line's *Skyways Inn* specked with swaying palms and sloping green lawns. Dark-skinned natives, called "Chamorros," who are American subjects, lined the quay to wave NC-02 in. Arriving and departing clippers were a big pastime for the fine Spanish-featured natives who lived close by. Stepping into a Pan Am launch, passengers and crew were motored to shore.

Humid and sticky, the weary hurried off for another shower. It was useless for comfort after the hour's hot drive north to Agana, Guam's principal city located 12 miles away. Agana was not much to view in 1940, a few bank buildings, two motion picture theaters, a couple of auto supply stores and other small shops, the majority of which had only thatched and tin-nailed roofs. Refreshing spirits were to be had at the *U.S. Navy's Officers' Club* perched high on a hill overlooking the sea.

At day's end, and back inside rooms before turning in for the night, was the chance to write another letter or postcard on Pan Am-printed stationery. Mail was sent to the U.S. on the next eastbound clipper. Before Pan Am established air mail service across the Pacific in 1935, mail coming into Guam was first sent to Manila by steamer and then back-tracked to Agana. Outgoing bags were sent first to Manila and then on to the U.S. and elsewhere. There was always a waiting list for the next shipment.

Next to table lamps and stationery was always to be found *The Guam Recorder*, a monthly magazine published in Agana. One of the chief writers was Margaret Saunders who wrote a Hedda Hop-

When loads were high to cut back passengers, the few aboard had more space to enjoy and relax in across vast Pacific. (*Photo Courtesy: Clyde H. Sunderland/Pan American World Airways*)

per-like gossip column entitled "Clippering Through." Saunders' articles not only told clipper fly-throughs who was aboard the most recent flying boat but their pertinent reasons for travel as well. News of clipper captains was also included from time to time. Aroused at 4:00 A.M., passengers were given breakfast and then enplaned to make seaway for Manila, 1,600 miles northwest of Guam.

Drinking coffee and watching clouds float past, any air-minded enthusiast had the opportunity to read general Pan Am PR Pacific clipper operational facts from pamphlets put aboard at Guam to help replace nearly one-week old magazines. Partial 314 coverage from the narrow-folded brochures told of the types of air express items flown to Manila out of San Francisco. Some included polo balls for Manila games; tree and shrub cuttings for transplant; seeds; fruits packed in dry ice; insured jewels; upper dental plates; artifical arms and legs; medical supplies and hard-to-come-by prescriptions; newsreels; cosmetics; flowers; catalogues; coconut oil; Agag weavings; shoes; and various types of apparel, such as baby clothes and wedding gowns for Manila brides.

When the 314s came into service, space for air express, inaugurated by the M-130 *China Clipper* on Feb. 22, 1936, was increased 500 percent for Pan Am's Pacific Division. Prices for shipped cargo differed depending from where one was vending. Between San Francisco and Honolulu the charge was 90 cents per pound, and from San Francisco to Hong Kong, $2.19 per pound. A first-class, half-ounced air mail letter to Manila from California cost 25 cents.

Along the 1,384 nautical-mile clipper route between Guam and Manila, stewards prepared a formally set luncheon in the salon from food-stocked supplies put aboard at Sumay. Passengers once more sat in shifts at the ultra-fine, linen-draped tables. Fine-printed menus stood upright in chrome-plated rings that revealed mouth-watering delights that included relishes, beef broth, hearts of lettuce salad, Swiss steak, steamed new potatoes, cut string beans, sliced peaches, assorted tinned cookies, cream cheese and crackers and coffee, tea, cocoa, lemonade or milk. Pre-lunch cocktails were also for the asking from assorted wines and beers to mixed drinks — a novelty for the day.

Land was spotted one hour after the salon and galley had been cleared and cleaned. Capt. Tilton lowered the NC-02 2,000 feet for calmer air and passed over the Islands of Samar, Bicol, Marinduque and Mindoro. Passengers changed into fresh clothing cleaned at Guam. Men wore uniforms or white suits and clutched matching military and Panama hats while ladies reappeared wearing summer dresses and straw-brimmed or flower-veiled hats, their gloves hung loosely over handbags. Soon, beneath flag-painted wings, a large expanse of tropical hills told mind-gazing eyes that their five-day flying hotel stay was drawing to a close that would climax in a heaven-to-earth splash-down.

Chewing gum, if desired, was passed out by stewards to aid ears during the descent. Farm lands and villages unfolded below through broken layers of clouds. Shortly, large white buildings in

Next stop Wake Island. Accommodations were same as those at Midway. Long-range directional finder system guided clippers on a navigational path across Pacific. Wake's DF center is shown in upper left corner. (*Photo Courtesy: Pan American World Airways*)

geometric arrangements showed up with hundreds of cars darting about like ants. Capt. Tilton circled the clipper over Manila Bay, thundered past the Gibraltar of the Philippines, Corregidor, and then Cavite, the American naval and Pan Am clipper base. Sending out a wide path of spray, the NC-02 punched into the muddy-green waters of Manila Bay at 2:30 P.M., Philippine time, after 11 hours of flight. For many aboard it was the end of the line when the flying boat was tied to the large dock in an inlet called Canacao Bay sided by the expansive, thatched-roofed terminal.

Cavite Seaplane Base was a hive of multifarious activity not unlike that found at Honolulu's Pearl City base. Uniformed soldiers and U.S. Navy personnel, under Gen. Douglas MacArthur, Far Eastern commander of U.S. Army forces, and Adm. Thomas Hart, U.S. commander of the Asiatic Fleet, were seen milling everywhere among the Filipinos. Boys with slanted eyes, and wearing Americanized shorts and sneakers, ducked in and out of the

crowd to take pictures of the arrivals. Reporters poked about the mass to get stories for local newspapers. Following a quick customs check, a one-hour car-shuttled drive around the shores of Manila Bay led to what was acclaimed in 1940 as the finest public lodging in the Far East, the *Manila Hotel*. Offshore from Dewey Blvd. a rusting Spanish warship sunk by Adm. Dewey in 1898 was seen.

Standing in the hot hotel's marble-lined lobby while waiting to register, numerous nationalities meandered and sat in small clusters at wicker tables babbling international banking and trade business and threats of war with Japan. Many held gimlets, the most popular drink in Asia. Politicians, businessmen and military brass made up the boisterous and clattering groups. What little afternoon time remained after showering was usually spent shopping or touring through a small section of Manila filled with bicycles, cars and mobs of pedestrians. Billboard signs in English, Chinese, French,

Tagalog (one of two Philippine dialects) and Spanish plastered fronts of buildings. The humidity was high and very displeasing. Bodies dripped with perspiration.

Dinner was served early at the hotel and then off to a night club or two. At 4:30 A.M., knuckles of Filipino houseboys rapped across door slats. It was time to arise, shower, dress, eat breakfast and take another hour's drive to Cavite to clear customs. Eyes were nearly shut as continuing passengers stumbled about preparing for their last day aboard the clipper.

Manila Bay swiftly fell away when the NC-02 soared upwards at 8:30 A.M. for a five-hour flight to Macao, only 638 miles northwest of Manila. Magnificent white thunder clouds rose into the eastern sky as the 314 winged out to sea. New faces were aboard: three Chinese National Airlines (CNA) directors bound for Hong Kong; three American business executives; an English colonel and major to be stationed in Singapore; a Chinese furniture exporter and wife returning home to Hong Kong after business in Manila; and two Catholic nuns being transferred to a Hong Kong mission.

One and a half hours into the flight, after having passed up coffee and sugar rolls for more sleep, passengers dined at another formally set buffet brunch. Drifting in a seemingly make-believe world, watches ticked to 2:00 P.M., Hong Kong time, when Cinderella's sky-pumpkin made a 30-minute stop at Portuguese-ruled Macao. Forty-three miles away — and 30 flight minutes later — the NC-02 was anchored in Victoria Bay, known as the "Harbor of Fragrant Streams," off Kai-tak Airport in Kowloon. Swarming about in the sea were junks, sampans, western and European ships and other sailing craft of all sizes and shapes. After some 60 hours of flight, and six days out of San Francisco, NC-02's passengers and crew were at the threshold of Asia in an area of high diplomacy and international intrigue outstanding in the some 400 years of European co-existence.

Walking up the dock towards the customs shed and cabs to the ferry to the Island of Hong Kong following a short launch ride to shore, the long-hauled personages showed facial expressions related to air fatigue. Despite the fact that many were relieved the long air trip was terminated, one still tended to stop, turn about and take in one more glimpse of the far-off *California Clipper*. Her mighty bow proudly displayed in paint the brilliantly colored American flags. So small, yet so big were the wavy cosigns that symbolized the courage felt in many a heart as all hastened to begin their adventures within the foreign port. Immediate thoughts hailed the flagship that had shepherded them 7,567 Pacific air miles to a land of uncertainty.

In May, 1941, the Pacific route was extended to Singapore at the southern tip of the New Territories. Once plans had been ironed out with the British, Pan Am's Manila-based Supt. Al Lewis was ordered to proceed to the Malayan island to prepare for 314 moorings, refueling facilities and for maintenance shops. Lewis was accompanied by Tolbert Rice, Pan Am's scheduling expert, and Owen Johnson, airline traffic representative in charge of setting up mail,

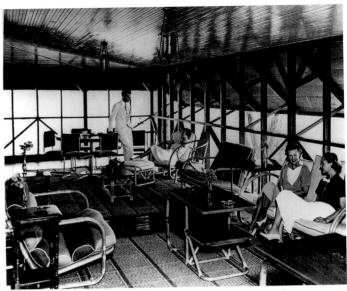

Tropical Art Deco-designed rattan furniture and grass-woven floor mats flashed social-gathering lanai at Guam's PAA hotel. Screens kept out flying insects. (*Photo Courtesy: Pan American World Airways*)

passenger and express services. The American defense aspect of the new link not only enhanced the U.S.' communication lines to the Far East, but also provided England with an air tie between Singapore and Hong Kong after the Empire's service had been shut down when French Indo-China stops had been taken over by Japanese forces in the autumn of 1940, referred to by Japan as an "incident."

On April 30, 1941, President Roosevelt signed into effect the CAA order that authorized the Pan Am route extension. "The current world conditions," Roosevelt said in part," and the importance to the United States of Malaya and the Nertherlands Indies require the establishment of service in the public interest."[129]

No resistance by the British was given when Singapore's government officials received in ceremonial standing the first clipper from San Francisco on May 10th. Long-experienced Capt. William J. Barrows, a nine-man crew and 19 passengers departed San Francisco on May 3rd aboard the *California Clipper*. One passenger was Pan Am's Pacific Division's Communication Supt. George Angus who acted as official observer. Passengers for the trip could be booked only as far as Hong Kong, as the non-stop 1,485-mile trip between Manila and Singapore had been authorized for the carrying of mail and officials only—a proving flight.

Five American-built RAF Brewster-Buffalo fighters flew in formation to escort the NC-02 into Singapore on May 10th while crowds stormed the waterfront to see the ship alight following a 10-hour flight from Manila. Capt. Barrows taxied the clipper into port and rested the flying boat just off the beach near the suburb of Tanjong Rhu at the city's Civil Airport where a formal welcoming party awaited the arrival. Stashed within the ship's storage bins was a small bulk of regular mail along with 25,000 first covers that weighed in at 570 pounds. Pan Am's announcement of the inaugu-

California, on first landing at Macao after cruise from Manila, and, same afternoon Hong Kong — seven days out of San Francisco. (*Photo Courtesy: Pan American World Airways*)

Capt. Barrows swishes NC-02 into Singapore to extend transpacific air route to Malaysia, 1941. (*Photo Courtesy: Pan American World Airways*)

ral flight had been given short notice and didn't allow philatelists enough time to prepare a specially designed envelope. It cost 70 cents to clipper a half-ounce letter from the U.S. to Hong Kong or Singapore. When the NC- 02 departed for the U.S., a local band played "California Here I Come." Capt. Barrows brought the NC-02 back into San Francisco on May 18th. Three days later, passenger and air express service to Singapore was inaugurated. The fare was $825 or $1,485 round trip.

The name of the 314 involved in the first passenger run was press-listed as the *California Clipper*, but the plane was not the NC-02. Boeing aircraft No. 2083, NC 18609 (NC-09), first A314 delivered to Pan Am, was the liner chosen to make the trip. Being the ninth 314 built, she was test flown on May 11, 1941, in Seattle, ferried to Astoria the following day, and taken to Treasure Island under the command of Capt. J. H. Fetters. The NC-02, after having established air mail service to Malaya, was given a major overhaul and then transferred to the Atlantic Division when an air emergency calling for additional commercial aircraft unraveled in Washington, D.C. Once on the east coast, the NC-02 was brought up to A314 standards and sent on a number of special mission flights to and from South America.

With the short-lived words *California Clipper* painted on her bow, NC-09 departed Treasure Island for Singapore with 15 passengers, five of whom were destined for the end of the line 9,472 air miles away. Following the plane's return two weeks later, and

lacking any ceremony, the NC-09 received her proper bow-painted name, *Pacific Clipper*.

Boeing 314 Clipper flights were conducted every other week to Singapore. One week a 314 would leave for Hong Kong, the next for Singapore. When the Malayan operation opened up, 314s were taken off the Manila-Hong Kong skyway. Overhead expenses in shipping spare engines and parts necessitated the rescheduling of the types of aircraft used to the Far East. In cutting back on costs, M-130 parts were sent to Manila and Hong Kong while 314 spares were shipped to Manila and Singapore. An S-42, flown first throughout the Caribbean and South America and later placed on the Bermuda run, was the only clipper making the shuttle flights between Manila and Hong Kong. The two M-130s terminated their Pacific flights at Manila where they made turn-around flights back to San Francisco whereas the 314s flew on to Singapore before beginning their turn-arounds. A second S-42, the *Bermuda Clipper* dubbed by crew as "Betsy," was to have relieved the 314s from flying beyond the Philippines. She was in Miami being primed for the Manila-Singapore run, and was to have been renamed *Singapore Clipper*, when the Japanese bombed Pearl Harbor.

Turning from the Pacific, we now focus on the Atlantic for a perceptible but shorter fanciful 314 flight from New York to Lisbon — that is if a 24-hour transatlantic air journey of yesteryear can be considered short as compared to a today's supersonic *Concorde* flight from New York to Paris in just under four hours!

21

Clipper to Lisbon

In order to recapture the once golden age of transatlantic commercial flight, we must turn back the clock to a period of time when stepping aboard a flying clipper ship was the latest sensation as compared to walking up the *Queen Mary's* gangplank that had, until 1939, been the epitome of super-fine travel for the ocean-going elite.

It's early October, 1941, priority-ticketed passengers cleared for travel by the U.S. State Department have gathered very early at LaGuardia's *MAT* before the 8:00 A.M. scheduled 314 departure. Some of the travelers appeared a bit nervous and apprehensive about their trip to a war-enflamed Europe and wondered if they could retreat in time if the peril became too great. Return space aboard a clipper had been confirmed by the best of Pan Am's ability giving the doubtful somewhat a sense of security.

Within the *MAT*'s large waiting room, 21 anxious passengers soon began to bid their good-bye to friends and loved ones, gave final statements to newsmen and smiled to ease their tensions when eyes of fellow voyagers met theirs. Listed on the clipper's manifest were two *NBC* radio executives destined for London; one *New York Herald Tribune* foreign correspondent also en route to London; a cardinal and secretary priest bound for the Vatican in Rome; an ambassador, his wife and two secretaries; an English courier and bodyguard; an American financier, wife, child and maid; an art his-

torian on his way to Madrid; an American millionaire and socialite wife from nearby Sands Point flying to Portugal on urgent business; two Red Cross managers off for London; and one American banker also destined for London.

Free clipper baggage allowance was first set at 25 kilos, or 55 pounds, and later raised to 77 pounds per person after the 314s were improved in their performance. Overweight charges were hefty and issued at one percent of the fare for 2.2 extra pounds, or about $3.25 per pound. But if money was not a concern, one cared less about the cost. Clerks at Pan Am's early Manorhaven Airport base told about extravagant passenger Anthony J. Drexel-Biddle who payed $2,000 more for his luggage. His 34 pieces of baggage had cost him nearly five times a one-way fare. One ticket to Lisbon from New York was posted at $375, equivalent to nearly $4,100 by today's currency rate. A good job in 1939 paid on the average of $50 per week.

Riders of the clippers were easy to spot. Male passengers were dapper in their dark suits, ties, down-coats and hats. Many a man's head in the crowd, as attested by the great number of 314 bookings by American and British males, were covered in bowlers and wide-brimmed felts. Women travelers were seen attired in either high-fashioned suits or knee-length dresses; gloves and eye-catching hats, some of which were draped with veils that nearly hid their made-up

All aboard *American Clipper* for Lisbon and beyond! Canopied walkway connected LaGuardia's *Marine Air Terminal*, pier and mooring float. (*Photo Courtesy: Pan American World Airways*)

High above Atlantic passengers sat in stateroom-appointed comfort. Note yacht-styled blinds. (*Photo Courtesy: Boeing Aircraft Co.*)

Out of New York while passengers relaxed in assigned cabins, stewards prepared sumptuous lounge buffet spread. Over the years many passengers wrote Pan Am for clipper recipes. (*Photo Courtesy: Pan American World Airways*)

faces. A few were always swirled in fox stoles and mink coats. Often the elite refused to carry their overnight flight bags, having requested that they be taken aboard the clippers and placed in their pre-assigned ststerooms. It was called "style;" the men looked like gentlemen and the women like ladies. Both sexes played their roles well. As former 314 First Officer Black commented in late 1995, "the men in their fine silk suits and the women, the women passengers with their furs and their jewels. It was really something to see."[130]

Two metallic-sounding bells soon rang out indicating it was time for the crew to board and prepare the plane for takeoff. About 30 minutes later one more bell sounded, signaling passengers to embark. Holding and wearing coats, furs and hats and lugging briefcases and waterproof flight bags stuffed with night gear and toiletries, the gathered trooped out through the *MAT*'s two opened rear doors and briskly walked down the lengthy pier to the swaying wharf and the moored *Yankee Clipper*, her outboard engines already purring to purge the chill and moisture from opened cowlings.

When the banded few reached the NC-03, base crew in white overalls assisted them onto the gangplank stretched across the clipper's starboard sea-wing. Passing over the railed walkway and under the ship's main wing that seemed to appear as an extended roof-like structure, the air adventurers disappeared down into the plane's posh lounge. Magical-dancing water reflections spun a ballet web across the shadowed boarding bulkhead. Once inside, all mingled in the surface ship-resembled parlor while awaiting direction. A slight rocking sensation was felt beneath feet; it was as though one were aboard an opulent yacht rather than an aircraft. Water reflections duplicated their movements through portholes upon in-

ner bulkheads. Then, with a check of his list, a smartly dressed steward pointed all to their assigned staterooms and seats.

Minutes passed. Passengers became settled. Flight bags were placed beneath the divan-fashioned seats and coats, furs and hats removed. The Sands Point couple occupied the expensive aft suite. Off-duty crew and stewards roamed through the staterooms asking for attention regarding safety drill procedures. Life jacket and emergency exit handling were thoroughly explained between reassuring smiles.

Looking out the portholes, bulkhead-seated passengers noticed the water level was close to the panes — the clipper's hull sitting deep below surface, the lack of human weight loss made up in cargo and mail of which the latter alone totaled 5,000 pounds. On the wharf the legs of ground crew could be seen moving about, the men undoing the lines that secured the vessel.

Vibration from the engines soon became more evenly paced when the power plants were opened up and the NC-03 began to move out across Bowery Bay. Tiny beads of water flecked porthole panes. Ten or so minutes later the clipper picked up taxi speed when she reached Rikers Island Channel. Streams of sea water now

Out of Bermuda a formal dinner was prepared. If a 314 had many passengers calling for more meal-sittings, four stewards were added to flight: one to prepare food, two to wait on tables and one to cater other passenger-cabined needs. (*Photo Courtesy: Pan American World Airways*)

splashed across the cabin windows. Slowing down, the wide-bod-ied sky boat turned and slipped into the wind, the splash of water heard against her hull and seen striking the sea-wings. Then a mo-ment of hesitation while the first officer cleared with a forward-positioned launch for takeoff. A few seconds later a thunderous clap of engine power was heard as far as two miles. Thud went the hull as the mighty *Yankee Clipper* surged forward. Streams of water beads against panes vanished, replaced by sheets of light green waves.

Less than a minute later the NC-03 broke surface without much sensation. Small whitecaps dropped quickly away; the regatta in the harbor sizing down to toylike objects and the ear-pounding throb of the engines turning to a moderate thrum-thrum-thrum after the clipper leveled off from her angled climb as she passed over Man-hattan and the Statue of Liberty and headed southeast for Bermuda, first stop on the long trek to Lisbon.

Time suddenly became unimportant; a fantasy kingdom was before peering passengers as an endless, sparkling sea, blue skies and puffy white clouds enveloped the flying palace. Jaws soon got tired from the chewing gum passed out by the stewards before take-off to keep ears from stopping up in the non-pressurized liner. Once out at sea at 8,000 feet, coffee and sugar rolls were offered. A num-ber of passengers turned down the latter as they were slightly full from the rolls, coffee and lemon tea offered them earlier in the *MAT*'s waiting room. First timers strolled the plane's interior. Some settled in the midship lounge, the only cabin where smoking was permit-ted. Conversations centered on the war and Hitler's intolerable acts of aggression.

One hour into the flight a buffet brunch was elegantly served in the lounge. A folding table with cloth was set up between the two facing port divan sections leaving only the starboard tables avail-able for seating passengers in three shifts. The spread was as lavish as aboard an ocean liner: assorted cheeses, crackers, fresh fruits, salmon with lemon twist, sliced ham and beef, tomatoes stuffed with chicken salad, tossed green salad with assorted dressings, rel-ish dishes and lemon meringue pie. Wine and beer were offered as were the usual coffee, tea and milk.

Approximately 20 minutes from Bermuda stateroom lights were turned on. Stewards strolled through the various cabins and ordered that all porthole blinds be lowered. The island's Royal Navy had its base secrets to guard. To land or takeoff from Bermuda with cabin blinds up was forbidden. By captain's direction, the third and fourth officers descended the spiral staircase to assist stewards in helping passengers prepare their landing papers. Five hours out of New York the *Yankee Clipper* landed.

Metal pounding on water beneath the decking was heard and felt as the 314 whisked across Hamilton Harbor towards the Darrell Island seaplane base. Once moored, passengers gathered in the ship's lounge and lined the promenade until a Bermuda official in white ducks came aboard to gather the individualized sealed envelopes from the purser that contained visas, passports and other traveling

A call for dinner or other lounged events gave passengers an opportunity to get in some exercise by using the extensive promenade. (*Photo Courtesy: Clyde H. Sunderland/Pan American World Airways*)

documents. Bermuda's British authorities required that all Lisbon-bound passengers have a visa. Everyone was ordered to deplane. Unknown to passengers and clipper crews, England's BSC secret service scouts at Bermuda had orders to thoroughly check luggage, search all clippers and scour through their tons of mail, the latter enforced to uncover any possible Nazi-coded espionage communi-cations.

For some time all clipper passengers, after exiting the 314s and walking up the long pier, viewed a Scottish soldier in a kilt who stood at attention at the dock's entrance with rifle and bayo-net. The sight made many quiver — to face the reality that they were edging closer to the land at war. Upon entering the terminal's custom office passengers were told to sit in stiff-backed rows of chairs. One by one names were called out over a loudspeaker. Though somber, the majority of clipper passengers who crossed the base's threshold had nothing more to fear than a common bag-gage check during the normal two-hour stop. However, there were times when some travelers never again saw a fellow companion, the ticketed Lisbon seat remaining empty for the remainder of the trip.

Examination over, the small gathering was shown to a waiting room where tea and lemon squash had been prepared. Then it was often a brief stroll around the small facility. If the weather in the Azores, second clipper stop, had been reported as being poor then a longer wait was imminent and passengers and crew were usually put up at the *Manor Hotel* near Hamilton where the stewards became social directors, setting up tours and bridge and golf tournaments to entertain their grounded and often-times frustrated flock. After war broke out, much of the island was placed off limits to tourists and it called for a great deal of imagination to keep sky patrons content.

At 3:00 P.M. sharp, Bermuda time, and the weather reported good off the Azores, the *Yankee Clipper* lifted away, her bow aimed for Horta. Many faces stared out of the exposed portholes watching for convoys. Spotting one was rare. Flight planning had been purposely arranged so that clippers stayed clear of any escorted ship movements. If for any reason sea-going vessels changed course and were spotted by a clipper crew, airline orders were to immediately alter air course to keep such sightings away from any unsuspecting fascist agent who may have been aboard the clipper.

High tea was served in the grand salon an hour after leaving Bermuda. Passengers snacked on tiny English-type sandwiches, assorted French pastries and tea poured from a silver-plated pot artistically displayed upon a matching-tabled tray. The service was to accommodate British diplomats and couriers who frequented the New York-to-Lisbon route and return. An hour later cocktails were offered in all cabins along with trayed hors d' oeuvres . Time was nearly forgotten in a darkening sky while some passengers played cards in the lounge. Others just conversed or read. Some glanced through the Pan Am-printed brochures telling about the 314s' historical and record-breaking flights—that the Atlantic was successfully crossed by airplanes only 19 times out of 86 planes that tried to do so before the advent of the 314 and that on April 1, 1940, the NC-03 had flown from New York to Lisbon in 18 hours, 56 min-

Female early-to-rise amenities to primp one's self for the Horta arrival were elegantly provided and well thought out when planning for sky-havened powder rooms. (*Photo Courtesy: Boeing Aircraft Co.*)

utes. Nine months later, on Jan. 21, 1941, the NC-04 flew non-stop from Bermuda to Lisbon in 16 hours, 30 minutes. Passengers, as well as the general public, were fascinated by such accounts.

At 6:30 P.M., mid-Atlantic time, stewards informed salon-seated passengers to return to their cabins — they needed to set up the lounge for dining. Beginning at 7:00 P.M., travelers were called back to cabin D in 14 person shifts. A special "captain's table" was always arranged for the first sitting. Female passengers dressed in short evening gowns. Males were requested to wear ties and jackets to the formal occassion.

A selected transatlantic course was given final touches in the galley: chilled Utah celery; consomme madrilene; crisp, chilled salad; grapefruit supreme; assorted salted nuts; breast of chicken with peas francaise; parslied potatoes and steamed asparagus; ice cream; petit fours; and assorted cheeses; after dinner mints; a bowl of fresh fruit; brandied dates; and the perennial coffee, tea or milk. Beer and wine were again available. Beautifully catered, the ambiance for dining was similar to that of a superb French restaurant. Tables were covered with the noted starched Irish linen and set with the fine flute-edged china, glaze-sealed with blue Pan Am monograms, the heavy crystal water goblets and Gorham' s sterling flatware, the latter having to be accounted for by the stewards

Meal hours allowed Atlantic-fared clipper patrons to exploit their Paris fashions, a time for suits, ties, hats and dresses. (*Photo Courtesy: Pan American World Airways*)

at the end of each meal. Then there was the ever-present fresh-vased flowers, their perfume scenting each table arrangement.

Back in their staterooms after dinner, passengers found ample time for an interlude with a book, newspaper or story from a black leather-bound magazine. Later, when all had finished dining, the salon was returned to its former day state where further conversations, a rubber of bridge, backgammon, checkers, chess or other card games were enjoyed. Brandy or more coffee was always available.

Getting late, it was off to bed in curtained-off upper and lower berths that were longer and wider then those found aboard the super deluxe U.S. rail liners *20th Century Limited* and *Super Chief*., and Europe's swank *Oriental Express*. It wasn't uncommon to find a few passengers continuing on with conversation and card-playing in the lounge throughout the night during some of the flights — as though they didn't want the trip to end. But for the majority it was to cuddle between sheets covered with royal blue blankets and to still find time for one last chapter, a postcard to someone back in the States to be mailed from Horta, or a glance out a porthole at the stars and moon.

About 2:00 A.M., New York time, 6:00 A.M. Azores time, passengers were awakened by the stewards. Putting on robes and slippers, a quick pace to hotel-sized restrooms was made while gripping toilet articles and clothing. Men went forward to wash, shave and dress. Women walked aft to the ladies powder room. White-caps, far beneath the 314's American flag-painted wings, told all that the sea was running rough. While passengers dressed, stewards arranged the cabins back to day-seated flying. Watches were reset. Varied fruit juices, sweet rolls and freshly brewed coffee were offered in the lounge where passengers turned over their landing papers to the purser.

Quickly the clipper descended through a stratus cloud cover, circled and came in for a bounced landing off Horta. Swathed in swells of sea water, the undulating bow of the NC-03 was sailed forward until safely behind a breakwater. A launch carried everyone to shore while the Pan Am-stationed tender refueled the anchored flying boat. Taxicab drivers wound passengers up the hill past white-sailed windmills to the club house, a small, low white building with an arched veranda and a glass entrance door where a full breakfast awaited them consisting of cereals, eggs, bacon, toast,

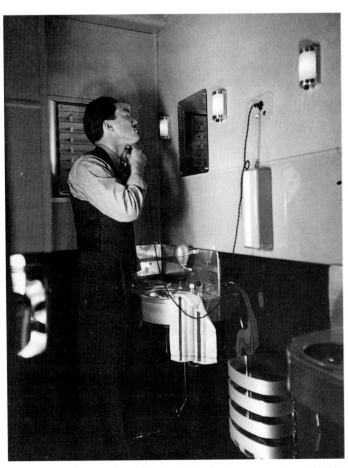

Free movement for a good-morning shave before landing was most appreciated by male travelers as compared to today's small-spaced, commercial jet-installed lavatories. (*Photo Courtesy: Boeing Aircraft Co.*)

Forceful Wright Cyclones helped wing-nip time across Atlantic when before the 314's advent it had taken days by ship. (*Photo Courtesy: Boeing Aircraft Co.*)

Chapter Twenty-one: Clipper to Lisbon

coffee and fresh fruit. A game of ping pong or a walk about the club's gardens smothered in chrysanthemums and hydrangeas followed. Word passed that waves had gotten worse. A five-hour delay was forecasted. Bridge, more ping pong and other past time events continued.

Cocktails and lunch at 11:30 helped to take minds off the dreaded prospect of a lengthy stay at Horta. Three and one-half hours later the news was good: waves had subsided to two feet. With no time to lose it was an eye-closed drive back down to the beach. Following a rough takeoff and a steep-arched climb the *Yankee Clipper* streaked for Lisbon at 3,000 feet. Sandwiches and coffee were trayed to cabined passengers. Somewhat bored and all talked out, a few just sat in the lounge and went into their own world of thought.

Gradually the clipper eased downwards. Stewards requested that passengers, if they had any, turn over their film-free cameras and landing papers for custom clearance and registering. Loaded cameras, due to war-time restrictions, were, for a time, prohibited by law in the Portuguese capital.

With a strong tail wind, NC-03 made good time in just over four hours. Ahead lay Cape Roco and blinking Sintra on the Iberian Peninsula, Europe's westernmost point. A few minutes later the giant air cruiser approached the wide estuary of the Tagus and was lowered to a 600-foot altitude. Flying east up river with landing lights ablaze, the sparkle of hilly Lisbon could be seen to port. With ease the *Yankee Clipper* was banked, circled and gracefully settled down onto the black carpet of water in a typical south-to-north landing. Seven glowing sea-runway lights strewn out by a *Panair* launch crew flashed past port windows in the darkness. Another adventure over the Atlantic had ended, then the safest mode of transportation across a U-boat-infested sea. Dead ahead lay twinkling Lisbon, the lights of which reflected atop current ripples forward of the taxiing 314. Behind the city's glitter was the ever-increasing interplay of international espionage. Secret developments of opposing German and Allied forces were hard at work, and the 314s, it was revealed later, played a major role in keeping the communication ties open between the dictatorial and democratic governments in a world partially at war and one headed shortly for a global conflict.

VIPs arrive Lisbon late afternoon aboard NC-06, circa 1940. Night landings on Tagus later became norm during war years. (*Photo Courtesy: Pan American World Airways*)

22

The Big Leap

Lisbon fast became the escape center for war-scarred Europe and to the free world by late 1939. By mid-1940, an estimated 80,000 refugees had poured into the Portuguese terminus in their flight from the ravages of Hitler's hell on earth. More trickled in with the average holding around 40,000 a year throughout the war. Besides the scurrying German Jews, most of the early arrivals came from Brussels, Paris and Warsaw in boxcars, available planes, buses or private limousines. Many of the uprooted and frightened souls who fled to Portugal ran ads in local Lisbon newspapers to sell all they had brought with them. Cars, furs and jewels provided exchange currency for transportation further west, if it could have been bought. Some had nothing while others hoarded millions in cash and costly ornaments. Two of the more fortunate refugees to get tickets on a 314 to America, along with their million dollars worth of precious gems, were the Baron and Baroness Édouard de Rothschild, one of Europe's highly regarded progenitors of wealth and world prestige.

A great number of U.S. citizens were helped out of Europe by Charles E. Shoemaker, Pan Am's chief traffic manager at Marseilles, and his assistant Édouard Houriet. Shoemaker, before being reassigned to Pan Am's base in New Orleans, hustled stranded Americans from Marseilles and Paris to Lisbon when the airline's Portugal-to-France clipper route was shut down after England declared war against Germany. Houriet was transferred to Lisbon to further assist Americans in getting seats on clippers destined for New York. As of August, 1941, 7,000 Americans were evacuated out of Lisbon on either 314s or surface ships. For many, the departure dates were slow in coming and nearly stagnant at times — even for priority clearances because both Pan Am and the steamship lines were obligated to honor those visas and tickets already acknowledged by authorities regarding the many bookings by foreigners prior to the crisis of England's declaration of war. Those persons lucky enough to acquire clipper tickets and American visas were told to report in person to Lisbon's Pan Am agents, such as Germano Serrao Arnaud, at the line's small traffic office on Rua Agousta in the business district, or at the clipper base the day before departure, to check luggage, weigh one's self in and to confirm reservations.

Cleared passengers waiting to leave soon found that Portugal's capital was a melting pot for the fearful and the uncertain, the brave and the calm. There were refugees who figured they had come as far as they could, trapped like foxes in a hunt if the Germans had taken over Portugal. Then there were the secret-opposing agents

who did their heroic deeds among the Portuguese populace who simply went about their daily lives in a peaceful and unconcerned manner. The relatively veiled calm among the Portuguese people was also seen and felt at the old European landplane airdrome at Sintra. Gathered were the flagships of the belligerents, parked about on the most international airport in the world. Airline signs read names of Aero Portuguesa, Ala Littoria, British Airways, Deutsche Lufthansa and Tráfico Aéro Español. At Pan Am's Cabo Ruivo base the German consul tried to meet each clipper arrival, no doubt to keep track of those who deplaned the world's foremost airliners.

Hotels were a hot bed of activity. The gleaming white *Aviz* had lost its sole transient position for Pan Am passengers in late 1939 when war was declared by England. As with the majority of Lisbon's hotels, the *Aviz* became a living quarters for the cream of refugees and a stop-over for diplomats, couriers and foreign correspondents. The ultra deluxe *Palacio Hotel* in Estoial was noted to be a German hangout. It was also reported to have served the best Manhattan cocktails in all of Europe. Modern in design with its exciting casino, the *Palacio* housed Portugal's Chief Gestapo Officer Biefurn who could, along with his band of civilian-clothed agents, observe Americans, Englishmen and Frenchmen waiting to get word their clipper, European landplane or ship was departing. Travelers were warned not to give up their passports or visas to the country's se-

Diplomats, couriers, newsmen and rich refugees hoarded 314 seats to America and spent long hours at Lisbon's small-spaced terminal located in city's refinery area adjacent to Tagus River to wait for few-scheduled departures and for any available ticket cancellations, the latter 99% nill. (*Photo Courtesy: Acme Newspictures, Inc./ Pan American World Airways*)

Coming and going transatlantic clipper mail sacks piled up on Lisbon's airway dock shortly after England declared war on Germany. Much of the mail was secret Axis-coded messages. (*Photo Courtesy: Pan American World Airways*)

cret "Policia" who supposedly were allied with the Gestapo because handed over documents were rarely returned.

Frequent clipper passengers passing through Lisbon were secret agent chiefs Donovan and Sir William Stephenson, the latter heading England's BSC, and Ernest Cuneo, President Roosevelt's special liaison officer. Harry Hopkins, special adviser to Roosevelt, made a covert 314 flight to Lisbon on his way to convene with England's Prime Minister Sir Winston Churchill in London in early January, 1941. Hopkins flew via the South Atlantic route to Guinea and then north to Portgual. After landing in Lisbon he was so tired he could barely rise out of his seat. On the return flight Hopkins was heavily guarded while carrying secret papers back to Washington, D.C. Diplomat and future Canadian Prime Minister Lester B. Pearson found himself extremely strained while in Lisbon in late December, 1940, after Stephenson asked him to secretly transport vital documents back to the British Security Coordination Unit in New York City. While at his hotel overlooking the Tagus River, Pearson encountered a German he once met in Geneva who, to his surprise, was one of the leading Nazi intelligence men working within Portgual and Spain. Pearson wasn't relieved of his anxiety until after he had flown across the Atlantic on a 314 and safely delivered his brown envelope to the proper authorities.

Foreign Correspondent and OSS agent Ben Robertson, Jr., told of a flight to Lisbon and what it was like to be in the "city of spies" in personal letters he wrote and mailed to family and friends in July and August, 1940, while en route to London to get first-hand war material for the then New York-based *PM* newspaper and during his covert OSS activities:

"I had a funny feeling getting in the clipper with all the ocean before it... We came across Long Island and headed east, and two hours later were told we would have to stop at Bermuda for the night as the weather was bad in the Azores. So instead of being on our way to a war, we found ourselves tourists in Bermuda. We got a thorough going over by the customs and spent the next 24 hours as guests of Pan American at the *Manor Hotel* near Hamilton.

"The next afternoon we left Bermuda about four in the afternoon, had dinner about six and then were told to put up our watches to nine o'clock as we would gain three hours during the night. We flew all that night at 11,000 feet; went to bed just as you do in a Pullman, and early the next morning we came down at Horta and stayed there about an hour refueling. In the afternoon we arrived in Lisbon...which was packed and jammed with thousands of the well-heeled, undamaged refugees who had come about as far as money would bring them... El de Wolfe came in disguised as a nurse — why, no one knows — and she brought along a couple of Rolls Royces. I was with Whitelaw Reid II* and we checked into town in a hotel at Estoril, 15 miles out of Lisbon. As we went to leave a couple of days later they told us they were very glad we were leaving; our room was wanted by the Baron de Rothschild.

"I have no idea how the mails are getting through to you. I hear that a hundred tons of air mail has piled up on the dock in Lisbon for the clipper, and that each clipper can take only five tons..."[131]

Together with the refugee situation regarding 314 travel out of Portugal was the network of secret agents who used the flying boats for communicating acquired German information across the Atlantic to Washington, D.C. Donovan had set up a spy organization on the Iberian Peninsula to counter possible invasion plans by Axis forces. The danger of a coup or invasion of Spain and Portugal remained a strong possibility from 1941 until the Spring of 1943.

In April, 1942, the first two OSS agents arrived in Lisbon by clipper to work under early Lisbon-based Col. Robert Solborg, former U.S. military attache in Paris. By late 1944, 20 OSS agents were spying in Lisbon with another 52 operating separately for the U.S. State Department. About 250 agents and sub-agents were stationed in Portugal and the Azores. Many of these freedom fighters, officiously intrusive figures to Hitler's cause, were transported overseas by the 314s. Any information regarding an Axis move, suspected Spanish aid to the Germans under the Franco-German co-operation scheme, or any vital background plans should the territory become a battlefield, were collected and sent to London and Washington, D.C. Top secret data was usually garbled to the U.S. and England over long distance phone calls. Less important, but still considered significant information was pouched by OSS couriers aboard clippers leaving Lisbon. In this crisis the 314s had become essential tools of aerial cammunication.

Whittling away at England's ground forces in North Africa during the time when espionage activities were being built up in Portugal and Spain was German Field Marshall Erwin Rommel's Panzer Division. "The Desert Fox's" men and tanks posed a threat

*Journalist and one of two sons of Ogden and Helen Reid.

to Egypt and the Suez Canal. An emergency lifeline of communications and supplies was eminent and foremost in the minds making up England's War Ministry headed by Churchill. Roosevelt and Churchill had secretly talked of setting up an American air assistance program to transport needed military planes, men and war materials to Egypt and the Far East, via Africa, to reinforce England's farthest outposts and to help keep China in the war. Caught in the defense web was Trippe and his 314 clippers.

Pan Am's chief left for England in June, 1941, shrouding the purpose of his journey under the cause of delivering a speech at a yearly "Wilbur Wright Memorial" dinner for London's Royal Aeronautical Society (RAS). Accompanying him was Gen. Arnold. The men first went to Lisbon aboard the *Yankee Clipper* and then to London on a KLM DC-3 "Dakota" previously used on the Holland-Batavia route. The plane had been taken to England before Amsterdam succumbed to Germany's tyranny and was operated by a half Dutch, half British crew.

Trippe gave his speech to devoted RAS members and British officers in an underground Air Ministry room. A uniformed Englishman then queried the honored guest if an American air supply system could be set up to help thwart Rommel's advances. Trippe believed so and outlined the possible trunk line on a map hanging from a wall. He traced the route with a finger down Pan Am's long-established run in the Caribbean and South America, and then suggested the new route across the South Atlantic to Leopoldville (now called Kinshasa) near the mouth of the Congo River dividing the Belgian Congo and French Equatorial Africa. From Leopoldville the route would V-branch north to include stops at Lagos, Nigeria, and east to Lake Victoria and north to Khartoum in Anglo-Egyptian Sudan and then into Cairo.

Later that night, while standing on the roof of his London hotel with Gen. Arnold, Trippe watched searchlights cut into the darkness and listened and viewed distant bombs explode about the city. A shadowy figure in the blackout approached and asked if the airline chief would have dinner with the prime minister.

At No. 10 Downing Street, and without Arnold present, Churchill and Trippe plotted an air system on maps after dinner and while tipping to mouths glasses filled with scotch and soda. England's sometimes obstinate and stout prime minister assured the U.S. executive he would hear from Roosevelt shortly after he arrived back in New York.

No sooner had Trippe stepped off a 314 at the *MAT* when he was militarily escorted aboard a landplane for Washington, D.C. From the Washington National Airport at Gravelly Point aside the Potomac River, Trippe was chauffeured directly to the White House where Roosevelt attentively listened to his account of Churchill's air supply needs. Report concluded, the President turned to future Secretary of the Navy James Forrestal and told him to financially set up aid for Pan Am to instigate the air support route tied in part to the "Lend-Lease Act" for emergency equipment. Thus was born the "Pan American Airways-Africa, Ltd." (PAA-AL) on July 15,

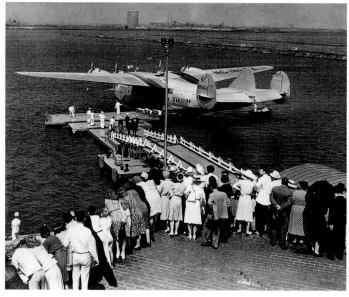

California Clipper, having undergone a major overhaul, draws attention from atop *Marine Air Terminal* before flying off to Miami base for more secret South American ADP surveys. (*Photo Courtesy: Pan American World Airways*)

1941, and the "Pan American Air Ferries, Inc." (PAAFI) on July 24th, both incorporated into the U.S. Army's "Air Transport Command" (ATC) in October, 1942, when Pan Am's contracts with the U.S. Government expired. The agreements would expand Trippe's empire, the biggest leap since establishing the Pacific route in 1935 and a route to be executed by 314 aircraft.

Three contracts between Pan Am and U.S. Government overlords were agreed upon and set into play on Aug. 12, 1941, that officially began the ferrying and transport services. The "Trans-African Transport Contract, DA W 53ac-415" provided for the institution and operation of Pan Am-operated 314 flights between the West Coast of Africa and Khartoum for the return of personnel in the ferrying system along with other desired African services. The second confidential document was issued as the "Ferry Contract, DA W 53ac-416" which gave Pan Am the authority to conduct its "PAAFI" supervision in the sending of coordinated military aircraft from the U.S. to and across the continent of Africa. The third and last written agreement, the "South Atlantic Transport Contract, W 535ac-21207," was entered for the authorization of 314 flights across the South Atlantic between Belem or Natal to Leopoldville, and other West Coast African bases, for the return of "PAAFI" personnel in conjunction with an established commercial transportation service as needed between Africa and the U.S. Gledhill, who handled the 314 sale with Boeing, was asked to provide the men and to organize and run the service at Pan Am's end. Gen. Arnold's assistant, hard-driving Brig. Gen. Robert Olds was placed in charge of the military aspect of the project and supervised the new route by working out schedules for the shipment of materials.

Two-hundred key Pan Am executives, flight and technical men, with another 300 employed airline personnel, were taken from their normal duties and sent to Africa as overseers in the directing of the air route base development. Gledhill and his Assistant Manager John H. Yeomans left from New York. From the Pacific Division came airport and maintenance experts Andrew D. Lewis and James A. Weesner. Brownsville and New Orleans-based men, such as Operation Manager George Kraigher, Chief Clipper pilot Henry C. Kristofferson, Supply Field Auditor John Forbes, Communications Supt. R. R. Fyfe, Senior Meteorologist George Matricians and Traffic Manager Shoemaker, were also drafted for the African commitment.

The majority of 1,500 additional handy men were drawn from all professions. There were radio operators, engine mechanics and construction workers, some of whom were non-technical. Four hundred American workmen and numerous African nationalities were contracted by Gledhill's and Arnold's offices to build landplane and seaplane bases at remote and unfamiliar port names, such as Accra, Fort Lamay, El Fasher, El Geteina, Kano, Khartoum, Maiduquire and Takoradi. A number of African bases, such as Lagos and Khartoum, were already in existence. They were stop calls for the early Imperial Airways' system, but were improved upon and incorporated into Gledhill's "PAA-AL."

Tropical Disease Specialist Dr. Lowell T. Coggeshall, heading a staff of doctors and nurses, took charge of the medical technicalities. Men going overseas to work on the airports had to be inocculated against diseases. Their first living quarters abroad were made of mere mud and thatched huts and the heat at many of the sites sizzled over 120 degrees Fahrenheit for days on end.

Beginning Oct. 5, 1941, chartered ships began to leave New York with tons of equipment to build both landplane and seaplane bases. Dynamite blasted away jungles and leveled hills. A rail bed of solid mahogany, the cheapest material available, was laid in West Africa to carry in equipment. English-based planes, trucks and camels were also used to haul about the precious supplies.

Eight of the 10 bases were operational 61 days after Roosevelt ordered Trippe to begin work. Completed in 1942, some 25,000 miles of trans-hemispheric airways were opened for military use, the largest task ever undertaken by an airline. What Pan Am had learned in constructing clipper bases in the Pacific had expanded tenfold in Africa and elsewhere.

No task seemed too great for Pan Am. America's only trans-oceanic airline was confronted by a Roosevelt demand in 1940 to secretly set up 25 landplane terminals and nine seaplane bases in the Americas to offset what was believed to be a German-Italian threat and a defiance of the Monroe Doctrine. Long-nesting foreign airlines of a suspicious nature operating to and from South America spurred the U.S. to counter any attempts of an Axis infiltration into Western soil. Two, Sociedad Colombo-Aleman de Transportes (SCADTA) of German heritage, and Italy's Lines Aerre Transcontinentali Italiane (LATI) were expressed as being a menace to U.S. security. Eventually SCADTA was neutralized and reformed into Aerovias Nacionales de Colombia (AVIANCA), whereas LATI was shut down after the U.S. entered the war.

At first Trippe refused to cooperate with Roosevelt on building bases in South America. He was justified in his reasoning in that if word leaked out that his airline was fronting a U.S. War Department scheme, governments of Central and South America could have revoked Pan Am's southern route system (Pan Am's financial right arm) thus jeopardizing America's defense system. Such a scandal could have been devastating to America's neutral world policy. But constant pressure from both Roosevelt and the U.S. State Department weakened Trippe's beliefs and he ultimately gave in. A contract was signed on Nov. 2, 1940, authorizing Pan Am to establish what other governments thought to be an expansion program and a turning away from flying boats for landplane operations.

Board member and Pan Am's Vice President Graham Bethune Grosvenor, a noted brilliant engineer, was entrusted by Trippe to take charge of base sites, yet replaced by Engineer Samuel F. Pryor, Jr., when Grosvenor was forced to resign due to serious illness. The bases, extending down to South America, had been coded by the U.S. Government as the "Rainbow Plan" and were referred to by Pan Am as the "Airport Development Program" (ADP), a prodigious effort expediated on Aug. 14, 1940. Within six months the organization had expanded to include an array of engineers and craftsmen that, together, hacked away jungles to form an aerial lifeline of secret government-funded ports-of-call.

Twelve million dollars were entrusted to Pan Am without any government auditing to build the airports some 550 miles apart. They stretched from Mexico and south to the airline's earlier Natal base on the eastern most touch of Brazil. By 1943, the world-scattered ADP totaled 90 million dollars that also aided in refurbishing and enlarging the original 25 airports already in existence. Another 25 were constructed to accommodate heavier landplanes in the mass ferrying under Gen. Arnold's ATC's Operational Comdr Maj. Gen.

Void of bow name, *California Clipper* became a common sight at Pan Am's Dinner Key base, Miami, during Pan Am-U.S. Government-sponsored ADP. (*Photo Courtesy: Pan American World Airways*)

Harold L. George.

Pan Am's Vice President of Management David S. Ingalls was put in command of the early PAAFI. Ingall's assistant and dispatcher John Steele put out the call for ferry pilots in the summer of 1941. America's neutral role kept young Army Air Corps flyers from participating. Steele's draw came from fly-by-night barnstormers, bush pilots from Alaska and Canada and the lobster flyers from Maine. There were Pan Am round-ups of aerial ranch hands, crop dusters, sport and stunt flyers, all wanting to get their pockets full of the $1,400 per-month salary wage, plus the 10 dollars a day expense gratuity. Those who hadn't already volunteered for armed air service poured into the command's headquarters located at the 97th Street's Art Deco-styled building at Miami's landplane airport.

Looking like many of Lisbon's refugees, the pilots came into town with all they had — some with only the clothes they wore. Tough and eager, a number of them rode in on motorcycles, in Model-Ts and other dilapidated vehicles. Others brought along their families and pets in rickety house trailers. A few even hitchhiked!

Ten-thousand air hours of experience placed one at the top as a

AMERICA'S NEW LIFELINE TO AFRICA

A 314 was chosen by artist to highlight airline's endeavors in constructing African bases which in turn gave U.S. a buffer against rising Axis tyranny. Ad appeared in many periodicals during ADP. (*Photo Courtesy: Pan American World Airways*)

captain, 5,000 hours as a co-pilot. Anything less required a 12-week navigation course set up by Pan Am in Miami. The training school was first thought of in the Spring of 1940, when Gen. Arnold called upon Trippe to have his company organize a series of courses to train young men in the aerial arts. The task, beginning in August, 1940, at Florida's University of Miami, required applicants to cram what Pan Am pilots, flight engineers and meteorologists had mastered in 13 years into a 350-hour time period. By November, 1941, 577 cadets were graduated. Of these, 166 were RAF students.

Pilot-training was headed by 314 Capt. Carl M. Dewey, veteran of all ocean divisions. Pan Am's Chief Navigator Charles J. Lunn, overseer of 20 instructors, schooled young pilots. The exact science of aerial navigation was conceived aboard the *Yankee Clipper* en route to Lisbon in the spring of 1940. Navigator Lunn was closely observed doing his work by Army Air Corps Brig. Gen. Delos C. Emmons, a passenger, who became so fascinated by Lunn's expertise that he asked Lunn if he could instruct young military flyers in the art of sky-reading. Thus was born the Pan Am school for navigation and meterology. Chief Meterologist Heaton B. Owsley, who assisted in pioneering weather forecasting, ruled over three other instructors skilled in teaching atmospheric variances.

Qualified cadets had to spend up to 50 air-hours, 16 of which were done at night, learning the complexities of dead reckoning, compass corrections, cloud formation, drift, radio (DF) coordination and the charting of sun stars.

Air courses were conducted aboard four antiquated flying boats, two twin-engined Consolidated Commodores previously used on the Miami-to-Panama run, and the former S-60 *American* and *Caribbean Clippers*. Aboard the Miami-based-overhauled planes were folding desks, chairs, sorted aerial navication equipment and a teacher's station located forward in the metal hulls. Between 10 and 12 students could be carried aloft at one time with an average of four hours of study given per flight over the Caribbean and Gulf of Mexico.

Graduated PAAFI pilots, one of which was David Binney Putnam, son of U.S. Publisher George Palmer Putnam, flew extra gas-tanked B-24s, North American-built B-25 "Mitchells" and Martin B-26 "Marauder" bombers from Miami to Trinidad, and then to Belem or Natal before the hop to Accra or Monrovia on Africa's Gold Coast. From West Africa the planes were ferried to such cities as Asmara, Ethiopia; Cairo, Egypt; Basra, Iraq; or Tehran, Iran. Many of the landing fields were still under developmont and in the rough. The once-called "girl-hugg'n, whisky-drink'n" mercenaries who flew for the air ferry's Atlantic Airways, Ltd., a fast-formed subsiderary set up betwen Pan Am and England's Air Ministry-governed BOAC in May, 1941[*], guided their radio-silenced planes with charts and close contour elevation calculations. Ingall's

[*]England's share of Atlantic Airways, Ltd., was incorporated into BOAC in December, 1941, whereas the ATC took over Pan Am's U.S. Government-sponsored interest in 1942.

Fifth 314 built at Robertsport, Fisherman's Lake, Liberia. Trippe had hopes 314s would encircle globe, but war and Washington politics halted his aim in Africa. (*Photo Courtesy: Pan American World Airways*)

recruited pilots delivered about 1,500 planes through Africa to the British, Dutch, Free French and Russians in the 22 months of operation before the PAAFI was absorbed by the ATC, the latter taking place on Oct. 15, 1942. Each delivery flight ranged between 2,500 and 16,600 miles.

Following the landmark ferry air-training program, classes were continued on into the war to teach navigation to U.S. Navy pilots. Navy courses, begun in October, 1942, were headed by Lt. Comdr. T. C. Brownell, a flight instructor from Annapolis. Some 5,000 cadets completed the prescribed schooling. A flight engineer training program for the Navy was also later set up by Pan Am at LaGuardia's *MAT* 314 hangar base. Fourteen-hundred flight mechanics, many of whom worked on 314s, were trained at the New York clipper base for war service.

Intricately a part of the international airport and ferry programs were two 314s, one of which was the NC-02 that had, as stated, been taken off the Pacific run in late May, 1941, and flown to New York where she was first upgraded to A314 standards, and then taken to Miami. Temporarily based at Dinner Key, the NC-02 was often seen whobbling in Biscayne Bay between long-hauled trips transporting ADP's Grosvenor, Pryor, L. L. Odell, Pan Am's superintendent of airport construction, base designer Andrew Lewis and other engineers to and from South America. Survey equipment, boxes of blueprints, charts, additional staff personnel and other supplies were carried aboard the *California Clipper*. The 314 began a pattern that became for 314s the U.S.' first "merchant marine ship of the air," a phrase linking airliners of the day to surface-floating vessels aiding the war effort.

Capable of flying long distances, the NC-02 was used to secretly survey for both landplane and seaplane bases from the air. When due for a major overhaul she was flown back to LaGuardia and then returned to Miami. At the end of her classified ADP support flights she was returned to Treasure Island for Pacific service.

Only two more A314s were purchased by Pan Am. Three of the second lot built, NC 18607 (NC-07), NC 18608 (NC-08) and NC 18610 (NC- 10), were sold to England. Boeing's production No. 2085, NC 18611 (NC-ll), was delivered to Astoria on July 2, 1941, and piloted to San Francisco by Capt. Gilbert B. Blackmore (1904-1997) for Pacific duty. Blackmore, who joined Pan Am in 1934, and who spent about 6,126.41 hours aboard 314s during their reign with Pan Am, had made a test flight around Lake Washington with Allen at the controls before taking over the ship.

Twenty-eight days after the experienced Blackmore, a senior captain who acted as first officer on the 314 inaugural passenger flight over the Atlantic and a graduate of Purdue University, flew the eleventh 314 built to Pan Am's Pacific Division, No. 2086, NC 18612 (NC-12), the last Model A314, was aired to Oregon and then to San Francisco under the expertise of former South American clipper, legendary and famed Capt. Steven Bancroft. Originally planned for Pacific service, NC-12 was instead sent on to Miami shortly after Sept. 18, 1941, to join her NC-02 sister in unique, quasi-commercial and military-roled flying to southern ports. She later became the first 314 to conduct scheduled flights (excluding the clippers operating out of Bolama during winter months) to the western shores of Africa carrying war VIPs, mail, express and air ferry pilots returning west across the South Atlantic for the long trek home to the U.S.

All exterior markings on the last six ships built were the same as on the first models when they left their Seattle plant (dubbed by Boeing upon departure as "fly aways") except for the prow numbers that had indicated the number of four-engine aircraft owned by Pan Am. The double digit figures were excluded on the second group of A314s to save time and ensuing labor costs since the airline removed the identification numbers prior to painting on bow names.

Boeing's eleventh Model A314, first test flown on June 30, 1941, and delivered to Pan Am from Astoria by Capt. Blackmoore, was, without ceremony, titled *Anzac Clipper* after the fighting men of Australia and New Zealand who comprised the shock troops for the British advance into Libya in 1940 that beclouded Hitler's outlook for southern conquest. A ceremonial maiden flight to New Zealand was planned by the Pacific Division for the NC-11 in June but Boeing was behind in their delivery timing, so NC-09 made the trip under the disguise of the *Anzac Clipper*. Then, at the last minute, flight schedules were again disrupted and the NC-09, still faking the name *Anzac Clipper* painted on the bow, left for Singapore instead. Unknown to the welcoming party at the other end of the line that the ship was really the *Pacific Clipper* rather than the *Anzac Clipper*, six Anzac officers stationed in Malaya greeted the NC-09's arrival where formalities were exchanged. Upon the NC-11's arrival at Treasure Island from Astoria, and the NC-09's return from Singapore, the clippers were each given their proper prow names.

No christening ceremonies were planned or given the last six-built models; the intrinsic qualities of war dominated the less im-

Next-to-last A314 on Elliott Bay before quick trial flight and delivery to Pan Am, July 1, 1941. (*Photo Courtesy: Boeing Aircraft Co.*)

portant social events of the period. Pan Am executives, as they had done with NC-05, NC-09 and NC-11, voted in the name *Capetown Clipper* for NC-12, a bow message clearly advertising Trippe's breakthrough into Africa — another leap towards his quest of an around-the-world American air service. A route linking Leopoldville and Capetown, the latter at the southern west tip of Africa, was in the making but had to be abandoned due to complications regarding the "Johnson Neutrality Act" (JNA) which forbid any commercial plane to fly in and out of belligerent territories.

Upon delivery of NC-12 following its test flight of July 28th, Pan Am had given serious consideration of leaving the aircraft on the Pacific and taking the one remaining Martin-built M-130s and placing it on the proposed South Atlantic run. Compared gross weight and power load tabulations proved, however, that one 314 could do the work of two M-130s. Regardless of the type of equipment used over the pond, the JNA posed a problem, especially for clippers that would operate near Bathurst on the Gambia River where a U.S. seaplane base was situated. It was an area surrounded by the Vichy French loyal to the Germans and only 85 miles from their Dakar headquarters. Yet Roosevelt was insistent on opening an aerial skyway to and along Africa's coast.

Concerning Trippe was the possibility of a 314 loss from enemy contact, and he did not want his company to bear the high insurance rate that was deemed necessary in the event of a clipper downing. Pan Am, per se, did not insure their aircraft through an agency. Instead they saved large amounts of revenue per year to cover any accidents. The U.S. Government compromised and provided a clause under the U.S. War Department's Aug. 12, 1941, South Atlantic Transport Contract whereby it would buy the *Capetown Clipper* at a reduced price of $900,000 and then charter it back to the airline at a dollar-a-day rental fee. By the War Department's purchase, the NC-12 was a state plane exempt from

the JNA restrictions, insured by the government and allowed free operation to and from Africa.

Trippe received some government flak for selling the plane over its across-the-board appraised value, but stood firm by stating that a 314 was worth more than the asking price. His assertion was correct, since Boeing had advised Pan Am in January, 1942, per the former's request, that if they were to undertake the same 314 building project, a rough estimate of 35.7 percent increase per boat over the original cost would be required. Not included in Boeing's analysis were the ever-changing inflationary costs in the material market since the time the 314 and A314 models were originally built. Management and profit fees, engines, propellers, in-flight equipment and certain other sub-contracted interior fittings were also not averaged into the percent raise.

West Coast African terminals built or modified for 314 service were four in number. Starting with Leopoldville (shared with BOAC), they extended north to Lagos, a BOAC flying boat port, Fisherman's Lake in Liberia, Bolama and Bathurst, the latter also established earlier by BOAC. Fisherman's Lake, a coastal lagoon adjacent to the Atlantic 53 miles north of Monrovia, Liberia, had been briefly surveyed by air and ground and chosen for the major U.S. military port-of-call. Pan Am needed an alternate northern base in the event British-occupied Lagos and Bathurst were attacked and Portugal fell to the Germans, taking with them Portuguese Guinea and the airline's winter stop at Bolama.

Separated from the Atlantic by sand dunes and dense jungle, swamps and thick reed to the east, north and south, the nearly round inlet six miles in diameter was selected for its fine year-round climatic conditions and relatively calm waters. Civilization at Fisherman's Lake was near nonexistant except for the small missionary village of Robertsport near the northwest mouth of the wide lagoon that fed into the ocean, and headed by Episcopal Father Harvey Simmons and wife.

Last A314 built on step before lift-off for trial flight over Puget Sound. Test pilot "Eddie" Allen was at helm. (*Photo Courtesy: Boeing Aircraft Co.*)

"Fish Lake," as it was later dubbed by clipper crews, was the last 314 base established on the Dark Continent's west coast. It wasn't even fully surveyed at the time when the government-owned *Capetown Clipper* made the inspection flight to the West African ports in November, 1941, prior to inaugurating regular air mail and proposed passenger service the following month. Not until mid-1942 was the base completely ready to fulfill its secret war-time duties along a dynamic aerial route system intended to stave further advancements of Nazi-dominated Europe.

Base establishment at "Fish Lake" first began shortly after Trippe returned to his New York office following talks with Churchill in London and Roosevelt in Washington, D.C. Calling a meeting of the minds, orders came down for Capt. Gray to quickly gather together a crew for a secret survey mission. Selecting a reliable lot that had been under his command during the 1937 S-42 Atlantic survey flights, Gray and men, that included Capt. Masland acting as first officer, departed July 4, 1941, aboard the NC-06 for Africa. Only Gray knew the purpose of the trip that he referred to as "it" — to scout and determine the best site available for a combination U

S. military seaplane/landplane base. Lagos, Bathurst and Leopoldville, like Bolama, were basically commercially orientated stops for both U.S. and English-operated aircraft. President Roosevelt was advised to establish an all-out secret U.S. jumping-off port where eventually C-47s could transport men and war materials further on across Africa to Kartoum and Cairo.

Flying south, Gray took the 314 to Natal, via Port of Spain, and across the South Atlantic to Bathurst where a number of American mechanics en route to Cairo to ready a group of damaged RAF P-40 fighters deplaned. The next day Gray and men flew to Bolama 150 miles down coast where Gray waited for a message from New York advising him of his next venturous stop. Four nights and three days later he winged the 314 500 miles further south, always flying low and making passes over inland bodies of water. It soon became evident to Masland that Gray was looking for a deep-watered inclave for clipper moorings. Then, for the second time along the aerial pathway, Gray spotted Fisherman's Lake nestled in a large flat area that he believed to be suitable for a U.S. military land-constructed runway — an area interrupted only by the 900-foot-high Cape Mount at whose base rested the village of Robertsport. Gray and men surveyed the area from the air by making several low passes and checked the location on maps. It was considered by all to be an ideal spot that would offer 314 crews a takeoff point of which would be the shortest distance between Africa and South America and, at the same time, would allow clippers to carry a sizeable payload using the least amount of fuel per crossing. Another advantage was the locale was within pro-American Liberia. Acquiring landing rights from the country's government would not pose to be a problem.

With observations correctly charted, Gray returned the 314 to Bolama, north to Bathurst to pick up a band of military personnel, and then was off for a non-stop flight to Belem and then north to New York to complete the mission. Times had become increasingly intense and some Washington officials began to take a harder look at the 314's capabilities that were far above and beyond the plane's original purpose for design — they began to think of the aircraft in military terms.

23

Three for England

The sale of the NC-12 to the U.S. Government had not been the first such type transaction. Three of the second lot of A314s, as previously noted, were sold earlier to Britain's Air Ministry for BOAC operations. Background of the sale began in early 1940 when a group of Royal Canadian Air Force and BOAC crews became involved in organizing the North Atlantic Ferry Service's Northern Wing Command, the former of which was entirely absorbed by BOAC on Sept. 24, 1941. The command had been formed to transport twin-engined Lockheed-built "Hudsons" and four-engined Consolidated B-24 "Liberator" bombers from Canada to the British Isles, via Newfoundland. Great Britain's back was to the wall in defense against Germany and the isle was in desperate need of long-ranged, four-engined equipment in which to carry air ferry crews and VIPS back to Canada following each such flight to the east. What few large flying boats England possessed were needed to secure their home Empire routes to the Far East and for patrolling the seas off England's coast in order to assist in the sinking of any menacing U-boats. The last BOAC commercial run across Europe was conducted on June 11, 1940. Emphasis by the line was then given to support the long-established "Horseshoe Route," a looped air highway that connected Africa, India and Australia.

In early August, 1940, two British delegates, Director Air General Representative and Under-Secretary of Air Capt. Harold Balfour, and England's high British Purchasing Commissioner (BPC) A. C. Boddis, proceeded directly to Canada and the U.S. aboard the English commercial flying boat *Clare* on behalf of their Air Ministry Command to open talks regarding the procurement of eight converted B-24s to be used either for landplane service across the Atlantic or for use on the Empire routes, both calling for long-range aircraft. At the meetings that followed, which included the successful purchasing of the "Liberators," the esteemed Pan Am 314 Atlantic operations came to fore and the possibility that maybe Pan Am would sell some of their world-acclaimed liners for the sake of England's dire plight. It was at that point of discussion that Balfour and Boddis contacted not only Pan Am but the U.S. Government as well, the latter of which was necessary for clearance of equipment under wartime conditions. The request was for the acquisition of two luxury-appointed A314s for carrying England's VIPS, not across the Atlantic, but to and from Africa. Roosevelt agreed for the sale.

With the U.S. Administration's approval for a sale, negotiations between Pan Am and the British officials, acting on behalf of the Air Ministry, were opened up in New York. Two A314s were sold to the British on August 22nd with an option for a third if Pan Am had to close down its Lisbon service in the event Portugal was occupied by the Germans. Eight days after the verbal agreement came to an end, a formally-printed contract was signed between Pan Am's Gledhill and BPC's Boddis. The 19-page document related to the purchasing of a third A314 as based on the needs of BOAC and not because of the threat of the possible Lisbon closure.

Each A314 was sold for $1,035,400, minus radio equipment which was an added expense of an unknown amount. Part of the agreement specified 12 additional spare Wright Cyclone GR-2600-A2A engines at $16,753 each, plus six Hamilton Standard propellers totaling $21,750. Payment was to be made in cash or check upon delivery. If the aircraft and parts were not ready by Oct. 15, 1941, buyer had recourse to cancel its end of the contract.

Under the terms, Pan Am agreed to the consignment of training a BOAC crew in A314 operations, and would fly the ships from Astoria to New York at their expense. Part of a secret cablegram sent by Boddis from the British New York Consul to the Air Minis-

Boeing's Allen (left) familiarizes British Capt. Kelly-Rogers with a NX-07's bow beaching gear-lock cable hook as tail of second-purchased A314 emerges from Assembly Building No. 3, Plant No. 1. (*Photo Courtesy: Boeing Aircraft Co.*)

try in England at the near close of negotiations on August 22nd read in part:

"We are inquiring into cost of insurance of boats during period of flights across America and training of crew... On present inadequate information, cost of insurance might be of the order of $30,000 in each case subject to our bearing 30 percent of a loss."[132]

Clause eight of the contract specified that if Pan Am lost one of their 314s, or one was damaged to the point of not being able to be repaired within six months, they had the right to buy back one of the clippers. Other related data included in the sale were 12 A314 handbook manuals covering maintenance procedures; one blueprint for each of the assembly and installation parts; one master assembly blueprint and accompanying list used as a key to figuring the installation of new or repaired parts; one set of blueprints covering general upkeep; and log books for BOAC crews and ground mechanics.

Stipulated in the "Reproduction and Resale" clause was the mutual understanding that BOAC was not allowed to manufacture any design features of the planes or use the word "clipper" in their operations. The foreign line was also not permitted to resell the ships outside the British Commonwealth of Nations, and if they did so that the future purchaser was held bound to the same agreements as outlined in the contract. Nearly six years later, in April, 1946, Robert N. Ward, aviation staff writer for the *Seattle Post-Intelligencer*, uncovered a twist in the story of the sale when he uncovered the following and wrote:

"The deal was closed, it is said, by an unauthorized under-executive of the British firm. His superiors were apoplectic and cooled down only when the clippers proved themselves an admirable bargain."[133]

And a stupendous transaction it was! When Balfour and Boddis were at closing agreements with Gledhill, other unnamed foreign powers inquired into the prospect of purchasing 314s, either from

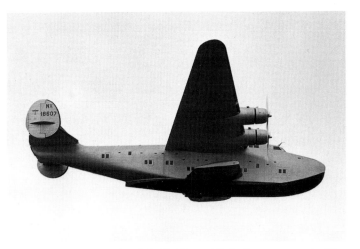

NX-07 undergoes brief trial period with Allen and Kelly-Rogers at controls. Allen showed British flyer tricks of flying 314A. (*Photo Courtesy: Boeing Aircraft Co.*)

Boeing or Pan Am, as they were the world's only aircraft, and likely to be the only ones available for some time to come, that could meet the emergency war needs of the period for use in transporting large quantities of priority payloads. The representative seekers were turned down. Indications for the rejections were that the asking price for an air queen was well above that which was squeezed out of the Air Ministry. Besides, commercial aircraft production in the U.S. was on the wane, and hence there were just not enough 314s to go around.

Meanwhile, back in England, BOAC began arrangements for delivery and in setting up crew assignments for their new service known as "The Boeing Flight," and renamed "No. Five Operating Division" near war's end. Placed in command was BOAC's top-ranking pilot, Capt. John Cecil Kelly-Rogers, who made the airline's last flight over Europe before war conditions closed down the vital route. Thirty-four-year-old Irish-born Kelly-Rogers, son of a ferry-boat captain, had served in the RAF in the 1930s before joining Imperial Airways. He flew England's first air mail to the U.S. with the S .23 *Caribou* in 1939, and made more news that same year when, under the most difficult conditions, took out the downed flying boat *Corsair* from a Congo swamp in which it had made a forced landing. For his brave effort he received the "Order of the British Empire," one of England's highest awards for valor beyond the call of duty.

BOAC's London Office of Operations held a confidential meeting on Jan. 8, 1941, to grant permission for the assignment of the first A314 crews. Twenty-five men were chosen that ranged from captains, first and second officers, to radio communicators — the procurement of ships and crew selections of which were considered secret information. Boddis stated in his August, 1940, cablegram:

"We have undertaken to keep the transaction as secret as possible and to avoid public disclosure. In view of importance attached to this by P.A.A., would you please ensure that our undertaking is

In civilian dress, BOAC's Capt. Kelly-Rogers (second left) and "Boeing Flight Crew No. 1" line up on test-mooring barge securing NX-07 before returning to San Francisco to await second phase of delivery flight to England. (*Photo Courtesy: Boeing Aircraft Co.*)

rigidly observed in the U.S... The parties hereto agree to deal with the subject matter of the agreement as confidential, and to use their best efforts to avoid public disclosure of the existence hereof; provided, by the parties hereto if required by a governmental rule or regulations, or, in their respective opinions, by the national interest of the United States or Great Britain."[134]

Since the sale was a separate entity, and not part of the lend-lease aid to Great Britain, those involved with the transfer thought it wise to keep all purchase information under cover. The boats, in general, were to be used for war business, an activity best kept confidential.

Able to select his own crew from the 25 qualified men assigned to "The Boeing Flight," Capt. Kelly-Rogers and party left England for New York in late January, 1941, after many time-scheduled delays at the Boeing plant. Upon their secret arrival by 314 clipper out of Lisbon, the men entered a training program under Pan Am's chosen Capt. Gray and his crew at LaGuardia. When the A314 air and ground-schooling was completed, the BOAC men proceeded by air to San Francisco under separate orders where they were to wait for further word. Meanwhile, Gray and his crew flew to Seattle whereupon Kelly-Rogers was notified and told to come north to observe order No. 2081 as she was launched into the Duwamish prior to her three-day taxi and two-hour CAB flight-testing period that occurred on March 3rd. Following a brief breaking-in period with test pilot Allen, Kelly-Rogers and crew returned to San Francisco to await delivery of the ship at Treasure Island by Gray who picked up the boat at Astoria on April 3rd.

The following day Gray checked-out the BOAC men once more in the skies above San Francisco that included a number of take-offs, landings and mooring techniques with the NC-07. Both crews then took the NC-07 to Los Angeles' San Pedro on April 5th, and the next day to Miami — a flight that marked the first non-stop crossing of the U.S. with a 314. On April 8th, Capt. Gray brought the boat into New York where Pan Am spent several days discharging itself of the intransigent contract obligation in checking out the foreign crew. Kelly-Rogers remarked many years later: "On the 18th of April, 1941, BOAC formally took delivery of the aircraft and payed over the final check. This was done by flying the plane from LaGuardia to Port Washington, the reason being to avoid the new sales tax which had been introduced by Mayor LaGuardia. The deal was completed at Port Washington, and then the aircraft came into British ownership on that day and was free to return to LaGuardia.

"However, there was one small snag because all the paper work hadn't been done. It was now a British-owned aircraft, but carried an American registration; and thus, under the CAB and CAA regulations of the time, it could not be allowed to fly until the necessary permission was forthcoming. It couldn't stay at Port Washington, so I had to taxi it all the way back to the *Marine Air Terminal* at LaGuardia. Needless to say, I wasn't slow about it! In fact I revved

Camouflaged *Bristol* wings away from New York to England, 1941. (*Photo Courtesy: British Overseas Airways/Gordon S. Williams Collection*)

her up so that I got her up on step and I taxied at high speed. I can assure you that I flew her most of the way, though only a foot or two above the water."[135]

Back at LaGuardia, the A314 was towed out of the water on a Pan Am-owned dolly and tractored into the base's hangar. For the next 33 days, at an undisclosed and additional cost to Britain, the plane underwent new registration markings and camouflage painting.

In that Britain was at war, the Air Ministry had ordered that all of their aircraft, commercial or otherwise, be concealed as best as possible from enemy planes or ships. Black paint on the ship's hull bottom was removed and replaced with a silver-lacquered coating that was later darkened. Sponson, wing and tail stabilizer undersides were at first left with their original Boeing finish but in time were also camouflaged, while the fuselage, propellers, wings, tail fins, and upper sea-wing and stabilizer surfaces were swabbed with mutable coats of dark green and blending earthy-brown colors. Drab looking, the final effect seemed to strip away the grace and sleek beauty that was once NC-07. Other markings included the name *Bristol* after the city in England which appeared in medium blue-painted letters outlined in white on the plane's bow panels.

Trimmed in white and underlined with stripes of red, white and blue, large black, and somewhat unappealing, G-AGBZ British civil registration letters were applied on both sides of the upper aft hull between the inward rear wings' trailing edges and tail. The outer tail fins were void of registration marks except for a small, square-shaped touch of Union Jack colors. Black port wing lettering took in the first two license characters as seen on both upper and lower surfaces. The last three registration letters appeared in the same locale on the starboard wing. A British flag was added to both sides of the forward hull section just below the bridge's side window panels.

Subdued in her war paint, *Bristol* was reboarded by Kelly-Rogers on May 22nd for BOAC's inaugural A314 flight over the

Chapter Twenty-three: Three for England

Atlantic, via Bermuda, Lisbon and Foynes. Accompanying the chief pilot and his crew were BOAC Captains Jack R. Alderson, of the *Cavalier* ditching and who later became BOAC's Director of Development, and A. C. Loraine, both of whom were earlier selected to head "Crews No. 2 & 3" of "The Boeing Flight." The trip was, as were all BOAC A314 voyages, numbered in sequence and designated "Mid-Atlantic Eastbound No. 1 (MAE-1). After two days in Ireland, the *Bristol* was taken back to Lisbon and south to Bathurst and Lagos. She returned to Foynes in early July with 800 kilos of mail, 44 passengers and a 11-man crew, then a record BOAC flight. From Foynes the former NC-07 returned to Baltimore, via Newfoundland, carrying ferry pilots, VIPS and tons of war mail. Once back in England, Kelly-Rogers and his original A314 crew began checking out the remaining assigned Boeing crews.

Clearance for the British-owned Boeing boats to land back in the U.S. had been worked out between BOAC, Pan Am and the CAB during the interval when *Bristol* was undergoing her dreary exterior modification work. England's international air line had secured the landing permit through the old reciprocal agreement of the late 1930s. BOAC had insured Pan Am they did not intend for pay fare competition at that time, but rather only wanted to have their new A314s overhauled in the U.S. after every 120-air-hours per ship (minor maintenance was done at BOAC's Hytha Marine Base in Poole, England). It was considered more economical to acquire the some 14,000 spare parts needed to maintain the crafts in the U.S., thus avoiding high insurance and shipment costs by freighter across Germany's submurged wolf packs seemingly sempiternal in the North and mid-Atlantic. Common sense had ruled at the discussions between the CAB and BOAC that a safer state existed if the A314s were serviced in America, a maintenance operation away from the unpredictable air-blitz attacks against England's ports and cities.

Baltimore was selected for the BOAC overhaul port for its basic ice-free conditions during winter. Trippe put out the welcome mat by chartering out his line's harbor facilities. A British-trained ground crew was sent from England to coordinate efforts alongside a group of technicians supplied by Pan Am. Boeing was requested to arrange for the shipment of the three beaching gears.

Only a tidbit of news regarding the sale was released to the public when Arthur Purvis, chief of the British Purchasing Commission stationed in Washington, D.C., returned from Britain on a Pan Am 314 in December, 1940. He broke silence of the sale from his headquartered offices after going abroad to confer with the Air Ministry regarding delivery dates along with other pertinent A314 information. Purvis had been deeply involved in implementing the arrangements and cleared the way for the transaction after he conferred with U.S. Under Secretary of State Sumner Welles who acted as the U.S.' intermediary sales spokesman.

Morris Wilson, British representative of the Minister of Aircraft Production in the U.S., issued Purvis' statement when he said, "We are pleased to announce that Pan American Airways has agreed to the transfer to Great Britain of three of their six new transoceanic flying boats which are now nearing completion in the Seattle plant of the Boeing Aircraft Company.

"The British Government are gratified that the United States has granted consent and approval for our purchase of these aircraft which are to be used to maintain essential lines of Empire communication.

"We also appreciate Pan American Airways' agreeing to the transfer of these new aircraft, notwithstanding the pressing needs of their own services."[136]

The dates and delivery port names (New York and Baltimore) were not released to the public as were other purchase details — all

Mirrored in Duwamish, last A314 for England is launched, June, 1941. (*Photo Courtesy: Boeing Aircrart Co.*)

In a British-havened port, war-painted *Bangor* awaits next trip. (*Photo Courtesy: British Overseas Airways/Gordon S. Williams*)

kept secret for reasons of national interests on both sides of the Atlantic.

The second A314 sold to BOAC was the eighth model built, construction order No. 2082. Lights blaring, she was launched into the night-blackened Duwamish on April 17, 1941, and, after dawn, given a brief CAA taxi and test flight on April 19th. Capt. Gray took out the American-registered NC-08 on April 23rd and arrived in Baltimore four days later after making the usual stops in Astoria, San Francisco, Los Angeles and Miami. Once inside the Baltimore hangar, the A314 was stripped of her U.S. registration plate numbers and camouflaged. She departed for service on June 21st under the command of Capt. Loraine who had been checked out by Kelly-Rogers on the *Bristol*. Loraine and four other BOAC crewmen had made the delivery flight with Gray out of San Francisco. When the liner left for Europe, the British-registered G-AGCA bore the name *Berwick* honoring the city in New Brunswick, Canada.

BOAC's last A314, order No. 2084, was test-flown on June 6th and also delivered to Baltimore by Capt. Gray. Joining Pan Am's skipper in San Francisco on June 10th, the day after Gray left Seattle and Astoria, was BOAC's Capt. Alderson and his four men. The two crews set the NC-10 down on the northern end of Chesapeake Bay on June 12th. Once camouflaged, G-AGCB took to the air for its first transatlantic flight on July 23rd. Her bow read *Bangor* after the U.S. city in upper-State Maine. The names of the three ships symbolically stood for the old unification between England, Canada and the U.S., and also for the bond represented in modern times against a common foe that stirred up clouds of war.

In that the bow titles only identified each A314, BOAC officials desired an overall service logo by which to label the craft. "The Boeing Flight" term was used strictly by the airline for flight scheduling and found unsuitable for public acceptance. What Britain's international airline desired was a short, one-word symbol that would catch the public's attention in the same manner as Pan Am had done with the word "clipper." In October, 1941, British newspapers ran want-ads in their editorial columns. Readers

were asked to submit a word that typified the A314 flights. Staff members of Britain's world air transport had previously been given the chance to select a catch word. Out of the submitted titles came "cutter," but it was too synonymous with "clipper," the latter being expressed by the British as relating to all large, commercial flying boats — even to their Short and Solent models. Shortly after the ads appeared, the word "speedbird" was coined, not only for the A314s but for all future BOAC skyliners. The "speedbird" logo first appeared in medium blue on the three A314 bows just above the individualized names, an artistic version depicting a bird in flight which, shape-wise, resembled the tropical flower bird of paradise.

A first-class service was maintained aboard the British-owned speedbirds for allied officials flying between Foynes, Lisbon, Bathurst and Lagos. Landplanes continued the service to Khartoum, north along the Nile to Cairo and beyond. To reduce the heavy weight load factor per flight, some of the A314 interior bulkhead panelings dividing staterooms were removed and replaced with stretched canvas viewed as athletic trampolines standing on end. When returning to Baltimore, starting in late September after the northern route became icebound, the ships were flown across the South Atlantic from Bathurst to Belem, north to Trinidad, Bermuda and into Baltimore. Often times the flights from Bathurst were made direct to Trinidad. During the summer months when overhaul was required, the Boeings were returned to Foynes across the North Atlantic, via Botwood or Gander, and flown back to England and Ireland in the winter, via the mid-Atlantic route through Bermuda, Lisbon, Poole and then Foynes. Each crossing carried tons of mail, cargo and non-paying government personnel.

Following a number of round-trip flights down the coast of Africa, BOAC was able to supplement the service with landplanes connecting England, Portugal and Africa. When Germany's threat of taking over Portugal dissolved, and the Mediterranean was still closed to non-military aircraft, the flying boat speedbirds became available to operate strictly across the Atlantic on the tri-route system as mentioned. The A314s, using the African run during the winter months, flew four times weekly in each direction and were the only British planes during the war to fly under non-austerity conditions. Maintaining such a service, especially the long way around, via the South Atlantic in winter, was wearisome to both crew and VIP passengers.

Kelly-Rogers said of the South Atlantic crossing, a route he surveyed for BOAC with a A314 in late 1941:

"It was a long 'ol trip, and we kept going continuously, but only with the help of what we called 'multiple crews.' We carried a double crew and really stood watches as one would do on a ship. On the long sectors we were always as heavily laden as possible because we took on as much fuel as we could. In that condtion, the A314s tended to be rather tail heavy. In fact we flew with the stick very nearly on the dashboard for the first few hours of the flight until we burned off some fuel and the trim improved."[137]

Chapter Twenty-three: Three for England

In that the Atlantic routes were basically the same for both Pan Am and BOAC, speedbird and clipper crews intermingled at the shared ports, many becoming lifelong friends across the sea. Capt. Masland wrote about a mutual flight period with Kelly-Rogers while at Foynes when both men were scheduled to take out their 314s across the North Atlantic at about the precise time:

"One noteable evening there were four of us in Foynes. I had just come up from Lisbon intending to refuel and cross the Atlantic for a return to New York by way of Botwood. The flight from Lisbon was most interesting... Outside of encountering the German off-shore patrol in clear skies, where heavy cloud cover had been forecast along with a dawn arrival (both wrong), the weather patterns that I had found were completely at variance with what the Foynes' meteorologist (met) service produced on my arrival there (It must be remembered that the met officers at neutral Foynes were denied access to all met services other than their own. I often wondered how they did as well as they did with little more than instinct and reports on the hour from Valencia at Ireland's western tip for forecasting North Atlantic weather).

"In this case I was sure they were wrong. Also it was beyond the normal time for shutting down the North Atlantic to the 314, as it could not handle any amount of ice. It must have been about Oct. 17, 1941. I elected to tie up at a mooring for the night. Kelly-Rogers decided to go and to take only the minimum 500 kilos, reserving the remainder for fuel — an operation that was required to keep going just as long as they could carry 500 kilos of payload. The flight time, based upon the forecast, came to about 14 hours to Botwood; so with 500 kilos, they had ample fuel reserve.

"Early the next morning Kelly-Rogers came into the *Dunraven Arms* at Adaire where we all stayed. He was both angry and exhausted, an unusual state, at least in the second part, for an Irish man of ample build. He had flown more than half-way to Botwood at a thousand feet under what he termed the worst turbulence imaginable. He decided that the rest of the trip would not be worth it at any price, so turned around and came back. From all the weather patterns that I reconstructed in my mind, and what Kelly-Rogers had reported, it would be a while before I could carry a load across the North Sea. So I fueled for Lisbon, loaded up and came back the middle route. We made it to New York before Kelly-Rogers, and with a lot more than 500 kilos of payload.

"This kind of flying was hard work, very hard work. But it also was good fun and most satisfying when you found that you had made a good judgment. And most of it was judgment, your own. In this particular case many or most of our passengers would have been left on the dock at Foynes had I elected to go across the north; or worse yet, dropped into the ocean at its coldest and least frequented spot east-north-east of Newfoundland. The passengers were also a concern of mine, and this concern was additional to the concern of getting the ship to its destination by what ever means I could devise.

Former registered NC-07 takes time out for Baltimore servicing. Testing or tuning of any one or simultaneously running of two engines while A314 sat on beaching cradle constituted operating at maximum power by mechanics to 30-inch Hg. manifold pressure as propeller(s) revolved in full low pitch. (*Photo Courtesy: British Overseas Airways/Gordon S. Williams Collection*)

"On this particular flight there were about 30, some seven times what we could have carried across the northern route, disregarding the mails which came first. But the passengers had to be more than numbers to me; they were people and had to be treated as such throughout the long trip back through Lisbon and Horta where we were once more delayed. And such a mixed bag of people they were! By great, good fortune Maury Maverick, one of the Texas 'mavericks,' was among them. With modest assistance from me he arranged diversions — Texas-style that found amused acceptance from even such unlikely sources as a pair of diplomats and the Knight of Glin and the Madame Fitzgerald, an English manufacturer and a tearful immigrant."[138]

Flying across the Atlantic during the war was considered, beyond poor weather conditions, a dangerous proposition for both airline crews, especially along the African coastline. Facing the ever-present danger of meeting the enemy, Kelly-Rogers remarked about the performance of the A314s when under the stress of long flights: "they were the sort of aircraft that gave one so much confidence that you didn't feel you were in peril at any time."[139]

When not carrying V-VIPS, the 314s flew unarmed and unescorted through enemy-patrolled skies. Their only defense was a small, black communication "IFF" box that operated automatically in answering interrogation by friendly aircraft. It received and sent out coded signals from and to other planes carrying the same equipment. Radio silence, a mania time for secrecy, was observed while flying far off the African shores between Bathurst and Lagos. Clipper crews carried 38 revolvers stored on the flight-decks for any unforeseen emergency. Capt. Masland quipped about those dark days of war, flying high in the skies to or from some strange, foreign port when he added, "It was my impression that we were fired upon more by our friends than by anybody else."[140]

24

World Crisis

Within the time span of an impending U.S. world war crisis, Pan Am's 314s continued their peaceful roles of commercial service. Flights from New York to Lisbon and return had increased from a thrice-weekly service starting in May, 1940, with the *Atlantic Clipper* which carried 18 passengers and 1,078 pounds of mail under the command of Capt. Blackmore to four flights per week beginning in early Summer, 1941, along with establishing more aviation historical firsts.

Regularly scheduled airplane air express over the Atlantic between New York and Lisbon was inaugurated by the *Dixie Clipper* on September 28th. Pan Am had intended the service to begin in 1939, but Hitler's abrupt actions across Europe delayed original plans. The cost was fixed at two dollars a pound. Minimum shipment was five dollars with insurance rates set at 25 cents for every $100 of valuation. Capt. Masland and crew, one of 11 314 teams based at LaGuardia, took out the first air express shipment that consisted of only 41.5 pounds, part of which was a Union Jack Afghan for England's Queen Mother Elizabeth. Although the first packages per trip were small in weight, large-scaled poundage had, by the end of October, 1943, scored a transported record of 4,300,000 pounds between the U.S. and Europe. Much of the priority stock safely flown over Germany's submarine-ravaged Atlantic included military machinery parts, foodstuffs, clothing, Red Cross blood plasma and much urgently needed medical war supplies.

Air shipments by all types of Pan Am-owned planes totaled 5,557,794 pounds sent out to 55 countries and colonies in 1940, a year that grossed 122,000 pounds of mail, 50,000 pounds of air express and 1,200 passengers carried across the Pacific by Boeing and Martin clippers. As of June, 1941, with the curtailment of surface ships riding the high seas, the pot-bellied 314s had transported about 20 percent of the mail between the U.S. and Hawaii and to and from Australia, and around 30 percent of all the bulk sent to and from Singapore.

Air express cargoes on the Pacific hit 270,792 ton-miles during the same 1940 time period. The Pacific Division's two M-130 and 314-based clippers each carried about 300 individual items per trip. Division Express Supt. Joe Passio and assistants had checked some 12,000 ton-miles of air freight a week out of Treasure Island for points in the Pacific. By the end of May, 1941, 1,400,000 miles were recorded at New York's Atlantic Division. In the first two years of operation, more than 6,000 passengers were carried

19,750,000 miles on 345 scheduled transatlantic crossings. The upsurge of war in Europe increased the mail to 750,000 pounds carried in 314s between New York and Lisbon between mid-1939 and mid-1941.

The second reguarly scheduled airplane Atlantic air mail anniversary was celebrated on May 20, 1941, when the *Yankee Clipper* departed LaGuardia's *MAT* with 25 passengers, an 11- man crew under Capt. P. J. P. Nolen, and 2,185 pounds of mail. New York Postmaster Albert Goldman, as he had done in 1939 for a PR pose, raised a sack of mail while standing on the NC-03's port sea-wing to gripping hands of a ground crewman reaching down through the main wing's underside hatchway.

Operational statistics at the Pacific Division, from August through December, 1941, showed that government operations totaled 51,000 miles flown with NC-01, NC-02, NC-09, NC-11 and NC-12. Mail-ton miles during the same months between San Francisco, Los Angeles, and Honolulu, a tri-port "shuttle" circle route begun August 10th by the Anzac Clipper under Capt. Tilton offering three flights every two weeks, reached the 34,673 mark with a record accomplishment of 31,025 express ton-mileage executed between the three ports alone. Passenger ton-miles covered in the

Flanked by crew at Treasure Island, Capt. Tilton (fifth from right) commanded first U.S. mail, express and passenger service to Fiji, November, 1941. (*Photo Courtesy: Pan American World Airways*)

Tilton slides NC-02 sky-beauty into San Pedro on route-opening flight to Fiji, first of three stops to Suva. (*Photo Courtesy: Pan American World Airways*)

Pacific peaked at l00,979 with a percent load factor registered at 86.91 with 929,563 passenger miles completed.

Mail, air express and passenger service was opened up to the Fiji Islands along the San Francisco-Auckland sector in November, 1941. Spectacular in ceremony, the inaugural flight, which departed Treasure Island in the early afternoon of November 5th, was commanded by Capt. Tilton who had taken leave of his strenuous duties as Pacific Division's Manager of Operations, a promotion accepted on Jan. 15, 1941. Accompanying famed Tilton, who was born in Washington, D.C., in 1893, and who first learned to fly in 1917 with the U.S. Navy before joining Pan Am in 1929, were nine-selected flight officers.

The NC-09 was to have made the first flight to Suva, just as she was to have maintained the bulk of travel to and from the South Pacific upon her delivery from Boeing. But the *Pacific Clipper* was no longer stationed at Treasure Island. During the second week of September, 1941, Capt. Sullivan and a crew of nine transferred the NC-06 back to San Francisco from New York, via Miami and New Orleans. The NC-06 was exchanged for the newer NC-09.

After bringing the NC-06 into San Francisco, Sullivan and crew took out the NC-O9 on September 19th and ferried her to New York. It was an unusual trip. Capt. Sullivan flew the A314 non-stop to LaGuardia, a Pan Am first despite the *Bristol*'s non-stop delivery flight. Flying south over the California Sierras and the deserts of New Mexico, Sullivan received a report near El Paso, TX., that a hurricane was whipping through Miami. To avoid the storm out of New Orleans, and with ample fuel aboard, the A314 was turned northeast to pass over Memphis, TN, Richmond, VA., Annapolis, MD, and Philadelphia. Eighteen hours out of San Francisco, the *Pacific Clipper* was landed at LaGuardia.

With the removal of the *Pacific Clipper* from the Pacific Division, a 314 name change occurred. Clippers flying south to Auckland, regardless of given names, were advertized and posted under the *Pacific Clipper* appelation. At LaGuardia, NC-09 was renamed the *South Atlantic Clipper* to commemorate the upcoming service between the Americas and Africa. It was, besides the *Hong Kong Clipper*, the second time a Pan Am plane bore a three-worded designation title.

The 314 assigned to make the Fiji trip was the NC-02 which had been returned to Treasure Island in A314 status. For the flight she was press-posted as being the *Pacific Clipper*. Fourteen passengers boarded the NC-02, either in San Francisco or Los Angeles. One of those aboard was Pacific Division's Young who was making the line's Fiji inspection tour. A total of 45,000 first-flight covers were carried during the round-trip flight that took in six points of call. More important than the official cachet-stamped mail was the military implications behind the new South Pacific base.

Before Fiji became a stop, 314s flying out of Canton Island were burdened with extra fuel for the 1,988-mile hop to Noumea, and were limited in their capacity for carrying large loads of air express and passengers. The cargo on earlier trips consisted of defense materials, such as grinding diamonds, roller bearings, binder cutting wheels, switches, cables, lathe machinery parts, military tank, aircraft and magneto tool drawings, drills and high-frequency electrode knife-blade tips. Many of the passengers consisted of defense executives to assist the British military buildup in the South Pacific. By bisecting the route between Canton and Noumea, the 314s were able to raise their essential cargo and passenger capacities.

The importance of the new service was evident by the first passenger list. Aboard were Leif J. Sverdrup, U.S. Army engineer consultant, and Sir Thomas Barrow, New Zealand's Air Secretary and Britain's High Commissioner for the western Pacific. Sverdrup, given the first ticket, and whose mission was secret, was headed for

Fiji for talks concerning U.S. Army assistance in the South Pacific. Barrow, on the other hand, was returning to New Zealand from a U.S.-Canada trip after setting up a program whereby 100,000 trained fighting airmen would be provided for the South Pacific by the end of 1941, and doubled by 1943.

"The inclusion of the Fiji Islands in Pan American's transpacific air services," Barrow said before boarding in San Francisco, "will mean much in Pacific basin affairs and will increase the importance of the contribution which Suva and the Fiji Islands can make in the present world crisis."[141]

When the flag-speckled clipper reached Suva, capital of the Fijian Islands at Viti Levus on November 8th, Tilton thundered the 314 in low passes over the town before setting the ship down. Hundreds of bushy-haired natives lined the defense's barbed wire shore-lined point as the NC-02 was moored to a barge in the harbor. Waiting on the float were British Governor Harry Luke, military and city dignitaries and Harold Gatty, Pan Am's South Pacific liason officer. It was a Sunday, a strictly observed Fijian day of reverence. Formal ceremonies were postponed until the NC-02 made its return trip from Auckland, via Noumea and Canton. A brief fete was held at the Town Hall after which Tilton wired Trippe in New York, "Routine and without incident."[142]

A drive around town was conducted followed later by a formal dinner hosted by Luke. The next morning the clipper was off to Noumea and New Zealand. Passenger Fred Laidlaw, Pan Am's philatelist expert, stayed behind to tediously stamp the many first covers. On the return flight Tilton and crew were beset with official ceremony. Under decorations of crepe-paper strung in the Town Hall, the native high chieftain and chiefs welcomed the crew with a Kava greeting, a royal Fijian toasting made from Kava root and served in a coconut shell.

Morning hour darkness prevailed when Capt. Harold E. Gray (left front) and crew rank-filed at end of *Marine Air Terminal*'s canopied walkway before boarding NC-12 for proving flight to and from Africa, Nov. 11, 1941. (*Photo Courtesy: Pan American World Airways*)

Rituals proceeded the ceremony before the nature-sculpted cup was passed to Tilton and crew — a warm exchange between tribunal land and clipper sky chiefs. This was followed by a native "meke" sitting dance with movements made by hands, shoulders and hips. Climax to the ceremony was in presenting a rare gift to Tilton — the "tambua," a whale's tooth. It was the most honored possession a chief could give, and was seldom presented to outsiders. Prior to the clipper's landing at Suva, the only known offerings to white men at the former head-hunting territory were two in number, one of which was given to Luke when he took office. When offered, the receiver, according to tradition, was held bound for a return gift. In 1887, a chief warrior gave one to a tribesman who then demanded in return the body of a missionary named Baker. Baker ended up as "bokola," his flesh cooked in a pot and distributed to natives as food.

Ceremonies ended, Tilton and his men were escorted to the hilltop *Defense Club* for better palate-tasting refreshments. The next morning the NC-02 was off for Canton, Hawaii and San Francisco. Fourth Officer William H. Grace later wrote:

"...we had time to stroll through town on our way to catch the launch for the plane. In market districts and back alleys, it was as neat and clean as the Town Hall porch, no filth and no smell. Beautiful-eyed Indians wrapped up in turbans and beards, or sheeted like ghosts; Fijians, with their clean, bushy hair, laughing and calling to us and each other in the bright morning. We sat for a moment on a bench under a great tree in the center of the street at the hub of the town. A huge black native with a terrible shock of hair came up carrying an axe edged like a razor. With one hand he grasped a branch and disappeared into the foliage above like Tarzan of the Apes. The tree shuddered and a chip fell at my feet, feet that were already carrying me across the street as fast as possible. Now I am not a nervous individual, but fun is fun and there is a limit to my cool daring amongst a pagan people. I was thinking of Missionary Baker. This fuzzy-wuzzy just might have been thinking of the same thing. How could I be sure he was just trimming up trees for the Park Board...?"[143]

Five days after Tilton left San Francisco on the historic flight to Fiji, Capt. Gray departed New York for the first-scheduled South Atlantic crossing. The inspection flight to the West Coast African bases was conducted with the *Capetown Clipper* that departed LaGuardia on November 10th. Thirteen crew members and 40 passengers were aboard, the latter consisting of 30 Pan Am employees assigned to the African ports, two airline executives and three CAA officials. Two full-fledged captains and two officers were added to Gray's crew to familiarize them with the new route.

Flying first to Bermuda, the NC-12 then headed south for San Juan, Port of Spain and on to Belem where an overnight stop was made. The next day Gray flew the ship to Natal, refueled and pointed the shark-nosed liner due east for Bathurst on November 12th. Four-

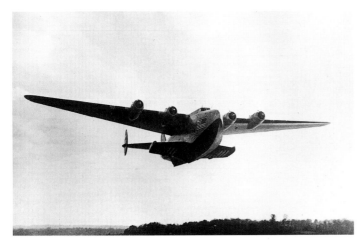

Gray ascends *Capetown Clipper* from Fisherman's Lake during long-hauled inspection trip along Africa's west coast. (*Photo Courtesy: Pan American World Airways*)

teen hours, 52 minutes later the A314 was landed 1,832 miles from Natal where an inspection tour of the upgraded BOAC base was conducted. Leaving November 14th, Gray flew the ship 1,715 miles south to Lagos for another thorough and tiring inspection tour whereupon all of the CAA, maintenance and radio specialists filed report papers.

At dawn, November 16th, the NC-12 headed south across the Bay of Benin, past the Portuguese Island of Sao Tome on the Equatorial line and then east to Leopoldville. Flying over and into the Belgian Congo's coastline, Pan Am's Transatlantic Manager John C. Leslie wrote in his diary after observing from his stateroom porthole, "It was the most interesting part of the entire trip. I have rarely seen anything more spectacular than that portion of the Congo River. We were flying at about one thousand feet directly over the river, which seems to be one cataract after another for almost the entire distance. Each new cataract seemed to cause the water to boil more violently than the last, making waves which were plainly noticeable even from our one-thousand-foot perch. It looked to me as if these waves were from 20 to 30 feet high. I was surprised to see no jungle along this stretch of the route. There is vegetation, of course, but generally speaking it is quite open and reminded me very much of what you see when flying over Southern California."

Six days and 9,370.3 statute miles away from LaGuardia, the *Capetown Clipper* was docked at Stanley Pool, Leopoldville. American flags waved from the port's frontage to welcome the first clipper and her emissaries of peace. Three days were spent touring the base. U.S. Consul Patrick Mallon gave a cocktail party; Vice Governor Paul Ermens hosted a formal dinner; Mayor Le Cont de Beaufort directed a sightseeing tour of the town; and M. Apel, general of river navigation, conducted a boat trip around Stanley Pool. In turn, Gray welcomed Leopoldville officials aboard the clipper for a tour. Upon entering with his wife, Ermens exclaimed, "Mon dieu, mais c'est magnifique!"[145] Another dignitary, an American stationed at Leopoldville who had not seen his homeland for some time,

showed tears when he saw the painted American flags on the clipper's bow.

Leaving the Congo at dawn on November 19th, Gray retraced the flight to Lagos on special orders. He was instructed to pick up the first official U.S. Government passengers to use the new South Atlantic service - Laurence A. Steinhardt, U.S. ambassador to Russia, and Douglas Brown, assistant to Steinhardt. Both men were returning to the U.S. from Kuibishev, Russia. Also taken aboard were 15 ferry pilots en route back to the U.S. to pick up another fleet of bombers destined for airfields in Africa and beyond.

The last stop on the African coast was made November 20th at Fisherman's Lake. Part of the afternoon was spent on Missionary Simmons' motor boat to check water depths for locating the best suitable spot for future clipper moorings and to wire New York to start sending equipment for base construction. From "Fish Lake" the NC-12 left for Natal, 1,828 miles away, thence to Port of Spain (longest single hop of the trip — 2,139 miles), and on to San Juan and New York.

Shortly after midnight, November 26th, the clipper circled down for a smooth landing after parachute flares had been dropped to light the way in. A large crowd of photographers, reporters and newsreel men were waiting. A *MAT* buffet had been prepared for the tired passengers and crew. The only incident encountered during the 15-day flight was when a small strip of bonding tape covering a wing seam had torn loose from a rear spar and Gray was forced to return to port for repair. With the logging of the first-scheduled flight completed to Africa, the CAB gave its permission to begin regular service in early December, a service President Roosevelt had earlier commented, "cannot be over estimated!"[146]

Roosevelt knew war was coming to the U.S. The question was how soon? He announced on Aug. 18, 1941, the importance of the South Atlantic air route in a special White House release that related the aerial network to national defense. A two-way commercial highway, to be turned into a military air system in the event of war, only strengthened the arsenal of democracy — a charted airway that would provide a direct and quick link for shipments of war materials and military personnel to the fighting fronts of Africa and the Far East. The times were heating up.

Six months earlier the threat of war had forced the U.S. State Department to clamp down on clipper passage and certain nonessential cargoes. Enforced by Pan Am, only those with a priority clearance could embark a clipper. Persons who met the four classifications for travel were cleared to leave. Washington's concern was set to ensure space allotments for essential materials and personnel. "Priority Number One" gave precedence to the President or for those traveling in the interests of the U. S. Government; "Number Two" was reserved for air ferry pilots; "Number Three" for those considered vital to the war effort, such as newsmen, but not of an extreme nature; and "Number Four" for passengers and cargo that rated some importance to justify travel by air. Military rank or civilian position did not necessarily give automatic priority rating.

While it was possible to get a seat on a clipper, there was always the chance one could be bumped. Priority V-mail and cargo had top billing over a non-priority passenger.

Likewise, working in conjunction with the U.S. State Department, Portugal enforced priority conditions on westbound flights out of Lisbon. A quota system was introduced for entry and exit through the control of issuing visas by the International Police who held a seat of authority in neutral Portugal. Only 13 percent of all travelers to and from Europe were transported by 314s as of August, 1941. Andrew Jackson Kelly, Pan Am's traffic representative in Lisbon, was often beseiged by U.S.-bound travelers who demanded they be on the next clipper. He was often seen by fellow employees to leave by way of the back door at day's end to avoid the pressing mob. Kelly had to personally turn down many ticket seekers while they screamed their heads off in defiance. One woman threatened to start a senatorial investigation when first rejected. Around 300 passengers per month, however, were cleared for New York on 314s. A high record load of 169 made the westbound trip during the last two weeks of July — an average of 28 per trip — an increase of 11 over the same 1940 time period. Similar conditions existed on the Pacific.

Many English families, Pan Am employees and U.S. Government officials stationed overseas were concerned with the safety of their children. They inquired for clipper space to get the youngsters out of warring Europe. Some of the toddlers traveled alone and without adult family supervision. The same held true in the Far East. In December, 1940, and before the priority clamp down was issued in February, 1941, U.S. Adm. Thomas C. Hart, Commander-in-Chief of the Asiatic Fleet, ordered home wives and children of Navy personnel and other Americans residing in the area of his jurisdiction. Hart had become increasingly alarmed over the crisis in the Far East. Clippers were the quick and sure way of providing safety for the young. Passenger lists increased rapidly with names of infants and pre-teenagers. A record load of 16 babies and children were aboard the *California Clipper* out of Singapore, Hong Kong and Manila in December, 1940. The two stewards on "Trip 436," piloted by Capt. H. J. Chase, were, beyond normal duties, up to their necks with baby sitting, helping to change diapers and warming different prescriptioned milk bottles in the galley's steam table. The unoccupied suite was turned into a nursery during the long flight to California.

A few newspaper correspondents, concealing their OSS affiliations, were given "Priority One" clearance. They used press credentials to shroud their real reasons for travel. But the majority of newsmen stuck to reporting, traveling abroad or returning to the U.S. to relate more accurately their personal accounts about the war in Europe, or the crisis in the Far East.

Clare Boothe Luce and her husband Henry R. Luce, president and owner of the *Time-Life* publishing empire, left by 314 for China in early 1941. Upon their return aboard the *California Clipper*, piloted by Capt. Blackmore under "Trip No. 498" in late May of the same year, Henry told pressmen at Treasure Island after the 314 landed June 4th that he wondered how much longer America could remain an isolationist country.

Two months later, and without husband, Clare was off again aboard the *Honolulu Clipper* to Manila to gather more material for print. She wanted to bring to the U.S.' attention the state of emergency that existed in the Far East and hoped for an interview with Gen. MacArthur. Her trip was briefly interrupted at Oahu. Coming into Honolulu, the NC-01 blew an engine head. A three-day delay resulted until the *Anzac Clipper*, which in turn had struck a reef at Guam, returned to Honolulu from Manila after repairs to pick up Clare and fellow-grounded passengers to resume the flight west. Stranded with Clare in Hawaii were Willys Peck and wife, newly-assigned American Minister to Thailand, and Alfred and Lady Diana Duff Cooper, recently-appointed coordinator of Britain's Far Eastern defenses. The Coopers, he in a dapper suit, she in a printed dress, brim hat and flashed in fur, had taken the *Atlantic Clipper* out of Lisbon en route to Singapore, via the U.S., in order to make the NC-01 connection.

Other notable writers continued to alarm the American public about impending war. Frank Gervasi, *INS*, a frequent clipper passenger, wrote following a trip from London and Lisbon, "Hitlerism is revolution in reverse. It is for the end of Liberty."[147]

Raymond Clapper, *Scripps-Howard* columnist, stated after his arrival in New York on the *American Clipper* before the ship's transfer to the Pacific Division, "I come back . . . more impressed than ever with the strength of the U.S.... The massive New York skyline appears through the windows of the incoming clipper like a great stone dam holding a reservoir of giant power."[148]

America, as if she were a sleeping tiger, slowly opened her eyes to the threshold of becoming involved in the war. The ties linking the U.S., Germany and Japan had worn down to mere threads

Priority No. 3 newspaper and radio journalists were seen more frequently boarding 314s for foreign ports when U.S. international relations began to wane. (*Photo Courtesy: Pan American World Airways*)

of strained peace by November, 1941. A U-boat west of Iceland in the North Atlantic torpedoed and sank the U.S. destroyer *Reuben James* on October 30th with the loss of 95 American lives. Another U.S. ship, her outer plates painted with four large American flags, was sunk off the west coast of Africa. In the Far East, Japaneae forces crossed the French Indo-China frontier into Thailand. America insisted that Japan pull back and agree to a multi-lateral pact of non-aggression or face serious trade and other sanctioned reprisals. Japan had other plans and stalled for time.

Negotiations between U.S. Secretary of State Cordell Hull and Japan's Ambassador to the U.S., Adm. Kichisaburo Nomura, had vehemently come to a near close. One last desperate attempt for reconciliation came when Hull cleared the path to accept Special Envoy Saburo Kurusu of Japan to Washington, D.C. Kurusu, who spoke fluent English and was married to a U.S. citizen from New York, was a veteran diplomat and former ambassador to Germany.

On November 5th, Kurusu and his secretary, Shiroji Yuki, flew from Tokyo to Hong Kong. Special permission was granted by the British to allow the Japanese airliner to traverse the route that had been previously shut down. Boarding the S-42B *Hong Kong Clipper*, which had been held over two days for the unique connection, Kurusu and Yuki continued on to Manila where they changed to the *China Clipper*. At Midway, the M-130 was delayed due to a faulty engine that had to be replaced and also to bad weather.

Arriving in Honolulu on November 12th, the diplomat and aid transferred to the *California Clipper* the next day at 5:55 P.M., Hawaiian time, and arrived at Treasure Island on November 14th at 9:15 A.M. (PST). Waving with his black homburg-styled hat as he walked up the dock with 22 other passengers that included William Keswick, a private secretary to Cooper, mustached Kurusu smiled, his eyes squinting behind a pair of spectacles. He had little to say except that the clipper trip was ". . .so nice."[149]

While waiting to clear customs inside the terminal, Kurusu autographed a Pan Am employee's broken arm cast per her request. At 6:45 P.M. the party of two left Mills Field for Washington, D.C., aboard a United Airlines DC-3 sleeper. Three days later, Hull, Nomura and Kurusu entered the White House to confer with Roosevelt.

Monday, Dec. 1, 1941:

A group of passengers boarded NC-06 at Treasure Island for a routine flight to Auckland. The 314 was listed under ship and clipper movements in San Francisco papers as being the *Pacific Clipper*. In the NC-06's high-perched bridge sat Capt. Robert ("Bob") Ford and First Officer John H. Mack. Ford, born in Cambridge, MA, became a business and engineering student at Harvard but remained a flyer at heart and so enlisted into the U.S. Naval Air Academy at Pensacola in 1929 after having spent the previous year as a U.S. Army cadet at Brooks Field, TX. In 1933, the slim-faced pilot was hired by Pan Am, worked up the ranks and earned his "Master of Transocean Flying Boat" status in 1939 while working out of the

Atlantic Division prior to being relocated west. Seated aft of Ford and Mack were seven crewmen, one of whom was the Pacific Division's chief Radio Officer John D. Poindexter. Poindexter was going only as far as Los Angeles — or so he believed! He was aboard to check out new radio equipment and had planned to fly back to San Francisco later that day. Before boarding the NC-06 he called his wife and told her to hold dinner Below deck, Stewards Verne C. Edwards and Barney Sawicki checked hats and coats and directed passengers to their assigned staterooms for "Trip No. 73."

Near noon, 35-year-old Capt. Ford (1906-1994) taxied the *American Clipper* out across the bay, opened power, lifted the giant into the air and headed down California's Great Valley for Los Angeles where an overnight delay occurred. Scheduled to replace Poindexter in Los Angeles was Harold G. Strickland, a second radio officer. Poindexter was told that Strickland was ill and that he would have to make the flight as far as Honolulu. Another phone call was quickly made whereby Poindexter told his wife he would return to San Francisco on an eastbound clipper in a couple of days.

Dec. 2, 1941:

Far west of the Hawaiian Islands an undetected Japanese strike force steamed eastward in a zigzag pattern. The fleet, commanded from Japan by Adm. Isoroku Yamamoto, chief of the Japanese Navy, was composed of six carriers screened by destroyers and submarines. Vice Adm. Chuichi Nagumo, sea commander of the First Air Fleet, received the secret order from Japan, "Climb Mount Niitaka," a coded notice to proceed with the long-planned attack against U.S. forces at Pearl Harbor.

Late in the afternoon, Los Angeles time, Capt. Ford directed the NC-06 towards Hawaii in turbulent air for a bumpy ride. In the galley, Edwards and Sawicki prepared high tea followed by the cocktail hour where the line's noted "South Seas Cocktail" and other drinks were served prior to a formal sit-down dinner.

Dec. 3, 1941:

Just past dawn Capt. Ford landed the press-labeled *Pacific Clipper* at Pearl Harbor after passing low over Ford Island, anchorage site for U.S. Navy ships. Inside the terminal's officers' quarters Poindexter was informed by operations that a replacement was not found — that he would have to continue on with the full roundtrip run to and from Auckland. The chief radio expert wired a cable to his wife stating he would not be home until about two weeks. In San Francisco at 3:45 P.M, long-admired Pan Am Capt. John H. Hamilton and First Officer William Washburn Moss gunned the M-130 *Philippine Clipper* away from Treasure Island, roared the boat skyward and headed for Hawaii. Aboard were seven additional crew and a small group of passengers. Hired in 1939, Moss, a former Navy pilot, was trained at Brownsville to fly DC-3s through Mexico and Central America and had recently been sent to the Pacific Division to navigate 314s where, after more training, he made first officership.

Dec. 4, 1941:

Ford, crew and on-going passengers transferred to the bowless-named *California Clipper* and departed Honolulu for Canton, Fiji, New Caledonia and New Zealand as Capt. Hamilton brought in *Philipplne Clipper*. In the afternoon, NC-06 was returned to San Francisco.

Dec. 5, 1941:

NC-06 arrived in San Francisco and Capt. Ford took the NC-02 to Suva from Canton Island. In San Francisco, Capt. Harry Lanier Turner and a crew of 11 reported to Treasure Island's base of operations to make a standard two-hour check-flight around the city with the *Anzac Clipper* before taking the ship on a scheduled run to Singapore the next day. Turner, who joined Pan Am in October, 1929, asked operations for a slight departure delay the next day so he could briefly attend his daughter's first piano recital in Oakland. Up until 1933, Turner commanded flights between Puerto Rico, Cuba and Miami. In 1933, he was transferred to the Rio-Buenos Aires-Belem-to-Miami sector, and, in 1938, sent to the Pacific Division. His first 314 command was with the NC-11.

Nearly three-thousand miles due east, Capt. Masland took out the *Capetown Clipper* from LaGuardia for its preliminary check before inaugurating U.S. air mail service across the South Atlantic to Africa the following day. Upon entering the control room, Masland noticed an odd document taped to the navigator's bookcase door. He copied down what it said and many years later wrote, "The amusing part to me was a letter under a sheet of plastic that read, 'To whom it may concern: This aircraft belongs to the U.S. Government. Signed/United States Government.' It was a signature I have never before or since seen. But it gave us license to wander all over and into unusual places."[150]

At around 8:00 A.M., Hawaii time, Capt. Hamilton lifted the *Philippine Clipper* away from Pearl Harbor and headed the M-130 for Midway Island. Passengers were few in number: a young pilot heading for China to become a P-40 "Flying Tiger" under Gen. Claire Chennault, a Pan Am mechanic assigned to an island base, an airline meteorologist, a U.S. Army colonel and his two assistants, and a U.S. Budget Bureau official. Besides a load of mail and air express, the main cargo load consisted of spare aircraft tires destined for Chennault's fighting airmen.

Dec. 6, 1941:

Ford, crew and passengers embarked the NC-02 for Noumea. In New York, Capt. Masland, with a double crew and a few passengers, departed aboard NC-12 on the U.S.' first designated "Foreign Air Mail Trip No. 22 (FAM 22)" for Africa, via Bermuda, Puerto Rico, Trinidad, Brazil and across the South Atlantic. Out of Miami a specially scheduled S-42 boat, used on the Caribbean and eastern South American routes, flew out to connect with the *Capetown Clipper* in San Juan. Her bins were stocked with 4,369 enveloped first-flight covers dispatched for Leopoldville, 2,424 stamped covers

Capt. Robert Ford made aviation history. The gallant airman later quit Pan Am to fly for a non-scheduled carrier out of San Francisco. (*Photo Courtesy: Pan American World Airways*)

destined for Bathurst, and 2,583 postmarked for Lagos. At San Juan, all mail was then conveyed to the NC-12. In addition to this load, plus the many-pounded covers out of New York and Bermuda, San Juan's postmaster sent aboard 1,970 letters for Leopoldville, 1,780 for Bathurst and 3,350 for Lagos. More cataloged mail was picked up at Trinidad before Masland struck out for Belem.

Across the U.S. in San Francisco, the *China Clipper* docked at Treasure Island early in the morning after a night flight from Hawaii. Disembarking in casual dress was Maxim Litvinoff, new Russian ambassador to the U.S. Litvinoff had boarded the M-130 at Manila following a flight from the Far East. With him aboard the clipper for his resumed air journey to Washington, D.C., were Ivy Low, wife, and Secretary Mlle. Anastasia Petrova.

No sooner had Treasure Island's ground crew unloaded the *China Clipper's* cargo and mail bins when they began to rapidly fill all holds of the silver-painted *Anzac Clipper*. Overlooking the sight, Capt. Turner and crew had gathered at the base's command center for last minute instructions. Signs of good weather prevailed along the route to Singapore. The NC-11's flight was scheduled to depart at 2:00 P.M. (PST), but was a half-hour behind. Approximately at 2:15 two bells signaled the 17 passengers to board, two of whom were Prime Minister U Saw of Burma and his First Secretary, Tin Tut. U Saw was returning home after holding important negotia-

Capt. H. L. Turner some 20 years after his perilous *Anzac Clipper* adventure next to jet-aged Boeing 707 Clipper. (*Photo Courtesy: Capt. Harry Lanier Turner*)

tions with Churchill in England and Roosevelt in Washington, D.C., pertinent to Burma's assured alliance. The Burmese director had arrived in San Francisco in November aboard a United DC-3 and waited nearly a month before tagging a seat on a clipper for the Far East.

The three mooring lines securing the *Anzac Clipper* to the float on that clear, beautiful day in San Francisco were shortly cast away. Capt. Turner headed the flying boat across Port of the Trade Winds, out into the bay and bolted the liner through small waves. Streaking skywards, NC-11 soared over and past the Golden Gate Bridge. High tea was served in the lounge, followed by highballs and the line's specialty, the "Clipper Cocktail." Dinner was announced at 6:00 by Stewards A. E. Harris and T. V. O'Leary whereupon Turner descended the staircase from the flight-deck to host U Saw and Tin Tut at the captain's table. While seated in star-studded-upholstered cushions, and facing into the flower-decorated table, the men exchanged words relevant to the European war and the crisis faced by the U.S. with both Germany and Japan. Through the portholes the sky was seen ablaze with color as the sun slowly set.

Later, in curtained-off berths, passengers tucked themselves under lightly starched sheets and deep blue-colored wool blankets. The *Anzac Clipper* droned onward through the dark but starry sky, her engines' exhaust systems shooting out short spurts of flame that seemed to evoke a foreboding of events to come. Far over the western horizon, Japan's flag, symbolic of a rising sun set against a white field, began to show its red rays of aggression. Adm. Yamamoto's fleet, directed by Vice Adm. Nagumo, approached its destination some 200 miles west of Oahu whereupon the escorted carriers were headed into the wind before sunrise to release their winged cargoes of death and destruction.

Earlier that same day at Midway, young Capt. Hamilton and First Officer Moss cleared the *Philippine Clipper* for Wake. During the 12-hour trip the M-130 cruised past the International Date Line, and for NC 14715 December 6th became December 7th. Within a few hours a world crisis was about to explode into an all-out global war.

25

The Clippers Go to War

Whispy clouds floated past the *Anzac Clipper* while stars faded and sun rays broke the night sky into daylight over the Pacific. Some of the passengers were already in the lounge snacking on sugar rolls, fruit juices, coffee or tea. A full breakfast awaited them at Pearl Harbor's *Pan Am Inn*. It was 19:00 (GCT), a crisp, clear day at 8,000 feet. Many of the passengers had set their watches ahead. The NC-11 was due to land at 8:30 A.M., Hawaiian time.

First Radio Officer W. H. Bell was at his post. He had just sent a dispatch to inform the Honolulu control officer that the clipper would arrive within the hour. Suddenly, a coded flash came over the ship's wireless. Pearl Harbor was under Japanese air attack! Stunned, Bell ripped the earphones from his head and rushed the message downstairs to his chief.

Capt. Turner was sipping a freshly brewed cup of coffee when Bell entered the lounge. The commander's face became drawn as he read the scribbled cryptic note. Remaining composed, Turner, who was chatting with passengers, excused himself and hurried back to the flight-deck. In an authoritative manner he tore the seal of an otherwise secret envelope marked "Plan A," a notice pertaining to orders calling for instant action in the event of war. Every clipper had been stocked with such an enclosure explaining emergency procedures to be followed.

Once opened, the papers revealed an alternate course to be taken by Turner and crew. The master took wheel command and sharply turned the craft to port towards Hilo, approximately 220 miles southwest of Honolulu. Amidship, cups, saucers and flatware rattled, but passengers were unconcerned — they believed the clipper to be bucked only by turbulent air.

Having stabilized the ship, Turner picked up the inner-cabin phone and ordered Purser O'Leary to report to the flight-deck. Once in the bridge the captain informed O'Leary of the attack but not to tell the passengers except that they were being diverted to Hilo. O'Leary was then instructed to page Army Lt. Harry Paller, a passenger returning to Honolulu from Washington, D.C. The master wanted to consult with Paller about the devastation taking place just minutes further west.

Paller, attired in his military uniform, and Turner went aft to the control room's conference station while First Officer E. P. Sommers piloted the NC-11 and Second Officer A. L. Charman rapidly plotted the new course. Lookouts were posted in the blister and at side portholes — a gleaming hull in open skies could be spotted for miles by crews of enemy aircraft. Broken clouds gave some concealment.

Like a razor across paper, the clipper cut through Hilo's calm and turquoise-reflected harbor and anchored near shore. No docking facilities were available at the remote air station. With passengers gathered in the lounge, Turner broke the shattering news. Before the startled group could react, they were whisked ashore by launch. The danger, however, was not over — Hilo, it was believed, was also vulnerable to attack. At the beach, FBI agents and local military officials took charge. Despite efforts to place a long-distanced call to Pan Am headquarters, Turner learned that all transpacific calls — unless of a military nature — were severed by the firm clamp of censorship. Proceeding with "Plan A," Turner and crew began to camouflage the *Anzac Clipper* as best they could to have the flying boat resemble a cloud when in flight.

Moving the liner as close to shore as possible near a large tree surrounded by shrubs, the master pilot and his men worked around-the-clock swabbing the mass bulk of metal with black and cream-colored paint secured by Hilo's military and port authorities. "This same color combination," Turner said, "was used in the old barn-storming days of flying to paint temporary advertising signs on aircraft." Meanwhile, dazed and frightened passengers had been escorted to the nearby *Naniloa* and *Volcano House Hotels*. A few lived on the island and fled in haste to be with their families. U Saw's secretary tried in vain to place a call through to U.S. Secretary of State Hull regarding further transportation to Burma It would be some time before the official was secretly taken to his homeland by the U.S. Navy. Young Lt. Paller reported to the Hilo's district commander for duty.

On the night of December 8th, after being refueled by hand since there were no pressure auxiliary pumps available, the blackened *Anzac Clipper*, her cargo consisting only of mail accepted by the Hilo postmaster, departed for San Francisco without passengers.

In the event San Francisco was under siege, Turner's "Plan A" ordered eastbound ships to fly some 80 miles north of Treasure Island to the alternate port located at Clear Lake in Lake County. The base was established in the late 1930s for the M-130s but never used until Nov. 8, 1941, when Capt. Max Weber was forced to settle the NC-11 in on Clear Lake after Treasure Island was socked under with a heavy blanket of fog.

Philippine Clipper slips into position for mooring, Midway Island, 1937. Four years later liner was caught at Wake and nearly destroyed by bullet-strafing Japanese aircraft. (*Photo Courtesy: Pan American World Airways*)

Maintaining radio silence, cruising at times just above the waves to scout for enemy ships and not knowing what to expect in San Francisco, Turner brought the NC-11 safely in on the morning of December 9th. The strain of the long ordeal showed on the crew's faces. Their eyes wore bloodshot and each wore a three-day growth of beard. The men had not slept in 72 hours. Tired as they were, one thought persisted: an additional 28 lives might have been added to Pearl Harbor's necrology list if the NC-11 had no delay departing Treasure Island on December 6th and had arrived in Honolulu on schedule at the precise time the attack began. The NC-11 would, without a doubt, have been blasted from the sky during its approach just northeast of "battleship row!"

Continued reports broadcasted the ever-increasing Japanese advances across the mid-Pacific that soon engulfed and destroyed U.S. strongholds, including Pan Am's aerial network of operations. Trippe was at home ill with the flu when his estate's phone rang. He was resting in bed in his spacious East Hampton house on Long Island, a residence located where arriving and departing 314s passed nearly overhead. Secretary of the Navy Knox told him of the bombing. Trippe quickly dressed and soon was at his *Chrysler Building* office to check on the whereabouts of his clipper fleet.

Germany had yet to declare war with the U.S. — the Atlantic-based 314s were not in immediate peril. Reports showed the *Atlantic* and *South Atlantic Clippers* were at LaGuardia undergoing maintenance; the *Yankee Clipper* was en route to Lisbon after a day's delay at Bermuda; the *Dixie Clipper* was moored in Bolama and ready to depart for Natal December 8th; and the *Capetown Clipper* was at Trinidad about to depart for South America and Africa. The Pacific Division-based clippers — at least two of them — were not as secure and this alarmed Trippe. The *Honolulu Clipper* was in shop at Treasure Island for a major overhaul and out of commission

until December 31st; the *California Clipper*, flying under the name *Pacific Clipper*, was somewhere between Noumea and Auckland; the *American Clipper* was back in San Francisco from Honolulu and being prepared for another trip to Singapore on December 14th; the *China Clipper* was also at Treasure Island having served the last incoming transpacific flight the day before; and the *Anzac Clipper* was temporarily safe at Hilo. The *Philippine Clipper* and the S-42B *Hong Kong Clipper*, docked in the city for which she was named, were the only two Clippers in dire straights due to their proximity to enemy air strikes.

Capt. Hamilton had just taken the M-130 off from Wake's lagoon and was two hours out heading for Guam when the flying boat's First Radio Officer D. V. McKay received a flashed message regarding the lethal blow and to turn back. After dumping some 3,000 pounds of gas to get the boat's gross weight down to the 48,000-pound safe-landing requirement, Hamilton alighted back at Wake whereupon he was requested by Navy Commander Winfield S. Cunningham and his assistant, Marine Major James P. S. Devereux, to make an aerial survey before evacuating the passengers and some airline base personnel back to Hawaii, via Midway. Just as Hamilton and crew were prepared to take out the refueled M-130, a swarm of G3M Nell bombers hove in sight and released their bombs. One exploded 20 feet away from foxhole-diving Hamilton and Airport Manager John B. Cooke.

After a short lull the planes reappeared and strafed the harbor and Peele Island. Gas storage tanks exploded, the hotel was set ablaze and Cooke's barracks-type house was shattered. Directional Finder masts were toppled and part of the Pan Am dock was ripped apart. Miraculously, the *Philippine Clipper* remained fast to the float. Hamilton and Flight Engineer T. E. Barnett examined the ship once the enemy had left. Twenty-three bullet holes riddled the clipper's fuselage and wing, but no vital areas were hit. Two of the crew lay injured on the flat, sun-baked soil. MacRay was struck in the calf and Steward Charles Relyea in the groin. Hamilton ordered the boat's mail and cargo to be removed, and the mail to be burned by the Marines. The clipper's flight log and other papers were set ablaze by Hamilton. About lay many dead and injured.

Three hours after the enemy departed, Hamilton taxied the M-130 away from the splintered dock. Thirty-six passengers and crew had boarded. Overloaded, the plane strained unsuccessfully during two takeoff runs, each time having to return to the dock to strip away more of the liner's refineries, food stock and personal items. On the third try, with everyone wondering if it could be done, Hamilton freed the ship from the water and headed at low altitude for Midway so as not to be spotted by any high-flying enemy planes.

Arriving at Midway at night, flames from Japanese Navy shelling guided them into port. Ninety minutes after landing, with all lights on so it would not be mistaken for a Japanese patrol plane, the refueled *Philippine Clipper*, keeping radio silence, was aimed once more into the eastern sky tor Honolulu. At dawn, the bullet-punctured ship was cleared to alight next to the untouched Pan Am base. Smoke and spurts of fire from crippled and sunken U.S. Navy ships still smoldered skyward. Thirty-six hours after toiling with their narrow escape, Hamilton and crew went to rest at the airline inn. MacKay and Relyea were taken to a hospital. Two days later the NC-15 continued on to San Francisco with a load of priority military personnel, cargo and mail.

In the Far East, the S-42B and its crew did not fair as well as did the NC-11, NC-15 and their crews. It was December 8th and the sun had just risen. Veteran Capt. Fred S. Ralph and his six officers had come in from Manila on a thrice-weekly shuttle flight the day before with "Myrtle." From the Kai-tek Airport, Capt. Ralph dialed a local number to the home of William Langhorne Bond, founder and vice-president of China National Aviation Corp. (CNAC), a subsidiary of Pan Am. The line had routes that extended north into China from Hong Kong to Shanghai, Peking, Nanking and Chungking. Bond, known to the Chinese as "Pan American's Number One Boy in China," answered his phone at his residence near Repulse Bay outside Hong Kong. Capt. Ralph, not knowing who else to call, told Bond he just heard from Manila instructing him to stay in Hong Kong, and, that Hong Kong officials told him to leave for Manila!

Bond was confused and did not know what to say. He gave Ralph his opinion: Hong Kong was a more dangerous area than Manila if there was to be trouble with the Japanese. Both men were perplexed over the varying orders. Bond then advised the captain to head for Manila. Ten minutes later Ralph called back and told Bond he just learned of the attack at Pearl Harbor and of Japan's declaration of war against Great Britain as well. Ralph was again advised by Bond to get the clipper out fast and fly inland to a lake near Kunming, and that he would order in a CNAC-piloted plane to guide him.

Capt. Ralph and men had just gotten into the S-42B when a wave of Japanese planes tore loose on the harbor and Kai-tek Air-

port. Hustling out of the flying boat, the men rushed up the dock as another formation dived six times for the moored clipper. Some of the crew ran towards the dockhouse. Others, including some horrified and puzzled passengers standing on the dock waiting to embark, a few maintenance men and Capt. Ralph, jumped into the sea — Ralph himself hiding behind one of the pier's concrete pillars. On the seventh run, while flying about 50 feet off the water, a tactic perfected by the Japaneae for the Pearl Harbor raid, a medium bomber's incendiary bullets tore into the clipper. Exploding into flames, the Sikorsky burned to the waterline and sank. That was the last anyone in the U.S. heard of Capt. Ralph and of his men until Jan. 10, 1942, when they arrived unscathed in New York aboard the *Capetown Clipper*. Fleeing to safety, the crew had made their way to India aboard a CNAC DC-2 after helping Bond arrange for a mass airlift evacuation plan with remaining CNAC planes. The men then caught the 314's return war mission flight out of Calcutta.

Before the NC-12 made the classified trip to India, it had completed the inaugural air mail flight across the South Atlantic at the time when the U.S. crisis turned into a blood-spilled, international war. Capt. Masland and some of his 11- man crew were standing in the lobby of Port of Spain's *Queen's Park Hotel* about to leave for the clipper base when Purser Edward Garcia hastily came up to Masland and blurted out the news of the attack he had just heard over a radio. He also told his chief that word revealed enemy ships 90 minutes away from New York. Without receiving any further orders from Pan Am's New York office, Masland proceeded to continue on with the first (FAM) mail flight to Africa.

"I had two concerns," Masland wrote, "one to keep the crew from thinking about what was happening on the other side of the world, and to pay attention to their jobs of the moment, and secondly to try to figure out what relationship there might be between Pearl Harbor and the task immediately in front of us — to get to the Congo and back. I laid it on hard with the crew so as to keep their thoughts on their present work—mine too!"[152]

Sailing into San Pedro on earlier trip to Hawaii, *Anzac Clipper* was just a short way out of Pearl City when hundreds of U.S. servicemen were slaughtered at Pearl Harbor. (*Photo Courtesy: Pan American World Airways*)

Chapter Twenty-five: The Clippers Go to War

Press-labeled *Pacific Clipper's* near 'round-the-world flight ends on Bowery Bay, New York. The first secret U.S. war-related clipper mission out of New York to the Far East ("SM No.1") occurred just before Pearl Harbor attack. Capt. R.O.D. Sullivan and a 16-man crew, without passengers, were ordered on a 11,500-mile 314 trek to Rangoon, Burma, via Miami, San Juan, Belem, Natal, Dakar, Lagos, Leopoldville, Port Bell, Kartoum, Aden, Karachi, and Calcutta, that carried tons of ammo and weapons loaded aboard at Miami for near-beleaguered AVG forces in China fighting Japanese invasion troops. While using dead reckoning navigation in a heavy dust storm between Port Bell and Kartoum, Sullivan instinctively yanked the 314 sharply to avoid striking a peaked mountain, the wing-on-end tilt of which spilled much of the stacked and bracketed passenger-cabined cargo load. (*Photo Courtesy: Pan American World Airways*)

After reaching Leopoldville on December 9th, Masland reported to the American consulate and querried about the state of war. Fretful discussions pertaining to Japan's attack were soothed by formalities of evening entertainment. A little more than 27 years later Masland communicated the following:

"...by the time we got there the entire African coast was a Rialto of rumor. None was more incredible than the attack on Pearl Harbor. If you believed that, you could believe any of the other stories. One of them was that the entire Vichy French fleet had come out of Dakar and was headed down the African coast."[153]

With a send-off likened to an ocean liner's maiden voyage, the NC-12 was lifted away the next day from the treacherous Congo River for Lagos. A French emissary representing Gen. Charles de Gaulle stepped aboard en route to Washington, D.C., while a military band blared and American flags lined the quay. Once in Lagos and while fuel was taken on, Masland spoke with a town official:

"The captain of the port of Lagos had no knowledge at all of such Vichy activities along the coast, but asked me to let him know if I met any strangers. I said that I would, but had no intention of seeking them out.

"Our next scheduled destination was Bathurst, from which we were to set out across the South Atlantic for Natal. Bathurst included the two banks of the Gambia River and was entirely surrounded by territory in the hands of the Vichy French... Under the circumstances I had no intention of going there if there were any other places to go. Our base at Fisherman's Lake was not by any means complete, but I made a late departure out of Lagos so as to

arrive over Fish Lake at dawn and leave maximum time for negotiation and minimum daylight flying.

"We dragged the main street of the tiny village of Robertsport and dropped a note on a parachute addressed to Father Simmons asking if he could stir up our representative to find us 2,000 gallons of fuel and 40 gallons of fresh water. Then we returned to the lake, anchored and waited. In less than an hour, Father Simmons came across the lake to us in his speed boat driven by his demon driver, George Washington. George, a native, always wore a white pith helmet. He clutched this to his head with one hand and drove wide out with the other.

"Father Simmons said that there would be no problem. Heuggens, our representative, who had been herding drums of aviation fuel, rowed up from Monrovia 53 miles in open surf boats. There was one problem that appeared later. The Liberian Government tried to collect air mail postage from Father Simmons for the message we had parachuted to him. One other problem was advising New York of our change in plans. It seemed that all of the codes had became prejudiced. So I invented one. I radioed New York that we were proceeding 'Simmonstown to Boydville.' 'Simmonstown,' of course, referred to Father Simmons of Fisherman's Lake, and 'Boydville' to Boyd, the airport manager at Natal. If Hitler broke my code, he never gave any sign of it. At any rate, we got off that evening at dusk for Natal with no further incident."[154]

Having cruised at 4,000 feet to Natal, Masland then headed the *Capetown Clipper* north with more passengers to Port of Spain and on to Miami where passengers, except for the French diplomat, disembarked. Within the 12-day scheduled air mail trip, the A314 finally approached LaGuardia as the first officer looked through binoculars and told Masland there were no signs of an invading fleet of war ships — that New York City was still intact.

The last of the clippers cut off by the sudden plunge into war was the NC-02 in the South Pacific. Poindexter's earphones flashed the news. Capt. Ford immediately checked his "Plan A," got out the clipper's .38 revolver, changed course 50 miles, posted officers as lookouts and continued on to Auckland. Upon landing, Ford went directly to the U.S. Consulate for his next move. He and his crew waited seven days until word finally came from New York directing them to proceed back to the U.S. in a westerly direction, and to do so the best way they knew how. Ford would have to improvise a route.

Without flight maps or weather data available, Ford estimated a near 31,000-mile hazardous trip back to New York. There had been no time to camouflage the 314 as Turner had done to his ship — all effort was spent mapping a course. It was clear the NC-02 could not return the way it came. Canton Island's Pan Am personnel had been evacuated and Hawaii might be invaded or hit again. For assistance, Ford turned to Bill J. Mullahey, Pan Am engineer who helped set up the Pacific island bases for the M-130s and 314s, and who would later work his way up to become Chief Base Director in the Pacific.

"We were ordered to get the plane back to its home base, " Mullahey said, "but to avoid routing it to any spot where it might face danger. We got hold of an eighth-grade geography book and, using advice from a Socony-Vacuum oil official who knew where fuel was available, mapped a course."[155]

Ford's first priority came from a second order: to fly back to Noumea and evacuate 23 airline employees to Gladstone, Australia, where they were to board a ship bound for the U.S. The NC-02, observing radio silence, left Auckland at 10:00 P.M., December 15th. Before departing, Poindexter managed to send a message to his wife, "Okay, Love John."[156]

Landing at Noumea at dawn with Auckland's Chief Mechanic Le Verne White aboard, Ford ordered evacuees to pack one bag apiece. Refueled, the clipper was off for a six and one-half-hour flight to Gladstone. Two men who were rescued out of Noumea were to stay aboard. In the clipper's holds were one spare 314 engine, one spare propeller and miscellaneous 314 parts. Orders from the Atlantic Division specified delivery of the equipment to Karachi. Unknown to Ford and crew, Pan Am had taken the NC-02's ordeal as an opportunity to chart and complete the airline's latest U.S. Government's "Contract 914" which stipulated that a new route extend beyond Cairo to India, Singapore and on to Australia. Ford was to assist in setting up new way stations in India and at Bahrain Island off Saudi Arabia in the Persian Gulf. Ranking Pan Am officials knew exactly where the NC-02 was every step of the way. The flight had become a secret mission.

One night was spent in Gladstone. Unable to secure gas, the clipper took off at 6:00 A.M. with tanks half full and flew northeast across upper Australia for Port Darwin. In the event of engine failure, Ford did not give much thought of where to set down when he later stated, "...we had lots else than a forced landing to be concerned about; we beat the Japanese to Surabaya, Java, by about three days, or thereabouts. We were in a hurry!"[157]

Eleven hours later the NC-02 reached Port Darwin. People of the town were panic-stricken about the war. A squall stormed sheets of rain adding to the sense of doom. Lightning and thunder flashed and sounded into the night as the plane was refueled. Ready for flight, Ford lifted the 314 into the stormy sky at 6:00 A.M. for Surabaya (Sunda Islands) in the Dutch East Indies. A British fighter plane rushed in to hover above the 314's tail as Ford approached for a landing under radio silence. Poindexter tuned in to the fighter pilot's conversation with the ground officer.

"What is she," demanded the C.O.?

"I don't know," replied the pilot, "but she is a big one. Might be a German or Japanese. Wait. There is part of an American flag on her side."

"That doesn't mean a thing," retorted the C.O. "Anyone can paint on an American flag."

"Then you'd better send up some more help," snapped the pilot.

Shortly, three more planes flocked about the incoming NC-02. From the ground the control officer radioed, "Stay on her tail. If she gets even a little way off the normal course for landing, shoot her down."[158]

In came the clipper — on a "conservative approach"—as the fighter planes circled closer overhead until the flying boat came to a halt. Obviously the British flyers had never seen a 314 before and were inadequately prepared in their friendly versus enemy silhouette-aircraft-identification chart training.

Only regular auto fuel was available for Ford's clipper. Without a choice, the captain authorized the loading of low octane for the next and longest hop to Trincomalee at Ceylon Island near the tip of India. Poindexter again wired his wife, "Okay, Love John."[159]

Leaving Surabaya December 21st following a two-day layover, Ford headed the liner for Ceylon. Just after takeoff the engines began to backfire from their poor fuel intake. Flight engineers kept their eyes focused on the panel and often crawled out into the wings to check the power plants. Crossing the Java Sea in daylight and the Bay of Bengal at night, Ford kept the ship at low altitude for better flying results. Inadvertently Ford took the 314 directly over a surfaced Japanese submarine, its men dashing for the deck gun. With a yank on the wheel, Ford pulled the boat's nose up and the flying boat disappeared into clouds. Nearly 21 hours since departure, Ford landed the clipper.

Three days were spent in Trincomalee. Poindexter sent another wire to his wife. Half an hour out on Christmas Eve, the clipper's No. 3 engine spurted oil and was shut down. Returning to Ceylon, repairs were required that called for a special tool that could not be found aboard the NC-02. A cylinder had broken loose trom its pins.

Anchored in the harbor was a British destroyer. Aboard was a lathe that enabled the clipper's flight engineer to hand-form the needed device. Then it was off again for Karachi on the morning of December 26th. Ford's takeoff was strenuous in a 100-degree calm that took 105 seconds to get airborne. Engines were held at full throttle for three minutes and 15 seconds across the glassy surface. Wright Aeronautical Corp. engineers were later astounded for normal 314 takeoff at full throttle was rated at 45 seconds. Anything longer could blow any number of engines.

Flying over India, the winged giant arrived in Karachi at 4:00 P.M, the same day. Some time was spent changing an engine piston and taking on more fuel. Poindexter again sent a wire. On December 28th, Ford, his crew and passengers flew on to Bahrain, an eight-hour, nine-minute flight. Before takeoff they bade farewell to the two mechanic passengers, the third of whom had departed at Karachi. Also left behind were the spare engine, propeller and other crated 314 parts.

Leaving Bahrain on December 29th, the clipper continued on to Khartoum. Ford had been denied permission by the Saudi Government to over-fly their territory. But once in the air above an overcast, Ford ignored the ruling of a flight plan submitted before take-off whereby he would have had to maneuver the metal bird a great distance south and around to Africa. Instead, he directed the ship southeast over Arabia and the Red Sea to Khartoum on the Nile. Engines coughed and sputtered with the new load of auto gas, again the only available supply at Bahrain.

Two days were spent in Khartoum, Anglo-Sudan. By no means an easy job, the stewards scurried about town — as they had done throughout the trip — to gather food provisions for the long trip to Leopoldville. During the takeoff for the Belgian Congo on New Year's Day, 1942, a section of exhaust pipe tore away from No. 1 engine. It ran rough and loud but did its job.

"The only part of the trip that gave us real concern," Ford wrote many years later, "was the flight from Khartoum to Leopoldville. We flew south of the Congo River over dense, tropical jungle. Surviving a forced landing there would leave one with a severe transportation problem, insects, snakes, hostiles. However, there was a lot of ocean flying too where conditions of the surface would have made a landing probably disastrous."[160]

Hot and muggy weather prevailed when the clipper reached Leopoldville. On January 2nd, NC-02 left Stanley Pool with 5,100 gallons of much-desired 100-octane fuel in her tanks. Ford poured on power in the windless air down the Congo River's slick, six-knot current towards the rapids. Forty-six seconds past normal lift-off time, while many watched from shore, the Boeing rumbled low into the western sky for Natal. The crew and ship were back on a regularly-scheduled Pan Am route — their first spirited feeling of security since leaving Auckland. Twenty-three hours and 35 minutes later they touched down in South America. It was January 3rd. Another three-worded wire was dispatched by Poindexter. For the next four hours the NC-02 was refueled, given a wired exhaust pipe for No. 1 engine and sprayed throughout with then-required insecticides.

Heading north, the sturdy 314, despite once more losing her exhaust extension shortly after takeoff, landed at Trinidad after more than 40 hours of constant operation out of Leopoldville. The next day the near globe-circling clipper and crew made their last takeoff for LaGuardia to arrive early on the morning of January 6th.

LaGuardia's landplane control officers were surprised when, at 5:45 A.M., the loudspeaker in the glass-enclosed tower crackled, "*Pacific Clipper*, inbound from Auckland, New Zealand, Capt. Ford reporting. Due to arrive, Pan American *Marine Terminal*, LaGuardia, seven minutes."[161]

It was still dark as the mighty flying boat circled overhead. Few of those on hand in the *MAT* knew of the arrival. The NC-02's epic flight had been kept secret for security reasons as related to the ports she had visited. The *MAT* was closed down as no clipper was due in or to depart for hours.

South Atlantic Clipper (ex-*Pacific Clipper*), seen on Bowery Bay, was briefly returned to Pacific Division after Pearl Harbor attack for emergency aid flights to and from Hawaii. (*Photo Courtesy: Pan American World Airways*)

At sunrise, Ford lowered the clipper, skimmed in and then got stuck in shallows while sailing into port. It was almost the last straw! Revving all four engines, the tired captain scraped the hull away from its entrapment and came to rest in Bowery Bay. Spray from the landing had turned into a thin sheet of ice that formed along the plane's wings and hull.

Sweeps of bitter cold wind blustered across Bowery Bay as the crew and three Pan Am-employed passengers stepped out of a launch and onto the dock. They wore tropical clothing, yet were wrapped in clipper blankets. Pan Am's Leslie, McVitty, Van Dusen and some military intelligence officers greeted the men. Leslie awarded each man with a hundred-dollar check. Two hours later the clipper story broke to hit many a front page. Newsmen considered the flight to be "unheralded" for the time and credited with encircling the globe for the first time with a commercial aircraft. This, however, was not correct since the plane and crew had not traversed the 3,000-mile leg across the U.S. Despite this fact, New York's *World Telegram* stated in part, "...the greatest achievement in the history of aviation since the Wright Brothers flew at Kitty Hawk."[162]

Including the use of the NC-06, the flight covered nearly 31,500 miles, 6,026 of which were spent over desert and jungle, in 207 hours and 22 minutes flying time. The NC-02 crossed the equator six times, spanned three oceans and touched all but two of the world's seven continents. So popular was the flight that one of the clipper's life jackets was purchased in November, 1942, by a Bronx banker at a war-bond rally for a whopping $35,000!

One down side to the flight occurred a few hours after arrival. Chief of Pilot Training and Operations Capt. Gray told the NC-02's crew they were now part of the Atlantic Division, that the Pacific Division would be down-sized in flying manpower and ships due to route cutbacks following the Pearl Harbor attack. Ford and his men were stunned in that their families were settled in and around San Francisco. In addition, Second Officer Roberick Brown was to have soon transferred to Miami where he expected to accumulate 1,500 necessary air-hours flying "home coast" DC-3s in order to become qualified as a prospective ocean division captain. Handsome Brown became so upset and angry with Gray that he stormed out of the master officer's office and went across the base to Amex's station where, with his extensive Pan Am experience, he was hired on the spot to fly the steamship company's three S-44s, and, at a much higher pay rate!

One of the more humorous aspects of Capt. Ford's heroic flight was when, at the end of the trip, Division Engineer McVitty went aboard to check the NC-02's interior. In a restroom a sign in red crayon called for water conservation. A Sudan Government-labelled bottle instructed the crew to take one tablespoon every four hours. An anticlimax to the trip came the same month when Poindexter and First Officer Mack were invited to the then *CBS* New York radio show *Take It Or Leave It*. Host Phil Baker, gagman and musician, queried the airmen about their long ordeal. Just about every question Baker asked was incorrectly answered due to censorship. Baker gave up his probing and quipped, "I know exactly what you boys mean. A year ago I went down to get my pilot's license, and the instructor said, 'You want an ordinary pilot's license, Mr. Baker, or do you want to make an ace of yourself?'"[163]

By the time Capt. Ford brought the clipper into New York, Pan Am's mid-Pacific island bases were under Japanese control. Two of Wake's airline personnel were taken prisoner along with the remaining Marines and civilian workers when the island's commander surrendered to Japanese forces on December 23rd. Forty of the clipper staff and their families were also rounded up by the Japanese in Manila as well as on Guam. In all, nine Pan Am employees were killed. Eighty-one were interned in camps, first at Manila then in Kobe, Japan, and Shanghai where they spent 37 anguished months of brutal treatment. One was shot and killed.

Four days after Japan's attack, Hitler officially declared war on America. More refugees fled to Lisbon that included many nearly entrapped U.S. citizens. Amongst the latter was 39-year-old Henry J. Taylor, last American newsman to abandon his Berlin post. After flying to Lisbon aboard the NC-04 on October 4th, and after completing a 72-day, 2,144-mile air journey throughout Europe that took him as far south as Gibraltar interviewing heads of state, *INS* North American Newspaper Alliance Foreign Correspondent Taylor rushed aboard a landplane for Lisbon just before the infuriated Fuhrer broadcasted Germany's death-throw upon the U.S. A shaky and prioritized Taylor, who carried vital U.S. information, reboarded the berth-stripped and heavily loaded *Atlantic Clipper* for New York, via Africa and the South Atlantic. By the end of December, 1941, 25,248 passengers had crossed the Atlantic in 314s.

With the outbreak of hostilities, Pan Am operations became scrutinized — and in a sense acquisitioned — by the U.S. Armed Forces. The Boeing, Martin and Sikorsky boats, as were a number of other U.S. commercial aircraft, were immediately drafted into military service. Three days after Pearl Harbor, the *American Clipper* departed for Hawaii, the only transpacific route left open. It was the first of many mercy flights, her holds filled to capacity with 1,465 pounds of serum and vaccines, 94 pounds of blood serum, 1,176 pounds of drugs, 834 pounds of triple typhoid serum, government officials and priority mail.

Roy L. Donham*, chief purser at the Pacific Division since 1937, and who accumulated more than 1,200 hours on 314s, was aboard.

"Looking down, coming into Pearl Harbor," Donham wrote, "was just one big mess — smashed aircraft, ships upside down and laying on their sides. Some were still smoking. A couple of U.S. fighter planes came up close to look the 314 over and followed us in."[164]

On the return trip, the NC-06 carried priority passengers, pregnant military wives, mothers and children ordered to leave the is-

---

*Left Pan Am in 1957 to start his own catering business.

The NC-09 storms away for one of many white-sprayed lift-offs from Riker's Island Channel while LaGuardia Field stretch-lined background. Patriotic flag-waving photo was taken from swerving *Panair* launch. (*Photo Courtesy: Pan American World Airways*)

lands. A nursing station was set up at Treasure Island to assist the arrivals.

William V. McMenimen, vice-president and general manager of Raymond Concrete Pile Co., recalled flying by 314 on government business to and from Honolulu during the dark days shortly after December 7th. On two of his trips berths had been eliminated, their weight allocated for emergency war cargo.

"Thirty-six women and children — mostly the latter -were aboard being evacuated from the islands. Some mothers had their own children and others besides because there wasn't enough room for additional adults. One of the children was a 10-week-old incubator baby. During the night all of us slept on the floor under most uncomfortable conditions, yet not once was there a child's cry to bother us. They seemed to sense that something unusual was happening and that it was no time to fuss. The taking of a suitcase on that trip meant that a child would be left behind, so I left Honolulu fully clothed, but with only a toothbrush for baggage!

"After December 7th, I enjoyed many flights between San Francisco and Honolulu, all of them with interesting compartment companions. One afternoon we left San Francisco for Hawaii with but three passengers aboard because of the heavy supplies of war cargo. One of them, a fine-looking soldier, introduced himself simply as Hurley. It was Gen. Patrick J. Hurley, who was starting out on a new assignment as minister to New Zealand...

"We reminisced until about eleven o'clock when, because the war emergency made it necessary to strip the plane of bunks, we decided to retire on blankets spread on the floor of the plane. A few hours later we were awakened and advised that we were on our way back to San Francisco because of bad weather ahead.

"The restrictions on the use of radio precluded our announcing the return and when we arrived in California, we found the city had

been alerted against the approach of a 'strange plane.' Fortunately no shots were fired upon us.

"We who flew over the Pacific by PAA planes during the war period after the Japanese attack on Pearl Harbor can well appreciate Pan American's service to our country. It was rendered under conditions that were always difficult and often seemingly impossible, but the clippers continued to fly."[165]

The clippers may have forged ahead, yet Pan Am's Pacific Division was crippled by the lack of available aircraft immediately following Pearl Harbor. Trippe's *Anzac Clipper* was being refurbished with a more professional camouflage paint job. The *Philippine Clipper* underwent a month's hull replating and camouflaging that included an inverted gold-painted chevron indicating the ship had been wounded in battle, and the *Honolulu Clipper*, as stated, was beached for major overhaul and out of commission until the end of the month. The only boats not bogged down in maintenance at the Pacific Division were the *American* and *China Clippers*. To offset this inadequacy, the *South Atlantic Clipper* was ordered back to San Francisco from New York to assist in the first emergency flights of urgently needed war shipments to and from Honolulu.

Military acquisition of the Boeing and Martin ships was ordered on December 12th and occurred the next afternoon, two days after the U.S. and Germany officially went to war. Early signs of possible armed takeover of America's commercial aircraft were brought to light by officials in Washington, D.C., a month before Japan struck out across the Pacific. U.S. Air Transport Association (ATA) President Edgar S. Gorrell, knowing war was inevitable, called together airline executives. At the Washington, D.C., session were such air leaders as C. R. Smith of American, Eastern's "Eddie" Rickenbacker, TWA's Jack Frye and "Pat" Patterson of United. Gorrell warned the men to mobilize for war — to pool their resources if they didn't want the government to take over their airlines lock, stock and barrel in the event of a military conflict. Commercial aircraft were not all that plentiful and the government, Gorrell warned, would mold them into whatever was deemed necessary for war use.

Gorrell was called to the White House shortly after war was declared. Roosevelt had drafted up an order authorizing the War Department to acquisition all commercial planes. Gorrell pleaded with the president to let the airlines run their own operations in conjunction with the U.S. Army Air Corps and Navy. Gen. Arnold was present and sided with Gorrell — that it would take too long for the bureaucratic and often divided offices of the government to set up its own air transport system. Roosevelt rescinded his order, tearing it to shreds. Nearly all commercial planes, however, would be called into duty, but allowed to function under their independent airline crews.

The sale of the Boeings and Martins was first carried out on December 13th under Army "Contract DAW535ac-914" which also provided for an extension of the South Atlantic route to Karachi and the Far East. Each of the Boeings were sold for the same price quoted Pan Am for their NC-12. The next day an emergency session was held in Washington, D.C., with Pan Am and the ATA, CAA, U.S. Army, Navy and War Department for a reasonable distribution of the 314s and M-130s to the Army and Navy. Retained by the Army were the NC-02, NC-06, NC-11 and NC-12 with the remaining boats assigned to the Navy. Justification was given by the Secretary of War Henry Stimson as approved by Roosevelt under a secret executive order issued on December 14th and finalized three days later.

Clippers taken over by the Navy were allotted by H. R. Stark, chief of Naval Operations in Washington, D.C., to the newly formed Naval Air Transport System (NATS) commissioned by Acting Chief Forrestal. Heading NATS was Lt. Cmdr. C. H. Schildhauer, liaison officer with the Army Air Corps Ferrying Command. Schildhauer ordered Boeings NC-03, NC-04 and NC-05 to be operated by Pan Am between the U.S., Lisbon and the British Isles with an Army stipulation stating that the planes could be diverted wholly or in part to such service as required by NATS. The NC-01 and one Martin were to remain at the Pacific Division under the same conditions with a possibility that the NC-01 could be pressed into service between Brazil and Portugal, via the South Atlantic and Africa, a *Honolulu Clipper* operation, for reasons unknown, that never materialized.

The Army-owned Boeings, under the direction of Col. Robert Olds, ATC Ferrying commander, were also to be flown by Pan Am

crews as established by the earlier contracts that required that communications be maintained between Miami and Malaysia, via Brazil, Africa and India. Judged reasonable and fair by the CAA in a confidential December 22nd directive from Olds to Schildhauer, the Navy reimbursed the Army for its share of the flying boats.

A new C-98 designation was given the four Boeings drafted by the Army. The "C" stood for "cargo" or "commercial" aircraft, and "98" for title catalogue listing. The clippers were tabulated according to serial numbers based on the Army's fiscal year-numbering system that corresponded to the order of acquired aircraft. Hence, the NC-12, even though purchased in early 1941, was given number 42-88632, NC-02, 42-88630, NC-06, 42-88631 and NC-11, 42-88632. Being the property of the Army before she arrived in New York from her long world flight, NC-02 was not returned to the Pacific Division and her original and proper *California Clipper* name was dropped in lieu of *Pacific Clipper*.

Schildhauer's command office kept Boeing's B-314 designation with classification numbers 48224 through 48228 for NC-01, NC-03, NC-04, NC-05 and NC-09, the numbers of which were used only for Navy filing. In addition, the 314s retained their original-painted commercial registrations on wings and tails to give them the appearance of being only civil-operated aircraft.

Importance of the Boeings to the war effort was evident in view of the U.S.' shortage of large, four-engined aircraft capable of flying long distances and carrying great quantities of war supplies.

For a short time grand clipper departures from San Francisco Bay that caused many slow-down traffic jams on *Oakland Bay Bridge* became fewer in number when Pan Am aircraft and transpacific routes were cut back following America's entry into World War Two. (*Photo Courtesy: Pan American World Airways*)

At the outbreak of war, the U.S. only had, besides the nine 314s, 23 other four-engined commercial planes that included three S-40s, six worn S-42s, two M-130s, three S-44s and nine B-307 Stratoliners — all of which did not compare in size to the 314s and to their super-sized cargo capacities.

Under the conditions set forth at the December meetings, the Army and Navy-owned clippers could be chartered out at a moment's notice on what became "Special Missions (SM)," of which 99 were made by 314s during the war, covering some 2,200,000 air miles. The Navy's 314s on the east coast were assigned to the VR-1 squadron at Norfolk, VA, but, for the convenience of maintenance, allowed to operate out of LaGuardia unless priority demanded an SM from Norfolk. Pan Am's NC-01 and M-130 *Philippine Clipper* were controlled by the VR-2 squadron at Alameda with service to Hawaii from Treasure Island. The M-130 *China Clipper* was taken to Miami, via Los Angeles, for LAD military service to and from Africa. Purchase of the clippers was kept confidential so they could assume civil status when flying over neutral countries or into foreign ports.

Like the clippers, Treasure Island was also taken over by the military shortly after Japan hit Pearl Harbor. The island base was in an expansion phase that was to include a domestic transcontinental land airport when war came. Rear Adm. A. J. Hepburn, Twelfth Naval District commandant, told the press in April, 1941, that the Navy had no intention of forming a training base on the island —

that they only wanted to house men and materials in the abandoned exposition buildings close to their Yerba Buena Island complexes.

Four months later, Pan Am extended its base facilities by constructing a new dock and walkway, extra waiting rooms, offices for government inspectors and an outside terrace on the backand south sides of the *Administration Building Terminal*. At the same time, the Navy began to settle workmen on the island with a promise to keep as many of the former faire's structures intact as possible. The Navy's invasion was based on a state of pre-war emergency allowed by San Francisco's Mayor Rosse who had opted for an act of state legislation for the final takeover as based on the pre-war crisis.

Beginning in early February, 1942, the Navy, which had taken title to Treasure Island after months of negotiations with city officials, stepped in with a wrecking crew. Down came the famous *Tower of the Sun*, its steel skeleton bulldozed away with all the other Art Deco-designed palaces that once housed industrial exhibits, to make space for a $15,000,000 compound consisting of drab, gray-painted barracks to quarter patrol and Coast Guard units, section groups and training schools. It was a costly takeover granted on a year-to-year basis that eventually became a permanently controlled military fortress. Contrary to the Navy's plans, the Pan Am station survived!

Meanwhile, sailing into the wild blue yonder, and unknown to the general U.S. and world populace, the clippers were off to war.

26

Flying 1942...

Regularly scheduled passenger service to Leopoldville and other African ports was automatically cancelled when Japan raised its sword of war against the U.S. All clipper flights to Africa became a secret, wartime nature. Captains and crews reported for SM trips without knowledge or reason as to their purpose. Many 314 round-trip cruises ranged between 10,000 to 20,000 miles. A certain amount of pioneering and danger surrounded each flight, and flying unchartered routes without CAB approval became routine.

Capt. Gray headed the second round-trip SM flight ever attempted from New York to Calcutta in early December, 1941. Leaving with the C-98 *Capetown Clipper* two days after the Pearl Harbor attack, Gray and crew transported crates of spare P-40 parts and tires to India for CNAC shipment to Gen. Chennault's "Flying Tigers" in China. The arrival of the equipment by A314 on Christmas Day, and shortly thereafter sent on to China, allowed Chennault's airmen to repair otherwise grounded fighters that soon downed 26 Japanese planes after the fall of Hong Kong, Singapore, the Dutch East Indies and Bataan in the Philippines. On the return flight out of Calcutta, Gray picked up stranded Capt. Ralph and his crew who had fled west from their strafed *Hong Kong Clipper*. Gray's SM No. 2 covered 29,801 miles in 209 hours that blazed the

In dull Navy colors, *Honolulu Clipper* at Treasure Island takes on tons of war cargo bound for Hawaii and beyond. The NC-01 became sole 314 on Pacific after NC-09, briefly returned to San Francisco to aid war effort immediately after Japan's sneak attack, was again taken back to Atlantic in early January, 1942. (*Photo Courtesy: Pan American World Airways*)

U.S. Army's aerial trail for what was to become an essential link to the ATC's global supply line to the Far East.

Special Missions Nos. 7 and 8, which left New York December 10th, carried 8,839 pounds of ammunition, extractors, engines and B-24 parts consigned to U.S. troops in Darwin, Australia. Nine SM operations were completed by Pan Am 314s within 8 days after the bombing at Pearl Harbor. At 8:00 A.M., Jan. 15, 1942, Capt. Masland and a 14-man crew lifted a C-98 away from New York to instigate SM No. 10. Destination was Bombay but later changed to Karachi. Two Pan Am employees, bound for Belem and Natal, made up the passenger list. With orders to get to India the best way he could, Masland was ordered first to Miami where his ship took on slightly more than three tons of war cargo appraised at $150,000 and then was off to Trinidad, South America, Africa and north to Cairo and Karachi out of Khartoum to conclude a nine-day trip. With a new load of cargo for the U.S., and 26 official passengers that included two Ferry Command crews, Masland retraced his route to New York. By the time Port of Spain was reached the clipper had covered 4,417 nautical miles in 34.5 hours during the return flight.

Just before leaving Trinidad, and while engrossed with weather maps and decoding a message, Masland was asked if the ferry pilots could take on a few crates of rum. Having figured the C-98 to be already over weight in load, Masland said "no." In an adjacent room the skipper shortly heard the sound of smashing crates and believed the matter closed.

Out of Trinidad the weather around New York turned for the worst forcing Masland to reroute to Bermuda. Blustering winds and 2,000-foot-ceiling stratocumulus clouds prevailed during the night arrival. Upon landing, Masland opened his side bridge window to check what he thought was only an eight-knot wind. Manuevering the clipper into a left crosswind taxi run, an unexpected 16-knot gust sharply raised the starboard wing to a point that it drove the port wing deep into the sea, submerging No. 1 engine until the inboard power plant also struck water. All aboard believed the end was near — that the clipper was going to capsize and sink. The 314, however, was too sturdy for such a happening.

Giving full right aileron and a quick right rudder, Masland uprighted the deluged C-98 but not before gallons of water had flooded through the dunked wing and rained down from overhead lounge panels to drench some horrified passengers who had rushed into the cabin believing it to be the safest point in which to evacuate. Once at the dock, and wrapped in blankets, the mixed patrons, one of whom was a Chinese ambassador and another a White House spokesman, staggered through the opened hatchway and onto the ramp. All were flush-faced, giggling and smiling. The first passenger to disembark toppled forward and fell. Another, feet dragging, was helped off by two swaying fellow comrades while still another never showed and had to be carried off. One clutched a bottle and was told by a ground crewman he could not bring it ashore. Taking one last gulp, he heaved the empty container into the bay. Splintered crates may have been left behind in Trinidad, but not the bottles of rum! Masland had been taken! Following a four-day weather and engine dry-out and grooming delay at Bermuda, SM No. 10 ended its long air voyage in New York on February 8th. The somewhat dank and cold-lounged C-98 had made it home once more.

In addition to Masland's whirl-winded trip, two more war-emergency flights raced off to the rescue in December, 1941, that transported full capacity loads of 150 cal. ammunition for Gen. MacArthur's battered Philippine-based forces. From Darwin, the cargoes were to have been flown to the islands by B-24s, but the 314 arrivals were too late. By the time the clippers reached Calcutta, they were ordered back across India to Karachi. MacArthur's forces had deteriorated and the two shipments were instead unloaded in Karachi whereupon the Boeings returned to the U.S., via Africa and the South Atlantic.

On January 15th, the NC-05 and NC-09 were ordered to proceed to Norfolk and thence to Bermuda. Prime Minister Churchill had sailed earlier to the U.S. from England aboard the *H.M.S. Duke of York* and arrived Dec. 22, 1941, under the escort of two destroyers. At the end of consultation with Roosevelt, and having addressed a joint session of the U.S. Senate and House of Representatives, England's leading statesman began arranging for his return trip. At the time the two clippers departed LaGuardia, Churchill and party boarded BOAC's *Berwick* at Norfolk for a flight to Bermuda where the men were to catch the *Duke of York* for the continued Atlantic crossing. The *Berwick* had just completed a major overhaul at Baltimore when its Capt. Kelly-Rogers was informed of the special mission. As Churchill approached the A314 at the dock, he hesitated and looked up at the operator in the control tower. Looking down from the post was former 314 Radio Officer Dalglish who, at first, did not recognize the person wearing the black bowler and black overcoat until the figure below raised his right hand and finger-signaled his noted "V" for "victory" sign.

Roosevelt was worried about Churchill's safety and thus demanded for the two backup 314s to escort the *Berwick* to Bermuda. Once safe in the British port the two Pan Am air boats were returned to LaGuardia. Meanwhile, Churchill, pressed by war developments in Malaya, and in a hurry to get home, had spoken to Kelly-Rogers en route to Hamilton about the possibility of continuing on to England aboard the *Berwick*—that is, if the flying boat could carry enough fuel. It was obvious Chruchill knew little of a 314's capabilities! The statesman was enthused about the plane's size and

A rare shot of a non-camouflaged 314 at Belem. Both Belem and Natal in Brazil were jumping off and setting in points for 314s flying across South Atlantic. Many air-unchartered rivers and harbors that clippers were forced to use, such as India's Ganges, were filled with large dead animals and other debris that could seriously damage a 314 or pull it away from its moorings—an ever in-port danger that kept strained and tired crews alert at all times. (*Photo Courtesy: Pan American World Airways*)

luxury, especially the suite where Kelly-Rogers had personally escorted him upon boarding. Once aloft, breakfast was served the Prime Minister in the suite at 8,000 feet. Churchill then visited the flight-deck where he sat for 20 minutes at the wheel puffing a cigar.

Kelly-Rogers assured Churchill the A314 could easily make the journey to England as the ship was built for just such a feat. A 40- mile tail wind was forecast out of Hamilton and the A314 could make the trip in about 20 hours. Churchill, who sat in the bridge, to watch the landing, discussed the matter with his Air Marshall, Sir Charles Portal, and the First Sea Lord, Adm. Dudley Pound, when once ashore in Bermuda. Arrangements were soon made after a clearance check with meteorologists.

After boarding by launch the next day, the *Berwick* departed for England at 2:00 P.M., Hamilton time, and lifted away in 57 seconds with a fuel load of 5,000 gallons, giving the ship a gross weight of 87,684 pounds. Churchill's disconsolated Flag Cmdr., "Tommy" Thompson, was left behind because of firmly set weight allocations allowed for Churchill's safety and protection. Thompson had begged a steward to switch places, but Kelly-Rogers intervened with a firm "no!"

Lunch was served in the salon where the captain joined Churchill for coffee. Following a sound nap in the suite, Churchill worked with his staff while periodically interrupted by Kelly-Rogers who informed his minister about the ship's progress. That evening, under a starlit sky and a darkened Atlantic below, a festive dinner of cold consomme, shrimp cocktail, filet mignon with fresh vegetables, dessert and coffee was welcomed by all. Brandy finished off the meal.

Rising early, Churchill told a steward his shoes were cold. To appease him, they were warmed on the galley's steam table and shortly returned. Once dressed, the stout statesman proceeded to the flight-deck to watch the sun break over the horizon. Sitting in the first officer's seat for nearly two hours, Churchill and the captain became anxious when England was not sighted between the cloud gaps below. Kelly-Rogers altered course under radio silence and flew north where he brought the liner over Mount Batten, Plymouth, to dodge ground-anchored interference war balloons before landing.

Churchill was later told that if Kelly-Rogers had continued on with the original course another five or so minutes in what was believed to be the approach to England from the southwest, the plane would have flown over German batteries in Brest, France. The sudden change to the north was reported by England's ground-air watch as a hostile bomber coming in from Brest. Six English Fighter Command Hurricanes were ordered up to shoot the A314 down, but failed to catch up with the *Berwick* before it arrived. A short-noticed mooring party stood by as the A314 taxied in to complete its 17-hour, 55 minute journey that covered 3,365 nautical miles. A fast- formed honor guard stood at attention on the dock to greet the country's first prime minister to fly the Atlantic. This was not Churchill's last 314 trip. On June 17, 1942, Capt. Kelly-Rogers again piloted the statesman on a round-trip to and from Washington, D.C., aboard the *Bristol* so that Churchill could once more address the U.S. Congress. At flight's end, the *Bristol* became the second commercial airplane to fly non-stop west across the North Atlantic.

"...on this particular occasion," Kelly-Rogers reported years later, "the government was anxious for security reasons that I should try and do the trip non-stop. I was to pick him up at Stranraer in southwest Scotland, and to drop him down in Washington, D.C. — in fact, on the Potomac River off the Naval Air Station at Ancostia. Well, I did do the trip non-stop, but it was pretty tedious... We left Stranraer at 8:12 P.M. and landed on the Potomac 27 hours and one minute later, the distance being 3,243 nautical miles. It was the longest trip I ever did..."[166]

Churchill's last 314 boarding occurred on May 26, 1943, after conferring with Roosevelt to set plans for Italy's invasion, increase air attacks on Germany and to step up efforts in the Pacific Theatre of war during the Trident Conference. He and his party skimmed off the Potomac for the long flight to Gibralter at 1238 hours, via Botwood, after sailing to the U.S. aboard the *Queen Mary*. Accompanying Churchill was U.S. Chief of Staff Gen. George C. Marshall.

The men were flown aboard the *Bristol* under the command of. Kelly-Rogers to Gibraltar where they arrived the next day at 1733 hours to begin inspection of the port's defenses. The only incident incurred en route was when while sleeping in the suite, Churchill had been abruptly awakened by a hard bump. Dressing and going to the flight-deck, Kelly-Rogers told the VIP passenger that the flying boat had been struck by lightning.

Before Churchill's January, 1942, trip back to England, 21 American republics began sending official delegates and newspapermen to Rio de Janeiro for a two-week anti-Axis alliance conference. Pan Am and its subsidiary PanAir, and affiliates, flew in 178

passengers from Argentina, Chile and Uruguay while others arrived by ship. Twenty-three U.S. newspaper, magazine and radio reporters were flown in clippers days before the conference began. On January 9th, the S-42 *Brazilian Clipper*, christened in Rio in 1934 by the wife of Brazil's President Getulia Vargas, left Miami with 17 passengers. Another S-42 shortly followed with 31 aboard.

Nearly 24 hours later the *South Atlantic Clipper* departed Miami with 26 delegates, secretaries and translators from the U.S. State Department to become the first 314 to fly south of Natal to the romantic and colorful port. The NC-09 had just been returned to the Atlantic Division from San Francisco.

Heading the U.S. delegation aboard the clipper, commanded by Capt. Wallace D. Culbertson who first flew for Pan Am in 1933 and became a master pilot in 1940, was Under-secretary of State Sumner Welles and wife who occupied the suite. In all, Pan Am required the use of three flying boats and 31 landplanes to transport the personnel and their parties to Rio.

A crowd reported in the thousands lined fences at Rio's Santos Dumont Airport to watch the first dramatic 314 arrival on beautiful Guanabara Bay. Capt. Culbertson swung the boat low over Sugar Loaf Mountain while the massed grouping below shouted "Viva America!"[167]

Churchill, England's first prime minister to fly Atlantic and to occupy a commercial captain's air post, later praised 314 comfort. (*Photo Courtesy: British Overseas Airways*)

In the melee upon disembarkation, some of the NC-09's passengers got disorientated by the crowd and had to go it alone to find their way to the hotels.

Pan Am's Maxwell Jay Rice, assistant to the airline's vice president, and PanAir's President Dr. Gauby C. Araujo, invited 45 of the conferees aboard the 314 the following day for a one-hour courtesy flight over Rio. Brazil's Minister of Aeronautics, Dr. J. C. Salvado Filho, was so impressed with the NC-09 that he sent two wires to Washington, D.C. The first went to U.S. Secretary of Navy Knox and to Secretary of Commerce Jesse Jones:

"PAA SOUTH ATLANTIC CLIPPER OVER RIO DE JANEIRO STOP FLYING OVER BRAZILIAN COAST STOP I CONGRATULATE YOUR EXCELLENCY ON THE EXCELLENT MEANS THESE SHIPS AFFORD TOWARD MORE CLOSELY UNITING OUR RESPECTIVE COUNTRIES."[168]

The second cable to U.S. Secretary of War Stimson extolled the 314:

"ON BOARD MAGNIFICENT PAA SOUTH ATLANTIC CLIPPER STOP I AM HAPPY TO EXPRESS TO YOUR EXCELLENCY MY CORDIAL REGARDS AS WELL AS MY ADMIRATION FOR THIS WONDERFTUL SHIP OF YOUR COUNTRY'S AIR FLEET."[169]

A short while later Capt. Culbertson departed for Europe, via the South Atlantic, to transport a group of U.S. Navy personnel assigned to help man captured Axis ships later used by the Allies to haul military cargo. At the conclusion of the Rio Conference, the NC-02 substituted the return of SM No. 11 that departed at 4:00 A.M., January 30th, carrying Welles and party. In a record-breaking trip, the *Pacific Clipper* made only two stops and reached Miami just past noon the following day. Twenty-eight and one-half hours were spent in the air, a then record for any plane flown over the route. Welles sent a message to Trippe, "Splendid trip every respect. Service could not have been better."[170]

About two weeks after the Rio Conference ended, Capt. Lodeesen called upon Operations Chief Capt. LaPorté at LaGuardia to ask for a week's leave of absence — that he had been flying continuously for months on end and desired a rest. Like out of a movie or TV script, LaPorté promised the vacation, but only after Lodeesen completed one more long and somewhat dangerous assignment. LaPorté had had Lodeesen in mind when given a top secret packet from British Air Marshall E. C. S. Evill addressed originally to Gen. Arnold. Authorization orders regarded a survey to be conducted in the Indian Ocean for a new military route far south of Egypt and India in the event the Japanese invaded and took over India. Conscientious Lodeesen was, by LaPorté's strict standards, the man chosen to handle the job. Lodeesen was apprehensive but had to follow orders.

For the next few days the well-experienced skipper checked out his assigned NC-12. Thirteen crew members selected to fly with Lodeesen questioned their captain about the mission so as to know what type of clothing to pack. Lodeesen, not revealing the clipper's destination, left such a choice to their imaginations. With only the briefest idea of where they were headed, but not the reason, the crew stocked provisions and took off from LaGuardia on February 22nd for Africa, via Miami, Port of Spain, Belem and Natal. Aboard were 25 U.S. Army Air Corps men led by Col. Clayton Bissell who were flying as far as Khartoum.

Crossing the South Atlantic at night, First Officer Lane Hurst spotted red flares on the ocean below. Lodeesen, dozing during his off-duty time, was called to the bridge. Hurst circled, flashed the clipper's landing lights, reported the position and continued east. Lodeesen took no chances on a night landing fearing a trick by a German sub.

The next morning the NC-12 alighted at Fish Lake and then flew south to Lagos and Leopoldville. Approaching the Congo's estuary, black clouds cudgeled with the incoming C-98. Lodeesen flew the ship low and under the air mass, passed the roaring cataracts and on to the semi-calm waters of Stanley Pool.

Generally speaking, Pan Am pilots disliked the west African ports. Without warning, squalls materialized severely buffeting clippers during takeoffs and landings. Wind shears were known to suddenly whip 314s to port or starboard while taxiing or turning that caused wing-dippings. Often times captains ordered crew to hobble out into the opposite wings for balance. There were also days, such as at Bolama or Fish Lake, when it became so hot and still it took up to three miles across windless, shimmering water before the Boeings could creep into the air, their hulls loaded down with cargo and mail. Many times pilots had to make their own waves by gunning 314s up and down the sea-runways so as to create enough friction to loosen keels from the sticking water.

Stanley Pool had its hazards as well. Besides the fast current, there were floating islands with clumps of trees and foliage, jutting rocks and half-submerged logs and other debris that continuously crossed the path of a taxiing 314.

It was while the crew were in Leopoldville that Lodeesen was allowed to tell his men the nature of their mission, a survey that extended far out into the Indian Ocean. Out of Stanley Pool the flight took on the designation of SM No. 16. Without radio contact or weather reports, the NC-12 was held at 1,000 feet over central Africa. Seeing a herd of elephants, the captain dropped the liner to tree-top level so all could observe the animals' stampede away from the monster air bird as if it were going to pounce down and devour them. Rising, the clipper was taken over jungle and plains to Port Bell and north to Gordon's Tree at a bend on the Nile near Khartoum. Lodeesen had never flown the route before and had no aids other then *National Geographic* maps to go by — a collected sort he stuffed into a briefcase before leaving New York.

Once in Khartoum, the 25 officers deplaned and were replaced by a survey party headed by a Col. Pohl and a Maj. Willis. After buying his men khaki wear, Lodeesen headed the clipper for Mombasa on the southeast coast of Kenya. Lift-off was made at midnight under a bright moon with 3,800 gallons of fuel, 500 pounds of galley stock and 450 pounds of survey equipment. River lights were unavailable and no specifically set sea-runway was provided. Lodeesen was warned to watch out for sandbars that could ground and severly damage a 314's hull. Two hours later, after flying past Mount Kenya, the C-98 was in Mombasa, a city with an Oriental influence set with a maze of winding, narrow streets and white-washed buildings roofed with tin.

Sitting in the bridge before striking out for the unknown, Lodeesen gave serious thought to the possible danger that lay ahead. The distance and hours of flight were calculated, but what of the safety of his ship and crew? A broken down engine with no parts to be found, a crushed bow from an unseen reef or a serious illness from which two of his men were just recovering — one from food poisoning and the other from an infected foot acquired after stepping on a sea urchin on Mombasa's beach — could ground or drastically delay the mission. There was a job to perform and Lodeesen hoped for the best.

Engines were switched on and the camouflaged C-98 slipped out into the harbor. Revving the engines to check the magnetos, Lodeesen looked out the side window. Water splashed over the sea-wing telling him the hull was deep into the sea. It would be a long takeoff — the length of the harbor estimated against the ship's 4,700 gallons of fuel plus nearly 1,000 pounds of cargo written into the

Historic English flight was basically "routine," a smiling Kelly-Rogers told reporters. (*Photo Courtesy: British Overseas Airways*)

ship's log. Overhead, six RAF bombers from the South African Air Corps circled waiting for the clipper to get airborne so they could partly escort the craft out to sea. With opened throttles, the powerful A314 stormed ahead. Lodeesen manuvered around a sail boat in his path and kept going, the keel stuck to the water with its heavy load. Seamen on a nearby freighter lined the rails to view the unique sight of an aircraft totally unfamiliar to the territory.

Ahead lay breakers. A pull back on the wheel groaned the A314 skyward for its next port-of-call, the Seychelles Islands. A few hours later the clipper was circled over Mahé Island lined with fine white beaches and lush palm trees and set down upon a large lagoon next to British-occupied Victoria, 1,000 miles east of Zanzibar.

Lodeesen posted a three-man watch and went ashore. That night Lodeesen, Pohl and Willis were the guests of the residing governor and his wife at the elegant magistrate's Victorian-styled residence. Over gin and tonic the governor and his assistants assisted the men in locating the site of a proposed air base and pin-pointed on a map to Coevity Island, 165 miles southeast of Mahé.

Coming down into the wind the next afternoon, Lodeesen skimmed the NC-12 over the rough sea off Coevity. Anchoring off shore, the survey team were rafted ashore with their equipment that included sleeping cots and two pitch tents. A steward went ashore to cook meals. Lodeesen returned the clipper to Mahé, came back to Coevity the next day but couldn't land as the sea was too rough. Returning to Mahé, crewmen took time to work on the clipper. Bilge water was pumped out, hull and wing corrosion sanded away and propellers filed down and oiled. Two days later a 75-foot British sub chaser came into port and rescued the sunburned survey team stranded on Coevity.

Before departing for the next secret port at Diego Garcia Island, a speck 14 miles long and six miles wide directly east of Mahé, a clipper officer broke security when he invited a local island girl aboard the clipper. She told authorities she was given — true or not — unwelcomed advances and was physically molested. The chief of police and the governor informed Lodeesen that by law they had to arrest the accused who had denied the allocations. Verbally chewing out the officer, Lodeesen avoided the arrest by telling the governor they were on a war mission — that the crewman involved would be charged by a U.S. military court. A grin crossed the governor's face — he was relieved of what could have been a nasty affair.

At Diego Garcia, the survey party began its work among the many coconut plantations while Lodeesen and crew sought fuel for the big boat. An Australian RAF officer stationed on the island supplied the needed octane, but all of it stored in many small cans. A whole day was spent transferring the stacked cans on the beach by rowboat out to the moored clipper that had to be poured by hand through a chamoix into the NC-12's tanks.

One of the island maidens, a girl friend to the RAF contingent, took a fancy to Lodeesen. She eyed him at a dinner given by the

Churchill-used *Berwick* made waves in a dead water, high speed taxi run before another Lagos fly-away while cockswain checked to spot any pathed debris. The A314s became a God-send to England's strapped Air Ministry. (*Photo Courtesy: British Overseas Airways/Gordon S. Williams Collection*)

Australian and later swam out to the clipper at night when Lodeesen was on watch duty. Hearing a voice, he opened the bridge's side porthole, looked down and spotted her plunked on the port sea-wing. Having avoided one near scandal, Lodeesen could not afford another and ordered her back to shore by boat.

Early morning darkness still shrouded the lagoon when the captain and his radio officer went out to the clipper to check weather reports around the Cocos Keelings, 1,500 miles from Diego Garcia, the next stop. Weather was unpredictable at the unsurveyed island chain and known to be usually socked in with hard rains at that time of year. There was also fear of a Japanese invasion at Batavia near the Cocos Keelings. Lodeesen ordered his subordinate to try and tune in to any Australian radio beam. It was an eery moment in time. The only light came from a radio's fluorescent bulb. Transmission dials were slowly turned by the officer. Earphones were tight against his head as he manipulated the set to try and hear any incoming messages. By coincidence, a flashed signal was picked up out of Melbourne addressed to the NC-12's crew. A Gen. Brett was trying to warn Lodeesen and his men not to proceed any further — to leave the area immediately and proceed back to the U.S. Japanese forces were advancing into the Dutch East Indies and enemy planes were reported close at hand. It was time to get the hell out!

That afternoon the *Capetown Clipper* was headed back towards Mombasa. Instinct told Lodeesen not to proceed until one last check was made. Leaving the bridge, he went below and walked aft to the deluxe suite and removed the rear bulkhead hatch cover that exposed cables and bell cranks that gave maneuverability to control surfaces. Seated on the curved under structure with her knotted cloth containing personal possessions was the island girl, her big brown eyes expressing disappointment in being found.

Five days later the NC-12 was back at LaGuardia after flying 91 hours with only three hours spent on the ground at nine refueling stops. Special Mission No. 16 lasted 34 days that logged 225 air hours. Evill's and Arnold's efforts to set up joint military bases in the Indian Ocean for connection on to Australia had failed to develop. But the aerial highway, known as the "Cannonball Route," through the heart of Africa to Cairo and east to India was kept open. By 1943, the ATC was flying C-47s and 25-ton, twin-engined Curtiss C-46 "Commandos" ("Dumbos") over the Himalayas ("Hump") into China on former CNAC routes. The camouflaged planes flew tons of supplies and ammunition to American and English forces that eventually helped to dispel Japanese forces in southeast Asia.

Camouflaging of the Atlantic-based 314s was first instituted by the Navy and then the Army starting in December, 1941. Graduated lines from off-white to blue-gray from the waterlines up marked the Navy-owned 314s that added about 200 pounds per aircraft. Early Army screening was of a briefly applied muted, non-reflective light brown paint, soon removed due to weight. License numbers were reduced half size on all 314s so as not to be distinguishable from a distance. Despite the attempted coverups, the large painted American flags were kept on the ships' bows, tails and wing surfaces.

Shabby in appearance, the coated military colors were not the first external change to occur with the Boeings since their peacetime launchings. As noted, war in Europe doubled the mail and cargo loads in 1940. To allow for more mail and cargo space, Atlantic 314s were each stripped of 1,700 pounds in December, 1940, which allowed 4,000 more pounds per trip than formerly stored. Silver-lacquered paint, added for beauty purposes, was removed that reduced each clipper's weight 93.5 pounds. Only flags, logos, bow names, license numbers and the wings' upper orange stripes were allowed to remain, the latter later blackened out. Coats of clear lanolin from sheep's wool was sprayed over the exposed alluminum skin for protection against the elements. Bolts and seam lines became more visible which gave the 314s a patch-quilt effect.

In the interior, 276 square feet (52 pounds) of carpet was removed from each 314. Additional weight-saving came from removing suite fineries and the stripping of two aft staterooms. Gone were the overhead panelings, canvas-backed partitions, seats, berth lights, heater regulators and berth supports and bedding, outside bulkhead panelings, porthole frames, blinds, molding and soundproof fiberglass paddings. Eighteen lock screws were also removed, a mite in the reduction effort. Galley weight was cut down when sterling utensils and fine bone china were replaced with lighter and more durable lucite serving ware. Additional weight was later eliminated in mail shipments when bulks of war documents and letters were filmed by a process developed by Kodak Camera, BOAC and Pan Am in 1941. Placed in small rectangular containers, the ingenious box-contained weight-saving invention was labelled "V-mail."

Boeing liners on the Pacific Division were left as luxury ships until Pearl Harbor. Then some of the NC-0l's cabins also became holds for war cargo and mail. All berths were removed after December 7th, but replaced for the number of passengers per flight starting in late March, 1942.

If camouflaging somewhat helped to hide clippers during day flight, night or early morning darkness sheltered arrivals and departures even more. To shroud SM trips, priority passengers and the loading of war cargo, 314s began to leave and arrive under the veil of darkness. When out at sea at night, wing tip and tail-running lights were extinguished and cabin blinds drawn. Blackouts existed in the air as they did in ports and cities around the world. No longer could the clippers and friendly surface-going vessels exchange blinking light signal greetings.

Clipper security became more intense after the U.S. entered the war. Schedules were changed to conceal all arrivals and departures. Daily clipper and ship movements were eliminated from newspapers. Booked Pan Am passengers were told to report the day before departure to save time — to bring in luggage, passports and visas and to be weighed in on new, unseen electrical scales. Agents told all to keep silent about the approximated flight schedules and to leave a phone number where they could be reached in the event of flight changes or delays.

Many passengers who dialed in to confirm flights or ask questions were given little if any feedback. Wartime regulations on 314 movements were kept confidential. Passengers Kenneth Fry, Charles A. Cole and Howard Bowman of Bell Aircraft made such inquiries while at Lisbon during their return trip to the U.S. after going to England on war business. They had become so frustrated with Pan Am that Bowman drew a cartoon to present the airline after they got back to New York. The sketch depicted Pan Am's Lisbon-based Traffic Agents Arthur G. Spenceley, Fred W. Bryant and Eugenio

Final extra luggage load is placed into a 314's anchor room. Darkness concealed the goings and comings of clippers as U.S. braced itself for long war. (*Photo Courtesy: Pan American World Airways*)

Gatto as the three carved monkeys from the 1636 Stable for Sacred Horses at the *Toshogu Shrine* in Nikko, Japan. With a play on words, the cartoon caption read, "Hear No Clipper, See No Clipper" and "Know No Clipper."[171]

Initial night landings were begun along the mid-Atlantic route in October, 1940. A number of them had been made at Bermuda, but only practiced without payload at New York and Lisbon. The first intentionally scheduled night touchdown occurred at Port Washington on October 11th with 33 passengers aboard the *Yankee Clipper* under the command of Capt. A. L. McCullough. Twelve days later, the *Atlantic Clipper* left New York two hours behind schedule to make a dark arrival at Bermuda. Cleared two hours later, Capt. Sullivan inaugurated the night takeoff from Bermuda. With beefed-up A314 gas tanks, Sullivan by-passed Horta the next day to make the first scheduled transatlantic night landing at Lisbon in addition to making the third non-stop hop between Bermuda and Portugal.

Night and early morning takeoffs were conducted with the use of 11 lights anchored to buoys and placed by a launch crew about 100 yards apart along a straight line. By 1943, only five such buoyed lights marked sea-runways. Clippers operating between San Francisco and Honolulu were usually flight-planned for daylight departures and arrivals. Improved sea-runway lighting hit a new peak in early 1944 when Willard G. Eldrige, assistant New York operations manager, developed a green fluorescent dry cell tube that was activated by storage batteries in a double-ended container five by three feet with an eight-inch draft. Eldrige's design was first tested on Bowery Bay in 1943 and then put into permanent use at New York, Eire, Lisbon and Fish Lake a year later. The lights gave captains and first officers a good gauge in measuring distance at night since the lit tubes were highly visible up to two or three miles away.

In-flight food service, despite weight cutbacks, was kept at a high standard. Cocktails were eliminated for a time because of bottle weight, but later reinstated. Pan Am had given serious consideration to serving just sandwiches, fruits and thermos mug soups and beverages to reduce the poundage per trip. Arguing in favor of maintaining full meals were base commissary superintendents that included Welch-born T. Kent Morris, dean of Pacific Division catering.

Morris and others contended that the weight saved in sandwiches and the like was in the ounces and insignificant compared to full-coursed meals. He argued that crews and passengers deserved the best on long flights for the sake of alertness and energy. Therefore, for crew and passenger efficiency, airline officials decided to keep the renowned quality that took in table linens, but no vased flowers. Passengers, it was believed, could at times, depending on the load, do without berths, but they expected good food!

An efficient organizer of catering and steward service since 1935, Morris developed in-flight techniques so far ahead of its time that in 1940 he became executive secretary to the International Stewards and Cafeteria Association. He ruled over 100 Pacific island-based men and 20 flight stewards and assistants at Pan Am's Treasure Island's kitchen before Pearl Harbor. Morris' career began at a London hotel. During World War I, he joined the British Navy to recondition merchant ships. At war's end he went to railroading in England and later catered in restaurants and aboard steamships for 10 years.

Chief Pacific Division Purser Donham was selected by Morris to head Pan Am's ground catering at Treasure Island while at the same time making periodic flights to direct and advise apprentice flight stewards. Donham and his ground-kitchened men had to gather all clipper food from local San Francisco markets where vegetables and meats were bought in bulk every 10 days. Eight hours before flight time, Donham and his men prepared the menus. Vegetables and meats were 90 percent pre-cooked and finished off to perfection in the clipper galleys.

LaGuardia's *MAT* flight kitchen was, by late 1943, staffed by 12 men and women under Supervisor Lester Murray. Three former flight Stewards, Joseph Raviol, Bruno Candotti and John Salmini, prepared clipper meals. The latter two men served aboard the NC-05 when it inaugurated passenger service to Europe. They had amassed nearly 10,000 flight hours, spoke seven languages and had years of experience working in hotels and beach clubs throughout the U.S before taking on their Pan Am wings.

When clipper flights over the Atlantic first began, 15 stewards had to purchase food from hotels and stores on both sides of the ocean — a difficult task before ground chefs were introduced. In December, 1940, Candotti sailed to Bolama to open Pan Am's first foreign commissary. He was replaced four months later by Abel Almeida so he could arrange similar kitchens elsewhere.

A new commissary dining room, first opened under Supt. C. C. Snowdown, was added to the *MAT* in January, 1943, to serve 314 passengers and guests by ground stewards. Prior to this event, flight stewards had to set up tables or chauffeur passengers needing a meal in airline limousines during delayed flights over to LaGuardia's landplane restaurant if taxies were not available. Chief Pursers Candotti, Raviol and Salmini were also in charge of providing games aboard the 314s out of New York. The men designed a kit less than a cubic-foot wide weighing under four pounds for playing backgammon, cards, checkers, chess, cribbage, poker, dice and a puzzle. Shoe shine kits, stationery, electric shavers (sterilized

Clipper flights, as with surface vessel voyages, became guarded secrets throughout war, and the defenseless flying boats were heavily painted — as seen on the NC-12 leaving San Juan — to blend in with clouds when airborne. (*Photo Courtesy: Pan American World Airways*)

after each use), newspapers and magazines were also a steward's responsibility.

Service on the clippers was often praised by the many who traveled on them throughout their existence with Pan Am. The 314s were the standard of excellence gauged by royalty and heads of state, the latter of which expected the highest state of luxury. In June, 1942, exiled Queen Wilhelmina of the Netherlands and her party of five flew on the NC-04 non-stop from Lough Erne, Uster, to Shediac. Wilhelmina came to Canada, and then the U.S. to visit her daughter, Princess Juliana, and two granddaughters where she spent the summer at an estate in the Berkshire Mountains near Lee, MA.

When the *Atlantic Clipper* landed, the elderly queen told Pan Am's Public Relations Manager E. Robin Little, "I thank you for your kindness. Yes, we had a very nice trip — so smooth. Your Capt. Harold Goodwyn and his crew have been so kind. I had a good sleep, but, you know, I looked so much out of the window upon the night sea that I did not rest as long as I should have. It was so beautiful."[172]

Before leaving the airport, Steward Francis L. Lopez wrapped six sandwiches for the queen in damp towels for her continued trip to Ottawa. Wilhelmina in turn autographed cards for Lopez and crew. Four months later the queen sent Goodwyn a gold-lined, silver-etched cigarette case and 11 gold stick pins topped by a silver crown over the letter W to be given the other crew members. Then, expressing a desire to return by 314 after visiting Roosevelt in Washington, D.C., the queen and party left again on the NC-04 in September. A year later Wilhelmina returned to the U.S. After a brief visit she once more clippered over the North Atlantic on America's Independence Day. For her comfort, as in the past, the suite had been reinstated. En route, Wilhelmina chatted with Capt. Lodeesen in their native tongue. Lodeesen was aboard in a supernumerary status making a routine, but mandatory check flight.

That evening, per her request, the queen dined with the NC-06's Capt. Howard M. Cone, Jr. The meal was specially prepared at LaGuardia by Ground Chef Joseph De Grande. Grande named his soup after Holland's monarch, "Consomme Wilhelmina." Other delights consisted of fresh grapefruit, olives, celery, salted nuts, breast of Chicken Stanley, new peas, parslied potatoes, mixed green salad with roquefort dressing, assorted French pastries, Mocha and coffee.

Stepping from the *American Clipper* at Foynes, Wilhelmina, who, in 1940, fled to London rather than submit to Nazi control, turned and looked back at the monstrous 314 and stated with a smile, "This, this is a good clipper!"[173]

The same month Wilhelmina journeyed to the U.S. in 1942, Roosevelt made a special request to transport exiled King George II of Greece to the U.S. His Highness, on a special mission to arrange for shipments of war materials under the lend-lease plan for his forces fighting in many theaters, embarked the NC-06 at Fish Lake. Capt. Winston and a crew of 10 flew under "SM No. 31" non-stop to Port of Spain where Archbishop Athenagoras, Greek Orthodox leader of North and South America, boarded. Capt. Winston then flew straight to Baltimore. A mass of U.S. officials greeted the special arrival on June 10th. Due to Greek legacy, the king, when with a traveling party, must sleep alone. Crossing the Atlantic, King George left the compartment set up for the royal party and slept on the deck of an adjoining stripped stateroom. In the haste of planning the trip, Pan Am had not provided for enough berths.

Queen Wilhelmina and King George were not the first royalty to fly by 314. Crown Prince Olaf of Norway clippered to New York from Lisbon in December, 1940. His Royal Highness Olaf tried to conceal his identity by going under the name of Pard Carlsen. His secret identity was revealed by a sharp, eagle-eyed vigilant press before the 314 arrived at the *MAT*. Capt. Haakon Gulbransen was not aware that Olaf was aboard until he took the clipper out of Bermuda.

Newsman and author Linton Wells, who circled the world 12 times and travelled some 2,200,000 miles, came into the *MAT* with his wife, aviatrix and writer Fay Gillis, in July, 1942, to board a 314 for Africa. While dunking Danish pasteries into coffee in the customs room before embarking on a special government mission, Linton acted like a child excited over a new toy. The Wells' had never, in all their travels, flown by 314. Linton told an interviewing reporter, "I can't wait to get on that clipper; I've been hearing about the Boeing 314s for years and this is the first time I've ever seen one close up."

And so it went, the 314s continued to be acclaimed as the world's most luxurious airliners. Their in-flight service was unequalled. In retrospect, however, it was the experiences entailed by the crews that formed the nucleus of interest for commercial aviation historians — always the lighter side associated to some of the clipper events while at the same time still forging ahead in a war-torn world.

27

Forging Ahead

Steward Donham could count his lucky stars. Before the 314s came about, he was scheduled aboard the M-130 *Hawaii Clipper* when it made its last, fateful trip in 1938. A steward on another flight took ill. Donham replaced him just as Ivan Parker did for Donham on the M-130. Other, but less-stinging memories of clipper life included striking a coral head at Midway on a 314, aiding a female passenger who fell in a 314's powder room and broke some ribs and helping a Frenchman on a Boeing flight from Noumea to Honolulu who tried to commit suicide over a lover's quarrel. The man had ingested something before boarding and lapsed into a coma while seated in the lounge.

"I pushed him around some, but he didn't respond," Donham wrote. "Finally, I mixed up some liquid soap, old coffee drainings, mustard and vinegar and slapped him around to stick a spoonful of my concoction down his throat. I got another crew member to help me, got the man stirring on his feet, dragged him to the men's room and held him up. He finally came around, but I had to walk him so he wouldn't go to sleep."[175]

Pacific Division-based Steward Gene Dunning, who began flying for Pan Am on July 15, 1942, and retired in March, 1985, re-called a humorous 314 event. It was common practice to hand-dump garbage from the clippers. Just as aboard surface-going ships, it satisfied all Department of Agriculture sanitation regulations to do so when out at sea. Part of a fourth officer's responsibilities was to let the stewards know exactly when to do away with the refuse during the last 45 minutes of flight. Coming into San Francisco, the officer was late in remembering when he hastened down the stairs and told the steward the plane was due to land in 20 minutes. The garbage, kept in large brown turkey bags, was rushed aft to the suite used to store cargo, mail and extra crew bedding. The star-board porthole exit panel was pulled away and the bags heaved out.

"Three, unfortunately, were linen," Dunning stated, "and even more unfortunately the navigator was way off because when the steward looked down after tossing the last bag, the fog parted and he was looking at Geary and Steiner Streets in San Francisco. We never did find out where they landed."[176]

Donham added to Dunning's comments by saying he enjoyed throwing garbage out a 314's suite window. He liked playing "bombs away," but nearly got his head air-blown off each time in the fast draft!

Regarding the frequent 314 wing-dippings, Dunning remarked, "Whenever we had a cross-wind takeoff, the captain would order both stewards and other crew inside the wing to hold it down to keep the other wing from hitting the water. We would sit behind the engines and watch the exhaust stacks turn red and then white hot. With no seat belt., we would pray, 'Don't abort.' As I look back now I do see humor, but mostly I think we were 'nuts!'"[177]

Honolulu Clipper, as were other 314s, was often stripped of cabin seats to make room for additonal carrying of war supplies to besieged U.S. Pacific forces that, after many such flights, bestowed the clipper with an incredible record by war's end. (*Photo Courtesy: Pan American World Airways*)

Fergusen J. Byars, Pan Am navigator on the Atlantic from February, 1942, to November, 1948, remembered, among other 314 experiences, a frightening time aboard the NC-02 between Lisbon and Foynes:

"We had just leveled off at cruise altitude and the flight engineer was standing between the pilots making some adjustments to the throttle settings when all four engines stopped. The only sound was the wind rushing by and the airplane began to lose altitude. Would we have to make a landing at sea at night? A few moments later the engines came to life with a tremendous explosion! I thought they had surely blown themselves apart, but they continued to run smoothly and the radio operator and I smiled at each other in relief.

"The flight engineer had inadvertently hit the master ignition switch with the peak of his cap, shutting off all engines. When he realized what he had done he reached up and pulled the switch back on and the engines started to run again. But unburned gasoline had gotten into the exhaust collector rings and it exploded in all engines simultaneously when the ignition switch was turned back on.

"One day while flying across the Caribbean, I was handling the controls in the captain's seat and the first officer's seat was empty. The first officer was practicing navigation and was taking sun sights through the navigation hatch.

"The captain brought a female passenger up to the flight-deck and introduced her to the crew. When he got to me he said, '... and this is our navigator, Mr. Byars.' I turned my head to smile and say hello when she impulsively raised her hand and her eyes widened. 'Oh,' she said, 'don't turn around!' She apparently thought that if I didn't keep my eyes straight ahead, I would lose control of the airplane."[178]

Byars, who checked-out on the *Dixie Clipper* in July, 1942, under Capt. Sullivan, continued with his 314 memories:

"During my check-out flight at night, the airplane made a very sudden but momentary climb. When I poked my head through the curtain, the captain said to me, 'I saw trees!' We were flying at about 6,000 feet and our course took us directly over the Madeira Islands which rise more than 6,000 feet out of the sea.

"At Botwood, while taxiing into takeoff position, a strong gust of wind got under our left wing and pushed the right wing into the water up to the outboard engine. We were delayed nearly two days while part of the right aileron was replaced.

"At Fisherman's Lake, while the captain was practicing an instrument approach during daylight behind curtained-off windows, we landed about 75 feet in the air. We hit the water at 2.8 g's, driving me to my knees.

"Making a landing in Flushing Bay one time, I noticed a telephone pole floating in the water and warned the captain in time for him to pull up and go over it. My most unusual flight was across the North Atlantic from Foynes to Botwood when we flew under 1,000 feet all the way to avoid stronger winds at higher altitudes."[179]

Capt. Black told of a tense westbound North Atlantic landing attempt in 1943 when flying as first officer under Capt. Frank M. Briggs with the NC-04 and a load of passengers. After prop-whirling from Botwood to Shediac the 314 was unable to safely put down on June 16th due to a thick cover of fog that had swept in over the area. Using the "howgozit" curve, power was cut back to reserve fuel for a continued flight to Boston. En route, the crew learned that the alternate base was also socked in forcing a decision to re-route back to Shediac. While the radio officer took manual bearings and Black the Direction Magnetic (QDM) instrument approach bearings, Briggs descended the NC-04 500 feet a minute through the thick cloud mass until he eased the flying boat into the port's bay with zero visibility. Upon landing Black remarked to Briggs, "If I could ever do what you just did I would consider myself an airline pilot."[180]

It took nearly an hour, according to Black, for launchmen to find the fog-shrouded clipper during which time the NC-04's third officer blew a fog horn while posted in the clipper's forward anchor hatchway.

Capt. Jack H. Curry, who began flying for Pan Am in May, 1940, and who retired in August, 1975, worked his way up to first officership and made his last 314 flight on Aug. 24, 1942, before his transfer to Brownsville where he made captain flying DC-3s. A reserve 2nd Lt. in the U.S. Army Air Corps during the war, Curry recalled a most humerous event when flying a Boeing out of New York:

"We were en route to Lisbon flying at about 10,000 feet (slightly above the freezing level.) We turned on the de-icers (a small stream of alcohol to melt the ice) and the ice started coming off the props in little chunks as usual. Sometimes it would hit the side of the hull with quite a 'bang.' The forward rest room was right in line with the propellers. There was a small window just above the 'throne' and, unfortunately, a small piece of ice came banging through this window like a cannon shot, and, again unfortunately, an elderly Portuguese gentleman happened to be peacefully sitting there... He exited the rest room screaming like a manic with his trousers at half mast trying to get out of the plane."[181]

Capt. Jim O'Neal, at the time a junior 314 officer hired by Pan Am in 1937, and who logged some 15 round-trip transatlantic flights in 500-plus hours with 314s, got a chuckle during a trip when he stepped into the bridge and found both captain and first officer asleep at their wheels. More alarming, but no endangerment to the flight per se, was the November, 1942 incident when, during a run between Miami and New York after a long haul from Africa, Capt. Black, amongst others, and then a third or fourth officer, witnessed a near serious injury to the first officer when the latter opened his side window and shot an identification code flare for coastal maneuvering U.S. Navy ship personnel. The gun was not all the

Treasure Island base crew toiled for hours to load NC-01 with single largest U.S. war cargo shipped by air during World War Two. (*Photo Courtesy: Phil Stroupe/ Pan American World Airways*)

way out the porthole when he fired, and shell phosphorous blew back to cover and burn an extensive amount of holes across the officer's uniform, barely missing his face! Black summed up 314 crew experiences when he stated, "That's the way we did it in those days!"[182]

In contrast to in-flight crew experiences were happenings within the ground bases. Clippers may have been manned by men, but their ports soon became employment centers for women. War shortages for skilled males opened once closed doors to females beginning at LaGuardia in January, 1942. Twenty-three women were hired to reskin wing control surfaces, do exterior retouch painting, check and repair emergency equipment, clean spark plugs, windows and instrument panels, assemble cowl brackets, splice ropes, renovate 314 bedding and make mosquito netting for the airline's African base inns.

Women in Pan Am's ground units were first introduced as hostesses in late 1940 when the line set up a Passenger Service Department at LaGuardia. Three gals were hired to soothe first flight jitters, answer questions, help passengers with immigration problems, and in general cater to embarking and arriving VIPS. By June, 1942, the efficient corps had grown to eight and rapidly spread to Miami and later Treasure Island. The young ladies (average age being 23) were all college graduates. Some spoke seven languages other than English. One, Vera May Dawes Covell, became a *MAT* radio control officer.

In the months that followed, more women joined airline staffs and aircraft factories across the country. New jobs opened up at the clipper bases that inducted women to work as junior airport managers, radio telephone and telegraph code operators, mechanics and fuel analysts. The number of female workers at Pan Am terminals had jumped from 387 starting Dec. 7, 1941, to 1,616 one year later.

Three-hundred and thirty-one were stationed at Treasure Island, 391 at New York, 449 at Miami and the rest dispersed at Brownsville, Seattle and Mexico City.

One of the fast-paced ground activities outside hangars was in the traffic departments located at airports and sub-offices within the heart of major free world cities. Traffic personnel, such as African-based Dick Carlson, Lisbon's and then London's Andrew Jackson Kelly and Natal's Henry Taft Snowden, were confronted with mounds of paper work to check and clear clippers, passengers and cargoes. Before the war, Pan Am had left much of this effort to transportation companies and to travel agencies that functioned on commissions. Pan Am traffic managers were held responsible only for correct departmentalization of passenger, mail and express traffic into sales, advertising and passenger service. General ticket sales, handling and servicing were left to individualized companies and travel agents. When war came, the nearly 3,000 travel agents dwindled to less than 100. Pan Am's traffic departments were then forced to take on the extra work loads.

Trafficmen were pressed into checking and working out priority lists, making bookings without the aid of pre-war time tables, cross-checking for enemy aliens and having their passages frozen, solving currency problems and keeping ahead of the many foreign travel laws that changed almost daily with the war. Added to their tasks were the preparation of hundreds of clearance papers and several duplicates for ports the clippers would call upon per trip. It was the traffic manager's responsibility to make sure captains signed departure papers and carried the proper documents for each port reached. Papers improperly filled out could delay both passengers and ships that could reault in severe penalties imposed against Pan Am from foreign authorities.

A big problem for traffic departments was to ensure that all travelers had correct visas and passports. Many, including top government officials, came into the *MAT* or the Miami terminal without visas. Long distance phone calls and radio messages then had to be made to foreign dignitaries. Only through the expertise of knowing their jobs were trafficmen able to undercut red tape procedures so priority-booked passengers could embark the clippers on time.

Two incidents, one a bit humorous, that occurred in 1942 were quickly handled by alert trafficmen. An eastbound 314 landed at an African port at night. Passengers were tired and thinking only of sleep. There was a problem in that a westbound clipper had landed earlier and all beds at the line's compound were taken. Trafficman Carlson put on his thinking cap. He took the eastbound passengers to a local night club to scatter their thoughts of sleep. About three hours before dawn, Carlson snuck out of the entertainment abode and rushed back to awaken the westbound passengers. He then ordered rooms cleaned, took the rested flock to the dock and saw them off. Going back to the club, Carlson gathered up the sleepy-eyed travelers and whisked them back to the inn for their long-awaited rests.

The second incident was when Trafficman Kelly's intergrity and knowledge of immigration procedures allowed a group of United Nations officials to continue their unabated flight between England, Portugal and the U.S. Flying in from England on a Short flying boat, the commission would have had to be cleared by Lisbon's authorities upon entry and then re-cleared when leaving, resulting in a great deal of lost time. The in-coming British plane was hours late due to bad weather. Any further grounding would cause the connecting 314 to hold over for 24 hours or for it to continue on without the delegates, thereby holding up an important conference in Washington, D.C.

Knowing how to cut through official red tape, Kelly went directly to the International Police and other Lisbon offices and arranged for a plane-to-plane transfer on the Tagus, thus avoiding health, immigration and baggage custom checks. The 314 took off just in time. A few hours later the Atlantic became unflyable when poor weather closed in for five days.

Even within the troubled times of war, wonderful remarks by passengers broke the tension of flying over large bodies of water. Leaving Nassau by clipper, an elderly lady was reminded in conversation with a traffic clerk how hot the weather was. He told her it would be much cooler once the flying boat was aloft.

"I'm sure it will be all right," she exclaimed. "I'm going to sit on deck anyway!"[183] Then in New York a 314 male passenger asked a Pan Am clerk in a serious tone if stewards ironed slacks en route to Lisbon.

Capt. Lodeesen was commanding the NC-04 to Lisbon with 38 passengers when, at Bermuda, Frances Ireland Foltz, wife of *AP* Correspondent Charles S. Foltz, and her five-year-old son Chip were clearing customs. Chip, jumping up and down with excitement, yelled out, "Passport 'specktion — that's to catch spies isn't it? 'Member when we came here on the boat before, they 'spekted passports, too, and even 'speckted some cabins? They're trying to catch spies, that's why we're here. Spies, real spies!"[184]

The next afternoon after the NC-04 took off, the youngster roamed the clipper talking to passengers and crew. Steward Leo LaMarre told Frances after landing at Horta for fuel, "This kid has broken the ice quicker than it's ever been broken since the war started."[185]

During a cross-country DC-3 flight out of Los Angeles, a toddler kept shouting, "Plane, plane, plane!"

"Doesn't he like to fly," inquired a fellow passenger?

"He loves it," the mother replied, "but he is spoiled. We flew from Honolulu to Los Angeles on the clipper and he won't believe that this is an airplane."[186]

As U.S. battle tactics became more intense on both fronts, so too did the 314 activities. Preciously-awaited war cargoes doubled within the 1940-41 period. More and more the 314s were called upon for SM flights. The Boeings began to make five round-trips per week between South America and Africa with takeoff. gross weights set at 87,000 pounds. A stripped 314, changed to a cargo

transport, resulted in an increase of available weight of some 1,200 pounds. Interior arrangements were such that each 314 on the run could handle 10,675 pounds 1,000 miles based on half cargo, half passenger accommodations. Many a trip between Miami, Natal or Belem transported between 90,000 and just more than 100,000 pounds, some 16,000 pounds beyond the 84,000-pound certificated 314 weight allowance. Pressures of war had pushed and waived the 314 beyond its maximum, unbelievable capabilities. Extreme loads, however, had to be lightened for the head-winded South Atlantic crossings when the boats took on extra fuel at the Belem or Natal ports. Cargo load space was held at weights ranging between 10,000 and 87,000 pounds.

Being a small fleet, complications soon arose among the U.S. Army, Navy and Pan Am in their use of the ships. The military needed the 314s for SM missions, Pan Am for their regularly scheduled commercial flights. Since the large load weights could be carried only a short distance, and flown only along the Miami-to-Natal route with intermediate stops, the War Department devised a plan. In June, 1942, C-47s and war-altered S-42As were put into service flying the Miami-to-Natal sector to absorb much of the heavy volume of supplies and increasing numbers of military personnel that gathered at Miami's terminal destined for Africa and beyond. This helped to aleviate the piling up of a large backlog at Belem and Natal, and the 314s were able to make extra shuttles over the South Atlantic before having to return to the U.S. for servicing. The plan also allowed more time use of the 314s for Pan Am's services across the mid-Atlantic.

Among the many SM flights made in 1942, 27 hauled 1,887,579 pounds of military cargo. Some of. the loads consisted of airplane landing struts, propeller hubs, blades, gas tanks, pumps, ailerons, whole engines, generators, tools, mechanical reports and drawings, radiators, first aid kits, serum, military documents, maps, mail and the like. "SM No. 27," that left New York on April 28th, carried 7,169 pounds of aircraft paraphernalia for pilots in Africa. The C-98 was, except for one stateroom, completely stripped. Airmen who accompanied the cargo were told to leave all possessions behind in order to accommodate the excessive load.

Three significant priority 1942 trips shipped tank parts, ammunition and dust filters to North Africa. The goods were the first of many such shipments flown by 314 to England's Eighth Army commanded by Gen. Bernard Law Montgomery just prior to the "Battle of El Alamein" that marked the first major defeat of German Field Marshall Rommel. The second momentous flight was made possible by the size of the 314's port bow hatchway that allowed the transporting of a captured German Army 88 milimeter anti-tank cannon taken in the Egyptian conflict. Both barrel and breach were shipped from northeast Africa to Baltimore for analysis at the U.S. Army's proving grounds in Aberdeen, Md.

Third noted charter flight carried a valued prize of war films from Lagos to Washington, D.C., in June. Maj. Elliott Roosevelt, one of four sons of President Roosevelt and the First Lady, cared for the footage aboard the *American Clipper* under Capt. Winston that showed developments in Africa and the Near East. The U.S. Army-directed flight was conducted just before Winston's return trip to Fish Lake to pick up King George II.

The largest single piece of war cargo carried by a 314 on the Pacific Division was in October, 1942. A crate, 11 feet long, two feet wide and high that weighed 2,064 pounds, was strapped down to the NC-01's lounge-decking. Treasure Island's Art Johnson, weight-space requirement manager, the bases's maintenance department and carpenter shops were all involved with how to load the secret and bulky item. A dummy crate was made for practice. When the time came to perform the feat, a truck carried the box down to the float. Then with blocks, tackle and an electric winch used for hauling clippers in and out of the water, the item was rolled across a flat ramp, onto the 314's starboard sea-wing, swung around and taken into the clipper's lounge. The job lasted two agonizing hours with the tide running even so the dock's float remained level with the 314's sponson. Only one lounge seat had to be removed in order to fit the article into place. With only a few passengers and 2,000 extra pounds aboard, the *Honolulu Clipper* lifted easily away for Hawaii.

Ton miles flown by both Navy and general Pan Am 314 operations between San Francisco, Los Angeles and Honolulu in 1942 totaled 1,896,672 with passenger miles set at 2,980,860. Some 50 round-trips to and from Pearl City were accomplished in the first month of 1942 by the B-314 *Honolulu* and M-130 *Philippine Clippers*. January's westbound flights had a 99.8 load factor made up mostly of mail, women and children, the latter ordered back to the U.S. by the War Department. Air mail, which accumulated at San Francisco's Post Office, came in at a rate of 1,500 pounds a day. Pan Am operations between Hawaii and the mainland involved only 30 percent less mileage flown on the full, pre-war Pacific routes.

On the Atlantic, 6,600,000 miles (3,161,959 for 1942) were logged by 314 Clippers in 1,219 crossings by year's end since 1939, as well as carrying 30 percent of all first-class air mail. Passenger

miles scored an all-time high of 55,679,972 with 1,000-pound miles recorded at 2,644,140 along with 8,043,076 1,000-pound cargo and freight miles executed. Two and one-half million pounds of mail was carried. V-mail had risen to 1,345,326 pounds. Express items totaled 3,183,544 pieces. One of the heaviest single cargo shipments weighed 7,363 pounds while another crated item scaled in at 2,200 pounds only to be later topped by a huge 21-foot-long, 2,750-pound crankcase sent to Bermuda for installation in a U.S. warship that otherwise would have been out of commission for an indefinite period of time. By year's end, the average month-to-month flights out of LaGuardia were up 125 percent over 1941.

Meeting deadlines within the quick turn-around maintenance procedures, 314s arrived and departed the *MAT* 12 times in a 48-hour August period. One flight, besides crew and cargo, took on 50 passengers, then the biggest passenger load flown over the Atlantic to Europe. In one month, express items reached 100,000 pounds, and in September, 1942, a single trip express record of three and one-half tons was recorded — 700 pounds more than the previous record logged the week before.

All through 1942, records continued to be broken. U.S. Chief of Staff Gen. Marshall and Hopkins flew on "SM No. 22" from Baltimore to Scotland for an April conference. The "SM No. 23" return flight the same month was noteworthy in that it marked the first non-stop westbound flight of a heavier-than-air commercial aircraft across the North Atlantic between the United Kingdom and the U.S. Six months later the *American Clipper*, on "SM No. 58," made the first Pan Am flight to Gibraltar shortly after the southern African invasion that carried U.S. Navy salvage personnel and equipment for the repair of vessels partially sunk or damaged in combat.

By the end of 1942, Capt. Sullivan had completed 100 Atlantic crossings when he brought in a camouflaged and oil-stained 314 at night with a crew of 12 without realizing his accomplishment. When asked by airport authorities and waiting newsmen about how he felt about his triumph, the 49-year-old skipper simply stated, "Well, I do feel kind of hungry!"[187]

In three and a half years of controlling 314s, Sullivan had scored more miles over the Atlantic than all the flyers amassed in 20 years of struggled transoceanic flying. He had commanded the last 314 flight out of Marseilles when war struck Europe, battled 50-mile-per-hour headwinds with a 314 for 20 hours during another trip and brought to 1942's end a perfect Pan Am Atlantic safety record. A total of 44,000 passengers were safely carried by the Boeings since 1939. Tied to Sullivan's record as all-'round top captain were four crossings in three days. Fourteen-thousand air hours were accredited to his fine file. Other praise-worthy records went to Capt. Gray who made nine Atlantic crossings in nine days, Capt. Masland with 10 crossings in 12 days and Capt. Richard ("Dick") Vinal who commanded six crossings in 12 days—records that don't take on much significance in today's jet-age world, but at the time a great achievement in that flying the Atlantic in the early 1940s was still considered somewhat new and daring, yet safe.

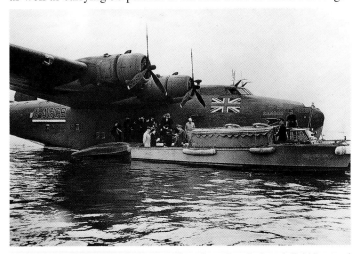

Poole-arriving *Bangor* passengers were often taken ashore by launch. British-owned A314s rapidly began to carry VIPS to and from America as war tempo increased. (*Photo Courtesy: British Overseas Airways*)

Thirty-five-year-old Capt. Joseph Hall Hart, Jr., also set a record — held to this day — in December by flying the Atlantic 12 times in 13 days, 15 hours using three different 314s. Hart beat his previous record in May when he flew the Atlantic six times in nine days, 15 hours. The young pilot began his flying career after earning a chemical-engineering degree in 1930 and then joined the Army Air Corps at March Field, CA, two days after graduation, after which he earned his wings at Rolly Field in June, 1931. He began flying for Pan Am along the Caribbean and South American sector in November, 1932, and changed to the Atlantic Division in 1938 where he attained his master pilot status in March, 1942.

Continued record-breaking 314 flights may have highlighted Pan Am's international service, but it was the acts of mercy that captured the hearts of many as the clippers crossed the trackless wastes of ocean between continents at war. Approaching San Juan after descending from eight to 1,000 feet, First Officer S. Gordon Wood scanned the ocean's surface from the bridge of the *Anzac Clipper* on an early May dawn in 1942. Three miles to port, Wood spotted the orange, brown and white sails of a lifeboat. He pointed out the blurred object to Capt. D. Lima who then banked the 314, circled and swept 100 feet off the turbulent sea for a closer look. To Wood it appeared that between 20 or 30 people had crammed the pitching boat. Only three were waving.

Finding it too rough to land, Lima continued to circle while the navigator took a fix. Lima wrote a note to inform those below of their 46-mile proximity to land and handed it to Wood who wrapped it in a life vest and dropped it from one of the clipper's underside wing-drift sight hatches where it landed 200 yards afront the lifeboat.

In 10 minutes of mercy action, the NC-11, with 19 passengers, 11 crew and a heavy cargo, was flown on to Puerto Rico. Lima reported the saga to U.S. Navy intelligence. He had been reluctant to do so from the air fearing a possible rescue interference from an alien sub that might still have been in the area. A few days later the Navy praised Pan Am in aiding the rescue of 16 survivors from the torpedoed U.S. freighter *Lammot Du Pont*. Eight of the 24 people in the boat had died after 23 days adrift in the open sea.

Wood's and Lima's actions were only one of many that resulted from sub attacks. Heroic in their efforts, 314 crews were often asked for outside assistance to deviate from their main course of flight and report on distressed vessels and to help North Atlantic ship movements in reporting the meanderings of deadly icebergs. In September, 1940, Capt. Ford, then stationed at the Atlantic Division, was radioed by Portuguese authorities after takeoff from Lisbon to search for survivors of a sunken ship while en route to Horta. Ford took the *Yankee Clipper* off its regular route, proceeded to the area and scouted about for 60 minutes. Unable to find anything other than a large oil slick, Ford was still honored for his brave effort in trying to save lives through the use of a clipper.

Even while masquerading at times as angels of mercy, the 314s also secretly played reversed roles of being winged demons to the

A Grumman-built PAA-training amphibian is dwarfed by war-coated *American Clipper* undergoing LaGuardia hangar maintenance. Numerous Navy seaplane airmen were trained at the Pan Am base. (*Photo Courtesy: Pan American World Airways*)

foe. Off-shore fishermen and clipper crews were requested by the U.S. Navy in April, 1941, to report sub sightings. Considered amateurish in the beginning, Pan Am devised a simple radio code captains could relay to clipper ports in New York, Baltimore and Miami whence they were coded on to the Third Naval District Headquarters. This procedure lasted until July 10, 1942, when the Navy ordered east coast commanders to take further action. Too much shipping was being lost to U-boats.

Responsible for fishery and clipper crew reports was Cmdr. B. M. Baruch, Jr., who was also in charge of contracting out the MAT's SM 314 Navy Flights. Pan Am captains and crew learned how to differentiate between friendly and unfriendly subs and taught other airmen how to rapidly deploy such information to said ports. On Sept. 15, 1942, ATC pilots were taken in as were 314 BOAC crews in November. By December, the Caribbean, North and South Atlantic air routes were covered. From April, 1942, to the end of 1943, clipper and other transocean-going pilots reported on the average of 10 to 12 sightings per month. Pan Am's Capt. Winston once reported a pack of 11 subs off Norfolk. Many a clipper spot-check report sent U-boats to "Davy Jones' locker!"

Even if the U.S. Navy's sinking of U-boats through clipper sightings was small in number, the Boeings and their crews had provided another strong arm to the United Nations defense system in more ways than one. The winged giants served the free countries in linking far outposts in a strategic network of aerial support. Governments placed their dependence and trust in the 314s knowing that the flying ships and their vital cargoes skirted the highways of the sky that spanned nearly around the world just for their vital needs in the effort to help defeat an encroaching and despotic tyranny aimed against mankind. Long distance operators were kept busy with calls such as, "Natal calling. Rush shipment by clipper.

Cairo calling. Decision awaits arrival of clipper. London calling. When does the next clipper leave Lisbon? Trinidad calling. Reserve four seats on the first available clipper."[188]

Financier Nelson A. Rockefeller said of Pan Am's 314 clipper fleet at a National Foreign Trade Council meeting in Boston in October, 1942, "...when it comes to the ships of the air, it's the 'Spitfires' and 'Fortresses' that make front-page news. But it is our overseas air transports that do the unspectacular but vital trucking and hauling in the air."[189]

Heavy war demands on the 314s were lightened somewhat in October, 1942, when Douglas Aircraft Co. began rolling out its four-engined C-54 "Skymasters," the military designation for the commercial DC-4. Giants in their day, but not as big as the 314s, the triple-geared planes had a wing span of 117 feet, eight inches with a fuselage length of 93 feet, 11 inches . The engines released 5,800 h.p. with a four-mile-a-minute speed. With a range of 2,600 miles, and a cargo capacity of 10,000 pounds, the ATC introduced the planes on the "Cannonball" run, thus alleviating the 314s from their many shuttle flights across Africa.

Land airports had sprung up in Africa, one of which was built next to Fish Lake, and the C-54s began out-flying the clippers in transporting men and materials to the Near East. Although 314s still flew the South Atlantic, the C-54s (many piloted by TWA crews) and later L-049 Constellations in 1944, spelled the sign of doom for flying boat operations. Regardless of the newer type aircraft that became available to the U.S. Armed Forces, the 314s failed to cease in their war effort operations. Return trips from South America transported cargoes of crude rubber, mica and beryllium, the latter for use in hardening metals in the production of war goods.

Adding to 1942's Atlantic air service was the reinstated Amex, despite Trippe's past objections. Under the December, 1941, acquisition sale, the Navy acquired the line's three S-44As to re-establish the steamship's overseas airline with civilian crews. Operations began in June, 1942, under military contract for service to Foynes and Lisbon with flights across the South Atlantic during winter months. The first trip was conducted with the christened S-44A *Excaliber* on June 22nd with Capt. Charles F. Blair in command. In October, 1942, the boat was wrecked shortly after lift-off from Botwood when it was believed by investigators that Capt. Joe Wilson's first officer accidentally flicked full down flaps that nosed the craft into the sea with a heavy loss of life to leave the other two S-44As to record tons of mail, cargo and VIPs over the Atlantic during the war.

Accommodations for Amex's operations was set up at the *MAT* where, until war's end, both S-44As and 314s were seen side by side on Bowery Bay and in the maintenance hangar. In August, 1942, Pan Am was forced to move its elated 314 mock-up out of the *MAT* to allow room for Amex's passenger and information counter, as well as for the shifting about of Pan Am's check-in station and for the construction of a new customs room. The mock-up had been a great attraction since October, 1940, when artist Paul

Lawler first assembled the three clipper-like compartments. It was taken apart and sent to New York's Museum of Science and Industry in Rockefeller Center where it remained intact until August, 1943, as a showcase for the latest Macy & Co.'s travel fashion attire seen adorning mannequins poised as passengers within the faked cabins.

In August, 1942, another accident befell a 314. Capt. Winston had just landed the NC-02 at Fish Lake after a flight from Natal and was taxiing the ship into port when a severe gust of wind that foretold the coming of a tropical storm caught under one of the 314's wings and swerved the big boat away from its marked sea-runway. Winston immediately applied full power to get the plane back on course when another strong swirl of wind blew the liner further off line and ground it to a halt atop a shoal. Overhead clouds darkened by the minute. Winston knew that in a fierce African pelting his clipper could be severly damaged where it lay stranded — or worse, torn apart unless posthaste action was taken.

Twenty-seven passengers, luggage, mail and 352 pounds of war cargo was quickly removed in a number of launch-to-shore runs after which Winston carefully worked the *Pacific Clipper*'s engines that eventually wrenched the plane free of its bind. Once afloat, the clipper was sailed to shelter to ride out the winds and strong rains.

Carpets and deck hatches were removed while waiting out the gale. Three amidship bilges were found flooded. When the storm abated, Flight Engineers Sylvester B. Tunis and Stephen P. McCrea, two of 12 crew aboard, stripped down to their shorts and jumped from a sea-wing into the murky brown water and went under to check the 314's hull. Unable to see anything through the murk, the two men felt along the keel with their hands. Surfacing, they informed Winston that the airliner had been torn from port to starboard just forward of the step.

Capt. Winston analyzed the situation and concluded temporary repairs could be made with the help of unskilled local labor while under the crew's keen direction. LaGuardia was contacted and three mechanics were sent aboard the next clipper bringing with them an array of tools and equipment. The next morning Tunis and McCrea again dove into the lake to make further inspections when they realized that diving gear was necessary. A helmet was made from a five-gallon flour can, its top removed and a hole cut into the side and sealed with a piece of pane glass. A 60-pound chunk of lead, taken from an old cable, was then soldered on top to give sink weight. Thirty more pounds of lead was tied to the engineers' waists when work was begun shortly after Burns English, the base's maintenance superintendent, rounded up port men to assist the crew. While the men were working the three mechanics from New York arrived hauling ashore a nautical helmet that became less useful than the conceived can device.

Air was fed to Tunis and McCrea from two hand-operated pumps taken from a base truck and later by a gasoline-driven pump as well as one from the 314's air compressor. An oxygen hose was

Capetown Clipper departs LaGuardia at dawn. Crews of 314s had many a war story to tell by end of conflict. One such narration began in a Lisbon bar when Clipper Radio Operator Walter Dalglish met an Italian ship's communications officer. Both men were leaving next day on same course to Horta and, having so much in common, agreed to send mutual dispatches when passing at sea. Upon seeing surface vessel, Dalglish sent salutations from the air but there was no response below. A short while later a message was flashed to Dalglish telling that Italy had declared war against the U.S.! (*Photo Courtesy: Pan American World Airways*)

provided by a local welding shop. Placed on a sea-wing, the motor-driven pumps allowed the men to work in the seven-foot water for up to an hour at a time.

Before the men went into the chilled lake, a tarpaulin was slipped under the clipper's hull and pulled tight. One by one the bilges were sucked clear and new plates, drilled with 1,000 screw holes, bolted into place. Seven-hundred of the holes were drilled from within and 300 from under water. Submerged lighting was shot by a sealed beam headlight removed from the truck and powered by a battery placed atop one of the clipper's sponsons. The last

step was mixing and pouring 1,500 pounds of concrete into the damaged holds that had been braced by two-by-fours shaped from nearby African timber. It took a week to complete the task wherein Capt. Sullivan, experienced in flying a concrete-filled 314 after his previous Horta episode, arrived on another 314 and flew the NC-02 6,000 miles back to New York for major repairs without passengers, mail or cargo.

With another year ended, and another clipper's misfortune reported to the CAB, the 314s flew on in their quasi-commercial military roles aimed towards a supposed peaceful world.

28

Casablanca and Around the World

Slowly at first, then picking up speed, the blind-drawn, five-car "Presidential Special" pulled out of Union Station, Washington, D.C., at 10:30 P.M., Jan. 9, 1943, and headed south to begin one of the best-guarded secret journies of World War Two. President Roosevelt and party were off to Morocco to attend the historic "Casablanca Conference . "

Roosevelt was cheerful as he sat in his private Pullman with Hopkins; Grace G. Tully, close associate and personal secretary; Capt. John L. McCrea, White House physician; and Adm. William D. Leahy and Rear Adm. Ross T. McIntire, chief Navy confidants. Seven other party officials also occupied the rail car. In another Pullman were quartered 11 advance personnel, seven of whom were secret service men. Despite the extensive cover-up surrounding the trip, word had leaked out to the press that the commander-in-chief was taking an extensively long journey to either Baghdad or as far away as Siberia.

Desirous of wanting to go abroad, and tired of sending special envoys in his place in order to convey U.S. political war policies, Roosevelt was firm that he alone was the only person who could meet and confer with Churchill, Russia's Premier Joseph Stalin and exiled Free-French leader Gen. De Gaulle regarding the unconditional surrender terms planned for Germany and Japan. Roosevelt also wanted to inspect U.S. Armed Forces that had landed in North Africa two months earlier. Capt. McCrea, on the other hand, was deeply concerned about the chief executive's health in undertaking the 16,965-mile trip. Roosevelt 's heart was not good and he looked older than he was with signs of great fatigue.

Winding its way south, the special-tracked conveyance, portered by five-trusted and cleared Filipino messmen from the president's ship, the *USS Potomac*, finally reached its Miami destination at 1:30 A.M., January 11th. Polio-crippled Roosevelt was carried off the train and quickly taken by a prearranged car to nearby Pan Am's Dinner Key base. Moored to two long docks extending far out into the darkened waters were the camouflaged *Dixie* and *Atlantic Clippers*, their crews having been ordered to attire themselves in U.S. Navy uniforms. The NC-05 was to carry Roosevelt and advisors while the NC-04 acted as a back-up transport that housed other party members. Since the flying boats were sold property of the U.S. Navy, all transportation details had been arranged through the U.S. Naval Intelligence Office and Pan Am's *MAT* base flight operations headquarters.

In preparing for the most momentous air voyage of the 20th century during a time of great peril, Pan Am was informed in early January to make ready two of its prized 314s for "SM Nos. 70 and 71." Dewey Long, White House presidential aid and organizer of the event, phoned Cmdr. Beruch, Jr., of the SM-planning division, who in turn notified Cmdr. C. H. ("Dutch") Schildhauer, past Pan Am Atlantic Division's chief operations manager. Schildhauer then got in touch with the airline's then Operations Manager Leslie to prepare two 314s for the missions.

Selection of the NC-04 and NC-05 was based strictly on the precedence that both aircraft had just completed major overhauls, given new coats of war paint, and had received minor interior renovations and cleaning. The only unusual request, stemming directly from Washington, was that Pan Am provide an extra abundance of linen and that one clipper be equipped with a double-thick mattress for a lower berth to be placed in a cabin adjacent to the flying boat's combination lounge/dining salon.

Immediately following the order, Pan Am's Chief Pilot Scheduling Manager Capt. LaPorté under Operations Manager John Leslie called in base Captains Howard Cone and Richard Vinal for no other reason then the men were scheduled to take out the next two flights. Both flyers were told by LaPorté to make sure that they and their crews wore U.S. Navy reserve uniforms and that the first leg of the flight was to fly the sky boats to Miami where further orders would await them, and, to be prepared to depart Dinner Key at 6:00 A.M., January 11th, with priority one passengers.

President Roosevelt (center with white hat) and half of party were U.S. Navy-launched back to waiting *Dixie Clipper*, Trinidad, following first stop en route to Africa. (*Photo Courtesy: United States Navy Archives*)

So secret and well-guarded by the military high command were the orders that even LaPorté and Trippe himself didn't know the exact reasoning behind the special SM trips. Masked in the disguise of a routine South Atlantic crossing, Capt. Cone with the *Dixie Clipper* and Vinal flying the *Atlantic Clipper* departed Riker's Island Channel late in the afternoon of January 7th for a seven, one-half hour cruise to Miami. Upon arrival both flying boats underwent three days of grueling and rigorous checking and prime servicing. On the fourth day the second set of top secret orders were handed to the pilots for flight briefing — to fly their passengers and each 10-man crew to Bathurst, via Port of Spain and Belem.

It was still dark when the crews double-checked their route planning at the line's meteorologist office. With flight plan cleared, Cone and Vinal were then given their passenger manifests. Capt. Cone was to carry nine passengers, the first of which was listed as "Passenger No. One." Twenty minutes before departure a second sheet was issued both pilots. Cone's updated sheet was headed by a "Mr. Jones" followed by Hopkins, Leahy, McIntire, McCrea and four other men Cone could not identify. Suspicion turned to reality—Cone couldn't believe what his mind assured him. He was to fly the President!

Approximately 2,200 pounds of luggage and 900 pounds of bottled water were put aboard the clippers. Red-tagged luggage went into the NC-05 while green-labeled pieces were stored on the NC-04. Each clipper had been loaded with 14 tons of fuel and given one last pre-flight check by their captains the day before.

Capt. Cone was standing in the NC-05's lounge when Roosevelt was rolled across the dock in a wheel chair, carried over the boarding ramp and lifted through the ship's main hatch and carefully lowered to the salon's deck. "Mr. President, I'm glad to have you aboard sir,"[190] Cone stated, flashing a sharp salute. Roosevelt responded with his usual broad smile, put everyone at ease with a handshake and his cordial "fire-side chat" appeal, and then was taken to cabin E just aft of the lounge.

Within minutes Master Pilot Cone taxied the NC-05 out into Biscayne Bay and throbbed the Boeing across the swelled surface along Bayshore Drive and into the pre-dawn sky at 6:05. Hopkins, as were all, sat buckled into his seat next to Roosevelt during the takeoff and later reported the President was so excited that he acted like a 16-year-old.

Twenty-nine minutes after the *Dixie Clipper* was cleared away, Vinal followed suit and stayed about 35 miles aft of the NC-05 to perform as the communication center and rescue ship in the event the NC-05 developed unforeseen trouble and was forced to ditch. Close at hand were 36 U.S. fighter planes that acted as a protective escort for a number of miles out to sea before having to return to base.

Forty minutes were spent in gaining a 9,000-foot altitude. Sunrise came at 7:40 and the flight path was altered 124 degrees and then again at 9:35 to 129 degrees. Before leaving the bridge to visit with the distinguished guest following breakfast in the salon, Cone

turned to First Officer Frank J. Crawford and quipped, "Let's not forget that this is just a normal operation..." Crawford answered, "That's right, but this will be something to tell our grandchildren!"[191]

Having finished breakfast, Roosevelt was assisted by his valet, Arthur Prettyman, in changing from a suit to a more casual and comfortable open-collared shirt, sweater and slacks. The chief then began going over navigation charts supplied him by Pan Am when Cone was permitted to pass into the presidential stateroom whereupon Roosevelt pointed with a finger out a window pane to the sea below where he once had been fishing. He then asked Cone if the clipper could be diverted to fly over the old Henri Christophe's Citadel off Haiti's coast, the second largest masonry structure in the western hemisphere. Roosevelt had visited the site in 1927 when he was Assistant Secretary of the Navy. Wish granted, Cone soon swung the 314 over the fortress for a view pass and then changed back to correct course in a turbulent free but cloud-scattered sky.

After a leisurely lunch in the grand salon, the chief executive took a two-hour nap before the flying boats began a slow descent. At 4:24 P.M., Trinidad time, both sky monsters sped up the Gulf of Paria and gracefully splashed down off Pan Am's U.S. Navy-controlled Cocorite Airport. The flight had maintained an average air speed of only 146 m.p.h. in just more than 10 hours when U.S. Navy-manned launches met the clippers.

Once ashore Roosevelt and party were hurriedly taken by auto to the *Macqueripe Beach Hotel*, a 15-minute drive from the clipper base. That evening the President dined with military dignitaries Leahy, McIntire, McCrea and Hopkins on his second-floored veranda overlooking the distant city and sea. Leahy was ill; he bucked a bad cold and ran a high temperature. McCrea informed Roosevelt of Leahy's health problem and the admiral was ordered by Roosevelt to be confined to the U.S. Navy's dispensary. Leahy's travel plans were cut short, and according to Hopkins glad of it. He was not up to the long trip but assured everyone he would rejoin the travelers on the return flight.

First takeoff was made by the *Atlantic Clipper* at 5:57 A.M. with its occupants having spent the night aboard trying to sleep in rocking berths caused by bay swells. Forty-five minutes later the NC-05 joined her sister ship and seven hours later both planes crossed the equator. A King Neptune initiation was held in the NC-04's lounge for four "pollywogs." All others were experienced "shellbacks." Capt. Cone signed a certificate for "Mr. Jones" as a cherished souvenir of the monumental sky voyage.

While cruising at 9,000 feet Roosevelt napped, played solitaire and occasionally glanced out a porthole at the seemingly endless carpet of South American jungle stretching as far to the west as the eye could see during the 1,227-mile run to Belem. At 2:45 P.M. the follow-up clipper set down on the River Para at Belem. Fifty minutes later the *Dixie Clipper* came in. During the time the planes took on fuel for the long hop across the pond, the President and party went ashore where they were greeted by, amongst others, Vice Adm. Jonas Ingram, USN commander of South Atlantic forces, and

High over Caribbean between Port of Spain and Miami, and before formal luncheon, were grouped from left to right, back row: Secret Service Agent Charles W. Fredericks, USN Capt. John L. McCrea, Secret Service Agent Elmer Hipsley, Lt. (TIC) George A. Fox, Adm. Ross T. McIntire and PAA Capt. Howard M. Cone, Jr., in Navy reserve uniform. Front row included from left to right: Secret Service Agent Guy Spaman, Adm. William D. Leahy and President Roosevelt. *(Photo Courtesy: United States Navy Archives)*

Brig. Gen. Robert L. Walsh, South Atlantic's U.S. Army Transport Command leader.

A tour of the U.S. Army-controlled Pan Am land-based airfield was conducted before afternoon cocktails were hosted at the quarters of Maj. L. E. Arnold, Belem's ATC South Atlantic Wing Station officer. Just past 6:00 P.M., the well-guarded group returned to the clipper base where they embarked for Bathurst at 6:30 P.M. The NC-04's Second Officer Mervin W. Osterhout had become ill and was replaced by a Pan Am man awaiting his next assignment. Several hours were spent at an altitude of 1,000 feet while some of the 4,600 gallons of fuel was burned away (three-fifths of a ton of gasoline was exhumed during each of the 19 hours estimated to make the crossing).

Pre-dinner drinks were served in the lounge. Stewards Albert Tuinman and Edward Garcia aboard the NC-05, and Gustove Garreau and Philip Casprini on the NC-04, prepared gourmet meals from the quality stocked food taken from the line's Belem commissary. Presented at the flower-decored tables was a past clipper passenger favorite consisting of fresh melon, celery, olives, Jelly Rosa, Florida salad, hot-buttered rolls, chateaubriand, string beans, parslied potatoes and a multi-selection of desserts menu-listed as peach melba, petite fours, Mocha and followed by coffee and brandy.

During the night rough weather was encountered by both clippers at 7,000 feet. Cone took his ship down to 4,000 feet where he managed to find comparatively smooth air for the sleeping President. Vinal, on the other hand, went down to a 1,000-foot altitude and then nosed back up to 5,000 feet for the remainder of the crossing. Following breakfast the next morning, brown-eyed, 52-year-old Hopkins read a mystery book and then taught McIntire how to

play gin rummy to help take the admiral's mind away from a persistant ear problem he suffered when the clipper's heating system malfunctioned and went out during the night.

Roosevelt slept in late and awoke in good spirits to work with Hopkins on the pending conference. Both Hopkins and Prettyman, being of civilian status, were required, other than just passports and visas, to have special travel documents. White House letters signed by Roosevelt included their names as members of the presidential party traveling on a U.S. Navy-owned aircraft operating on an official military mission.

Relaxed, and seemingly in no hurry other than what the clipper's speed could provide, the VIPS roamed about the NC-05's plush cabins in pajamas, robes and slippers and didn't fully dress until a late hour just prior to a formally set salon luncheon. At 4:30 P.M., Bathurst time, both flying boats lowered flaps, circled and cut water off the African coast. Once anchored, all were taken ashore by motored whaleboats from the *USS Memphis*, a light cruiser sailed from Natal under the direction of Capt. H. Y. McCown used as a temporary quarters for the President and his immediate aide before leaving for Casablanca the next morning. McCown escorted his Commander-in-chief, Hopkins, McIntire and McCrea on a 30-minute boat tour of the harbor passing oil tankers, barges and a net tender, the sailors of which were working atop decks and unaware of the sightseers passing below. Later, while lifting Roosevelt back aboard the *Memphis*, an aid slipped and lost his handling grip to cause Roosevelt to drop onto his posterior without injury.

Eighteen miles outside Bathurst, three camouflaged ATC C-54s waited at Yundum Field to transport the delegates to Casablanca. One C-54 was used as the executive plane, the second to carry secret service personnel and the third as an emergency back-up craft. The two envoy-carrying planes were piloted by military-inducted TWA pilots Otis Bryan and Don Terry who departed at 9:00 A.M., January 14th, with the spare plane taking off last. Bryan flew Roosevelt and associates past Dakar on the African coast at 8,000 feet, went inland over the barren Sahara and snow-capped Atlas Mountains at 11,500 feet and landed at Casablanca's Medouine Airport at 6:20 P.M. local time, thus culminating a six-hour flight. Clipper Captains Cone and Vinal were ordered to remain posted at Bathurst, and then at Fish Lake, to await the return of the party for "SM No. 71" back to the U.S.

Roosevelt was met at Casablanca by White House Secret Service Agent Michael Reilly of the advance party and taken by automobile to a rented villa in the southern residential section of town. Security was tight, the area surrounded by barbed wire, a large number of armed guards plus an artillery command. For the next 12 days Roosevelt attended the summit conference. Among his many conferrees were Lt. Gen. Dwight ("Ike") D. Eisenhower, later appointed by Roosevelt and Churchill as Europe's supreme war commander and future 33rd U.S. president, and First Armored Corps Chief Gen. George S. Patton, a somewhat arrogant individual who later became victor in Belgium's "Battle of the Bulge," Hitler's last devastating and futile offensive against U.S. forces in December, 1944.

While in Casablanca Roosevelt also met with his sons, Lt. Col. Elliott and Lt. Franklin, Jr.; inspected U.S. Army forces near Rabat, 85 miles northeast of town, and Fort Lyautey; traveled 150 miles by car to Marrakech; and flew back to Bathurst on a C-54 that arrived at 3:30 P.M., January 25th. Churchill, dressed in pajamas, bathrobe and slippers, accompanied Roosevelt to the airport to give his diplomatic friend personal au revoirs.

During his stay in Casablanca, and during the time spent at his Villa No. 2 (*DAR es SAADA*), Roosevelt entertained the then Sultan of Morocco who in turn gave the President a gold-mounted dagger set in an inlaid teakwood case, two gold bracelets and, most stunning of gifts, a high-tiered gold tiara for the First Lady. Reciprocating in less extravagance was Roosevelt's personally autographed photo engraved with the presidential seal and encased behind glass in a sterling silver frame.

Running a slight fever after his tiring travels, Roosevelt kept pushing himself to take an excursion up the Gambia River upon his return to Bathurst. He sat in a deck chair on the fantail of the 560-ton *USS Aimwell*, sold by the U.S. to England's Royal Navy under the lend-lease program. Another 690-mile round-trip C-54 air trip out of Bathurst followed that took the U.S.' leading politician to Roberts Field near Monrovia. Upon arrival he met with Liberia's president Edwin Barclay. Following lunch a review of U.S. troops was held plus a tour of a Firestone rubber plantation. Roosevelt was back aboard the C-55 for a 3:25 P.M. takeoff and back in Bathurst by 7:00 P.M. and aboard the *Memphis* for dinner 90 minutes later. Pilots Bryan and Terry and their crews departed west across the South Atlantic for Natal with the two C-54s to await further flying orders.

Nearby, Cone and Vinal waited for their special passengers after flying back from Fish Lake. At 10:25 P.M., Roosevelt was taken to the moored clipper. A few minutes before 11:00 he was carried aboard the NC-05, its interior glow shimmering forth from portholes to ripple across the inky black water. Far out in the harbor a string of buoyed lights were laid from a launch to mark the sea-runway. At 11:36 the NC-04 sped away first and disappeared into darkness. A water-thrashing NC-05 soon followed.

For most of the night the presidential plane, in essence the first *Air Force One* even if under U.S. Navy jurisdiction, encountered turbulence. Stewards had a difficult time serving late snacks to buckled-in personages. Vinal, after first flying at 7,500 feet, descended to smoother air at 1,000 feet whereupon he held the clipper for the duration of the 1,841-mile leg to Natal. Some miles out from the South American coast on the morning of January 28th the NC-04's No. 3 engine acted up. Oil spat aft to strike the wing's trailing edge and tail. Flight Engineer Donald R. Fowler told Vinal to shut the power plant down and to feather the prop. A piston had blown.

Capt. Cone landed first at 7:50 A.M., Natal time, after having passed the faltering *Atlantic Clipper*. Twenty-five minutes later, and after both aircraft had gained three hours with tail winds, Vinal executed a perfect touchdown with his crippled flying boat. Roosevelt and rank were taken directly to the anchored *USS Humboldt*, a seaplane tender brought in for the President's comfort while he conferred with Brazil's President Getulio Vargas, talks that had been prearranged before leaving the U.S. Being old acquaintances, the men chatted for some time on deck before having lunch while motion news pictures were taken and later shown in theaters across the U.S. and Canada. A week later Brazil declared war against the Axis powers!

That afternoon Roosevelt and Vargas rode in a Jeep to inspect U.S. and Brazil military shore installations that took in the U.S. Navy Patrol Squadron 74 adjacent to the Pan Am base. Officers and men stood at attention resplendent in white uniforms. After conferring briefly with commanders, Roosevelt and Vargas transferred to a sedan and rode through the city and 10 miles beyond to Parnamarim Field, headquarters for ATC's South Atlantic Wing and the Ninth Ferry Group under the command of Brig. Gen. Robert L. Walsh. A long row of twin-engined B-26 bombers sat idle until dawn for the next fly-off to Africa and the Far East. Nearby the U.S. Navy maintained its Patrol Squadron 83 under Lt. Cmdr. G. Loomia.

U.S. Ambassador Jefferson Caffery joined Roosevelt and Vargas for dinner on the *Humboldt*. Both left by 9:45 P.M. so the aging Roosevelt could get a good night's sleep. Meanwhile, Vinal's NC-04 had been replaced by the *American Clipper* that had been sent under U.S. Navy orders. It was estimated that repairs of the *Atlantic Clipper*'s blown piston would take two days. Roosevelt couldn't wait that long — he was needed back at the White House. Issued orders directed Cone and Vinal to Port of Spain to await the parties who were scheduled to continue north to Trinidad aboard the two C-54s.

A surprised and jubilant Roosevelt starts to cut his post-lunch birthday cake in NC-05's dining salon while Adm. Leahy, next to his chief, Hopkins, across from President, and Master Clipper Pilot Cone, Jr., look on. (*Photo Courtesy: United States Navy Archives*)

Leahy and Roosevelt inspect bound collection of fine Trinidad prints after joyous birthday party, one of three gifts presented to Chief Executive by passenger flight party. (*Photo Courtesy: United States Navy Archives*)

At 4:00 A.M., January 29th, the President and his staff ate breakfast and left for Parnamarim Field at 5:10 A.M. Roosevelt's plane, piloted by Bryan, was airborne at 6:00 A.M. with the second C-54 aloft 15 minutes later. White banks of clouds had rolled in along the coast while blue expanses of water glittered to the east as the planes flew north between 8,000 and 10,000 feet at 180 m.p.h. During the trip north, C-54 No. 2 passed C-54 No. 1 to circle for half an hour over Trinidad's Waller Field before the President's plane came into view. Capt. Terry landed five minutes ahead of the executive plane, the latter setting down at 4:15 P.M. after flying 2,135 miles from Natal in 11 hours and 15 minutes. Adm. Leahy, feeling in better health, welcomed Roosevelt who had to be manually hoisted off the C-54 on a special ramp built just for that purpose.

An automobile tour was undertaken to and from Waller Field and Fort Read before Roosevelt was escorted back to the *Macqueripe Beach Hotel* 30 miles outside town. Another formal dinner with military brass was held that evening on the President's expansive veranda overlooking the bay. Just before 7:00 A.M., January 30th, the entourage arrived at Cocorite Airport. Capt. Cone had done himself proud by hoisting international signal flags from atop the *Dixie Clipper* as attached to the flying boat's radio antenna that extended from above the cockpit aft to the tail. In code the flags read, "DNW, CAX ELV" and "GUB" meaning "CinC, Birth, Day, Greetings."[192] Roosevelt was to celebrate his 61st birthday aloft over the Caribbean:

Capt. Cone plowed the NC-05 away at 7:10 A.M. with Capt. Vinal following with the NC-06 two minutes later. When high over Haiti a few minutes past noon, Cone circled his clipper over Port au Prince for a short time to afford Roosevelt a more pleasing aerial view from the otherwiae empty and boring tracks of sea.

About 12:00 the President was carried into the 14-chaired dining salon and seated next to a porthole on the port side facing for-

ward. Preparations for a birthday party had been in progress since early morning. Tables were covered with starched linen. Bright red and yellow-pistiled tropical antheriums stemmed from vases to add festive color while tall champagne glasses glistened aside each place setting. Across the promenade, between two starboard tables, and perched on a padded folding chair, rested a linen-wrapped cooler filled with ice and topped by a large bottle of vintage champagne.

As planned, everyone raised their glasses at 12:30. McCrea passed a message to Roosevelt from Pan Am's Navy-uniformed Operations Chief Lt. Cmdr. Leslie who trailed behind aboard the *American Clipper*. Leslie, the only Pan Am employee knowing of Roosovelt's trip, made the flight to and from Africa as the airline's reprsentative to insure perfect service for the president and staff.

"Passengers and crew of Clipper No. 2 request you to inform the President that they will drink to his health and happiness at 1620 GMT, wishing him many happy returns of his birthday. That our Commander-in-Chief should, for the first time, be celebrating his birthday in the vast freedom of the sky seems to us symbolic of the new day for which we are all fighting with one mind and heart."[193]

Capt. Cone, who was seated at the President's table, refrained from consuming his poured alcoholic beverage while on duty as stipulated by airline regulations. Stewards Tuinman and Garcia brought in lunch from the forward galley that consisted of crackers and caviar, celery sticks, olives, roasted turkey, cranberry sauce, peas, buttered mashed potatoes and coffee. A candled birthday cake, brought aboard at Trinidad by McCrea, was then set before Roosevelt. Smiling and laughing, the Chief Executive was handed a cake cutter to make the first slice at 8,000 feet above the expansive Caribbean. Nicely wrapped gifts were presented to the surprised chief that contained a bound collection of rare Trinidad prints, a carved cigarette box and two fancy egg cups. Shortly after lift-off, and after having leveled the ship in the upper atmosphere, Cone gave Roosevelt three envelopes from the crew. One contained money for the President's Birthday Ball Fund, a second held donations for the Infantile Paralysis Fund and the third sealed individual letters written to Roosevelt by the airmen.

Gliding down, the NC-05 soon punched into turquoise-shaded Biscayne Bay at 4:35 P.M. whereupon the VIP travelers were met by an honor guard presided by Rear Adm. J. L. Kauffman, Seventh Naval District commander. Departing congratulations were warmly given by secret flyer "Mr. Jones" to both clipper crews. Carried ashore and rolled away, Roosevelt was taken to his waiting train that left for Washington, D.C., at 6:00 P.M. Capt. Cone later said of the unique round-trip flight experience, "The men and women in Pan American's shops, the crews at every station, had every detail set up. The Army Air Force and the Navy stood constant guard. The cooperation was wonderful. We take off our hats to those we had behind us. They did the hard work. Our job was easy. All we did was fly."[194] The last day's entries of "SM No. 71" in the *Dixie Clipper*'s log were entered with a red pencil under the heading, "President's Birthday."

Historically noted was that the *Dixie Clipper* had swept aloft the first U.S. President to leave his country by air; the first Chief Executive to fly an ocean; the first to touch three continents by air; and the first to cross the equator four times by air. Of the total miles covered, 70 hours and 21 minutes of the trip had been spent aboard the NC-05. From Miami the flying boats were returned to New York to continue maintaining commercial passenger and mail schedules to and from Europe as well as future-called-upon SM flights.

Roosevelt was safely home in the White House the very same day the clippers arrived back at the *MAT* base. His "Presidential Special" pulled into Union Station at 6:30 P.M., January 31st. Slush and four inches of snow chilled the air, but the European war news was good. The "Battle of Stalingrad" in Russia was stilled. Infamous German Field Marshall von Friedrick Paulus and 16 other generals had been captured that in turn forced the capitulation of all surrounding Nazi forces.

Directly connected with "SM No. 70" was "SM No. 72" that originated out of LaGuardia on Jan. 14, 1943. This mission was so well guarded by the Pentagon and Pan Am that even just the mentioning of the flight was not released to the public until Dec. 15, 1944, and the purpose of which kept secret until long after war's end.

The same day Cone and Vinal took the NC-04 and NC-05 to Miami for the start of "SM No. 70," Capt. Masland, scheduled to take out the next SM, was ordered by operations to take a night train from New York and by noon the next day report directly to a Col. Milton Arnold in the Pentagon. Done, Masland was joined by Pan Am's Atlantic Division's Air Security J. M. Van Law of coding and Communications Specialist Bob Dutton. Maps of the Indian Ocean were laid out on a table by Arnold. Could a flight, with a fuel stop at the Keeling Islands, be safely executed from the RAF base at Trincomalee, Ceylon, to Port Hedland on the northeast shores of Australia? Masland, who was told by Arnold the mission was planned to transport a 1,000-pound secret cargo, needed time to calculate such a trip based on a 314's capabilities. Masland told Arnold he would refuse the refueling stop at the Keelings because he believed the islands to be under Japanese control. Arnold gave the men 24 hours for a yes or no answer to the proposed flight.

On the train back to New York the same day, the airline men discussed the request. Back at LaGuardia Masland went to the port's hydrographic office, library and navigational chart room where he spent the night researching all available climatology Indian Ocean data to chart a figurative and somewhat feasible route that would require precise navigation, some knowledge of northeast and southeast trade winds, and an exact study of a 314's capabilities based on the weight carried versus plane weight calculated to fuel consumption curves along the projected trek to Australia. Only after plotting a 314's wing lift against its drag characteristics, settling for a stripped ship cruising at a seven, one-half-degree attitude with 50 percent power and low thrust prop pitch to conserve fuel, was Masland convinced that a non-stop flight could be accomplished. Nearly one-half of the Indian Ocean crossing would be made at 1,000 feet, then up to 8,000 for nearly the rest of the voyage until a gradual descent into Port Hedland. With a thumb's up for a go, Arnold, who had come to the *MAT*, set plans into motion.

Out one of the terminal windows that overlooked the beaching ramp, Masland noticed the NC-12 coming in for service. He hoped it wouldn't be the assigned ship. He had experienced poor power climb performance with what he called the "clunker" during the previous air mail flight to and from Africa.

Within minutes the skipper was guaranteed another 314, the NC-11, out of Ceylon — a back-up plane to the NC-12 as far as Trincomalee. Meanwhile, he was to take the NC-12 to Fish Lake under the guise of a regular commercial operation where, upon arrival, the NC-12 would be stripped for better power-rating on to Ceylon. En route, a stop was also to be made at Miami to pick up a spare 314 engine and other possibly needed parts in the event of an emergency. At Ceylon he and his selected crew could then switch to the NC-11 for a better power-performanced aircraft over the Indian Ocean. The crew of the NC-11 would return the NC-12 to New York. As for the 1,000-pound secret load, Arnold only told Masland that it consisted of three VIPs and their personal gear, and, that three seats and one berth were to remain in the otherwise stripped clipper. When asked who should prioritize the berth, Arnold, in a matter-of-fact tone, told Masland he would know when he saw his passengers. The suave, low-keyed Masland thought immediately of Roosevelt and how very dangerous such an ill-planned trip could be for the chief executive.

With two Pan Am engine mechanics aboard, Masland climbed the NC-12 off Rikers Island Channel on January 14th with reliable First Officer John Auten at his side plus an 11-man crew. All except Masland believed they were off for a routine flight to and from Africa, and had told their wives they would be home in about 18 days. At Miami, U.S. Army hands loaded the boat with 314 parts before the skipper proceeded the ship on to Natal, via Trinidad and a night flight to Belem during which time Masland had the navigators practice their charting without the use of radio fixes. Passengers, one an Indian woman in sari, were taken on at Natal for the darkened crossing to Fish Lake after an ignition and cylinder change to engines No. 2 and 3 that had run rough along the way south.

Before departing Fish Lake the next evening for Lagos, Arnold had ordered Masland and men to change into Army khaki uniforms while base personnel painted out the airline's name and logo and marked the rear fuselage with two large Army star insignias. The *Capetown Clipper* was turned into an ATC transport, the change of which was deplored by Masland when said application gave the military full credit to a mission laid out and flown by Pan Am.

Without water lighting, and cloaked in heavy fog covering the lake, the NC-12 was roared away for an eight-hour flight south to Lagos with engines running full power. Incorrect signals were flashed to the clipper's crew for entrance into Lagos. Unable to correct the matter while circling off shore, Masland gambled and

Secret Service staff also enjoyed the benefits of 314 luxury travel. Seated foreground from left to right were Hipsley and Spaman. Next to bulkhead were Fredericks and James M. Beary. (*Photo Courtesy: United States Navy Archives*)

came in over armed batteries without a shot fired. After a night's stay at BOAC's base club, and an incoherent ATC briefing of land airports to be used by the flying boat along the way to Khartoum, Masland got a weather forecast and headed the clipper for the Sudan. In less than a 10-knot wind against a 91-degree Fahrenheit surface, takeoff was registered as poor and one compared to be made under the same circumstances out of China Bay. It took Masland 4,600 feet to get the "clunker" onto the step and into the air for a slow climb that took 12,000 feet to reach an altitude of only 250 feet. Capt. Masland did not like the NC-12:

During the long 15-hour flight north, Masland briefed his men on the mission's general destination but left the supposition of carrying Roosevelt to himself. The men were then drilled to calibrate the ship's performance by practicing different climbs (altitude step-climbing) and airspeeds without using too much fuel. Masland and his fourth officer, who was holding and studying the second officer's only major map of the area and on first officer watch, opened the bridge's two side windows. The map blew out the porthole!

Khartoum was reached at the crack of dawn. Throughout the trip the NC-12's engines and instruments had given the crew problems. Codes and cyphers had also perplexed the men, never to be matched with ground stations. At Gordons Tree a continuous watch was posted aboard the clipper until the next morning's departure while Masland toiled with the 13th Air Ferry Command on security matters, part of which was to syncranize codes, radio frequencies and to collect any available weather data. With new maps, a Very pistol and star shells to be used to code signal ground stations, the refueled NC-12 was airborne again at 5:59 A.M. to wing northeast for Bahrein, the British protectorate base in the Persian Gulf, that took the flying boat directly over the Nubian Desert, Red Sea and Arabia. Before leaving Khartoum, Masland received a message from Saudi Arabia's King Ibn Saud, via the U.S. State Department, giv-

ing authorization for clipper clearance across the Arabian Desert. Holy cities had to be avoided, and if for any reason the NC-12 or NC-11 had to force land, King Saud would disclaim all knowledge of his note. Arabia, at the time, played a double diplomatic role with the U.S. and Germany in selling its oil and tried to abstain the best way possible from becoming politically involved with such minor territory incidences as clipper downings or over-flies.

Masland was three days ahead of schedule when he plunked the NC-12 down at stormy cumulonimbus-skied Bahrein. Not until the 28th did an extremely late U.S. Army liaison officer team show up to further confer about the special flight. From January 24th through the 25th special radio watches were posted on the NC-12 for word of the NC-11's arrival. Finally, on January 27th, at 1:40 P.M. local time, Capt. Charles S. (Chilie) Vaughn and his crew of 11 came into port with the *Anzac Clipper*. Vaughn had been delayed three days leaving New York as a result of NC-11 engine problems and bad weather. Throughout the flight, however, the NC-11 performed well which both pleased and relieved Masland in that the ship he was to take across the Indian Ocean would live up to his previous calculations.

The next day a U.S. Army captain informed Masland and his stunned crew that they were to fly Roosevelt, Churchill and Stalin to Australia after the "Casablanca Conference" for a meeting with China's Generalissimo Chiang Kai-shek. In preparation for the trip the NC-11's engines were run every 48 hours while both crews awaited further orders. Familiarization courses in rope knot-tying, emergency procedures and equipment checks and radio ground station schedules were given and hashed over. Navigation classes on star identification were also conducted on a rooftop quarters at night. Even stewards were instructed on how to start engines!

It wasn't until January 28th that Masland and Vaughn met with U.S. Army Lt. Col. John Steele, a former Pan Am employee, and Lt. Gil Kerlin who flew in from Cairo on a Lockheed Loadstar. Steele was to fly ahead to Trincomalee to clear the NC-11's arrival and departure while Kerlin was to accompany Masland into port as liaison officer. All were well prepared when both crews flew on to Trincomalee, the rendevous port to pick up the three world leaders.

Days passed. Unbeknownst to any of the crews, Roosevelt was already back in the U.S. hard at work when word came on February 9th to move on to Trincomalee. Whisking eastward the following afternoon, both C-98s arrived safely through a heavy squall on the morning of the 11th at BOAC's Malay Cove moorings on mountain-encircled China Bay. There Steele told Masland that a communique from Col. Arnold (had flown to Australia from San Francisco on military aircraft to await the arrival) told of a destination change from Port Hedland to Exmouth Gulf further west. The next morning the NC-11 was given a practice takeoff run from tricky China Bay followed by a reporting that the special 1,000-pound human cargo lift was cancelled. Security violations prevented the connection when ATC's liaison representative efforts were forced to dissolve the plan.

"They changed their minds," Masland stated years later, "because the Japanese got wind of it. I have never known whether the Prime Minister knew of the project. In one of his books describing the Casablanca Conference he makes oblique reference to it. In the years that have followed, it was my plan at some suitable moment to write to him and request a meeting in order to clear up this point. My object in writing would have been both simple and obvious; to talk with a man whom I had long admired, occassionally seen, but never met...

"It was obvious that President Roosevelt knew of the project. On his return to the States after the conference, he made a radio report to the nation. In this broadcast he said how pleased he had been to have had the opportunity to visit some of the troops in the North African area, and how disappointed he had been to have missed the chance to visit the forces in the southwest Pacific.

"Of Marshal Stalin, I have no knowledge. It is my recollection that it was his 'niet' that cancelled the trip, at least as far as the three leaders were concerned. Somewhere, perhaps in the east, the security was broken. Enemy interceptors patrolled the routes leading to our intended destination, Port Hedland...".[196]

Capt. Masland's heroic air deed for the Pentagon scrunched Capt. Ford's earlier near-world-encompassing journey by setting the first commercial airplane flight around the world that demands a change in air record annals. (*Photo Courtesy: Capt. William M. Masland*)

In his coded message, Col. Arnold had also told Masland to hold back on the flight until further word due to bad weather around northeast Australia. What Arnold did not crypt was that enemy interceptors had been reported flying about the planned Indian Ocean route the day the special air journey was to have taken place! Not wanting to worry or frighten the Pan Am skipper, the ATC's regional command covered up the delay by falsifying a poor weather condition until better security was recouped to advance "SM No. 72." Masland noted later that if he had known of the true reason for the temporary postponement he would have, as a civilian-prescribed captain, authorized an abort for the safety of his crew and ship. In the course of events he had been requested to replace the "big three" with a general and his two aides plus their 900 pounds of luggage.

At 8:58 A.M., Trincomalee time, February 14th, Masland and crew crept the *Anzac Clipper* away with two-cabined Army majors and Gen. Albert C. Wedemeyer, Southeast Asia's deputy chief of staff who, in 1944, became Chiang Kai-shek's chief of staff. At boarding one major asked Masland if 500 pounds of canned food could be taken aboard. Quickly analyzing his long-prepared load limitations, Masland responded with a flat "no!"

Stabilizing the clipper into its required flying attitude and cruise control took extreme effort. Takeoff was good for the dead-reckoned flight. Airspeed was set at 1,000 feet and engines pulled back to maximum power. Flying the C-98 by hand at its expected airspeed did not keep the ship up and the boat slipped in 40 minutes to a scary 240-foot altitude. Masland was worried. Then slowly, ever so slowly at its air-cushioned low level minus the 500 pounds of canned food that would have taken the boat into the sea, the sky beauty climbed back with set airspeed to 1,000 feet. It took six hours to do so! Three hours past sunset, and without a weather forecast out of Ceylon, the NC-11 was at 8,000 feet.

Radio silence and the darkness of night were the only guardians that concealed the NC-11 from later-learned searching enemy aircraft. Masland pioneered the lightless clipper 360 miles east of Sumatra, 365 miles east of Java and Bali and 200 miles east of Japanese-occupied Christmas Island at midnight. Not far away in New Guinea, U.S. and Australian forces were engaged in heavy combat with the Japanese on Buna and Gona Islands.

After a long and frustrating night working with gibbish-garbled Syko code machine cards, the NC-11's automatic pilot brought the 4,084 gallon gas-burned ship over Australia's Norwegian Bay, across green-laden hills and above Exmouth Gulf where Masland set the ship down next to the *USS Childs*, an arranged fueling tender. Col. Arnold was waiting with Pan Am's Charles Ruegg and a naval officer to tell Masland to fly 600 miles down coast to Perth to discharge Wedemeyer and aides and to pick up a Pan Am radio operator and 314 parts and return to New York from whence they came. Perth, yes, but to return across the Indian Ocean, no!

A heated argument between Masland and Arnold insued with the air chief winning out. The NC-11 was due for an overhaul after its prescribed and more than 200 air hours and was closer to the

U.S. where she lay being refueled by a floating tender line then it was going eastward. Besides, recrossing the Indian Ocean was too dangerous and Masland was not about to jeopardize his crew or war-valued ship.

With gas tanks filled, and Col. Arnold aboard, it was off to Perth where, on the afternoon of February 16th, the clipper took on a new load of passengers — 26 U.S. Navy officers bound for the U.S. — after leaving off Arnold, Wedemeyer and others. From Perth the clipper was arched southeast across Australia for a night flight to Brisbane to pick up Pan Am Capt. Art Peters who brought with him the NC- 11's Pacific island security clearance papers. Lining up with the old Pan Am South Pacific route, Masland flew the flying boat on to Noumea, Suva, submarine-shelled Canton Island and into Honolulu four days later.

After a festive night at Waikiki's old but elegant *Moana Hotel*, its beach closed by curled strands of barbed wire, the C-98 was struck east for San Francisco only to return to Pearl Harbor an hour into the flight when an engine broke down. Greeting Masland was a peremptory message to hasten to the island's ATC commander who ranted and raged over the crew's easy coming and going in wartime and for not reporting the flight upon the first arrival the day before. Masland told the fired-up general the landing had been reported. Without further conversation the skilled aviator pulled from his pocket a clearance letter he had carried since leaving New York for just such a reason at hand. It was addressed to all ATC posts informing them of a secret mission, to assist Masland in any way possible and signed by Maj. Gen. H. L. George, ATC's senior commanding officer. Without argument or further delay the NC-11 headed stateside late in the afternoon for an overnight cruise to the city by the bay where the victorious crew occupied two rooms at the classic *St. Francis Hotel* for the following night for a mere $18.

The next day, after wives had been wired of a pending homecoming and clearance given, Masland again took the NC-11 aloft and flew it some 20 hours non-stop to New York, a path that lumbered the giant south over California's San Bernardino Mountains, southeast across Arizona, New Mexico, Texas, north of Atlanta to swing northeast to New Jersey's Cape May, upwards along the coast passing Atlantic City, Asbury Park, Sandy Hook, and finally up New York City's East River to alight off LaGuardia at 9:20 A.M., EST, February 23rd, 16 hours after Vaughn had brought in the NC-12. Only McVittie was on hand to meet the arrival.

As successful as the trip was, it had taken a toll on the exhausted crew. Along the way an engineer and steward were hospitalized with malaria while others suffered skin irritations, diarrhea and dysentery. There was a lighter note as well when a large pile of wet laundry was taken aboard at Trincomalee before departure and hung on inner-winged-ribbing to dry by radiating engine heat.

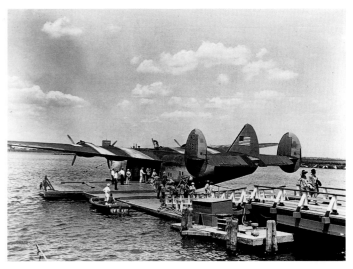

Excluding flag markings, and missing large-painted white stars on rear fuselage, *Anzac Clipper*, seen at *MAT* base with disembarking passengers, is about how she was seen under Masland's command during the world-encircling flight. (*Photo Courtesy: Pan American World Airways*)

Most outstanding was the fact that the 30,000-mile trip registered the first commercial airplane flight to encircle the globe and fly non-stop across the Indian Ocean between Asia and Australia in accordance with a scheduled operation. Pan Am's three divisions later agreed "SM No. 72" was their superior war flight, yet the public relations departments remained close-mouthed. To the end of his days, Masland was miffed about the squelching of such an important aviation feat — that possibly the voiding was related to Col. Arnold's tempered argument with him or, for some unexplained reason, nullified by a higher Pentagon authority to insure an ATC claim-to-fame mission. For sure, someone or some group stole Pan Am's and Masland's parade!

"From a strictly technical point of view," Masland wrote, "this was the first 'round-the-world flight.* Bob Ford flew from San Francisco westward to New York after Pearl Harbor. The ship he flew had once been in New York, so this was a complete circumnavigation for the ship. But ours, for what it is worth, was the first time ship and crew had made a complete circumnavigation. Incidentally, we did it the long way with four crossings of the equator."[197]

In late 1985 a clipper article mentioning Capt. Ford's flight was published in a popular magazine followed by a printed letter to the editor from Capt. Masland who once more asserted, "Without in the least belittling Bob Ford's superb flight in the *Pacific Clipper*, it was not the first 'round-the-world... The first flight completely around the world was in February, 1943, under my command."[198]

*The first lighter-than-air (dirigible) passenger-carrying craft to circumnavigate earth was made by the *Graf Zeppelin* LZ-127 in 1929.

29

"Trip No. 9035"

"Everything is arranged and I'm expecting to get off at any time... Am off by clipper again, will go to London. You can always get in touch with me through Miss Kay Phelps, the managing editor's secretary at the *Herald Tribune* in New York..." So wrote newspaperman Ben Robertson, Jr., on Feb. 16, 1943, in a typed letter to his ailing father and sister Mary "B" in Clemson, N.C., as he sat in New York's *Hotel Piccadilly* while waiting word from Pan Am on the exact day and hour of departure.

Robertson had just accepted a new post as chief of the *New York Herald Tribune*'s London bureau, a cover for his *OSS* activities. Traveling to the "Big Apple" from Clemson he had stopped over in Washington, D.C., for briefing on his latest secret mission — to carry a coded message to London's *BBC* headquarters. In New York he met with the owners of the *Herald Tribune*, the Reids, to clarify his role with the paper's *OSS* affiliations and activities therein as it pertained to his concealed purpose for travel.

Over dinner and conferences, Helen Reid took an immediate business-related liking to the well-known book writer and reporter. She told Robertson she would feel more at ease if he would wait and fly to Europe under her trusted pilot, Capt. Sullivan. Having no objections, the Reids then projected their influence through the airline channels to switch an earlier passage to one scheduled under Capt. Sullivan in late February.

Old-gloried NC-03, shown in more pristine times with, ironically, Capt. Sullivan peering forward out bridge window, was the pride of Pan Am's 314 fleet. (*Photo Courtesy: Pan American World Airways*)

As Robertson put his priorities in order, so too did 28 other people booked on the same 314 for Europe. Across town popular radio, movie and stage personality Jane Froman was wrapping up a long engagement at the *Roxy Theatre*. Her rich, combination contralto-soprano singing voice had given her a meteoric rise to fame in the early 1930s when she starred in the showing *Ziegfeld Follies* and later in the films *Stars Over Broadway* and *Music City Revels*. Froman's 1938 album recording of *Gems From Gerswhin* and the successful Oct. 9, 1941, recorded adaptation of Tchaikovsky's piano concerto *Tonight We Love* kept her husband and composer agent Don Ross busy negotiating engagements at the swankiest hotels and night clubs in Chicago and New York. The singer's last big success was just a few months before her *Roxy* show when she captivated audiences in the 1942 Broadway play *Laugh Town, Laugh*. Beautifully gowned with a face, figure and voice to match, Froman, while at the *Roxy*, received a special letter from the White House. It was from Roosevelt, an ardent fan, requesting her immediate service to entertain troops overseas.

Accepting, Froman's closing performance at the *Roxy* was on Saturday, February 20th. In the audience sat another admirer, John Curtis Burn, a Pan Am fourth officer who had just been assigned his first Atlantic flight. In a local newspaper off-duty Burn had seen an ad that featured his favorite singer whom he had never seen in person. At a matinee he was so impressed with her beauty and style he stayed on for two additional performances.

Joining Froman on the Camp Shows, Inc. (USO) tour were six additional show people that included Russian-born stage, radio and screen star Tamara Drasin. Known for her husky, haunting singing voice and fine strumming of guitar, Drasin was most remembered for her introduction of Jerome Kern's immortal song *Smoke Gets In Your Eyes* in the 1933 musical comedy *Roberta*. From *Roberta* came the 1934 movie *Sweet Surrender* with singer Frank Parker followed by numerous stage productions from which she first sang the standards *Love For Sale* and *Get Out Of Town*. She was married to Erwin D. Swann, then vice-president of the Park Avenue-based advertising firm, *Foote Cone & Belding*. In addition to Drasin's booking there were Grace Genevieve Drysdale, noted New York night club puppeteer and daughter of Grace W. Drysdale, owner of New York's *Knickerbocker Hotel*; Gypsy Markoff, renowned accordionist; Jean and Roy Rognan, husband-and-wife dance team who appeared under Lorraine and Rognan since 1937; and Elsa ("Yvette") Harris Silver, radio singer.

Also approved for travel to Europe by the U.S. State Department were William Butterworth, returning to his Lisbon post as First Secretary of the American Legation; Frank J. Cuhel, *Mutual Broadcasting System* reporter and 1928 Olympic track team member en route to a North African assignment; Manual Diaz, co-owner of the Garcia & Diaz steamship agency off to Spain on business; George T. Hart, newsman on a foreign assignment; T. W. Lamb, U.S. official engaged in government business; Arthur Lee, president Artee Corp. representing British motion picture firms, returning to his London office and to visit his son, an RCAF sergeant assigned to the RAF near London; H. G. Seidel, Standard Oil executive for European interests and marketing, also returning to his London war office; James N. Wright, U.S. official on government business; and Clifford Heldon and Spicle Lee flying to London on priority one war business. Another 10 all-male passengers bound for Europe were not listed by name, two of whom were bodyguards for Robertson.

In the interim before departure, and sheltered in a North Carolina mail box from the driving snow, was another letter from

Last known picture taken of Ben Robertson, Jr., photographed in family home from whence he was raised, shows him going over speech papers before addressing Clemson College's student body, December, 1942, and wearing war-press uniform he adorned for ill-fated flight two months later. (*Photo Courtesy: Mrs. Julian - Mary "B" - Longley*)

Robertson addressed to his father and sister Mary "B" which said in part, "I'll be leaving some time soon, probably within two or three days. Do not grieve for me if I do not return. I've done what I wanted to do with my life..."[200]

Two days after Robertson mailed the letter, "Trip No. 9035" was scheduled to depart LaGuardia's *MAT* for Foynes, via Bermuda, Horta and Lisbon. Passengers going on to Foynes and London were to transfer to a British airliner at Lisbon while the 314 returned to the U.S. by way of Africa and the South Atlantic.

Thermometers had dipped to 39 degrees when passengers arrived early for the 8:00 takeoff on Sunday, February 21st. Every seat was taken but only 28 were ticketed for Europe because of the additional heavy load of war cargo and V-mail. The majority of passengers were booked only as far as Bermuda.

In the customs room the usual Danish rolls and coffee were served. To one side Froman bid her husband farewell. He had driven the singer to the terminal from their plush apartment on East Sixty-Eighth Street. Billed in the 1930s as the "Number One Lady of Song," Froman's success was evidenced by her mink coat. Among the items she carried in her purse was a gold chain and cross sent her by a fan she had never met. Froman had tucked it into her handbag at the last minute believing it to be a good omen for a safe trip.

Two bells signaled all to board. Carrying small overnight flight bags and other personal items, passengers passed through the *MAT's* rear-swinging and security-guarded doors to the canopied, wire-fenced walkway that led to the dock and float. Cuhel, Hart and bodyguarded Robertson wore their military press uniforms, the latter carrying a portable typewriter concealing a top secret *OSS* message. Drasin held a cased guitar.

At the far end of the pier sat the camouflaged *Yankee Clipper*, its two outboard engines in operation. Pan Am's queen of the 314 fleet was credited with 240 Atlantic crossings and had broken seven Atlantic air records. The month before she had become the first airliner to complete more than a million miles of transatlantic flying in 8,505 hours.

On the flight-deck with Capt. Sullivan were nine officers, to the right of which sat First Officer H. Stanton Rush. Born in Mindanao, Philippines, in 1915, Rush was the son of a U.S. Army officer. He graduated from Virginia Polytechnic Institute in 1940, and became a U.S. Army Air Corps pilot while continuing his studies at the Parks Air College in St. Louis. Rush, desiring a flying career, joined Pan Am on July 7, 1941, and rapidly worked his way to first officership. He held a commercial pilot's certificate with a 0-825 h.p. single engine land-rating and had logged 1,706 hours as a first officer with 1,454 hours aboard 314s. Aft of the bridge were positioned David M. Saunders, first radio officer; Robert J. Rowan, assistant radio officer; Joseph F. Vaughn, first engineer; William H. Manning, assistant engineer; William Osterhaut, second officer; Leonard A. Ingels, supernumerary navigator; Andrew R. Freeland, third officer; and Burn. Below deck to greet passengers were Stewards Casprini and Greg H. Robinson.

The air voyage to Bermuda was noted as smooth and pleasant. Coffee and sweet rolls were offered, followed later by a brunch. Burn could hardly believe Froman was aboard and at every opportunity went below to gaze at her from her cabin's forward doorway aft of the galley. Both Froman and Drasin were situated to starboard in stateroom C at the window seats with Froman facing the stern. Eight males filled the compartment's remaining seats, one of whom was Robertson who sat to port across the promenade.

Just before arriving at Bermuda, Burn assisted stewards in explaining to the travelers how to fill out landing papers and to get another look at his dream gal. Froman found the young, blond-haired officer humorous when he continuously blushed during their one brief encounter.

Out of Bermuda there was a slight reduction in poundage when a male passenger, booked through to Lisbon, did not reboard. He was never seen again by either the crew or passengers after entering the customs shed. Burn said he and the crew believed the man was arrested for being a spy. The seat that became available remained unoccupied. Pan Am agents in Bermuda found it too late to contact Ken Willard, U.S. Army Air Corps officer, who was waiting to catch a 314 to continue his classified mission to Europe. Willard had arrived earlier on a clipper from New York, but his passage was interrupted when heavy seas swelled at Horta. His clipper returned to LaGuardia and Willard was told he would be placed aboard the next Lisbon-bound 314. Then "Trip 9035" was reported full and an angered Willard was bumped once more.

En route to Horta the entertainers gathered in the NC-03's lounge for a light song fest. Drasin accompanied the festivities with her talented guitar playing. That night, according to Casprini, passengers dined on steamed vegetables, pork chops, rolls and a dessert. No berths were assembled. Those who wished to rest simply stretched out on the many available cabin divans.

At 10:12 A.M. (GMT), the *Yankee Clipper* alighted at Horta whereupon it was serviced and refueled. Channel swells rose from two to three feet when, at 11:43 A.M. (GMT), the flying boat bounced across the open sea into an eight-knot southern wind, climbed and headed for Portugal at 7,000 feet.

Six hours and 52 minutes later Capt. Sullivan switched on the clipper's navigational running lights and nosed the boat down to 600 feet above the ocean as he approached the Tagus River's esturary for the last 11 miles up river to the landing area off Lisbon. The airliner was 15 minutes ahead of its expected arrival time.

About 15 or 20 minutes earlier, Casprini and Robinson informed passengers they were approaching Lisbon and to return to their assigned staterooms and seats and prepare for the landing. Upstairs, crew checked watches. Burn, having again helped with landing papers, returned to the flight-deck. Froman put on her hat and began to do the same with her mink coat when Drasin began to excuse herself for inadvertently taking the wrong divan seat. Smiling, telling her to stay put, that it didn't matter who sat where, Froman occupied Drasin's assigned position. Casprini was standing in the

A broken starboard wing and hull section protrude from Tagus. Some 54 years since the crash, survivor John C. Burn stated, "The B-314 has a special place in the memory of all of us who were fortunate enough to fly it. It represented a remarkable achievement in aircraft design, and was truly 'a pilots' airplane.' No other had so much appeal until the arrival of the B-747, which I also had the privilege to fly." (*Photo Courtesy: Civil Aeronautics Board*)

galley looking out the large square-shaped porthole while Robinson was somewhere in an aft cabin assisting passengers.

Upstairs, Sullivan controlled the ship at level flight in a northeasterly direction. To port the lights of Lisbon glittered like bits of flame, their glare reflected down across the river's rippled surface. A thunderstorm had just passed to the south at 6:00 P.M, local time and a light rain fell from scattered 2,000 foot-high clouds. Intermittent lightning broke the western darkness when the sun set at 6:20. Visibility was seven miles with a surface wind hitting six knots against an ebbing two-knot tide.

First Officer Rush was at his post, eyes straight ahead. Burn, as part of his training and with one foot in the stair well, stood behind him to observe the landing. Behind Sullivan, also watching the approach, was Freeland. Between the men, and standing further astern, was Osterhaut. Manning was at the engineer's station; Saunders was seated at his station; Vaughn was in a rear jump seat; and Ingels stood at the navigator's table. According to Burn, Saunders "...had put on his top coat and hat before the approach, an odd thing to do since we never did that until after landing..."[201]

The time was about 6:36.

Approximately three miles southeast of Cabo Ruivo Airport, Sullivan made his last radiophone communication with the airport's control tower officer. Communication was then switched to the Pan Am lanuch whose crew, headed by Scott Goddard, assistant airport manager, had laid a string of five landing lights that extended in a south-to-north direction for about 4,500 feet. The northern most light glowed red, the southern supposedly to have been green but had burned out and was replaced with a white bulb yet did not confuse Sullivan for a correct landing approach. Sullivan intended to pass over the lights in the maintained northeasterly direction, make a 180-degree turn, return south parallel to the lights, again bank to port, line up with the flickering bulbs and settle in facing north.

When the NC-03 came over the landing site Rush spoke with the launch officer requesting flares be sent up the moment the signal was given by his blinking the clipper's landing lights. A communicated response gave Rush the barometric pressure and confirmed the glide path. At that point Sullivan roared the flying boat past at 500 feet abeam of the center light to about one, one-half miles east before starting his north-to-west-to-south circle.

The first inkling of trouble was indicated by Sullivan the moment the clipper winged past the middle of the landing lights when the ship's bow slowly dropped. Not alarmed, Sullivan continued the plane eastward. To everyone else aboard all seemed normal. A plane-to-launch report was given that a right turn was about to be executed. Rush had errored and meant to say a left turn. It was only when Sullivan banked NC-03 north and then west did he realize they were in danger. A fast glance at the board showed air speed had dropped to 135 knots at 400 feet and that the angle of bank had increased 45 degrees with the bow dropping by the second.

Without speaking to Rush or anyone standing by, Sullivan pulled back hard on the yoke in an effort to raise the bow. Out of the corner of his right eye he noticed Rush — seeming to be aware of the trouble — grab onto his wheel in an effort to help. Sullivan then quickly throttled the engines and applied left aileron control.

He knew the clipper was out of control and put the port wing down, as he said, "to absorb some of the shock."[202] Casprini saw the wing in almost a vertical position to the water, the sharpest angle he had ever seen. Even at that point the other crew and passengers didn't seem to be experiencing any sense of danger.

Below, in an aft port cabin, the Rognans were holding hands and enjoying the city's view before the turn. Silver, also in an aft compartment, reached into her purse, removed a tube of lipstick and started to apply the color when a series of vibrations began to quake the aircraft — the wing started to drag across the surface.

In the control cabin Manning looked forward towards Sullivan to wait for any final instructions on engine control. He too didn't experience any steep banking, but knew they were close to the river while in the turn because he glanced out both sides of the flight-deck's aft windows. Out the north was water, out the starboard clouds.

"Everything appeared to be perfectly normal in every respect," Manning later reported, "including the airplane and the engines... He had made a turn and apparently, to my sense, had leveled off and was proceeding to land and had closed the throttles. That is why I looked up to see whether it was time to give him power or not, because of the throttles being closed."[203]

It was about that moment when the Rognans saw the wing touch the water. Knowing a crash was inevitable, and still buckled into his seat, Roy yelled to his wife to hold onto their briefcase while he attempted to remove his trousers, thinking he could swim better without them. The 314 was in a steep bank, the water had taken up most of the port view and ground lights from the Tagus' southern

Engines torn away, port wing was crane-lifted from depths of merky Tagus. Remains were guarded by both Pan Am crewmen and Maritime Police. (*Photo Courtesy: Civil Aeronautics Board*)

shore seen just moments before along the starboard side had vanished from view. Then came a mass of confusion as the wing dug in, pulled the NC-03's nose down and the ship impacted with the water and cartwheeled. Swirls of water began to fill the detached cabin as the Rognans undid their belts. Jean desperately pulled at a window emergency hatch. Within seconds she was flushed out the plane's opened exit. Her husband called out her name and Jean saw his waving hand. She screamed out his name, but Roy vanished from sight when the broken clipper section went under in 10 minutes.

The impact was more violent towards the bow. Casprini, who joined Pan Am in April, 1941, came around under water, bobbed to the surface and thought it odd he could see the tail high out of the water and yet believed he was still on the plane yet unaware of how seriously injured he was. Burn had been looking out the bridge windows when "...whether I heard something, whether someone spoke to me or whether I was just looking around, I turned my head to the right and I heard a crash, and that was the last thing I recalled..."[204]

Manning heard a snap. Sullivan had cut the power. He glanced at the engineer's panel to see the throttles moving back. It was the last Manning remembered until he regained consciousness in the water. Froman said she first felt a hard bump. "The crash itself I remember as a sudden shocking confusion of noise and violence. I was conscious of being flung across the compartment, of the sound of ripping, crumpling metal and breaking glass and then I was in the water fighting to keep myself alive."[205]

When the clipper struck nose down in a tumultuous cascade of water at 6:47, the hull's once impermeable decking stridently disintegrated. Stateroom partitions and outer bulkheads splintered into flying particles of twisted metal that uprooted seated passengers and crew. The force bashed them through crumbling outer bulkheads and spilled them into the chilly Tagus. The port wing was shorn away outboard of engine No. 1 as were both port propellers, cowlings and nacelles. Also torn away were the hydrostabilizers of which the port one struck and sheared away the tail's left fin.

Two major breaks parted the hull, one just aft of the rear wing spar and the other at the tail bulkhead in the former suite. Three-fourths of the bow's anchor room disintegrated as did the bridge and control room overheads. Seated and standing crew were whiplashed and flipped out the ripped-away overhead into the river like discarded match sticks. Rush was killed instantly, his chest crushed by colliding with the wheel when flung forward at the same time his control column backlashed. Freeland was also killed after striking his head against a hard object. Burn and Osterhaut survived. Other crew killed were Ingels, Robinson and Vaughn. Fortunately for Saunders, the coat he had put on trapped air and inflated to keep him afloat until his rescue nearly an hour later.

Froman, also unaware of how seriously injured she was, regained consciousness under water and fought free of the sinking wreckage with a determination not to give up. She heard a man swearing nearby and called out for help while gasping for air and trying to swim in a confused state of mind. The man was Burn. He thought, in his intransitive state of shock, that he had been stupid enough to have fallen out of the clipper! His senses came back only when he saw the *Yankee Clipper*'s tail sticking out of the water, its silhouetted angle similar to that of the *R.M.S. Titanic* when it made its final plunge into the depths of the North Atlantic after striking an iceberg on a cold April night in 1912.

Upon hearing Froman's plea for assistance, Burn swam to her side and kept her head above water even though his back was broken. Both talked about their careers while grappling onto floating debris awaiting rescue 45 minutes later. Not too far off, Casprini held tight to a floating mail bag.

Portuguese launches were immediately dispatched to the crash site as was Pan Am's launch stationed at the northern end of the landing lights. Sirens reverberated across the inky black water giving an eery touch to the mask of tragedy that blanketed the Tagus during the search for life and death. Numerous harbor trawlers of all sizes crisscrossed the area, their beaming and widesweeping lights focusing in on the cries for help. Burn called out when he heard the motor of a boat. Two Portuguese men tumbled overboard trying to get Froman out of the winter-chilled water. The boat drifted away into the darkness. Twenty minutes later all four were picked up by another craft and rushed to the clipper dock where they were wrapped in blankets by local fire fighters and placed onto stretchers. Froman had little clothing left on her body. The nightmarish impact tore away her coat, skirt, blouse, shoes and seamed nylon stockings.

Silver, who clambered out from one of her cabin's emergency exits that had become an overhead escape hatch when the compartmented hull had gone over on its side, swam to the north shore. Her clothes were torn to tatters but she still clutched her tube of lipstick when picked up by poople standing near the water's edge. After being placed on a stretcher she finally got around to applying the make-up.

Not hurt, but suffering from shock, Butterworth helped attendants with the injured before he himself walked to an ambulance. Ambulance attendants and others attempted to save more lives by giving artificial respiration. During the search, three bodies were taken from the Tagus, two of which were Diaz's and Rush's.

Red Cross ambulances screamed their sirens and raced through rain-slickened Lisbon streets carrying survivors to *San José Emergency Hospital*. The driver carrying Casprini forgot to close the door! At the hospital Dr. Mendes Ferreira, a Hindu physician assigned to the critical cases, was concerned about Froman's and Casprini's conditions. The singer incurred three broken ribs, a compound fracture of the right leg, left leg cut to the bone beneath the knee, a crushed ankle and dislocated back, two severe breaks in her right arm and multiple bruises and cuts with small pieces of the plane embedded in her body. Delerious Casprini, who served on the back-up clipper during Roosevelt's flight to and from Africa, was in deep pain with a broken left hip and arm, two cracked vertebrae and four smashed ribs.

Glen M. Stadler, a *CBS* reporter, and later an Oregon State Senator, was en route to Madrid and dining at a restaurant in nearby Estoril when word came that a clipper had crashed. Stadler hurried to the flying boat base but found the survivors had long since been taken away. Anxious for a story, he went to the hospital and came across an alert Froman who peered at him through two blackened eyes. They talked about her USO tour until she interrupted to ask Stadler if the doctors were going to amputate her right leg. Becoming her interpreter, Stadler spoke in French to a young Portuguese physician and told him to say "no" regardless of the diagnosis.

Stadler rolled Froman's cot into the operating room, leaned over and was kissed and thanked by the singer. Rushing off to the American Legation to see George Kennan, Lisbon's American counselor, Stadler was surprised to see Butterworth, who filled in more details of the crash for his report. Amongst other things, Butterworth told the reporter he had, as Burn had done with Froman, saved Markoff's life by keeping her afloat until they too were rescued. Stadler used Kennan's typewriter to work out a cable story intended to be sent to his New York office. An American censor in Lisbon blue-penciled the entire copy.

Injuries to the eight surviving psasengers ranged from serious to minor. Four were uninjured. Markoff sustained injuries to the head and body. Jean Rognan had a broken leg. Drysdale and Silver were treated for shock, cuts, bruises and then released. The seven surviving crew members also had injuries that ranged from minor to serious. In all, 16 persons were landed alive but one died during the night. Froman and Casprini were taken off the critical list some 24 hours later. Froman's leg was saved.

Reported among the missing passengers, and presumed dead, were Cuhel, Drasin, Hart, Lamb, A. Lee, Robertson, Seidel and Wright. Heldon and S. Lee were rescued. All hopes that boats had picked up some of the missing and transported them to Cacilhas on the south shore of the Tagus rapidly faded by the hour.

Unauthorized to say much, Sullivan related to newsmen from a hospital bed that he was unable to explain the crack-up.

As for himself he said, "There is nothing broken but my heart."[206]

Salvage operations were begun at low tide after the first rays of dawn broke over Lisbon. Removing the wreckage from the river was a grueling task. Swift currents hampered all efforts. Large portions of the wreck lay hundreds of feet apart with debris scattered across the surface. Sections of the 314's cockpit floated upwards during the afternoon of February 23rd. An extensive portion of the broken wing protruded atrociously from the Tagus' low tide. Cranes hoisted the deluged dross onto a barge and then transferred it to the nearby *Cais De Santa Apolonia Dock* for subsequent examination. Two bodies were found within the tangled and twisted fuselage, one being Freeland's. A third was retrieved seven miles down river.

Recovered from the plane and river were a number of mail bags, a leather brief case with the initials "JR" (picked up at Cacilhas with signs of being forced open and contents believed stolen), a bashed guitar, a broken typewriter, a small gold chain and cross from a lady's crushed purse and pounds of soaked and torn lug-

gage. One of the most concerned about items was a lost diplomatic pouch searched for by Lisbon's maritime police and later found.

There were rumors of sabotage, that possibly enemy agents had dropped heavy floating objects into or near the sea-runway. Another rumor was that the flight crew, including Sullivan, were distracted in their landing procedures after inviting some of the USO members to the flight-deck to watch the touchdown. Both suppositions were based only on rumor and discounted as a possible cause to the crash.

Robertson's *OSS* message was retrieved and eventually turned over to proper authorities. Froman was given back her cross and chain, the only personal possessions worth returning which she considered a symbol of faith and courage. Following the find, she felt her life had been spared for a greater cause. If Froman had not switched seats with Drasin she would have been the one killed as were the other eight passengers sharing her cabin.

Portuguese Government secretaries were sent to the hospital, and later to a Middle Park nursing home on the outskirts of Lisbon, to offer the survivors their sympathy and assistance. Women received flowers and the men expensive English pipes and tobacco. A bottle or two of whisky was also smuggled into the hospital for an additional cheering up!

Other visitors included Bert Fish, U.S. Minister to Portugal, Kennan and wife and Pan Am personnel that included pilots and crews during their runs to and from Lisbon. Burn said his and other officers' suspicions were aroused when a group, supposedly cleared by Pan Am, requested an interview. They didn't come back when a check was made with the airline's New York office that wired no such permission had been granted. Drysdale told reporters of how fearful she was of not being able to free herself under water when she finally saw the sky and how terribly cold the water was.

At the time of the crash, Pan Am's then third Officer Bill Nash was dining in Lisbon with Capt. Max Weber and crew before they were to go to the airport to relieve Sullivan and his crew and fly the NC-03 back to the States via Africa. Weber was called to the phone and came back to the table in total disbelief to relate the stunning news. More dazed was Nash; he had been scheduled for "Trip 9035" but had been ordered to replace an ill officer on Weber's run to Lisbon two days before the NC-03's ill-fated flight.

For the next three weeks Nash and crew acted as the line's official guardians to the wreckage. Deeply saddened they visited and cheered hospitalized comrades and other victims and spent hours at the dock sifting through the clipper's remains to gather, carefully disassemble and safely pack into barrels the retrieved instruments and other vital parts that could be studied by the CAB's investigative team. Pan Am asked the men to identify their dead friends at the city's morgue, to witness finger-printing and the signing of maritime police documents. Freeland and Nash had been close friends six years before the buddies both went to work together for Pan Am.

Clipper dross was deposited on nearby *Cais de Santa Apolonia Dock*. Nothing in wreckage could determine cause of crash. (*Photo Courtesy: Civil Aeronautics Board*)

"Some of the bodies had not been easy to identify," Nash claimed. "Identifying Andy at the morgue was one of the times in my life that this grown man cried."[207]

Twelve days after the crash the bodies of Drasin and Hart were found in the Tagus. In mid-March the river remissed another badly decomposed vicitim who's chest had been crushed. Washed ashore some distance from the downing, it was identified by papers in the ripped military clothing as that of Robertson. From New York Pan Am telegramed the next of kin whenever a body was identified. Bixby sent personal remorse letters along with death certificates issued by the State Department and signed by Hull. Many of the missing were believed swept out to sea. The bodies of Drasin, Hart and Robertson were shipped back to the U.S. in sealed metal coffins in the holds of the Portuguese freighter *San Miguel*. Each was interned in their home town. Five-hundred people attended Drasin's funeral in New York on April 16th. She was eulogized by film and stage actor Luther Adler, founder of the 1930's *New York Group Theater*.

Pan Am soon faced the inevitable investigation into the cause of the NC-03's loss. Lisbon authorities notified the CAB on the night of the accident. Two board members, Howard B. Railey, technical consultant, and Allen P. Bourdon, chief investigator, left by clipper for Lisbon on February 28th, arriving March 4th to study the wrecked plane, its recovered pieces laid out on the dock and guarded by Lisbon's maritime police.

On March 5th, hospital-released Sullivan faced Bourdon, Railey and Cmdr. Paulo Teixeir Viana, a Portuguese Government representative, for his first formal statement regarding the crash. During the time spent in Lisbon, Bourdon and Railey took quoted statements from the survivors and eight Pan Am ground personnel.

At stake was Sullivan's flying career. The first strike against him ensued when passengers and crew agreed that the plane's course and attitude seemed normal up to the time of the crash. Sullivan disagreed. He said that when he pulled back on the yoke there was no pressure, even with Rush's assistance. Sullivan maintained that when at 400 feet he knew the clipper was going in, and at that point decided to put the wing down after cutting power and applying left aileron control. He was sure he had left aileron but was not sure of rudder control because he did not use it. When asked why, Sullivan didn't know. He was also queried by the authorities why he didn't apply more power instead of cutting it.

"I don't think it would be a wise thing to try the motors at that altitude,"[208] he responded.

On the morning of April 17th back in New York, Sullivan accompanied a 314 test flight out of LaGuardia with CAB members aboard. A angle of bank was taken using the bridge portholes where he last saw Portugal's shore going out of view. Sullivan's angle registered 45 degrees. He couldn't remember when asked what he did to regain control of the ship when he noticed the plane nose down to the degree mark. He was then asked if it would have helped it he had changed the stabilizer setting?

Bridge and bow section was one of largest pieces recovered. Opened hatch (left) once gave access to anchor room from cockpit. Only a few aboard knew clipper was going to crash. (*Photo Courtesy: Civil Aeronautics Board*)

"If I did not, I should have," the commander remarked. "That really would have been the first thing I should have done. I don't know whether it was changed, or whether it was not. I don't remember doing it... It always acted very quickly to the tab, to the control."[209]

Lisbon's airport manager, John J. Anderson, seemed to confirm Sullivan's statement regarding the sharp angle of the clipper before it hit the water. Anderson saw the plane come in at an estimated 20 degrees, but because of darkness could not clearly detect if there was any leveling off or not. Pan Am's Portuguese radio telephone communications representative was standing next to Anderson in the control tower when he overheard the conversation between the launch and Rush. Rush told the launchman a right turn was about to be made. Sullivan testified he had no intention of making any landing other than in the direction so described. He was correct, for when the NC-03 struck the water it was north of the landing lights and banked in a southwest direction. The control tower's radio assistant saw the clipper bank left, not right, and noticed the wings were turned in about a 45-degree angle until the clipper disappeared. He then stated he heard a "distant boom."

The CAB concurred in its September, 1943, issued report of the accident that if the clipper was at a 20 or 45-degree bank during descent, the NC-03's crew and passengers would have become alarmed. Because of this factor the CAB didn't believe Sullivan's account. However, the board took note of passengers viewing the wing skim the water that indicated the plane was, in fact, in a steep banking angle. One passenger added, "Even to that point nothing made me think we were crashing."[210]

Examination of the wreckage showed no failures in the ship's cable control system, especially the two cable-connecting links that, according to the CAB, were the only items that could have made the elevators inoperative. Both cable links were recovered undamaged and intact. Detailed studies by the CAB's technical staff of the Safety Bureau were conducted in New York and Washington, D.C., covering elevator control and horizontal tail surfaces. The 314's outboard section of the port elevator was never found. Studies made by the Safety Bureau and the Division of Metallurgy of the National Bureau of Standards on the recovered flight-deck's instruments and control settings added nothing to the explaination of the crash. According to the CAB findings, the elevator control system was operative before the crash. The only item found broken before the accident was the lower starboard spring cartridge rod. Tests were conducted by Pan Am when one or more of these cartridges were disconnected, but, according to the findings, did not interfere with the proper functioning of the elevator control system.

Some eyewitnesses walking along the north shore near the airport told of how they saw flames shoot out of the flying boat just before it went down. What in fact they saw was the exhaust stream. There was no fire or explosion indicated by the recovered wreckage. The *Yankee Clipper* just disintegrated upon impact with the water.

One possible contribution to the cause of the crash was a sudden down draft. Vertical velocities inside thunderstorms frequently exceed one-mile-a-minute. There was turbulence reported in the area and the air was highly charged with electricity. These factors were eventually ruled out because survivors reported that all was well up to the time of impact — that there was no sudden drop or lurch prior to the crash.

Four of the five board members, L. Welch Pogue, Edward Warner, Oswald Ryan and Josh Lee, involved in the investigation, suggested that Sullivan intended to make an east-to-west landing rather than the projected south-to-north approach. Because of this hyperthetical theory, the plane was lower to the water, and when

Some survivors saw empennage sticking upward from Tagus. Second Steward Robinson, a young aspiring artist, was looking forward to doing some sketching during the upcoming Lisbon layover. (*Photo Courtesy: Civil Aeronautics Board*)

Sullivan banked the plane, he inadvertently misjudged his altitude which resulted in the port wing to strike the water. Board member Harllee Branch did not concur.

Two major issues seem questionable regarding the CAB's report. First, if the control system was found operational, how could a 100 percent accuracy be asserted when, in the same report, the following was stated, "All rudder and elevator control cables had either parted during the separation of the empennage from the major portion of the wreckage, or remained intact and were pulled through the stabilizer structure, carrying with them portions of the elevator control mechanism." And secondly, "The extent of the damage to the aircraft structure, as it existed immediately following the accident, could not be determined with accuracy, as the action of the tide on the wreckage while submerged, together with the subsequent salvage operations, undoubtedly contributed somewhat to its further destruction."[211]

There was no mentioning of a possible jamming in the CAB's findings. Could Sullivan have used trim tab control but it stuck and, due to shock, couldn't recall? Burn wrote, "Neither radio officer was injured and yet neither has ever been able to recall any part of the accident or any event of the last two hours of flight."[212]

Hence, Sullivan's recollection of professional and correct procedures taken on his part up to the last second before the splash-in could, and probably was, distorted or forgotten due to severe mental trauma.

Capt. Masland, who said he talked with Sullivan from time to time after the wreck, was one of those who did not go along with the CAB's report. Masland told how Sullivan stuck to his account that the yoke did not respond to his pressure of pulling back and that the nose of the plane continued to settle.

"...Sullivan," Masland wrote, "was the only inarticulate Irishman I ever knew. He seemed to me to be totally unable to defend himself... Is it possible that a bracket that carried a pulley on the elevator control system gave way at that unfortunate moment?"[213]

Destroyed bridge showed a violently twisted yoke and crunched leather-upholstered seat, the angles of which decidedly killed First Officer Rush. Third Officer William ("Bill") Nash, who was to have been on clipper, told of how Sullivan once said that control column suddenly went forward then left from his gripping hands. Could behind-standing Officer Freeland's foot accidently activated auto pilot by pushing handle while possibly resting a foot on captain's seat dais? (*Photo Courtesy: Civil Aeronautics Board*)

Last of the Flying Clippers

Aboard as Yankee Clipper Crashed in the Tagus River at Lisbon

Tamara
(missing)

Yvette
(injured)

Jane Froman
(injured)

Jean Rognan
(injured)

Gypsy Markoff
(injured)

Captain R. O. D. Sullivan
(injured)

The Yankee Clipper during a take-off at LaGuardia Field

Associated Press

Arthur A. Lee
(missing)

Crash news was carried for days by leading New York newspapers, one of which bannered the event to overshadow the torpedoing and sinking of a U.S. troop ship that resulted in a heavy loss of life. (*Photo Courtesy: New York Herald Tribune*)

Nash, who later made captain, believed Freeland to be the direct cause of the NC-03's fatal plunge when, while standing behind Sullivan, rested a foot up on the captain's seat dais that accidently activated the auto pilot knob during the critical point of flight which froze the controls. "More than once, while flying the B314, I had found a crew member's foot moving that valve, so had formed a habit of keeping an eye on any feet that got near it. I fully explained my theory to my superiors. I was thanked, but that was the last I ever heard of 'autopilot' in connection with the crash. I do not know if it ever was brought up at the hearing."[214]

The CAB's supposition that Sullivan intended to land in another direction other than that which was required was the basis of a suit filed against Pan Am by Froman and Markoff. Pending more than 14 years since the crash, the action was taken before a State Supreme Court jury in 1953 by Attorney Harry Gair who argued that Sullivan "...willfully disregarded landing instructions and regulations for safe night landing over water."[215] Froman sought $2,500,000 for her injuries against the $400,000 in medical bills incurred through more than 25 operations in an effort to keep her right leg and for loss of her career-earning capacity during recuperation. Markoff sought one million in damages.

Froman married Burn in 1948 following her divorce from Ross. Unfortunately, the storybook romance between hero and heroine broke up in 1955 and ended in divorce on June 14, 1956, four years after the award-winning movie, *With A Song In My Heart,* highlighting the singer's career, was released starring Susan Hayward as Froman. Only through a successful comeback was Froman able to pay off her heavy doctor and hospital debts. Her small compensatory court settlement of $138,205, recommended and passed through a special bill by the House Judiciary Committee in 1957, hardly covered the nearly insurmountable amount owed. Markoff, who also resumed her career, was awarded only $33,236.

Throughout the rest of her life Froman wore a light weight leg brace and walked with a slight limp. In 1962, she married Rowland Smith, an old friend and former newspaperman, and retired from show business. On April 22, 1980, Smith found his 72-year-old wife dead in their Columbia, MO, home of congestive heart failure.

As for Sullivan's career as a pilot, it ended shortly after the CAB report was released. He was fired by Capt. Gray. Even if the CAB report was somewhat ambiguous in never fully explaining the exact cause to the crash, it was used as an excuse to dump a man who was in conflict with some higher Pan Am personalities — an enigma. Ten years after the downing during Froman's and Markoff's suit, and long after Sullivan's dismissal, it was noted by the press that Pan Am's defense denied any negligence. In retrospect, Burn, who flew as an officer with Sullivan, said the captain was a remarkable airman, but a practical joker — a trait not admired by some higher authorities. Burn said one of Sullivan's pranks was to pull the separate height adjuster lever on the first officer's seat as he walked behind the bridge to either go aft or below deck. The seat would snap up or down to jar its occupant.

Sullivan once kidded around once too often with this trick. He pulled the lever on a pilot of equal rank acting as first officer. Later in the flight the pilot retaliated, and, to the horror of the crew on the flight-deck, an out-'n-out brawl ensued between the two men.

In contrast to his often irritable antics and unappreciated sense of humor, Sullivan was a superior pilot. The famed captain had spent about 11 years with the U.S. Navy as a test pilot and instructor at various naval air stations around the country. He knew his planes like the back of his hand as well as what they could or could not do. He was Pan Am's most accumulative-houred pilot at the Atlantic Division with an airline transport pilot's certificate listed at 0-7200 h.p. single and multi-engine land and sea-rated operation. The airman had flown 55 round-trip Pacific clipper trips with some 3,278 hours of his total 14,332 hours flying 314s.

Sullivan was well-admired by many, including passengers. While in the recovery home Rognan told the press "she would be willing to fly back home with the same pilot"[216] Chief Engineer Borger said Sullivan was one of the best captains of the day.

"True, or not, I've often wondered," Nash added, "if, when the opportunity presented itself to dump R.O.D., his enemies took it. I liked him. I know he was an excellent boat pilot, and I know being

Capt. R.O.D. Sullivan was, many believed, railroaded out of Pan Am because of his disfavor with the hierarchy — that the *Yankee Clipper's* crack-up was an excuse to dump him. Photo from first Atlantic revenue flight, 1939. (*Photo Courtesy: Pan American World Airways*)

blamed for the accident broke his heart."[217] It seemed, however, Sullivan carried a touch of hemlock humor in his flight bag not admired by some airline hierarchy who went strictly by the book!

Following Sullivan's Pan Am dismissal it was press-reported that the U.S. Navy who trained him as a pilot wanted him back in their ranks. Other airlines also welcomed him for his experience and expertise, but the skipper refused all offers. When reporters tried to locate Sullivan he couldn't be found — he had temporarily left the country. Airmen told newsmen they heard the flyer had become the captain of a Portuguese steamer, or that he went to Africa to work for the *Liberian American Development*, a subsidiary of Pan Am. Eventually the controversial pilot of sea and sky retired to his many-acred farm in North Carolina, a haven previously managed by his wife when he was away flying. Sullivan died in 1955 at the age of 62.

30

Wings Towards Victory

Exactly 1,225 Atlantic 314 flights were scored at the time of the *Yankee Clipper*'s demise with 44,000 passengers and 2,500,000 pounds of mail flown a total of 6,600,000 miles without previous incident. As tragic as the Atlantic Division's crash was, the Pacific Division was also marred once more 33 days prior to the Lisbon incident.

Under Navy flight "No. V-2-1104," the M-130 *Philippine Clipper*, while in a wide, early morning holding pattern under Capt. Robert M. Elsey, who had come up the ranks since being a junior flight navigator aboard the NC-03's inaugural air mail flight to Europe, struck a hilltop near Boonsville and Ukiah north of San Francisco in a heavy rain storm. All eight crew and 10 passengers inbound from Honolulu were killed, including Rear Admr. R. R. English, submarine commander flying to a naval headquarters meeting. Through its years of service, alteration forms and bullet-riddled repair, the modified M-130's log book was closed with a 14,628-hour, five-minute flight record. Befitting to Elsey's memory were his own words that echoed from his first 314 trip aboard the *Yankee Clipper* in 1939, "Over wave, with wind, through cloud, out of the night!"[218]

Twenty-eight days after the M-130 wreck, the 314's test pilot and a crew of nine were killed in a fiery crash with the then secret B-29 prototype bomber. Allen was desperately trying to return the crippled plane back to Boeing Field when two of its four engines caught fire shortly after takeoff. Numerous eyewitnesses saw the bullet-shaped bomber faulter and then smash into a five-story fish-packing plant that also took the lives of 20 ground workers. Allen and his crew were buried with honors in American flag-draped coffins following the most extravagant funeral ever sponsored by Boeing for veteran employees.

The year 1943 seemed a period of grief in the aviation world. Pan Am again suffered when the S-42B *Bermuda Clipper*, former *Pan American Clipper III*, was destroyed without injury or death while docked at Manaos, Brazil, on July 27th. A stressed flight engineer inadvertently pulled the gas dump valve instead of the fire extinquisher knob to put out a burning engine. Spilled fuel intensified the flames that engulfed the flying boat that marked the third S-42 sinking in two years.

Because of the M-130's destruction, and hence the insufficient number of clippers on the west coast, the Navy, at Pan Am's request, returned two 314s to the Pacific Division in May, 1943, in an effort to balance out backlogged loads between San Francisco and Honolulu. Chosen for the cross-country return flights were the NC-02 and NC-05. When the NC-05 left in mid-May, she had accumulated 293 transatlantic crossings. Most hailed by Treasure Island personnel was the return of the *Pacific Clipper* on May 4th. Capt. Chase and a crew of nine, who had flown east to pick up the NC-02, departed New York the previous morning. Within the liner's staterooms were 27 Pan Am representatives. Security measures were observed during takeoff and blinds had to be drawn and later removed when the ship broke through dense overcast on its path to Miami.

From Miami the clipper was flown towards Texas and on to California where many airline employees and wives of the crew greeted the night arrival.

"I'm so glad to see her back I could kiss her," said W. B. ("Shorty") Greenough, Treasure Island's assistant chief of ground services. A few seconds later Greenough did just that while standing on the plane's starboard sea-wing. With a pat from mouth-to-hand, he smacked the hull just aft of the opened hatchway.

A short time later the Pacific's NC-05 and Atlantic's NC-11 exchanged titles. The *Dixie Clipper* became the *Anzac Cllpper* and visa versa. It was at this time that many 314s, especially those on

Pacific Clipper's night return to San Francisco after nearly two years away from Treasure Island base. To right a wife waits for crew member husband as white-ducked "Shorty" Greenough passes to rear. (*Photo Courtesy: Eugene "Gene" J. Dunning Collection*)

the east coast, began flying without bow designations. War demands and the quick turn-arounds didn't allow paint crews enough time for name applications.

Despite the loss of so many aircraft within a relatively short span of time, Pan Am was able to keep astride in meeting its war-scheduled commitments. Activities soared to an all-time high in 1943 when Army and Navy requirements made it necessary to increase the carrying of V-mail, war VIPs and secret-labeled cargoes to the far distant destinations in the shortest possible time. Working around the clock, the 314s went on to break more records in their push to transport tons of materials through the execution of SMs.

Six outstanding 314 Atlantic cargo trips, conducted in January, May, July, August, October and December, 1943, hauled 14,114 pounds of emergency supplies and equipment. Stashed in cargo and stripped passenger compartments were diving gear apparatus for the Free French Navy to assist in the salvage of ships damaged by mines off Africa; insulin and metquine tablets for Lisbon's Red Cross; transmitters and generators for the U.S. Navy at Fort Lyautey; and Cynogas A. powder to thwart a vermin that had reached a plague stage in the Far East and consigned in May to Gen. Joseph W. Stilwell's China-Burma-India theatre of operations.

Among other essential 314 cargoes carried over the Atlantic in September and October, 1943, were two loads (7,500 pounds) of maps and charts for Lt. Gen. James Doolittle, Mediterranean commander of the Fifteenth Air Force, and famed for his 1942 B-25 bomber raid on Tokyo. The maps were used in the planning of the North African invasion in November, 1943, and the charts for the intensified bombing of Europe and Africa by U.S. aircraft as approved by Churchill and Roosevelt at the Trident Conference held in Washlngton, D.C., in May. Additional 1943 war cargo consisted of first aid equipment, more dust filters later installed on African-based aircraft for desert warfare, secret radar plans and parts, machine guns, entire radio stations with operators, beryllium, mica and rubber. In October, 1943, two 314s were completely stripped to move 11,600 pounds of dry cell batteries labeled for London's Signal Property Command.

Perhaps the most concentrated effort made by a 314 during the war was conducted in March, 1943. The *American Clipper* accomplished 20 transoceanic crossings between Natal and Fish Lake, plus two round-trips to LaGuardia for overhaul. She had traveled 55,000 miles and carried 213,000 pounds of war cargo at the peak of the South Atlantic run. At month's end, the NC-06 had a utilization factor of 12.58 hours per day. The same month the *Atlantic Clipper* carried 18,000 pounds of freight from Natal to Monrovia.

Mail loads continued to be on the rise. Ten million letters were carried across the Atlantic in 1942, and more were estimated for 1943. U.S. Postmaster Albert Goldman announced in mid-March that surface vessels had been commissioned to carry tons of the bulging bags to help alleviate the 314s' extra loads. Priority one was given official transmissions, second to V-mail and third, if space allowed, to regular postage not weighing in excess of two ounces

Two passengers (left) and NC-02 *Pacific Clipper*'s return-flight crew safely home from Atlantic Division are, from left to right: Bill A. Del Valle, Pan Am's liaison engineer with Boeing Aircraft, G.T. Ramsey, Pacific Division's assistant operations manager, Clipper Capt. J. H. Chase, First Officer A. E. Pfau, Second Engineer J. D. Scouten, Second Officer W. K. Harris, Second Radio Officer P. C. Canham, Supernumerary William Miller, First Radio Officer L. D. Paulson, First Engineer J. W. Zeigler and Chief Steward Eugene ("Gene") J. Dunning. (*Photo Courtesy: Eugene ("Gene") J. Dunning Collection*)

per letter. Since Pearl Harbor, mail loads multiplied ten times. Four thousand or more pounds was common for an outgoing transatlantic 314. Single loads ran as high as 13,620 pounds.

Between the military and Pan Am's scheduled hauls, BOAC's three A314s had chalked up their own records. Paul Bewshea, Baltimore's BOAC PR director of operations, called Boeing's Public Relations Jack Carson on July 9, 1943, to inform him that their three 314 Speedbirds had flown more than a million miles and carried some 44,000 pounds of cargo during the first two years of service.

Along the 11,500-mile Africa-Orient "Cannonball" route, and the Natal-Fish Lake route, Pan Am crews often stayed on the job 40 hours at a stretch without rest. For many months the clippers and other Pan Am-operated craft averaged 17 crossings a day. Between the U.S. and Europe, air express and freight had reached 5,480,010 pounds by December, 1943. Cargo, however, was only part of the tremendous job undertaken by the 314s. Eight million miles were flown between the two hemispheres in 1,550 crossings. More than 50,000 passengers and 2,600,000 pounds of air mail passed through the *MAT* en route to and from Europe. Since the U.S. had entered the war, 5,000 Pan Am flights were scored over the Atlantic as of Nov. 17, 1943. Of these, about 900 were made by 314s, the rest attributed to Pan Am crews flying the M-130 *China Clipper*, Navy-owned PB2Ys, and ATC's C-54s and B-307s.

By December 1st, the Atlantic Division reported 1,250,000 miles a month were flown carrying cargo at the rate of 3,500,000-ton miles every 30 days. Seven-hundred special missions were also completed by 314s by the end of December. Departures reached the 187-mark running up 2,276,000 314 miles flown since the at-tack on Pearl Harbor. At year's end, 1,700 314 transatlantic flights were scored since service began in 1939. Passenger miles with the Boeings came to 37,107,355. Cargo-ton miles with the clippers reached 38,916,244, including 416 tons of mail. Pan Am schedules reached around 3,100 at LaGuardia with 600 more at stations in South America, Europe, Africa and way-island ports-of-call.

An analysis of 314 miles flown by Army, Navy and commercial Atlantic operations totaled 1,871,148 in 1943. Thousand-pound miles covered reached 2,445,056. The three Pacific-based 314s had an equally remarkable 1943 record. Their trips to and from Honolulu (Pearl City) registered 1,301,830 miles with mail ton-miles set at 1,306,986. Overall cargo ton-miles flown was 873,748. Each 314 had a utilization factor of 8.58 hours per day throughout 1943, and flew 13,965,228 passenger miles. The NC-01, NC-02 and NC-05 carried 5,814 passengers with the largest share going to the *Honolulu Clipper*. Pan Am crews completed 1,221 314 flights in 1943 between San Francisco and Hawaii.

Air-shipped cargo and mail beyond the Honolulu sector was mainly sent by NATS in PB2Ys. Pan Am crews and ground personnel functioned alongside the Navy with many clipper captains commanding the Consolidated-built boats and smaller twin-engined Martin PBM-3Rs. Airline skippers and crew flew 520 flights over the South Pacific route in 1943, not to mention the many flights along the Aleutian chain west of Alaska under the joint Navy-Pan Am Pacific-Alaska Division with headquarters located in Seattle. NATS, solely organized to function as a Pan Am extension service, had some of their PB2Ys fitted with plush accommodations for military brass. It was aboard one of the PB2Ys that Adm. William ("Bull") Halsey, Allied South Pacific naval forces and U.S. Third Fleet commander, flew in style on a special 1944 mission.

Acting as aerial sub chasers, patrol bombers and mini-passenger-carrying clippers for military personnel, the PB2Ys and PBM-3Rs kept the vital communications airway system open to New Zealand and Australia. But it was the back-breaking 314 Atlantic flights that made the 314s so famous as exemplified in February, 1943, when Capt. Black was part of a crew that accomplished 10 round-trips between Natal and Fish Lake to transport secret east-bound cargo consisting of iron mats used atop African desert sand for strengthening landplane runways during their construction.

In July, 1943, Pan Am announced plans for a larger clipper base at Mills Field, now San Francisco International Airport. Vice Adm. John C. Greenslade, 12th Naval District commander, stationed at Treasure Island, told of the Navy's need to expand its facilities at Port of the Trade Winds and in turn appropriated $3,500,000 for Pan Am's new facility. Treasure Island would be NATS-controlled in conjunction with the military V-2 transport organization at Alameda. Already the Navy had begun construction on the island by building a 337-by-130-square-foot twin hangar complex with three rows of shops and offices. The exquisite Art Deco-styled air-line *Administration Building* became NATS' Pacific headquarters.

Supervising the change was Frank McKenzie, airport engineer, who joined Pan Am in 1934. Born in Scotland, and a graduate of the University of Glasgow, McKenzie'a past experience hailed him as one of the world's greatest airport designers, including Port of the Trade Winds. Under William S. Grooch, Pacific Division's base development operations chief, McKenzie had assisted in the construction of Alameda, Midway, Wake, Canton Island, Noumea and Fiji bases as well as Pan Am's Ketchikan and Juneau docks in Alaska. He was en route to establish another flying boat haven between Manila and Singapore when the Japanese stopped him at Wake. McKenzie was one of the fortunate few who fled aboard the *Philippine Clipper* with an injured elbow after being struck by a chunk of shrapnel.

Pan Am'a transfer to Mills Field was forecast in June, 1943. But due to the exigencies of war, the availability and final move was not completed until September, 1944. Nine-tenths of Pan Am's maintenance staff had been transferred by mid-1943 to the site previously occupied by the U.S. Coast Guard. The new clipper compound included a hangar, an administration building, terminal and two 314 cove-sheltered piers.

Doc Savage, head of Treasure Island's cable shop, and later a 314 flight engineer, was sent to Honolulu's Pearl City base in the summer of 1943. Upon his return some two months later Savage found his shop moved to Mills Field. More than half of his personal tools had vanished. The last Treasure Island departure was on April 18, 1944.

Facilities at LaGuardia were also enlarged to accommodate the quick turn-around demands for both Navy PB2Ys and 314s. New quarters were opened March 31, 1943, when Bixby, acting on behalf of Trippe, officiated at ceremonies limited to 225 city and airport officials. Doubled were hangar additions containing welding, paint, machine, propeller, engine and accessory shops within a 219,000 square-foot area that surpassed the original 107,000-square foot space. The project came to a near stand still in early 1942 when a shortage of steel reached an all-time low. Engineers tore down the abandoned clipper hangar at Port Washington and salvaged 1,000 tons of steel. Some 100-foot-long span trusses and parts were transported 20 miles by truck to LaGuardia, cleaned and resurrected for the new additions.

Elated with their new quarters, Pan Am offered NATS faster servicing for the PB2Ys and for the four ATC 314s turned over to the Navy in August and October, 1943. The Army, stocked with a large fleet of landplanes, resold the clippers at a devaluated price to the military's seaplane operator that reclassified the ships with file numbers 99081 for NC-02, 99082 for NC-11, 99083 for NC-06 and 99084 for NC-12.

Protection of the clippers on the ground and in the air was given top security. Base guards patrolled with guns at off-limit zones around hangars, terminals and docks. In-coming and departing passengers had to follow designated walkways and were not allowed to wander. Fear of the enemy finding out the nature of SM flights and their concealed cargoes was always pertinent in the minds of Pan Am and military-concerned officials. It was believed if Hitler had known the flying ships were owned by the military and used for the exporting of war materials he might have ordered the downing of every Atlantic-flying 314.

Hitler, upon finding out that the super liner *Queen Mary* was being used as a troop ship, offered a cash reward to the sub commander who could find and sink her. Clipper base personnel were therefore sworn in under "The Espionage Act," an oath created for the protection of preventing information leaks relating to arrivals, departures, routes flown, passengers and cargo carried and all other pertinent 314 matters considered secret or confidential.

Pan Am's 1929-employed, U.S. Navy-trained and Atlantic-based Security Officer Van Law held tight reins. At his secret-papered office behind closed doors were volumes of codes for 96,000 messages cataloged under 2,096,000 cyphers used for the many transmissions sent to in-flight transatlantic planes. Within the confines of his secretive office, nicknamed "Iron Lung," nine cryptologists were staffed under Van Law's ruling. The only outsiders allowed in were the division's manager and the air captains programmed for departure. Van Law's "Iron Lung" housed confidential progress flight charts plus all other operational material in locked filing cabinets and a safe. Ground communication messages were passed to and from the "Iron Lung" through wall slots near iron-grilled windows.

Two secretly guarded aids to in-flight 314 navigation were introduced in late 1943 to supercede the DF system. War made the DF a somewhat impractical method of transmitting information as it allowed the enemy to pick up on signals and pin-point clipper positions.

Taking the DF principle, the military devised an electronic radar scope for transoceanic planes called the *Loran*, an abbreviation for *Long Range Navigation*. Small in size, the *Loran* took up little space at the navigator's station on 314s and other aircraft. *Lorans* were connected to aircraft radio antennas and instantly calculated positions. By turning and tuning five knobs the device automatically recorded on a scope the variances in time between receptions of ground signal stations located at strategic spots along the air routes. Special charts with colored lines that matched those on the scope permitted navigators to determine a plane's location as transmitted by ground stations regardless of night flying or density of fog. A clipper's exact location was found where two separate colored lines intersected on the chart.

Another secret war-developed instrument was the radar altimeter. This fool-proof piece of equipment gave both navigators and captains a visual indication of their plane's height over sea and ground. It recorded altitude in the form of a green light on a calibrated dial by way of powerful radio waves bounced from solid objects below. Radio waves were focused and the radar set sent out frequency pulses through new antenna affixed to the wing's aft-tipped edges.

Clipper crews found the new navigational aids a great asset when regularly scheduled mail, passenger and express service was, beyond SM flights, resumed on the northern route during summer months beginning May 17, 1944, with the NC-11. Even during the summer fog blanketed the fishing villages at Shediac and Botwood. The 3,089 mile flight between the U.S. and Foynes required mail stops be made on the Northumberland Strait in Shediac Bay and on the Bay of Exploits, 63 miles inland from New foundland's cove-dotted coast. With the advance in technology, fewer flights were grounded due to fog.

Though not related to top secret technological developments, clipper captains asked their airline in 1943 for an improved 314 control synchronization, a task achieved in October by Frank Taubl, LaGuardia's plane maneuverability supervisor. The 314's throttle and mixture system installed in the bridge and at the engineer's station that turned the engines at an uneven recorded pace when activated was worked upon. Mixture controls, connected to throttles by metal rods called quadrants, and joined to control cables run on spools, were altered which gave a perfectly aligned movement to both the throttle and mixture controls.

Taubl also recommended in October, 1943, that a new jig in the hangar be designed to exactly reposition a clipper's four ailerons from the former trial-and-error type. His suggestion was to cut time in reconnecting aileron cables from the cockpit through four gear boxes in the wings during overhaul. Between 300 and 400-man hours per ship were saved during each check after the improved jig was devised and put into place.

From 1939 to June, 1944, 314s had carried 60,000 passengers in 10,000,000 miles traversing the Atlantic with 2,000 flights. Among the many famous personalities who crossed and re-crossed

By mid-1943, LaGuardia Airport's *MAT* facilities handled maintenance for Navy's Atlantic-flying PB2Y3s as seen on Bowery Bay. Pan Am crews often flew Navy boats dubbed and painted "G.I. Clippers." (*Photo Courtesy: Pan American World Airways*)

the Atlantic were Hollywood USO entertainers such as crooner Bing Crosby; America's best-loved comedian Bob Hope; songstress Frances Langford; comedians Keenan Winn and Martha Ray; actors Joe E. Brown, Jimmy Durante, William Gargan; and actresses Linda Darnell, Paulette Goddard and Ilona Massey. Goddard, along with four other entertainers, flew by 314 to Karachi in April, 1944, and then by C-47 over the "Hump" for a 38,000-mile troop tour to China and back. She visited 15 countries during her extended 130-show coverage. Goddard, a favorite among movie fans, had left New York with 55 pounds of luggage and returned 45 pounds lighter having given the rest to refugees, American nurses and other women deprived of such clothing luxuries.

Not only did 314s carry film and radio notables abroad, but one, the NC-11, became a featured part of a USO publicity film partly shot at LaGuardia on Nov. 4, 1943. The movie short, made by the Army Signal Corps, was a visual record of how the USO functioned in preparing for an overseas trip. But it was behind such glamour that 314s flew on in their more important military missions. Two weeks before D-Day, America's invasion of Europe at Normandy, France, June 6, 1944, 314s and other Pan Am planes carried 23,000 pounds of lead weights, tow lines, bridles and other invasion gear for use on landing boats concentrated in the south of England. Gun magazines, electrical equipment, live depth bombs, smokeless powder and medical supplies made up other priority 314 cargoes. Two whole generators, weighing 1,800 pounds each, were flown to North Africa on a 314 . More crude rubber from Brazil's Amazon basin, replaced by rubber siezed by the Japanese when they overran Malayan plantations, was rushed to Belem and then by 314s to the U.S.

On another mission in early April, 1944, one 314 winged into liberated Dakar with 3,155 pounds of B-17 parts for a Fortress that had made a forced landing near Bolama and was sold to the Portuguese authorities under conditions that they be given the parts to rostore the downed plane. Then, above and beyond secret flights, BOAC's Capt. Gordon Store established another Atlantic record on July 27, 1944, by flying the *Bangor* from Foynes to Botwood in 11 hours, 33 minutes.

An unusual special mercy flight, and one of the last known made by a 314, occurred in February, 1944. Alfredo de Carbalho, director of Portuguese Air Services in Bolama, made an urgent plea to Louis Boyd, Pan Am's Bolama airport manager, to rush a deployment of serum by 314 for his son dying of diphtheria. No serum was available in Bolama and Carbalho was desperate. Taking action, Boyd radioed Natal where a 314 was scheduled to depart. Clipper Capt. John M. Mattis and airport officials went into conference, wired New York about their change of flight plans to Bolama rather then Fish Lake, procured the needed serum, and headed out across the South Atlantic. Stewards Vilante Gerbi and Ernest Boudreau placed the precious anti-toxin in a gallon thermos packed in ice and stored in stateroom A. Every two hours new ice was added. Boyd met the clipper at Bolama's Bolola Channel and rushed

the container to the ailing child. His life was spared. Another 314 had come to the rescue in the nick of time.

Near the end of 1944, an even greater number of C-54s were assigned to Pan Am's Africa-Orient Division at Miami. A new route across the Atlantic between New York, Miami and Casablanca were established to replace the Cannonball aerial supply line. From Casablanca, Army-operated C-54s carried men and supplies eastward over Africa to far-flung Pacific conflicts. The war-weary 314s had begun a decline in their priority cargo demands and being the number one world air transport.

As of Oct. 31, 1944, 1,595 Atlantic crossings were recorded by 314s since America went to war with 53,717 passengers carried on 6,561,534 plane miles. During the same period, 314s on the Pacific made 1,299 flights between San Francisco and Honolulu and carried 18,904 passengers in 3,348,692 miles. The Atlantic-based 314s accomplished 286 flights across the North Atlantic alone in 1944.

The small fleet of four Boeings carried 12,846 passengers and 9,820,003 pounds of cargo, mail and express. From June 24, 1939, to Dec. 31, 1944, the 314s made 2,136 crossings of the Atlantic, carried 68,033 passengers, 5,481,735 pounds of express cargo and 4,338,268 pounds of mail. Also, a new human load record over an ocean by plane was set in December, 1944, when 64 passengers and 11 crewmen flew west in a 314 across the South Atlantic.

During the war years there were times the 314s were in peril. Capt. Basil L. Rowe, first Pan Am skipper to carry engineers to survey the "Cannonball" route bases at Leopoldville, Lake Victoria, Khartoum, Cairo and Karachi with the NC-12, had three crucial experiences aboard the Boeings. Twice he was shot at by Nazi submarines but able to maneuver through the flak. Then, after landing from another crossing bullet holes were found in the underside wings. Another time in North Africa, Rowe dropped his 314 to tree-

Anzac Clipper got star status when Hollywood Director Shepard Traube (center) regulated U.S. Signal Corps-produced USO movie at *MAT*'s docking pier, 1943. (*Photo Courtesy: Pan American World Airways*)

top level after spotting German aircraft. Rowe, who joined Pan Am in 1928, often escorted fighter planes across the South Atlantic with 314s by "follow-the-leader" principle. Once he spanned the Atlantic six times in five days flying 314s.

Navigator Ferguson Byars remarked about a frustrating time while aboard the *Capetown Clipper* in September, 1944 (his last trip on a 314), when flying the circuit route from New York to Natal, via Bermuda, Azores, Portugal and West Africa and then return in the reverse direction under Capt. Wallace D. Culbertson:

"...more things happened on that trip it seems then on any other. We were delayed out-bound and on the return trip for a total of four days waiting for landing conditions to be right at Horta. In mid-ocean between Africa and South America, No. 2 engine blew a cylinder which hung half way out of the cowling. We were again delayed two days in Natal for an engine change. Between Bolama and Dakar we lost a section of an exhaust collector ring and were delayed four days waiting for parts from Lisbon and Fisherman's Lake."[219]

BOAC's Capt. Kelly-Rogers revealed in the late 1960s what he considered two perilous 314 flights during his flying career:

"I got a fright on one occasion when I was doing a non-stop flight from Bathurst straight to Trinidad. Halfway across the South Atlantic one engine ran away on me... It was an outboard engine, so it was effecting the performance of the aircraft. I had to shut it down immediately. But fortunately, the flight engineer could get to the back of each engine. The throttle rod had broken. He was able to effect a repair and therefore, when the throttle was reconnected, I was able to make use of the engine after about half-an-hour. We were heavily laden at the time, and I'd lost a good deal of height before I got the engine going again.

The only other fright — real fright — I got was during the war. It was our practice to cross the Bay of Biscay for safety reasons at night. On this occassion we were in a hurry and I was urged by the British Embassy in Lisbon to get home as quickly as possible. So I did it in daylight. About halfway across the bay I came out of a rain storm flying somewhere around two or three-thousand feet. And there, right ahead of me, crossing my bow, was a big Fokker-Wolfe Condor, probably one of those the Germans previously used on their meterological flights across the Atlantic.

I gave the 314 full throttle and stood her on her tail and tried to climb back into the clouds again — not too successfully I may say, because she wasn't a high-performanced airplane. But I think the German was nosed down headed for home looking only in front of him because he never swerved at all. And, I think, as he was crossing my bow, he wasn't keeping a very sharp lookout around him. And once he got across my bow he wasn't looking behind, and I was safe... Nothing happened, but I was very frightened for the moment."[220]

Steward Dunning, although not aboard, recalled another terrifying 314 incident during a flight from San Francisco to Honoululu

when a clipper lost all engine power. "Engineer Nels Wicklund had just switched over to the sea-wing tanks. Suddenly, the plane began a very steep glide. Wicklund threw himself down the stairs, crawled back to the lounge, removed the floor board hatch under the carpet and found the problem. He discovered the fuel valve had been wired in the 'closed' position and opened it. All the engines caught and the flight proceeded to Honolulu."[221]

Whereas only male 314 crews experienced the thrill and danger involved in commercial transoceanic flights during the war, there was an alteration in Pan Am's hiring beginning in March, 1944, when stewardesses were introduced. Equal rights for air-minded women came about when hostesses began to supplement stewards between the U.S. (Miami), Havana, Nassau, Mexico and Guatemala City in old S-42s, DC-3s and Lockheed Lodestars. After a three-month training course in meal preparation, life-saving techniques, first aid and manifestation of passport and general paper work, the average five-foot, three-inch tall women were assigned to trips in the western hemisphere.

The first Pan Am transoceanic-going stewardess began work on Sept. 15, 1945. Madeline Cuniff, former ground passenger service representative at the *MAT* since 1940, was dressed in her trim, powder-blue tailored coat and skirt with winged Robin Hood-styled cap, white blouse and brown shoes when passengers embarked the *American Clipper* at LaGuardia for a flight to Bermuda. Cuniff held a Bachelor of Science degree from the University of Alabama, her home state. An aviation advocate, she attended New York University's aviation ground school where she obtained a pilot's license before starting work with Pan Am.

Recalling her first 314 flight, Cuniff said mid-way to Bermuda she went to chuck lunch garbage down the galley's chute. Not using Capt. Beer's specially designed "jammer" correctly, the garbage backed up and spewed all across her new uniform. Cuniff later went on DC-4 flights to Botwood and then Foynes when the northern summer route reopened to regular peacetime service on May 15, 1946. Between flights she and Betty Stark, second Pan Am transatlantic stewardess, continued as ground service agents at LaGuardia's *MAT*.

"The male pursers didn't like having us. They did half the work for twice the pay," Cuniff remarked, who then took home about $160 a month. "We were limited to certain flights. It was thought unsafe for women to fly to Europe during the war. People were really afraid to fly in those days, and I wanted to take the job to show them what it was about."[222]

Joseph Raviol, Pan Am's eastern flight service superintendent, directed the stewardesses' training. Flight hostesses at first flew only on trips to and from Bermuda and had equal duties as junior stewards with guidance given by Senior Flight Stewards Verbe Edwards and Anthony Grajirena.

Cuniff remembered many a time at Bermuda during 314 layovers before returning to New York when she had to organize dances, tours, and bridge and golf tournaments to keep transient passengers from becoming bored. Among her patron passengers were celebrities and members of royalty. After a number of later DC-4 flights across the Atlantic, Cuniff returned to ground duty where, by 1980, she had made chief hostess at Pan Am's *Clipper Club* at Kennedy International Airport.

Eight months before Cuniff stepped aboard the NC-06 for her first hostess flight, another tragic accident marred the over-water clipper fleet. The legendary *China Clipper*, returned to Pan Am by the Navy on Oct. 13, 1943, was destroyed in a crash during a night landing at Trinidad. With her war paint removed for regular commercial service to and from Africa, the M-130, which had been transferred to Miami shortly after Pearl Harbor by Pan Am's Capt. Max C. Weber, was reported in excellent condition.

Under "Trip 161," the *China Clipper* left Miami on the last scheduled flight to Leopoldville, via San Juan, Port of Spain, Belem and Natal, on Jan. 8, 1945, with 30 occupants. At San Juan, the craft was refueled and given a brief routine mechanical check. Taking off, the flying boat proceeded to Port of Spain. First Officer L. W. Cramer, employed by Pan Am since April 1, 1942, and having about 7,034 hours to his credit, was seated in the captain's seat. Commander G. A. Goyette, a nine-year clipper veteran with some 7,040 hours behind him, was seated to starboard. About 10 miles from the south coast of Trinidad, Coyette instructed Cramer to remain in the captain's seat to make the approach and landing at the Corcorite Airport.

Cramer began his final descent with excellent visibility after having lined up with the string of seven launch-placed lights. Goyette's eyes were on the clipper's dash dials, Cramer's on the surface lights. Unaware the bow was in a steep angle, the clipper made an abrupt contact with the surface, lurched and broke apart. Twenty-three were killed or died in a hospital after consuming gasoline and oil from broken tanks. Many of the victims were children.

Resolved to find a probable cause to the accident, the CAB fixed blame to Cramer's misjudgment of altitude to the water and to Capt. Goyette's lack of supervision during night-landing procedures. Also, according to the CAB investigation, Cramer was inexperienced in landing flying boats during night hours. When the *China Clipper* slipped below the surface she closed her books with 20,545 flying hours.

Despite the tragic loss of old NC-16, the 314s kept alive — at least for awhile — the line's flying boat era. But their days with Pan Am were limited.

Looking forward to a world of calm, the 314s' exterior luster was restored beginning in February, 1945. Removed from the hulls, tails and wings were 260 pounds of war paint per clipper that saved 960 man-hours a year since late December, 1941. First to be renewed to its lanolin coating, christened name plate and airline logo markings was the NC-11.

Not fearing the Germans any longer, crews began to fly 314s over the Atlantic in peacetime colors. The war in Europe had begun to grind to a shattering end by March. German defenses disintigrated when the entire Allied front was posed east of the Rhine. Russian forces started their final drive into Berlin on April 16th. Fourteen days thereafter Hitler was dead from a self-inflicted gun shot wound to the head in his Berlin bunker. Collapse of the proclaimed "Thousand-Year Reich" finally came on May 7th. Grand Adm. Karl Doenitz, U-boat commander and Hitler's successor, unconditionally surrendered on May 6th. Doenitz ordered his Chief of Staff, Col. Gen. Alfred Jodl, to meet with Gen. Eisenhower at Rheim. Crowds went wild in cities and towns throughout the free world two days later. "V-E Day" had come and the war in Europe was history.

With peace secured on the Eastern Front, Van Dusen issued a public notice placed in the *New York Times* on August 7th foretelling the return of normal commercial air operations. Illustrated with a 314 drawing, the ad read:

"Now you can fly to Lisbon by Clipper. Space available for civilians. This news is of special interest to subjects of Portugal, Spain, France, Italy and other Mediterranean countries. Non-military, one-way transatlantic passage is now available aboard the big, four-engine Pan American Clippers from New York to Lisbon."[223]

Two days before travel restrictions were lifted, the NC-04, under Capt. Calvin Y. Dyer, and a crew of 11, got another human load record over the Atlantic when it left New York for London, via Shediac, Botwood and Foynes. The majority of the 56 passengers were American delegates headed for a conference on the future United Nations relief and rehabilitation activities. The month before, on July 24th and 25th, three 314s carried 191 passengers in and out of New York. Then on September 10th, the *American Clipper* lifted 64 peasengers and a crew of 13 to Bermuda to break the previous August 5th northern route record.

About 75,000 war-related passengers had flown by 314 over the Atlantic as of May 16th in 2,500 crossings. Nearly three million pounds of cargo and seven million pounds of mail in a little more than 11 million air miles was also recorded by the 314s. The four Atlantic-based Boeings had flown 2,200,000 miles. One of the last big Pan Am 314 cargo loads over the Atlantic was made on August 13th when 2,610 pounds of penicillin was sent to Foynes for transshipment to Berne, Switzerland.

Long before war's end, Pan Am began to market for new postwar aircraft to compete against what Trippe realized would be a great influence of international air carriers into the U.S. The master-minded air champ played another trump when he organized for reduced fares through the use of faster landplane equipment that would cut ocean-going flight time nearly in half. It was a new world, a time for expansion and growth. Slower and less feasible flying boat service was doomed. To begin his long-range landplane planning, Trippe first looked to the war-proven DC-4 and pressurized L-049 to get his program off the ground. His keen awareness and excellent PR practices through Van Dusen gave Trippe a lead into the post-war air market.

Camouflaged *Anzac Clipper*, docked at Botwood, reopened the northern route to scheduled passenger and mail flights in 1944. (*Photo Courtesy: Pan American World Airways*)

There was only one side kick to Trippe's new philosophy of flight. He had to sacrifice luxury for speed. Douglas DC-4s and Lockheed L-049s were not the luxury liners when compared to the volumnious 314 interiors. Side-tracking this aspect by promising giant new landplanes, Trippe and staff studied the six-engined Consolidated-Vultee CV-37 with its 204-passenger capacity with a prospective 4,200-mile range and a 342-m.p.h. cruising speed

Having a blueprinted span of 230 feet with a hull length of 182 feet, the global pusher-type prop liner awed the air traffic public into thinking they could be content flying DC-4s and L-049s until the CV-37s appeared on the scene. However, it would not be until 1949 when the Boeing 377 Stratocruiser with its lower-decked lounge appeased disenchanted DC-4 and L-049 world-traveled passengers. The B-377 had become Pan Am's earlier-promised "Wings of Tomorrow."

Trippe's reduced fare program began the confined seating arrangements on transoceanic planes prevalent to this day, even in the largest of jumbo jets. A 314's sky luxury fast became a lost art, a commodity of the past.

To help ease many bored post-war air customers during the long trips, Pan Am introduced in-flight movies on Nov. 15, 1945, on DC-4s flying the Atlantic. Porthole curtains were drawn while modified 16 mm projectors, shock-mounted in the aft sections, reflected film images onto 27-by-38-inch screens attached to brackets at the forward ends of the aircraft just aft of the cockpit. The forerunner of air movies was developed by Pan Am's traffic and engineering departments with the aid of Joe Karpchuk of air service who adapted the equipment for aircraft use. Ironically, the first movie shown aloft was the 1945 *FBI* thriller *House On 92nd Street* that incorporated the word "clipper" into the script which referred to the 314. Although movies helped to pass time, many a former 314 passenger missed the spacious cabins, elegant lounges and overall 314 ambiance. Also gone were the wonderful dining salons. Landplane-prepared meals, served on trays, were set on pillows in the laps of cramped passengers who often disembarked more tired than after a 314 trip.

Transatlantic landplane service was begun by Pan Am on Sept. 15, 1945. The airline sent aloft one of its 17 war-reconditioned DC-4s on a route-check flight from New York to Shannon, via Newfoundland, in 14 hours and 29 minutes, nine and one-half hours shorter than a 314's time. As it left LaGuardia's runway it passed over Bowery Bay between two moored 314s, one of which was the *Capetown Clipper*. The DC-4 returned to New York six days later. Then, on October 27th, the first post-war landplane revenue flight departed the U.S. for England, via Gander and Shannon. The same day a 24,000-mile DC-4 route-check flight was conducted between San Francisco and Tokyo, via the old Pacific island-hopping track. A 'round-the-world service had become foremost in Trippe's mind.

Official U.S. Government priorities on all Pan Am routes, except for the San Francisco-Honolulu sector, had been done away with on October 15th. Exactly a week later the last westbound Pan Am 314 flight from Lisbon across the mid-Atlantic was completed. High waves at Horta diverted the few remaining Boeing flights to use the South Atlantic route. The last North Atlantic 314 run under the Pan Am flag was made on Oct. 29, 1945, bringing the total crossings of the Atlantic since 1939 to 2,098.

One of the passengers aboard the *Atlantic Clipper*, piloted by Capt. Gulbransen, was 83-year-old George Rice, president of the Roberts Machine Tool Co. of Brooklyn. Rice had been a passenger on the first flight to Foynes six and one-half years earlier. He and fellow travelers brought the number to approximately 6,400 passengers who passed through Foynes in the four and one-half years of summer 314 operations.

In commemoration of the last 314 flight on the northern route, a "Pan American Day" was celebrated with a luncheon at Foynes' clipper base restaurant for Capt. Gulbransen and crew, Capt. Wallace Culbertson and his men, airline officials and guests. The next day Capt. Culbertson relieved Gulbransen to continue the flight to Lisbon after making one last grand circle over Foynes and the Shamrock city of Limerick. From Portugal the NC-04 returned to New York, via the South Atlantic, to bring the number of passengers carried across the Atlantic to 83,000 in 11,100,000 314 air miles. The clippers had transported some 5,720,000 pounds of express and over eight million pounds of mail in 3,650 Atlantic crossings.

On November 13th, 38-passenger DC-4s began two weekly trips to Bermuda's Kindley Field. Pan Am's last flying boat to the British-mandated isle departed the *MAT* on December 22nd. Three subsequent 314 trips were cancelled when Bowery Bay froze over. Sikorsky S-42 operations to and from Bermuda had been curtailed since July 6th. When the NC-04 arrived at Hamilton, Capt. Masland and his 10-man crew were winging home after taking over the *Capetown Clipper* from Capt. Joe Hart and crew at Lisbon with 25 passengers aboard that marked the last Pan Am 314 transatlantic flight. In the early morning of December 24th, Masland brought the NC-12 into New York.

"Before the commencement of the flight," Masland communicated, "I sent a wire from Lisbon asking what sort of a schedule they wanted for this last return flight. The answer was that they didn't care, anything we chose. So we came straight through, or as straight as the winds would let us; three days and three nights via Africa and South America. From a public point of view we chose a poor time to arrive — 2:00 A.M. But all hands, and especially the passengers, wanted to be home for Christmas, and we made it."[224]

Two days later the *Atlantic Clipper* arrived back from Bermuda and the *MAT*'s doors to Pan Am flying boat traffic were closed. Earlier, the U.S. Navy had asked Pan Am if the line wished to repurchase the Boeings for $50,000 apiece. Turning down the offer, NC-04, NC-09, NC-11 and NC-12 were, along with their beaching cradles, shifted to Floyd Bennett Field in Brooklyn for military storage. The fifth Atlantic-based 314 (NC-06) was flown to the Pacific Division in mid-November to replace another 314 that had met with misfortune the same month. A short while later, NC-04 joined the San Francisco 314 fleet to meet what was considered an increase in tourist traffic since war restrictions were lifted on the run to Hawaii.

Resting on their beaching gears under Brooklyn's sky, the three remaining Atlantic-based 314s were put up for sale by the end of January 1946, by the War Assets Administration (WAA), a temporary U.S. Government agency geared to dispose of antiquated war machinery, for the same price offered Pan Am. Still bearing American bow flags, the 314s showed great wear. Keels were dented from years of hard water poundings, and corrosion had begun to eat hull bottoms. Yet despite their momentary silence, their days of service had not ended. Gone, however, were the envied captains and crews. Their valor, courage and flight records were praised by both the military and Pan Am. Capt. Winston, for example, had filled 17 log books by November, 1943, with 14,000 flying hours on both the Pacific and Atlantic 314 routes. He was also remembered to have entertained many a 314 passenger during his off-time flight duty

Pan Am's first DC-4 landplane clipper on proof-flight to Europe flew over Bowery Bay-moored *Capetown Clipper*, 1945, the introduction of which spelled doom for future flying boat services. (*Photo Courtesy: Pan American World Airways*)

with his repertoire of card tricks. A master at shuffling the deck, he could deal himself four aces without being detected.

Capt. Gulbransen was another pilot who held an impressive 9,000 air record by December, 1944. His log at that time was equivalent to 1,170,000 miles flown, or 45 times around the world at the equator. A graduate of Columbia University in the early 1930s, Gulbransen enlisted into the U.S. Naval Reserve at Pensacola. He began Pan Am pilot training in 1933 flying throughout the Caribbean and later mastered M-13Os to Manila. In 1940, Gulbransen transferred to the Atlantic Division and retired in April, 1969.

Concerning his 314 adventures, Gulbransen remarked, "Although I flew this airplane for five years on the Atlantic, from May, 1940, to April, 1945, I apparently was too close to the forest to observe the trees. I knew practically nothing about the history of the airplane except that we used it to maximum advantage!"[225]

Third and last example of excellent Atlantic 314 captainship was the record of Basil Rowe, who, by early 1946, had recorded 25,000 flight hours in three million miles since he first began flying in 1911 at the age of 15. Rowe became an instructor when the U.S. entered World War I, and later barnstormed throughout the U.S., Mexico, West Indies and Central America. He became, in his spare time, the winner of the "Town and Country Club Trophy" of Dayton, Ohio's International Air Races' "Allen Hinkle Trophy" and "Glenn Curtiss Trophy."

Beginning with survey trips to the West Indies in 1928, Rowe flew nearly every type of Pan Am plane, from the Fokker F-7 to the early 1960-introduced B-707 jet. Rowe had, by January, 1946, accumulated 2,700,000 air miles after flying both 314s and C-54s during the war. According to Pan Am, Rowe's flight record was one of the world's most honored.

Many 314 Atlantic-based crew recalled the ships of sea and air with great fondness. The majority of flight officers were sad to see the boats go. Only one Atlantic 314 flight officer gave a negative outlook towards the Boeing boats. Scott Flower, a 314 engineer, and by 1965 Pan Am's chief technical pilot, wrote, "Thank good-

While Pan Am 314s scored record war loads, so too did BOAC's A314s. As a result of the lack of men called to battle, BOAC trained a number of English women in general flying boat ground-servicing. (*Photo Courtesy: British Overseas Airways*)

ness, that as a result of the Second World War, numerous adequate landing fields for large aircraft were constructed, world-wide, to allow the elimination of water-based equipment...

"The B-314 played a great role in opening transatlantic air service. However, because of its slow speed, it broke backs to accomplish some of its missions. Spending 24 hours or more on one of these craft at low altitude (one thousand feet) in order to make the range requirements is not what the undersigned considers a desirable machine. The mere mention of the words 'Boeing 314,' until this day, brings about a great sense of weariness rather than nostalgia."[226]

Three examples of many positive impressions regarding the 314s came from Pan Am's Capt. Burn, saver of Froman's life in the Tagus, BOAC's Capt. Kelly-Rogers and Capt. Gray:

"I really enjoyed flying on the 314s," Burn commented. "They were good planes, easy to handle and very roomy."[227]

Kelly-Rogers voiced, "Did we like the ships; did they operate well? The answer to all that is positively yes! We loved those aircraft, and I'd love to get my hands on one now. They are what we call a 'pilot's airplane.' They were not, of course, very fast, but they could go a long way"[228]

Distinguished Capt. Gray stated in 1963 when then executive vice-president of Pan Am, "one of my favorite flying machines"[229]

Boeing flights were still going strong between San Francisco and Honolulu when the Atlantic Division shut down its flying boat services. The war in the Pacific came to a quick end after B-29 "Superfortress" bombers dropped two atomic bombs on Hiroshima and Nagasaki, Japan, on August 6th and 9th, the uranium of which

One long and narrow DC-4 cabin with its close-quartered seats was the start of "no frills" flying so prevalent within today's global-spread commercial airliners. (*Photo Courtesy: Pan American World Airways*)

was used to develop the weapon secretly flown to the U.S. from Leopoldville aboard the *China Clipper* in 1944 under Capt. Lodeesen.

On September 2nd, Gen. MacArthur presided at surrender ceremonies aboard the *USS Missouri* in Tokyo Bay. Japan's Premier, Adm. Baron Kantaro, signed over his country to MacArthur's administration. From the White House President Harry S. Truman announced "V-J Day." World War Two had ended.

With victory in hand, the U.S. Navy ended its military contract with Pan Am, and on November 15th lifted the Pacific Division's travel restrictions. The following day the first post-war, regular Pacific commercial flight was scheduled for Honolulu at 5:00 P.M. Van Dusen's public relations adjunct office in San Francisco had prepared a statement welcoming the public to view the takeoff of the *Pacific Clipper* from the base at Mills Field. The NC-02 was, as were all 314s after the war, refurbished with its original interior luxuries, including the tail suite. A bottle of champagne was given to all who reserved space in the clippers' deluxe compartments. Over the NC-02's two egress hatches was painted *Pan American World Airways System*. The word "world," a first-time application on a Pan Am plane, advertised the line's upcoming global service.

Walking across the gangplank that evening were honeymooners John Wayne, actor, and latest bride Esperanza Bauer. Void of the American flags on its bow, the NC-02 splashed away and flew out past the Golden Gate to begin the 17,060th Pan Am flight over the Pacific since Nov. 22, 1935. During the war, the military-dominated airline flew 177,343 hours (enough time to keep one plane airborne for nearly 20 years) in 3,370 Pacific flights that included the use of PB2Ys and PBM-3Rs. Twenty-five million air miles were compiled in the four years of war-expanded operations.

Meanwhile, the four Pan Am and three BOAC 314s still in operation continued to hold their queen-of-the-skies crowns.

Madeline Cunniff, Pan Am's first Atlantic-going stewardess, had many jobs to perform, one of which was to spray cabins and 314 flight-decks with insecticide before leaving ports-of-call. The gracious sky lady retired in 1984 after 44 years with Pan Am. Former Treasure Island Traffic Department employees Mary Lyman and Beverly Mogensen were first stewardesses to fly San Francisco-Honolulu run aboard 314s starting in August, 1945. On her first flight, Mogensen severely cut a finger with a galley knife and had to be attended to by Purser Roy Donham. During off-duty time, flight attendants would, if unoccupied, often use the clipper's tail suite to relax in. (*Photo Courtesy: Pan American World Airways*)

31

Down and Out

It was Saturday, Nov. 3, 1945, when nine crew under Pan Am Capt. Sannis E. ("Robby") Robbins of Palo Alto, Calif., and 13 passengers, two civilian technicians and 11 U.S. Navy men, enplaned the *Honolulu Clipper* at the NATS' seaplane base situated at John Rogers Airport, Oahu, for a routine military flight to San Francisco. Good tail winds were forecasted when Robbins took off at 3:30 P.M. for the overnight cruise.

Trailing about 150 miles behind NC-01 on another regular run to the Mainland was the NC-05 piloted by Capt. Fred C. Richards. Aboard the renamed *Dixie Clipper* (i.e. the *Anzac Clipper*) ship were nine passengers, one of whom was C. Niles Tavares, Hawaii's attorney general en route to Washington, D.C. The NC-05 had also departed from John Rogers Airport 90 minutes after the NC-01 swept away.

Plotting the *Honolulu Clipper*'s flight was Second Officer William O. Buchanan, later to become Pan Am's maintenance administration manager at John F. Kennedy International Airport. Engineer Officers Dan Broadwater and Robert J. Dernberger kept power plant watch while First Officer Wallace W. Reed, a Pan Am man since 1940, and a former U.S. Army flying instructor, assisted Robbins. First Radio Officer Jack B. Crawford, Second Radio Officer Edward W. Ancell, and Third Officer Dunbar Carpenter also kept a tight- posted vigil. Below, Stewards H. George ("Tommy")

Quatsoe and Ferdinand McKee began to prepare the usual sit-down salon dinner.

Everything was normal at 7,000 feet. Both clipper captains had tuned in to the oceanic airway traffic control to keep abreast of rescue attempts underway 450 miles east of Oahu. An ATC Consairways L-B30, a converted B 24 bomber, had ditched and broken apart with 27 passengers and crew aboard just before the two 314s left Oahu.

At about 9:00 P.M., the NC-01's No. 3 engine began to backfire and run rough. From the starboard flight-deck windows the crew noted sparks and flames shooting out in the vicinity of No. 8 cylinder. Smoke soon engulfed the wing station along the inner catwalk. Fearing a dangerous fire, Robbins cut the engine's power and feathered the prop. He then notified traffic control at 10:20 following the two engineers' failure to correct the problem. Ten minutes later Capt. Richards received a MAY DAY signal from the *Honolulu Clipper*'s Radio Officer Crawford when the ship was between 700 and 850 miles out to sea and east of "aqua-time," the point of no return. Robbins had decided to abort the flight and return to base.

About 20 minutes after the turn-around, engine No. 4 started to sputter and again Capt. Richards of the NC-05 was notified. Gages on the NC-01's engineer panel indicated No. 4 was consuming oil

With its war paint removed, Mills Field-moored *Honolulu Clipper* helped to reinstate post-war regularly scheduled passenger service to and from Hawaii. By this time war-weary 314 galleys and compartments showed signs of much wear. Berth rod supports were badly worn and difficult to assemble. Metal fatigue was also spotted in some 314 wing spars where ends to cracks had to be hole-bored by ground maintenance to prevent spreadings. (*Photo Courtesy: Gordon S. Williams*)

Chapter Thirty-one: Down and Out

Downed by engine failure, a still sturdy *Honolulu Clipper* is spotted wallowing endlessly in wind-tossed Pacific. (Photo Courtesy: United States Navy Archives)

at the alarming rate of six gallons an hour. Eighty minutes later Robbins was forced to shut No. 4 down and feather its prop when the engine also began to backfire. Another message was sent to Richards.

Robbins applied full power to the two remaining power plants. Danger came to the fore when the NC-01 began to lose 100 to 150 feet a minute despite Boeing's assurance that a 314 could stay aloft with only two of its engines in operation.

Further attempts at in-flight repair were to no avail. Robbins ordered stewards to inform passengers of the turn-around, to don life vests and to belt down. Broadwater and Dernberger were then told to stand by to jettison fuel. At 11:00 P.M., a radio message was sent out. "We are going to dump the plane. We are signing off at 300 feet."[230]

While fuel was being dumped, other flight-deck crew heaved out cargo and 500 pounds of mail from opened under-wing hatchways. But even with an estimated 5,000-pound lighter aircraft it was calculated by the NC-01's navigators that the clipper would never make port. Robbins had to ditch!

With no visual horizon reference to help guide the clipper down, Robbins relied only on the ship's altimeter and the boat's powerful landing lights. Darkness enveloped the 314 within a cloak of pending doom, the dipping hull angled to an unseen turbulent sea with swells whipping upwards between five and eight feet.

A wind direction was quickly taken. Last minute ditching procedures were given passengers, who, Buchanan later said "...were calm, cooperative and confident as one would expect from officer Naval personnel in a time of emergency."[231]

Landing lights blinked on in the moonless sky as the mighty clipper glided down in zero visibility. The Pacific Ocean raged and waited.

At 11:07, without much sensation, the NC-01 bounced in. An almost hysterically joyous message was phoned from the downed

NC-01 and picked up by Capt. Richards. "We are on the water. Hurray. There are no leaks."[232]

Buchanan remarked many years later about the precarious touchdown when he wrote, "In spite of a total darkness landing, Capt. Robbins managed to bring the clipper down to the open-sea landing without cracking a single rivet in the hull. This is about the highest commendation one could give the skill of the skipper and the structural integrity of the aircraft. I am sure that every member of Capt. Robbins' crew on this occasion shared with him, as I do, the utmost respect and admiration for the integrity, performance and seaworthiness of the 314s."[233]

Robbins' skill as an air-ocean master was backed by 27 years as a pilot. It was during World War I that he learned how to fly in an OX Jenny. He joined Pan Am in 1931, and in 1941 was assigned to the Pacific-Alaska Division. During the war Robbins flew many military-oriented missions for the government-sponsored airline throughout Alaska and the Aleutian Islands. But it wasn't until that November, 1945 night that his perfected training and years of experience came to the test.

"Accordingly," Buchanan added, "the skill with which he executed this particular landing was miraculous."[234]

Touchdown was made 650 miles east of Oahu and about 200 miles northeast of the ditched and wrecked B-24. Robbins and crew determined that all available rescue ships were at or near the location of the crash site from which seven bodies were found among eight survivors.

While the NC-01's flight engineers checked for leaks throughout the plane, Robbins kept Crawford working on messages to Honolulu and San Francisco. Replies advised that help was on its way.

With nothing else to do, Robbins relaxed a bit and said to his crew, "What we need while we are waiting is a little diversion."[235]

Aware that Broadwater's wife in Palo Alto was expecting a baby, Robbins thought it appropriate to send her a message stating

'Twas a touch-and-go rescue operation. Clipper tended to return to Hawaii on its own when nature's tide and winds favored a westerly direction. (Photo Courtesy: United States Navy Archives)

that her husband was safe and not to worry. Radio Officer Crawford sent the coded wire to Pan Am's San Francisco base that in turn relayed it on to the expectant.

About an hour later Capt. Richards zeroed in, guided by a flare shot aloft from the NC-01. It was a few minutes past midnight. Most of Richards' passengers, such as Tavares and wife, Mother Superior Mary Joseph of the Maryknoll order and Navy officers, were alseep in berths. One, T. Clifford Melin, a Honolulu businessman, was awake and aware of the situation. He soon tired and went back to sleep as the NC-05 continued its wide-arched circling.

Staying within a 10-mile radius, Richards made contact with Hawaii's Air-Sea Frontier Navy Rescue Service which reported several ships in the area. Richards increased his circling radius and notified the nearest vessel, the 7,000-ton Army transport *John Henry Payne* sailing to San Francisco and only about 35 miles beyond the sea-tossed clipper,

The second ship Richards contacted was the U.S. Navy *USS Manila Bay*, an escort carrier 60 miles away. Each ship altered its course and steamed at full speed toward the stricken 314.

Continuing to circle, Richards had his radio officer keep the communication key open with the men aboard the rescue ships and those on the NC-01. At 12:24 A.M., November 4th, the *Payne's* dispatcher reported sighting flares over the horizon. Two other ships, the *Englewood Hills*, a merchant tanker, and *Copahee*, also an escort carrier, were ordered to the rescue by Pearl Harbor's watchful command. A Consolidated PBY amphibian was sent out from Kancohe, a naval air station near Honolulu. Upon learning the *Manila Bay* was only 30 miles from the clipper, the *Copahee* was turned away to resume her course towards Pearl.

Towards morning some of the NC-01's crew and passengers became seasick. Jokingly, Richards phoned Robbins, "Do you want me to drop ham sandwiches?"

"Yea, but go easy on the pork,"[236] Robbins jested back.

It was 5:30 A.M. when the *Payne* came in sight of the bobbing and pitching 314. Two and one-half hours later the *Manila Bay*, bound for Honolulu to pick up servicemen and transport them back to the Mainland, sailed into view. Ahead of the *Payne*, and the first

to arrive, was the *Englewood Hills*. Meanwhile, the seas had calmed down considerably. Whale boats were lowered at the crack of dawn and were carefully manuvered towards the NC-01 where, without much difficulty, passengers were removed from clipper rafts and taken back to the tanker. Robbins and crew remained with their ship.

By 8:00 A.M., the *Englewood Hills* signaled Pearl Harbor that all passengers were safely aboard. Those wanting to return immediately to San Francisco were transferred to the *Payne*, and those desiring to go back to Honolulu were taken aboard the *Manila Bay*. Only one, Lt. Cmdr. Edwin Harrett, decided on the latter.

Shortly after the passengers were removed from the clipper, a crew of aviation mechanics from the *Manila Bay* were sent by boat to board the wallowing flying boat. For three hours they toiled in vain to repair the engines. Giving up for the time being, the clipper's crew joined the seamen back on the carrier.

During the next two hours the *Manila Bay's* mechanics worked in worsening weather to hook tow lines from the plane's bow to the carrier's stern. At one point the 314 and ship nearly collided when the NC-01 drifted too close atop heavy swells. By 1:00 P.M., lines had been secured and the flying boat was in tow.

For the remainder of the day and part way into the night the towing operation went well. Then rain began to fall, winds picked up and swells capped higher. Seaman First Class Phillip F. Assarito, along with other shipmates, were watching an evening movie aboard the carrier when an announcement came that all members of the second division were to report to the ship's fantail.

"We knew something was wrong," Azzarito later told reporters, "and upon reaching our positions we learned that the lines attached to the plane gave way and the plane was drifting helplessly."[237]

After only seven hours under tow 700 feet to stern, the rough sea had caused havoc. Little could be done that night to recover the 314. Seas were too high. Searchlights from the *Manila Bay* beamed down on the NC- 01 for a few hours until the carrier's captain decided to track the clipper by radar.

Adrift and absent of human life, the flying boat was monitored against the blackened curtain of sea, its separation between sea and sky indiscernible to the naked eye. Performing its own ballet, she danced over waves as if directed at the helm by some ghostly stagehand.

For nearly two more days the *Manila Bay* followed its prey. It was considered too dangerous to try to snag the queen with ropes, and the carrier's chief, Cmdr. Leon Johnson, radioed Pearl for assistance. Sent to rendezvous with the carrier was the seaplane tender *San Pablo* that arrived on the scene at noon, Tuesday, November 6th. Her job finished, the *Manila Bay's* bow was pointed towards Pearl.

For the rest of the day, attempts by the *Pablo's* crew were made to latch onto the rocking clipper. From the point of landing to where the *Pablo* took over, the NC-01 had been swept 125 miles closer to

Hawaii by strong currents. Radar kept the unsinkable plane in sight for the next night.

Near noon on November 7th, tragedy struck the unapproachable 314 which had made more miles towards Hawaii. After snagging the rascal, and while tirelessly trying to hoist her out of water, a huge wave carried the sturdy plane into the *Pablo's* fantail with a resounding crash. The Boeing sky bird was just too big and too heavy to be lifted.

Ripped from its extreme outer roots were the starboard wing tip and engine No. 4, the latter of which tore through the plane's bow as the hull swayed to the right. Adrift again, the *Pablo's* captain ordered his radio officer to contact Vice Adm. Sherwood A. Taffinder, Pearl Harbor's sea frontier commander, to inform him of the predicament. Taffinder wired back authorization to sink the crippled plane by gunfire. The NC-01's death warrant was sealed. Based on the time and effort to save her, plus the high cost for repairs, it was best to destroy her as she was now a derelict, a menace to surface navigation.

The *Pablo's* men commenced firing once the tender was positioned about a mile away from the port-dipping clipper. The first round of lobbed shells didn't do the job. Only after 30 minutes of intense firing — the shooting of 1,300 20 mm explosive capsules — did the grand lady of sea and air surrender to the elements. Crackling in fire and spewing forth smoke, the NC-01 slid beneath the surface and vanished into the depths of the blue Pacific.

Since its 1939 debut to her last day in 1945, the *Honolulu Clipper* had flown an incredible 18,000 hours, 11,595 of which were conducted by NATS. This was enough time to circle the globe 80 times! Among her many famous passengers were, besides Henry and Clare Booth Luce, Howard Cone, publisher; Thomas Kinkeid, U.S. admiral; Peter Fraser, New Zealand's Prime Minister; Chester Nimitz, U.S. Pacific fleet admiral; and Edward V. Rickenbacker, U.S.' prime WWI flying ace and then iron-ruling chief of now defunct Eastern Airlines. He took the NC-01 to Hawaii en route to New Guinea in 1942 on a mission to see MacArthur.

An epitaph for the sunken air queen was seen later floating miles away from her grave. It was a container of boxed leis and orchid corsages once destined for a San Francisco flower shop.

Robbins and crew met with newsmen at a pre-planned press conference after disembarking the *Manila Bay* at Pearl Harbor on the morning of November 8th. The highly skilled captain praised the Navy for their fine support, but remarked that he and his men were glad they didn't have to watch the NC-01's destruction and added,

"I never was sold on the superiority of seaplanes over land-type planes for ocean flying until my experience."[238]

As a result of the ditching, an investigation was carried out by the CAA. Although the 314 was owned by the Navy, the aircraft was commercially registered. Chief CAA Airlines Inspector R. V. Keeler, and CAA Air Carrier Maintenance Inspector Oliver A. Rosto, conducted one of the shortest inquiries recorded in commercial air

disasters. Completed two days after the sinking, Keeler reported: ". . .we have concluded that the flight was conducted with good operating practices and the Pan American crew executed duties and responsibilities even beyond the line of duty. The crew has contributed a great deal of valuable information relative to emergency equipment which should be carried or designed for future use in aircraft flying the routes of the world."[239]

Pan Am wrote a letter to Rosto on Dec. 19, 1945, informing the agency to close the NC-01's files. The action was finalized on March 4, 1946.

Five months after the NC-01's sinking, Pan Am phased out its flying boat service. On the morning of April 9, 1946, Capt. S. Denton ("Dent") Terrell, a veteran skipper who mastered 314s under Capt. Beer, and a crew of nine landed the *American Clipper* off Mills Field after a night flight from Honolulu. Not much attention was given to Pan Am's last 314 trip that carried only 24 passengers. Across the lagoon at the land terminal a new L-049 triple-finned Constellation clipper had arrived from Hawaii four hours earlier with 42 passengers after a record-breaking flight of nine hours, nine minutes. The NC-06's flight, originating the day before, took 16 hours and 39 minutes to reach San Francisco.

Pacific landplane service, introduced with a L-049 flight to Honolulu on April 8th, was in the news. Bemoaning the end of the Pan Am 314 flights was ground chief Greenough. He had serviced the Pacific-going air boats since their conception and was photographed in the NC-06's bridge with Capt. Terrell while hashing over the ending of an era.

Once passengers, cargo and mail were removed, the NC-06 was towed into the lagoon and anchored between her retired sister ships whereupon the Navy put the four Pacific 314s up for sale through the WAA. For a little more than four months NC-09, NC-11 and NC-12 were seen parked atop cradles at New York's Floyd

All hands on *San Pablo's* decks viewed another one of many futile attempts to tow stricken clipper 700 miles to port. Picture captured by crewman in a circling B-24 observation plane. (Photo Courtesy: United States Navy Archives)

Bennett Field while out west clippers NC-02, NC-04, NC-05 and NC-06 were taxied by Pan Am captains across San Francisco Bay and moored at the U.S. Navy's Alameda depot.

Pacific Division Capt. Robert ("Bob") C. Howard, hired by Pan Am in Miami on Nov. 16, 1936, and sent to the Pacific within a year as a young fourth officer of six crews stationed at San Francisco, was one of those who turned the gallant 314s back to the Navy.

Howard was an old hand with the 314s. He was on the delivery flights of NC-01 and NC-02 between Seattle and San Francisco in 1939, and also aboard the NC-01 when it nearly crashed into Lake Washington during the stall-landing test.

A captain on 314s since 1942, Howard wrote, "I had the nostalgic honor of commanding the delivery of the NC-02 from old San Francisco Airport to Alameda Naval Air Station. The boat was no longer insured by the airline, so orders were to taxi it across the bay. At one point we taxied too fast and I flew it 10 feet high for my last feel of the loveable old craft."[240]

Van Dusen wrote in part in May, 1946, "We've just been saying 'good-bye' to an old friend of yours — and ours. She's the last of Pan American's famous flying boats that carried the American flag on flying wings to all the seven seas. Leaving the airways now, she takes something with her that we'll probably never see again in aviation — a character of courage, a symbol of enterprise that dared the deep unknown for the first time...

"The global routes of the air age were turned into reality by the pioneering enterprise of the flying boats. It was the clippers that took the mystery out of ocean flying and set the pattern for wartime multiple schedules...

"Sure, the sky's full of four-engine transports now. But... those 12 Boeing boats were the only airplanes, under any flag, capable of carrying a sizeable load safely across an ocean stretch. These boats made America first on the airways of the world. We can't very well — and shouldn't — forget that. They were big, too big to go wrong, timid passengers used to be convinced...

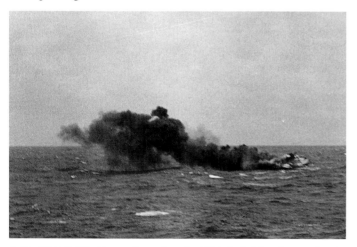

A sky queen is killed by gunfire and a prized historical airliner is gone forever. (Photo Courtesy: United States Navy Archives)

"They contributed a chapter in the annals of flying that'll still be thrilling reading for generations to come. They bred a new breed of airmen — who talked and thought and worked in the lingo of the air and sea. They left an indelible mark. And they'll take with them some of that glory, some of that sense of accomplishment, some of that excitement of the 'first,' some of that thrill of 'men against the sea,' some of that bold adventure of the explorer and pioneer — yes, some of the faith and the hope and the courage of all those who fly!"[241]

Along with the adventure, the pioneering, and the "firsts" also went an impressive record. Combined, the Pan Am-owned 314s compiled more than 12,500,000 air miles on some 5,000 ocean flights that averaged 3,340 miles per flight. It divided equally, each 314 had more than 18,000 flying hours. During the war the Boeings carried in excess of 84,000 passengers, some 300 of them admirals, generals and commodores. For such a very small fleet, it was, to say the least, the most incredible and outstanding commercial air record established in the 20th century:

When the Pan Am 314s were retired, the Pacific-based captains and crew, as did those on the Atlantic, took with them their years of 314 experiences — priceless, individualized stories more valuable than any materialistic souvenir. Examples, based on memories, are many and varied, but four, told by three captains and a steward, stand out as being both exciting and whimsical.

"I can relate a few things that were amusing," said Capt. Beer some 36 years after the last Pan Am 314 flight terminated at Mills Field. "At one time when we were stationed in Manila, there was a forecast of a typhoon. So, they sent the crew and the airplane to the southern Island of Mindanao. On our way down we visited all the side islands — we didn't stop, but we flew low where we could see what the countryside looked like on those islands.

"We arrived at a bay on the western side of Mindanao, and there we landed. It was a bay surrounded by jungle. We just dropped the anchor... We were in contact with Manila and knew what was going on, and so we just stayed there until the forecast of the typhoon had passed.

"It rains very hard in those islands. After spending two or three days in a sweaty airplane, because of the tropical climate, we decided to take a shower in the next rain storm. So when the rain came, up on the wing to shower in the rain. Just about the time we were all soaped and ready to clean off the rain stopped. We had to dive into the bay in the salt water to get the soap off and that leaves you kind of 'gummy'...

"On our return trip we encountered a rain storm that was so heavy that the water on the windshield gave the appearance of being in a submarine. We had to increase the horsepower of the engines in order to stay level. It only lasted 15 or 20 minutes, but it was the heaviest rain that I have ever encountered and I've been in numerous hurricanes and typhoons."[242]

Capt. Blackmore recalled his most humorous 314 incident while commanding the *California Clipper* on a flight from the Far East to San Francisco in 1941 when Clare Boothe Luce was aboard. At one point along the route, Blackmore and his first officer opened the bridge's side windows at low altitude to get fresh air which caused a decompression-type suction throughout the 314. According to Blackmore, Luce, who occupied the suite, had gone "...to the head in her section and, because of the draft, everything flew back at her!"[243]

Blackmore went on to tell about his 314 days as being "... great as long as it lasted. There was great glamour, the crew marched aboard to music and passengers followed - - great combination of flying and sea travel. It was Pan Am at its zenith, and fun to be part of the pioneering years."[244]

Besides being aboard the inaugural flights to Auckland and Singapore, Capt. Howard added an unforgettable 314 experience when he wrote, "The unique design of the 314, and our thorough training on it, saved one aircraft and its occupants. We were just past the mid-point between Honolulu and San Francisco when No. 3 engine failed and was shut down. A few minutes later No. 2 dropped power to 'idle' but did not stop. To reach shore under those conditions became impossible. As we slowly descended toward the

Draped in flowered leis, last Pacific Division B-314 passengers were momentarily held back by clipper's ground hostess for historical picture-taking. (Photo Courtesy: Pan American World Airways)

ocean I walked out into the left wing, took the clam-shell off No. 2 engine and located a broken throttle rod link. I was able to manually hold the throttle open to regain power until the flight engineer could locate a spare link (which we fortunately carried) and make permanent repairs. We had about five minutes of airborne time left over a dark, stormy night. I couldn't hear properly for a week from the noise in the wing."[245]

Steward Dunning also remembered with zest one of his 314 Pacific trips, and the sometime problems attendants encountered when serving meals during rough weather where china 'n all toppled off tables and onto the laps of passengers or onto the decking.

"It did happen, but not quite as often as one might think. I do recall a trip when I was pouring a cup of coffee behind an admiral who was seated with our captain. We ran into the only cloud buildup within 500 miles. The guys in the cockpit weren't watching (it was night) and went right through it. The coffee landed on the admiral's head, the captain headed for the flight-deck and you can guess the rest!"[246]

While awaiting their WAA disposition, the U.S. Navy arranged to fly the Alameda-moored 314 castaways to San Diego where the weather was more condusive against corrosion which had already begun to take effect. For a short time, until the cradles were shipped, the 314s sat poised in San Diego Bay off old Lindbergh Field near Shelter Island at the Navy's seaplane bases. Once the cradles arrived by rail the Boeings were tractored out of the water onto the near-abandoned Convair flying boat ramp, parked and aired out.

Meanwhile, in Washington, D.C., the WAA's Director of Information Huly E. Gray ran newspaper and aviation magazine ads telling of the 314 sale. Interested parties were asked to submit a letter of intent to purchase with a 10-percent down. Checks were to be made out to the WAA's Aircraft Sales Division and mailed to the

Holding Pacific-Divisioned end-of-the-line achievement certificate, Capt. Terrell and Greenough shared a NC-06 bridge moment for mutual-yeared 314 jobs well done. (*Photo Courtesy: Pan American World Airways*)

With hat removed in salutation, Greenough sorrowed Pacific Division's 314 stifling as well as viewing last captain to man such a ship leave *American Clipper*. (*Photo Courtesy: Pan American World Airways*)

End of Pacific 314 flight, last of Pacific 314 crew line-up, was headed by Capt. Terrell (far left). On flight was Chief Steward Eugene J. Dunning (center, front row). (*Photo Courtesy: Pan American World Airways*)

Railroad Retirement Building, 425 Second St., Washington, D.C. Prospective buyers from a foreign country had to apply through the U.S. State Department's Foreign Liquidation Commission. Eight parties responded with interest to purchase.

On Aug. 20, 1946, all seven U.S.-owned 314s, including spare engines and other assemblages, were sold to Universal Airlines for $325,000. Universal, the highest bidder, and one of many non-scheduled ("non-sked") airlines to sprout forth at war's end, was an east coast charter firm. Their headquarters was located on Hudson Street in New York, and by November, 1946, had moved to the city's *Lincoln Hotel* at 45th Street and 8th Avenue.

Universal desired to use the 314s on their route linking New York, Newark and Miami with San Juan in the West Indies. Near month's end the line initiated a brief non-stop service to and from Miami. The clippers had been mortgaged to General Phoenix Corp. (GPC), a brokerage company on East 42nd Street, N.Y. A second mortgage was obtained by Universal on Dec. 20, 1946, from a Nate Madell, also of New York.

Three months after the purchase, Universal's Marine Division Manager at the *MAT*, S. C. Huffman, notified the Department of Commerce:

"One of these boats was received in such a damaged condition that we have decided to salvage same for parts. This damage was incurred during a wind storm before this company acquired ownership of the planes, and while in the custody of the United States Navy."[247]

The wrecked boat was the NC-09, still based at Floyd Bennet Field. A wing tip had been crushed. Since clipper spares of any kind were hard to come by, Pan Am's former *South Atlantic Clipper* was stripped of all essential parts and equipment. The remain-

der of the boat's hull, wing and tail surfaces were then sold for scrap. Huffman sent the NC-09's registration certificate (Form 500), its airworthiness certificate (Form 308-A) and the plane's operational records (Forms 309-A-1, 309-A-2 and 309-A-3) to the Commerce Department on Nov. 23, 1946. Another 314 file was closed by the CAA on Dec, 13, 1946.

Universal had barely acquired the 314 fleet when it ran into financial trouble. Just more than five months after Huffman mailed the NC-09's papers, the line was adjudged bankrupt on May 28, 1947, and a trustee appointed to the material assets. The equipment was picked up by another charter firm, American-International Airlines, Inc. (ATA), a Delaware corporation with headquarters located on Lexington Ave., N.Y., and later at 1440 Broadway, N.Y.

Registered as a contract air carrier, AIA was not granted a regular operating certificate as listed under section 42 of the then CAA's regulations manual. A dispute arose between AIA and the CAA in July, 1947, over the line's intent to operate unlicensed aircraft for non-sked charter operations. The company could, as granted, only charter out its planes to other air carriers. On June 18, 1947, AIA registered the 314s with the CAA.

Prior to the second sale of the clippers for $500,000, the liners were subject to liens imposed by GPC, Madell and to U.S. Government taxes. Only five of the ships were cleared to fly.

During the summer of 1947, AIA was called upon for three of the clippers. Only one, however, was leased out. It was the NC-12, renamed the *Bermuda Sky Queen*. The San Diego-cradled 314s were, at the time, still undergoing refurbishing. By early October, 1947, AIA planned to use all remaining one-time Pan Am 314s for private 10-to-30-day charter air cruises to Bermuda and the West Indies. Originating out of New York, AIA's President J. Stuart Robinson listed such a holiday air cruise as a "Houseparty In The Sky."

Out-of-service clippers lay stilled, Mills Field, San Francisco Bay, May 22, 1946. (*Photo Courtesy: Boeing Aircraft Co.*)

In early October, 1947, AIA contracted the NC-12 out to London-based Air Liaison, Ltd., to fly English emigrants and a number of British delegation employees to New York and the United Nations. The plane Capt. Masland disliked so much had been reconditioned and furnished with its pre-war luxury fittings. She was taken from Floyd Bennet Field in July and flown to the BOAC base in Baltimore, hauled out of the water, groomed and inspected. Sister ship NC-11 then became the sole Floyd Bennet Field beached 314.

On October 2nd, the last built Model A314 was ferried back to New York and landed on the Hudson River off 79th Street in view of awe-struck thousands. Six days later the flying boat departed for Poole, England, under the command of 26-year-old Capt. Charles M. Martin of Miami. Martin had flown 2,000 hours, 162 of which

were with 314s. He was checked out for a commercial air license with single and multi-engine land and seaplane instrument ratings.

To Martin's right sat 34-year-old First Officer Addison Thompson, also from Miami. Addison held the same rank status as Martin and had accumulated 8,000 airhours, 102 of which were aboard 314s. He was the only qualified, certificated celestial navigator amongst the crew and Martin would rely on his experience. Aft and below-deck were Second Officer Jack Shafer, First Engineer Walter Yaramishyn, Assistant Engineer Robert Hamilton, Radio Officer Willard Keith Woodmansee and Steward Charles Penn.

When the *Bermuda Sky Queen* took off from the Hudson River near Floyd Bennet Field for its North Atlantic flight to England, its engines made so much noise that the New York Police Department

First L-049 Constellation Clipper (NX 88836) to replace Pacific 314s gets engine testing at California's Burbank Airport-based Lockheed Aircraft plant before delivery to San Francisco and inaugurating landplane passenger service to and from Hawaii. (*Photo Courtesy: Lockheed Aircraft Corp.*)

With part of airline name-wording removed above main midship hatches, worn-looking and former *Atlantic* (foreground) and *American Clippers* sit out temporary storage, Mills Field, San Francisco, 1946. (*Photo Courtesy: Fred Nott Collection*)

called AIA headquarters and demanded that the airline not bring the aircraft into the area again. There had been too many public complaints.

Three days later Martin landed the NC-12 at Poole. On Sunday afternoon, October 12th, 62 passengers and 3,651 pounds of baggage were taken aboard. The 314's suite, sometimes referred to in the past by Pan Am crews as "the tail room," was remodeled into a standard passenger compartment to accommodate the large human load factor. Many who stepped aboard recalled the 314s and their fame when under Pan Am rule. An account reported some of the passengers were excited and thrilled to learn they were flying on a former clipper. Nine of those who embarked were U.S. merchant seamen, homeward-bound after delivering a tanker to an English firm.

Around noon the same day the NC-12 alighted at Foynes, one of two pre-planned stops. Expecting to get off that evening, Martin had to temporarily postpone the flight until the next day when reports of bad weather over the North Atlantic route were forecasted.

Cast-off was made at 3:40 P.M., Foynes time, October 13th, for the long hop to Gander, second refueling port. Martin, Thompson and Shafer had gone to the meteorological station at Shannon in the morning to obtain weather information. Conditions appeared to have improved. Reports, however, indicated a high pressure existed along the route with headwinds averaging 26 knots at the planned 8,000-foot cruising altitude. Martin filed his flight course and left.

With 4,000 gallons of fuel in its tanks, the former *Capetown Clipper* was climbed and leveled on course over billowing clouds. The point-of-no-return was computed to be 11 hours and 36 minutes away from lift-off time. Calculated into the flight plan was enough petrol for 22 hours (180 gallons burned per hour) with a five-hour reserve after reaching Gander. Below, passengers had settled in the lounge or in their staterooms to read, converse, sip beverages and play card games, unaware the flight would never reach Gander.

32

Bermuda Sky Queen

Ex-World War Two Navy pilot Martin proceeded west across the North Atlantic in calm weather for the next five hours and 50 minutes. Sunset came at 5:40, Greenwich time, just after the NC-12 encountered the first of many headwinds.

First Officer Thompson assisted Shafer in taking the first celestial observation fix when the stars began to show their twinkle and just before an overcast blacked out the sky at 9:30. Before leaving his post for off-duty time, Thompson told Martin the ship would pass "Ocean Charlie," a weather-stationed U.S. Coast Guard ship anchored 809 miles east of Argentia, Newfoundland, at 0200 hours. Calculations had placed the *Bermuda Sky Queen* 45 minutes behind schedule before reaching "Ocean Charlie," 961 miles west of Foynes. Winds picked up.

Thompson left the bridge and retired to a bunk reinstalled in the crew's aft station. Shortly after midnight, October 14th, icing conditions were encountered. About an hour later Woodmansee contacted the Moncton Ocean Air Traffic Control requesting permission to descend 2,000 feet. A weather forecast was received from Gander revealing headwinds had increased 12 more knots.

Winds continued to be strong at 6,000 feet as Martin continued west without another fix until about 1:55 A.M. when the 314's radar blip picked up "Ocean Charlie's" U.S. Coast Guard cutter *George*

M. Bibb, a 327 foot-long, 6,200 h.p.-driven ship, 68 miles away on an 80-degree bearing. The NC-12 had flown 892 miles since leaving Foynes, was nearing the half-way mark to Gander and had consumed 10 hours and 25 minutes of the 22-hour estimated fuel range. In the lower-decked cabins the majority of passengers tried to sleep in their upright seats. There were no berths on this trip. Twelve of the passengers were children, one a one, one-half year old baby.

Shortly, the *Bibb* was contacted and informed that the flying boat would arrive at Gander about 0930 hours, 52 minutes behind schedule. One hour, 11 minutes away the craft was to reach the point-of-no-return. Winds of 40 to 45 knots at 6,000 feet were reported by the *Bibb*'s radio operator. Then at 0232 hours the Boeing was tracked between 15 and 20 miles south of the *Bibb*, one hour, 17 minutes later from the original plane's calculation and 32 minutes more than the amended estimate.

Martin lowered to 4,000 feet hoping to find less headwinds. At 3:27 A.M., 11 minutes past the mid-point, Gander sent out another weather forecast. Headwinds were forecasted between 250 and 260 degrees at 38 knots for the remainder of the flight.

At 5:00 A.M., the weather cleared and Thompson was awakened to affix an accurate location from the weather data received earlier. The computations were devastating!

Future-titled *Capetown Clipper*, hugging Elliott Bay after 1941 trial takeoff, ended her fabulous air career as the *Bermuda Sky Queen*. (*Photo Courtesy: Gordon S. Williams*)

According to Thompson's charting, gale force headwinds in excess of 60 knots had existed along the route. The NC-12's time checks showed a position considerably behind dead-reckoning with a ground speed west of "Ocean Charlie" set at a snail's pace of 59 knots! Flight Engineers Yaramishyn and Hamilton quickly computed the remaining fuel load for the last 550 miles to Gander.

They wouldn't make port!

Continuing west, and while double-checking their fixes, a position report was sent Gander at 6:00 A.M. A decision was made to return to the *Bibb* where rescue facilities were available. At about 460 miles east of Gander, and 300 miles west of the *Bibb*, Martin turned the ship about at 7:58 A.M. Gander was told of the re-routing at 8:40 A.M. The NC-12 had two hours and 45 minutes of remaining fuel at 100 miles west of the *Bibb*.

Passing near the *Bermuda Sky Queen* was a DC-4 freight plane that intercepted the NC-12's distress call. Three-hundred miles eastward another Pan Am passenger-totting DC-4 also picked up the urgent call. Homing in, both planes joined the NC-12's plight like chicks to a mother hen. Radio traffic alert signals crackled out first to Halifax, then to Coast Guard stations in New York, Boston, Newfoundland and Canadian ports as well as to all North Atlantic shipping lanes. A BOAC plane's radio operator notified the *Bibb* at 6:47 A.M. that Martin would execute an emergency landing near the ship at about 8:00 A.M.

It had been quite a night for the Bibb's crew. Assigned to a 10-mile radius, the ship was one of three in the North Atlantic that augmented air travel safety. Besides giving out constant weather information to passing aircraft, "Ocean Charlie" tracked planes with radar and assisted their crews with correct aerial positions. The meteorological data gathered by the *Bibb* and two sister ships was also given shore forecasters who in turn could, if necessary, reroute flights where strong headwinds prevailed.

Throughout the last 72 windy hours, the *Bibb's* men aided many planes bound for Gander, Shannon, Prestwick and London. The ship's commander, Capt. Paul B. Cronk, USCO, a 10-year Navy man before joining the Coast Guard, had just fallen asleep after having spent many hours at watch when he was awakened by his quartermaster and told of the NC-12's plight. On edge, and sounding grumpy over the lack of sleep, Cronk told the seaman to order the preparation of rescue gear and to have his steward brew up some coffee and then fell back to sleep.

At 7:30 A.M. the plane was again contacted. Cronk was awakened and ordered that all rescue stations be manned. Still groggy, he could hardly believe when told that 69 persons were aboard the troubled plane. He later remarked that he couldn't comprehend a passenger plane to be large enough to carry such a high figure. The biggest plane he knew about was the 42 passenger DC-4. Puzzled, stunned and still sleepy-eyed, Cronk dressed and went out on deck.

One hour and 38 minutes from the proposed arrival time, the A314 was sighted by the *Bibb's* crew. Three minutes later Martin swept the monster over the cutter. Cronk and his topsided men

couldn't believe their eyes — they were stunned by the plane's size compared to the two smaller and circling DC-4s.

Strong winds whipped the sea's surface into 30-foot waves that rose and tumbled, spewing crests of foam. It was an angry sea, as if to demonstrate itself against the flying boat's encroachment. Cronk and his crew visualized the possible outcome — the horror of it all — when the powerful waves, acting like walls of stone, would tear the Boeing to bits upon impact. Already some of the *Bibb's* men were fitted in rubber suits and webbed flippers. They stood poised to dive for any attempted rescue — a futile and deadly choice if undertaken in an eternity of a wild and havoc-whipped ocean.

Cronk left the bridge wing and stepped inside the chart room where he phoned Martin who continued to circle the air boat. Wind direction and lengths of waves were noted. To have Martin skim the flying boat over the wave tops and settle in was to ask for a miracle. Cronk suggested that the *Bibb* could calm the sea down a bit by circling, thus enabling Martin to nestle in the ship within the circled area. Martin, however, preferred to find his own niche.

For 20 minutes, from the time he first flew over the *Bibb*, Martin kept the NC-12's wings dipped so his crew could survey from portholes the nearly three-storied waves. A calm spot was soon spotted and Martin, in a matter-of-fact tone, phoned he was coming down.

Banking, the *Bermuda Sky Queen* glided seaward. Near the crest of a huge wave the plane shot up and circled again as if to tease the savaged ocean. Passengers, unaware of the pending danger, remained calm. In general, the trip had been a disappointment for many. The service was shoddy and had much to be desired. One steward was unable to meet the demands of 62 passengers. By early morning many complaints were voiced about the lack of reclining seats and the over-crowded conditions. Steward Penn served only orange or tomato juice for breakfast. It was later reported he "...told passengers tartly that he 'had other things to do beside cook food.'"[248]

Perplexing attempts to reach the gleaming speck caught in storm-ravaged North Atlantic gave *Bibb* crew cause to believe a heavy loss of life was evident. (*Photo Courtesy: United States Coast Guard*)

Chapter Thirty-two: Bermuda Sky Queen

According to 27-year-old passenger Lillian I. Lewin, Penn came into her cabin and announced, "'You'd better break up your card game because we're going down to get a weather report.' We thought it was odd but everyone just sat there calmly."[249]

On his second pass Martin again leveled the plane, cut power and plunked down at a spot where the waves were opposed to each other resulting in a somewhat smoother surface. The NC-12 slipped past a big wave and stalled, struck a second tumbler just behind the crest and skirted down across the trough to plow into a third mountain of sea. Engulfed by water and spray, it was first thought by many viewers the ocean had been the victor. But to their astonishment, including those in the above-flying DC-4s, the grand old Boeing popped to the surface like a cork unscathed and without a single leak. Then, like a toy duck in a tub, the flying hotel bobbed about with each succeeding crest.

"It was a wonderful landing," Lewin added. "There wasn't a bump. We just rode the waves, it was beautiful."[250]

Communication was reestablished between plane and ship. Martin thought the best way to start evacuation procedures was by first connecting a six-inch thick Manila hemp tow line to the cutter. A forward-stationed port crew aboard the *Bibb* climbed into a surfboat and prepared to be lowered away into the slashing sea in order to make the connection, a precarious effort in that the cutter rolled between 35 and 45 degrees.

To assist, Martin switched on the 314's engines and maneuvered the flying boat towards the *Bibb*'s lee side. The scheme worked well until a massive wave carried the plane straight for the cutter. Engines were cut in a desperate but futal attempt to brake. Nearly repeating the *Honolulu Clipper*'s end, strong winds uncannily sailed the NC-12 into the *Bibb*'s steel plating. A sickening crunch of metal against metal was heard. Seconds later a second wave raised the aircraft higher where No. 3 engine ripped into a boat davit 25 feet above the *Bibb*'s waterline, bending the prop and cowling and caving the davit inboard.

As the *Bibb* rolled back into the sea, the A314's starboard wing tip smashed into the cutter's catwalk, 10 feet above the weather deck. On the next pitch of the *Bibb*, the NC-12, angled by another strong wave, hit again with its port wing tip. Only after repeated orders were the *Bibb*'s engines finally reversed from full astern to forward pitch. Riding high on waves, both plane and ship parted company. Damage to the flying boat's port wing was slight, but her prow was staved in about three feet.

Martin and his crew controlled the rolling plane by manipulating the stabilizers while keeping the bashed bow into the wind. At 10:37 A.M., Cronk ordered out a ten-oared surfboat to survey the plane's behavior and to practice various approaches. Oil had been laid to help calm the immediate area but didn't seem to help. The *Bibb* began to drift away from the plane at about 3.4 knots while the plane came downward at about 4.2 knots in a 30-knot wind.

Wave upon wave carried both plane and surfboat from high atop a crest to deep into a following trough. It was too dangerous to get close to the plane on its lee side in fear the flying boat would crash down onto the boat. Approach to the weather side was also periled by the possibility the boat would be carried beneath the 314's hull or flailed by a dipping wing. Passengers were seen peering out portholes between washes of 50-degree water beating over sponsons and against the fuselage. Children in the plane started to cry. Many passengers became seasick.

After an hour of battling the elements, the surfboat's tired crew waited for the cutter that eventually hoisted them to safety. While waiting for a special weather report from Washington, D.C., Cronk poured more oil slicks to help the 314 ride the sea better while at the same time trying to shelter it from ravaging waves. When the report finally came it was bad news. A new gale and cold front was expected from the northwest. There was, however, to be a short lull between storms.

Cronk suggested to Martin by phone that when the air captain thought the time was right to abandon ship, that passengers be put to sea in the nine, five-person plane rafts or to have them jump into the water where they would be picked up by the cutter. Martin was seasick and could be heard retching over the phone. How much more the occupants of the plane could take was anybody's guess. Many were near panic stage.

Strong and virile and nonchalantly eating sardines and crackers from the galley, the nine merchant seamen aboard the NC-12 took the roller coaster ride in stride. They roamed the plane's cabins to reassure passengers and helped seasick parents tend their children by making bibs from torn linen. Staterooms were stuffy and smelled of vomit. Porthole exit panels couldn't be opened for fear the compartments would be swamped by sea water.

Passenger Cwendolen Ritchie said, "I believed there was no escape from the plane... The babies' screams just tore every mother's heart to pieces. Every woman would say, 'There, there.' But that was about all they ever said. A three-year-old son, Gordon, spent hours on his father's knee...never saying a word. We said 10,000 good-byes with our eyes that day."[251]

Cronk's second rescue suggestion was to have both plane and cutter launch a raft on a line. When done, both rafts blew off into the wind like kites. The cutter's men next sent out a 15-person raft. It also proved fruitless. More practice approaches by the *Bibb* were made to determine drift and relative motion of both plane and ship. Oil slicks were again laid, but this time ahead of the plane's wind direction while figuring how close the cutter could get broadside to and ahead of the flying boat, as well as how much shelter the cutter could offer without encountering another collision.

Between Martin and Cronk, the rescue plan was to get everyone off the plane after all the *Bibb*'s lifeboats were lowered and then drift the cutter down and near the floundering aircraft where the *Bibb*'s crew could cast out lines, life preservers and more rafts.

Frogmen were on stand-by to rescue any who fell overboard. Martin signed off to save battery power.

That afternoon at 3:30, Martin phoned Cronk. The plane's tail and sponsons were weakening and the hull was taking on water. People were getting sicker by the minute, some reported to be in a semi-coma. Martin requested if they could be taken off before night fall. When rescue operations were begun, Cronk asked Martin to get three strong men to get into a raft, their weight possibly holding down an otherwise flying rubber kite. If the test worked, the raft was to be cut loose, and, if not, the men were to be taken back on board. Three of the plane's merchantmen volunteered.

From the *Bibb*'s decks, sailors saw the raft set loose from the Boeing as the cutter crossed the ship's bow on its second pass. The operation was unsucceastul due to the cutter's distance and the partially deflated raft burst while the pilot tried to put more CO2 gas into its valve. A second try was made after the cutter spilled a three-mile downwind streak of oil, came in at 15 knots across the plane's prow, reversed engines and waited until another raft was set loose. At 3:57 P.M., the first three passengers were plucked from the sea.

Martin found it difficult to control the raft launching and requested Cronk to send a larger 15-person raft. Daylight dwindled just as the work pace picked up. The next effort was also to no avail when a raft leaked, a second destroyed when caught in the *Bibb*'s propeller and a third torn apart against the cutter's side.

Cronk conferred with his officers on the bridge. They would launch a 5,800-pound self-bailing motor surfboat built with floatation tanks and made of a buoyant material. It was the most durable of the *Bibb*'s vessels.

Before lowering away, the 26-foot-long boat was damaged when its rudder was accidently torn off. Hurriedly repaired, it was sent downwind, first towing the rubber rig then cradling it next to its stern. At 5:30 P.M., two minutes before sunset, the raft, held as close as possible to the plane's forward port hatch, took on more desperate and frightened passengers. Families went first. Seven people, one a held baby, jumped into the raft when a swell carried the rubber device close to the 314's bow hatchway. A nine-year-old boy jumped at the wrong time just when the hatchway was between 20 and 40 feet above a trough. He landed in the swirling water, was quickly rescued and only complained about the ruining of his suit.

Passengers were transferred to the surfboat, taken to the cutter's port landing nets and hauled aboard the *Bibb* by lines tied under their arms. By 6:34 P.M., two more operations were carried out under floodlights. Twenty-one passengers had been saved.

Trying for one more run, the *Bibb*'s quartermaster reported the gale at its worst. Waves, cresting in a 45-knot wind midway between ship and plane, turned to breakers that tore through the oil layer. More oil was dumped towards the drifting plane. A line was passed from the surfboat to the aircraft by shoulder-gun to maneuver a raft close enough to the pitching flying boat.

When the raft was secured, Martin and Thompson pushed hesitating passengers out the hatchway. A scramble was then made back to the boat and then back to the *Bibb*. During the last attempt the raft was battered against the *Bibb*. Three of the 16 rescued had to

Bermuda Sky Queen made *Bibb* contact with resounding crash. (*Photo Courtesy: United States Coast Guard*)

transfer back to the raft when the surfboat began to sink with its heavy load. During the run people were piled atop each other and gear casing snapped when stray raft lines tangled. Waves poured over both raft and boat while the *Bibb*'s five volunteers desperately tried to keep balance.

Once at the cutter's life nets, seamen clamored down or jumped into the sea to help pull up the bruised and soaked passengers while searchlights zeroed in over the scene that resembled a part out of a Cecil B. DeMille movie. Screaming, some were washed away into the darkness but miraculously retrieved by stern-positioned crew teams. One male passenger incurred a scalp injury after hitting his head against the plane when jumping into the raft. About 100 *Bibb* crewmen tied lifelines to themselves with more lines tied to the helpless. After nearly everyone had been pulled to safety the badly damaged raft and surfboat were cut loose and sent adrift.

Lewin reported, "I left in the last boat that night, the one that was swamped. We knew something was wrong with the boat because we were told to keep still so we could balance the boat. But they didn't do it. When the water was coming in one side they kept hopping over to the other side. I had someone's feet around my neck so I couldn't move... Then we saw the ship; gosh it looked good with all those lights...

"I tried to get hold of a line but it slipped through my fingers. After that I felt a terrific shock. I was in the water. Some woman tried to get hold of me but I went under. Someone got me by the scruff of the neck and got me back in... Finally they got the line through one arm and then another arm. I was lying there feeling pretty sick. Anyway, they pulled me up. They were just getting me over the rail and my dress was coming up and I kept trying to pull it down. One of the sailors said, 'Don't worry lady we're not looking!' Two of them carried me into the sick bay. I had a fur coat on. It was saturated..."[252]

Chapter Thirty-two: Bermuda Sky Queen

Cronk worried over the loss of the motor surfboat, the one he and his crew depended on to complete the rescue. A line-pulled boat could not tow a raft fast enough in the roaring sea. More time was given for thought.

The next rescue attempt came when the line-tied boat and raft were dropped ahead of the plane's drift with intentions of shooting a raft line to a flight officer aboard the 314. Cronk called for volunteers and just about everyone aboard the *Bibb* came running to the starboard wing of the bridge. Six fresh men were chosen, ones that had not manned an earlier boat or had worked less shift hours since the episode began. Apprehensive, but full of courage, they remained adrift for 66 minutes in total darkness. Now and then the brave were spotted by searchlights one-half-mile away high on crested waves.

Several lines were shot out to the plane from the runner before one was finally secured. The *Bibb*'s oarsmen waited an hour for the raft to return with passengers before calling Cronk to tell him of their failed attempts. The boat returned empty. A conference was held and finalized to shut down the night's work unless Martin thought the plane might sink.

Cronk tried to reach Martin but the 314's radio had gone dead. He tried Alder lamp code but there was no acknowledgement. Both wind and sea continued to howl as the *Bibb* circled within 50 feet of the plane. Again the *Bibb* flashed a coded message about remaining on the plane for the night. An affirmative answer was sent back by the 314's landing lights using a dot followed by a dash. Then darkneas; all lights in the flying boat went out. It was 11:30 P.M. A searchlight continued to play upon the rolling Boeing.

Before turning in for the night, Cronk made a round of his ship. In the sick bay the rescued were given sugar, water and whisky. Many were in shock and remained in a semi-coma from extreme seasickness. Water sloshed across the deck to soak even more the pile of wet clothing taken from the passengers. Fortunately no one was badly hurt. Cronk payed his respects and left.

Sunrise came at 6:45 on October 15th, along with the expected lull. Winds had subsided to a mere breeze. A bad sea swell concerned Cronk, but over-all the ocean had bowed to the sturdy 314. The *Bibb*'s captain ordered his personal 10-oared gig be sent out to rescue the remaining 16 male passengers and crew. In the event the gig's engine quit, and it did, only four oars were provided to make more room for the rescued.

At 7:03 A.M., the captain's gig was sent to the plane. Twenty-three minutes later it was back with eight happy souls. On the second try at 9:46 A.M., six more were brought back. During the third run the engine gave out and the gig drifted. Restarted, it was motored towards the raft attached to the plane from which it took on six more people. At 10:10 A.M., the raft was cut adrift from the floundering NC-12, The last two of the flying boat's crew, Martin and Thompson, jumped into the sea and were picked up at 10:35 A.M. All 69 lives had been prayerfully saved.

Wallowing about on her own, the NC-12 remained well afloat. Martin conferred with Cronk and told the sea captain his flying ship was definitely unflyable. Considered a derelict by U.S. Coast Guard standards, Cronk was given permission to sink the *Bermuda Sky Queen*. At 1:20 P.M., the first round of 20-millimeter explosive tracer bullets were fired towards and into the Boeing. Flames soon shot out from the hull, the wings dropped, the tail broke away and the bulk of the once great plane sank in 20 minutes.

Strange as it was, the sponsored mid-section refused to go under as did the finned tail. More explosives were shot until the remnants disappeared beneath the swelled sea at 2:30 P.M. Gone in a blaze of glory, the NC-12 took with her the fine 12,000 air-hour record and service accumulated since her 1941 construction.

After having followed the drifting flying boat for nearly 100 miles in the 24-hour rescue period, the *Bibb* was turned west for Boston. Aircraft flew out from tho U.S. and dropped relief comforts, including a supply of baby diapers. On October 19th, the cutter reached port ending one of the most dramatic rescues recorded in Coast Guard annals. Thousands of spectators lined the waterfront to see the vessel come in. Whistles blew from passing boats and ships. Tugs sprayed the air with water. A broom was tied to the *Bibb*'s mast, a sign of a clean rescue sweep. Once docked, Coast Guard brass and city officials greeted Cronk, his crew and the plane's occupants while a horde of reporters sought stories for their latest editions.

Eleven days later an inquiry was opened at the CAB's Washington, D.C., office. The investigation into the forced landing was begun immediately after the board was informed of the accident on October 20th, and public hearings were held in New York from November 7th through the 11th.

Between the time of the ditching and the hearings, newspaper accounts praised and rebuked the A314. Some of the NC-12's passengers, as reported by the press, wondered why people were al-

Another one down — another 314 lost! (*Photo Courtesy: United States Coast Guard*)

lowed to travel on such an out-dated flying machine. One of the rescued, 41-year-old William H. Bostock of the Shell Oil Co., told a newsman that a declaration against the use of the A314 had been signed by all but three of the plane's adult passengers.

Beall, who followed the incident closely, and who read about the signed affidavit, was irked about the spreading accounts that his 314 was unsafe. From his Seattle office he wrote a letter to D. B. Martin, Boeing's New York public relations representative, with copies to the company's News Chief Harold Mansfield and PR staff member Florence Teets. Concerning the difference of reported opinions on whether or not the A314 was safe, Beall, in part, wrote the following on October 22nd:

"This division of opinion has caused several people around here to suggest that we volunteer to supply witnesses to the CAB hearings which will be held in New York... I do not think we should have anyone officially representing the Boeing Aircraft Company until such time as the hearings themselves develop some misinformation that needs to be straightened out. In other words, if convenient, I would like to have you attend the hearings as a spectator and only volunteer to become a witness if and when derogatory misinformation is presented on the design and construction of the Model 314"[253]

Regarding the signed passenger statements, Beall remarked:

" . . .This, of course, implies that the airplane themselves are not safe. Actually, if operated properly, they are no doubt safer than many modern airplanes that I can name.

"One of the many reasons that the *Bermuda Sky Queen* stayed afloat so long in such a monstrous sea after having been bumped by the *Bibb* is that she was unique in her design and construction. She had multiple watertight compartments and a watertight lower deck. You will recall that she had 11 compartments — a nose compartment isolated from the rest of the ship by a watertight so-called 'collision' bulkhead, nine bottom compartments and a tail compartment. I have forgotten the exact figures, but over one-half of these compartments could be completely flooded and the flying boat would still stay afloat. Further, she was of extremely sturdy and heavy construction. She had weight and extra strength in the hull which in these days of extreme competition we could not afford to put into any airplane. The only reason that she is obsolete is that modern airplanes have more speed and range. I do not know the reasons why she ran out of fuel, but from the meager information that we have from the newspaper accounts, it appears that it was a matter of poor dispatching, which of course was no fault of the airplane."[254]

Boeing tried its best to back up its superbly-built product — to save face against a rising tide of injustice, especially since three of the models were still operating across the Atlantic by BOAC, a prospective buyer of Boeing's new double-decked Model 377 "Stratocruiser." Many PR hours were spent by Boeing writing de-

fending news copy, one of which was released to the *Seattle Times* on Nov. 5, 1947:

"Boeing officials still are hearing words of praise on the sturdiness of the Seattle-built flying boat *Bermuda Sky Queen*...Last week the following telegram arrived from Cienfuegos, Cuba: 'Only a Boeing could ride Atlantic while Coast Guard saved *Bermuda Sky Queen* passengers. Am proud my son is a Boeing engineer. Monzon-Aguirre.'"[255]

Five men, Joseph J. O'Connell, Jr., Oswald Ryan, Josh Lee, Harold A. Jones and Russell B. Adams, made up the CAB's investigation team. In the beginning the men were somewhat hampered in that they were unable to obtain substantial, concrete evidence. Destroyed with the NC-12 were the ship's weight and balance manifests, engine, radio, navigation and engineering logs, essential records to the inquiry. Only partial records were acquired from AIA. The probable cause of the accident could only be determined from the crew's testimony.

Established was the fact that the A314 was in good mechanical condition when it left Foynes. The last major repair done to the air boat was in November, 1946, when new fabric was installed on her wings' trailing edges. Filed engine manifests showed proper maintenance procedures and that they were in good operating condition. Also the plane's airworthy state had proper safety provisions for passengers and crew, such as life jackets, safety belts, proper amount of life rafts, emergency radio transmitter, a Very pistol, smoke bombs, flares and other equipment deemed necessary for transoceanic flight.

Flight Engineer Yaramishyn's statement that the A314's weight, prior to leaving Foynes, was about 98,710 pounds, 5,710 pounds over the maximum 84,000 allowed, opened doors to delve deeper into the allegations of improper flight-planning. Yaramishyn told the board the weight was distributed properly in accordance to the aircraft's c.g. within approved limits. Contrary to the "approved limits," were statements taken from the passengers as to the aircraft's attitude. Throughout the flight the 314 was tail heavy, giving question to the proper weight distribution. Martin added that he found it difficult to trim the plane for even flight. Under such conditions an aircraft is likely to burn more fuel.

Martin's weather and wind velocities were accurately determined from other flight records taken from planes flying the same route and from reports sent out of Shannon, Gander and the *Bibb*. Recorded westerly winds were known to prevail at an average velocity of 39 knots. The actual airspeed of the A314 was 130 knots, the speed used to compute the flight plan. But Thompson said an average airspeed of only 105 knots was maintained out of Foynes. The 105-knot speed, when calculated with altitude and temperature, came to 118 knots. Martin's and Thompson's discrepancy showed the flying boat was cruising 12 knots slower than planned.

When the effective headwind component to compute the flight plan was used, the five-man board found the plane cruised not at 39 knots, but at 26 knots, 13 knots slower than estimated by the crew.

And with the increase in wind along the route, and the crew's failure to compute the planned indicated airspeed, the NC-12 flew 25 knots slower than originally planned — a ground speed not of 104 knots as figured, but one of only 79 knots!

The board stipulated that Martin should have found his true ground speed at the time the A314 received a radar fix from the *Bibb* after which time the flying boat had been in the air for 10 hours and 25 minutes after flying 892 nautical miles. At that point the plane's ground speed was estimated to be 86 knots. If it had remained constant, an 86-knot ground speed would have taken the plane 20 hours and 12 minutes to complete the 1,730-mile hop from Foynes to Gander. With 4,000 gallons of fuel aboard, a reserve of only one hour and 48 minutes would have been the rule rather than what the crew believed to be a five-hour reserve.

In computing their fuel consumption, the flight engineers told the board that 180 gallons per-hour was in the flight plan for the 22-estimated hour flight. The error was shown after the plane was airborne for 17 hours when it reported only two hours and 45 minutes of fuel left. Thus, the 4,000-tanked fuel supply, when analyzed, was adequate for only 19 hours and 45 minutes. This meant that the average hourly consumption of fuel was 202 gallons per hour instead of the earlier projected 180 gallons. There was insufficient fuel to complete the flight as planned at Foynes (Shannon).

When the board asked the crew if they had arranged for long-range cruise control as developed by Pan Am for flying boat flight, their answer was in the negative. Long-range cruise control was used by pilots who planned for low fuel consumption. The board believed the low airspeed of the NC-12 was due to a 5,000-pound overload. There was also no Pan Am-fostered cruise control graph drawn out before leaving Foynes. The crew indicated they made no attempt to systematically plot or chart the fuel consumption during the trip in relation to time versus distance. Had such a chart existed,

Photographed from an approaching lifeboat in 50-degree waters, NC 18612's staved bow and weather-beaten, flag-painted hull is visually evident following a roller coaster-like ride. Immediately after plane and ship collided, the A314's captain wanted to abandon ship in 10-person rafts, but was told by *Bibb's* master not to do so unless flying boat started to break up. (*Photo Courtesy: United States Coast Guard*).

and periodic fuel-versus-distance notes been taken, the board decided the crew would have realized they had used more fuel than planned after the first one or two hours of flight and might have, at that point, opted for a turn-around to Foynes with a strong tail wind.

Another lead to the probable cause to the downing came to light when Yaramishyn testified that engine power settings were at 1,750 rpm with 28.8 inches of manifold pressure at 8,000 feet that resulted in 818 h.p, with a fuel flow of 290 pounds per hour. Hour-wise, the fuel consumption was 192 gallons. With these figures compared to the 4,000 gallons of fuel, the aircraft could have flown only 20 hours and 18 minutes rather than the estimated 22 hours.

Called in by the board was an engineer from Wright Aeronautical Corp. He was informed of Yaramishyn's account. The engineer stated that at such power settings, fuel flow would have been 340 pounds per hour with a consumption of 228 gallons. This would have kept the A314 in the air for only 17 hours and 30 minutes, some four hours and 30 minutes less than what Yaramishyn figured. If the fuel flow reading had been 290 pounds per hour, as Yaramishyn stated, the Wright engineer said the A314 would have had less than 650 h.p.

After all the evidence and testimony was presented, the CAB men convened to discuss the results. They concurred that part of the testimony given by Martin and Thompson was that both men were aware of the A314's maximum gross weight as placarded on the flight-deck, but thought they could make the flight with the approximate 5,000-pound overload. Considering the 4,000 gallons of fuel, the flight engineers should have figured it would not be adequate and thus ignored proper aircraft operational procedures. Instructions were available to the men in the operating manuals provided both by Boeing and Wright. They clearly showed that the

A refusal to submit called for more gunfire. (*Photo Courtesy: United States Coast Guard*)

engine settings for the flight would not have allowed the plane to reach its destination.

A third factor revealed and discussed was Martin's and Thompson's estimated true air speed set between 128 and 132 knots. The board surmised that it had been based on the eastward trip without the heavy payload. Also, during the most critical point of the flight, Thompson was asleep and Martin did not bother to get a fix from the *Bibb* nor any wind reports from Gander that would have informed him the A314 was not cruising at the correct speed so necessary to complete the flight with the remaining fuel aboard.

In conclusion, the board found the crew negligent in practicing fundamental planning for oceanic flight and hence violated certain CAA safety regulations. Without proper air speed estimates as related to the available weather and wind reports, and the proper figuring of the insufficient fuel against the plane's heavy load, as well as not planning and maintaining correct cruise control, the aircraft was forced to ditch. In summation, the probable cause of running low on fuel was given as improper flight-planning for an airliner laden with an excessive gross weight.

Along with the board's findings, adopted Dec. 14, 1948, and released the following day, the A314's reputation was reinstated as being a dependable and safe plane given proper handling. The NC-12 was found to be in good shape from June 18, 1947 — the date it was granted its AIA operations certificate — to the time of its demise. Her registration was terminated by the CAA on Oct. 24, 1947.

Regardless of the faults brought against Martin, he had been highly praised by passengers, Cronk and others for his fine piloting skills. Unfortunately, he and his crew were found temporarily out of a job. American-International Airways had its services suspended

Its plight caught by camera from the decks of the rescue cutter *Bibb*, a staunchly built *Bermuda Sky Queen* was tossed and dipped for hours atop gale-stricken North Atlantic. It took, however, more than a wild ocean to sink the last model constructed in the 314 fleet. (*Photo Courtesy: United States Coast Guard*)

by the CAB three days after the incident along with a cancellation of its charter permit. As for Cronk, he was awarded a Gold Star by John W. Snyder, then U.S. Secretary of the Treasury, for his rescue leadership and gallant service. Sixteen additional awards for bravery were also presented to *Bibb* officers and enlisted men.

Once more, and still parked atop their beaching gear in San Diego and New York, the 314s NC-02, NC-04, NC-05, NC-06 and NC-11 were up for sale by GPC. Robinson, AIA's former owner, was not, however, put under by the recision of his operating air license nor by the loss of his remaining 314 equipment to the mortgage company. In time he would come to the fore with a new 314 charter outfit entitled World Airways, Inc.

33

End of an Era

Exactly one month before the NC-12 was destroyed by gunfire, BOAC announced to the news media the possible sale of their three A314s. Negotiations for the release were held at the airline's Baltimore base between negotiating BOAC and Compania Aeronautica Urugay S.A. (CAUSA) representatives. The South American airline, quartered in Montevideo, considered purchasing the world's historically famed flying boats for their country's major services. Long-houred talks, however, lulled to a close when CAUSA learned that parts for the planes were scarce and hard to come by. For CAUSA to safely maintain the well-noted liners had become nil.

A year before BOAC officials broke the news of their A314 retirement (services were outdated when the line ordered three L-049s to compete against Pan Am's then excelling landplane operations), a wave of affection for the A314 swept through BOAC staffing. Between the lines a sad hint of the boats' abandonment was expressed in early 1946 when Charles Abell, BOAC's Baltimore operations chief remarked:

"The main problems of flying boat maintenance, as opposed to landplane maintenance, are the continual battles with salt water and corrosion, the inevitable damage which occurs when small boats come alongside in rough weather, and the beaching and landing operations. However, the Boeing 314s were designed and built with all these problems in mind, and they have achieved their purpose to a truly remarkable extent."[256]

Vernon G. Crudge, BOAC's Baltimore-based regional director added, "...these ships have given magnificent service. Their combined record. . . of the Atlantic under all weather conditions, and at all seasons of the year, is something of which the workers, the cosigners and the manufacturers can all be justly proud."[257]

Towards the end of September, 1946, each BOAC A314 had logged more than 1,250,000 miles over the Atlantic. With the military restrictions lifted at war's end, the flying boats were returned to their peacetime colors in July, 1945, and flown across the Atlantic on regular, four-time commercial flights per week between Poole and Baltimore, an incredible record-breaking prop-planed pace for just three aircraft.

Known for their luxurious appointments and service, the British-owned A314s carried only 20 passengers and about 9,100 pounds of cargo and mail per trip. For the first time, starting in the summer of 1945, the flying boats carried paying passengers when Pan Am and the CAA waived BOAC's war restrictions in transporting noncommercial loads and allowed the full and promised reciprocal service as guaranteed by Trippe and the U.S. Government. At that time, Pan Am and BOAC (now British Airways) became Atlantic competitors.

In July, 1943, *Berwick*'s crew at Baltimore chalked up an incredible two-year, one-million-mile BOAC A314 service record. (*Photo Courtesy: British Overseas Airways*)

Flying an English-in-port flag, camouflaged *Bristol* flying hotel clearly shows Speedbird logo. (*Photo Courtesy: British Overseas Airways/Gordon S. Williams Collection*)

A thrice-weekly A314 service was begun by BOAC to Bermuda on Oct. 18, 1945. Tourists had begun to flock to the once off-limits island by any mode of transportation available. Within a year the three boats, each seating 55 passengers for the five-hour ride out of Baltimore, had carried 14,500 people round-trip.

Beginning March 7, 1946, and terminating three days later, the last BOAC transatlantic A314 flight was made with the *Bristol* from the United Kingdom to the U.S. under the command of black-haired, blue-eyed Capt. J. W. Burgess who had 5,000 314 air hours credited to his fine record. From 1941, the year purchased, to March, 1946, the three BOAC A314s totaled 596 Atlantic crossings. The *Bristol* flew the Atlantic 203 times, the *Berwick* 201 and the *Bangor* 192. Between the ships, 15,630 passengers were carried, as were 291 tons of cargo and 141 tons of diplomatic and GPO mail. The 314s' manifests during the war were composed of allied officials, chiefs of staff and England's royalty line.

More than 200 engines were replaced to keep the giants going, and after every 220 hours of flight each A314 was grounded for a major overhaul. On the average of every five months, each air boat had flown about 10 hours and 18 minutes per day with every flight arriving nearly always on schedule. Cancellations or turn-arounds were reported few in number.

Beall and his wife Jean flew aboard the *Bangor* with Boeing's President William M. Allen and BOAC's Bermuda Manager M. D. Morrissey and wife in late 1946. It was, for Beall, a part business, part pleasure trip. The 314's designer knew his boats wouldn't be around too much longer, and he wanted to travel on one for, as they say, "'ol-times-sake." While in Bermuda, Beall's and Allen's work hours centered on selling the latest B-377 design to BOAC that appeared on the market two and one-half years later.

England's three Boeings were kept in service between Baltimore and Bermuda after they had been taken off the transatlantic run in 1946. As of Sept. 30, 1946, 2,600 arrivals and departures were scored at the Baltimore base. Fourteen months later, BOAC retired the grand air ladies when their certificates of air-worthiness ended. To renew the licenses, the boats would have had to be completely overhauled, an expense BOAC did not wish to foster, especially when parts were far and few between and too costly to produce through Boeing.

After six and one-half years of operation the planes had flown 4,250,000 miles, carried 40,042 passengers (transatlantic and Bermuda services combined) and had made 682 round-trips to Darrel Island. In the last two years of service, the ships were credited with carrying 24,412 tourists to and from Bermuda before being replaced by three L-049s that bore the A314 names.

Capt. Kelly-Rogers commanded the last BOAC A314 in-bound flight from Bermuda with the *Bristol* on Jan. 27, 1948, with 55 passengers. Years later he remarked about the nostalgic flight, "It is interesting to note that one of the passengers aboard on that occasion was Sir Richard Ferry who founded the Ferry Aviation Co. It so happened that I had the honor of carrying the first transatlantic

To reduce weight, BOAC stripped stateroom dividers to resemble standing tarpaulins. As seen, VIPS were often allowed to line promenade with their luggage that contained secret government documents. (*Photo Courtesy: British Overseas Airways*)

passengers for Britain in one of the Short flying boats in the summer of 1940. In those aircraft, payload consideration and fuel limited us to a total of four passengers west-bound. And Ferry was one of the four on the first trip."[258]

As for Kelly-Rogers, he had been in charge of all BOAC's North Atlantic A314 operations during the war, including landplane "Liberator" flights, and with post-war L-049 flights. He left BOAC in 1947 to become, at the invitation of the Irish Government, chief pilot and technical manager of Aer Lingus and deputy general manager of both Aer Lingus and Irish International Airlines. England's most honored transoceanic commercial pilot retired in 1965 and died at the age of 75 at his Dublin estate on Jan. 29, 1981.

Patrick F. A. Griffin, former BOAC steward, said of the 314 flights to and from Bermuda in 1977, "Those planes were really wonderful. I just started work with BOAC and they placed me on the Baltimore-to-Bermuda 314 run. I remember one trip — it was so scary. Our captain flew into a frightful storm and we had to cancel serving lunch to the passengers in the lounge because we were bouncing about so much. I know now what they mean when they

Bristol over Baltimore. Deep-shaded camouflaging gave A314s a more squatty-looking appearance. (*Photo Courtesy: British Overseas Airways/Gordon S. Williams Collection*)

talk so much about the 'Bermuda Triangle' stories... It was so black outside we couldn't tell if we were right-side up or upside down!

"I was really frightened. I kept thinking I shall never fly again if we made it into Bermuda. We did though, we came out of the 'stuff' and landed OK. Any other plane would have been torn to part in that storm. But the 314 made it through it. You know, they were really strong airplanes. That 314 gave me confidence to keep on flying as a steward. And I did, until I retired.

"One time when I was in Bermuda waiting for a flight back to Baltimore, a speedboat struck one of our 314s. It made a big hole in the plane's side and was sticking out of the hull. I don't know if the driver of the boat was hurt. I think he was killed! They patched up the 314 and it was as good as ever."[259]

After BOAC's A314 services were curtailed in early 1948, the planes were beached on cradles at Baltimore's Harbor Field. British Overseas Airways then moved its offices from the seaplane base to the land terminals at Baltimore Municipal Airport and LaGuardia.

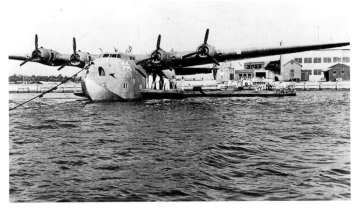

Bristol gets Baltimore fuel for next air voyage. (*Photo Courtesy: British Overseas Airways*)

For three months the A314s sat idle before being sold. One interested party had speculated on buying one of the boats for living quarters as had been done in Miami in 1946 with the old S-42 *Brazilian Clipper* (i.e. *Colombia Clipper*).

Picking up each giant for a moderate $6,949.74 on April 16th (about 14 cents a pound), was the usual GPC bidder. The deal was cinched following negotiations initiated through Mendes & Mount, English U.S.-quartered representatives for Lloyd's of London, BOAC's A314 insurance agency.

Immediately following the sale, the ships, along with the NC-11, were financed out to World Airways, Inc. (WA), Robinson's newly formed airline headquartered at the old BOAC base in Baltimore with other offices at New York's *Lincoln Hotel* and at the *MAT*. The amount of money involved in the transaction was not released. Robinson made a down payment for the 314s with the unknown amount of insurance money collected after the NC-12 was sunk.

World also mortgaged out the four San Diego-based 314s through GPC in an effort to carry forth their remodification work in an attempt to place all ships on the reestablished New York-San Juan route. Meanwhile, the former BOAC boats had been reassigned their original U.S. serial numbers, NC-07, NC-08 and NC-10.

In order for WA to get the Harbor Field-beached 314s up to airworthy condition, GPC cleared for parts to be taken from NC-05 and NC-06. Registration for the remaining 314s had been filed with the CAA and granted three days after the sale.

Robinson's WA operated the NC-07, NC-08, and NC-10 for a very short time out of Baltimore and LaGuardia's *MAT*. Woodmansee, the NC-12's last radio operator, was re-employed and recalled flying aboard the NC-07 and NC-10 between New

In peacetime colors, *Bristol* strikes for a Baltimore Harbor takeoff for routing flight to Bermuda, 1947. (*Photo Courtesy: British Overseas Airways*)

York and San Juan. He later flew for Pan Am as a flight engineer and, by late 1993, was a second officer on United Airlines' B-747s.

As for the NC-11, she too was scrapped for essentials in order to keep the former BOAC-owned ships in the air for WA. Seemingly forgotten, the NC-11's registration was not cancelled until 1954. In 1948, according to Bart Benedict, freelance writer, researcher and public relations consultant, a newspaper article stated that a WA 314 had been literally beached by its pilot somewhere off Florida's coast following a bad storm while en route from San Juan.

Illegal immigrants were aboard, and after the emergency landing and subsequent beaching, U.S. officials confiscated the A314. There remains, however, no concrete evidence to confirm or deny Benedict's claim. If, on the other hand, the account was (is) true, the incident probably led to WA's downfall.

By early 1949, the three former BOAC A314s were seen back on their cradles at Harbor Field where two remained for more than a year. The same held true for NC-02, NC-04 and NC-05 in San Diego. The shell of NC-06 had been sold off for scrap. World's NC-02 and NC-04 were in relatively good condition. It is believed Robinson had intended these two ships to be placed into charter operations out of New York and Baltimore.

E. R. McGregor, former FAA general aviation operations inspector, said he recalled seeing the Boeings at Lindbergh Field, and that the NC-02 was test-flown as far as Laguna Beach, a resort sailing port about 70 miles north of San Diego, when it developod engine trouble and was forced to return to San Diego. The one-time *Pacific Clipper* (i.e. *California Clipper*), as with the remaining 314s, never flew again:

By early 1949, WA had either gone financially into the red or was forced out of business by the CAA following its unorthodox and shady beaching episode. The following year WA underwent an ownership and management change. Financier Edward J. Daly rebuilt what was left of WA into a leading U.S. charter airline that lasted well into the late 1970s, and was once highly admired for its outstanding coordinated U.S. military service operations during the Vietnam conflict. Daly stated that when he stepped in as new owner and president of WA in 1950, the 314s were no longer part of the old WA's meager fleet of planes.

It was learned that a few months before Robinson's WA went belly up, he had authorized needed parts from the beached and block-supported NC-08. What was left of the former *Berwick* was then sold in the fall of 1949 to Baltimore's Tomke Aluminum Co. for scrap.

Back in GPC's possession after the original WA went under in early 1950, NC-07 and NC-10 were sold to the Baltimore Lumber Co. (BLC).

It was believed BLC intended to use the two 314s as fire fighters, much the same as had been done with the remaining Martin JRM-1 flying boats (one left) stationed on Victoria Island, B.C., Canada. Unable to bring them up to flying condition, BLC sold NC-10 for $2,000 to the Tomke Aluminum Co. for junk. The once elegant *Bangor* was torn apart by a wrecking crew during the first

Anzac Clipper waits for new owner, Floyd Bennet Field, New York, August, 1946. (*Photo Courtesy: Boeing Aircraft Co.*)

week of April, 1950. While the stripped A314 rested atop its dolly, Tomke workers again came to Harbor Field, tore away the NC-10's tail and outer wing panels and then smashed the inner wing stubs, nacelles and hull to yield enough recycled material to cast 580 50-gallon barrels, or, one and one-sixth miles of stove-piping, or 10,000 one-gallon pails.

In an effort for a more profitable return, BLC extricated themselves of the NC-07 through a sheriff's sale which put the past *Bristol* once more on the block. With some work, it was figured, the NC-07 could be placed back into flying status. Once advertised in papers, BLC received a number of expressed interests in the old boat. Before the month was over, BLC had sold NC-07 to a man from Richmond who went by "Master X." The self-proclaimed minister was described as everything from a wizard to "...father confessor to half the Negro population of tidewater Virginia."[260]

"Master X" told the press he wanted the flying boat to ferry Jordan River water to the U.S. for his followers. After having paid an undisclosed amount of cash for the Boeing, the A314 sat on its cradle and then in Baltimore Harbor for more than a year while "Master X" hired workers to recondition the flying ship.

Baltimore's 1968 Director of Aviation, John F. R. Scott, Jr., reported, "'Master X' employed several local mechanics to work on the airplane, and could frequently be seen arriving in his large Cadillac to inspect the progress of their work..."[261]

During the summer of 1951, a sudden squall hit the Baltimore area. Torn from her moorings by strong winds, the NC-07 drifted out into the harbor and struck an object that ripped a long gash along the starboard prow below the water line. Water poured into the forward holds and the near-refurbished NC-07 sank bow first in 20 feet of water, her mid and aft sections and port wing angled above the surface similar to the sinking of a torpedoed troop ship.

According to Scott, the minister and his son attempted to raise the A314, but their diving gear, assembled from an old soup kettle for a helmet, a gas mask valve and a discarded convertible coupe top, proved unsuccessful. "Master X" had hoped to repair the former sky queen so he could, in addition to gathering holy water, fly the plane to Moscow for peace talks with Premier Stalin.

Unable to reclaim his winged property, "Master X" gave up his salvage rights when port officials claimed the half-sunken derelict a menace to harbor navigation. A barge with a large crane moved alongside the deluged liner, attached lines, lifted the A314 from the sea and took it to shore where it was later scrapped.

When GPA disposed of the NC-07, NC-08 and NC-10 in 1950, they also dumped NC-02, NC-04 and NC-05 in San Diego. Aviation buff and San Diego resident Hank W. Arnold said he saw the three ships as late as 1951 still perched high on their cradles at Lindbergh Field.

Both Arnold and McGregor heard rumors the ships were to be overhauled. Arnold recollected they were to be sold to a foreign airline and put into service in Siam (Thailand), but the skeptical transaction failed to materialize.

Gathered at a Baltimore boarding for clipper designer's last 314 flight were, from left to right: M. D. Moorissey, Bermuda's BOAC manager, and wife, Jean Beall, Wellwood E. Beall, *Bangor*'s flight steward and William Allen, president, Boeing Aircraft Co. (*Photo Courtesy: British Overseas Airways*)

The NC-05 was in poor disrepair with many missing parts, including trailing wing fabric, port tail fin rudder and porthole emergency hatches. Arnold recalled he went out to the field to check the parked ships. Hull bottoms were badly corroded and the 314s were, over all, in a sad state. Arnold walked about the abandoned "Pullmans of the sky" with his camera to take what he did not realize were some of the final known pictures capturing the stilled giants. A short while later the planes, he said, were scrapped, the last being the NC-05 in 1952. Certificates of registration for NC-02, NC-05, NC-06, NC-07, NC-08, NC-10 and NC-11 were finally cancelled by the CAA on May 5, 1954, for non-compliance regulations.

By some quirk of fate the NC-04's re-registration had been overlooked in 1951. Needing an update on the plane's condition for its files, Daly informed the regulatory commission that the NC-04 had passed into obilivion — was scrapped — and therefore on Jan. 17, 1951, the CAA closed the book on the former *Atlantic Clipper*.

Throughout their relatively short span of service, limited when compared to other commercial aircraft, the 314s had few faults. Ventilating the cabins with fresh air when berths were assembled was one of the more critical problems passengers had to contend with during night flight. Sleeping passengers were often exposed to strong drafts when vents were opened and a "stuffiness" when not. During day flight, overhead ducts forced air into the cabins so strongly that it often times "parted hair" or alarmed those who unwarily walked beneath the ducts. In addition, it was difficult to control the heat and passengers often found it too hot while in their curtained-off berths.

Some passengers complained about the mattresses being uncomfortable when the bedding settled a bit between cushions. An aluminum brace, used to support day and night arrangements, ran across the middle of the lower bunks that could be felt enough to annoy many passengers. Also, due to the arrangements of the berths, the noise level was greater at the head position rather than at the foot base for those sleeping in port- stationed berths which suggested to designers that the making up of beds should have been reversed. A simple alteration by stewards could have solved this particular problem but was never implemented.

In planning for future transoceanic aircraft, be they land or sea-type airliners, Capt. Masland was asked by the U.S. Airline Planning Commission to write a report on the human traffic flow aboard 314s as a base to study future airline designs. Masland noted that the men's restroom, galley, staircase and forward crew's quarters in stateroom A were all too close in proximity to each other and often caused steward service interference from the congestion centered around each of the stations. The Pan Am captain recommended that the galley, forward restroom and crew's off-duty stations be separated, and that the galley and any lavatory be apart from each other to prevent the mingling of unpleasant odors.

Problems related to flight-deck operations were found to be minimal aboard the 314s when addressed to human comfort and proper functioning. Some navigators experienced a great deal of airsickness when flying the North Atlantic where turbulent weather is common at altitudes between one and 15,000 feet. Standing and bending over the navigation table in opposition to the forward ship movement caused frequent upsets. One officer heaved 14 times on one trip and had to be relieved of his duties for the duration of the flight.

Cause for navigators to get so sick on 314s was believed related to stooping sideways for a long period of time while charting

that resulted in a circulatory restriction of the neck, much eye irritation after long hours affixed to the slightly vibrating table, and, as stated, riding sideways accompanied by occassional glimpses out the side portholes that resulted in more abnormal stimuli.

Two additional problems were also noted. Bridge officers expressed the seats were limited in back positions, that the adjustable chairs were not provided with enough aft direction in accordance to foot control on the rudder pedals. The last major difficulty experienced by 314 crews was the extreme distance between captain and flight engineer stations. Because of the simplicity of the bridge's two control panels, the large portion of engine control was situated at the aft engineer's panel. The space between captain, first officer and flight engineer was extensive to the point where, at times, it caused a communication problem, despite the two-way-connecting phone system. Crew members, through Pan Am request, advised aircraft designers that future-planned oceanic planes have the two posts situated in a more desirable proximity to each other.

The disappearance of the 314s marked the end to major commercial transoceanic flying boat flight and the trend to economically keep seaplanes in the fiercely competitive post-war field of international air transport. A few threads of the once golden era of overseas air travel lingered on when BOAC reinstituted a two-year service using Short S-45 Solent flying boats between Southampton and Johannesburg in 1948. Construction of the 21 planes began in 1946. The model had a length of 87 feet, eight inches, with a wing span of 112 feet and flew the route in four and one-half days.

In 1950, the S-45s were replaced by landplanes and the boats were used by Tasman Airways to link South Seas islands. Each plane was able to carry 30 passengers on two decks and were noted

Flaps down, Kelly-Rogers brings in *Bristol* from Bermuda for BOAC's final A314 landing, January, 1948. On ground is the *Berwick*. (*Photo Courtesy: Boeing Aircraft Co.*)

Poor photo reflects *Bangor*'s bad ending, the only known visual record of a 314 scrapping. (*Photo Courtesy: Capt. John Cecil Kelly-Rogers Collection*)

for their plush appointments. As of September, 1958, all British commercial flying boat services ceased.

Bigger and better flying ships appeared following the demise of the 314s, such as the U.S. Navy's Convair-built XP5Y, costing two million dollars each, Saunders-Roe's 45-A *Princess* and Howard Hughes' HK-1 *Hercules*, better known as the "Spruce Goose." Only one of these, England's *Princess*, was designed as a 105-passenger-carrying Goliath capable of flying non-stop across the Atlantic to either the U.S. or South America on BOAC routes.

Three 45-As were built at East Cowes, England, for more than eight million pounds. Each of the double-decked, pressurized boats weighed 140 tons, had a wing span of 219 feet, six inches; a length of 148 feet and cruised at 380 m.p.h. at 40,000 feet. Air-conditioned for passenger comfort, a 45-A was equipped with 10 Bristol gas-turbined Proteus engines of 3,500 h.p. each (five to each wing in two groups of two-driving twin contra-rotating propellers) with a 5,500-mile range in still air with a fuel load of 49 tons (15,000 gallons).

One 45-A, considered the largest all-metal airplane hull ever produced to carry passengers, was calculated in cubic feet to be equal to three and one-half L-049 Constellations. Two and one-half miles of longitudinal members, 1,469 square yards of metal plating and three million rivets went into each 45-A hull.

Designed by Saunders-Roe Engineer H. Knowler, the first *Princess* was test-flown for 30 minutes on Aug. 22, 1952, by the company's leading pilot, Geoffrey Tyson. During further tests the craft was found to be under-powered for its size, too late in production for BOAC service, and, too expensive to maintain. The British Government cancelled its order for four more and then beached and cocooned the ships at Galshot, England. In May, 1957, there had been speculation the Ministry of Supply, owners of the 45-As, was to reactivate the flying boats for experimental work in supplying the ships with nuclear-type power plants. The idea was eventually abandoned and the 45-As remained shelved for a time and then were torn apart for scrap.

Scrapped along with the *Princess* ships were the construction plans by Great Britain's Saro Aircraft for the *Duchess*, the world's first proposed jet-powered commercial flying boat. Tasman Airways had considered taking on the boats in the early 1950s for their

Australia-New Zesland routes. Pressurized with a payload set at 25,000 pounds, the 138-foot winged flying boat was to have been powered by 7,200-pound-thrusted PR Avon jet engines. But when land airports began to sprout throughout the South Seas, Tasman cancelled its order for the plane and the boat, like the *Princess* liners, became part of aviation history. The *Duchess* was the last of man's planned big sea-air ships considered for commercial production.

Now and then one is taken back to that exciting time of 314 flight through the movies or by way of the "tube." Hollywood Producer Francis Coppola's April, 1983 release of *The Black Stallion Returns* featured — even if out of correct Pan Am 314 operation time period — a 314 scene. A life-sized exterior 314 mock-up was built in Italy. After all the painstaking research that had gone into the model's construction, round portholes dimmed its accuracy. But then "That's Hollywood!"

Television, too, at times, has had its fling with the 314s, such as in the 1982-83 adventure series *Tales Of The Gold Monkey*. Actual 314 film footage, models and sets were used to add the adventure and romance needed to support the exploits of a dare-devil seaplane pilot flying the South Seas in a Grumman "Goose" amphibian. A more serious side to 314 activity was seen in the British production of *Diamonds In The Sky*, a TV special featuring the evolution of commercial flight. An impressive collection of 314 clips highlighted the program that related to man's struggle to conquer the Atlantic by air. Also most impressive were the 314 shots used in the 1990s TV productions of *Airports* and *Wings'* series, *The Big Ones*, that brought back to life the elegance of the Boeing Clippers.

It seems a producer, director or research writer is forever contacting Boeing for 314 information. Boeing's former PR chief Williams stated in a 1982 letter, "Had an interesting phone call just yesterday — someone wanted to know if Boeing knew 'where he could find a 314 flying boat.' I told him we only wish we had one ourselves, sorry!"[262]

About the only so-called major artifacts left intact to remind one of the 314's greatness are the architectural splendors of LaGuardia's *MAT*, Treasure Island's *Administration Building*; Miami's Dinner Key *Clipper Terminal* and the small Foyne's base terminal now an air museum housing the original ground-to-air communications equipment and other clipper-related paraphernalia. But its the grandeur of the terminals that spark the imagination.

The *MAT*, specifically built for the 314s and for the ships that never followed, was to international flight what New York's *Grand Central Station* was to the early U.S. railroad industry. And similar to the decline of the independently run U.S. commercial rail services, the *MAT* too diminished in rank at clippers' end as being the Atlantic's main aerial gateway to the U.S.. Striving for new business, New York and New Jersey port authorities began an expensive and extensive renaissance for LaGuardia Airport in 1952. Included in the refurbishing project was what was thought to be a face-lift since the building was used for small interstate and north-

War-weary and abandoned *Pacific Clipper* (foreground) on blocks and *Atlantic Clipper* on dolly wait out last days, Lindbergh Field, San Diego, 1951. (*Photo Courtesy: Hank W. Arnold*)

eastern air-feeder services as well as for private and corporate aircraft charter flights. The *MAT*'s natural brick exterior facade was gobbed over with layers of beige and brown paint. "McCarthyism," the American inquisition, was at its peak!

Senator Joe McCarthy, a radical who stopped at nothing to keep his influential power seat, claimed he was saving the U.S. from Communism. Thousands of ordinary and innocent Americans lost their livelihoods and homes without a thread of substantial evidence after being dragged under by McCarthy's anti-Communist attacks. During this slanderous period, American contemporary artist James Brooks lost his mural in the *MAT*. It was said that someone passing through the terminal saw a hammer and sickle, symbol of Communist Russia, in the Rorschach of the painting Brooks called "Flight." Coats of deep blue-green industrial paint, a popular color of the early 1950s, were applied over three of the painting's panels in the rotunda. The four-year project by one of America's most renowned abstract impressionistic painters had vanished from sight. A friend of the artist told him of the loss. Going to the *MAT*, Brooks was saddened and hurt. On a nearby wall was a sign he had installed describing the first of three panels. With his mural gone, Brooks took a screwdriver, removed the plaque and departed.

Twenty-four years later the *MAT*, holding its own, but with port officials desiring to revamp and enlarge the famous terminal, was changed to restore Brooks' fine work and to have it designated as a historical landmark. Young Geoffrey Arend, publisher and editor of the aviation newspaper *Air Cargo News*, had moved into the *MAT*'s old radio room in 1976 for reasons of needing more space for putting out his monthly publication. Being a follower of avia-

tion history, Arend struck up a friendship with two other MAT occupants, Tom Walker, vice president of Butler Aviation, and Dennis Wrynn, Air New England's station manager. Wrynn showed Arend his collection of 314 photographs and told him about the *MAT*'s lost art treasure, photos of which were kept by Tim Peirce, LaGuardia'a manager.

Arend borrowed the pictures and did a spread of the mural in his paper. Reaction was swift. Letters and phone calls came in from many who asked why Brooks' mural had been "greened out" and how they could help to restore it. A photo display was mounted in the *MAT* by Arend and his brother to draw attention to the $80,000

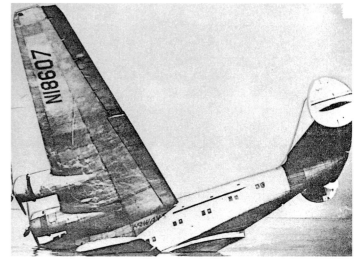

Angled somewhat like the *R.M.S. Titanic*'s sinking, former World Airways' NC-07 was storm-sunk in Baltimore Harbor. (*Photo Courtesy: John Tepler/Gordon S. Williams Collection*)

restoration plan. One day Financer Laurence Rockefeller and his friend DeWitt Wallace, philanthropist and founder of the *Reader's Digest*, walked through and spotted the photo exhibit after missing a connecting flight. Action was taken by both men when they split the cost with port authorities to restore Brooks' work. Arend had already spent $4,000 of his own money to further the cause.

Restoration expert Alan Farancz, and his co-worker Denise Whitbeck, began the long, slow process of removing the heavy coat of green paint from a 40-foot-high scaffolding partially hidden behind draped canvas. Using a special solvent, the mural was gradually revealed in 20-foot sections. Some earlier graffiti was found after the overpaint was removed as were old EXIT signs that had been bolted to some of the mural's painted figures. Many additional hours were spent filling in bored holes and matching Brooks' original paint colors.

On Sept. 18, 1980, a dedication ceremony was held in the terminal's rotunda. Among the prominent officials present were Arend, Brooks, Rockefeller and New York Port Authority Executive Director Peter Goldmark. Arend's work wasn't finished. He went to all the officials and told them of the need to preserve the *MAT* for future generations, a monument to America's first transatlantic air terminal. New York's Port Authority opposed Arend's program; they felt the site was needed for a bigger facility to handle the more than 19 million people who then passed through LaGuardia each year.

Arend's determination to succeed was pushed by his editorial coverages in the *Air Cargo News*. In November, 1980, New York's Landmarks Preservation Commission proclaimed the *MAT* a historical landmark. From the rotunda's ceiling hangs a six-foot model of the *Yankee Clipper*, a compliment, not only to Brooks' last painted panel depicting an in-flight 314, but to all those who continue to cherish the golden era of flight and the memory of the 314s.

Across the country from New York is the second monument to 314 history, Treasure Island's *Administration Building*. Built before the *MAT*, the Art Deco edifice is the U.S.' second great transoceanic air terminal. In its own way it is just as appealing as the *MAT* with its grand staircases of brass-lined railings and Art Deco-designed French-styled entrance doors of brass and glass. For years occupied by the U.S. Navy, it was, in October, 1997, closed for three months for interior revamping for new offices for the city's mayor and staff. Repainted in its original white color from the Navy's drab beige hue, the building still stands much in its grandeur of old. The huge Pan Am globe, once stored at Pan Am's San Francisco International Airport offices, and temporarily replaced in 1984 for a historical display honoring the building's past use and the island's history, is, of course, gone, as is the Pacific air mural map that years ago graced the terminal's upper inner grand hall. The control tower once used to direct many a clipper flight into and out of San Francisco still remains, a glass-enclosed room where one can still look down and see the massive hangars where the M-130s and B-314s were maintained.

Outside Miami at Dinner Key stands the first-built *Clipper Terminal*, constructed in 1930 and opened to the public on Feb. 1, 1931, whereupon it quartered Pan Am's Eastern Division for nearly 14 years. In 1945 the striking Art Deco edifice was sold to Miami's city officials for $1,050,000 to become the City Hall after the last Pan Am clipper flying boat arrived from Port-au-Prince on August 9th. Another splendid reminder of the flying boat era, the structure remains nearly as it was when under the Pan Am flag with touches of the line's old winged logo adorning upper walls. The winged clock is but one example. Interestingly enough, many former employees of the now defunct Pan American World Airways System

Missing many parts, once-exhalted *Dixie Clipper* nears its crushing end, Convair seaplane tarmac, Lindbergh Field, 1952. Airport expansion programs over the years have long since vanquished beached storage site. (*Photo Courtesy: Gordon S. Williams*)

Larger flying boats, such as Hughes' colossal HK-1 *Hercules* seen on only takeoff run, Long Beach, California, were to have followed the 314s in commercial transoceanic services but were never built. Final, and short-existed, revenue operations with the "big boats" was with Air France's six-engined sky liner Latecère 621 between France and Caribbean, via Canary Islands, beginning in 1947. (*Photo Courtesy: Hughes Aircraft*)

former employees of the now defunct Pan American World Airways System who are active members of the *Clipper Pioneers, Inc.,* are presently striving towards having the building turned into a Pan Am museum. Miami's government officials are planning for a more commodious and much-needed new City Hall.

It doesn't matter which of the air terminals one visits. Upon entering, one cannot help but to contemplate on its purpose for construction—to reflect on the days of flying ships, especially the beautiful machine-sculpted Art Deco-lined 314s. It is another one of man's follies not to have, in some way, preserved a Boeing Clipper for posterity's sake and for the pure enjoyment that could have been afforded commercial aviation historians and enthusiasts alike for decades to come.

As for the 314s themselves, not much remains. Pan Am's vanquished *Clipper Hall Museum*, once at New York's Kennedy International Airport, contained a propeller tip from the NC-02, an engine valve head and some 1939 314 flute-edged china serving pieces . There are numerous models on the market, a piece of lounge bulkhead fabric, an anchor, a rare set of original salon cushions with the star-studded pattern in the author's private collection, some clipper flags, and additional memorabilia, such as privately held log books, first-flight menus, film and newsreel clips and an abundance of photographs and first-cover mail envelopes. Seattle's *Museum of Flight* houses, amongst other small items, a license-marked piece of fabric. Combined, it does not amount to very much. Truly, the 314s have vanished forever!

'Tis only across the vastness where sky and sea meet the horizon at that imaginable isle will one find a 314 poised in majesty upon a blue-speckled lagoon. There, and only there, does the former "queen of the skies" await another takeoff destined for only a memory in time and space.

And therefore, in conclusion, to a most gracious, short-reigned liner of the clouds, your charming and romantic profoundess within the mercantile branch of historical flight — a period in the more dreamy, magical world of air travel in its oceanic beginnings-has come to a recorded close. And to those persons who cosigned (Beall), built, tested, commanded and maintained the last of the flying clippers of sea and air goes a grand salute evanescence of a superbly aero-staged era long since gone.

Color Gallery

NCI8601

THIS IS THE CLIPPER SHIP THAT WILL FLY ATLANTIC

The 86,000-lb. Atlantic Clipper which will carry Pan American passengers across the Atlantic is shown here in cross section. At the bow of the plane (above) is the *Anchor and Gear Room*, which also holds a mooring post which slides out when the hatch is opened. From this room a gangway leads up to the *Bridge* which is entirely lined with black to eliminate glare. Here two pilots handle controls which fly the plane. Back of the Bridge is *Navigation and Radio Room*, directive brain of the ship. Here are (left to right) the radio officer, the flight navigator and the flight engineer, all of whom have telephone communication with the bridge. *Captain's Office* is just behind, curtained off. In back of this is the *Cargo Hold*, whose main contents will probably be mail. Below, are the *Galley* and *Dining Lounge*. Stretched along the length of the ship are seven *Passenger Compartments*. The one in the ship's tail is a *De Luxe Compartment* corresponding roughly to a ship's bridal suite. At the bottom of the plane, pumps force gasoline stored in sponsons up to the wing tanks and engines. On the plane's very top, showing in cross section at right, is the *Celestial Observation Turret* from which position is checked by sun and stars.

Boeing artist Kenneth W. Thompson's 314 cutaway rendering helped to promote and popularize the then up-coming 314 Atlantic service through its 1938 multi periodical reproductions. (*Photo Courtesy: Boeing Aircraft Co.*)

Shimmering in its newness, NX 18601 was moored to barge at opening of test period, Fauntleroy Cove, Elliott Bay, June 1, 1938. (*Photo Courtesy: Boeing Aircraft Co.*)

In her final tail configuration, future-named *Honolulu Clipper* at bay between tests, Lake Washington, 1938. (*Photo Courtesy: Boeing Aircraft Co.*)

An aircraft artist's impression of the *Yankee Clipper* flying high, wide and handsome over a sun-specked Atlantic. (*Photo Courtesy: Boeing Aircraft Co.*)

California Clipper is locked onto sunken beaching cradle, Port of the Trade Winds, Treasure Island, 1939. (*Photo Courtesy: Gordon S. Williams/Boeing Aircraft Archives*)

A graciously formed liner lifts away from one royal-hued element into a lighter-shaded blue one for a Summer, 1939, air voyage to Europe, Port Washington waters. (*Photo Courtesy: Pan American World Airways/Boeing Aircraft Archives*)

Yankee Clipper arrives Lisbon, late afternoon, under threatening skies following a 1939 flight from New York. (*Photo Courtesy: Pan American World Airways/Boeing Aircraft Archives*)

Sailing Port Washington waters, 1939. By late 1941, the Boeing Clippers had become so famous through their aviation breakthroughs and pre-war U.S. strategical African-routed flight operations that one ship was photographed to grace the Oct. 20th, 1941, cover of *Life* magazine. (*Photo Courtesy: Pan American World Airways/Boeing Aircraft Archives*)

A 314 at anchor, Bowery Bay, just forward of Pan Am's elegant *Marine Air Terminal* as spectators line its observation deck, Summer, 1940. In upper right is Riker's Island Channel, takeoff and landing area for the Boeing sky ships. (*Photo Courtesy: Pan American World Airways/Boeing Aircraft Archives*)

With one in for servicing and three at anchor, the entire Atlantic Division's 314 Clipper fleet is in port, Bowery Bay, 1940. When introduced to the flying public, the 314s soon became the most elite international club in the world. (*Photo Courtesy: Pan American World Airways/Boeing Aircraft Archives*)

Already secretly owned by the British Government, first-ordered A314 model undergoes 1941 engine testing, Puget Sound, as City of Seattle forms backdrop. Note fore and aft-breaking hemp lines to keep clipper in position while engines were run. (*Photo Courtesy: Boeing Aircraft Co.*)

Over Puget Sound, NC 18611 was briefly test-flown before being turned over to Pan Am, 1941. (*Photo Courtesy: Gordon S. Williams*)

In addition to the original contracted price and overhead expenses per 314 was the $756,450 Boeing charge for extra parts and spare engines that didn't include A314 improvements, such as the additional expense for 10-inch steel diameter prop extensions over the 1937-1939 14-foot prop dimensions. (*Photo Courtesy: Gordon S. Williams*)

A sometimes beautifully viewed pause in Bermuda lasted hours or days when seas swelled at Horta in the Azore Islands, second stop along mid-Atlantic route to Europe. (*Photo Courtesy: Pan American World Airways/Boeing Co. Archives*)

Crew kept long-dutied hours to keep 314s on correct sky routes. It was not unusual during the war when westbound that clipper night trips between the Azores and Bermuda were kept at an unbelievable altitude of only 200 or 500 feet with landing lights on so captains wouldn't fly the boats into the sea. Westbound headwinds were stronger, and the lower the altitude the better the flying speed. On the average, however, westbound flights held a 1,000-foot altitude and an 8,000 going eastbound where winds were more favorable. (*Photo Courtesy: Pan American World Airways/Boeing Co. Archives*)

Navigator kept tabs on projected course as captain and first officer conversed forward in bridge. Flights over great expanses of sea during the war were arranged so that the majority of flying time would be at night to hide 314s from the foe and most importantly so navigators could rely on the heavens for starfixing through celestial navigation to more easily guide the flying boats along their projected skyways. (*Photo Courtesy: Pan American World Airways/Boeing Co. Archives*)

To assist shielding the NC-12 from German Luftwaffe pilots that periodically patrolled off the shores of West Africa following the air boat's sale to the U.S. Government, Pan Am removed the upper wing-painted "International Orange" stripe as seen during an after-sale Bermuda stopover. (*Photo Courtesy: Pan American World Airways/ Boeing Co. Archives*)

If a slight delay occurred at Bermuda before the outbreak of hostilities, passengers were allowed to stroll along the tree-lined path, have refreshments or even take a brief swim in the clear turquoise-shaded bay alongside their moored clipper. (*Photo Courtesy: Pan American World Airways/Boeing Co. Archives*)

Bermuda's unusually designed clipper port control tower became a noted landmark for constant-going Atlantic air travelers during the long-yeared course of 314 flight. Strong-galed winter storms and pelting rain sometimes made stop nearly unbearable. (*Photo Courtesy: Pan American World Airways/Boeing Co. Archives*)

Six-foot-long *Yankee Clipper* model hangs motionless from the *MAT*'s rotunda, illuminated by the original many-windowed skylight. The replica and a few-posted pictures with text are about all that reminds one of the building's purpose for design and the once famed B-314 Clippers. (*Photo Courtesy: author*)

An American bald eagle spreads its mighty wings over one of a royal liege, the 314 Clipper. (*Photo Courtesy: Pan American World Airways*)

Notes

1. Luce, Clare Boothe, "Destiny Crosses the Dateline," *Life*, Nov. 3, 1941, Vol. II, No. 18, p. 99.

2. Shawe, Victor, "Wellwood E. Beall, Creator of the Pan American Clipper," *U.S. Air Service*, October, 1940, p. 23.

3. *Ibid.*

4. "Dreamboat — Wellwood Beall and the Boeing Clipper," *Pacific Northwest Aviation Historical Foundation*, Seattle, Wash., 1979, p. 2 (pamphlet).

5. Clipper Proposal Made to Pan Am, 314 File, *Boeing Aircraft Co.*, Seattle, Wash., June 22, 1936 (letter).

6. "André A. Priester Marks 25th Anniversary with PAA," *Pan American World Airways System*, copy 072952, New York, N.Y., 1952 (PR release).

7. *Ibid.*, p. 2.

8. *Ibid.*

9. "André A. Priester," *Pan American World Airways System*, New York, N.Y., May , 1943 (PR release).

10. *Ibid.*

11. Gledhill, Franklin J., B-314 Contract Notification, 314 File, *Boeing Aircraft Co.*, Seattle, Wash., June 22, 1936 (letter).

12. Borger, John, Personal long distance phone interview with author, June 18, 1980.

13. Beall, Wellwood E., "Clipper of the 40's; 314 — The Most Vital Designing Job of the Generation," *Yale Scientific Magazine*, Winter, 1940, p. 3.

14. Gall, R.S., "Wright Aeronautical Announces Development of 1500 H.P., Double-Row Cyclone 14," *Curtiss-Wright's Public Relations Department*, New York, March 3, 1938, p. 2 (PR release).

15. Cram, Ralph L., "Propeller Study - Boeing Model 314," Boeing Engineering Department, 314 File, *Boeing Aircraft Co.*, Seattle, Wash., Nov. 27, 1936, p. 1.

16. "André A. Priester," *Pan American World Airways*, New York, N.Y., May 26, 1943, p. 8 (PR release).

17. Beall, Wellwood E., "Design Aspects of the Boeing Trans- Atlantic Clipper," 314 File, *Boeing Aircraft Co.*, Seattle, Wash., November, 1938, p. 11.

18. *Ibid.*, p. 14.

19. *Ibid.*

20. *Ibid.*, p. 15.

21. *Ibid.*, p. 13.

22. Trippe, Juan Terry, "Ocean Air Transport," 29th Wilbur Wright Memorial Lecture Delivered Before The Royal Aeronautical Society, London, *Pan American World Airways*, New York, N.Y., June 17, 1941, p. 7.

23. McCrea, Capt. Stephen, Personal interview with author in upstairs B-747 lounge, Pan Am Flight No. 002, Los Angeles to Tokyo, Aug. 16, 1971.

24. Beall, Wellwood E., "Design Aspects of the Boeing Trans-Atlantic Clipper," 314 File, *Boeing Aircraft Co.*, Seattle, Wash., November, 1938, p. 5.

25. Mansfield, Harold, "Control Room of Boeing Clipper," *Boeing News Bureau*, 314 File, Boeing Aircraft Co., Seattle, Wash., Dec. l6, 1938, p. 4 (PR release).

26. Black, Capt. Edward Matthew, Personal letter to author, Feb. 18, 1994.

27. Jarboe, Jr., W. T., Employment offer letter to Col. Walter M. Dalglish (copy sent to author by Dalglish in 1994), *Pan American Airways*, Baltimore, Md., March 6, 1939.

28. Dalglish, Col. Walter M., Handwritten notes mailed to Chris Driscoll, staff writer for *Red Rock News*, Sedona, Ariz. (copy sent to author), Dec. 2, 1993.

29. Masland, Capt. William M., Personal letter to author, Sept. 26, 1964.

30. Lodeesen, Capt. Marius, "The Difficult We Do Today...Tomorrow, The Impossible," *Popular Aviation*, Vol. 1, No. 4, September-October, 1967, p. 57.

31. Masland, Capt. William M., Personal letter to author, April 27, 1965.

32. Lodeesen, Capt. Marius, "The Difficult We Do Today...Tomorrow, The Impossible," *Popular Aviation*, Vol. 1, No. 4, September-October, 1967, p. 58.

33. Bermane, R. B., "Huge Atlantic Clipper Ship Launched Here," *Seattle Post-Intelligencer*," June 1, 1938, pp. 1, 2.

34. "Chanute Award To Eddie Allcn," *Boeing News*, Boeing Aircraft Co., Seattle, Wash., January, 1940, p. 5.

35. Allen, Edmund T., "Tons Aloft; Test Piloting the Transatlantic Clipper," *The Saturday Evening Post*, Sept. 17, 1938, pp. 12, 13 (courtesy: The Curtis Publishing Co.).

36. Hill, Al, "Dixie Clipper's 25th Anniversary Flight Noted," *Boeing News*, Boeing Aircraft Co., Seattle, Wash., July 2, 1964.

37. Allen, Edmund T., "Tons Aloft; Test Piloting the Transatlantic Clipper," *The Saturday Evening Post*, Sept. 17, 1938, p. 13 (courtesy: The Curtis Publishing Co.).

38. "Cameramen Lose Clipper," *Seattle Post-Intelligencer*, June 8, 1938.

39. Bermann, R. B., "Huge Boeing Plane Makes Maiden Trip," *Seattle Post-Intelligencer*, June 8, 1938, p. 1.

40. *Ibid.*, p. 3.

41. "Cameramen Lose Clipper," *Seattle Post-Intelligencer*, June 8, 1938.

42. *Ibid*.

43. Allen, Edmund T., "Tons Aloft; Test Piloting the Transatlantic Clipper," *The Saturday Evening Post*, Sept. 17, 1938, p. 88 (courtesy: The Curtis Publishing Co.).

44. *Ibid*.

45. *Ibid.*

46. *Ibid.*

47. *Ibid.*

48. Berman, R. B., "Huge Boeing Plane Makes Maiden Trip," *Seattle Post-Intelligencer*, June 8, 1938, p. 3.

49. "Vivid Memory — Boeing Paid Him To Saw Off Clipper Tail," *Boeing News*, Boeing Aircraft Co., Seattle, Wash., Nov. 25, 1953.

50. "Consolidated Flight Test Report, Model 314," *Boeing Aircraft Co.*, Seattle, Wash., 314 File, Sept. 20, 1938, p. 1.

51. Kylstra, J., "Confidential Engineering Procedure Memorandum: Changes Model 314," *Boeing Aircraft Co.*, Seattle, Wash., 314 File, Sept. 22, 1938.

52. Williams, Gordon S., Personal letter to author, March 26, 1982.

53. Beall, Wellwood E., "Design Aspects of the Boeing Trans-Atlantic Clipper," *Boeing Aircraft Co.*, Seattle, Wash., 314 File, November, 1938, p. 4.

54. "From Windjammers to Flying Clippers," *Boeing News*, Boeing Aircraft Co., Seattle, Wash., Nov. 3, 1938, p. 2.

55. Beall, Wellwood E., "Clipper of the 40's; 314 — The Most Vital Designing Job of the Generation," *Yale Scientific Magazine*, Winter, 1940, p. 4.

56. Sloan, R. L., Personal interview with author, Feb. 18, 1965.

57. Klemmer, Harvey, "Lisbon — Gateway to Warring Europe," *National Geographic*, Vol. LXXX, No. 2, August, 1941, p. 259.

58. O'Neal, Jim, "One Captain - Two Captains," *Clipper Pioneer Newsletter*, Vol. 26-4, Dec. 23, 1994, p. 6.

59. Teets, Florence, "The Little Flower's Folly," *Pegasus*, October, 1954, p. 1.

60. Keith, P. J., Personal interview with author, Sept. 3, 1964.

61. *San Francisco Chronicle*, Feb. 7, 1939, p. 3 (photo caption).

62. Hill, Al, "Dixie Clipper's 25th Anniversary Flight Noted," *Boeing News*, Boeing Aircraft Co., Seattle, Wash., July 2, 1964.

63. "314s Make News," *Boeing News*, Boeing Aircraft Co., Seattle, Wash., March, 1939, p. 4.

64. "Plane Christened by Mrs. Roosevelt," *New York Times*, March 4, 1939, p. 17.

65. "Hail To California Clipper," *Pan American Airways*, Vol. 10, No. 2, April, 1939, p. 14.

66. "Three New Clippers of Transocean Fleet Are Christened," *Pan American Airways*, Vol. 10, No. 2, April, 1939, pp. 4, 5.

67. *Ibid.*, p. 5.

68. *Ibid.*, p. 7.

69. *Ibid.*, p. 8.

70. *Ibid.*

71. *Ibid.*

72. *Ibid.*, p. 9.

73. *Ibid.*

74. "Aviation Day Calls Throngs To Fair," *New York Times*, May 21, 1939, p. 38.

75. *Ibid.*

76. *Ibid.*

77. *Ibid.*

78. *Ibid.*

79. "Delayed Clipper Reaches England," *New York Times*, June 29, 1939, p. 1.

80. "Ocean Air Service Begun By Clipper," *New York Times*, June 29, 1939, p. 1.

81. "Office Division," *Pan American Airways*, Vol. 10, No. 4, September, 1939, p. 19.

82. "Los Angeles Is Scene Of Naming American Clipper," *Pan American Airways*, Vol. 10, No. 4, September, 1939, p. 3.

83. "To New Zealand — Clipper Poised For Takeoff," *San Francisco Chronicle*, July 19, 1940, p. 13.

84. Trippe, Juan T., "Ocean Flying Is Routine," *Flying and Popular Aviation*, October, 1941, pp. 60, 100.

85. Gunnison, Royal Arch, "The Pacific — a Pond," *San Francisco Chronicle*, July 19, 1940, p. 13.

86. *Ibid.*

87. "Those First Flights To New Zealand," *Pan American Pacific Division News*, Pan American Airways, Vol. 1, Nov. 1, 1940.

88. "Minshall Receives Trophy," *Boeing News*, Boeing Aircraft Co., Seattle, Wash., July, 1940, p. 3.

89. Beall, Wellwood E., "Unsatisfactory Items — Aircraft Serial Nos. 1989 (NC 18602) and 1990 (NC 18603) Model 314," Boeing Aircraft Co., Seattle, Wash., 314 File, Feb. 18, 1939.

90. _____, "Overnight Test Trip — Aircraft Serial No. 1989 (NC 18602), Model 314," Boeing Aircraft Co., Seattle, Wash., 314 File, Feb. 17, 1939, p. 4.

91. *Ibid.*, p. 6.

92. Martin, George C., Memo to George Snyder, *Boeing Aircraft Co.*, Seattle, Wash., 314 File D18P, Feb. 9, 1940 , pp. 1, 2.

93. Kelsey, Al F., Letter to Wellwood E. Beall, *Boeing Aircraft Co.*, Seattle, Wash., 314 File M2P, Aug. 4, 1939.

94. Martin, George C., Memo to George Snyder, Boeing Aircraft Co., Seattle, Wash., 314 File D18P, Jan. 3 , 1940.

95. Schairer, George S., Personal letter to author, May 12, 1980.

96. Snyder, George, "Failures On NC-05 Report To Beall," *Boeing Aircraft Co.*, Seattle, Wash., 314 Docket File No. D18E-1, April 15, 1940, p. 1.

97. *Ibid.*, p. 8.

98. *Ibid.*, April 17, 1940, p. 3.

99. *Ibid.*, April 26, 1940, p. 1.

100. *Ibid.*, p. 4.

101. Snyder, George, "Report Of Inspection And Repair To Airplane NC-01's Cracked Spar Chord," *Boeing Aircraft Co.*, Seattle, Wash., 314 Docket File No. D18E-3, Dec. 23, 1940, p. 2.

102. Luce, Clare Boothe, Personal letter to author, Jan. 15, 1980.

103. "Design Notes - Miscellaneous, Model A-314," *Boeing Aircraft Co.*, Seattle, Wash., A-314 Docket File No. D-2358-01, February - July, 1940, pp. 1, 3.

104. Borger, John, Personal long distance phone interview with author, June 18, 1980.

105 "Flight 262," *New Horizons*, Vol. XI, No. 6, March, 1941, p. 14.

106. *Ibid.*, p. 17.

107. *Ibid.*

108. *Ibid.*

109. *Ibid.*

110. Luce, Clare Boothe, Personal letter to author, June 18, 1980.

111. Dodd, Jr., Allen R., "Air Travel's Glamour Era; Brother Can You Spare A Ride On The Golden Skyway?," *Signature*, December, 1973, pp. 46, 47.

112. Luce, Clare Boothe, Personal letter to author, June 18, 1980.

113. "Flying to Europe in the Yankee Clipper," *Look*, May 23, 1939.

114. Whitiker, Bruce, Personal interview with author, San Fernando Jr. High School, San Fernando, CA, May 14, 1979.

115. Colton, F. Barrows, "Aviation in Commerce and Defense," *National Geographic*, Vol. LXXVIII, December, 1940, p. 686.

116. Rice, Elmer, "To Write a Play," *New Horizons*, Vol. XI, No. 5, February, 1941, p. 6.

117. "Flight To The West," *New Horizons*, Vol. XI, No. 7, April, 1941, p. 24.

118. *Boeing News*, Boeing Aircraft Co., Seattle, Wash., October, 1940, p. 6.

119. Hodson, George, "The Steward Said...," *New Horizons*, Vol. XI, No. 1, Oct. 1, 1940, p. 6.

120. "Life Flies The Atlantic — America To Europe in 23 Hours by Clipper," *Life*, Vol. 8, No. 23, June 3, 1940, p. 16.

121. "Casablanca," *Warner Bros. Studios*, Burbank, CA, 1942 movie script lines.

122. Pemperton-Billing, Noel, "Are We Too Proud To Learn?," *Aeroplane*, London, England, Aug. 16, 1939.

123. *Ibid.*

124. *Ibid.*

125. *Ibid.*

126. "Shipping and Mails, Foreign Air Mail," *New York Times*, N.Y., July 1, 1939, p. 33.

127. "Crowds Of Visitors Meet Every Clipper At Manorhaven," *Port Washington News*, Port Washington, Long Island, N.Y., Aug. 4, 1939.

128. Luce, Clare Boothe, "Destiny Crosses the Dateline," *Life*, Nov. 3, 1941, Vol. II, No. 18.

129. "Air Link To Singapore," *New York Times*, New York, May 4, 1941, p. 34.

130. Black, Capt. Edward Matthew, Personal interview with author over dinner, Nov. 10, 1995.

131. Robertson, Jr., Ben, Personal letters written to family and friends from the *Waldorf Hotel*, London, July 28, 1940, and Aug. 5, 1940 (courtesy: Mary "B," Robertson's sister, Dalton, GA, 1967).

132. Boddis, A. C., "Air Ministry DCAF NZZ" (cablegram from British Consul, New York), 314 File, *Boeing Aircraft Co.*, Seattle, Wash., Aug. 22, 1940.

133. Ward, Robert N., "Seattle's Sky Queen Makes Last Flight," *Seattle Post-Intelligencer*, Seattle, Wash., April 14, 1946.

134. "Agreement Relating To Sale of Three Boeing Model 314 Flying Boats," Contract No. A-967, Requisition No. U.S. 65/40/390, *Pandick Press, Inc.*, for Pan American Airways and BOAC, New York, N.Y., Aug. 30, 1940, pp. 6, 7.

135. Kelly-Rogers, Capt. John Cecil, Personal tape letter to author, Aug. 15, 1968.

136. "All Aid...," *New Horizons*, Vol. XI, No. 4, January, 1941, p. 10.

137. Kelly-Rogers, Capt. John Cecil, Personal tape letter to author, Aug. 15, 1968.

138. Masland, Capt. William M., Personal letter to author, July 16, 1968.

139. Kelly-Rogers, Capt. John Cecil, Personal tape letter to author, Aug. 15, 1968.

140. Masland, Capt. William M., Personal letter to author, July 16, 1968 .

141. "Fiji Opening," *New Horizons*, Vol. XII, No. 3, December, 1941, p. 23.

142. *Ibid.*

143. Grace, William H., "Firsthand From Fiji," *New Horizons*, Vol. XII, No. 3, December, 1941, p. 6.

144. "Africa and Return," *New Horizons*, Vol. XII, No. 3, December, 1941, p. 12.

145. *Ibid.*

146. *Ibid.*

147. *New Horizons*, Vol. XII, No. 1, October, 1941, p. 31.

148. *Ibid.*

149. "Rush from Japan " *New Horizons*, Vol. XII, No. 3, December, 1941, p. 10.

150. Masland, Capt. William M., Personal letter to author, July 16, 1968.

151. Turner, Capt. H. Lanier, Personal letter to author, March 4, 1966.

152. Masland, Capt. William M., Personal letter to author, Aug. 21, 1982.

153. *Ibid.*

154. *Ibid.*

155. Hamby, Bruce, "Flying to Macao in the Early Days," *Los Angeles Times*, Part VII, April 13, 1980, p. 17, col. 1.

156. "Pursued Ships," *Boeing News*, Boeing Aircraft Co., Seattle, Wash., January, 1942, p. 9.

157. Ford, Capt. Robert, Personal letter to author, Dec. 13, 1981.

158. "Epic," *New Horizons*, Vol. XII, No. 4, January, 1942, p. 13.

159. *Ibid.*, p. 12.

160. Ford, Capt. Robert, Personal letter to author, Dec. 13, 1981.

161. "Epic," *New Horizons*, Vol. XII, No. 4, January, 1942, p. 11.

162. "The Year," *New Horizons*, Vol. XII, No. 4, January, 1942, p. 1.

163. "Air Version," *New Horizons*, Vol. XII, No. 6, February, 1942, p. 25.

164. Donham, Roy L., Personal letter to author, July 15, 1982.

165. "PAA Clipper Commuters," *New Horizons*, Vol. XIV, No. 14, October-December, 1945, p. 25.

156. Kelly-Rogers, Capt. John Cecil, Personal tape letter to author, Aug. 15, 1968.

167. "History at Rio," *New Horizons*, Vol. XII, No. 4, February, 1942, p. 23.

168. *Ibid.*

169. *Ibid.*

170. *Ibid.*

171. "Advice," *New Horizons*, Vol. XII, No. 6, March, 1942, p. 31.

172. "To The Queen's Taste," *New Horizons*, Vol. XII, June, 1942.

173. "Queen's Flight," *New Horizons*, Vol. XIII, No. 12, August-September-October, 1943, p. 20.

174. "Wells' Farewell," *New Horizons*, Vol. XII, No. 11, August, 1942, p. 30.

175. Donham, Roy L., Personal letter to author, July 15, 1982.

176. Dunning, Gene, Personal letter to author, June 17, 1982.

177. *Ibid.*

178. Byars, Fergusen J., Personal letter to author, Oct. 29, 1981.

179. *Ibid.*

180. Black, Capt. Edward Matthew, Personal interview with author over dinner, Nov. 10, 1995.

181. Curry, Capt. Jack H., Personal letter to author, Aug. 19, 1994.

182. Black, Capt. Edward Matthew, Personal interview with author over dinner, Nov. 10, 1995.

183. "On Deck," *New Horizons*, Vol. XI, No. 2, September, 1940, p. 39.

184. "Ice Breaker," *New Horizons*, Vol. XII, No. 1, October, 1941, p. 14.

185. *Ibid.*

186. "Must Be a Clipper," *New Horizons*, Vol. XI, No. 5, February, 1941, p. 34.

187. "100," *Newsweek*, January, 1943.

188. "The Most Watched-For Ship In The World," *Pan American Airways* (ad), 1941.

189. "Presidential Pronouncements," *New Horizons*, Vol. XIII, No. 1, November, 1942, p. 9.

190. "The Month; Passenger No. 1," *New Horizons*, Vol. XXII, No. 3, January, 1943, p. 7.

191. *Ibid.*

192. "The Log of The President's Trip to the Casablanca Conference — Jan. 9-31, 1943," *U.S. Navy Historical Center*, File No. Op-09B93, Washington, D.C., p. 49.

193. *Ibid.*, p. 50.

194. "The Month; Passenger No. 1," *New Horizons*, Vol. XXII, No. 3, January, 1943, p. 8.

195. *Ibid.*

196. Masland Capt. William M., Personal letter to author, Feb. 12, 1965.

197. *Ibid.*

198. "China Clipper," *Smithsonian*, Vol. 16, No. 10, January, 1986, p. 18.

199. Robertson, Ben, Personal letter to family, Feb. 16, 1943, courtesy of Mary "B," Robertson's sister.

200. *Ibid.*, Feb. 19, 1943.

201. Burn, Capt. John Curtis, Personal letter to author, June 5, 1979.

202. "Report of the Civil Aeronautics Board: Investigation of an accident, involving aircraft of United States registry NC 18603, in the Tagus River, Lisbon, Portugal, Feb. 22, 1943," *Civil Aeronautics Board*, Washington, D.C., Docket No. AC- 5, File No. 2143-43, September, 1943, p. 7.

203. *Ibid.*, pp. 10, 12.

204. *Ibid.*, p. 10.

205. Froman, Jane, "I Lived It," *The American Weekly* (supplement to the *Los Angeles Herald Examiner*), March 30, 1952.

206. Press, United (UP), "Jane Froman Tells How Clipper Officer Saved Her From River," *New York Daily News*, N.Y., Feb. 25, 1943, p. 4.

207. Nash, W. Bill, "R.O.D. Sullivan and the Yankee Clipper Crash," *Clipper Pioneer Newsletter*, Vol. 18-7, Dec. 12, 1986, p. 6.

208. "Report of the Civil Aeronautics Board: Investigation of an accident, involving aircraft of United States registry NC 18603, in the Tagus River, Lisbon, Portugal, Feb. 22, 1943," *Civil Aeronautics Board*, Washington, D.C., Docket No. AC-5, File No. 2143-43, September, 1943, p. 7.

209. *Ibid.*

210. *Ibid.*, p. 8.

211. *Ibid.*, pp. 13, 11.

212. Burn, Capt. John Curtis, Personal letter to author, June 5, 1979.

213. Masland Capt. William M., Personal letter to author, Aug. 21, 1982.

214. Nash, W. Bill, "R.O.D. Sullivan and the Yankee Clipper Crash," *Clipper Pioneer Newsletter*, Vol. 18-7, Dec. 12, 1986, p. 7.

215. Press, Associated (AP), "Pilot Disobeyed Orders; Froman Case Jury Told," *Valley News*, Los Angeles, CA., March 10, 1953, Part I, p. l.

216. "Survivor Depicts Wreck of Clipper," *New York Times*, N.Y., Feb. 25, 1943, p. 6.

217. Nash, W. Bill, "R.O.D. Sullivan and the Yankee Clipper Crash," *Clipper Pioneer Newsletter*, Vol. 18-7, Dec. 12, 1986, p. 7.

218. "First Flight Echo," *New Horizons*, Vol. XIII, No. 7, May, 1943, p. 18.

219. Byars, Jr., Ferguson, Personal letter to author, Oct. 29, 1981.

220. Kelly-Rogers, Capt. John Cecil, Personal tape letter to author, Aug. 15, 1968.

221. Dunning, Gene, Personal letter to author, June 17, 1982.

222. "Madeline Cuniff: stewardess pioneer," *Pan Atlantic Clipper*, Pan American World Airways System, New York, October, 1980, p. 1.

223. "Now you can fly to Lisbon by Clipper," *New York Times* (Pan Am ad), Aug. 7, 1945, p. 16.

224. Masland, Capt. William M., Personal letter to author, Sept. 26, 1964.

225. Gulbransen, Capt. Haakon G., Personal letter to author, July 11, 1969.

226. Flower, Scott, Personal letter to author, April 19, 1965.

227. Burn, John Curtis, Long distance phone call interview with author, Aug. 23, 1982.

228. Kelly-Rogers, Capt. John Cecil, Personal tape letter to author, Aug, 15, 1968.

229. Gray, Capt. Harold E., Personal letter to author, May 13, 1963.

230. "Second Clipper Located Downed Plane, Brought Ships To Rescue," *Honolulu Star-Bulletin*, Honolulu, Hawaii, Nov. 5, 1945, Part I, p. 4.

231. Buchanan, William O., Personal letter to author, April 15, 1970.

232. "Second Clipper Located Downed Plane, Brought Ships To Rescue," *Honolulu Star-Bulletin*, Honolulu, Hawaii, Nov. 5, 1945, Part I, p. 4.

233. Buchanan, William 0., Personal letter to author, April l5, 1970.

234. *Ibid.*

235. "Wife Is Advised Husband Aboard Clipper Is Safe," *Honolulu Star-Bulletin*, Honolulu, Hawaii, Nov. 5, 1945.

236. "Second Clipper Located Downed Plane, Brought Ships To Rescue," *Honolulu Star-Bulletin*, Honolulu, Hawaii, Nov. 5, 1945, Part I, p. 4.

237. "Carrier's Fight To Save Stricken Clipper Is Told," *Honolulu Star-Bulletin*, Honolulu, Hawaii, Nov. 5, 1942, Part I, p. 4.

238. "1,300 Rounds of Gunfire, Half Hour Required To Sink Stricken Clipper," *Honolulu Star-Bulletin*, Honolulu, Hawaii, Nov.10, 1945, Part I, p. 4.

239. *Ibid.*

240. Howard, Capt. Robert ("Bob") C., Personal letter to author, May 11, 1984.

241. Van Dusen, William, "Magellans Of The Air," *Boeing Magazine*, Boeing Aircraft Co., Seattle, Wash., June, 1946, pp. 7, 8, 13.

242. Beer, Capt. Kenneth V., Personal tape letter to author, September, 1982.

243. Blackmore, Capt. Gilbert B., Personal letter to author, Oct. 14, 1982.

244. *Ibid.*

245. Howard, Capt. Robert ("Bob") C., Personal letter to author, May 11, 1984.

246. Dunning, Gene, Personal letter to author, June 17, 1982.

247. Huffman, S. C., Letter to Department of Commerce, Nov. 23, 1946, 314 File, *Federal Aviation Administration*, Tulsa, Okla.

248. "Broomstick at the Mast," *Time*, Oct. 27, 1947.

249. First eye-witness account, Bermuda Sky Queen File, *U.S. Coast Guard*, Public Information Division, Washington, D.C., Oct. 16, 1947, p. 1.

250. *Ibid.*

251. "Broomstick at the Mast," *Time*, Oct. 27, 1947.

252. First eye-witness account, Bermuda Sky Queen File, *U.S. Coast Guard*, Public Information Division, Washington, D.C., Oct. 16, 1947, pp. 2, 3.

253. Beall, Wellwood E., Letter to D. B. Martin, *Boeing Aircraft Co.*, Seattle, Wash., 314 File, Reference E711-261, Oct. 22, 1947.

254. *Ibid.*

255. "Boeing 314 Praised By Cuban," *Boeing Aircraft Co.*, Seattle, Wash., News Bureau release to *Seattle Times*, 314 File, Nov. 5, 1947, p. 1.

256. Saunders, Keith, "Three Great Boeings," *Boeing News*, Boeing Aircraft Co., Seattle, Wash., October, 1946, p. 11.

257. *Ibid.*

258. Kelly-Rogers, Capt. John Cecil, Personal tape letter to author, Aug. 15, 1968.

259. Griffin, Patrick F. A., Personal interview with author, London, England, July 18, 1977.

260. "One Flying Boat, Slightly Sunken, May Visit Stalin," *Boeing News*, Boeing Aircraft Co., Seattle, Wash., Aug. 8, 1951, p. 1.

261. Scott, Jr., John F. R., Personal letter to author, May 15, 1968.

262. Williams, Gordon S., Personal letter to author, Aug. 3, 1982.

Bibliography

Books:

Bender, Marylin; Altschul, Selig, *The Chosen Instrument, Juan Trippe - Pan Am*: Simon And Schuster, New York, 1982.

British Ministry of Information, *Merchant Airmen, 1939- 1944*: His Majesty's Stationary Office, London, 1946.

Brock, Horace, *Flying The Oceans; A Pilot's Story of Pan Am, 1935-1955*: The Stinehour Press, Lunenburg, Vermont, 1978.

Brown, Cecil, *Suez To Singapore*: Random House, New York, 1942.

Cheney, Sheldon & Chency, Martha Candler, *Art And The Machine*: McGraw-Hill, New York, 1936.

Coward, Noel, *Future Indefinite*: Doubleday & Company, Inc., New York, 1954.

Cooke, David C., *Seaplanes That Made History*: C. P. Putnam's Sons, New York, 1963.

Craven, W. P.: Cate, J. L., *The Army Air Forces In World War II; Part I, Plans & Early Operations - January, 1939-August, 1942*: University of Chicago Press, Chicago, 1948.

Daley, Robert, *An American Saga - Juan Trippe and His Pan Am Empire*: Random House, New York, 1980.

Davies, R. E. G., *History of the World's Airlines*: Oxford University Press, 1964.

Dunning, Eugene J., *Voices Of My Peers - Clipper Memories*: Clipper Press, Nevada City, California, 1996.

Editors of American Heritage, *The American Heritage History of Flight*: American Heritage Publishing Co., Inc., 1962.

Emery, Edwin, *The Press And America*: Prentice-Hall, Inc., New Jersey, 1954, 1962, 1964.

Educational Director, *The Pacific-Alaska Flying Clippers*: Pan American Airways, New York, 1947.

Grooch, William S., *From Crate To Clipper*: Longmans, Green and Company, New York, 1939.

_____, *Skyway To Asia*: Longmans, Green and Company, New York, Toronto, 1936.

_____, *Winged Highway*: Longmans, Green and Company, New York, 1938.

Hatch, Alden, *Glenn Curtiss; Pioneer of Naval Aviation*: Julian Messner, Inc., New York, 1942, 1962.

Heinmuller, John P. V., *Man's Fight To Fly*: Funk & Wagnalls Co., New York, London, 1944.

Hoare, Robert J., *Wings Over the Atlantic*: Charles T. Branford Printing, Great Britain, 1957.

Hood, Joseph P., *Skyways Round The World*: Charles Scribner's Sons, New York, 1968.

Jablonsky, Edward, *Sea Wings - The Romance of the Flying Boats*: Doubleday & Co., Inc., New York, 1972.

Jackson, Ronald W., *China Clipper*: Everest House, New York, 1980.

Josephson, Matthew, *Empire Of The Air*: Harcourt, Brace and Co., New York, 1943.

Lester, Valerie, *Fasten Your Seat Belt! - History and Heroism in the Pan Am Cabin*, Paladwr Press, McLean, Virginia, 1995.

Mance, Osborne, *International Air Transport*: Oxford University Press, London, 1943.

Masland, William M., *Through The Back Doors Of The World In A Ship That Had Wings*: Vantage Press, New York, 1984.

McFarland, Ross A., *Human Factors In Air Transport Design*: McGraw Hill Co., New York, London, 1946.

Morison, Eliot Samuel, *The Battle of the Atlantic - History of United States Naval Operations In World War II - September, 1939 - May, 1943: Vol. X*: Brown & Company, Boston, 1961.

Munson, Kenneth; Taylor, John W. R., *History of Aviation*: Crown Publishers, Inc., New York, 1977.

Nay, Carol, *Timmy Rides The China Clipper*: Albert Whitman & Co., Chicago, 1941.

Palmer, Jr., Henry R., *This Was Air Travel*: Bonanza Books, New York, 1974.

Richardson, Capt. Holden C.; Beall, Wellwood E.; Manly, Charles W., *Flying Boats*: National Aeronautics Council, Inc., New York, 1942.

Robertson, Ben, *I Saw England*: Alfred A. Knopf, New York, 1941.

Rose, Barbara, *American Art Since 1900; A Critical History*: Frederick A. Praeger, New York, Washington, D.C., 1967.

Roseberry, C. R., *Challenging Skies*: Doubleday & Co., New York, 1966.

Scribner, Capt. Kimball J., *Adventures In Aviation*: Wimmer Brothers, Memphis, Tennessee, 1990.

Sherwood, Robert E., *Roosevelt and Hopkins - An Intimate History*: Harper and Brothers, New York, 1948, 1950.

Sikorsky, Igor I., *The Story of the Winged-S*: Dodd, Mead & Co., New York, 1952.

Snyder, Louis L., *The War, A Concise History, 1939-1945*: Julian Messner, Inc., New York, 1960.

Solberg, Carl, *Conquest Of The Skies - A History of Commercial Aviation in America*: Little, Brown & Co., Boston, Toronto, 1979.

Stevenson, William, *A Man Called Intrepid*: Ballantine Books, New York, 1976.

Taylor, Frank J., *High Horizons*: McGraw-Hill, New York, 1951.

The School of Education, *Aviation Education Source Book* (prepared tor and in co-operation with the CAA): Hastings House, New York, 1946.

Trippe, Betty Stettinius, *Pan Am's First Lady - The Diary of Betty Stettinius Trippe*: Paladwr Press, McLean, Virginia, 1996.

Wright, Monte Duane, *Most Probable Position; A History of Aerial Navigation to 1941*: University Press of Kansas, Kansas City, 1972.

Documents:

"Acoustic Treatment for Model 314 Dry Zero vs. Stonefelt by Electrical Research Products, Inc.," *Boeing Aircraft Co.*, Seattle Wash., 314 File, Box 314-D, Feb. 25, 1938.

Allen, E. T.; Cram. R. L.; Beall, W. E., "Consolidated Flight Test Report - Serial No. 1988 - Model 314," *Boeing Aircraft Co.*, Seattle, Wash., 314 File, Sept. 20, 1938.

"Aircraft Accident Report - NX 18601," *Boeing Aircraft Co.*, Seattle, Wash., 314 File, Feb. 20, 1939.

"Aircraft Operation Records, NC-01 - NC-12," *FAA*, 314 File, Tulsa, Okla., Storage.

"Air Safety Board of the Civil Aeronautics Authority; Preliminary Report of the Disappearance of an Aircraft of Pan American Airways, Inc., in the Vicinity of Latitude 12° 40' East, on July 29, 1938," *CAA*, Washington, D.C., Nov. 18, 1938.

Allen, E. T., "Test Report - Model 314; Test No. 5, Flight No. 1," Boeing Aircraft Co., Seattle, Wash., 314 File, June 7, 1938.

Allison, John M., "Tank Tests of a Model of the Hull of the Boeing 314 Flying Boat (NACA TANK MODEL 72)," *NACA*, Sept. 16, 1936.

"Aloha, Boeings," Boeing Aircraft Co., Seattle, Wash., 314 File, April 15, 1946 (PR release).

"America's Largest Airliners Nearing Completion For Atlantic Service," *Boeing Aircraft Co.*, Seattle, Wash., 314 File, Aug. 20, 1937 (PR release).

"André A. Priester," Pan Am, New York, May 26, 1943 (PR release).

Beall, Wellwood E., "Design Aspects Of The Boeing Trans-Atlantic Clipper," *Boeing Aircraft Co.*, Seattle, Wash., 314 File, Nov. 18, 1938.

_____, " Launch Service at Astoria - Delivery Flight - Model 314," Boeing Aircraft Co., Seattle, Wash., 314 File, Feb. 2, 1939 (memo to Boeing).

_____, Memo to Chief Engineer Jack Kylstra, *Boeing Aircraft Co.*, Seattle, Wash., 314File, Feb. 7, 1939.

_____, "Propeller Installation - Model 314 - Serial No. 1989," *Boeing Aircraft Co.*, Seattle, Wash., 314 File, Feb. 2, 1939 (memo to Boeing).

_____, "The CAB Hearing on the Accident of the 'Bermuda Sky Queen,'" *Boeing Aircraft Co.*, Seattle, Wash., 314 File, Oct. 22, 1947 (letter to D. B. Martin, PR chief, Boeing's New York office).

_____, "Unsatisfactory Items - Model 314, Serial No. 1989," *Boeing Aircraft Co.*, Seattle, Wash., 314 File, Feb 7, 1939 (memo to Chief Engineer Jack Kylstra).

_____, "Unsatisfactory Items - Model 314 - Aircraft Serial Nos. 1989 (NC 18602) and 1990 (NC 18603)," *Boeing Aircraft Co.*, Seattle, Wash., 314 File, Feb. 13, 1939.

_____, "Unsatisfactory Items - Aircraft Serial No. 1989 (NC 18602) Model 314," *Boeing Aircraft Co.*, Seattle, Wash., 314 File, Feb. 10, 1939.

_____, "Overnight Test Trip - Aircraft Serial No. 1989 (NC 18602) - Model 314," *Boeing Aircraft Co.*, Seattle, Wash., 314 File, Feb. 17, 1939 (memo to Jack Kylstra).

___, "Unsatisfactory Items Aircraft Serial Nos. 1989 (NC 18602) and 1990 (NC 18603) - Model 314," *Boeing Aircraft Co.*, Seattle, Wash., 314 File, Feb. 18, 1939 (memo to Jack Kylstra).

Bedinger, R. D., regional CAA supervisor. Letter to Jack Kylstra regarding CAA personnel reorganization for 314 flight tests, *CAA*, Nov. 4, 1938.

Bixby, H. M., Letter to Mrs. Frederick Wagener, second sister to Ben Robertson, *Pan Am*, April 10, 1943 (courtesy: Mrs. Julian -Mary "B" — Longley, Sr.; sister to Robertson).

"BOAC Reports Sale Of Three Boeing 314 Flying Boats," *Boeing Aircraft Co.*, Seattle, Wash., 316 File, April 16, 1948 (PR release).

Ibid., *British Overseas Airways*, New York, April 16, 1948.

"Boeing Clippers - Six Years of Service," *Boeing Aircraft Co.*, Seattle, Wash., 314 File, 1945 (PR release)

"Boeing Crews," Confidential BOAC memo to Capt. Kelly-Rogers, *BOAC*, London, Jan. 10, 1941.

"Boeing Model 314 - ATC 704," *Boeing Aircraft Co.*, Seattle, Wash., 314 File (PR release).

"Boeing A314 Flying Boats," *British Overseas Airways*, London, May 20, 1946 (PR release).

"Boeing 314 Praised By Cuban," *Boeing Aircraft Co.*, Seattle, Wash., 314 File, S-982, Nov. 5, 1947 (PR release).

Boudwin, J. E., "Certification of Flight Test Data, Model 314," *CAA* , Nov. 14, 1938.

___, "Flight Test Board - Boeing Model 314," *CAA*, Nov. 9, 1938 (letter to Jack Kylstra).

Bradley, R., "Dates of first 6 Clipper (314) flight tests; Dates of 314A Clipper test flights," *Boeing Aircraft Co.*, Seattle, Wash., 314 File, Aug. 25, 1944.

"B-A314 Sale to Pan American Airways," *Boeing Aircraft Co.*, Seattle, Wash., 314 File, Oct. 3, 1939 (PR release).

CAA License & Delivery Schedule, *Boeing Aircraft Co.*, Seattle, Wash., 314 File, Dec. 9, 1938 (telegram from R. J. Minshall to Franklin Gledhill).

CAA Testing, *CAA*, Dec. 9, 1938 (letter from CAA Adm. Clinton M. Hester to Fred Collins).

"CAB Accident Investigation Report; American International Airways, Inc. - 'Bermuda Sky Queen,' North Atlantic Ocean," *CAB*, Washington, D.C., SA- 152, File No. 1-0088, Dec. 14, 1948.

Casprini, Philip, "Biographical Sketch," Aug. 19, 1994 (courtesy of Roland H. Usher, personal friend of Casprini, and former B-314 second officer).

"Changes Necessary to Reduce Wing Dihedral Angle - Model 314," Boeing Aircratt Co., Seattle, Wash., 314 File, Oct. 28, 1938.

"Change Request Order No. 1 - Change Request Order No. 299," Boeing Aircraft Co., Seattle, Wash., 314 File, Docket No. D-1590, Aug. 4, 1936 - Oct. 19, 1940.

"Chronology, Transpacific Operations," *Pan Am*, San Francisco, 1945.

"Chronology: Inauguration of Transatlantic Service by Pan American Airways," *Pan American World Airways*, New York City, NY, 1964 (PR Release data sheet).

"Chronology of Pan Am's 1937-1939 Transatlantic Survey Flights," *Pan American World Airways*, New York City, NY, 1964 (PR Release data sheets).

"Civil Aircraft Allocations," *U.S. Navy Archives*, Washington, D.C., Dec. 22, 1941 (memo from Col. R. Olds to Lt. Cmdr. C. H. Schildhauer) .

Bibliography

Cleveland, Carl M., "Clipper Statistics," *Boeing Aircraft Co.*, Seattle, Wash., 314 File, May 20, 1943 (letter to Thomas F. Collision, director of Boeing's New York advertising company, N. W. Ayer & Son, Inc.).

"Clipper Begins Fourth Year of Trans-Atlantic Flying," *Pan Am*, New York, 1943 (PR release).

"Clipper War Record," *Boeing Aircraft Co.*, Seattle, Wash., 314 File, November, 1943 (PR release).

Ibid., 1946.

Collins, Fred B., "Inquiry, American Export Airlines for Model 307 and Model 314," *Boeing Aircraft Co.*, Seattle, Wash., 314 File, April 17, 1939 (memo to Beall).

___, "Model 314 Proposal, Mitsubishi," *Boeing Aircraft Co.*, 314 File, Oct. 12, 1939 (memo to Beall).

Ibid., Oct. 6, 1939.

Contract - A314 Clippers, *Boeing Aircraft Co.*, Seattle, Wash., 314 File, Box 388j, Jan. 31, 1940.

Cram, R., "Propeller Study - Boeing 314," *Boeing Aircraft Co.*, Seattle, Wash., 314 File, Nov. 27, 1936.

"Crew For New Zealand Survey," *Pan Am*, San Francisco, 1940 (PR release).

"Crew Members Of Coast Guard Cutter 'Bibb' Get Awards For 'Bermuda Sky Queen' Rescue," *U.S. Coast Guard*, Washington, D.C., 1947 (PR release).

Crews, Marion P., "Boeing Model 314 Temporary and Final Revised Hydro-stabilizer Connections," *Boeing Aircraft Co.*, Seattle, Wash., 314 File, Oct. 20, 1938 (letter to CAA).

___, "Boeing Model 314 - Flutter Prevention Measures," *Boeing Aircraft Co.*, Seattle, Wash., 314 File, Oct. 12, 1938 (letter to CAA).

___, "Boeing 314 - Proof and Operation Tests for New Vertical Tail Surface Control Installation," *Boeing Aircraft Co.*, Seattle, Wash., 314 File, Aug. 29, 1938 (memo to Jack Kylstra).

___, "Official CAA Aircraft Inspection Request," *Boeing Aircraft Co.*, Seattle, Wash., 314 File, Nov. 22, 1938 (memo and report to Jack Kylstra).

"Design Notes - Power Plant - Model 314A," *Boeing Aircraft Co.*, Seattle, Wash., 314 File, Docket No. D-2458, January - September, 1940.

"Detailed Flight Test Program - Boeing Model 314," *Boeing Aircraft Co.*, Seattle, Wash., 314 File, June 3, 1939.

"Excerpt From Official Assistance Report; Rescue Operations - Flying Boat - 'Bermuda Sky Queen' (NC 18612) - Sequence of Events," *U.S. Coast Guard*, Washington, D.C., 1947.

"Exhibit A to Agreement Relating to Sale of Boeing Model 314 Flying Boats Between Boeing Aircraft Company and Pan American Aviation Supply Corp.," *Boeing Aircraft Co.*, Seattle, Wash., 314 File, Document No. D-1590, No. 20, Aug. 6, 1936.

"Eye-witness Account," *U.S. Coast Guard*, Washington, D.C., 1947 (PR release).

"Fin, Rudder, Stabilizer, Elevators - 314; Notes From Stress," *Boeing Aircraft Co.*, Seattle, WA, 314 File, June 30, 1938-July 1, 1938.

"Finished Specifications For The Model 314 Airplane," *Boeing Aircraft Co.*, Seattle, Wash., Docket File D-1600, No. 78, Sept. 22, 1937.

Gall, R. S., "Wright Aeronautical Announces Development of 1500 H.P., Double-Row Cyclone 14," *Wright Aeronautical Corp.*, Aug. 21, 1936 (PR release).

Gentry, Letha, Boeing librarian, Letter to Florence Teets regarding BOAC's 314 statistical record of passengers and miles flown, *Boeing Aircraft Co.*, Seattle, Wash., 314 File, Feb. 13, 1948.

Gledhill, Franklin, Postal Telegraph notification of 314 contract, *Boeing Aircraft Co.*, Seattle, Wash., 314 File, July 22, 1936.

Goeschel, Nancy, "Marine Air Terminal Interior - Marine Air Terminal, LaGuardia Airport," *New York's Landmarks Preservation Commission*, Designation List 138, LP-1110, New York, 1981.

"Handbook Of Instructions For Operation Of The Boeing Model A-314 Flying Boat," *Boeing Aircraft Co.*, Seattle, Wash., 314 File, Document No. D- 3207, 1941.

"Handbook Of Instructions, Maintenance, Boeing Model A-314 Flying Boat," *Boeing Aircraft Co.*, Seattle, Wash., 314 File, Document No. D-3206, Oct. 13, 1941.

"High Spots In The History Of The Boeing 314 Clippers," *Boeing Aircraft Co.*, Seattle, Wash., 314 File, 1945 (PR release).

Hill, Al, Boeing News Bureau manager, Letter to Huly E. Bray, director of Information, War Assets Administration, regarding 314 sale, *Boeing Aircraft Co.*, Seattle, Wash., 314 File, May 3, 1946.

"History of Pan American World Airways, 1927-1945," *Pan Am*, New York, 1945 (mimeo).

Hull, Cordell, "American Foreign Service Report Of The Death Of An American Citizen," *U.S. State Department*, Washington, D.C., March 31, 1943 (courtesy of Mrs. Julian—Mary "B"—Longley, Sr., sister to Robertson).

"Investigation of Failure of Station 8 Vertical - Model 314," *Boeing Aircraft Co.*, Seattle, Wash., 314 File, Report No. D-5970, June 1, 1944 .

"Itinerary Route of the 'Pacific Clipper' On 'Round The World Flight (Capt. Robert Ford)," *Pan Am*, New York, 1945.

"Juan T. Trippe, President, Pan American World Airways," *Pan Am*, New York, 1959 (PR release).

Kelsey, A. P., "Hull Bottom Damage Report - Model 314 NC-04," *Boeing Aircraft Co.*, Seattle, Wash., 314 File, Aug. 3, 1939 (letter to Beall).

Kenworth Motor Truck Corp.& Boeing Agreement, *Boeing Aircraft Co.*, Seattle, Wash., 314 File, April 29, 1937.

, "A Report On the Testing of Model 314 Beaching Gear," *Boeing Aircraft Co.*, Seattle, Wash., 314 File No. M51, Nov. 15, 1937.

Kerber, L. V., "Flutter Prevention Measures," *Boeing Aircraft Co.*, Seattle, Wash., 314 File, Nov. 23, 1938 (letter to M. P. Crews).

Ketcham, Howard, "Color Specifications For Interior Plan of Pan American Airways' Boeing Model 314," *Boeing Aircraft Co.*, 314 File D-1622, No. 11, Nov. 24, 1936.

___, "Specifications for Interior Fabrics & Decorative Materials - Boeing Model 314A," *Boeing Aircraft Co.*, Seattle, Wash., 314 File, March, 1940.

Krahenbuhl, Marguerite, "Boeing Clipper Specifications," *N. F. Ayer & Son, Inc.*, New York (PR release).

Kriendler, J. F., "Fifty Years of Pan Am Transatlantic Technology," *Pan Am News*, Docket No.. 150189, New York, June, 1989 (PR release).

___, "Impressions Of Passengers Aboard First Transatlantic Flight, Fifty Years Ago," *Pan Am News*, Docket No. 050189, New York, June, 1989 (PR release).

___, "The First Transatlantic Passenger Flight, 50 Years Ago, Was De Luxe All The Way," *Pan Am News*, Docket No. 050189, New York, June, 1989 (PR release),

Kylstra, Jack, "Application For ATC - Model 314 Airplane," *Boeing Aircraft Co.*, Seattle, Wash., 314 File, Oct. 11, 1938 (letter to CAA).

___, "Dept. of Commerce Inspection - Model 314," *Boeing Aircraft Co.*, Seattle, Wash., 314 File, Sept. 22, 1938 (memo to Beall and Egtvedt).

___, Letter and 314 alteration form sent CAA, *Boeing Aircraft Co.*, Seattle, Wash., 314 File, Oct. 14, 1938.

___, Memo to Beall, *Boeing Aircraft Co.*, Seattle, Wash., 314 File, Feb. 9, 1939.

___, "Model 314 - Flutter Prevention Measures," *Boeing Aircraft Co.*, Seattle, Wash., 314 File, Nov. 7, 1938 (letter to CAA).

___, "Model 314 - Seaworthiness Tests," *Boeing Aircraft Co.*, Seattle, Wash., 314 File, Nov. 29, 1938 (memo to CAA regional supervisor).

___, "Model 314 - Serial No. 1988, Ground Inspection," *Boeing Aircraft Co.*, Seattle, Wash., 314 File, Dec. 29, 1938 (letter to CAA).

___, "Model 314 - Summary of Offiaial Flight Tests," Boeing Aircraft Co., Seattle, Wash., 314 File, Nov. 16, 1938 (letter to R. D. Bedinger, CAA).

___, "Report - Delivery and Test - Model 314," *Boeing Aircraft Co.*, Seattle, Wash., 314 File, Feb. 10, 1939 (memo to Beall).

___, "Structural Testing - Model 314; Twin Rudder Installation," *Boeing Aircraft Co.*, Seattle, Wash., 314 File, July 25, 1938 (memo to Boeing).

___, "Trouble Reports - Model 314," *Boeing Aircraft Co.*, Seattle, Wash., 314 File, Feb. 10, 1939 (memo to Beall).

___, "Unsatisfactory Items - Airplane Ser. No. 1989," *Boeing Aircraft Co.*, Seattle, Wash., 314 File, Feb. 15, 1939 (memo to Beall).

___, "Weighing Procedure and Certificated Weight - Model 314," *Boeing Aircraft Co.*, Seattle, Wash., 314 File, Nov. 15, 1938 (letter to CAA).

Laudan, Fred P., "Model 314 Contract - Necessary Facilities," Boeing Aircraft Co., Seattle, Wash., 314 File, July 22, 1936.

"Letter CNO to Chief, Dec. 18, 1941," *U.S. Navy Archives*, Washington, D.C.

"Letter, Secretary of Navy to Secretary of War, Dec. 20, 1941," *U.S. Navy Archives*, Washington, D.C.

"Machining Parts for Aerial Giants," *Boeing Aircraft Co.*, Seattle, Wash., 314 File, Feb. 23, 1940 (memo).

Manners, E. Hlinko, "Pan Am Celebrates 50 Years Of Transatlantic Service With 50 Years Of Unlimted Travel Sweepstakes," *Pan Am News*, New York, 1989 (PR release).

Mansfield, Harold, "Boeing 314 Clipper," *Boeing Aircraft Co.*, Seattle, Wash., 314 File, 1939 (PR release).

___, "Boeing 314 Clipper - Largest airplane ever built for service on any of the world's Airways," *Boeing News Bureau*, Boeing Aircraft Co., Seattle, Wash., 314 File, November, 1939 (PR release).

___, "Clipper Tests," *Boeing News Bureau*, Boeing Aircraft Co., Seattle, Wash., 314 File, Nov. 3, 1938 (PR release).

___, "Control Room of Boeing Clipper," *Boeing News Bureau*, Boeing Aircraft Co., Seattle, Wash., 314 File, Dec. 16, 1938 (PR release).

___, "Facts About Boeing 314 Clipper," *Boeing News Bureau*, Boeing Aircraft Co., Seattle, Wash., 314 File, 1939 (PR release).

___, "For Howard Rice, United Press," *Boeing News Bureau*, Boeing Aircraft Co., Seattle, Wash., 314 File, 1937 (PR release).

___, "Memorandum on Boeing 314 Test Program," *Boeing News Bureau*, Boeing Aircratt Co., Seattle, Wash., 314 File, June 3, 1939.

___, "Passenger Accommodations of Boeing 314 Clipper," *Boeing News Bureau*, Boeing Aircraft Co., Seattle, Wash., 314 File, 1939 (PR release).

"Manufacturing Schedule, Model 314," *Boeing Aircraft Co.*, Seattle, Wash., 314 File, Aug. 21, 1936 (memo from Supt. Fred P. Laudan to all Boeing shop personnel).

Minshall, R. J., "CAA Procedure In Issuing a Final-Type Certificate For Aircraft," *Boeing Aircraft Co.*, Seattle, Wash., 314 File, Oct. 14, 1938 (letter to C. L. Egtvedt).

"Miscellaneous Reports Received From the Service Showing Failures and Difficulties - Model 314," *Boeing Aircraft Co.*, Seattle, Wash., 314 File, June 16, 1939.

"Model 314, Pilot's Daily Flight Test Reports," *Boeing Aircraft Co.*, Seattle, Wash., 314 File, Report Nos. D- 2007 - D-2038, from Test No. 1 - Test No. 46, June 2, 1938 - Dec. 28, 1938.

"No Sprained Ankles," *British Overseas Airways*, New York, May, 1948 (PR release).

"N-12 - 'Capetown Clipper' Schedule; Around The World Flight," *Pan Am*, New York, 1944 (PR release).

"Pacific Clipper - Flying Crew," *Pan Am*, New York, 1942 (PR release).

"Pan American Airways Co. and His Majesty's Government In The United Kingdom Agreement Relating To Sale Of Three Boeing Model 314 Flying Boats," Aug. 30, 1940, Courtesy, *Royal Air Force Museum*, Hendon, England,

"Pan American To Start U.S. Air Service Across South Pacific To Australia," *Pan Am*, New York, July 31, 1940 (PR release).

"Partial List of Satisfactory Items - Model 314," *Boeing Aircraft Co.*, Seattle, Wash., 314 File, 1938.

"Ponceti, H. D., "Control Cable Tensions; Boeing Model 314, Airplane NC 18602 at San Francisco," *Boeing Aircraft Co.*, Seattle, Wash., 314 File, June 21, 1939.

"Press and Radio Briefs," *Boeing Aircraft Co.*, Seattle, Wash., 314 File, Feb. 1, 1946 (PR release).

Price, N. C., "Reports on Heating and Ventilating System - Model 314," *Boeing Aircraft Co.*, Seattle, Wash., 314 File, Box 314-D, 1937.

"Proposal Made To Pan American, Exhibit II," *Boeing Aircraft Co.*, Seattle, Wash., 314 File, March 3, 1938.

"Radio Broadcast On KJB From Boeing Clipper No. 17," *Boeing Aircraft Co.*, Seattle, Wash., 314 File, Feb. 8, 1939.

"Report of Around The World Flight," *Pan Am*, New York, Document Nos. CM51244 and CM121144, Dec. 15, 1944 (PR release).

"Report of the CAB on the Investigation of an accident, involving aircraft of United States registry NC 18603, in the Tagus River, Lisbon, Portugal, on Feb. 22, 1943," *CAB*, Washington, D.C., File No. 2143-43, Docket No. AC-5, Sept. 7, 1943.

"Report On Clippers," *Boeing Aircraft Co.*, Seattle, Wash., 314 File, D-480, Feb. 18, 1946.

"Report On Hull Bottom Damage - Model 314 (NC-04)," *Boeing Aircraft* Co., Seattle, Wash., 314 File, August, 1939.

Reynolds and Reynolds, Patent Attorney letter to Boeing, *Boeing Aircratt Co,,* Seattle, Wash., 314 File, June 25, 1936.

Robertson, Ben, Letter to family, Feb. 16, 1943 (courtesy, Mrs. Julian - Mary "B"- Longley, Sr., sister to Robertson).

Roosevelt, President Franklin D., "Executive Order, Dec. 14, 1941," *U.S. Navy Archives*, Washington, D.C.

"Silver Anniversary of Transatlantic Flight: 25 Years Of Flying The Atlantic," *Pan Am*, New York, 1964 (PR release).

Sneed, A. N., "Request for Data on 314 Disposition," *Boeing Aircraft Co.*, Seattle, Wash., 314 File, Jan. 28, 1963 (letter to H. V. Brackin, Jr., FAA, Tulsa, Okla.).

Snyder, George, "Failures & Repairs to Hull & Hydrostabilizer; Boeing Model 314, Airplane NC 18605," *Boeing Aircraft Co.*, Seattle, Wash., 314 File, Report No. D-18E-1, April, 1940.

___, "Inspection & Repairs to Model 314 NC 18601 Wing Chord," *Boeing Aircraft Co.*, Seattle, Wash., 314 File, Report No. D-18E-1, April, 1940.

___, "Study Effect On Hull Structure of Increased Sea-Wing Span - Boeing Model 314," *Boeing Aircraft Co.*, Seattle, Wash., 314 File, Feb. 9, 1940.

___, "Study Revisions to the Wing Due to Use of Wing Floats and Roll Stability Investigation," *Boeing Aircraft Co.*, Seattle; Wash., 314 File, December, 1939.

Stark, H. R., "Establishment of Naval Air Transportation Service," *U.S. Navy*, Washington, D.C., Document Op-38-H-Ag/ks, (SC) A21-1/121, Serial 0123438, Dec. 12, 1941.

Symington, F. J., "The Contribution To The United States War Effort Made By Government-Owned Boeing Clippers Operated by Pan American Airways," *Pan Am*, New York, 1945.

"Synopsis of Purposes and Provision of the Federal Aviation Act in Relation to the CAB," *CAB*, Office of Information, Washington, D.C., 1979.

Teets, Florence, "Boeing 314 Statistics" *Boeing Aircraft Co.*, Seattle, Wash., 314 File, Feb. 19, 1945 (PR release).

___, Letter to Al Hill, Boeing's News Bureau chief, regarding 314 passenger and miles statistics, *Boeing Aircraft Co.*, Seattle, Wash., 314 File, Feb. 9, 1948.

___, Letter to Gordon S. Williams regarding American International Airways' flights, *Boeing Aircraft Co.*, Seattle, Wash., 314 File, Oct. 14, 1947.

___, Letter To Robert Ward regarding sale of BOAC 314s, *Boeing Aircraft Co.*, Seattle, Wash., 314 File, Feb. 12, 1948.

___, Letter to Harold Mansfield, *Boeing Aircraft Co.*, Seattle, Wash., 314 File, July 27, 1944.

___, Telegram reply to inquiry by Gordon S. Williams regarding 314 construction in "Bermuda Sky Queen" ditching, *Boeing Aircraft Co.*, Seattle, Wash., 314 File, Oct. 21, 1947.

"The Boeing Model 314," *Boeing Aircraft Co.*, Seattle, Wash., 314 File, Nov. 25, 1952 (PR release).

"The Log of The President's Trip to the Casablanca Conference," *U.S. Navy*, Historical Center, Washington, D.C., January, 1943.

"Trans-South-Pacific Flight Schedule," *Pan Am*, New York, 1940 (PR release).

"Trans-South-Pacific Preview (Press Flight)," *Pan Am*, New York, 1940 (PR release).

"Uruguayan Aviation Company Negotiating Purchase of BOAC's Boeing Flying Boats," *British Overseas Airways*, New York, Feb. 9, 1948 (PR release).

Ward, Bob, Letter to Florence Teets regarding sale of BOAC 314s, Feb. 9, 1948.

"Wellwood E. Beall, Senior Vice President, Boeing Airplane Company," *Boeing Aircraft Co.*, Seattle, Wash., Docket File No. S-6265 (PR release).

Williams, Gordon S., Memo to Florence Teets regarding "Bermuda Sky Queen" ditching, *Boeing Aircraft Co.*, Seattle, Wash., 314 File, Oct. 8, 1947.

___, Telegram to Florence Teets regarding information on General Phoenix Corp., *Boeing Aircraft Co.*, Seattle, Wash., 314 File, April 20, 1948.

___, Telegram to Florence Teets regarding 314 construction following "Bermuda Sky Queen" ditching, *Boeing Aircraft Co.*, Seattle, Wash., 314 File, Oct. 20, 1947.

"Wind Tunnel Test - Preliminary Data Model 314," *Boeing Aircraft Co.*, Seattle, Wash., 314 File, Box 388-c, June 7, 1936.

"Wind Tunnel Tests - Report of. Aerodynamic Tests of 1/25 Scale Model of 314 in the NACA 7' x 10' Wind Tunnel," *Boeing Aircraft Co.*, Seattle, Wash., 314 File, Sept. 2, 1936.

"Work Order - To Cover All Engineering & Shop Work for Reworking of the Hydro-Stabilizer Installation and Changes in the Tail Surfaces as Required," Boeing Aircraft Co., Seattle, Wash., 314 File, Work Order No. 9087-XX-89, June 13, 1938 (includes nine tail modification sketches).

"50,000 Atlantic Crossings - 2,000,000 Passengers," *Pan Am*, New York, June 28, 1955 (PR release).

PERIODICALS :

"A Great Ship Is Born," *Boeing News*: June, 1938.
"A Look Inside The Big '314," *Boeing News*: September, 1937.
"A New Kind Of College," *Boeing News*: May, 1938.
"A Spar...And a Spar," *Boeing News*: June, 1937.
"A-1 Performance," *New Horizons*: Vol. XIII, No. 9, July, 1943.
"Absolute Approached," *New Horizons*: Vol. XII, No. 5, February, 1942.
"Advice," *New Horizons*: Vol. XII, No. 6, March, 1942.
AEA christening, *New York Times*: June 21, 1939.
"Africa & Return," *New Horizons*: Vol. XII, No. 3, December, 1941.
"Africa: The Record," *New Horizons*: Vol. XII, No. 5, January, 1943.
"Aircraft...The Coronodo - Air Battleship and Freighter," *New Horizons*: Vol. XIV, No. 4, February, 1944.
"Air Express," *New Horizons*: Vol. XI, No. 4, February, 1941.
"Air Version," *New Horizons*: Vol. XII, No. 5, February, 1942.
"Air Link To Singapore," *New York Times*: May 4, 1941.
"Air Mail Schedule," *Los Angeles Times*: Sept. 12, 1940.
"Air Passengers Reach Marseille," *New York Times*: July 1, 1939.
"Airway Inn," *New Horizons*: Vol. XI, No. 2, November, 1940.
"All Aid...," *New Horizons*: Vol. XI, No. 4, January, 1941.
"All Eyes On the Clipper," *Boeing News*: May, 1938.
"All in the Family," *Boeing News*: February, 1939.
"All-Out Cargo," *New Horizons*: Vol. XII, No. 13, November, 1942.
"Allen, Clipper Test Pilot, Helps Builders Plan Planes," *Seattle Times*: Sept. 13, 1938.
"Allen, Edmund T., "Tons Aloft," *The Saturday Evening Post*: Sept. 17, 1938.
"Allen's First Job as Boeing Officer To be 307 Tests," *Pan American Airways*: Pan Am, New York, April, 1939.
"Allen Named to CAA Advisory Group," *Boeing News*: October, 1940.
"America Recaptures a Lost Sea Glory," *San Francisco Chronicle* (magazine section): April 16, 1939.
"American Clipper Hops for New Zealand With 11 Aboard," *San Francisco Chronicle*: Sept. 12, 1940.
"An Airport for the City of the Future," *San Francisco Chronicle*: Feb. 17, 1939.
Anend, Geoffrey, "Marine Air Terminal Should Be Designated Landmark," *Air Cargo News:* September, 1980.
___, "We Must Never Allow This To Happen Again," *Air Cargo News*: October, 1980.
"Angels of Mercy From Above," *New Horizons*: Vol. XIV, No. 10, October - December, 1944.
"Another Clipper," *Boeing News*: April, 1941.
"Another Trail Is Being Blazed - Clipper Leaves for New Zealand," *San Francisco Chronicle*: July 13, 1940.
"Another Trans-Atlantic Clipper Is Launched," *New York Herald Tribune*: Feb. 5, 1939.
"Annual Report," *New Horizons*: Vol. XIII, No. 12, August - October, 1943.
"Army Bomber Crashes Into Packing Plant - Test Pilot Is Among the Victims," *New York Herald Tribune*: Feb. 19, 1943.
"Ashore," *New Horizons*: Vol. XI, No. 3, December, 1940 .
"At Auckland's Dock," *New Horizons*: Vol. XI, No. 9, June, 1941.
"At Night," *New Horizons*: Vol. XI, No. 1, November, 1940.
"Atlantic Airmail," *San Francisco Chronicle*: Aug. 9, 1940.
"Atlantic Clipper Has Modern Interiors," *Life*: Aug. 23, 1937.
"Atlantic Life Line," *New Horizons*: Vol. XII, No. 3, December, 1941.
"Atlantic Shuttle," *Boeing News*: June, 1943.
"Australasia," *New Horizons*: Vol. XI, No. 1, Oct. 1, 1940.
"Australasia Reached," *New Horizons*: Vol. XI, No. 1, Oct. 1, 1940.
"'Aviation Day' Calls Throngs To Fair," *New York Times*: May 21, 1939.
"Aviation Honors Allen and Crew," *Boeing News*: February, 1943.
"Aviation - Ocean Transport Notes," *Time*: March 14, 1938.

"'Aviation' Shows Leadership In Air Belongs to U.S.," *Pan American Airways*: Pan Am, New York, April, 1939.
"Avigator Anniversary," *New Horizons*: Vol. XII, No. 11, August, 1942.

"Baby Business," *New Horizons*: Vol. XII, No. 5, February, 1942.
"Back From The Philippines," *New Horizons*: Vol. XIV, No. 13, July - September, 1945.
"Bad Luck Mars First Tests of World's Biggest Airliner," *Life*: June 20, 1938.
"Banishing Corrosion," *Boeing News*: September, 1939.
"Basil L. Rowe; Veteran of Global Airplanes," *New Horizons*: Vol. XV, No. 1, January - March, 1946.
Bayles, William D., "Lisbon: Europe's Bottleneck," *Life*: April 28, 1941.
Beall, Wellwood E., "Clipper of the '40's," *Yale Scientific Magazine*: Winter, 1940.
"Beall Writes Of Clipper Design," *Boeing News*: December, 1938.
Belcher, Jerry, "It Was Lovely The Day Before The Day of Infamy," *San Francisco Examiner Chronicle*: Dec. 4, 1966.
Bermann, R. B., "Huge Atlantic Clipper Ship Launched Here," *Seattle Post-Intelligencer*: June 1, 1938.
"Bermuda again, at last!," *New Horizons*: Vol. XIV, No. 14, October - December, 1945 (ad).
"Bermuda Service Sets New Record," *Pan American Airways*: Pan Am, New York, April, 1939.
Bess, D., "Four Continents in four days; from London to New York by way of Lisbon, Liberia and Brazil," *The Saturday Evening Post*: June 19, 1943.
"Best Times To See The Clippers Down At PAA Airport, Manorhaven," *Port Washington News*: July 7, 1939.
"Beyond the Figures," *New Horizons*: Vol. XIII, No. 9, July, 1943.
"Big Plane's Wing Dips Into Sound," *Seattle Post-Intelligencer*: June 4, 1938.
"Big Putt," *New Horizons*: Vol. XII, No. 11, August, 1942.
"Big Wind," *New Horizons*: Vol. XI, No. 3, December, 1940.
"Bigger Than Ever Grows the 'Clipper'," *Boeing News*: July, 1937.
Blair, Jr., William D., "Last Of Historic Flying Boats Again Is Offered For Sale," *Baltimore Sun*: April 5, 1950.
"Blue Ribbon," *New Horizons*: Vol. XIII, No. 7, May, 1943.
Blum, Walter, "The Fairest Of The Fairs," *San Francisco Sunday Examiner & Chronicle*: Aprll 15, 1979.
"BOAC Stratocruisers," *Boeing News*: September, 1946.
"Boarders," *New Horizons*: Vol. XIII, No. 5, March, 1943.
"Boeing-Built Model 314 Clippers Blaze Seven-Year Trail of Skyway Pioneering," *Boeing News*: Vol. 5, No. 5, Jan. 31, 1946.
"Boeing Clippers Bring Express Rate Cuts," *Boeing News*: September, 1938.
"Boeing Clipper Engines Tested In Elliott Bay," *Seattle Times*: June 1, 1938.
"Bolama Round-up," *New Horizons*: Vol. XI, No. 8, May, 1941.
"Bomber Falls on Factory, 14 Killed," *New York Daily Mirror*: Feb. 19, 1943.
"Bombers to the East," *New Horizons*: Vol. XII, No. 11, August, 1942.
Borner, Hank, "The Renaissance At LaGuardia: Once Dubbed 'Airport Without A Future', It Now Fills Jet-Age Needs," *Long Island Commercial Review*: Plainview, L.I., New York, Feb. 16, 1966
Bowers, Peter M., "The Great Clippers," *Sentry Magazine*: Vols. 6, 7, No. 6, November - December, 1977
Bredin, Dee, "Java Assignment," *National Geographic*: January, 1942.
"Broomstick at the Mast," *Time*: Oct. 27, 1947.
"Building a Ship The Modern Way," *Boeing News*: November, 1937.
"Bureau of Air Commerce Visitors," *Boeing News*: January, 1937. Busch, Noel F., "Juan Trippe," *Life*: Oct. 30, 1941.
"Busman's Holiday," *New Horizons*: Vol. XI, No. 9, June, 1941.
"CAA Officials Begin Tests," *Boeing News*: November, 1938.
"CAA Speeds Clipper Tests," *Boeing News*: December, 1938.
"C.A.B. and Radio," *New Horizons*: Vol. XI, No. 5, February, 1941.
"California Clipper Ready For New Zealand Flight," *New York Times*: Sept. 1, 1939.
Callender, Harold, "Clipper At Auckland After 8,000-Mile Trip," *New York Times*: Aug. 16, 1940 .
"Cameramen Lose Clipper," *Seattle Post-Intelligencer*: June 8, 1938.
"Canton Island Base Finished In Record Time," *Pan American Airways*: Pan Am, New York, September - October, 1939.
"Cargo - Various," *New Horizons*: Vol. XII, No. 1, October, 1941.
"Catering Aloft," *New Horizons*: Vol. XI, No. 5, February, 1941.
"Catering To Efficiency," *New Horizons*: Vol. XII, No. 10, July, 1942
"Cavalier Survivors Arrive Praising Heroisim of Crew; Tell of Long Ordeal in Sea," *New York Times*: Jan. 23, 1939.
"Chamber Will Sponsor Program Inaugurating PAA European Flights," *Port Washington News*: June 16, 1939.
"Change for Express," *New Horizons*: Vol. XII, No. 11, August, 1942.
"Chanute Award To Eddie Allen," *Boeing News*: January, 1940.

"Clearance Grows Up," *New Horizons*: Vol. XI, No. 5, February, 1941.
"Clipper," *San Francisco Chronicle*: Feb. 9, 1939.
"Clippers At War," *New Horizons*: Vol. XV, No. 1, January - March, 1946.
"Clipper Cleaning," *New Horizons*: Vol. XIV, No. 11, January - March, 1945.
"Clippers Click," *Boeing News*: March, 1942.
"Clipper Climaxes 22 Years," *The Seattle Star*: June 8, 1938.
"Clipper Crash at Sea," *San Francisco Chronicle*: Nov. 5, 1945.
"Clipper Crash In The Tagus River," *Newsweek*: March 8, 1943.
"Clipper Crashes At Lisbon; 4 Aboard Killed, 20 Missing," *New York Times*: Feb. 23, 1943.
"Clipper Crashes In Portugal," *PM*: Feb. 23, 1943.
"Clipper Crew Back; Interview Not Allowed," *Honolulu Advertiser*: Nov. 9, 1945.
"Clipper Ends Singapore Run," *New York Times*: May 13, 1941.
"Clipper Finished Flight Survey of Southern Pacific," *Pan American Airways*: Pan Am, New York, September-October, 1939.
"Clipper Finishes 2-Way Ocean Trip," *New York Times*: July 1, 1939.
"Clipper Fleet...Fire-Fighting Demonstration by PAA Men; Chinese Crew Services the Clippers," *New Horizons*: Vol. XIV, No. 5, March, 1944.
"Clipper Fleet . . . Prop Women; Weighing the Clipper," *New Horizons*: Vol. XIV, No. 3, January, 1944.
"Clipper Fleet...Stewardesses Join Clipper Flight Crews," *New Horizons*: Vol. XIV, No. 6, April, 1944.
"Clipper From U.S. Arrives At Singapore," *New York Sun*: May 23, 1941.
"Clippers Fully Equipped," *New York Times*: Jan. 25, 1939.
"Clipper Held Back as Fog Hides Port," *New York Times*: June 25, 1939.
"Clipper Heads for Europe with Mail," *New York Journal-American*, NY, p. 1.
"Clipper Hops on New Zealand Trip," *San Francisco Chronicle*: Aug. 11, 1940.
"Clipper Hull Emerges," *Boeing News*: February, 1938.
"Clipper in New Caledonia," *New York Herald Tribune*: Aug. 29, 1939.
"Clippers in Service Over Two Oceans," *Boeing News*: April, 1939.
"Clipper Kitchens," *New Horizons*: Vol. XIV, No. 14, October- December, 1945.
"Clipper Leaves First Flight to Singapore," *San Francisco Chronicle*: May 22, 1941.
"Clipper Makes Flights And Makes Records," *Boeing News*: September, 1938.
"Clipper No. 19 Hops For Hong Kong," *San Franciaco Chronicle*: March 14, 1939.
"Clipper Opens Regular Mail Line To Europe," *New York Herald Tribune*, NY, June 11, 1937.
"Clipper Passengers Here," *Hilo Tribune Herald*: Dec. 8, 1941.
"Clipper Pilots Rehearse World-Wide Flights in the Link Trainer," *New Horizons*: Vol. XIV, No. 5, March, 1944 (ad).
"Clipper Plane Lands at Honolulu," *San Francisco Chronicle*: March 31, 1939.
"Clipper 'Plumbing' Fills a Room," *Boeing News*: July, 1938.
"Clipper Progress," *Boeing News*: October, 1937.
"Clipper Progress Gratifying; Government Tests Begin Soon," *Boeing News* : October, 1938.
"Clipper Record," *New Horizons*: Vol. XIII, No. 12, August- October, 1943.
"Clipper Soars Over The Atlantic, Inaugurating Pan American Line," *New York World Telegram*, NY, May 20, 1939, p. 1.
"Clipper Tail..." *Boeing News*: December, 1937.
"Clipper Will Land at Treasure Island Today," *San Francisco Chronicle*: July 24, 1940.
"Clipper With 29 Leaves U.S. for New Zealand," *New York Herald Iribune*: Aug. 23, 1939.
"Clipper 18; Ship Hop for China Today," *San Francisco Chronicle*: Feb. 22, 1939.
"Closed Doors," *New Horizons*: Vol. XIII, No. 12, August- October, 1943.
"Cold Fright," *New Horizons*: Vol. XII, No. 6, March, 1942.
Colton, F. Barrows, "Aviation in Commerce and Defense," *National Geographic*: Vol. LXXVIII, No. 6, December, 1940.
"Concentric Curriculum," *New Horizons*: Vol. XII, No. 13, November, 1942.
"Condors of 1943," *New Horizons*: Vol. XII, No. 5, January, 1943.
"Constellation," *New Horizons*: Vol. XIV, No. 8, June, 1944.
"Constellation Service to Hawaii Begun; Boeing Seaplanes Retired from Service," *The Clipper*: Vol. 3, No. 39, April 15, 1946.
"Co-Pilot at Pan Am," *Newsweek*: July 20, 1964.
"Crash Proved Paradoxical Blessing for Jane Froman," *Los Angeles Times*: April 28, 1980.
"Crash Victims Now Total 29," *New York Sun*: Feb. 19, 1943.
Cronk, Capt. Paul B., "The Rescue On Station Charlie," *The Atlantic Monthly*: 1950.
Crosson, John & Dixon, George, "Pacific Clipper In; Ends 24,686-Mile War Flight," *New York Daily News*: Jan. 7, 1942.
"Crowds of Visitors Meet Every Clipper At Manorhaven," *Port Washington News*: Aug. 4, 1939.
"Delayed Clipper Reaches England," *New York Times*: June 29, 1939.
De Manche, Don, "Not a Chinaman's Chance," *The Clipper*: Vol. 25, No. 24, Dec. 1, 1966.

"Diaper Special," *New Horizons*: Vol. XI, No. 4, January, 1941.

Dillon, Richard H., "Treasure Island: Our Other 1939-40 World's Fair," *American History Illustrated*: Vol. XXV, No. 2, May-June, 1990.

Dodd, Jr., Allen R., "Air Travel's Glamor Era; Brother Can You Spare a Ride on the Golden Skyway," *Signature*: December, 1973.

"Double Record," *New Horizons*: Vol. XII, No. 1, October, 1941.

"Downed Clipper Parts Tow Line; Due In Today," *Honolulu Advertiser*: Nov. 6, 1945.

"Dreamboat - Wellwood Beall and the Boeing Clipper," *Pacific Northwest Aviation Historical Foundation*: 1978 (pamphlet).

Driscoll, Chris, "Atlantic Clipper carried 74 passengers with an 11- man crew—It was the largest plane in the world in 1940," *Red Rock News*, Sedona, AZ, Jan. 5, 1994.

"Easter Parade," *New Horizons*: Vol. XIII, No. 4, February, 1943.

"Eddie Allen One of World's Noted Flyers," *Seattle Post- Intelligencer*: Feb. 19, 1943.

Edwards, Ron, "Martin Mars Flying Boats," *Air Classics*: Vol. 17, No. 11, November, 1981.

"End Of Sikorsky," *Time*: July 12, 1943.

"Engineers in Training," *New Horizons*: Vol. XI, No. 2, November, 1940.

"Epic," *New Horizons*: Vol. XII, No. 4, January, 1942.

"Event of The Month...Waves Visit NBA," *New Horizons*: Vol. XVI, No. 6, April, 1944.

"Eyewitnesses In South End Tell of Crash," *Seattle Post- Intelligencer*: Feb. 19, 1943.

" Expansion," *Boeing News*: November, 1936.

"Exposition Extra," *San Francisco Chronicle*: March 15, 1939.

"Exposition Visitors Will See Clippers," *Boeing News*: November, 1938.

"Express to Cargo," *New Horizons*: Vol. XII, No. 12, September, 1942.

"Facts About New Boeing Clipper," The Seattle Star: June 8, 1938.

"Ferry for War," *New Horizons*: Vol. XIII, No. 2, December, 1942.

"Fiji Opening," *New Horizons*: Vol. XII, No. 3, December, 19410

"First Air Mail Leaves Via Yankee Clipper For Europe From Manorhaven," *Port Washington News*: May 23, 1939.

"First Big Bermuda Flight Brings In Sixty Passengers," *Port Washington News*: April 7, 1939.

"First Clipper Nears Completion," *Boeing News*: February, 1938.

"First Flight Echo," *New Horizons*: Vol. XIII, No. 7, May, 1943.

"First Hand News Of European War Comes by Clipper," *Port Washington News*: Sept. 1, 1939.

"First Passenger Flight Today On Northern Route to England," *New York Times*: July 3, 1939.

"First World Flyer Norman C. Lee Made Trip in 21 Days," *Port Washington News*: July 4, 1939.

"Firsts," *New Horizons*: Vol. XI, No. 6, March, 1941.

"Five Years," *New Horizons*: Vol. XI, No. 3, December, 1940.

"Flag Tags," *New Horizons*: Vol. XI, No. 12, September, 1941.

"Fledgling Clippers," *New Horizons*: Vol. XI, No. 8, May, 1941.

"Fleet Movement," *New Horizons*: Vol. XI, No. 10, July, 1941.

"'Flight' Gets Back in the Picture," *Air Cargo News*: July-August, 1980.

"Flight to Nowhere," *New Horizons*: Vol. XI, No. 2, November, 1940.

"Flight To The West," *New Horizons*: Vol. XI, No. 7, April, 1941.

"Flight Watch," *New Horizons*: Vol. XII, No. 2, November, 1941.

"Flight 262," *New Horizons*: Vol. XI, No. 6, March, 1941.

"Floatless," *New Horizons*: Vol. XI, No. 6, March, 1941.

"Flying Boat Begins Cross - Sea Surveys," *New York Times*: July 1, 1939.

"Flying Boat Leader Hauled Mail, Churchill," *Los Angeles Times*: Feb. 2, 1981.

"Flying Boats: Plane sailing," *Upper Class*, World Publications, Ltd., Virgin Atlantic Airlines, Spring, 1991.

"Flying Classrooms," *New Horizons*: Vol. XI, No. 2, November, 1940.

"Flying to Europe in the Yankee Clipper," *Look*: May 23, 1939.

"From Windjammers to Flying Clippers," *Boeing News*: November, 1938.

Froman, Jane, "I Lived It!," *The American Weekly*: March 30, 1952.

"Furnishings Luxurious," *The Seattle Star*: June 8, 1938.

"Gala Holiday Declared By Chamber As Clipper Starts Passenger Trips," *Port Washington News*: June 23, 1939.

"Gambit," *New Horizons*: Vol. XIII, No. 9, July, 1943.

"Giant Boeing Treats Seattle," *Boeing News*: September, 1938.

"Giant Clipper Hops for S.F.," *San Francisco Chronicle*: March 4, 1939.

"Giant Clipper Moves Slowly Down Duwamish," *Seattle Times*: March 17, 1941.

"Giant Clipper Reaches Manila," *San Francisco Chronicle*: March 4, 1939.

"Giant Clippers to Fly 204 Passengers Abroad," *New Horizons*: Vol. XIV, No. 12, April-June, 1945.

"Giant Land, Sea Planes Compared," *The Seattle Star*: June 8, 1938.

"Glamour Girl," *New Horizons*: Vol. XIII, No. 8, June, 1943.

"Global Geography," *New Horizons*: Vol. XIV, No. 13, July- September, 1945.

Grace, William H., "Firsthand From Fiji," *New Horizons*: Vol. XII, No. 3, December, 1941.

Graham, Frederick, "Air Express To Europe; Ocean Cargo Service By Pan American Airways To Start Thursday," *New York Times*: Sept. 21, 1941.

"Gray Lady," *New Horizons*: Vol. XII, No. 7, May, 1943 (picture caption).

"Greek Thanks," *New Horizons*: Vol. XII, No. 9, June, 1942.

"Greek Welcome," *New Horizons*: Vol. XII, No. 9, June, 1942.

Gross, Kenneth, "Mural restored, but the Hurt Remains," *Air Cargo News*: Vol. 6, No. 9, October, 1980.

Gunnison, Royal Arch, "The Pacific - a Pond," *San Francisco Chronicle*: Aug. 11, 1940.

Hager, Alice Rogers, "Atlantic Clipper Returning," *New York Times*: June 25, 1939.

"Hail To California Clipper," *Pan American Airways*: Pan Am, New York, April, 1939.

Hamby, Bruce, "Flying to Macao in the Early Days." *Los Angeles Times*: April 13, 1980.

"Harold Gray Dles; Ex-Head Of Pan Am," *New York Times*: Dec. 24, 1972.

"Help From Home," *Boeing News*: Deeember, 1946.

"High Praise from Rickenbacker," *Boeing News*: October, 1937.

Hill, Al, "Dixie Clipper's 25th Anniversary Flight Noted," *Boeing News*: July 2, 1964.

"Historic Firsts," *New Horizons*: Vol. XIII, No. 3, January, 1943.

"History at Rio," *New Horizons*: Vol. XII, No. 5, February, 1942.

"History Is Made In the Keel Jig," *Boeing News*: May, 1937.

Hodson, George, "The Steward Said," *New Horizons*: Vol. XI, No. 1, Oct. 1, 1940.

"Hong Kong Drama," *New Horizons*: Vol. XII, No. 5, February, 1942.

Hulse, Jerry, " On the Go; Bottoms Up at Top of Mark," *Los Angeles Times*: Section K, April 7, 1968.

"Hut Sut," *New Horizons*: Vol. XI, No. 10, July, 1941.

"Ice Breaker," *New Horizons*: Vol. XII, No. 1, October, 1941.

"Incredible Rescue," *New Horizons*: Vol. XII, No. 4, January, 1942

"Industry Here Aided By Pan Am," *The Seattle Star*: Juno 8, 1938.

"Incident at Guam," *New Horizons*: Vol. XII, No. 1, October, 1941.

"Ingenuity in Africa," *New Horizons*: Vol. XII, No. 12, Septsmber, 1942.

International, United Press (UPI), "Clipper Resumes Flight," *New York Times*: Aug. 13, 1940.

___, "Jane Froman Tells How Clipper Officer Saved Her From River," *New York Daily News*: Feb. 24, 1943.

"Island Babies," *New Horizons*: Vol. XI, No. 7, April, 1941.

"Island Drafted," *New Horizons*: Vol. XII, No. 5, February, 1942.

"Japanese Sabotage Attempt Is Charged By Pan American," *Honolulu Star-Bulletin*: Nov. 9, 1945.

Jones, Grahame L., "Crew Recalls Dixie Clipper's Flight Into History," *Los Angeles Times*: Part VII, June 25, 1989.

Keen, Victor, "Clipper Arrives at Singapore; British Welcome New U.S. Tie," *New York Herald Tribune*: May 11, 1941.

Kehr, Ernest A., "Aid To Clipper Navigation," *New Horizons*: Vol. XV, No. 3, July-September, 1946.

___, "Fifty Jungle Airports," *New Horizons*: Vol. XV, No. 4, October-December, 1946.

Kelly-Rogers, Capt., "The Churchill Flight," *Life*: Feb. 2, 1942.

Kershner, Howard E., "A Fantasie in the Sky," *New Horizons*: Vol. XIV, No. 4, February, 1944.

Klemmer, Harvey, "Lisbon - Gateway to Warring Europe," *National Geographic*. Vol. LXXX, No. 2, August, 1941.

Kocivar, Ben, "Six Ways To Make The Going Really Great," *Holiday*: Vol. 46, No. 1, July, 1969.

"L.A. Terminal," *New Horizons*: Vol. XI, No. 10, July, 1941.

"Laboratory Aloft," *Aviation*: December, 1938.

"Land Clippers Fly to Bermuda," *The Clipper*: Vol. 3, No. 28, Nov. 16, 1945.

"Last Boeing Transit Marked At Foynes," *The Clipper*: Nov. 22, 1945.

"Life Flies The Atlantic - America To Europe In 23 Hours By Clipper," *Life*: June 3, 1940.

"Lifetime of Gas For Automobile," *The Seattle Star*: June 8, 1938.

Lindbergh, Anne Morrow, "Flying Around the North Atlantic," *National Geographic*: Vol. LXVI, No. 3, September, 1934.

Little, E. Robin, "Transatlantic Circuit," *New Horizons*: Vol. XIII, No. 2, December, 1942.

"Lodeesen's Leopard," *New Horizons*: Vol. XI, No. 8, May, 1941.

Lodeesen, Marius, "The Virgin of Diego Garcia," *Explorers Journal*: March, 1968.

Loning, Grover, "Make My Supersonic Jet a Flying Boat," *Holiday*: Vol. 46, No. 1, July, 1969.

Long, George, "Christmas in the Azores," *Air & Space*: Vol. 1, No. 5, Smithsonian, Institute, Washington, D.C., December 1986-January, 1987.

"Los Angeles Is Scene of Naming American Clipper," *Pan American Airways*: Pan Am, New York, September-October, 1939.
"Loss & Recovery," *New Horizons*: Vol. XII, No. 4, January, 1942.

Lubsen, Walter, "Last Lap," *New Horizons*: Vol. XIV, No. 1, November, 1943.

Luce, Clare Boothe, "By Clipper To African Front," *Life*: March 30, 1942.

___, "Destiny Crosses the Dateline," *Life*: Vol. II, No. 18, Nov. 3, 1941.
"Luxury Aloft," *Boeing News*: January, 1939.
"Madeline Cuniff: stewardess pioneer," *The Clipper*: October, 1980.
"Manila, March 2," *San Francisco Chronicle*: March 2, 1939.
"Massive Framework For Ocean Cruiser," *Boeing News*: September, 1937.
"Matthews Beach," *Boeing News*: February, 1939.
"Matthews Beach Test Base," *Boeing News*: December, 1938.
"Men of the Meal-Line," *New Horizons*: Vol. XIV, No. 1, November, 1943.

Merrell, Creighton, "Weight Predictor," *Boeing News*: November, 1938.

Miller, Burke William, "Flying The Pacific," *National Geographic*: Vol. LXX, No. 6, December, 1936.

"Minshall Receives Trophy," *Boeing News*: July, 1940.
"Mock-up Christened," *New Horizons*: Vol. XI, No. 2, November, 1940.
"Mock-up Moves," *New Horizons*: Vol. XII, No. 12, September, 1942.
"Model 314A Clipper Assemblage," *Boeing News*: November, 1940.
"Modern Version Ocean Liners," *Boeing News*: November, 1936.
"Monarch Remembers," *New Horizons*: Vol. XII, No. 13, November, 1942.
"Monster Sea Bird Poised for First Flight," *Seattle Post-Intelligencer*: June 1, 1938.

Moore, Ward, "Planes Don't Trust To Luck Any More; Aerial Navigation Born In Miami, Is a Science," *Miami Herald*: Miami, FL, May 13, 1945.

"Morrison Joins Boeing; Minshall, Kylstra Promoted," *Boeing News*: January, 1939.

Morton, Robert S., "Air Empire," *Flying*: November, 1942.

"Mother Carey Corps," *New Horizons*: Vol. XII, No. 11, August, 1942.
"Movies in the Clouds; Another PAA First," *New Horizons*: Vol. XV, No, 2, April-June, 1946.
"Moving Month," *New Horizons*: Vol. XI, No. 11, August, 1941.
"Must Be a Clipper," *New Horizons*: Vol. XI, No. 5, February, 1941.

Nash, W. Bill, "R.O.D. Sullivan And the Yankee Clipper Crash," *Clipper Pioneer Newsletter*: Vol. 18-7, Dec. 12, 1986.

"NATS," *New Horizons*: Vol. XIV, No. 3, January, 1944.
"Navy," *New Horizons*: Vol. XI, No. 4, January, 1941.
"Navy Starts, RAF Finishes," *New Horizons*: Vol. XII, No. 13, November, 1942.
"'NC' Ships Airworthy," *The Seattle Star*: June 8, 1938.
"Need Lumber In Building of Giant Clipper," *The Seattle Star*: June, 1938.
"New Clipper," *New Horizons*: Vol. XI, No. 7, 1941.
"New Clippers," *Boeing News*: October, 1939.
"New Clippers," *New Horizons*: Vol. XI, No. 4, January, 1941.
"New Clipper Run Over Pacific Begun," *New York Times*: July 13, 1940.
"New Clipper To Arrive Soon," *Port Washington News*: March 3, 1939.
"New Crew," *New Horizons*: Vol. XII, No. 11, August, 1942.
"New Name," *New Horizons*: Vol. XI, No. 5, February, 1941.
"New Order at Lisbon," *New Horizons*: Vol. XI, No. 11, August, 1941.
"New Passenger Clipper Under Construction," *Port Washington News*: Aug. 20, 1937.
"New Planes," *New Horizons*: Vol. XI, No. 5, February, 1941.
"New Plane Service Goes Into Singapore," *New York Times*: May 1, 1941.
"New Play," *New Horizons*: Vol. XI, No. 4, January, 1941.
"New Quarters,". *New Horizons*: Vol. XIII, No. 6, April, 1943.

"New School," *New Horizons*: Vol. XI, No. 3, December, 1940.
"New Star-Gazers," *New Horizons*: Vol. XI, No. 7, April, 1941.
"New Super Clipper Will Arrive Soon," *Port Washington News*: Jan. 20, 1939.
"New Transpacific Service Hailed," *New Horizons*: Vol. XV, No. 2 April-June, 1946.
"New Zealand Air Service," *Treasure Island's Clipper News*: Pan Am's Pacific Division, San Francisco, Vol. 1, No. 6, July 26, 1940.
"Newly Named American Clipper Goes Into Service," *Los Angeles Times*: July 7, 1939.
"News Names . . .Codeman, Crossword Expert; Captain Chalks up 10 yrs ," *New Horizons*: Vol. XIV, No. 2, December, 1943.
"News Names . . . PAA Lady Flight Dispatchers; Clipper Captain Aloft 9000 Hours," *New Horizons*: Vol. XIV, No. 3, January, 1944.
"News Names...Twice War Bond Winner; China's Contribution," *New Horizons*. Vol. XIV, No. 1, November, 1943.
"North Beach Gets Dedicated, But Clippers Still Use Port," *Port Washington News*: April 5, 1940.
"North Haven Sails For Canton Isle To Set Up Base," *Pan American Airways*: Pan Am, New York, April, 1939.
"Now the Atlantic," *Time*: Vol. XXXIII, No. 22, May 29, 1939.
"Now you can fly to Lisbon by Clipper," *New York Times*: Aug. 7, 1945 (Pan Am ad).
"Ocean Air Service Begun by Clipper," *New York Times*: June 29, 1939.
"Ocean Liner of the Air," *Boeing News*: March, 1940.
"Ocean Master," *New Horizons*: Vol. XI, No. 12, September, 1941.
"Officials Fly To Ceremonies," *Pan American Airways*. Pan Am, New York, April, 1939.
"On Deck," *New Horizons*: Vol. XI, No. 2, November, 1940.
"On Stage," *New Horizons*: Vol. XI, No. 6, March, 1941.
"On the Pacific," *New Horizons*: Vol. XI, No. 10, July, 1941.
"One Flying Boat, Slightly Sunken, May Visit Stalin," *Boeing News*: Aug. 9, 1951.
O'Neal, Jim, "One Captain - Two Captains," *Clipper Pioneer Newsletter*: Vol. 26-4, Dec. 23, 1994.
"Orders from a Woman," *New Horizons*: Vol. XII, No. 4, January, 1942.
"Out of the clipper kitchens," *New Horizons*: Vol. XIV, No. 10, October-December, 1944.
"Over the Hump," *New Horizons*: Vol. XIV, No. 8, June, 1944.
"Overland Express," *New Horizons*: Vol. XII, No. 1, October, 1941.
"Overseas Airmail Sent Partly by Ship," *New York Times*: March 18, 1943.
"PAA Clipper Commuters," *New Horizons*: Vol. XIV, No. 14, October-December, 1945.
"PAA Introduces Flight Movies At Press Party," *The Clipper*: Nov. 22, 1945.
"PAA Resumes Commercial Operations Today: Div. 10th Anniversary, Nov. 22," *The Clipper*: Vol. 3, No. 28, Nov. 16, 1945.
"PAA Sets New Records; Clippers Clip Time Over Atlantic, Pacific Routes," *New Horizons*: Vol. XV, No. 2, April- June, 1946.
"Pacific Air Express," *New Horizons*: Vol. XI, No. 6, March, 1941.
"Pacific-Alaska...PAA Crew in Daring Pacific Rescue; Air Transport Proves Its Versatility," *New Horizons*: Vol. XIV, No. 7, May, 1944.
"Pacific Clipper Off to Hong Kong," *San Francisco Chronicle*: March 27, 1939.
"Pacific Fares Help Downward Trend," *New Horizons*: Vol. XV, No. 3, July-September, 1946.
Palmer, Gretta, "Clipper To Lisbon," *Coronet*: March, 1942.
"Pan American Airways Goes Into Singapore; Flights To Alternate With Hong Kong Run," *New York Times*: May 1, 1941.
"Pan American Airways received permits from Great Britain, Canada and the Irish Free State," *Los Angeles Examiner*: April 21, 1937.
"Pan American Commercial Operations To Be Resumed Nov. 16 From S.F. Airport," *The Clipper*: Vol. 3, No. 27, Nov. 4, 1945.
"Pan American Compensation Set," *New York* Times: April 2, 1939.
"Pan American Plane Named 'California'," *San Francisco Chronicle*: March 27, 1939.
"Pan American To Double Sailings On South Atlantic," *Port Washington News*: Sept. 6, 1939.
"Passenger Plane Arrives Lisbon," *New York Times*: June 30, 1939.
"Passenger Service," *New Horizons*: Vol. XI, No. 3, December, 1940.
Pemperton-Billing, Noel, "Are We Too Proud To Learn?," *The Aeroplane*: London, England, Aug. 16, 1939.
"Perpetual Motion College," *New Horizons*: Vol. XI, No. 8, May, 1941.
"Philately," *New Horizons*: Vol. XI, No. 5, February, 1941.
"Photos by Cable," *San Francisco Chronicle*: April 5, 1939.
"Pilot Program," *New Horizons*: Vol. XII, No. 13, November, 1942.
"Pilot's Heartbreak," *Time*: Vol. XLII, No. 12, Sept. 20, 1943.
"Plane Ahoy," *New Horizons*: Vol. XIII, No. 9, July, 1943.

Bibliography

"Plane Christened by Mrs. Roosevelt," *New York Times*: March 4, 1939.

"Plane Talk," *New Horizons*: Vol. XIII, No. 8, June, 1943.

"Portal Performance," *New Horizons*: Vol. XI, No. 12, September, 1941.

"Port Receives Last Look At The Clippers," *Port Washington News*: March 29, 1940.

Prass, Jr., Marc R., "Merchant Marine of the Air; Pan American Blazes New Diplomatic Relations," *The Scientific Magazine*: Vol. XIV, No. II, Winter, 1940.

"Presidential Pronouncements," *New Horizons*: Vol. XII, No. 13, November, 1942.

Press, Associated (AP), "Clipper Explodes in Lisbon Landing; 5 Die," *New York Daily News*: Feb. 23, 1943.

___, "Jane Froman Divorces Flier Who Saved Her Life in Plane Crash," *Los Angeles Times*: June 15, 1956.

___, "Jane Froman Stills Voice to Study Art," *Los Angeles Times*: June 23, 1963.

___, "Jane Froman, Who Inspired 'With a Song in My Heart,' Dies," *Los Angeles Times*: April 23, 1980.

___, "Pilot Disobeyed Orders; Froman Case Jury Told," *Valley Green Sheet*: Los Angeles, March 10, 1953.

___, "15 Safe In Clipper Crash; 4 Known Dead, 20 Missing," *New York Daily News*: Feb. 24, 1943.

"Promotions," *New Horizons*: Vol. XI, No. 5, Fobruary, 1941.

"Prince," *New Horizons*: Vol. XI, No. 4, January, 1941.

"Purchasing Department," *Boeing News*: April, 1938.

"Pursued Ships," *Boeing News*: January, 1942.

"Queen's Flight," *New Horizons*: Vol. XIII, No. 12, August-October, 1943.

"Quick Turn-Around," *New Horizons*: Vol. XI, No. 1, Oct. 1, 1940.

Ibid., Vol. XIII, No. 3, January, 1943.

"Radio School," *New Horizons*: Vol. XV, No. 1, January-March, 1946.

Ranpau, Clem J., "Around the Pacific," *New Horizons*: Vol. XI, No. 2, November, 1940.

"Record," *New Horizons*: Vol. XI, No. 5, February, 1941.

"Record in War," *New Horizons*: Vol. XII, No. 12, September, 1942.

"Record Load of Mail Expected On First Transatlantic Flight," *Pan American Airways*: Pan Am, New York, April, 1939.

"Record Set in Development," *The Seattle Star*: June 8, 1938.

"Reflections on Vanity," *New Horizons*: Vol. XIII, No. 8, June, 1943.

"Refugees in Reverse," *New Horizons*: Vol. XI, No. 12, September, 1941.

"Research Chief," *Boeing News*: May, 1939.

"Rescue Ship Due Here Today With 10 Saved From Plane; Search Ends For 3 Missing," *New York Times*: Jan, 23, 1939.

"Return," *New Horizons*: Vol. XI, No. 12, September, 1941.

"Review of The Week - Transport," *San Francisco Chronicle*: Feb. 12, 1939.

Rice, Elmer, "To Write a Play," *New Horizons*: Vol. XI, No. 5, February, 1941.

Rovanpers, Brad, "He captured history from the Sky," *Contra Costa Times*: Walnut Creek, Calif.., May 20, 1982.

"Rush from Japan," *New Horizons*: Vol. XII, No. 3, Decernber, 1941.

"Safety Over the Seas," *Sunday World-Herald*: Omaha, Neb., June 21, 1939.

"San Juan Flight," *New Horizons*: Vol. XI, No. 4, January, 1941.

"Sargassa Saga," *New Horizons*: Vol. XII, No. 9, June, 1942.

Saunders, Keith, "Three Great Boeings," *Boeing News*: October, 1946.

Saunders, Margaret, "Clippering Through," *The Guam Recorder*: Guam Island, Vol. XVI, No. 10, January, 1940.

Scammeli, Henry, "Pan Am's Pacific," *Air & Space*: Vol. 4, No. 3, Smithsonian Institute, Washington, D.C., August-September, 1989.

"Scientific Flight Control," *New Horizons*: Vol. XIII, No. 3, January, 1943.

"Sea Airline Votes Wide Expansion," *New York Times*: Oct. 4, 1939.

"Sea-Legged Airmen," *New Horizons*: Vol. XIII, No. 8, June, 1943.

"Search," *New Horizons*: Vol. XI, No. 1, Oct. 1, 1940.

"Second Boeing Clipper Makes Initial Flight," *Boeing News*: December, 1938.

"Second Clipper Located Downed Plane, Brought Ships to Rescue," *Honolulu Star-Bulletin*: Nov. 5, 1945.

"Second Plane Down At Sea In 24 Hours," *Honolulu Advertiser*: Nov. 5, 1945.

"Secret Turn-Around," *New Horizons*: Vol. XII, No. 4, January, 1942.

Seilder, Michael, "Airline Pioneer Juan Trippe Dies; Made Pan Am a Giant," *Los Angeles Times*: April 4, 1981.

"Seven Boeing Clippers To Fly Airline Routes," *Boeing News*: Sept. 12, 1946.

Shawe, Victor, "Wellwood E. Beall; Creator of the Pan American Clipper," *U.S. Air Services*: October, 1940.

"Ship Model Is First Atlantic Air Express," *Pan American Airways*: Pan Am, New York, April, 1939.

"Shipping And Mails," *New York Times*: Nov. 5, 1941.

"Ship Sails to New Air Base," *San Francisco Chronicle*: April 30, 1939.

"Shuttle; Non-Productive; Cargoes of 1941," *New Horizons*: Vol. XI, No. 11, August, 1941.

Simpich, Frederick, "Return to Manila," *National Geographic*: Vol. LXXVIII, No. 4, October, 1940.

"Singapore Surprise," *New Horizons*: Vol. XI, No. 12, September, 1941.

"Singapore Greets Clipper's Arrival," *New York Times*: May 11, 1941.

"Sketches of Some on Clipper; Noted: Entertainers Were Aboard," *New York Herald Tribune*: Feb. 24, 1943.

Slattery, Desmond, "The Wildest Men in the Air," *Argosy*: Vol. 336, No. 2, February, 1968.

"Something New Has Been Added: It's Stewardesses For Atlantic," *The Clipper*: April 5, 1945.

"So. Atlantic & Africa," *New Horizons*: Vol. XII, No. 1, October, 1941.

"South Atlantic & Africa," *New Horizons*: Vol. XI, No. 12, September, 1941.

"Sparks," *New Horizons*: Vol. XI, No. 4, January, 1941.

"Stars on the Clippers," *New Horizons*: Vol. XIII, No. 4, July, 1943.

"Start of the 4th," *New Horizons*: Vol. XII, No. 8, May, 1942.

"'Startlers' About the Clipper," *Boeing News*: March, 1938.

"Stewardesses," *New Horizons*: Vol. XIV, No. 9, July, 1944.

"Strato Path To Alaska," *Boeing News*: August, 1938.

"Strip," *New Horizons*: Vol. XI, No. 4, January, 1941.

"Submerged Clipper Comes Up; Tamara, Ben Robertson Missing," *New York Herald Tribune*: Feb. 24, 1943.

"'Super-Clipper' Being Built for Atlantic," *Los Angeles Examiner*: April 21, 1937.

"Super Clipper Now At Baltimore Until Port PAA Base Is Ready," *Port Washington News*: Feb. 24, 1939.

"Survivor Depicts Wreck of Clipper," *New York Times*: Feb. 25, 1943.

"System Spotlight," *New Horizons*: Vol. XIV, No. 5, March, 1944.

Tabes, Isabella, "Courage Unlimited," *Reader's Digest*: October, 1952.

"Tagus Surrenders 2 Clipper Victims," *New York Times*: March 7, 1943.

Talbert, Ansel E., "Clipper Blazing Pacific Trail To New Zealand," *New York Herald Tribune*: Aug. 11, 1940 .

"Tamara Gained Theater Fame With 'Smoke Gets in Your Eyes,'" *New York Herald Tribune*: Fob. 24, 1943.

"Tamara Reported Missing In Lisbon Clipper Crack-up," *New York Times*: Feb. 23, 1943.

"Tavares, Aboard Second Clipper, Tells How Assistance Was Given," *Honolulu Star-Bulletin*: Nov. 5, 1945.

Taylor, Henry J., "Wartime Crossing," *New Horizons*: Vol. XII, No. 5, February, 1942.

Teets, Florence, "The Little Flower's Folly," *Pegasus*: October, 1954.

"Test Pilot For the XB-15," *Boeing News*: May, 1937.

"Test Run," *New Horizons*: Vol. XI, No. 3, December, 1940.

"The Boeing 314A Clipper," *Boeing News*: June, 1946.

"The Day," *New Horizons*: Vol. XI, No. 4, January, 1940.

"The 'Edwin C. Muscick,'" *New Horizons*: Vol. XIV, No. 5, March, 1944.

"The Last Link - Transatlantic Service," *Boeing News*: June, 1939.

"THE MONTH - Back To Ireland," *New Horizons*: Vol. XII, No. 3, December, 1941.

"THE MONTH - Character Confirmed, " *New Horizons*: Vol. XII, No. 12, September, 1942.

"THE MONTH - Passenger No. 1," *New Horizons*: Vol. XXII, No. 3, January, 1943.

"THE MONTH - The Year," *New Horizons*: Vol. XII, No. 4, January, 1942.

"THE MONTH - The Year, The Day," New Horizons: Vol. XI, No. 4, January, 1941.

"The Name Clipper," *New Horizons*: Vol. XI, No. 5, February, 1941.

"The Scenic Route," *New Horizons*: Vol. XIII, No. 9, July, 1943.
"The Yankee Clipper Completes Final Inspection Trip," *Pan American Airways*: Pan Am, New York, September-October, 1939.
"The Year," *New Horizons*: Vol. XI, No. 4, January, 1941.
"The Year," Vol. XIII, No. 3, January, 1943.
"The Year; Passengers, Air Express," *New Horizons*: Vol. XII, No. 4, January, 1942.
"The Women," *New Horizons*: Vol. XII, No. 5, February, 1942.
"The 200th," *New Horizons*: Vol. XI, No. 1, Oct. 1, 1940.
"Theodore P. Wright Writes Of Flying On Bermuda Clipper," *Port Washington News*: April 21, 1939.
"Third Big Ship Lands at Fair," *San Francisco Chronicle*: March 3, 1939.
"This Is The Clipper Ship," *Life*: Aug. 23, 1937.
"This World," *San Francisco Chronicle*: Aug. 11, 1940.
"Those First Flights To New Zealand," *Treasure Island's Clipper News*: Pan Am, San Francisco, Vol. 1, No. 8, Oct. 1, 1940.
"Three New Clippers Of Transocean Fleet Are Christened," *Pan American Airways*: Pan Am, New York, April, 1939.
"Throng at Airport Sees Clipper Off., Opening City Base," *New York Times*: April 1, 1940.

Tilton, Capt. Jack H., "California Clipper Covers 2,000 Miles," *New York Times*: Aug. 29, 1939.

___, "Clipper At Honolulu On A Survey Flight," *New York Times*: Aug. 24, 1939.
___, "Clipper At New Zealand," *New York Times*: Aug. 24, 1939.
"Time Is Ripe," *New Horizons*: Vol. XI, No. 2, November, 1940.
"To The Queen's Taste," *New Horizons*: Vol. XII, No. 9, June, 1942.
"To New Zealand - Clipper Poised For Takeoff," *San Francisco Chronicle*: July 19, 1940.

Tobey, Banks, "Random Route Reflections," *New Horizons*: Vol. XIII, No. 7, May, 1943.

"Tokyo Envoy Kurusu Due Here Today," *San Francisco Chronicle*: Nov. 14, 1941.
"Traffic at War," *New Horizons*: Vol. XII, No. 11, August, 1942.
"Tragedy in Lisbon," *New Horizons*: Vol. XII, No. 5, January, 1943.,
"Transatlantic...Clippers Complete Five Years of Transatlantic Service; Twelve Planes in Air Sets Daily Record," *New Horizons*: Vol. XIV, No. 9, July, 1944.
"Transatlantic...Division Administrative Reorganization Made," *New Horizons*: Vol. XVI, No. 6, April, 1944.
"Transatlantic...Mercy Flight to Bolama; Prams Guide Clippers to Safety," *New Horizons*: Vol. XIV, No. 5, March, 1944.
"Transatlantic...NATS Officials Tour NBA; Clipper is Scene for Movie on USO," *New Horizons*: Vol. XIV, No. 2, December, 1943.
"Transatlantic...NATS Officials Visit NBA; Bermuda Lilies Shipped By Air," *New Horizons*: Vol. XIV, No. 6, April, 1944.
"Transatlantic...Northern Route Opens; Youngest Passenger Arrives At NBA," *New Horizons*: Vol. XIV, No. 8, June, 1944.
"Transatlantic...PAA Men Honored by Queen Wilhelmina; Clipper Crew Marooned on Bowery Bay," *Now Horizons*: Vol. XIV, No. 4, February, 1944.
"Transatlantic Sky Ferry," *New York Times* (*Rotogravure Picture Section*): July 2, 1939.
"Transatlantic,..Transatlantic Cargo Third Year; Visual Education Inaugurated," *New Horizons*: Vol. XIV, No. 1, November, 1943.
"Transatlantic...Transatlantic Year; NBA Trains Brazil's Foremost Aviatrix," *New Horizons*: Vol. XIV, No. 3, January, 1944.
"Transatlantique!," *Air Trails Pictorial*: February, 1946.
"Transpacific...China Clipper Anniversary; Letters Prom Jap Prisoners," *New Horizons*: Vol. XIV, No. 1, November, 1943.
"Transpacific...Transpacific's Year; News from the Orient," *New Horizons*: Vol. XIV, No. 3, January, 1944.
"Transportation's Studies; In Air and on Highway," *San Francisco Chronicle*: Feb. 12, 1939.
"Trans-Sea Flying Open to All Lines," *Los Angeles Examiner*: April 21, 1937.
"Treasure Island," *San Francisco Chronicle*: Jan. 31, 1939.
Ibid., Feb. 19, 1939.
"Treasure Island Airport," *New Horizons*: Vol. XI, No. 8, May, 1941.
"Trip 500," *New Horizons*: Vol. XI, No. 10, July, 1941.

Trippe, Juan T., "Ocean Flying Is Routine," *Flying and Popular Aviation*: October, 1941.

"Two Years," *New Horizons*: Vol. XI, No. 9, June, 1941.
"Tyrone Powers Are Greeted By Throng As Clipper Docks," *Port Washington News*: Sept. 8, 1939.
"Unique Auction," *New Horizons*: Vol. XII, No. 13, November, 1942
"Urge Painted," *New Horizons*: Vol. XII, No. 13, November, 1942.
"U.S. Mail, Ships, Planes Again Go Through Bermuda," *San Francisco Chronicle*: Aug. 23, 1940.

Van Dusen, William, "Magellans Of The Air," *Boeing News*: June, 1946.

"Wake Escape," *New Horizons*: Vol. XII, No. 4, January, 1942.
"Wanted - A Name," *New Horizons*: Vol. XI, No. 12, September, 1941.
"War Correspondents," *New Horizons*: Vol. XI, No. 7, April, 1941.
"War Pioneer," *New Horizons*: Vol. XII, No. 13, November, 1942.

Ward, Robert N., "Seattle's Sky Queen Makes Last Flight," *Seattle Post-Intelligencer*: April 14, 1946.

Wavy flag design (pix caption), *San Francisco Chronicle*: Feb. 7, 1939.

Welch, Doug, "'We're Coming In; A Wing's On fire'," *Seattle Post-Intelligencer*: F'eb. 20, 1943.

"'Well Done' Says The Navy," *New Horizons*: Vol. XV, No. 1, January-March, 1946.
"Wells' Farewell," *New Horizons*: Vol. XII, No. 11, August, 1942.
"Where Are They Now?," *Newsweek*: Aug. 29, 1966.
"Wife Is Advised Husband Aboard Clipper Is Safe," *Honolulu Star-Bulletin*: Nov. 5, 1945.
"Wilbur Wright Lecture," *New Horizons*: Vol. XI, No. 9, June, 1941.

Wiljerson, Reba, "Return To Wake," *American History Illustrated*: Vol. XXII, No. 8, December, 1987,

"Wings That Fill a Hall," *Boeing News*: January, 1938.
"Winter & the Atlantic," *New Horizons*: Vol. XI, No. 2, November, 1940.
"Winter Preparations," *New Horizons*: Vol. XI, No. 3, December, 1940.
"Who's Who," *New Horizons*: Vol, XII, No. 11, August, 1942.
"Women of the Year," *New Horizons*: Vol. XII, No. 2, December, 1942.

Woodmansee, Willard Keith, "Was There Life After Pan Am?," *Clipper Pioneer Newsletter*, Vol. 25-6, Dec. 31, 1993.

"Wound Stripe," *New Horizons*: Vol. XII, No. 9, June, 1942.
"Yankee Clipper's Dead Hunted, Show Folk, Writers Among Them," *New York Times*: Feb. 24, 1943.
"Yankee Clipper Reaches French Port," *San Francisco Chronicle*: April 3, 1939.
"Yankee Clipper To Start Today For First Atlantic Trip," *Port Washington News*: March 24, 1939.
"Yankee Clipper Visited By Many," *Port Washington News*: March 17, 1939.
"Yankee Clipper, With 21, On First Flight to Europe," *New York Herald Tribune*: March 27, 1939.
"Your Chance to Name a Clipper," *The Clipper*: Nov. 22, 1945.
"1st of New Clipper Planes Launched," *Seattle Times*: March 17, 1941.
"1-Way Air Mail From Bermuda Closed to U.S.," *New York Herald Tribune*, NY, June 11, 1937.
"3-Fold Art," *New Horizons*: Vol. XIII, No. 3, January, 1943.
"7 Killed in Plane Crash Off Hawaii," *San Francisco Chronicle*: Nov. 4, 1945.
"11 Short Years From Lindy's Plane to the Boeing Clippers," *The Seattle Star*: June 8, 1938.
"14 Die, 13 Hurt as Crashing Bomber Fires Plant," *New York Daily News*: Feb. 19, 1943 .
"15 Passengers Aboard Clipper Off For Europe," *Port Washington News*: July 7, 1939.
"23 On Clipper Saved at Sea," *Los Angeles Times*: Nov. 5, 1945.
"44 Are Rescued From Flying Boat," *New York Times*: Oct. 15, 1947.
"300," *New Horizons*: Vol. XI, No. 7, Aprll, 1941.
"'314s Make News," *Boeing News*: March, 1939.
"500 Attend Service For Tamara Swann," *New York Times*: April 17, 1943.
"1,300 Rounds of Gunfire, Half Hour Required To Sink Stricken Clipper," *Honolulu Star-Bulletin*: Nov. 10, 1945.
"5,000 Flights," *New Horizons*: Vo. XIV, No. 2, December, 1943.
"5,000 See Clipper Leave Here On First Passenger Trip From U.S. To Europe; Port Sends Greetings," *Port Washington News*: June 30, 1939.